AS Level
Applied Business
for EDEXCEL
Double award

John Evans-Pritchard • Margaret Hancock
Rob Jones • Alan Mansfield • Dave Gray

Causeway
Press

edexcel

Acknowledgements

Dedication

To Sheila, Amanda Jane, Oscar and Cleo, Jan, Natalie, Holly and Ellen.

Cover design by Caroline Waring-Collins. Illustration © Tiit Veermae/Alamy.

Graphics by Caroline Waring-Collins and Kevin O'Brien.

Cartoons by Alan Fraser.

Photography by Andrew Allen and Dave Gray.

Proof reading by Sue Oliver, Heather Doyle and Mike Kidson.

Reviewer - Stuart Kneller.

Typing - Ingrid Hamer.

Acknowledgements

The publishers would like to thank the following for the use of photographs and copyright material. Other copyright material is acknowledged at source. Campbell/TopFoto p88; Charles Sturge/Rex Features p408; Corel pp75, 84, 200, 207, 224, 232, 292, 362; Dennis Stone/Rex Features p255(l); Digital Stock pp60, 79; Digital Vision pp22(r), 48, 96, 105, 115, 117, 164, 223, 245, 252(r), 267(r), 276, 278(t), 326, 330, 374(l,r), 377(b), 399; Graham Burns/Photofusion p277; Ilpo Musto/Rex Features p37; Jane Haralambos p129; John Tickner/Rex Features p47; Lucy Pateman/Giles Hancock p228; Marty Hause/Rex Features p301; Nils Jorgenson/Rex Features pp255(r), 409(t); PA/EMPICS p278(b); PA/TopFoto p314; PhotoDisc pp25, 30, 43, 44, 59, 64(t), 70(t,b), 86(t,b), 93, 97(t,b), 101(t,b), 104, 105, 114, 134, 177, 187, 196(l,r), 215, 216, 220, 230, 233, 267(l), 299(t,b), 302, 359, 374(t), 377(t), 400, 412, 417(l,r); Photofusion pp123, 142; Rex Features pp8, 61, 260; Sally-Anne Baker p202; Shout/Rex Features p46; Sipa Press/Rex Features pp379, 384; Stafford Sumner p199; Stockbyte pp22(l), 35, 50(b), 120, 128, 163, 251, 252(l), 257, 281(t), 316(t), 338, 380; TopFoto p409(m); TopFoto/EMPICS pp20, 41, 179, 188, 323(t); TopFoto/ImageWorks pp50(t), 55, 109, 147, 261; TopFoto/National p178; TopFoto/UPPA p145; Topham/Chapman pp283, 290; Topham/PA pp54, 69, 284, 372.

Office for National Statisitics material is Crown Copyright, reproduced here with the permission of Her Majesty's Stationery Office.

Every effort has been made to locate the copyright owners of material used in this book. Any errors and omissions brought to the notice of the publisher are regretted and will be credited in subsequent printings.

British Library Cataloguing in Publication Data

A catalogue record for this book is available from the British Library.

ISBN-10: 1-4058-2115-9
ISBN-13: 978-1-4058-2115-5

Contribution © John Evans-Pritchard, Margaret Hancock, Rob Jones, Alan Mansfield, Dave Gray.

Pearson Education, Edinburgh Gate, Harlow, Essex CM20 2JE.

First impression 2005
Typesetting by Caroline Waring-Collins and Anneli Jameson, Waring Collins Ltd.
Printed and bound by Scotprint, Haddington.

Contents

Unit 1 Investigating people at work

1	Business aims and objectives	5
2	Types of ownership	10
3	Business functions	16
4	Organisational structures & job roles	21
5	Reasons for recruitment	27
6	The recruitment process	31
7	Methods of training employees	36
8	Legal and ethical responsibilities – discrimination and equal opportunities	41
9	The importance of motivation and de-motivation	45
10	Motivation theories	48
11	How businesses motivate	52
12	Legislation and employees' well-being and motivation	55
13	Environmental issues	59
14	Social and ethical issues	63
15	Legal and self regulatory constraints and issues	68

Unit 2 Investigating business

16	Setting up a business	73
17	Business planning	77
18	Business resources	81
19	Monitoring quality and performance	85
20	The profit and loss account	89
21	The balance sheet	94
22	Cash flow forecasting	98
23	Budgeting	102
24	Break-even	106
25	Spreadsheets, word processing and databases	111
26	Specialist software	116

Unit 3 Investigating marketing

27	Understanding customer needs and wants	121
28	Developing new products	125
29	Improving profitability	130
30	Improving market share	135
31	Diversification	140
32	Increasing brand awareness	143
33	Market segmentation	147
34	Primary research	154
35	Secondary research	161
36	The marketing mix	166
37	Product	171
38	Price	175
39	Place	180
40	Promotion	184
41	Other constraints on the marketing mix	189

Unit 4 Investigating electronic business

42	What is electronic business?	193
43	On-line presence and business aims and objectives	197
44	The impact on a business of its website	201
45	The impact of a website on customers, suppliers and competitors	205
46	E-business, legislation and industry standards	209
47	Financial costs of a website	213
48	E-business – the opportunities	217
49	E-business – the threats	221
50	Effective websites	225
51	Establishing a website	229

Unit 5 Investigating customer service

52	The importance of customer service for organisations	234
53	Internal and external customers	237
54	The needs of different customers	244
55	The degree of customer service expected	250
56	Staffing for effective customer service	255
57	Premises and product	260
58	Effective communication	266
59	Customer service and the needs of the organisation	271
60	Measuring the quality of customer service	276
61	Monitoring methods	280
62	Maintaining and improving customer service	286
63	Customer service legislation	291
64	Health, safety and security	296

Unit 6 Investigating promotion

65	How promotion is used by businesses	301
66	Sales promotion	303
67	Advertising	308
68	Public relations	313
69	Direct marketing	317
70	Sponsorship	323
71	Print media	327
72	Audio media	331
73	Moving image media	334
74	Ambient and out-of-home media	339
75	New media	343
76	Internal constraints on promotion	346
77	External constraints on promotion	349
78	Analysing promotional campaigns	352
79	Evaluation of promotional campaigns	357

Unit 7 Investigating enterprise

80	Company formation	360
81	Choice of product	365
82	Planning processes	370
83	Wider business issues	374
84	Company officers	379
85	Team working, communication and role evaluation	384
86	Monitoring human resources	389
87	Monitoring production, quality and purchasing	394
88	Monitoring financial performance	399
89	Monitoring sales and promotion	404
90	Winding up a company	409
91	Evaluating the success of an enterprise	414

Index	419

Preface

AS Level Applied Business for EDEXCEL (double award) is one of a series of books written to follow the EDEXCEL Advanced Subsidiary GCE and Advanced GCE in Applied Business (single and double awards). Other books in the series include:
- **AS Level Applied Business for EDEXCEL (single award)** containing Units 1-3;
- **A2 Level Applied Business for EDEXCEL (single and double awards)** containing Units 8-14;
- **Applied Business for EDEXCEL Teachers Guide**.

AS Level Applied Business for EDEXCEL (double award) contains Units 1-7 of the specification. Units have the following features.

Content coverage Units provide comprehensive coverage of 'What you need to learn' in Units 1-7 of the EDEXCEL specification. They give the content knowledge for Units 1 and 6 external assessment and essential background information for internally assessed Units 2, 3, 4, 5 and 7.

Meeting the assessment criteria Units 1 and 6 contain sample questions in the style of the external examination, with sample marks. They clearly show the expected answers and how marks are allocated in the externally assessed examination. Understanding how questions are answered and marked will enable students to achieve examination success. Units 2, 3, 4, 5 and 7 provide suggested student responses in internal assessment at Mark Bands 1, 2 and 3. Understanding the type of response required for different Mark Bands will allow students to meet the assessement criteria effectively. Answers are not meant to be comprehensive, reflecting all of a student's internal assessment, just the part that relates to the content covered in that section.

Examination practice Units 1 and 6 provide sample questions which reflect the style of question asked in the externally assessed examination. Completing all the examination practice questions will allow students to practise and develop the skills for examination success.

Portfolio practice Units 2, 3, 4, 5 and 7 provide questions which allow students to practise the knowledge, application, analysis and evaluation skills which they need to demonstrate in internal assessment.

Research activity Units 2, 3, 4, 5 and 7 provide suggested research and investigation activities. They allow students to practise the research skills required for their internal assessment.

Business examples Many examples are given of actual businesses to illustrate how their operations relate to the EDEXCEL specification.

The publication has been endorsed by EDEXCEL.

Author team for the series
- **John Evans-Pritchard** is Chief Examiner with a major awarding body and an experienced author and teacher.
- **Margaret Hancock** is Principal Examiner with a major awarding body and an experienced author and education consultant for Business Studies.
- **Rob Jones** is an Examiner with a major awarding body and an experienced author and teacher.
- **Alan Mansfield** is Principal Examiner with a major awarding body and an experienced business and education consultant.
- **Dave Gray** is an experienced author and teacher.

The authors would like to thank Stuart Kneller for acting as a reviewer and for his comments and advice in the development and production of the series of books. They would also like to thank all those business representatives who spent time researching and supplying information for use as case studies.

1 Business aims and objectives

Aims and objectives

All businesses have something that they are trying to achieve which explains the purpose of the businesses and why they are here. For many businesses the long-run purpose is to make profits for their owners, but there are many other purposes as explained below. First it is necessary to distinguish between aims and objectives.

There is a difference in the meaning and use of the two words, although in some cases businesses may not make any distinction between them. The words do, after all, both indicate the purpose of what is being done.

The technical difference and the one that will be used for this unit is:
- an aim is what the business is trying to achieve in the end - what the final target is;
- an objective is what needs to be done in order to achieve this aim. This is illustrated in Figure 1.

Identifying a business's aims and objectives

Sometimes a business will state what its aims and objectives are, but often the real aims and objectives are hidden away. In other cases the business will state what its aims and objectives are to mislead people and only careful research will reveal what the actual aims and objective of the business are.

Companies often openly publish their main aims and objectives, sometimes as part of their 'mission statement'. A mission statement states the basic fundamental purpose of a business and so it should include what the main aims are. Unfortunately, it is sometimes used to try to convince customers that the business is only interested in what is good for the customer.

Major business aims

The major aims of businesses will depend on why they are in business and what they are producing. Businesses in the public and private sectors tend to have different reasons for being in business and, therefore, different aims. These differences are considered in section 2. Section 1 considers general aims and objectives and how they can differ depending on what is being produced and sold. Some examples are shown in Figures 1 and 2.

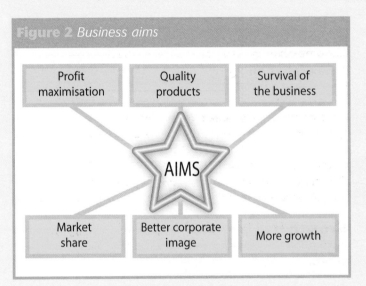

Figure 2 *Business aims*

Making sales and profit

For most businesses selling their products is vital, otherwise they will not have the money necessary to buy raw materials, pay their employees and stay in business. For many businesses the primary aim is to make profits for their owners. In reality it may be difficult to find a business that will state that making profit is its major aim. Making the maximum profit, profit maximisation, is often a major aim although some businesses are prepared to 'satisfice' and make only satisfactory profits.

For example, *The Independent* reported in April 2001 that:

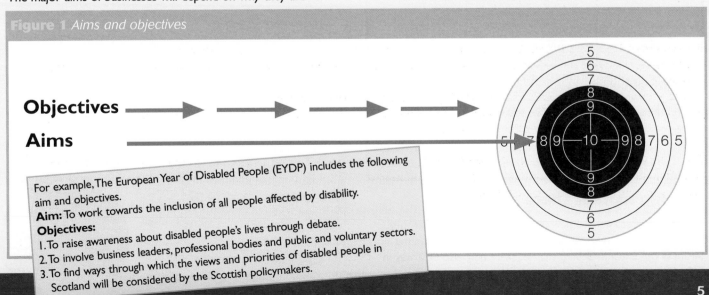

Figure 1 *Aims and objectives*

Objectives

Aims

For example, The European Year of Disabled People (EYDP) includes the following aim and objectives.
Aim: To work towards the inclusion of all people affected by disability.
Objectives:
1. To raise awareness about disabled people's lives through debate.
2. To involve business leaders, professional bodies and public and voluntary sectors.
3. To find ways through which the views and priorities of disabled people in Scotland will be considered by the Scottish policymakers.

'Tesco broke through the £1bn profit barrier for the first time yesterday but was immediately criticised by farming groups for making 'obscene' returns while the industry is in crisis and the foot-and-mouth outbreak continues'. Some objectives needed to achieve profit maximisation are shown in Table 1.

Table 1 *Profit maximisation*	
Business aim	**Typical objectives needed to meet that aim**
Profit maximisation and high sales	Find new markets through effective market research.
	Increase promotion through media such as the Internet.
	Revise pricing policies to meet customers' expectations.
	Improve customer service through better complaints procedures.
	Set performance targets for all employees.
	Reduce costs wherever this can be done without affecting quality or performance.

Growth

The easiest way for a business to increase it sales and its profits is to get bigger. This can be done in a number of ways.
- Internal growth, where the business grows simply by selling more products to more customers, increasing the number of outlets and building new factories.
- Moving into new markets, e.g. abroad.
- Diversifying by selling different products.
- Taking over other businesses.

Some objectives needed to achieve growth are shown in Table 2. Figure 3 shows how Caffè Nero has grown.

Table 2 *Growth*	
Business aim	**Typical objectives needed to meet that aim**
Growth	All of those listed for maximising profits and sales.
	Achieve a wider customer base.
	Research and develop new products to replace declining products.
	Ensure that additional funds are available to meet any increase in demand.
	Establish the business name as a market leader, perhaps by creating a brand.

Gaining market share

When businesses enter a new market it is important that they gain market share so that their product is recognised and the business can expand. Gaining market share may also be a way in which existing businesses expand.

Many markets, such as basic groceries and food, have relatively fixed total sales, so the only way to expand is by taking market share from other businesses. There is another benefit of gaining market share. When businesses become market leaders or even monopolies this gives them great power, which in the long run will allow them to earn higher profits.

For example, in 2005 the supermarket group J Sainsbury took over 114 convenience stores from Jacksons. Convenience stores are now recognised as one of the key growth areas in UK retailing and Sainsbury is keen to attract a greater share of the market for those consumers wishing to shop locally. Some objectives needed to gain market share are shown in Table 3.

Table 3 *Market share*	
Business aim	**Typical objectives needed to meet that aim**
Gaining market share	All of those listed for maximising profits and sales.
	Achieve annual growth in sales of (say) 5-15%.
	Ensure that prices are set at levels equal to or below those of competitors.
	Reduce the number of competitors in the market through takeover or merger.
	Use aggressive promotion to show the strengths of the business's products and the weaknesses of competitors' products.

Figure 3 *Caffè Nero growth*

Caffè Nero Group Plc founded in only 1997 was, by 2004, the largest independent coffee retailer in the UK, with over 198 outlets. This expansion has come from setting up new outlets, and buying competitors' outlets.
- March 2001 – Raises £7.5m from Stock Exchange flotation to fund expansion.
- Feb. 2001 – Buys 26 of its Aroma coffee bars from McDonald's for £3.5m, taking the Caffè Nero chain to more than 100.
- June 2001 – Opens first coffee bar at easyInternet Cafe's High Street Kensington branch in London.
- Aug. 2002 – Aimed to open up to four coffee bars a month over the next 12 months, having secured a new £7m funding facility.
- Feb. 2003 – Announces plans to expand its chain of 111 coffee bars to 125 during 2004.
- Sept. 2003 – Announces plans to expand its chain of 131 coffee bars to 150 by January 2004 and to 300 within five years. Target increased to 400 in Feb. 2004.
- June 2004 – acquired eight stores in the south of England from Coffee Republic for £0.7m, taking its chain to 171 sites.

Source: adapted from www.caffenero.com.

Quality goods and services

For many businesses the quality of the good produced or service provided will determine how successful they are. This is especially true in competitive markets. Being ranked as the best in the business is a very powerful marketing factor.

Many businesses achieve this aim through modifying and improving their products. Others achieve this through branding their products. If the branding is very strong there will be no other business in the market and their product will therefore, automatically, be the best. Branding is discussed in section 32.

For example, the Soil Association checks UK farms to ensure a farm that claims to be producing organic arable or livestock products meets the customers' expectations. Its requirements are the highest in the world. Aberhyddnant Farm in the Brecon Beacons National Park is an example or a farm that sticks rigidly to this standard as it produces organic beef and lamb. Some objectives needed to achieve quality products are shown in Table 4. Figure 4 shows how Denby Pottery ensures quality.

Table 4 *Quality goods and servcies*

Business aim	Typical objectives needed to meet that aim
Better quality goods and services	Carry out market research to find out what customers really want.
	Carry out research and development into new products.
	Set internal minimum quality standards.
	Seek external recognition of quality as with the BS 7000 and ISO 9000.
	Provide customers with fast and effective solutions whenever products fail to match their expected quality.

Figure 4 *Denby Pottery quality*

- Started in 1806 because of the quality of the clay at Denby in Derbyshire.
- Expanded through its international reputation for quality bottles and jars.
- As glass production became cheaper Denby changed to producing quality kitchenware.
- In the 1930s Denby introduced classic giftware ranges.
- In the 1950s Denby changed to producing high quality tableware, employing the best designers.
- In the 1970s Denby introduced its revolutionary oven-to-tableware.
  Why is Denby unique? Its mark of quality is shown through:
- versatile and stylish tableware for entertaining and everyday use;
- distinctive shapes and rich colours to create a unique look;
- practical tableware that goes from the oven to the table - effortlessly;
- the highest standards of English craftwork for nearly 200 years;
- exceptionally durable and safe for use in the oven, microwave, freezer or dishwasher.

Source: adapted from www.denbypottery.co.uk.

Improving the corporate image

Corporate image is about how a business is seen by its customers and the general public. In today's highly competitive world of business it is often not enough just to have a high quality product available at a competitive price. More and more, customers are beginning to question how businesses behave and how what they do affects not just their direct customers, but also society, the environment and their employees. Businesses need to provide good publicity and avoid negative publicity.

Businesses use the following ways to ensure a positive public image.
- Having environmentally friendly products and methods of production.
- Treating employees fairly, with no discrimination.
- Contributing to charity.
- Supporting the local community through sponsorship.
- Providing customers with top of the range products at a fair price.
- Becoming the market leader that all other businesses try to copy.

Some objectives needed to improve corporate image are shown in Table 5. Figure 5 shows how Red Bull has attempted to improve its image.

Table 5 *Corporate image*

Business aim	Typical objectives needed to meet that aim
Improving the corporate image	Create a meaningful corporate aim in the form of a mission statement.
	Assess the general public's expectations of the business.
	Ensure all government requirements in terms of environmental, social and ethical standards are met and surpassed.
	Raise public awareness of the business through press releases and sponsorships.
	Engender a feeling of corporate identity in all members of staff.

Survival

For some businesses survival can become the most important aim. This can occur as the business is first launched into a competitive market and struggles to make a name for itself against established competitors. It also regularly happens to established businesses and even very well known ones. There are many reasons why demand for a business's products might decline and make survival the primary aim.

- Out of date products.
- The entry into the market of major competitors.
- A downturn in the business cycles.
- Negative publicity about the business or its products.
- Poor management of costs.

Some objectives needed to achieve survival are shown in Table 6. Table 7 shows the number of incorporated companies closing in Great Britain over a six month period. Mainly these are companies which have failed to meet their primary aim of survival. There are even more sole trader businesses that had to close in the same period.

Figure 5 *Red Bull's sponsorship and corporate image*

On the 6th March 2005 Red Bull hit a major part of the sporting big time as Red Bull Racing competed in Formula 1 for the first time. Scotsman David Coultard secured 4th place in the first race of the season, but the smaller events have not been forgotten.

From the 5th to 10th of April the Zed Rooms at The Old Truman Brewery in East London will be hosting the 'Red Bull Art of Can' exhibition. Here 'cans will imitate art'. The entries will be displayed for a week and judged by artist Tracey Emin, presenter Sara Cox, art critic Nick Hackworth and fashion designers Basso & Brooke.

Source: adapted from http://www.redbull.co.uk/ which shows the ranges of events that Red Bull supports.

Examination practice · Dasani

Dasani was launched by Coca-Cola in the UK in 2004 to offer a healthy alternative to their standard Coca-Cola products. It boasted pure water based on a 'highly sophisticated purification system'.

The press then reported that the water was simply being piped in from Thames water, put through a similar purification system to that found in many houses and the price being raised from 0.03p/litre to 95p/litre. Bromide was then added and oxidised into bromate at twice the legal limit, making it very much less healthy than ordinary tap water.

Coca-Cola had to recall all of the bottles of Dasani but claimed that the incident would not affect the brand name of Dasani or Coca-Cola.

Source: adapted from various sources.

(a) **Suggest an aim which Coca-Cola was trying to achieve by launching Dasani. Justify your answer.** (3 marks)

(b) **Suggest another aim which Coca-Cola should have been trying to achieve, yet failed to achieve. Explain your answer.** (3 marks)

(c) **This incident affected the reputation of Coca-Cola in the UK. List and justify actions that the company should have taken in order to ensure that its reputation would not have been affected in the long run.** (6 marks)

(d) **Explain the effects that this incident may have had on UK employees working in the Coca-Cola bottling plant.** (4 marks)

Table 6 *Survival*

Business aim	Typical objectives needed to meet that aim
Survival	Establish the cause of the loss of sales.
	Reduce costs to allow effective competition.
	Secure long term financial backing.
	Change or improve the product if this is felt to be sub-standard.
	Implement an effective marketing strategy.

Table 7 *Company Liquidations (Great Britain)*

Month	Total
Jan 2005	1,104
Dec 2004	1,886
Nov 2004	1,324
Oct 2004	1,492
Sep 2004	1,367
Aug 2004	1,375
6 month total	**8,548**

Source: adapted from Companies House.

Meeting the assessment criteria

When Stuart Rose, Marks & Spencer's Chief Executive, looked at the problems of falling sales facing the company in 2004 he identified, amongst many other problems, that it has let rivals steal its core business.

His solution was that M&S needed to win back the 35 to 55 year-old women shoppers from cheaper clothes chains and supermarkets and that this should be done by getting the right goods on the shelves, in terms of style and quality, at the right price. For the food business he stressed that M&S needed to focus on quality and innovation as they had done in the past.

Source: adapted from *The Guardian*, July 2004.

(a) From Stuart Rose's comments identify **ONE** aim that M&S has for the future and list **TWO** objectives that would help to meet this aim. **(3 marks)**

Expected answers
- *Gain back market share from competitors (aim) – win back 35-55 year olds (objective) – set the right price (objective).*
- *Increase sales of food items (aim) – ensure quality is what customers expect (objective) – find new innovative products (objective).*

Mark allocation
1 mark for identifying aim.
1 mark for each related objective. **(3 marks)**

(b) Stuart Rose identified rival firms stealing M&S's business as a major cause of the company's problems. How important, therefore, is it to:
(i) 'win back the 35 to 55 year old women shoppers'?
(ii) 'get the right goods in terms of style and quality'? **(6 marks)**

Expected answers
(i) *Rivals taking away core customers – the core customers are the 35 to 55 year old women so the problem is major – winning back these customers should, therefore, have a major positive effect on M&S's sales and profits.*
(ii) *M&S has lost customers because its styles and quality are not considered adequate by customers – supermarkets are making inroads on M&S's sales (e.g. George) – improving style and quality will help to make M&S appeal to its core customers so that they reject the competitors.*

Mark allocation
1 mark for recognising the problem (should be different for (i) and (ii)).
1 mark for quantifying the problem (it asked for 'how important').
1 mark for how the suggested strategy helps to solve the problem.
(1 + 1 + 1) x 3
(6 marks)

2 Types of ownership

Ownership

The aims and objectives that a business has will depend on a variety of factors. Some of these have been covered in section 1. The organisational structure and functions will be covered in sections 3 and 4. This section considers the effects of three main factors and also what impact they may have on such aspects as the size of the business. The three main factors are:

- what sector of industry the business is in;
- whether it is profit making, non-profit making or a not-for-profit business;
- what type of ownership it has.

Industrial sectors

Businesses in different sectors of industry operate in very different ways. Whilst most will share the same basic aims of making profits, increasing market share and survival some aims and many objectives will be different.

Primary Industry Primary industry is involved with directly using what nature has provided in order to produce goods.

- **Farming or agriculture.** The UK has a wide range of agricultural businesses including arable farming, livestock farming, organic farming and horticulture. All of these require use of land, so having the right kind of land, improving the land the business has and ensuring that is it not polluted, become vital objectives.

  For example, www.organicfarmfoods.co.uk states that 'The aim of every organic farmer is to produce the highest possible quality of food in optimum quantity and seeks to co-exist and work with nature rather than to dominate it'. Each of the needs shown in Table 1 will create its own objective for the business involved.

- **Fishing.** This covers two main sectors of business - sea fishing, for example in the North Sea, and fish farming, such as trout and salmon farms. The major requirements and objectives here include ensuring sufficient stocks for the future, reducing water pollution, working within EU restrictions on fishing and marketing the benefits of fish over other food.

Table 1 *Aims and objectives in primary industry*

Type of farming	Examples of aims and objectives
Arable	Good soil, good seeds, right climate, sufficient water.
Livestock	Good pedigree, correct feed, shelter, virus protection.
Organic	Unpolluted soil/livestock, customer awareness.
Horticulture	Fertile soil, local markets, new strains of plants.

- **Forestry.** Specific concerns here may be what type of trees to grow, as they grow at different rates and have widely differing values, what the market value will be in the future, as they take so long to grow, and what government support is available
- **Mining.** These tend to be large scale operations and ones that require high expenditure before anything is produced. Concerns may involve where the funds will come from, the effects of cheaper imports and what responsibilities the owners have when the mines are finally closed down.

Secondary Industry Secondary industry covers all manufacturing and construction businesses. Here businesses are using raw materials from the primary sector to produce a very wide range of goods. Businesses are likely to have different aims depending on what is being produced.

For example, in the highly competitive world of vacuum cleaners Dyson has, yet again, come up with another innovation, meeting its aim to stay ahead of the field. Instead of the conventional wheels, Dyson is using a single ball which is designed to make the vacuum cleaner easier to handle and to move into and out of confined spaces.

Some examples of industries are shown in Table 2.

Table 2 *Aims and objectives in secondary industry*

Type of industry	Examples of aims and objectives
Chemical industry	Ensuring harmful waste products are disposed of safely.
Car industry	Developing a cost effective alternative to petrol driven vehicles.
Tobacco industry	Diversifying into new non-tobacco products as smoking in public places is banned.
House building industry	Planning to build more smaller houses as the government raises the stamp duty threshold to £120,000.

Tertiary Industry Tertiary industry provides services to both the general public and to other businesses. This is now the largest sector of UK production and includes a very wide range of services' from personal services such as hairdressing and plumbing to major commercial services such as banking and retailing. Because the types of service being provided are so diverse, the aims and objectives are also often very different. Examples are given in Table 3.

The profit motive

Businesses can be divided into those that have profit as a major aim and those that do not.

Profit making businesses Many, if not most, businesses have the

Table 3 *Aims and objectives in tertiary industry*

Type of service	Examples of aims and objectives
Supermarkets	As essentially all of the goods are the same, the aim becomes providing a service that is significantly different to that of competitors.
Premier League Football teams	Qualifying for European competitions.
Computer services help lines	Providing accurate and rapid solutions to customers' problems.
Advertising agencies	Ensuring each business's message and image is put across effectively.

primary aim of making profits. These are called profit-making businesses. They include most of the well known businesses such as BP, Virgin, Sainsbury, British Telecom and HSBC. There are, however, two other major sections of business where making profit is either not an aim or it is only a way of reaching a more important aim.

Non-profit making businesses These orgnaisations have little or no interest in making profits, so this is not one of their aims. Their only concern, as far as profits are involved, is that they may need to make enough money to cover costs. Examples of these types of businesses include:

- local sporting clubs;
- most schools and colleges;
- charities;

Figure 1 *The Ramblers' Association objectives*

- Safeguarding Britain's unique network of public paths.
- Providing information to help you plan your walk and enjoy it in safety and comfort.
- Increasing access for walkers.
- Protecting the countryside and green spaces from unsightly and polluting developments.
- Educating the public about their rights and responsibilities and the health and environmental benefits of walking so that everyone can enjoy our wonderful heritage.

Source: adapted from www.ramblers.org.uk.

- interest groups, such as the Countryside Alliance.

With State funded businesses, such as schools, costs are paid by the State and nothing is being sold, so profit is irrelevant. Other businesses, such as local clubs, take in subscriptions to pay for providing the facilities and staff, but make no profits. This is done because they were set up for a more important reason. Local clubs are there to provide their members with leisure and recreation. Figure 1 shows an example of a non-profit making business organisation.

Not-for-profit businesses These are businesses that do make profits, but this is not for the benefit of the owners. Typical examples of this kind of business are charity shops, such as Oxfam, Scope and Age Concern.

Public and private sectors

One method of classifying business by ownership is into private and public sectors. Businesses can be classified by how they are owned. This has important effects on how the businesses are run and on their aims and objectives.

The public sector

State owned businesses should have the primary objective of providing goods or services that benefit the public. Examples are shown in Table 4.

Because the businesses are owned by the state it is the state that decides how they will be run and how they will be financed.

Table 4 *Aims of state owned businesses*

State owned business	Major aims
The National Health Service	'The aim of the Department of Health (DH) is to improve the health and wellbeing of people in England.'
Department for Education and Skills	'Our aim is to give children an excellent start in education enable young people to equip themselves with life and work skills, and encourage adults to achieve their full potential through learning.'
British Nuclear Fuels Limited (BNFL)	'To be trusted as a quality supplier to deliver safe, environmentally sound and profitable nuclear services and products.'
HM Treasury Aims and Objectives	'Aim: To raise the rate of sustainable growth and achieve rising prosperity and a better quality of life, with economic and employment opportunities for all.'
Copmanthorpe Parish Council	'Our aim: Your Parish Council is committed to retaining our traditional village life and representing the whole village in matters that affect us all.'

Figure 2 *Private and public sector ownership*

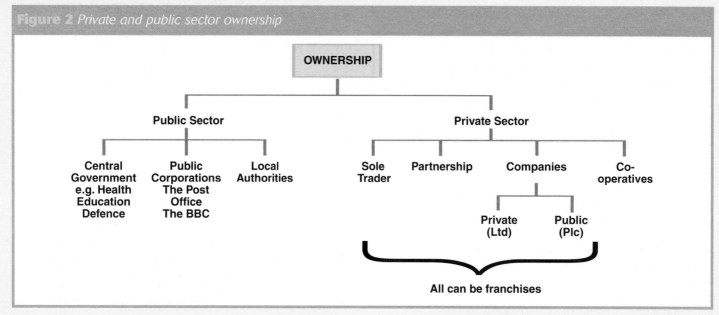

Most schools, for example, are financed by money that has come from central government and has been passed first to the Local education authorities and then to the schools and colleges themselves. How much an individual school will get is decided by government, as is the general way in which it can be spent.

Public private partnerships

In the past many major sections of UK industry were owned by the state including gas, electricity, coal, railways, telephones and steel. Today most of these are in the private sector. However, there are also many examples where the state still owns the business but produces in partnership with private companies. These can be found in education, the health service and in the transport system.

Where these partnerships exist there will be different aims for each of the partners. The public sector part is interested in providing services that benefit the general public and the private sector part will be interested in making profits. If the partnership works, both aims can be achieved through efficient production and the reduction of costs.

For example, in the 1990s London Underground was unable to cover all of its costs and important investments of up to £1.2 billion had not been made. In 1998 the government announced a Public Private Partnership (PPP) through which the track, signalling, bridges, tunnels, lifts, escalators, stations and trains would be transferred to three private companies. Contracts were signed in 2002 with Tube Lines and in 2003 with Metronet. Publicly owned London Underground Ltd has overall responsibility for the underground system and has, as its major aim, 'To perform to the highest possible standard, and to deliver a world-class Tube service for the three million customers who rely on us each and every day'.

The private sector

The aims and objectives of both public and private sector businesses will be determined by certain basic factors. These include how they are owned, how many owners there are, how they are financed and how much money is available, how easy it is to set them up, how they are controlled and what risks are involved in running the business and hence whether limited liability status is needed.

Sole traders These are businesses owned by one person. They tend to be, but do not have to be, small businesses. Typical sole traders are shown in Table 5.

Table 5 *Examples of sole traders*

- Window cleaners
- Minicab drivers
- Mobile hairdressers
- Stallholders
- Writers
- Farmers
- Plumbers
- Artists

The owner has complete control over the business so the aims and objectives tend to reflect his or her personal interests. These may be expansion, survival, or providing the best customer services. But they may also be simply working for oneself without unwanted pressures. As sole traders usually have limited financial backing some aims may be out of reach, such as becoming a multinational business, and some may only be possible in the long run.

Partnerships These are businesses where two or more people, usually to a maximum of twenty people, own the business together. They are not, however, companies. Typical partnerships are shown in Table 6.

Table 6 *Examples of partnerships*

- Doctors
- Architects
- Solicitors
- Dentists
- Estate agents
- Stockbrokers

With more and more risks involved in running business, many firms are now becoming companies in order to benefit from limited liability. Businesses that remain as partnerships tend to provide services, where they are not likely to run up heavy debts. They may not, therefore, need the protection of limited liability although some large accountancy firms may become limited liability partnerships. Aims are likely to include:

- providing customers with high quality services;
- ensuring that partners' funds in the business are safeguarded;
- expanding through efficiency and a good reputation.

Companies Companies can be **private limited companies (Ltd)** or **public limited companies (PLC)** but in both cases they are owned by private individuals, not the state. Both types of companies are set up through Companies House in London (http://www.companies-house.gov.uk/). Companies are treated by the law like individuals, which is why the companies and not the owners will have claims against them for debt. The owners have **limited liability**.

Companies frequently have owners who do not actually run the business, so a major aim is to protect the owners' investments and make them increase in value.

Control in companies is generally decided by how many shares a shareholder has, usually one vote per share. Major decisions, such as taking over other businesses, selling off parts of the business, or changing from a national to an international or even global business are usually put to all the shareholders for them to vote on. They will, therefore, be creating new aims together.

When registering with the Registrar of Companies these businesses have to complete Articles and Memorandum of Association documents. In the Memorandum the company must state, in the object clause, what type of business it will be involved in. This provides a basic aim for the business and it will not be allowed to do anything that is not listed in the object clause.

Private limited companies (Ltd) These are usually owned by one or a small number of shareholders. Shares can only be sold privately so the owners have control over what can happen to the business. Many small businesses which have high levels of raw materials or make products over a long period of time before they sell them may be private companies because of the danger of getting into debt and having to sell personal possessions in order to pay for them. Examples of private limited companies are shown in Table 7.

Many private companies are owned by just two people and frequently one of the owners has most of the shares. It is also possible to have single owners of companies. With these two types of company, the single, or main, owner will set the aims and objectives. With larger private companies the major shareholders will work together to set the objectives.

Table 7 *Examples of private limited companies*

• Builders	• Garden centres
• Local grocery stores	• Merchant banks
• Local garages	• Large farms

Public limited companies (PLC) These are called 'public' because any member of the general public can buy shares in the company. The general public can do this because the company's shares are available to buy on the Stock Exchange. There are some fairly small companies, in terms of capital value and turnover, on the Stock Exchange, but most PLCs are very large companies and generally ones that are very well known, as shown in Table 8.

Table 8 *Examples of public limited companies*

Company	Industry
Barclays	Banking
British Oxygen Company (BOC)	Chemicals
Dixons	General retailing
Tate & Lyle	Food processing
Weatherspoons	Leisure & hotels
Rio Tinto Zinc	Mining
Vodafone	Telecommunications
easyJet	Transport
Severn Trent Water	Utilities

For these very large companies the major shareholders can be other companies. These other companies include insurance businesses, investment businesses, such as unit trusts, and pension companies. The major reason why these companies buy shares on the Stock Exchange is to generate funds so that they can pay out insurance claims, give their customers the increase in value on their investments that they promised and pay pensioners what the promised as they retire.

To achieve this they need profits because this provides an income for them. They also need capital gains because this means their shares will be worth more when they sell them. Where these **institutional investors** have a major part of the shares, the PLCs have to set, as major aims, high profit levels and an increase in the capital value of the business.

There is a significant number of PLCs which are so powerful that they can ignore their individual shareholders and set their own aims and objectives. Usually these businesses have aims that include:

- being the market leader;
- capturing market share;
- taking over other businesses in the same market or forcing them to close;
- moving from national to international to multinational;.
- cutting costs in order to increase profits;
- establishing a good public image.

Franchises A **franchise** is a contractual agreement between two businesses. It is not a separate form of ownership. All franchises are sole traders, or partnerships or companies. The **franchisor** is a business which has an idea to sell to other businesses. The **franchisee** is a business that wants to use this idea and is willing to pay the franchisor for the right to use their name and idea. Well known franchises are shown in Table 9.

Table 9 *Examples of franchises*

• McDonald's	• Dyno-rod
• Subway	• Cash Converters
• Prontaprint	• Thorntons

When a franchisee takes on a franchise, it agrees to run it in a particular way. This usually dictates what the main aims will be. For example, it could be to:

- promote the image of the franchise;
- maintain the quality expected by the franchisor;

- make sufficient profits to pay what is owed to the franchisor and what is a reasonable minimum for the franchisee;
- expand by taking on additional franchise units.

The franchisor will also have specific aims related to the nature of franchising, such as:

- providing advice and support, including financial support, for the franchisees;
- expanding through establishing new franchised outlets;
- maintaining and promoting the image of the franchise on a national and even international level.

Although Mothercare owns its own stores in the UK it has expanded internationally by selling franchises. The main aim is to 'work with its franchisees to build profitable retail businesses around the world'.

Co-operatives Co-operatives are businesses that are either owned by members who are workers or by members who are consumers. The first co-operative was the Fenwick Weaver Co-operative Society in 1769 although the Rochdale Pioneers Society in 1844 was the inspiration for many others. Now co-operatives can be found across the world. They follow certain basic principles.

- Membership is open and voluntary - all those who qualify for membership must be allowed to join.

- Equal control, by members only - one member one vote.
- Outside investors do not have control and receive only a limited return.
- Any profits distributed among members should be done so fairly.
- There are educational and social objectives, not just commercial ones.
- Co-operatives try to co-operate with each other.

These principles mean that co-operatives have very specific aims and objectives that make them different from other types of business. There are two main types of business co-operatives.

Worker or producer co-operatives These are companies that are owned and controlled by the people who work in them. They will still have profit as a major motive, but the profits will be shared by the workers rather than being given to outside shareholders who do not work in the business. Most of these co-operatives are private companies, but there are also partnerships.

Consumer or retail co-operatives These are businesses owned and controlled by members who are consumers. They were set up so that the people who were shopping would be charged a fair price for their goods. Prices were set at the same level as those of competitors, but any profits made were then given back to the members. Generally this was done on the basis of how much they had spent in the shop.

Figure 3 *Worker and retail co-operatives*

Sheffield Co-operative Development Group
South Yorkshire has a successful worker co-operative sector, employing nearly 200 people and a combined turnover of £4-5 million. Businesses include:

- Boat Builders and Chandlers;
- Computing Services;
- Contract Cleaning and Property Maintenance;
- General and Precision Engineering;
- Nursery Day Care;
- Pre-Cast Concrete;
- Printers and Typesetters;
- Theatre Groups and Actors' Agents;
- Wholefood Suppliers;
- Woodworkers.

The **Co-operative Group** is the largest retail co-operative in the UK, with all of the following retail outlets:

- over 1,700 food stores;
- over 380 branches of Travelcare arranging holidays.
- over 500 branches of Co-operative Funeralcare, the largest funeral business in the country;
- the Co-operative Bank, Co-operative Insurance Society (CIS) and 'Smile', the Internet bank;
- over 300 branches of Co-op Pharmacy.

Source: adapted from www.co-op.co.uk.

Examination practice · Dennis Publishing Ltd

Dennis Publishing Ltd is one of the world's leading independent publishers, publishing magazines such well known titles as *Auto Express, Bizarre, Maxim, Viz, Computer Buyer* and *Computer Shopper*. The company is privately owned and aims to deliver what customers and advertisers want, as well as demonstrating independence, risk–taking and innovation in its choice of magazines and its editorial approach. The company has consistently identified, launched and developed new titles, creating fresh markets and opportunities for advertisers.

The business started in 1974 in the UK and then joined with an American publisher. Group turnover has increased dramatically in the last few years, mainly in the USA.

Source: adapted from www.dennis.co.uk.

(a) **Does Dennis Publishing operate in the primary, secondary or tertiary sector of industry? Justify your answer.** **(2 marks)**

(b) **Explain what aim Dennis Publishing was most likely trying to achieve when it formed an agreement with an American Publisher.** **(2 marks)**

(c) **Explain why being a private limited company can help Dennis Publishing to remain independent, risk-taking and innovative.** **(9 marks)**

(d) **Every year staff vote for the seven most deserving employees who then receive an all expenses paid trip to the island of Mustique. Explain how this is likely to help the business to meet its objective of delivering what customers and advertisers want.** **(5 marks)**

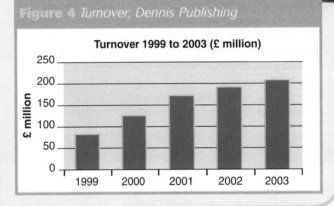

Figure 4 *Turnover, Dennis Publishing*

Meeting the assessment criteria

Trident Water Garden Products Ltd of Coventry is the world's largest manufacturer of water garden products, such as pumps, pond liners and filters. The business exports to twenty three countries around the world.

The company's stated aim is to manufacture 'products of the highest quality using only first-class components and state of the art technology'. All products and services are supported by a dedicated after sales and technical support team.

Source: adapted from www.tridentwatergarden.com.

(a) Which major sector of industry does this business operate in? **(1 mark)**

Expected answers
• *Secondary.*
• *Manufacturing.*

Mark allocation
1 mark for identifying sector. **(1 mark)**

(b) This business is a private limited company. Considering what it produces, why would it be important for Trident to have limited liability? **(4 marks)**

Expected answers
• *Limited liability will limit the debts of the owners (term) – the company is manufacturing (what is produced) – it will make goods before it can sell them (situation) – it could, therefore, run up large debts and not sell anything (why needed).*

• *Making pumps and filters (product) costs a lot of money (situation) and the company is likely to spend money producing the pumps before it gets paid (situation) – it might therefore make a loss and need protection if it is sued (implied term).*

Mark allocation
1 mark for showing understanding of the term (may be implied).
1 mark for identifying what is being produced.
1 mark for why limited liability is needed because of the product/or business situation (maximum 2 marks). **(4 marks)**

(c) The stated aim of the company is to manufacture products of the highest quality using only first-class components and state of the art technology. List **TWO** objectives that would help to make sure that this overall aim was met. For each objective state why it would help to meet the overall aim. **(4 marks)**

Expected answers
• *Check all products to ensure there are no faults – faults will be identified and corrected so only highest quality products will be sold.*
• *Identify suppliers who produce high quality components – this should ensure that when used in pumps or filters they do not fail.*
• *Ensure continuous research into new production techniques – will help to improve quality as new technologies are developed.*

Mark allocation
1 mark for objective.
1 mark for how this helps aim.

(1 + 1) x 2
(4 marks)

3 Business functions

Functions and departments

Understanding the difference between the terms **functions** and **departments** is important, although sometimes people use the terms as though they were the same thing and often the major functions are the names given to the departments.

The **functions** of a business are what are carried out in order to make and sell products. Producing, financing and selling are all functions.

Departments are the names given to the different sections of a business, such as Production, Finance and Marketing. These departments are carrying out the function of the business.

Frequently a department is responsible for a particular function in a business, but this is not always the case. Some functions, such as administration, can be found in most departments. In small businesses more than one major function is often carried out by just one department.

There is a number of major functions that need to be carried out by nearly all successful businesses. These are shown in Figure 1.

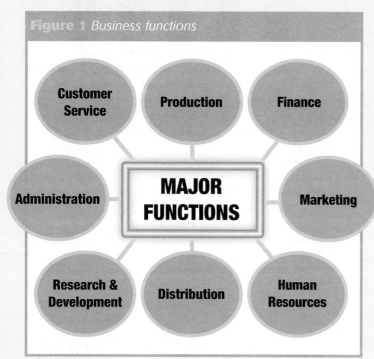

Figure 1 *Business functions*

Production

Production is the process of combining factors (inputs) together so that a product is made (output). This product might be a good, such as a car, or a service, such as banking. This is shown in Figure 2.

The actual inputs will depend on what is being produced and this will vary significantly depending on whether goods or services are being produced and what sector of industry the business is in.

Examples are given below of different production processes from inputs to the final product. At each stage value is being added.

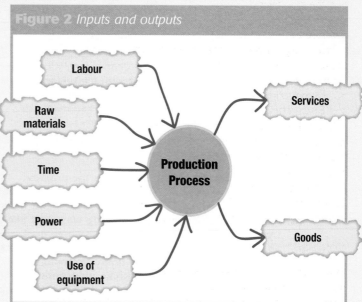

Figure 2 *Inputs and outputs*

Dairy farmer Inputs (cattle feed, straw, tractors, farm labourers) ⇨ breeding cattle ⇨ milking the cows ⇨ storing milk in churns ready for collection by the dairy.

Pottery manufacturer Inputs (clay, labour, electricity) ⇨ making clay into pottery ⇨ painting and decorating pottery ⇨ firing the pottery in kilns ⇨ packing pottery ready for wholesalers and retailers.

House builder Inputs (wood, bricks, cement, cement mixers) ⇨ digging out and making the foundations ⇨ building the basic structure out of breeze blocks, bricks and wood ⇨ fitting the floors and ceilings ⇨ installing the plumbing and electrics ⇨ plastering, painting and decorating.

Clothes retailer Inputs (labour, stocks of clothes) ⇨ Placing clothes on display ⇨ Serving customers.

Banker Inputs (Labour, stationery, use of telephones, money transfer systems) ⇨ providing services for saving and borrowing money ⇨ allowing customers to pay in or take out money ⇨ transferring money from one account to another ⇨ advising customers on the bank balances ⇨ providing a range of other financial services.

Human Resources/Personnel

Human Resources (Personnel) management is the function of managing the employees of a business and will include:
- recruitment;
- training;
- retention;
- appraisal and monitoring performance;
- dismissal;
- ensuring the laws relating to employment are followed.

It is important that human resources are managed to meet needs. For example, in March 2005 *The Herald*, reported that

Sainsbury's improvement coincided with the recruitment of 3,000 extra staff in order to address customer complaints about poor product availability.

Marketing

It is the employees who produce the goods or services and they will feature in all of the functions. However, it is not just enough to produce the products. They must also be marketed.

Marketing is a very diverse function because it deals with all aspects of identifying who a product should be targeted at through market research, to how to promote and sell the product that has been produced. It also applies to all organisations, e.g. businesses and government.

In 2004, for example, a number of businesses ran successful marketing campaigns aimed at students. They included Endsleigh, NatWest, STA Travel, Red Bull, Malibu, *The Guardian*, Barclaycard and Orange.

Marketing will involve all the elements in Figure 3. Marketing is covered in detail in Unit 3 of this textbook which explains why marketing is so important for businesses.

Finance

In the past the finance function tended to relate to providing monies for running the business and recording all transactions. Today the planning side of the finance function has become far more important. Finance can be divided into the following specific functions.

Management accounting This deals with company budgets and strategic planning, such as:
- preparing business plans;
- monitoring performance against set targets;
- suggesting ways in which the financial performance of the business can be improved;
- giving advice on how decisions in other departments, e.g. production or marketing, will affect the business financially.

Financial accounting This deals with the keeping of the business's financial records, such as:
- keeping records of all financial transactions in the business;
- monitoring cash flow;
- ensuring that the accounts are managed correctly;
- checking that monies owed to and by the business are paid on time;
- checking customers' credit positions if customers are being offered credit.

Internal auditing This involves checking the finances of each department and how the departments are managing their finances.

Payments This includes:
- wages and salaries;
- calculation and payments of taxes;
- payments to suppliers.

Raising finance This includes:
- negotiating loans and overdrafts with the bank;
- dealing with government for grants and subsidies;
- establishing leasing agreements with other businesses;
- managing the profits of the business for re-investment;
- dealing with share issues.

Details of how many of these functions operate within a business are covered in unit 2.

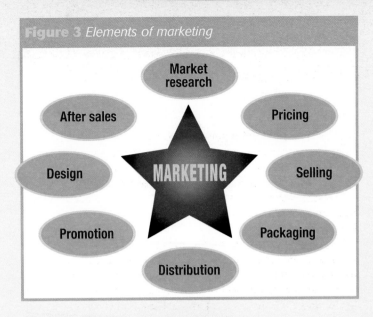

Figure 3 *Elements of marketing*

Research and Development

For many businesses the improvement of existing products or the creation of new products is vital for the expansion and even survival of the business. This is especially true of highly competitive markets where these innovations give a business a major competitive advantage.

The role of research and development is to look at actual products. The role of researching the market to find what customers want and where there may be new markets to sell into is a function of marketing. They are closely linked and marketing may be able to tell research and development what products will be worth developing.

For goods the research and development is likely to be technical, such as:
- making computers faster;
- manufacturing safer cars;
- building environmentally friendly houses;
- finding ways of growing vegetables that stay fresh longer;
- creating new media for recording music on.

For services the research and development is likely to be about how the service is delivered, such as:
- providing banking by phone or the Internet;
- offering air passengers no frills very cheap travel;
- supporting buyers of computers with a 24 hour helpline;
- providing gas, electricity and telephone services from a single supplier;
- offering customers an 'eat-all-you-can' option in a restaurant.

Some types of production, especially in the realm of new drugs, require very heavy investment in research and development as shown in Figure 4.

Administration

Administration is the management of services that help to support the smooth running of departments.

All departments will need administration and frequently this function will be carried out by the individual departments. In a larger business there is often a separate Administration Department. Either way, the following functions will be carried out somewhere in the business.

Figure 4 *Research and development spending (£ million)*

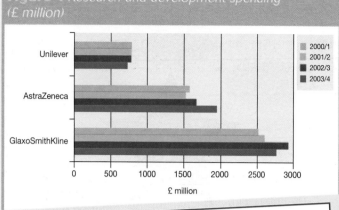

Company	Products
GlaxoSmithKline	Pharmaceuticals
AstraZeneca	Pharmaceuticals
Unilever	Food/homecare

Source: adapted from Dti.

- Reception - greeting people visiting the business, checking who they are and who they will be visiting, taking outside telephone calls and connecting people to the right departments.
- Receiving and distributing mail from outside.
- Security of the building, property and staff.
- Cleaning, maintenance and catering or arranging for outside contractors to carry out these jobs.
- Clerical work - making records and managing records, filing and photocopying.
- Organising meetings and keeping minutes.
- Internal communications, through post, intercoms, e-mails and memos.
- Monitoring staff - clocking staff in and checking pay against attendance.

Distribution and Logistics

For many businesses the efficient distribution of their products to their customers is so vital that it becomes a major aim and function. This function is now often referred to as 'logistics' and can be summarised as 'having the right thing, at the right place, at the right time'.

The Distribution Department will normally carry out all the following functions.
- Preparing packing lists of the goods to be moved.
- Packing the products into boxes, crates and then into lorries or vans.
- Working out delivery schedules, showing where and when goods are to be distributed.
- Delivering the goods if the business has its own vehicles or arranging for another firm to deliver them.
- Receiving any returned goods and dealing with replacements.
For example, it was reported in 2005 that New Look, the high street fashion retailer, would have its new, automated national distribution centre at Newcastle-Under-Lyme completed in the autumn. The centre would provide warehousing and transport and distribution to other 'outbases' located throughout the UK. The centre would respond to orders with automatic sorting and distribution to packing areas.

Customer services

All businesses need to ensure that their customers are being provided with good service. In many businesses this is considered so important that a separate Customer Services Department is set up. This is particularly important when the business is dealing with the general public.

Customer service is both internal and external.

Internal customer service This is about providing supportive services for the people who work in or own the business. Internal customers include:
- employees;
- managers;
- different departments;
- providers of internal services, such as catering;
- owners.

Each of these internal customers will require support which in many cases will come from existing departments as with appraisal and training for staff by the Human Resources Department, the setting up and running of meetings by Administration and the payment of profits to shareholders by the Finance Department.

External customer service This is about providing good service to people or organisations which are outside of the business. External customers include:
- individuals;
- families;
- other business customers;
- suppliers;
- the state and society.

The kinds of customer service that these external customers may expect include:
- a wide range of value for money products;
- good after sales care;
- prompt payments if they are suppliers;
- correct payments of taxes;
- production which does not harm the environment.

Other functions

In many businesses the functions described above are divided up and placed into their own departments. There will also be distinct and different functions that are needed because of the type of product being produced and the type of business involved.

For example, many businesses rely very heavily on **purchasing** large quantities of raw materials that are vital for their businesses and so they have created separate Purchasing Departments. Such businesses include:
- supermarkets;
- major chain stores;
- hospitals;
- the armed services.

Information and communication technology is now so common and important in business that setting up and running systems for the benefit of the business have become major functions in their own right. Many businesses also now have websites that need to be created and maintained.

How the business functions work together

For businesses to operate successfully all of the functions mentioned above need to work together and support each other. Typical links can be shown by tracing through how particular products are produced, as in Figure 5.

Figure 5 *Developing a new breakfast cereal*

- Market Research identified a gap in the market.
- R & D develops and trials the new product.
- Finance decides budgets for new product and provides funds.
- Marketing decides on a suitable price and where to sell the product.
- Sales representatives approach retailers with samples of the product.
- Human Resources arranges for training of staff to produce the new cereal.
- Production starts producing the new cereal.
- Marketing designs the packaging to appeal to customers.
- Distribution provides lorries for transporting products to retailers.
- Finance sends out invoices to retailers for payment.
- Marketing provides TV advertising to coincide with the launch.
- Customer Service contacts retailers to ensure they are happy with the product and the service.
- Finance and Marketing monitor the success of sales.

Table 1 shows other examples of when each function needs to work with another function. Details of the support from Administration have been given before.

Table 1 *Functions working together*

Function	Situation
Marketing & Production	Marketing will identify what Production needs to produce. Production will tell Marketing when the product will be ready for promotion campaigns.
Marketing & Finance	Marketing will inform Finance of likely level of sales. Finance will approve Marketing's promotional budget.
Finance & Production	Finance will pay for the raw materials and equipment. Production will monitor production costs and keep Finance informed.
Human Resources & Production	HR recruits employees for producing the goods or services. Production provides details of staff absences for HR.
Marketing & Human Resources	Marketing provides details on the likely size of new markets that will need staffing. HR provides training for new sales representatives.
Human Resources & Finance	HR provides Finance with details of all employees. Finance pays all employees.
R & D & Production	R & D provides Production with details of new products. Production runs trials on the new products.
Sales & Production & Distribution	Sales informs Production and Distribution when customers need products. Production informs Distribution when products are ready. Distribution delivers goods to customers.
Customer Services & other departments	Customer Services provides Marketing with customer feedback on in-store promotions, Production with details of complaints about products and HR with requests for training in handling difficult customers.
ICT & other departments	ICT provides web pages for Marketing, EDI facilities between branches so sales figures go direct to Finance, Staff databases for HR, CAD and CAM support and training for R & D and Production, and recording facilities so that Administration can check security.

Examination practice · Anthony Alan Foods Ltd

Anthony Alan Foods Ltd is the UK's leading supplier of low fat cakes and pastries, sold under the Weight Watchers brand. In 2005 it launched a brand new range of Weight Watchers savoury pastries, including Sausage Roll, Pork & Apple Roll, Cheese & Onion Slice and Chicken & Stuffing Slice. The new products were tested for satisfaction using consumer panels and then supported at their launch with extensive advertising. This successful launch was achieved with the full involvement of the company's highly trained and motivated staff at its Barnsley premises.

Source: adapted from www.aafoods.eu.com.

(a) From the data, describe how the marketing function would have been involved in the launch of the new Weight Watchers savoury range. (4 marks)

(b) Explain what contribution each of the following functions is likely to have made to the new savoury range of products.
(i) Research and development. (3 marks)
(ii) Finance. (3 marks)
(iii) Production. (3 marks)

(c) Explain how the fact that the staff at Anthony Alan Foods are highly trained and motivated will help the business to introduce this new range. (6 marks)

Meeting the assessment criteria

Ford's Halewood plant on Merseyside was totally modernised in the late 1990s, ready for production to switch from producing high-volume Escorts to the prestige Jaguars. More than £300 million was invested in the plant. Part of this modernisation was to prepare for the production and well publicised launch of the new V6 X-Type Jaguar. Workers also agreed to new working practices to help ensure that the plant was competitive.

In 2004 Jaguar took on 600 extra workers to help produce the X-Type. Of these 600 workers, some 200 were to be laid off in 2005, as they were only temporary workers. Half of these were offered re-deployment to the West Bromwich plant.

Source: adapted from various sources.

(a) Identify **THREE** major functions referred to in the data and say how each has helped to make the new Halewood plant a success. **(6 marks)**

Expected answers
* *Production – changing production from Escorts to Jaguars.*
* *Finance – providing £300 million for the modernisation.*
* *Marketing – publicising the launch of the X-Type Jaguar.*
* *Human Resources – recruiting 600 extra workers in 2004/negotiating new working practices with staff.*

Mark allocation
1 mark for each function.
1 mark for how that has helped the Halewood plant/production of Jaguar. **(1 + 1) x 3**
(6 marks)

(b) As part of the modernisation a rail terminal has been built nearby, which allows 90% of cars destined for export markets to leave the plant by rail rather than road. Explain how this will affect the Distribution Department. **(4 marks)**

Expected answers
* *Distribution will have to decide how cars get to customer – now 90% will go by train – less lorries will be needed – drivers may need to be laid off.*
* *Distribution needs to arrange transport – main method will now be by train – will need to buy/rent rail transporters – also need to keep some road transporters for the 10%.*
* *As most of the transport is now by rail – need to ensure that rail schedules are known – have cars ready to meet these schedules (understanding has been implied).*

Mark allocation
1 mark for showing understanding of the distribution function (may be implied).
1 mark for recognising changed situation.
1 mark for how Distribution will be affected (maximum 2 marks).
(4 marks)

(c) Explain how the fact that Jaguar cars are being exported will affect:
   (i) the Finance Department?
   (ii) the Marketing Department? **(4 marks)**

Expected answers
Finance
* *Dealing with different currencies – foreign buyers may wish to pay in their own currency.*
* *Should check what government support is available – exports receive specific help from the government/Export Credit Guarantees may be available.*
Marketing
* *Will need to work out appropriate prices – exports need to be priced in the other country's currency/prices need to be set in relation to the foreign country's income.*
* *Advert will need to be changed – export countries may have other languages/cultures/advertising laws.*

Mark allocation
1 mark for how affected.
1 mark for why that comes from exporting. **(1 + 1) x 2**
(4 marks)

4 Organisational structures & job roles

Organisational structures

This section examines the way in which businesses are structured and the major job roles in those structures. Section 3 explained that businesses have various functions that need to be carried out. These often become the responsibility of specific departments, with the different parts of the main function being divided up within that department. Specific roles and responsibilities are given to different sections and people within each department. As the business makes these divisions into departments, it is creating a structure through which the functions of the business operate.

These structures can be divided in various ways, as in Figure 1, although the main one is often division by function. The usual way of showing how the structure of a business is divided is through an **organisation chart**. This shows the structure in the form of a diagram.

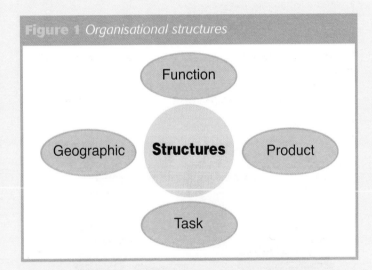

Figure 1 *Organisational structures*

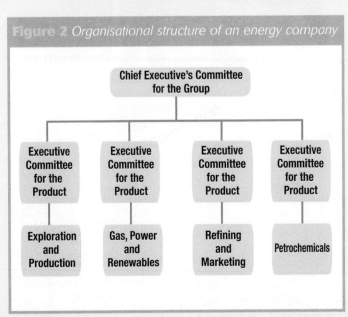

Figure 2 *Organisational structure of an energy company*

Division by product

Where businesses produce a range of very different products they are sometimes divided in terms of these products. The basic break-down for an energy company by product is shown in Figure 2. Division by product allows the business as a whole to pass over the running of the individual sections to managers who are experts in those types of production.

Geographical division

Many businesses have production units in different parts of the country and even in different parts of the world. Often these businesses will divide their operations on a geographical basis. This allows the managers in the different regions to run the production in the areas where they are, rather than having it run by managers who are a long way away.

For example, Arts & Business (A&B) is a not-for-profit business set up to promote links between business and the arts. It runs, events, seminars and training throughout its 18 offices which are divided by region across the UK. Its structure is shown in Figure 3.

Figure 3 *Regional structure for Arts & Business*

Division by function

Even where there is a basic division by product or geographical area, it is still normal for the business's activities to be further divided by function. This also involves levels of authority, showing who is in charge of whom and who is responsible to whom.

Three basic structures are common in business – flat, tall or hierarchical and matrix.

Flat structures These are ones where there are very few levels in the way the business is structured, usually only two, but never more than three. A flat structure shows that the manager, in small businesses often the owner, is directly linked to the staff. Because of this there are certain characteristics that flat structures are

likely to have.
- The business is likely to be fairly small, otherwise it would be difficult for the manager to deal with everyone at the lower level.
- Communications are likely to be good because the manager is in direct contact with the staff.
- The direct contact with management is likely to make control more friendly and less formal.
- The cost of management is likely to be fairly low because there is only one level of management.
- The burden of management falls on only one person.

Tall structures These tend to have a minimum of three levels and frequently have more. A tall structure separates the senior managers from the staff at the bottom of the structure and this also leads to certain characteristics.
- The business is likely to be fairly large, otherwise there is no point in creating many layers of management.
- Communications between one level and the next may be good because each person is likely to be dealing with only a few people below them. Communication from the top of the structure to the bottom can, however, be poor because of the number of stages involved.
- Control and decision making is likely to be very formal with each person having clearly set out responsibilities and authority. This can lead to a less friendly working environment.
- The cost of management as a whole may be high because there are so many levels.
- Each person in the organisation will have a distinct role and this will allow people to specialise in what they are best at.
- There is usually a clear route for promotion and this may act as an incentive to work hard.

These tall structures are usually **hierarchical** because they also place staff in different grades, with the major decisions being made at the top and lesser decisions being made at lower levels.

The span of control This refers to how many people someone in the structure is directly responsible for. It is estimated that a span of control of more than six people starts to become inefficient in terms of managing what they are doing. Typical narrow and wide structures would be as shown in Figure 6.

Figure 5 *Hierarchy in an organisational structure*

Board of Directors
Senior Management
Department Manager
Department Deputy Managers
Supervisors
General Staff

Control greatest at the top
Responsibility greatest at the top
Decisions passed down from the top
Communications up and down

Figure 4 *Flat and tall organisational structures*

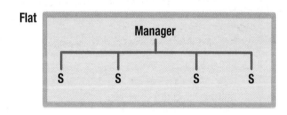

Flat

Manager
S S S S

Tall

Manager
Assistant Manager
S S S S S S S S   S S S S S S S S

S = member of staff

Figure 6 *Span of control*

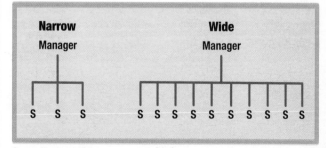

Narrow
Manager
S S S

Wide
Manager
S S S S S S S S

S = member of staff

Figure 7 *Matrix structures*

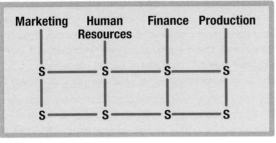

Figure 7 *Matrix structures*

| Marketing | Human Resources | Finance | Production |

S = member of staff

Matrix structures A matrix structure is one that allows the business to operate across different levels of authority and across different functions. When decisions need to be made, a group of people work together to decide what is best for the business. It is called a matrix structure because everyone in the structure is linked to everyone else in the structure. This is shown for four main departments and two levels of staff in Figure 7.

Often these groups are formed to look after one particular product, project or section of the business. Such groups are known as **project groups** or **task groups** as in Figure 8. Where the aim of the group is to look at the quality of the product and try to find ways of improving it, they are known as a **quality circle**.

Matrix structures tend to have the following characteristics.

- Although the main control still rests with senior management many important decisions are made lower down the structure.
- Work is often carried out in teams with members jointly making decisions.
- Decisions may take longer to be reached.
- Because all staff are involved in the making of important decisions the staff may be more motivated and may work harder for the business.
- Communication takes place directly between all levels in the business.

Major job roles

This section will look at only the major job roles, some of which have been shown in the organisation charts above. It will not deal with specific job roles, which vary considerably from business to

Figure 8 *Task groups*

Finance Manager
R&D Manager
Production Manager
Marketing Manager
TASK
Human Resources Manager
Marketing Staff
R&D Staff
Production Staff
Finance Staff

Figure 9 *Advertisements for jobs roles*

Sales & Marketing Director

As a member of the leadership team reporting to the Managing Director, you will be responsible for developing and implementing the commercial strategy, including the creation of a professional sales and marketing team focused on achieving and sustaining profitable growth.

DISTRICT MANAGER

As a District Manager, you will be responsible for the activities of about ten of our stores, providing leadership to all the store managers within your district and ensuring standards are maintained and store expenses are kept to the agreed budget. You will also get involved with the merchandising of your stores, the training of staff and will oversee all loss prevention policies.

STORE MANAGER

Each Superstore has a Store Manager in charge. His or her role covers both operational effectiveness and team leadership. Because of the diversity in each store, we always need Section Managers for areas such as fresh food, produce, deli, dairy, bakery, café and stock control and Non-Food Managers to supervise and motivate staff in everything from clothing to cook shops. Every Superstore also employs Customer Service Managers, Personnel Managers and experienced specialists in a number of other areas to ensure that the whole operation runs smoothly right round the clock.

Stock Supervisor

Join us as a Stock Supervisor and you will be responsible for ensuring all our shelves are full to ensure every customer is truly satisfied. From day one you will enjoy the responsibility of leading others to deliver exceptional customer service.

Payroll Supervisor

Main responsibilities. To supervise and develop the payroll team. To ensure the monthly payroll and associated procedures, meet all required deadlines, accuracy and quality targets. To monitor, evaluate and develop internal payroll procedures. To manage implementation of new systems and procedures when these occur. To provide management information and payroll administration for the practice.

business and nor will it look at the major job roles in terms of specific functions, i.e. it will look at the role of the manager rather than the role of, say, a Marketing Manager.

The following roles will be considered, with examples - directors, managers, supervisors, professional staff, operatives and general staff. Examples of advertisements for these job roles are shown in Figure 9.

Directors Directors are appointed by the shareholders of a business. Their primary function is to ensure that the business is being run for the benefit of shareholders - the owners. Where there are more than just one or two directors they will meet and make decisions about the business as the Board of Directors. Major decisions in the business, ones which have a major impact on the shareholders, will be decided by the Board, or put to the shareholders by the Board for them to vote on.

Some directors, called Executive Directors, will be involved in running the business, although the day-to-day running of a business is the responsibility of the managers. Others take very little part in running the business and are non-executive directors. Some of these are appointed simply so that the business can say that it has someone famous as part of the business.

Managers Managers are the people who run businesses and make most of the important decisions. Where directors make decisions about how the business should be run and instruct other people what to do, they are also acting as managers.

It can sometimes be difficult to identify exactly what management involves because it can, and does, operate at many different levels within a business. A major national business may well have all of the following managerial roles.

- Managing Director – who manages all of the other directors.
- Executive Director – who will manage one aspect of the business on behalf of the shareholders.
- District or Regional Manager – who will be responsible for all branches in a certain area.
- Branch or Store Manager – who will be responsible for the operation of a specific branch.
- Departmental Manager – in charge of a specific function or major department such as marketing or finanace.

Department Manager – in charge of a section of the business within the branch, e.g. food, bakery, restaurant, clothes.

Managers will be in charge of staff and responsible for what they do. They will also generally be in charge of financial budgets and decide how these will be allocated and used. It will be managers who decide many of the policies and strategies of the business.

Supervisors Supervisors also have a management role, but at a lower level than the senior managers. They will be in charge of a particular department or unit and the staff that work in there. In some businesses these junior roles are described as supervisors and in others they are still referred to as managers.

Professional staff Professional staff are those staff who have been trained or have qualifications in a particular profession. In the past this applied to jobs in which academic skills were expected or ones which require a long period of apprenticeship. Examples of jobs are shown in Table 1. Today many more jobs require specific qualifications, skills or training, Examples of such jobs are also shown in Table 1.

Professional staff tend to be respected because of their qualifications and skills and they tend to be fairly well paid. Most professions also have a hierarchy through which staff rise because they have gaining additional qualifications, have greater experience, and sometimes simply by staying with the business long enough.

Operatives Operatives are skilled workers, especially in industry. Some of the skills require basic qualifications, others require experience, but many will be taught on-the-job. Examples include:

- Installation Operative – tasks could include unpacking and assembling the equipment in Hospitals, Health Centres, Clinics, Care Centres, Schools and Colleges and also at customers' homes.
- IT Helpdesk Operative – tasks could include taking and logging support calls, performing appropriate diagnostics on operating systems and referring complex issues where necessary.
- Production Operative (textiles) – tasks could include producing high quality cloth on rapier looms and replacing the cones for weft as required.
- Warehouse Operative – tasks could include dealing with goods in/out, picking, packing, and despatch as well as having a licence to drive both counter balance and reach forklifts.

General staff In many businesses there are also staff who have no specific skills or qualifications when they enter the business. With training they gain skills and are able to perform their duties effectively and gain promotion to more senior jobs, such as operatives, supervisors and managers.

Examples of general staff positions in retaling and in other industries are shown in Table 2.

Table 1 *Traditional and modern professionals*	
Traditional professionals	
• Doctors	• Dentists
• Nurses	• Barristers
• Architects	• Teachers
• Solicitors	• Stockbrokers
• Accountants	• Printers
• Army Officers	• Pilots
Modern professionals	
• Broadcasters	• Chefs
• Landscape gardeners	• Plumbers
• Footballers or golfers	• Prison warders

Table 2 *General staff*	
Retailing	
• Shelf stackers	• Waiters
• Checkout staff	• Cleaners
• Shop floor staff	• Receptionists
• Bar staff	• Paper delivery staff
Other industries	
• Farm labourers	• Road sweepers
• General building labourers	• Refuse collectors
• Leaflet deliverers	• Market research interviewers

Examination practice · Chesterham Golf Club

Table 3 shows a list of the staff working at Chesterham Golf Club.

Table 3 *Job roles at Chesterham Golf Club*

Housekeeper	Front House Supervisor	Housekeeper	Gardener
Barperson	Housekeeper	Operations Manager	Receptionist
Chef	PGA Golf Professional	Waiter	Head Chef
Trainee Manager	Front House Supervisor	Gardener	Business Director
Managing Director	Admin. Manager	Head Housekeeper	Function Supervisor
Waiter	Farm and Golf Director	Chef	Greenkeeper
Head Greenkeeper	Kitchen Domestic	Head Receptionist	Chef
Restaurant Manager	Chef	Marketing Director	

Source: adapted from author research.

(a) Choosing an appropriate structure, draw an organisation chart to include all of the listed staff. **(8 marks)**

(b) From Table 3 identify TWO different examples of each of the following job roles.
 (i) Professional staff.
 (ii) General staff. **(4 marks)**

(c) From Table 3 select ONE example of each of the following job roles.
• Directors.
• Managers.
• Supervisors.
• Explain what each job role selected is likely to involve. **(6 marks)**
(ii) Explain how the roles will differ because they are referred to as directors, managers, or supervisors. **(4 marks)**

Meeting the assessment criteria

The organisation chart in Figure 10 is a fairly typical chart for a secondary school. Figure 10 shows part of the structure.

(a) (i) Explain why this organisation would be described as hierarchical. **(2 marks)**

Expected answers
• *Hierarchical structures have many levels – chart shows up to 8 levels.*
• *Hierarchy suggests levels of authority/status – here there are heads and deputies, etc.*

Mark allocation
1 mark for showing meaning of term.
1 mark for explanation related to the chart. **(2 marks)**

(ii) Using appropriate examples, explain how being hierarchical would affect the way in which the school was run. **(5 marks)**

Expected answers
• *What schools must teach is dictated by government (authority) shown by being at top of the structure (hierarchy) – examples include Maths, English and ICT (example).*
• *Head of Department in charge of a specific subject area (authority) – Departments have deputies and subject teachers (hierarchy) – Head of Department will decide who teaches which classes (example).*

Mark allocation
1 mark for recognising the authority element (may be implied).
1 mark for example (maximum 2 marks).
1 mark for how that shows the hierarchy (maximum 2 marks).
(1 + 2 + 2) 5 marks)

(b) Using appropriate examples, explain when staff on the curriculum side of the organisation would need to communicate with staff on the pastoral side.

(3 marks)

Expected answers
* *When writing reports - subject staff will write reports - form tutors will collate them/discuss overall reports with students.*
* *When there has been a disciplinary incident in class - subject teacher will report to form tutor/head of year - form tutor/head of year will contact parents.*

Mark allocation
1 mark for situation.
1 mark for why each side would need to be involved (2 marks).

(3 marks)

(c) Which job role listed on the chart does not require professional staff? Justify your answer. **(2 marks)**

Expected answers
* *School Governor – No specific qualification is required/they are not staff in the school.*

Mark allocation
1 mark for role.
1 mark for justification.

(2 marks)

(d) Give TWO examples of administrative tasks that would be carried out by the school office and explain how each of these could help teachers.

(4 marks)

Expected answers
* *Photocopying – providing class copies of exercises.*
* *Manning telephones – teachers able to ring in and arrange cover if they are late.*
* *Collecting and banking money for trips – allows teachers to concentrate on planning the trips.*

Mark allocation
1 mark for each task.
1 mark for how that helps teachers.

**(1 + 1) x 2
(4 marks)**

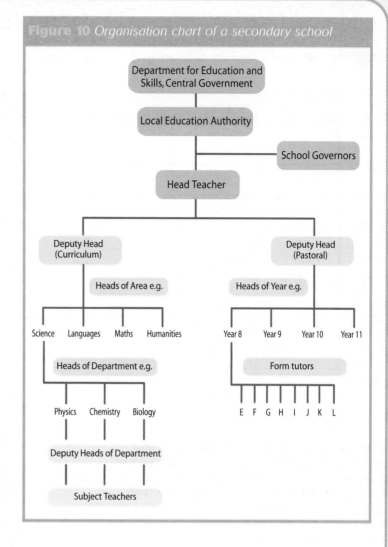

Figure 10 *Organisation chart of a secondary school*

5 Reasons for recruitment

Who are employees?

All businesses require some form of labour so that they can operate. With very small businesses there may be only one person working, the owner. In the UK there are many people who do work for themselves and alone. They are **self-employed**.

This section deals with people who are employed by the business itself. As an **employee** a person is employed as a specific named person by the business, with a contract of employment. The business will decide what the person does and how much they will be paid. In this section the terms employee and staff will be used interchangeably.

In many businesses people may be paid to do specific jobs for the business, but they are not actually employees in terms of the law. They will have a contract to carry out a specific job but they will not have a 'contract of employment'. For example, many builders will have contracts with self-employed plumbers, carpenters and electricians to carry out specific parts of the building of a house. These people are sometimes referred to as workers and this category would also include agency workers, contractors, freelancers and volunteers.

Reasons for recruiting

There are many reasons why staff need to be recruited, but the basic reason is that there is a vacancy to be filled. Recruitment can be **internal**, i.e. from staff already in the business, or **external**, from people outside the business. Which of these is most appropriate will depend on why the vacancy has arisen and factors such as cost, time, and the importance of having experience of how the business operates.

The reasons why there may be a vacancy include the following.
- The business is starting up and needs staff.
- The business is expanding and needs more staff.
- Staff have been promoted internally and new staff are needed to take their place.
- Existing staff have left and need to be replaced.
- The job roles in the business have changed and staff with different skills are needed.
- Other reasons, for example getting a better ethnic balance in the workforce.

Starting up

New businesses will be recruiting staff for the first time. It will, therefore, be very important that they get the right kind of staff and ones that will help to rapidly establish the business in the market place. It may also be the case that the owners or managers recruiting employees have not done this before and, therefore, need to consider very carefully how to recruit effectively. For example:
- what job roles need to be filled?
- what structure will the business take? For example will managers or supervisors be needed?
- which jobs need to filled immediately and what recruitment will be needed in the future?

- where and when to place advertisements?
- how to select the right people for interview?
- how much training they will need to provide?

For example in 2004 a Barclays Bank survey stated that 453,000 new businesses were started in the UK of which 40,000 were in the construction industry. Other sectors of industry that had the most number of new businesses were leisure, transport and communications. The number of new catering businesses was around 20,000. Researchers concluded that this was because TV chefs have made dining out more trendy, with around a fifth of consumers now eating out more than once a week and experimenting with different dishes.

Expanding businesses

As businesses expand they will generally need additional staff. The main difference between these businesses recruiting staff and businesses setting up is that the management should know the type of staff they will need and they will already be experienced in the recruiting process.

There will, however, still be important decisions to be made because this is expansion and more staff in total are being employed. For example:
- should internal staff be promoted into the new jobs or would experienced staff from other businesses be more suitable?
- will the new staff be dynamic and ready to exploit new markets?

Recruitment decisions will also depend on how the expansion is taking place, as shown in Table 1. For example *The Belfast Telegraph* reported in April 2005 that the city could gain up to 750 new jobs as a leading UK operator opened a new call centre in West Belfast. LBM, one of the UK's largest privately owned direct marketing companies, was setting up a new contact centre that

Table 1 *Recruitment decisions*

Method of expansion	Examples of decisions
Internal growth on site	1. Are new levels of management needed? 2. How well will new staff fit in with existing staff?
Moving into new markets at home or abroad	1. Should national or international advertising be used? 2. Will foreign language speakers be needed?
Taking over business	1. Will it be necessary to replace another some of the staff in the other businesses with new staff loyal to this business?
Expansion through diversification	See the section on changed job roles below.

was expected to create 300 new jobs in the medium term and potentially as many as 750.

Promoting internal staff

When staff are promoted internally to fill spaces created by someone leaving or to fill newly created posts, this will leave vacancies for the more junior posts. The business will then have to answer the following kinds of questions in addition to the usual questions about where to advertise.

- Do we fill the post from our existing staff or do we recruit from outside the business?
- What experience did the person have in the business and how much training will be needed to replace the person?
- How quickly does the post need to be filled?

> **Figure 1** *Internal promotion*
>
> ### Branch Manager
> Due to promotion, the role of Branch Manager at Milton Keynes with Robert Half Ltd is available. Robert Half is a NYSE traded international staffing firm specialising in finance and accounts.
>
> Source: adapted from roberthalf.co.uk.

Staff have left

The **turnover of staff** in a business refers to how many staff are leaving compared to how many staff are normally employed. When staff leave there may be a considerable cost involved in advertising for, selecting, interviewing and training new staff. It is therefore important for the business to establish why staff are leaving, as shown in Figure 2.

Retirement When staff retire, they are frequently older and more experience staff. They may also be in a more senior position than younger staff. The business will therefore need to consider the following specific questions.

- Is the post still required or would this be a good time to scrap it?
- Do we recruit internally or externally?
- Do we look for someone with the same level of experience or train someone?

- Do we look for a young person who will be in post for many years?

Promotion Internal promotion has been dealt with above. When promotion takes place because a person has left for a better job in another business, the business needs to consider the following questions before trying to recruit a replacement.

- Did the person leave because there were no internal promotion prospects and is that likely to happen again?
- Did the person leave for higher pay and should we, and can we afford to, raise our pay?

De-motivation Staff may be de-motivated for many reasons. The business needs to think about what the actual reason was and try to improve the situation before recruiting replacements. If the underlying causes are not dealt with, it is highly likely that the same problem will arise again. The factors that might lead to de-motivation and hence staff leaving are dealt with in sections 9-12.

Family commitments Family commitments are generally outside the control of the business and would include such factors as:

- illness and the need for staff to leave in order to take care of someone;
- a husband or wife moving out of the area because of his or her job and the partner is moving as well;
- the family is moving so that the children can attend a better school;
- staff are leaving to have children.

  Although the business can often do little about the person leaving, it will need to consider the following sorts of questions.

- Is the vacancy temporary or permanent? The law states that staff on maternity leave must have their job kept open for them.
- Would higher rates of pay prevent this happening in the future?
- Would it help future retention of staff if part-time work, flexible hours or job sharing was offered?

Dismissed Staff may be dismissed because their jobs are no longer needed **(redundancy)**, in which case recruitment of new staff will not be an issue. However, they may have been dismissed because they have done something wrong. If that is the case, it is vital that the business works out why this has happened so that it can ensure that, when new staff are appointed, the same thing does not happen again. Legislation states the situations where dimissal might be legitimate and legal, without breaking employment legislation conditions on unfair dismissal. These are shown in Table 2.

> **Figure 2** *Reasons why staff leave*

> **Table 2** *Reasons for dismissal which do not break legislation*
>
> - Where the employee's conduct has been unacceptable and even criminal.
> - Where the employee has been unable to provide work of a satisfactory quality.
> - If the employee is made redundant because there is not enough work to be done.
> - Where it would be illegal for the employee to continue work, e.g. if a bus driver had lost his/her licence.
> - Where a job had only been offered for a set period of time, e.g. until a member of staff returned from maternity leave.

Changed job roles in the business

In many cases, what businesses produce and sell and how this is done change over time. Most businesses now use computers somewhere in their business and this means that they will need staff who understand both the hardware and software involved. It may be possible to recruit staff internally if they have the basic skills, but if people within the business cannot be re-trained to deal with these changes then new staff will have to be recruited.

Job roles within a business can change for many reasons.
- The introduction of new technology, e.g. computers and marketing through web-sites.
- Changing what is produced, e.g. new ranges or totally new types of product as when Tesco started to sell petrol.
- Changing the structure of the business, e.g. introducing a new layer of District Managers.

As the job roles are new it will be a vital starting point for the business to very carefully consider what is involved in the role so that the right staff for the job can be recruited. An example of changing roles is shown in Figure 3.

Other reasons

Because businesses are so different in terms of how they are owned and run, what they produce, whether they are expanding or contracting and their size there are many other specific reasons why staff are recruited.
- Businesses that only operate or have increased production at certain times of the year, as with some fun fairs, summer schools and farmers harvesting their crops.
- Family businesses that want to pass the business on to their sons or daughters and recruit them so that they can learn how it should be run.
- Businesses that are trying to achieve a representative ethnic balance. For example, in December 2004 Warwickshire had just 32 ethnic minority officers in a force of more than 1,000. Warwickshire Police Force urged people from minority ethnic communities to attend a recruitment event in Coventry. The session was open to anyone interested in a career in the police service, but the force were keen to encourage more people from ethnic minorities to apply.

Figure 3 *How job roles changed in farming*

Farmers in England made almost £300 million from new ventures such as tourism, sports and recreation in 2004. Defra's Farm Business Survey shows that:
- 48 per cent of full-time farmers have diversified;
- average earnings were £5,000 per farm from diversification;
- turnover from diversification had risen to £550 million (£425 million in 2002-3);
- 2,200 farms had turnovers of more than £50,000 from diversified businesses;
- the amount of diversification varies across England. 68 per cent of farms in the South East have diversified, compared to 37 per cent in the North. Farmers in the South East earned most, more than £111 million, from new enterprises.

Source: adapted from Defra, January 2005.

Examination practice · Global Resources

Figure 3

Are you Ex Management, Redundant, Self Motivated, Ambitious, Ready for a Change? If you are then we need to talk!

We need people with the following experience:-
Network Marketing, Senior Management, Trainers, HR Managers, Logistics and Supply Chain Professionals, Sales Executives, Business Development Managers, Marketing Managers, Team Builders, ex military, Teachers.

We are looking for motivated ambitious people to fill Trainee Manager, Manager, Senior Manager and Leadership Manager positions in several locations around the UK & in Europe. We have just started phase two of our UK growth and we expect our turnover to move from £30million last year to £100million within the next 3-4 years and then £200million five years after that. This has created massive opportunities at all income levels in several locations around the country.

Source: adapted from Global Resources (natural health products industry).

(a) Identify ONE job role that is being specifically advertised in Figure 3. **(1 mark)**
(b) Justify why 'expansion' is the main reason why Global Resources is recruiting in the UK. **(4 marks)**
(c) The advertisement suggests that some job applicants may have left other businesses or may still be with other businesses. Identify ONE example of each and explain why it shows this.
(i) Have left other businesses.
(ii) Still with other businesses. **(4 marks)**
(d) Some of the new jobs will be in Europe. Explain how this may affect the kind of people Global Resources would want to recruit. **(4 marks)**

Meeting the assessment criteria

Figure 4 shows the main reasons why staff left businesses in 2003 as a percentage of all staff leaving. The figures are taken from all businesses returning details.

(a) (i) The pie chart shows that by far the greatest number of staff left their jobs voluntarily. Give **TWO** different reasons why people, in this case 71%, may have left their jobs. **(2 marks)**

Expected answers
- *Seeking promotion outside the business.*
- *Looking for higher pay.*
- *Family commitments, e.g. husband/wife moving to new job in another area.*
- *Pregnancy.*
- *Looking for a more interesting job.*
- *(Do not accept 'retired'.)*

Mark allocation
1 mark for each clearly different reason. **(2 marks)**

(ii) For each of the reasons you have given in (i) above, explain how the business could successfully encourage staff to remain with the business and state why this might be difficult. **(6 marks)**

Expected answers
(Three examples are given below)

Promotion – provide better jobs within the business – staff may be leaving because of lack of opportunities – there may simply be no posts available.
Higher pay – increase pay – will now be paid as much as in other jobs – additional cost/other employees will want the same.
Husband/Wife moving – offer to pay travel costs – may be prepared to travel if no personal extra cost – if move is to, say, another country could be impossible in terms of time.

Mark allocation
1 mark for method.
1 mark for why that would encourage staff to stay.
1 mark for why it may be difficult. **(1 + 1 + 1) x 2
(6 marks)**

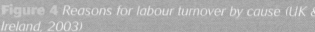
Figure 4 *Reasons for labour turnover by cause (UK & Ireland, 2003)*

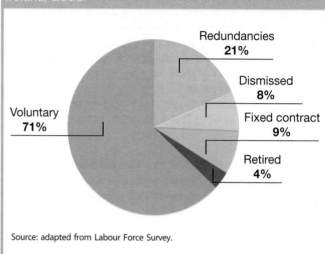

Redundancies
21%

Dismissed
8%

Fixed contract
9%

Retired
4%

Voluntary
71%

Source: adapted from Labour Force Survey.

(b) For each of the following reasons for staff leaving:
1. Redundancy
2. Dismissal
3. Fixed contract
4. Retirement
   (i) state whether or not the business is likely to be seeking to recruit new staff;
   (ii) explain why it will or will not be looking for new staff;
   (iii) and if it is recruiting new staff state **ONE** way in which the reason for staff leaving is likely to affect the recruitment process. **(10 marks)**

Expected answers
Redundancy – will not – staff being made redundant because less staff are needed.
Dismissed – will – if staff dismissed for wrong doing/poor work the post will still exist – need to be more careful when selecting replacement.
Fixed contract – will not – staff were probably employed to get a specific job done and that is no longer needed.
Retirement – will – when people retire the job usually still needs to be done – may need to consider the level of experience needed to fill the post.

Mark allocation
1 mark for likelihood of recruitment.
1 mark why recruiting or not.
1 mark for how this will affect new recruitments.
**(1 + 1 + 1/0) x 4
(10 marks)**

6 The recruitment process

The basic steps in recruitment

When businesses recruit staff they should consider carefully what post needs to be filled, the kind of person needed to fill it and how this can be successfully achieved. For some posts the process will be very short. For example, a newsagent employing a delivery worker could involve advertising in the window and having a short talk with the boy or girl to explain the job, starting work the next day. Others may be much longer, as with civil service jobs or senior management which may have many rounds of interviews and tests.

Figure 1 shows a typical list of steps a business might go through when recruiting and selecting the right person for a vacancy.

Identifying the vacancies to be filled

It could be suggested that it should be obvious to a business if there is a vacancy that needs filling. However, it really depends on why the vacancy has occurred and how any recruitment fits in with the overall strategy of the business.

As explained in section 5, the reason why a vacancy occurs may affect how the business should think about new vacancies. For example, when vacancies occur because the business is starting to produce a totally different product, the first step must be to think about the skills that will now be needed. On the other hand if a supervisor in a supermarket is promoted, the supermarket should know exactly what type of person is needed to fill the vacancy.

When deciding on which vacancies need to be filled the business must also look at the overall business strategy.

- Is the business expanding or contracting? If it is contracting perhaps the vacancy does not need to be filled.
- Is the businesses trying to reduce the number of levels of management (**delayering**)? If so, perhaps some management vacancies do not need to be filled.
- Is the business becoming an international or multi-national business? Will recuitment need to be made abroad? Will speakers of foreign languages be needed?

Planning ahead when filling vacancies is very important. Figure 2 shows on average how long it takes for vacancies to be filled in various industries.

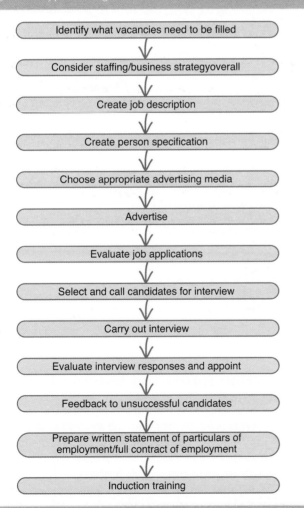

Figure 1 *Typical stages in recruitment and selection*

- Identify what vacancies need to be filled
- Consider staffing/business strategyoverall
- Create job description
- Create person specification
- Choose appropriate advertising media
- Advertise
- Evaluate job applications
- Select and call candidates for interview
- Carry out interview
- Evaluate interview responses and appoint
- Feedback to unsuccessful candidates
- Prepare written statement of particulars of employment/full contract of employment
- Induction training

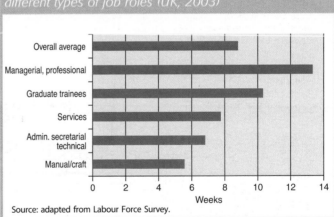

Figure 2 *Number of weeks taken on average to fill different types of job roles (UK, 2003)*

Source: adapted from Labour Force Survey.

Job descriptions and person specifications

When a business has decided which vacancies need to be filled, the next step is to create a job description for the post to be filled and a person specification to identify what sort of person would be best.

Job description A job description gives details of the duties and responsibilities associated with a particular job. Job descriptions do vary from job to job and from business to business, but they will tend to include the following categories:

- job title;

- who the employee is responsible to;
- where the job is located;
- a brief description of what the job entails;
- a list of duties and responsibilities;
- hours of work;
- the working conditions and pay.

Figure 3 shows a possible job description for the position as Team Leader at Little Chef.

Job descriptions are important because they:
- make the business think about what the job really involves;
- make it clear to the employee what is expected;
- provide a basis for measuring job performance;
- state clearly what duties must be carried out if there was a dispute.

Figure 3 *Job description for Little Chef post*

Job Title: Team Leader
Salary: £10,000 - £13,000
Location: Nationwide

Job Description

Job Purpose To effectively organise and control front of house activities and when required to open or to close the restaurant. To act as a key team member, consistently delivering the highest standards of customer service.

Principal Accountabilities
- To supervise Front of House activities ensuring that the highest levels of service are delivered in accordance with the required standard of hospitality and customer care.
- To adhere to legislation, company standards and procedures in a consistent manner.
- To demonstrate active selling skills, leading by example within the restaurant.
- To adhere to all cash handling procedures, ensuring the security of all company assets contained within the unit.
- To efficiently carry out all duties required of fully trained team members.
- To support the Manager and Assistant Manager/s in the achievement of company objectives.
- To undertake specified tasks/responsibilities when required and to support the Management Team by taking full shift responsibility to cover periods of absence.

Source: adapted from www.little-chef.co.uk.

Person specification A person specification gives details of the characteristics that would be expected of the successful applicant. It will be very closely related to the duties and responsibilities listed in the job description.

Person specifications usually set down requirements under the following headings:
- skills and experience;
- education, qualifications and training;
- personal qualities.

The personal qualities are likely to be very wide and will depend very heavily on the type of job.

- Farm labourers may need to be physically fit.
- Teachers in primary schools need to have a good rapport with young children.
- Army officers may need to be able to show authority.
- Part-time workers may need to be flexible about their hours.
- Employees in fast-food restaurants usually have to be happy to work in a team.

It is now common to split basic requirements into those which are 'essential' and those which are simply 'desirable'. Figure 4 shows an example of a person specification for the job of Police Driving Instructor for the Devon & Cornwall Constabulary.

Creating person specifications are important because they should:
- help to decide where and how to advertise the vacancy;
- give a set of standards against which the job applicants can be measured;
- tell the applicants, very clearly, what the minimum requirements are in terms of their own personal qualifications, experience and attitudes.

Figure 4 *Person specification for a police driving instructor*

Job Title: Police Driving Instructor
Main duty: Carrying out driving instruction and assessment to a Police Standard and Advanced level, including specialist courses, e.g. Stinger, TPAC, where necessary.

Person specification

Essential

Qualified to Police Driving Instructor Class 1 Level or equivalent

Excellent communication skills

Up-to-date knowledge of current legislation and Police procedures

Excellent inter-personal skills

Prepared to undertake further training and development in order to achieve and maintain National Standards

Knowledge of National Police Training working practices

Experience of working unsupervised

Desirable

PCV and LGV licence

Experience of Skid Car training and other specialist driver training qualifications e.g. TPAC, Surveillance, VIPEG

ADI

IT skills

Stinger Instructor

Assessing/teaching qualifications, i.e. D32/33.

Application forms and letters of application

Many businesses produce their own job application form for job applicants to fill in. The benefit of doing this is that the form can be set out so that it asks applicants to provide details that will be particularly useful to that specific business.

Application forms can, however, be fairly general and ask for:
- name and address of the applicant;

- personal details such as age;
- the post applied for;
- education and qualifications;
- present post and previous employment;
- relevant skills, knowledge and experience;
- the names and addresses of referees.

This information would be required for the job in Figure 5.

Figure 5 *Job requirements of a sales ledger assistant*

SALES Ledger Assistant required immediately by small London publishing company. Must have experience of customer liaison (private and trade customers) and of computerised ledger system. Varied, demanding full-time permanent position.

Because application forms usually cover many different jobs in a business, job applicants are often asked to complete a **letter of application**. This is used by the applicant to explain why they want the specific job on offer and why they would be particularly suitable for the job.

Sometimes there is no application form and job applicants should then send a letter of application and a **curriculum vitae**. Curriculum vitae sum up most of the information that would be put on an application form, although not the references, but would also have a short section for main interests. Many potential employers expect this information to be put on no more than one side of A4 so that it is easy to read, although this would depend on what job is being applied for.

Advertising

Advertising available posts needs to be thought about carefully to ensure that the message reaches the right people. Internal recruitment might use notice boards, memos, company intranets, newsletters and even word of mouth.

External recruitment may be highly targeted if the business knows specific people who would be good for the job. This includes:

- **head hunting** – where specific individuals are invited to apply;
- **'The milk round'** – where businesses visit universities to try to persuade students to apply as they approach their final examinations.

Other advertisements and approaches will be more general, using newspapers, trade magazines, the Internet, recruitment agencies, radio and in-store leaflets and for smaller or more local firms, window displays, local newspapers or leaflet drops.

It is important to get the right information into the advertisement so that it will attract the right people, and stop unsuitable people from applying.

Selecting candidates for interview

When it has been decided that job applicants should be called for an interview, the business needs to ensure that the right candidates are invited. The following steps should then be followed.

- Decide how many candidates will be invited.
- Read through each of the job applications.
- Compare them to the job description and the person specification.
- Consider other criteria, such as the notice needed in the current job, where they live and potential costs of moving and ensure that there is no illegal discrimination taking place.

This process of selecting the people to be considered for interview is call **short listing**. With some jobs there will be a number of interviews or tests and at each stage a smaller and smaller short list will be created. Sometimes businesses create a long list and then reduce it to a short list

The Interview

Where a business calls candidates for interview and then decides which person to appoint on the basis of the interview, it needs to think very carefully about how the interview is going to be conducted.

There are legal issues that need to be understood, especially in terms of potential discrimination. These are considered in section 8. There are also very important practical issues which should be planned.

Providing details Each interviewee should be given full details about:

- where, when and how the interviews will be carried out;
- details of the costs that will be covered by the business, e.g. travel;
- copies of job descriptions, person specification and the business ethos if they have not already been provided;
- informing them of any tests they may be expected to take as part of the interview process.

The nature of the interview Deciding if the interview will be:

- one to one – the interviewer and the interviewee;
- a panel – a group of interviewers and one interviewee;
- a group interview – a group of interviewees with one or more interviewers.

Selecting the interview panel This should include:

- the person with authority to make the appointment;
- a senior member of the department in which the person will be working;
- other experienced interviewers who know how to get answers that will make the decision easy and correct.

Conducting interviews effectively is a skill. The interviewees needs to be put at their ease. But at the same time the interviewer needs to find out just how good the applicants are for the job, what their real feelings are about the job and whether they are answering questions truthfully. Asking the right questions in the right way is important for a successful interview. This often means that the interviewers need to give applicants space to develop their answers.

The interview stage in many businesses will include tests. The two most common tests that are used are as follows.

Aptitude tests. These are designed to find out if an applicant can actually do the job. They would include the following common examples:

- secretarial jobs – being asked to type or take shorthand to test the speed at which they can carry out the specific duty;
- teaching jobs – being asked to teach part of a lesson to assess how well it was planned and delivered;
- senior civil service or management jobs – where problem solving tasks are set.

Psychometric tests. These test the way the applicant thinks and feels about things and they can also test basic skills, as with intelligence tests. They would include tests to show the following.

- The way people think.
- How motivated they are.
- Their attitudes to other people.
- How they would approach problems.
- Intelligence.
- How open they are to new ways of doing things.

These tests may be very structured and formal like an examination. They may be filled out at, before or after the interview. Their purpose is the same, to get useful information from the applicants. It is equally important that the right questions are asked at the interview itself and in the right way.

Some questions will be asked to put the interviewee at their ease, such as 'How was your journey here?' Some questions will want specific answers and may be **closed questions** with set answers expected, such as 'Have you worked with Microsoft Word before?'

Other questions will be **open questions** which invite the person to develop answers in the way they want, such as 'What skills do you think you could bring to this job?' Each type of question is trying to find out information in a different way so that the right final choice can be made.

Figure 6 *Job requirements of a sales ledger assistant*

'Interviews are never easy, but some can be much worse than others. Being scrutinised and assessed is rarely going to feel comfortable, but if you've never had a truly dreadful job interview, you haven't lived. If you have, don't let it dent your confidence. Thinking about what you can learn will help you to move on.'

Irene Krechowiecka

Source: http://www.ivillage.co.uk/workcareer/findjob/interviews/articles/0,,186_167095-1,00.html.

After the interview

In some cases the successful and unsuccessful applicants will be told immediately after the interview. With other jobs the applicants have to wait to be told later on.

Whichever way is used, the business will think carefully about what was said in the interview, check the results of any tests, possibly look at the application forms, letters of application and the CVs and then decide on the best candidate for the job. Usually applicants have been asked in advance whether they would take the job if it was offered to them, so informing the successful applicant creates the appointment.

Most businesses will also give some feedback to the unsuccessful applicants. This is the courteous thing to do, but it also makes business sense because these may be people that the business might like to work for it in the future.

All employees require, by law, a written statement of the particulars of their employment within two months of starting work. This needs to be drawn up. For more details see section 15 on legal issues. Most employees will have some kind of induction training to introduce them into the business. For more details see section 7 on training.

Examination practice · Job research

With reference to a specific job that you have studied answer the questions below. The job must be one in which an important interview stage took place.

(a) (i) Name of the business.
    (ii) Name of the job.
    (iii) Details of the main duties of the job.   **(4 marks)**

(b) Identify which of the following documents were used for recruiting for this job important for this specific job.
    (i) Curriculum vitae.
    (ii) Application form.
    (iii) Letter of application.   **(6 marks)**

(c) Describe the type of interview used (one-to-one, panel or group) and explain why that type of interview was used.   **(4 marks)**

(d) Give TWO examples of an open question and TWO examples of a closed question used in this interview and explain why that type of question was used for the questions you have given.
    (i) Closed.
    (ii) Open.   **(8 marks)**

Meeting the assessment criteria

Figure 7 *Job advertisement for Sales Administration Assistant*

> # SALES ADMIN ASSISTANT
> We are looking for a hard working individual with good keyboard and telephone skills to assist our Sales Manager in a variety of duties at our Head Office in London.
> - *Excellent working environment*
> - *Interesting and varied role*
> - *Attractive package*
>
> Write in the first instance to
> **Jason Freeland at Kapland Ltd**
> **125 New Way, London, WC20 4RR**

Figure 7 shows an advertisement placed in a London magazine. Before the advertisement was designed and created a job description and person specification would have been created.

(a) Explain the main purpose of each of the following in the recruitment process.
   (i) A job description.
   (ii) A person specification. **(4 marks)**

Expected answers
(i) Job description
- *Gives details about what the job involves – allows the business to match applicants' details against the job.*
- *Gives basic details of what the job involves – will tell the applicant if it is worth applying.*
(ii) Person specification
- *Gives details of the type of person required – allows the business to reject unsuitable applicants.*
- *Gives details of skills/personality needed to do the job – could form the basis of aptitude or psychometric tests.*

Mark allocation
1 mark for what it is/description.
1 mark for its basic purpose in the recruitment process.
(1 + 1) x 2
(4 marks)

(b) From the advertisement shown in Figure 7, identify TWO details that would come from the Job Description and TWO details that would come from the Person Specification.
(4 marks)

Expected answers
(i) Job description
- *Job title/Sales Admin. Assistant.*
- *Location/London Head Office.*
- *Responsible to/Sales Manager.*
(ii) Person specification
- *Skills/good keyboard/telephone skills.*
- *Personal qualities/hard working.*

Mark allocation
1 mark for each detail.
(1 + 1) x 2
(4 marks)

(c) Someone interested in the job should contact Jason Freeland. He may then ask them complete a document that he sends out to them and possibly send in two documents that they have created. What are these three documents and what are their basic functions? **(6 marks)**

Expected answers
- *Application form – a standard form which will list the main details that the business needs.*
- *Curriculum Vitae/CV – provides personal details of the applicant in terms of address, education and qualifications.*
- *Letter of application – gives details of why the applicant feels the job is specifically suited to them.*

Mark allocation
1 mark for each document.
1 mark for its basic function/main points it will include.
(1 + 1) x 3
(6 marks)

(d) If you were designing tests for an applicant for this job, what aptitude and psychometric test would you create? Justify your answers.
   (i) Aptitude.
   (ii) Psychometric. **(6 marks)**

Expected answers
(i) Aptitude
- *Will test specific skills – test how fast they can type – good keyboard skills are required.*
- *Will test if applicant can do job – ask them to work for fifteen minutes in the office taking telephone calls – good telephone skills required for the job.*
(ii) Psychometric
- *Will test personality – a test where applicants are faced with a wide range of tasks – test ability to deal with a varied role.*
- *Will test attitude to work – ask them to carry out demanding tasks – should identify hard working individual.*

Mark allocation
1 mark for showing understanding of the term (may be implied).
1 mark for identifying a specific suitable test.
1 mark for justifying why this is aptitude/psychometric or why it is valuable for this job.
(1 + 1 + 1) x 2
(6 marks)

7 Methods of training employees

Training

At some stage in employees' lives they will need training for the job they are doing or going to do. Some employees may have skills from their education or from previous jobs and therefore need little additional training. Others will need extensive training.

How much training and what kind of training is needed will depend on the type of job involved and the amount of training that has already been given through education and courses and the natural skills of the person employed. This section will be looking primarily at the type of training provided by businesses to their employees.

Reasons for training

Businesses train staff for a number of reasons, as shown in Figure 1. When asked by a client 'What if you train staff and they leave' a manager replied 'What if you don't train staff and they stay'. This suggests that businesses with untrained staff can have problems and the benefits of training staff outweigh the possible problems.

Figure 1 Reasons for training staff

New staff joining There are very few jobs where absolutely no training is required when staff join a business. Even for a very basic job, such as washing up plates and dishes in a restaurant, the employee will need to be told where the washing up materials are kept, where to stock dried plates or where to put dish towels ready for the laundry.

In other jobs extensive training will be needed when new staff join. This would be for the following reasons.
- The type of job is new to the person.
- The equipment, e.g. a software package, is unique to the business.
- The business wants to recruit inexperienced people so that it can train them as it wants.
- The training is a continuous part of their education, as with junior doctors in a hospital.

- The work is very technically difficult, as with flying a fighter aircraft.

Most new staff will be given some kind of induction training (see below) when they join. For the more technical and professional training mentioned above this will be delivered through continuous training.

New jobs in the business Most businesses are developing all the time, introducing technology and developing and selling new products. When this happens, new jobs will be created in the business and often a business will decide that the easiest way to staff these jobs is to train people already in the business.

New equipment In many cases in business the job being done does not change very much but the equipment on which it is being done does change. Staff then need to be trained to use this new equipment effectively so that they can carry on doing their job. Examples of this would include:
- new photocopying machines in an office;
- new forklift trucks in a warehouse;
- new fast speed passenger trains on the railways;
- new cookers in a restaurant.

Keeping staff up-to-date Many jobs have frequent changes in their products or the way that jobs are expected to be carried out. This would include:
- learning how to use new software packages;
- training staff in new health and safety procedures;
- explaining new electrical products to sales staff so that they can advise customers.
- Providing teachers with training when examination syllabuses change.

Multi-skilling There are many definitions of multi-skilling. One is multi-skilling means you've been trained to cover a range of different jobs in your workplace.' The main benefit for the business is that staff can move from one job to another and that will help to cover unexpected absences, provide additional staff when demand for a particular activity is especially high or, move staff when someone leaves. This provides the business with added flexibility.

The main benefit for the staff is that they will now have additional skills which can improve promotion prospects and make it easier for them to move to new jobs in different businesses if they wish. Figure 2 shows an example.

To keep staff motivated Training can be an important motivator for staff. It makes them feel that someone is thinking about what they need. It can also lead to higher rates of pay, promotion prospects and greater job satisfaction, all of which will act as motivators.

Training for promotion In many businesses the way in which staff progress and move to higher pay scales is through promotion. Figure 3 shows a possible promotion route for staff in a supermarket.

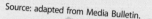

Figure 2 *Training for promotion and retirement*

Barclays Bank implemented a multi-skilling strategy in its call centres, known as Barclays contact centres, as a direct response to employee demands for career progression and a more varied workload. The new training structure aimed to address a major problem affecting call centre staffing - high turnover rates.

Source: adapted from European Finance Director.

The Warwick Business School was commissioned by the FA Premier League, the Football League, the Football Association, and others, to provide a training programme to develop the management skills of footballers who wanted to move into club management positions.

Source: adapted from Media Bulletin.

At each stage of the promotion process staff will need to learn new skills and techniques so that they can deal with the different duties and added responsibilities of the higher post. Most businesses will provide training to help staff make the move.

Preparing staff for leaving Some businesses will specifically train staff to help them when they leave. There are two main reasons why they do this.

- Because the staff are only employed for a fixed period of time and providing them with training for other jobs will help

Figure 3 *A promotion route for staff in a supermarket*

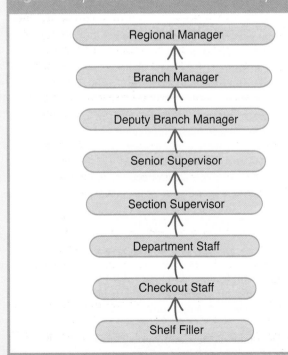

with initial recruitment and keep staff motivated. This is a common practice in the armed forces.
- Helping staff to cope with retirement. Most people who retire have a very significant fall in income and need to adjust to not going out to work. Some businesses help their staff to make this transition. An example is shown in Figure 2.

Types of training

The exact type of training given will depend on what the job is, the current level of skill and experience of staff and constraints such as cost and time.

Induction training Induction training takes place when new employees join a business. The main purpose of this is to ensure that they know what they are doing and to make them familiar with the business itself. The following are all typical elements in an induction training programme.
- Meeting senior staff.
- Conducted tour of the premises, including toilets, canteen, recreation facilities.
- Details of basic health and safety procedures.
- Use of internal and external communications systems.
- Main company aims and objectives.
- Company policies, e.g. on smoking.
- Dress code.
- Disciplinary procedures.
- Meeting people that the employee will work with.
- An introduction to the job itself.

On-the-job training On-the-job training takes place as someone is actually doing his or her job. Because the training takes place as someone is working, it has various benefits and drawbacks as shown in Table 1. Training for many job roles is done on-the-job, especially where the required skills are fairly limited, as with fast food restaurants, or where the employee is highly skilled and is simply learning new techniques, as with computer programmers.

Table 1 *Benefits and drawbacks of on-the-job training*

Benefits
- Work is being done so something is being produced.
- The trainees learn by actually doing the job.
- Practice should help to improve skills.
- Often easy to arrange.

Drawbacks
- If the trainee gets it wrong the product, or customer, may be lost.
- Difficult for the trainee to concentrate whilst working.
- Dangerous for others, e.g. surgeon, airline pilot.
- Trainers may have to stop their jobs to do the training.

Off-the-job-training Off-the-job training takes place when the person is not actually doing the job. This may or may not take place at the workplace. The benefits and drawbacks of off-the-job training tend to be the opposite of on-the-job training as shown in Table 2.

Table 2 *Benefits and drawbacks of off-the-job training*

Benefits
- If a trainee does something wrong an actual product will not be affected.
- Easier to concentrate.
- Does not put customers in danger.
- Can be done after the normal hours of work.

Drawbacks
- No work is being done so it costs more.
- Problems and how to deal with them may only appear when real work starts.
- It needs to be organised and may take time.
- Can disturb other employees if training involves watching them.

On-and off-site training On-site training means that the training is taking place where the person works. It may or may not be on-the-job. Off-site training means that the training is taking place away from where the person is working. It will, therefore, automatically be off-the-job.

The decision as to whether to train staff on or off site will usually depend on whether or not the business has the facilities to train on-site. The comparative advantages of the two methods of training are shown in Table 3.

Table 3 *On-site and off-site training*

On site
- Usually cheaper.
- Trainees can see the job they will actually be doing.
- There is no time lost in travelling or staying overnight.
- Likely to be less worrying for staff as it is in familiar surroundings.

Off site
- Special training facilities can be used.
- Staff may see the training as a special privilege.
- Unlikely to be distracted by daily work commitment.
- Can meet with other businesses. staff.

In-house training This is used to describe training that is provided by the business itself. It may be any of the four types of training mentioned above. Today, however, the term in-house is also used for training that is supplied by outside providers and is tailored for the specific needs of the business.

Apprenticeships Apprenticeships are jobs in which training forms a major part of the agreement between the employer and the employee. In these agreements the employees are trained on-the-job, actually doing the work, but they are also often trained both off-the-job and off-site in local colleges. This may be through day release, where the person spends, say, one day a week at college or through night school after work.

There were over 234,000 apprentices in UK businesses in 2005 and many major businesses and many companies used this method of training with younger staff. British Gas, which has over 7,000 engineers, planned to recruit at least 50% of these through apprenticeships by 2010.

Many apprenticeship schemes come from government initiatives. The main benefits to the apprentices are:
- they are trained;
- usually they gain additional qualifications.

The main benefits to the businesses are:
- they finish up with well trained staff;
- many of the schemes receive some kind of monetary support from the government.

On-going training The majority of training that takes place in a business is on-going training. This is training that continually supports the member of staff and helps him or her to progress. It also helps to ensure that the members of staff will be able to perform duties efficiently.

If on-going training is going to be effective it is vital that the business first of all assesses the need for training and how that fits with the needs of the individual member of staff and the main aims and objectives of the business, as shown in Figure 4.

Figure 4 *Aims and objectives of on-going training*

Meeting the business's objectives.
- Review aims and objectives.
- Establish staff training needs to meet these.
- Cost the training needed.
- Provide suitable training to increase staff's effectiveness.

Meeting employees' needs.
- Monitor employees' performance.
- Assess employees' needs through appraisal interviews, discussion and observation.
- Agree targets and establish training needs.
- Check training needs against business aims and objectives.
- Plan and implement training.
- Evaluate the success of the individual's training.

To ensure the best training for individuals it is important that line managers establish a close professional relationship with their staff. In some businesses a mentoring system will be established. In other businesses the approach taken is coaching.
- Mentoring means acting as a trusted advisor. In business this means that the mentor must understand what is best for the person they are mentoring and ensure that that person gains the best advice and training possible.
- Coaching means giving specific instructions and training to staff in order to achieve a specific outcome. In businesses that needs to be matched to the aims and objectives of the business or to the aspirations of the individual member of staff.

Government training schemes

The Department for Trade and Industry (Dti) states that:
A well-trained and professional workforce is better equipped to:
- work effectively with minimal supervision, helping to raise productivity;
- improve customer satisfaction by giving knowledgeable responses to enquiries;

- be flexible so staff can be employed on related jobs and cope with work-level fluctuations and absences;
- take a creative approach to business problems and develop new products and services;
- appreciate the value of developing their personal skills and be highly motivated.

The government believes that all businesses should provide regular and on-going training for their staff. It has, therefore set up various schemes to encourage and support businesses.

Investors in People 'Investors in People' (IiP) is the national standard that sets a level of good practice for the training and development of people. It was created by leading businesses and business organisations such as the CBI and TUC and the Employment Department.

The standard lays down a set of conditions that a business

must meet in terms of its training provisions before it can be award the title of Investors in People. These standards relate to each of the ten indicators shown in Figure 5.

Skills Strategy The government's first Skills Strategy was launched in July 2003. In March 2005 the government published a white paper, *Skills: Getting on in business, getting on at work*, to build on the original strategy. The White Paper emphasises two main aims:

- ensuring that employers have the right skills to support the success of their businesses;
- helping individuals to gain the skills they need to be employable and personally fulfilled.

The White Paper sets out proposals and reforms designed to:

- put employers' needs centre stage in the design and delivery of training. This will be met through a new National Employer Training Programme (NETP) and Skills Academies;
- support individuals in gaining the skills and qualifications they need to achieve the quality of life they want. This will include, from 2006/7, an entitlement to free tuition for a first Level 2 qualification;
- reform supply. This aims to improve the provision of training in schools and colleges and from other training providers.

Apprenticeships policy The Learning and Skills Council supports businesses in England who take on apprentices in a variety of ways. Apprenticeships are managed nationally through 47 local offices and a network of learning providers. Large businesses are supported by National Contracts Service which can put them in touch with a suitable learning provider and works with them to find suitable training programmes for their apprentices. Details can be found at http://www.apprenticeships.org.uk.

Changes to the existing Apprenticeship scheme were announced in May 2004. In summary, these:

- removed the upper 25-year age limit on Apprenticeship training;
- introduced a new Advanced Apprenticeship award at Level 3;
- created Young Apprenticeships to give school pupils at Key Stage 4 the opportunity to experience real work environments;
- brought in pre-Apprenticeship courses for young people who were not yet ready for the full-blown award.

Figure 5 *Investors in People standards*

1. A strategy for improving the performance of the organisation is defined and understood.
2. Learning and development is planned to achieve the organisation's objectives.
3. Strategies for managing people are designed to promote equality of opportunity in the development of the organisation's people.
4. The capabilities managers need to lead, manage and develop people effectively are clearly defined and understood.
5. Managers are effective in leading, managing and developing people.
6. People's contribution to the organisation is recognised and valued.
7. People are encouraged to take ownership and responsibility by being involved in decision making.
8. People learn and develop effectively.
9. Investment in people improves the performance of the organisation.
10. Improvements are continually made to the way people are managed and developed.

Details can be found at http://www.investorsinpeople.co.uk.

Examination practice · Training in the UK

Figure 6 shows the percentage of all employees receiving job related training as collected by the Labour Force Survey. The total has then been divided to show the percentage of that total in each age group.

(a) **Explain, using examples of on-site and off-site training, what job related training is.** (5 marks)

(b) **Explain why the 16 to 17 sector is so small when compared to the other sectors.** (3 marks)

(c) **Which sectors could the Learning and Skills Councils support through its Apprenticeship programmes? Justify your answer.** (2 marks)

(d) **Figure 6 shows that all groups of working age receive some job related training. Outline how this training is likely to benefit:**
   (i) the business;
   (ii) the individual employee. (10 marks)

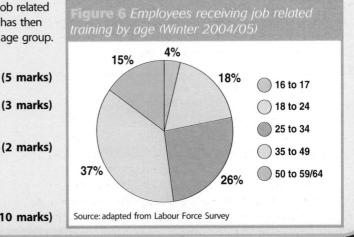

Figure 6 *Employees receiving job related training by age (Winter 2004/05)*

4%
18%
15%
26%
37%

- 16 to 17
- 18 to 24
- 25 to 34
- 35 to 49
- 50 to 59/64

Source: adapted from Labour Force Survey

Meeting the assessment criteria

(a) Identify from Figure 7 which parts of the training programme were likely to have been conducted:
(i) on-the-job;
(ii) off-the-job.
For each, explain why they would have been on-the-job or off-the-job. **(6 marks)**

Expected answers
* *Classroom tutoring - off-the-job - it is taking place in a classroom not producing chemicals.*
* *Safety training could be either - may be shown how to handle chemicals on-the-job - may be shown fire exits off-the-job.*
* *Written assessments could be either - if a line manager is assessing, this could be done whilst watching staff work, if staff are writing the assessment they cannot do this whilst producing chemicals.*

Mark allocation
1 mark for identifying part and on or off.
1 mark for reason why on or off.

(1 + 1) x 3
(6 marks)

(b) Explain the meaning of the following terms and for each explain how they might help the business.
(i) Multi-skilled.
(ii) Self-directed teams. **(6 marks)**

Expected answers
Multi-skilled
Having more than one skill – provides staff flexibility – can move staff to other jobs as they have the additional skills.
Self-directed teams
* *Teams which plan and carry out their own work – more production – providing individuals with responsibility acts as a motivator.*
* *Team chooses how to work – encouraged additional investment – investors could see improved on-site culture.*

Mark allocation
1 mark for showing meaning of term.
1 mark for benefit to business.
1 mark for explaining how this comes from the initiative.
(1 + 1 + 1) x 2
(6 marks)

(c) Health and safety is likely to form a major part of the induction training for BASF plc. State why this is likely to be so important for BASF and explain the kind of training that could be included. **(8 marks)**

Expected answers
Meaning and basic reason
* *Training provided when employee joins the business – chemical firm so more potential health and safety issues.*

Figure 7 *BASF training*

Figure 7 *BASF training*

BASF training programme saves £4m

One of the world's leading chemical companies, BASF plc, recognised the benefits of training through improved business performance.

At its Seal Sands site near Middlesborough, the implementation of a major training programme included classroom tutoring, safety training, and written assessments.

The benefits were numerous and included the development of 150 employees towards multi-skilled self-directed teams, secured savings of £4m for 2001 due to improved performance, increased staff morale, and an improved on-site culture that attracted investment and secured the company's future in the region.

Also, other companies now use BASF plc as a good practice benchmark for adopting new training processes.

Source: adapted from www.dti.gov.uk.

Likely elements of training
* *Fire drill procedure – tells staff what to do if fire breaks out/fire is a real possibility where there are chemicals.*
* *What protective clothing to wear – show staff how to prevent damage from chemical spills.*
* *How to handle/store dangerous chemicals – tries to ensure staff will not be injured whilst working.*
* *What to do if accidents do occur – help to limit the injuries that might be caused by this.*

Mark allocation
1 mark for showing understanding of the term (may be implied).
1 mark for why so important to BASF.
1 mark for each item likely to be included (maximum 3 marks).
1 mark for why this will be included (maximum 3 marks).
1 + 1 + [(1 + 1) x 3]
(8 marks)

8 Legal and ethical responsibilities - discrimination and equal opportunities

What is discrimination?

Businesses have many ethical and legal responsibilities towards their employees. A major responsibility is to prevent discrimination at work. Discrimination is about choice. In the work environment the term discrimination usually refers to the unethical or illegal choice of one person rather than another.

What if a business required an experienced sales assistant to work in an office in London? When making the selection the business:

* chose a male candidate rather than a female and argued that a male was required to work with customers, even though a female could do the job equally well;
* people from ethnic minority groups were rejected as the job was in London;
* a candidate in a wheelchair who was not able to drive was rejected even though driving was not required for the job.

In this case the business is unlikely to be meeting its legal and ethical responsibilities. It is likely to be discriminating against certain people.

What are equal opportunities?

Equal opportunities are when everyone has the same chance and everyone is treated the same. It is important for businesses to ensure that there are equal opportunities and equality of treatment when recruiting and selecting employees. If equal opportunities exist in a business then there is a greater chance that discrimination can be prevented. Figure 1 shows an example of equal opportunities at the Virgin company.

Figure 1 *Equal opportunities at Virgin*

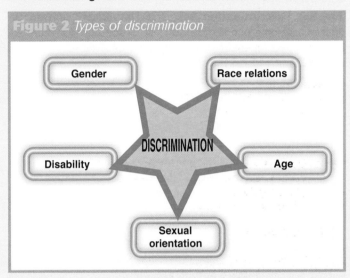

We strive for equal opportunities for all present and potential employees

* There is a diverse workforce and an equal opportunities policy in place. We aim to employ people who reflect the diverse nature of society and we value people and their contribution irrespective of age, sex, disability, sexual orientation, race, colour, religion, marital status or ethnic origin.
* We do not discriminate against anyone for their membership or affiliation to any trade unions or political parties.
* We do not tolerate any sexual, physical or mental harassment of our employees.
* Procedures are in place to respond to accusations of workplace discrimination, harassment and victimisation.
* An effective employee grievance procedure is in operation, and the policy is properly communicated to our people.

Source: adapted from www.virgin.com.

Types of discrimination

Employers are ethically and legally bound to prevent discrimination in business. It is often suggested that certain types of discrimination must be prevented in business. These are shown in Figure 2.

Figure 2 *Types of discrimination*

Gender

Race relations

DISCRIMINATION

Disability

Age

Sexual orientation

Gender or sex discrimination This is discrimination against one sex or another. An example might be employing a male director rather than a female director when the gender of the director has no influence on the job.

Racial discrimination This is discrimination against a person on the basis of their race. An example might be refusing to employ a bank assistant because he is from an Asian ethnic minority group.

Disability discrimination This is discrimination against disabled people. An example might be refusing to employ a person with hearing difficulties when this does not affect their performance in the job.

Age discrimination This is discrimination against people of a certain age, usually older people. An example might be refusing to employ a 61 year old just because of their age.

Sexual orientation discrimination This might include refusing to employ a person because of their sexual preference.

There is a variety of legislation that affects businesses. This legislation will affect the ways in which a business recruits and selects its employees.

Gender discrimination legislation

Gender discrimination legislation aims to prevent discrimination against one gender or another. It is usually used to prevent discrimination against women, but it can apply to men. Certain legislation in the UK and the EU promotes gender equality.

The EU Equal Treatment Directive This states there must

be equal treatment of men and women as regards access to employment, vocational training and promotion and working conditions. In 2002 it was amended to prevent sexual harassment.

Equal Pay Act, 1970 This states that employees are entitled to the same pay and conditions as others doing broadly similar work. It was amended in 1983 to relate to equal pay for work which makes the same demands.

The EU Equal Pay Directive This states that men and women should receive equal pay for equal work. Equal work is work which is of equal value determined by job evaluation.

The Sex Discrimination Act, 1975 This makes it unlawful to discriminate on grounds of sex or marital status or for there to be sexual harassment at work. It makes it unlawful to discriminate:

- directly - treating someone less favourably than another person because of their gender;
- indirectly - where women have less chance of meeting employment conditions.

Employees who feel that they have been discriminated against can take their case to an employment tribunal, to court or to the European Court of Justice. These bodies rule whether discrimination has taken place and have the power to force business to comply with legislation. The Equal Opportunities Commission is a government body set up to advise and help employees who feel that they have faced discrimination. Table 1

shows how ethical and legal responsibilities regarding gender might affect businesses.

Race relations discrimination legislation

Race relations discrimination legislation aims to prevent discrimination on the grounds of:

- colour;
- race;
- nationality;
- ethnic, national or religious origin.

The **Race Relations Act, 1976** is the main legislation in the UK designed to promote racial equality. It states that it is unlawful to discriminate directly or indirectly on the grounds of colour, race, nationality or ethnic origin. In 2002 it was amended to include nearly all public functions such as the police force and health service. The **Race Relations (Amendment Act) 2000** includes a right to claim against ethnic harassment and the **Employment Equality (Religion and Belief) Regulations** outlaw discrimination on religious grounds. Again, people who feel that they have faced discrimination can take their case to an employment tribunal. The Commission for Racial Equality is a non-government publicly funded body which helps to promote racial equality in the UK.

Disability discrimination legislation

Disability discrimination legislation aims to prevent

Table 1 *Gender - how ethical and legal responsibilities might affect businesses*

Situation	Possible effects
Clothing for administration employees	Do not prevent women from wearing trousers in the office if males do.
Advertising for a Refuse Collector	Use non-gender based terms in advertisements, for example Binman should not be used and replaced by Refuse Collector.
Designing person specifications for a machine operator	Carefully word the person specification, for example do not state only people over 6'4'' as few women are this tall. This is a form of indirect discrimination.
Pay rises at a travel agent	Do not pay a male travel agent more than a female doing the same job.
Promotion of a manager	Can not chose a single male for promotion rather then a married woman because of the possibility of leave to have children.
Work situation	Training will be required to prevent sexual harassment and encourage equality of treatment.

Table 2 *Race relations - how ethical and legal responsibilities might affect businesses*

Situation	Possible effects
Clothing for employees	Do not prevent Sikhs from wearing turbans in the office.
Advertising a post	Cannot state generally that people of certain nationality, colour or ethnic origin may not apply.
Designing person specifications	Carefully word the person specification, for example cannot state generally that the post must be held by someone born in the UK.
Conditions at work	Take into account religious holidays of all ethnic groups.
Interviews	Do not discriminate against certain nationalities with language in written tests or questions.
Selection for training	Cannot refuse to select people from particular nationalities.
Work situation	Training will be required to prevent racial harassment and encourage equality of treatment.

Figure 3 *Possible changes that a business might make to comply with disability discrimination legislation*

Modifying telephone handsets for people with gripping difficulties

Adding a ramp to the building for wheelchair access

Allowing absences for physiotherapy for people with mobility problems

Creating wider workspace for workers in wheelchairs

Modifying computer software or hardware for people with sight or hearing difficulties

discrimination against people with disabilities. The **Disability Discrimination Act, 1995** makes it illegal to discriminate against employees with disabilities unless there is a substantial, relevant and justified reason. For example:

- not selecting a candidate for a position in a call centre because they use a wheelchair might be discrimination as only minor changes to work conditions may be required;
- not selecting a candidate who uses a wheelchair for a job as a roofer might not be discrimination because there may be a justified concern for safety, the person may be unable to carry out the job and major changes may be needed to the conditions.

The Disability Rights Commission is an independent organisation set up by government to prevent disability discrimination. Part of its duties includes producing a code of practice for businesses to show how they can meet the requirements of legislation.

Age discrimination

Protection for older employees in the past was mainly in the form of conditions of service in their employment contracts. This is dealt with in sections 12 and 15. However, all EU countries must introduce laws to comply with the EU **Employment Framework Directive**. This aims to prevent all workplace discrimination. By 2006, the UK must introduce legislation that will make discrimination on the basis of age illegal. A business can not reject an applicant under 25 for not being mature enough or someone over 50 for being too slow to train. Possible examples of effects on businesses are shown in Table 3. There are a situations where differences in treatment related to age may be allowed. For example, a business may be able to set a seniority level before an employee can become a director.

Sexual orientation discrimination

The **Employment Equality (Sexual Orientation) Regulations 2003** makes discrimination on grounds of sexual orientation illegal. Both direct and indirect discrimination and harassment are unlawful.

Reasons to prevent discrimination

There are reasons why a business may want to prevent discrimination at work.

The well-being of employees Good employers are concerned about the well-being of their employees. They want them to be as happy and motivated as possible in work and are

Table 3 *Effects of complying with age discrimination legislation when recruiting and selecting*

Situation	Possible effects
Application forms	Cannot state that people over 50 can apply in applications.
Interviews	Assumptions can not be made about candidates who look old or young, for example and older looking candidates will be less enthusiastic.
Experience	A business cannot be able to state how many years experience are needed as this might disadvantage younger candidates.
Work situation	Training will be required to prevent harassment on the basis of age and to encourage equality of treatment.

concerned about their welfare. Preventing discrimination is a way of helping employees feel that the business takes their interests into account.

Motivation Increasingly, businesses are recognising that people are an important asset. Well-motivated employees are likely to be productive at work. This will help the business to be profitable. So it could be argued that preventing discrimination will help a business to be profitable. Staff are also likely to stay with a business that takes their interests into account. This can reduce staff turnover, which is cost. It also helps the business to retain important personnel and their skills.

Other methods used to motivate employees and protect their well-being are dealt with in section 12.

Public image Ensuring that discrimination does not take place will improve the image and reputation of a business in the eyes of customers. They may buy more products as a result. It may also help to attract the best candidates for a post. They may be attracted by statements such as 'We are an equal opportunities employer'.

Financial issues Businesses that break laws regarding discrimination may face fines or compensation, or a court may impose conditions on them, which are costly. Preventing discrimination cases will help to reduce these costs.

Examination practice · Sidell Construction

Sidell Construction is a construction company which builds roads and other infrastructure. It has recently won a government contract for work in the Midlands area. It has decided to advertise for a new project manager to handle one of the construction teams working on road clearance.

The main role of the project manager will be to monitor progress of the work and ensure that deadlines are met. A number of important characteristics that the business wanted from the job holder were identified in the person specification. The business decided to place an advertisement in national newspapers and trade journals. It was keen to stress in the advertisement that it was an equal opportunities employer.

The business interviewed three applicants for the post. At the interview they were asked about their previous experience and given problem solving activities which the business felt would help to make a decision about the most suitable candidate.

(a) What should the business mean when it says that it is an equal opportunities employer? **(2 marks)**

(b) Suggest TWO reasons why a business might want to state that it is an equal opportunities employer. **(4 marks)**

(c) Explain how the:
(i) Equal Pay Act;
(ii) Race Relations Act;
would affect the advertisement for the post. **(4 marks)**

(d) Advise the business on TWO ways in which it might avoid discrimination when recruiting and selecting the candidate. **(6 marks)**

Meeting the assessment criteria

Sara responded to an advertisement for a job as a clerical assistant in a London firm of solicitors. She was invited for an interview which she felt went well. When she got home she received a call from the firm to ask her whether or not she was Jewish. She said that she was. She was then asked whether she intended to take all the Jewish holidays, but explained that she planned to take only one, as part of her leave.

Sara waited to hear whether she had been successful. After four days with no response she rang the company who said that she had not been offered the job. She was told that the successful candidate 'had different circumstances'. Sara decided to take her case to an employment tribunal.

Source: adapted from Commission for Racial Equality, www.cre.gov.uk.

(a) Suggest TWO pieces of legislation, other than the Race Relations Act, that might affect the advertisement of a post for a clerical assistant at a firm of solicitors and for each Act suggest how the wording of an advertisement might have broken the Act. **(4 marks)**

Expected answers
* *The Sex Discrimination Act, 1975 – if the advertisement had said only women should apply.*
* *Disability Discrimination Act, 1995 – if the advertisement had said no facilities for wheelchairs, when there were facilities.*

Mark allocation
1 mark for naming a relevant Act.
1 mark for examples of how the wording would contravene the Act.
(1 + 1) x 2
(4 marks)

(b) Discuss whether or not the London firm of solicitors is likely to have broken the Race Relations Act in its dealings with Sara. **(5 marks)**

Expected answers
Reasons why and counter point
* *She was asked if she was Jewish – but all candidates may have been asked this as part of checking ethnic origins.*

* *She was asked if she was taking all the Jewish Holidays – may have been asked this to help with staff planning.*
* *Successful candidate had different circumstances which might mean they were not taking Jewish holidays – the exact difference was not stated.*
Conclusion
* *Taken together the references to the particular position of Jewish people sounds like discrimination, so Act broken.*
* *There could have been a valid explanation for all the apparent discrimination, so Act not broken.*

Mark allocation
1 mark for reason why the Act may have been broken (maximum 2 marks).
1 mark for argument of why Act not broken (maximum 2 marks).
1 mark for reasoned conclusion
(2 + 2 + 1)
(5 marks)

(c) If Sara had been employed, the Employment Rights Act, 1996 would have required that she was given:
(i) a written statement of particulars of employment within two months of starting work.
(ii) a written itemised pay statement every time she was paid.
Explain what each of these requirements means and how each protects Sara. **(6 marks)**

Expected answers
* *(i) Details of the terms on which Sara will work must be written out for her – for example when employment begins/how much the pay will be/the expected hours of work – Sara will have written details in case there is any dispute.*
* *(ii) Details of how Sara's pay has been worked out – rates of pay per hour and hours worked/details of deduction such as income tax, NIC – will allow her to check that she has been paid correctly.*

Mark allocation
1 mark for showing understanding of requirement.
1 mark for likely details in requirement.
1 mark for how that protects Sara.
(1 + 1 + 1) x 2
(6 marks)

9 The importance of motivation and de-motivation

Why motivate?

It is sometimes argued that staff motivation is the most important factor for the success of a business. For some, the key role of motivation is expressed in the following formula:

$$Performance = ability \times motivation.$$

Frequently the ability that one member of staff has is the same as other members, but the levels of motivation are different. The effect is usually very clear. Motivated staff, generally, work harder than de-motivated staff and, therefore, tend to produce more, provide better quality products and encourage staff around them to work harder.

In 2004 the Learning and Research Council, which is responsible for post-16 education and training outside universities, surveyed 72,100 employers in England. The results showed that 2.4 million workers were classed by their employers as not being proficient in their current jobs. Lack of skills was the main cause, but 33% of the employers also stated lack of motivation as a cause.

This section looks at what happens if staff are de-motivated. If staff are well motivated these negative effects will be reversed.

Effects of poorly motivated staff

Five important effects of poorly motivated staff are examined below, although there are many more. For each negative effect, the opposite will be the case with well motivated staff.

Figure 1 *Effects of poorly motivated staff*

- Poor working environment
- Lower production
- More absenteeism
- POOR MOTIVATION
- Less innovation
- Higher staff turnover

'It's often difficult for managers in a functional areas, like dealing with mail, to keep their employees motivated. There are several factors that lead to this, including relatively low pay, working in what is often considered a low-status department, and the high turnover of personnel. You're now faced with another phenomenon that works against you - the rapid rate of change in the technologies used to do your job. To counter these obstacles, you must motivate your employees by instilling pride in their jobs.'

Source: adapted from The Berkshire Company.

Lower production

When trying to identify poorly motivated staff the following definition has been used.

'They are people who often don't try to do their best and who are rarely willing to spend extra time and effort to get the job done.'

De-motivated staff tend to feel that their jobs are not important and management does not respect them. They, therefore, see little point in working hard. The result is that they produce less than they could and respond negatively to what management is asking them to do.

Poor working environment

De-motivated staff may suffer in silence. But normally they are only too willing to voice their dissatisfaction to other staff, their family and friends and even to the customers.

This can create a negative impression of the business to those outside. It can cause loss of sales and a reluctance in people to look for jobs in the business. It can also affect other people in the business. Negative effects could include:

- other staff becoming de-motivated and working less efficiently;
- pressure put on managers who may react negatively and either blame themselves and become de-motivated or openly blame the staff and create a confrontational atmosphere in the business;
- creating a general atmosphere of negativity, where getting anything done is difficult and, in extreme cases, pointless.

Figure 2 *Motivation and the work environment*

Tackling bullying and harassment at work is the topic for the latest guide for trade unionists from the Labour Research Department (LRD). Bullying and harassment remain widespread in UK workplaces, despite improved legal protection for the victims. One-in-five workers reports being bullied in the last five years and more than one-in-ten in the last six months. Often it is linked to poor management and high workloads, and men and women are just as likely to be bullied and to be bullies.

Source: adapted from Unison, Feb 2005.

Greater absenteeism

When staff are de-motivated they do not generally think that there is very much point in going to work, except that they will be paid.

In many cases staff can take days off, claiming to be sick and still get paid for them. De-motivated staff, therefore, have relatively high levels of absenteeism. Some of these are genuine

and some are not. If staff are not motivated:
- they may become depressed and need absences to cope with this;
- they may prefer to be at home and simply take days off when they feel like it;
- they may feel that any minor illness becomes a good reason for not going to work.
- staff can feel that the business is exploiting them and therefore taking days off is a justified way of getting a fair level of payment for the work done.

According to Susan Rhodes, Associate Professor emeritus of human resource management at Syracuse University, employees miss work for two reasons:
- either they can't come to work;
- they don't want to come to work.

Those who can't come to work usually have legitimate reasons such as illness, transportation problems or childcare/eldercare responsibilities. However, those who lack the motivation to come to work pose the greatest challenge.

Higher staff turnover

Many staff who are de-motivated will simply leave the business. When this happens staff turnover will rise. The level of staff turnover is often a good indication of the level of motivation in the business.

High staff turnover can also lead to additional motivation problems.
- De-motivated leavers usually make the reasons for leaving clear to other colleagues.
- Remaining staff may feel that they should also get out and feel demoralised if they cannot.
- New staff are likely to ask why people left and may pick up on the feeling of negativity.

Less innovation

Many businesses operate in highly competitive markets and finding new products, new promotions, new customer service or provisions is what makes the business stand out. In order to achieve this, however, businesses generally rely upon the inspiration and innovation that comes from their staff.

When staff are de-motivated this inventive flair is one of the first things to go. Staff reactions to a new challenge go from 'This sound interesting, let's see what I can do with it' to 'Who cares'. Firms which have poorly motivated staff often have uninspiring and out-of-date products.

The Employers Council argues that 'Suggestion boxes are making a comeback. More and more companies are taking their boxes into cyberspace - creating suggestion boxes that can be accessed with computers. Suggestion boxes can strengthen your employee's communications and retention efforts. Suggestions -

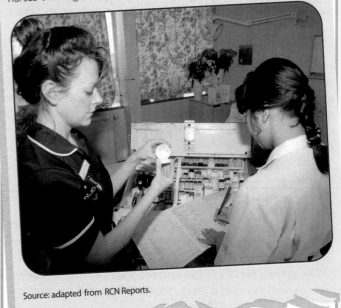

Figure 3 *Turnover of nursing staff*

In 2004 about 50,000 UK trained nurses left the profession. 15,000 of these retired but the rest left for a number of reasons including violence of patients, rigid working hours and dissatisfaction with the pension scheme. These reasons for leaving reflected a worrying level of de-motivation in the profession. With only 20,588 UK trained nurses entering the profession in 2004, that left a huge shortfall.

Source: adapted from RCN Reports.

the ones that don't get ignored by management - can improve employee morale and foster a sense of cooperation between employees and management and reduce the level of employee discontent.'

Positive effects of motivation

Generally, the positive benefits of well motivated staff are that the problems listed above should not happen.
- Motivated staff will be happy to work for the objectives of the firm and production and output per employee should be high.
- The working environment will be positive and workers will support each other and want to improve performance.
- Staff will look forward to coming to work and so absenteeism will be low.
- Staff will be committed to the business, feel part of it and want to stay. Staff turnover will, therefore, be low.
- Staff who are motivated and feel valued by their businesses want to be involved with its development. They, therefore, contribute to the innovation process.

Examination practice · Sainsbury's 'us and them' bonuses

J Sainsbury's new boss was to get share options worth around £1.5m, just as staff have learned they are to lose a long running Christmas cash bonus. The firm confirmed that for the first time in 25 years, full-time staff would not be getting their festive bonus in 2004, worth around £100. Instead the supermarket chain's staff would have to make do with a 5% extension in their store discount. The decision to end the Christmas bonus would affect 100,000 full-time Sainsbury's staff.

Staff reaction

'I work for Sainsbury's and am disgusted that hard-working staff like me are to lose our Christmas bonuses.'

'I work for Sainsbury's at the moment and worked there previously for eight years. It is amazing how much staff moral has gone down in the last eight years – they simply don't care about the general staff, only the fat cats in their suits.'

Source: adapted from BBC News, 21.5. 2004.

(a) **Identify TWO decisions by Sainsbury that are likely to de-motivate staff. Explain why each could de-motivate. (4 marks)**

(b) **Explain the likely effects that these decisions might have on general staff at the business in terms of:**
(i) production;
(ii) the working environment;
(iii) absenteeism;
(iv) staff turnover.
For each of these, justify why it might have that effect. (12 marks)

(c) **Examine whether these decisions might cost the business more than it will save. (9 marks)**

Meeting the assessment criteria

In 2004 the Royal Mail introduced an incentive system for its workers, specifically designed to reduce the level of absenteeism. This included rewards for not taking days off for sick leave. Rewards included new cars (37 workers), £2,000 holiday vouchers (70 workers) and other £150 vouchers (90,000 workers). The Royal Mail recorded a fall in sickness absences from 6.7% to 5.7%.

Source: adapted from various sources.

(a) State TWO likely reasons, other than sickness, for absenteeism at the Royal Mail. **(2 marks)**

Expected answers
- *Dissatisfaction with the job/de-motivation.*
- *Staff extending their weekends.*
- *Family issues, e.g. a child is sick.*
- *Hangovers after a heavy weekend.*
- *Person experiencing stress.*
(The reasons should reflect the fact that absenteeism can be both habitual and occasional).

Mark allocation
1 mark for each reason. **(2 marks)**

(b) Explain why it may be difficult for the Royal Mail to tell the difference between sick leave and other forms of absenteeism. **(3 marks)**

Expected answers
- *Staff may lie about why they are absent – with sickness they will be paid, for other reasons they may not be paid – may show they are sick when they are not.*
- *Some causes of absences are difficult to categorise – feeling stressed/de-motivated may or may not be sickness – the figures may, or may not, be recorded as sickness.*

Mark allocation
1 mark for basic reason.
1 mark for how this relates to sickness or example or development of reason.
1 mark for why it is therefore difficult to tell the difference. **(3 marks)**

(c) With reference to the data about the Royal Mail, explain why the incentive system was so important for the business and why it was successful. **(5 marks)**

Expected answers
- *Absenteeism was very high/6.7% – this would cost the business in terms of lost production/sickness payment – incentives offered looked very generous/new car – rewards only offered if no sick days were taken off – staff saw incentives as sufficient to actually go to work every day.*

Mark allocation
1 mark for why it was needed (maximum 2 marks).
1 mark for example of an incentive scheme from the data.
1 mark for explaining how the incentive schemes achieved this effect (maximum 2 marks). **(5 marks)**

10 Motivation theories

Motivation theories and practice

Section 11 deals with the ways in which businesses actually motivate their staff. In many cases the businesses are putting into practice some of the best know motivational theories dealt with in this section. The theories have developed slowly over time and are continuing to develop. This section will look at the theories of:

- Taylor – Scientific Management;
- Mayo – Behavioural Management;
- McGregor – Theory X, Theory Y;
- Maslow – Hierarchy of Needs;
- Herzberg – Motivation-Hygiene Theory.

F.W. Taylor (1856 - 1915)

Fredrick Taylor believed that the main factor that motivated workers was money. He argued that providing workers with the opportunity to earn more money by producing more efficiently would be beneficial to both the workers and the business.

Taylor, working in the steel industry, noticed that many workers were producing well below what they were capable of. He noted three reasons for this.

- The belief amongst the workers that if they produced more individually some would lose their jobs.
- Pay systems that did not motivate them to work harder.
- Producing products in an inefficient way.

He then set about trying to find the most efficient way of producing products. He used a stop-watch to time each part of the production process and to check how quickly it could be done. This became known as time and motion study. When he had worked out the most efficient way to produce, he then changed the work practices at the business. This involved the following changes.

- Using specialist equipment.
- Breaking jobs down into very simple tasks.
- Devising a set procedure for workers which they had to stick to.
- Training workers in these specific jobs.
- Using piece rates to encourage people to produce more.

This approach essentially treated the workplace and the workers as though they were part of a scientific experiment which is why Taylor's approach is known as **Scientific Management**.

The main drawback of Taylor's approach was that it treated workers as just a basic factor of production with no choice as to how they would do their work. The manager was autocratic and decided exactly how the worker would work. It also ignored the fact that workers are not just motivated by pay.

An example of this scientific approach is shown in the calculation of the minimum wage for piece workers in Figure 1.

Figure 1 *Piece rate rewards*

Whilst the National Minimum Wage (NMW) ensures that all workers receive a basic rate per hour £5.05/hour from October 2005, it is more difficult to protect workers who are paid for 'rated output work' (piece rate). The law now requires that workers on piece-rate will be paid as follows.

The employer must work out how many pieces can be made by the average worker in one hour and then set the rate of pay so that the average worker will get at least 120% of the minimum wage (i.e. £6.06). Faster workers will get paid more but really slow workers could get paid well below the NMW.

Source: adapted from DTI, *Guidance on new system for 'fair' piece rates.*

Elton Mayo (1880 - 1949)

Elton Mayo's studies of how people worked started with experiments on changing physical conditions in the workplace, for example giving workers longer breaks. At the Hawthorne Works of the General Electric Company in Chicago he expanded this work to find out what effect fatigue and monotony had on job productivity and how to control them through varying rest breaks, work hours, temperature and humidity.

Part of this research involved interviewing all 10,000 employees to find out why some worked better than others even when the rest periods were reduced. What he discovered was that what really determined how well people worked was not so much their physical environment as how well motivated they were and their social interaction with other workers.

He came to certain conclusions.

- Work is a group activity.
- The need for recognition, security and a sense of belonging is more important in determining workers' motivation and productivity than the physical conditions under which they works.
- Informal groups within the workplace have a major effect on work habits and attitudes of the individual worker.

To ensure that workers work efficiently, it becomes necessary to manage the way they behave, including managing the environment so that they will be motivated and want to work. This is why his approach is referred to as **behavioural management**.

Douglas McGregor (1906 - 1964)

Taylor had put forward the theory that workers are motivated solely by money and need to be told what to do. Mayo showed that other factors affected how people work, especially the social environment and whether or not they felt valued.

Douglas McGregor essentially summed up these two theories when he described two opposing ways of managing workers. McGregor saw two extreme styles of management which he called **Theory X** and **Theory Y**. The style of management chosen depended on what the managers felt was the attitude of their workers to work. The characteristics of the two management styles are shown in Table 1.

Table 1 *Theory X and Theory Y management styles*

Theory X	Theory Y
1. The average worker dislikes work and avoids it whenever possible.	1. Workers see work as a natural activity which can be enjoyable.
2. Most people have to be persuaded, controlled, directed and even threatened with punishment to achieve goals.	2. Working conditions will affect how workers feel about their work so the right conditions need to be provided.
3. Security of environment is important.	3. Workers can be committed and this should be recognised and rewarded.
4. The average worker dislikes responsibility and needs supervision.	4. Motivated workers will seek additional responsibility and need less directing.

- Theory X Managers. They use close supervision and dictate how workers should carry out their jobs, monitoring them carefully to make sure they do the work set.
- Theory Y Managers. They will give workers more responsibility and praise and will ensure that they have a positive working environment.

Abraham Maslow (1908 - 1970)

Abraham Maslow was a psychologist who originally studied the way in which monkeys behaved and then applied these studies to an examination of how humans behaved and what motivated them. He saw a hierarchy of needs, where it was generally necessary to meet one set of needs before the next and higher set of needs could be met. Typically these needs are shown in the form of a pyramid as in Figure 2.

For employers and managers, recognising these needs and providing for them was the way to motivate workers and increase productivity and efficiency and improve the working

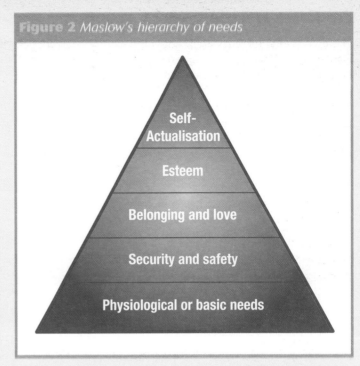

Figure 2 *Maslow's hierarchy of needs*

environment. Some examples are shown in Table 2. In one way or another, Maslow's theories and approach can have an impact on all businesses.

Table 2 *Meeting Maslow's hierarchy of needs in business*

Need	Employer provides
Physiological The basic needs of hunger, thirst and warmth.	Pay and sometimes food and accommodation.
Security The need to be protected from danger and feel secure.	Job security and a safe and healthy working environment.
Belongingness The need to feel part of something and be accepted.	Opportunities to be part of a team, in a friendly working environment.
Esteem The need to be recognised and praised for achievements.	Opportunities to make decisions, and rewards for and acknowledgement of success.
Self-actualisation The need to find self-fulfilment and to achieve one's potential.	Challenges for employees and the freedom to carry out employees' own ideas.

Frederick Herzberg (1923 - 2000)

Maslow's studies were generally not in the workplace. Frederick Herzberg, like Taylor and Mayo, researched actual workers. He interviewed employees in a number of different jobs about what they felt about their work.

Herzberg concluded from his studies that there were two elements needed for people to succeed in their work. Motivation was vital. However, before that was possibly certain basic needs, which he called hygiene factors, had to be met. If not, motivation would be negatively affected. These are shown in Table 3.

In his interviews with employees he asked them what pleased and displeased them about their jobs. He found that what pleased people were the **motivators**, and what displeased them were negative aspects of the **hygiene factors**.

The importance for employers and managers is that, if they want their employees to be motivated, they must first of all provide an acceptable level of basic hygiene factors. Then they must provide the motivators. An example is shown in Figure 3.

Table 3 *Motivators and hygiene factors*

Hygiene factors	Motivators
• Salary • Security • Working conditions • Position in the business • Company policy • Supervision • Interpersonal relationships	• Achievement • Recognition of achievement • Interesting work • Responsibility • The chance of advancement

Figure 3 *How hygiene factors are important*

A survey carried out in small and medium sized enterprises (SMEs) found that a third of employees felt that they were unable to improve their own performance because of lack of effective training. As many as 80% wanted the training to provide them with more flexibility in terms of their jobs. They also wanted the training to involve more face-to-face contact as part of the training.

Source: adapted from Bizhel p24, April 2005.

Examination practice - new leadership style in local authorites

Traditionally local authorities are managed from the top down. In the 1990s there was an attempt to change, to a fairer and more democratic approach, where motivation of staff was considered equally important. Unfortunately, in the end, these leaders ultimately regarded themselves as the font of power and knowledge.

The Rosen Group in the USA, studying a similar situation, compared one team led by an Interactive Leader and other teams in the same organisation led by traditional leaders. It found that the only team to be able to be consistently successful in the long-run was the interactive team, where employees were 'customer-focused, agreed a shared purpose and consulted other employees on their ideas'. They were ecouraged to take risks, strive for the best solutions and received praise for their efforts. They out-performed all other teams in the company.

Source: adapted from Employers' Organisation for Local Government '21st Century Leadership'.

(a) Explain, giving an appropriate example from local government, what is meant by:
(i) 'managed from the top down';
(ii) 'Interactive Leader'.
(4 marks)

(b) Identify which parts of the Rosen Group's study match different needs identified by Malsow. Justify your choices. **(8 marks)**
(c) Evaluate whether the management style in UK local authorities is closer to McGregor's Theory X or to his Theory Y. **(8 marks)**

Meeting the assessment criteria

When label manufacturer, MTM Products Ltd, was made Joint UK Small Employer of the Year it summed up its approach to employee/manager relations. 'We work on the basis of mutual trust between managers and employees and are now benefiting from the extra commitment and innovative ideas generated by many of our employees.'

The business also employs a work-life balance policy, ensures involvement of all staff in policy decisions and actively practices equality of opportunity. The result has been excellent staff retention, lower absenteeism, higher motivation and increased profitability.

Source: adapted from www.workingfamilies.co.uk.

(a) Identify which elements of the work at MTM Products Ltd. fit the following sections from Maslow's hierarchy of needs.
   (i)   Security and safety.
   (ii) Belonging.
   (iii) Esteem.
   (iv) Self-actualisation.   **(4 marks)**

Expected answers
(i) Practices of equality of opportunity.
(ii) Trust between managers and employers.
(iii) Involvement in all policy decisions.
(iv) Innovative ideas from employees are encouraged/work-life balance policy.

Mark allocation
1 mark for each element.   **(4 marks)**

(b) Using Mayo's approach to human resource management, and information in the article, explain why there was increased profitability at MTM Products Ltd.   **(7 marks)**

Expected answers
Basic reason
• *Increased motivation.*

Explanation with reference to Mayo
• *Group activity – staff involved in all policy decisions – helps to encourage innovation – new ideas could be profitable.*
• *Sense of belonging – mutual trust between managers and employees – employees will feel part of the business – employees will work to make it a success and increase profitability.*
• *Receive recognition – involved in policy decisions – feel their ideas are being listened to and become more committed/work harder.*

Mark allocation
1 mark for basic reason without reference to Mayo.
1 mark for Mayo approach (maximum 2 marks).
1 mark for identifying appropriate feature at MTM (maximum 2 marks).
1 mark for how this would lead to increased productivity (maximum 2 marks).   **(7 marks)**

(c) As part of its overall employee policy MTM allows employees to change working hours during school holidays and it also offers, part-time and home working. Staff repay this caring approach by offering to work when additional staff are needed urgently. Explain why this approach does **not** match Fredrick Taylor's view of what motivates workers.   **(6 marks)**

Expected answers
• *Workers primarily motivated by pay according to Taylor – but staff have other concerns such as their children – MTM caters for these other needs.*
• *Staff should be told exactly what to do according to Taylor – staff are allowed to innovate – staff involved in policy making.*
• *Decisions are made by management according to Taylor – staff negotiate some of their working condition – flexibility is offered by both sides/holiday arrangements & willing to work extra when needed urgently.*

Mark allocation
1 mark for Taylor's view (maximum 3 marks).
1 mark for why each view is not the approach in MTM (maximum 3 marks).   **(6 marks)**

Motivation in practice

Many students reading this book have part-time jobs and for them there may be two main motivators:
- pay;
- job satisfaction.

In contrast, for businesses the two most likely reasons for their choice of the way in which they will motivate employees could be:
- which way will gain most profits for the business;
- which way will keep employees motivated and producing efficiently.

This section will be looking at the real factors that motivate staff and real incentives that businesses use. Many of these factors will show that the theorists in section 10 got it right. Other factors will show that in the real world simple explanations of why people work, e.g. pay, pressure, family commitments, are more significant.

Real motivators

Research carried out in 2004 found that what actually motivates staff to go to work is very different to what motivates them when they are at work. 1,500 staff were questioned. The results are shown in Figures 1 and 2.

This survey shows that pay is the primary drive, which is not surprising and matches the first level of Maslow's hierarchy of needs. Pay also provides security, the second level, and in many cases the level of pay also shows recognition.

Whilst at work and actually doing the job, pay is less important because that has already been sorted out, which was the main reason why the person took the job in the first place. Now Maslow's higher levels come into effect, with esteem needs being met by responsibility and recognition.

The list of what the staff felt motivated them at work also

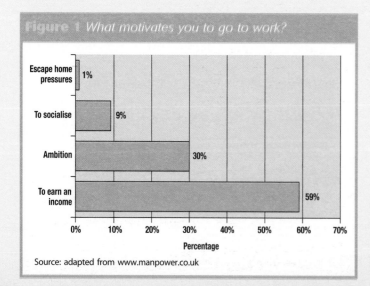

Figure 1 *What motivates you to go to work?*

Source: adapted from www.manpower.co.uk

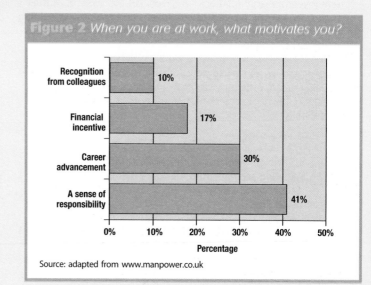

Figure 2 *When you are at work, what motivates you?*

Source: adapted from www.manpower.co.uk

matches many of the motivators identified by Herzberg.

What motivates individuals either to go to work or in their work depends on the nature of the job and individual circumstances.

The nature of the job

Most people need to take a job so that they are paid and can afford to buy the necessities and sometimes the luxuries of life. But there are many different types of job, ranging from charity work to dealing in the financial markets in London and these frequently show that people are motivated by very different factors. Table 1 shows some general examples.

Table 1 *Examples of jobs and their motivations*	
Charity work, e.g. Oxfam	The main motivation here is to help to make other people better off. In Oxfam shops some staff are even unpaid.
Vocational jobs, e.g. teaching and nursing	Here the motivation is generally the belief that the job is worth doing and there are positive results in terms of examination grades or patients getting better is a major motivator.
Inspirational jobs, e.g. performing music.	Creating something worthwhile and being recognised for that are likely to be major motivators.
Jobs in highly competitive businesses	Here success is vital and people are likely to be motivated by succeeding, receiving recognition, gaining higher pay and achieving promotion.

Individual circumstances

In reality every individual is likely to have their own set of factors that motivate them and therefore it is difficult to pin down exactly what motivates people at work unless each person was given a lengthy individual interview.

It is, however, possible to suggest some general motivators which typically fit with people in different circumstances, as shown in Table 2.

Table 2 *General motivators*	
Students	They frequently have a relatively low income and pay will be a major motivator.
People over the age of retirement	Again, they may be relatively poorly off and need the money to supplement their pensions. For the better off keeping active and being with other people is often a major motivator.
Mothers with young children	Flexible working and fitting round school hours will be important as will be, for many people, continuing to progress in a career.
People taking out mortgages for the first time	They will need a reasonable level of pay, but also job security and hopefully promotion prospects so that they can comfortably pay off their mortgage.

What businesses offer

When most businesses provide jobs they do recognise that motivating staff is vital. This is needed in order to keep staff productive and to ensure that they stay with the firm. Businesses therefore offer a range of incentives and benefits. An example is shown in Figure 3.

Figure 3 *Benefits for a Business Development Manager*

Business Development Manager
(Oxford): Kitchens
THE PACKAGE:
Basic Salary : £25-30,000
Commission/Bonus : £7,000 Commission
Company Car : Peugeot 407
Benefits : Mobile, Laptop, BUPA,
Pension, Lunch Allowance

Benefits and incentives

In many cases the basic motivations are clear to the business and it provides these as a matter of course. They may include the following.
- A good rate of pay.
- Promotion prospects.
- Generous holiday provisions.
- A company pension scheme.
- On-site facilities, such as a staff canteen.

Many more specific benefits are related to the type of business involved. Examples of these are shown in Table 3.

Although these kinds of benefits do not usually make people choose to work for that business, they can help to motivate staff who are already there.

Table 3 *Motivators for particular occupations*	
Banks	Cheap loans and mortgages.
Airline companies	Cheap or free flights for staff and for their immediate families.
Car salesroom	Use of demonstration models to get to and from work.
Fast food restaurants	Free meals and drinks.
Public schools	Reduced fees for children of staff.
Clothes retailers	Discounts on clothes.

Providing the right working conditions

Many businesses will provide staff with good working conditions in terms of a pleasant working environment, practical furniture, the right equipment and canteens or at least access to facilities to make hot drinks. They will also provide a safe working environment because that is a legal requirement.

Other businesses will think more about how people work and how to provide motivation. This may involve providing the following kinds of environment.
- The possibility of working in teams.
- Open access to senior management so that staff can discuss problems and ideas.
- Regular appraisal sessions.
- Flexible working arrangements.
- Planned career development.

An example is shown in Figure 4.

Figure 4 *Motivation at Lyreco UK*

Relationships throughout the company are good. When the managing director eats lunch in the low-cost canteen, employees 'plonk' themselves next to him for a chat. He must be a good talker, as 82% think he is full of positive energy.

Source: adapted from www.business.timesonline.

Negative motivators

Generally motivators are thought of as being positive incentives that make staff want to work harder because they will be better off because of this. There are, however, also negative motivators which are threats rather than rewards that make staff work harder. These negative motivators may include:

- the threat of being sacked if staff do not work harder;
- insisting on unpaid overtime if jobs are not completed on schedule;
- possibly bullying.

In some cases what looks like a motivator, such as performance-related pay, may simply be a clever way of the employers getting more out of their employees with little thought about their welfare. Performance-related pay can often lead to additional pressure, stress and even illness.

These two approaches are sometimes referred to as the carrot and stick approach. The carrot motivates workers positively (an incentive or reward) and the stick motivates workers negatively (a punishment or threat).

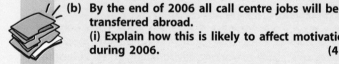

Examination practice · Motivation at First Direct

First Direct, the telephone and Internet bank, owned by HSBC has a majority of female staff, about 70%. 53% of staff are under 35 years old and staff turnover is 12%. To support working mothers there is an on-site crèche and facilities for children of school age during the holidays. Staff are also offered flexible shift patterns, overtime if additional money is needed and at least 25 days holiday a year.

HSBC has decided that the 4,000 call centre jobs will be transferred to India, China and Malaysia by the end of 2006 and this has greatly reduced the confidence staff have in their senior management.

Source: adapted from *The Sunday Times,* 100 Best Companies to Work For.

(a) Considering the type of staff that work for First Direct, assess how appropriate the support is that the business provides. **(6 marks)**

(b) By the end of 2006 all call centre jobs will be transferred abroad.
(i) Explain how this is likely to affect motivation during 2006. **(4 marks)**

(ii) Explain what measures First Direct could introduce to ensure that during 2006 motivation in the business is kept at a high level. **(6 marks)**

Meeting the assessment criteria

Pinnacle has a strong team spirit. 81% of staff say they have a laugh with colleagues and 83% believe they make a valuable contribution to the company's success. A 'take it to the top' initiative allows staff direct access to the chief executive at pre-advertised monthly visits. They can raise any issue they like and 82% describe him as 'full of positive energy'.

Staff are given the choice of a wide variety of working options, including job sharing, part-time working, flexible working hours, occasional and permanent home working and team-based self-rostering. Holidays are set at 25 days for everyone, but staff can sell or buy five days. Life insurance is offered at four times salary and employer contributions to the pension scheme are 7% for staff and 10% for directors, with an employee contribution of 2.5%.

The company offers performance-related pay. Other awards include employee of the month and best suggestion of the year where the employee is rewarded with a week's holiday in the executive chairman's villa in Italy.

Source: adapted from The *Sunday Times,* 100 Best Companies to Work For.

For each of the following benefits for staff explain why they would motivate staff and outline ONE problem that providing staff with that benefit might create for the business.

(i) A 'take it to the top' initiative.
(ii) Team-based self-rostering.
(iii) Life insurance at four times salary.
(iv) Employee of the month awards. **(12 marks)**

Expected answers

- *Allows staff to approach senior management on a regular basis – staff will feel their views are valued by senior management – may tie up valuable time for senior managers.*
- *Teams can choose between themselves when they will work – allows staff more flexibility – may not match when management wants staff to be working.*
- *Life insurance cover provided at four times current salary – will give staff a sense of security for their family – premiums will have to be paid by business.*
- *One employee will be selected each month as the best employee – will satisfy the esteem need/achievement will be recognised – staff who never get the award may feel de-motivated and work less.*

Mark allocation

1 mark for showing understanding of the benefit.
1 mark for why it would motivate.
1 mark for why it would cause a problem for the business.

(1 + 1 + 1) x 4
(12 marks)

Protecting employees

Section 8 explained that businesses have legal and ethical considerations to take into account when recruiting and selecting employees. These affect the equality of treatment of employees. Once staff have been employed, businesses then need to ensure that staff are happy in work and well motivated. Well motivated employees are likely to work hard for the business and help towards its success.

Contracts of employment

When employees are first appointed to a post they are given a contract of employment. This is either a verbal or written agreement by the organisation to employ the worker.

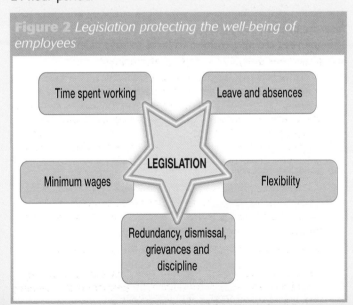

Figure 1 *Written statement of terms and conditions of a CNC machine operator*

You
Darren Hayles
began employment with
Peabody Engineering
on
1 April 2005
Your previous employment with
Jones Ltd
does count as part of your period of continuous employment which therefore began on
25 August 2002
You are employed as
A machine operator responsible for operating CNC machinery
Your place of work is
Peabody Engineering, Unit 135 Ainscough Trading Estate, Newcastle
And the address of your employer is
As above
Your pay will be
£18,000 annually
You will be paid
On 24th of each month for work in the previous month
Your hours of work are
9am – 5pm each day
Your holiday entitlement is
25 days plus statutory holidays
Particulars of any terms and conditions relating to incapacity to work due to sickness or injury, including any provision for sick pay, can be found in
The company handbook
Particulars of terms and conditions relating to pensions and pension schemes, can be found in
The company handbook
Particulars of the amount of notice of termination of your employment you are entitled to receive and are required to give are given in
The company handbook
Your employment is permanent - subject to above and to general rights of termination under the law
You are not expected to work outside the UK (for more than one month)
The disciplinary rules which apply to you can be found in
The company handbook
If you are dissatisfied with any disciplinary (or, from 1 October 2004, dismissal) decision which affects you, you should apply in the first instance to
Your line manager, Mrs J Sheering

Source: adapted from www.dti.gov.uk.

- The **Employment Rights Act, 1996** states that employers must then provide a written statement of employment within two months, stating the terms and conditions of employment. An example of a written statement is shown in Figure 1.
- The **Wages Act, 1986** sets out conditions for payments to workers and any deductions, such as National Insurance contributions, income tax or pension or trade union membership payments.

The terms and conditions of employees shown in their contract of employment will affect their well-being and motivation. There is a variety of legislation in the UK and the EU that exists to protect employees in a number of areas. Employees are given certain rights at work by these laws. Areas where they may be affected are shown in Figure 2.

Time spent working

The amount of time that employees spend at work is influenced by legislation. Workers must be protected from working for too long, so maximum amounts of continuous time that employees can be made to work are often set out in legislation. This could be:

- the number of hours worked at one time;
- the number of hours worked in a week;
- the number of days worked in a year.

The **European Working Time Directive** limits the maximum amount of continuous time that employees can be made to work in a week to 48 hours. There are some exceptions, however. These include executives and junior doctors. Employees must also be given a 20 minute rest break after every 6 hours worked. Workers who work at night may be particularly affected. Their work time is limited to 8 hours in any 24 hour period.

Figure 2 *Legislation protecting the well-being of employees*

- Time spent working
- Leave and absences
- Minimum wages
- Flexibility
- LEGISLATION
- Redundancy, dismissal, grievances and discipline

Figure 3 *Problems in working too long*

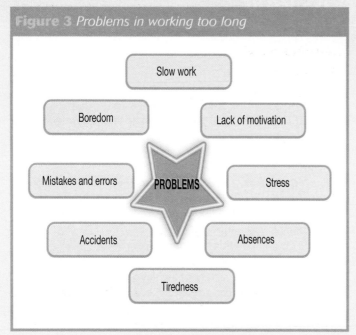

If employees work too long they may experience certain problems, as shown in Figure 3. This can be a problem for both employees and businesses.

Employees Employees who work too long may become tired, bored and stressed. This may result in slow work or errors. Workers may have accidents or be off work with stress, losing earnings.

Businesses Errors and slow work can be costly for the business. Output may fall, errors may be costly to replace and their reputation may be affected.

Leave

Employees are entitled by law to regular leave. This is often in the form of a number of days each year. The **European Working Time Directive** states that employees are entitled to 4 weeks' annual paid leave a year. They are also entitled to statutory holidays as well, such as Christmas Day, Boxing Day and bank holidays. Employees who work too long are likely to face the problems in Figure 3.

Employees are also entitled to leave to have children. The **Employment Act, 2002** states that employers must give:

- maternity leave to mothers having children;
- paternity leave to fathers whose partners or wives are having children.

The Act states that parents and adoptive parents are entitled to a period of leave when children are born and sets rates of pay. Mothers are also given the right to return to work as long as this is within one year.

Minimum wages

The **Minimum Wage Act, 1998** states that employees must be guaranteed a minimum wage. This is the minimum amount that they must be paid each hour. It is unlawful for businesses to pay employees less than the minimum wage. Table 1 shows how the rate has changed over a number of years.

It is argued that employees will benefit from a minimum wage because:

- they will be guaranteed a minimum level of payment which could prevent poverty and perhaps sickness and absences;
- they will be more motivated knowing that they are earning a fair wage;
- it helps to reduce wage differences by erasing the pay of lower paid workers;
- it may encourage people to take jobs that they might not have otherwise taken due to low pay.

Minimum wages do increase the costs of businesses. But a better paid and more motivated workforce could be more productive for the business and offset these costs.

Table 1 *Changes in the minimum wage rate, per hour*

	2000	01	02	03	04	05*	06*
18-22 year olds	3.20	3.50	3.60	3.80	4.10	4.25	4.45
22 year olds +	3.70	4.10	4.20	4.50	4.85	5.05	5.35

* Future rates in April 2005.
Source: adapted from www.dti.gov.uk.

Flexibility

Employees may have a number of opportunities to work flexibly. Certain legislation protects employees in this area.

- People job share. This is usually where two employees do one job. One employee might do the job in the morning and the other in the afternoon. An example could be a rail tickets sales person, where one person sells tickets in the morning and the other in the afternoon.

Figure 4 *Minimum wage rates*

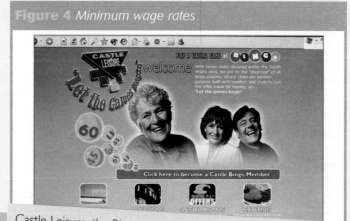

Castle Leisure, the Bingo Hall operator, aims to maintain a 25 to 30 pence differential between its rates and the national minimum wage. In 2004 its lowest starting rate was £4.75 an hour rising to £5.25 an hour.

In 2004 HSBC amalgamated its lowest clerical grades, increasing the minimum rate by 22% from £10,000 a year to £12,500.

Source: adapted from www.unison.org.uk and Low Pay Commission.

- Shift work. In some businesses, such as car manufacturing, employees work different shifts. There might be three shifts (early morning start, afternoon start, night shift).
- Annualised hours. This is where an employee's contract states they will work a certain number of hours a year. But they may be able to vary the number of hours they work each day, week or month.
- Part time work. This is where employees only work part of the day or week. The **Part-Time Workers (Prevention of Less Favourable Treatment) Regulations, 2000** and the **Employment Relations Act, 1999** prevents part-time workers from being treated less favourably than full-time employees over pay, conditions, leave, pensions and holidays.
- Flexible hours. The **Employment Act, 2002** gives certain employees, such as parents with children under 6 or disabled children under 18, the right to request flexibility in their terms of employment, such as working flexible hours. This must be granted by employers unless there are valid business reasons.

Employees and businesses may benefit from working flexibly. Example are shown in Table 2.

Table 2 *Effects of flexibility*

Employees	Employers
Better work/home life balance	Motivated employees
Work when they want	Work takes place at times that suit conditions
Can change work to suit conditions	May reduce costs
Reduced stress	Less stress and absences

Redundancy, dismissal, grievances and discipline

Laws exist to protect employees in the areas of redundancy, dismissal, grievances and discipline.

Redundancy Employees can be 'made redundant' by a business. But a business cannot simply tell a person that they no longer 'have a job'. Employees have certain rights under the **Employment Rights Act, 1996**.

- Redundancy can only take place if there is no job or insufficient work. Employees can not be made redundant one day and another person employed to do the same job the next.
- Employees who have worked for a certain period are entitled to redundancy or severance pay.
- A period of notice must be given by the business.

Table 3 *Legal and unfair dismissal – possible examples*

Legal dismissal
- Incapable of doing the job.
- Unqualified for the job.
- Deliberately providing false information during the selection procedure.
- Serious misconduct such as theft.

Unlawful dismissal
- Joining a trade union.
- Pregnancy, although able to do the job.
- Following incorrect procedures.
- Breaking legislation regarding gender, race or age. This is dealt with in section 8.

Grievances Employees sometimes have complaints or grievances at work. If these are not dealt with the employee may become demotivated, take days off or look for another job. Examples of grievances might be:
- being overlooked for promotion when qualified and the best candidate;
- being singled out for unfair criticism;
- being continually selected for difficult tasks or those which are not part of the job.

The **Employment Act, 2002** introduced minimum grievance procedures that businesses must have.

Dismissal Employees can not just simply be 'dismissed' and told that they have no job. Legislation protects the right of employees in this area. The **Employment Act, 2002** sets out conditions in which employees may be dismissed. Employees must have worked for one year to qualify. Dismissal may be legal or it may be unfair dismissal. Examples are given in Table 3. Before dismissal takes place, employees must be given verbal and written warnings. Employees who feel that they have been unfairly dismissed can take their case to an employment tribunal. It has the power to reinstate employees and pay compensation.

Discipline Employees must comply with the terms and conditions of their contract. If they break these they may be liable for disciplinary procedures. The **Employment Rights Act, 1996** sets out the conditions and rules of these procedures. Employees must be:
- informed of these procedures;
- the consequences of breaking them;
- investigations of complaints;
- rights of appeal.

Examination practice · Whitbread plc

Whitbread PLC is a leading UK hospitality company. It manages a number of hotels, restaurants and health and fitness clubs. These include:
- Premier Travel Inn;
- Brewers Fayre;
- Beefeater;
- Costa;
- T.G.I. Friday's;
- David Lloyd Leisure.

It also has a strategic investment in Pizza Hut (UK).

Whitbread has around 67,000 employees. The leisure industry accounts for one in every ten jobs. It will account for one in every five new jobs created. So recruitment is a big issue. In order to attract and retain the best staff Whitbread's commitment to caring for and developing its people is one of the company's most important concerns.

Whitbread recognises that commitment to its employees also has a direct impact on the business. In short, content and satisfied people equate to satisfied customers, which equals happy shareholders. Whitbread treats its people according to three basic principles.
- It cares for them.
- It makes clear what is required from them.
- It treats people as individuals.

There are, of course, a number of things that Whitbread has to do for its people. Most of them legal requirements, such as the Minimum Wage and the Working Time Directive. David

Lloyd Leisure, for example has a commitment to pay more than the minimum wage.

Source: adapted from www.whitbread.co.uk and www.unison.org.uk.

Really nice family rooms for four from just £46.95

That's great value, whichever way you look at it.

So it is!

Go to premiertravelinn.com or call 0870 242 8000

premier travel inn

Good night, after night, after night...

(a) State FOUR pieces of information that should be contained in the contract of employment of an employee at Whitbread. **(4 marks)**

(b) Examine THREE ways in which employees at the business might be affected by its approach. **(6 marks)**

(c) Considering the service offered by the business, identify THREE pieces of legislation that would particularly affect it in terms of its employees. Explain why the legislation is so important. **(9 marks)**

Meeting the assessment criteria

Connahs Quay Antiques is a business that restores and then re-sells old prices of ceramics and furniture. It scours the markets around the UK or attic clearances looking for unusual pieces that may be a little damaged but sell for a cheap price. The business has three shops in the North Wales area. Repairs are carried out at its repair centre in Flint. It employs three specialist repair workers. The oldest is aged 40 and has spent many years working in the trade. The other two are 21 and 18, with little experience, but are important to help share the workload. One works part-time. The other has a child under 6.

In the summer of 2005 the business bought a number of 'job lots' from attic sales. This has meant working hard in a very short period to repair the pieces. The business has spent a lot of money buying these 'lots' and needs to sell the products as quickly as possible. It was concerned about the impact of holidays that the two younger employees might take, although it wanted to be flexible. Working long hours also meant that the two younger repair workers did not always have enough time when they needed it. They asked whether they could work less at other times or they may consider looking for other jobs.

Source: adapted from company information.

(a) From the data identify THREE pieces of legislation that might affect the business and say why the legislation would apply. **(6 marks)**

Expected answers
- *Minimum Wages Act, 1998 - states the minimum wages to be paid to different age groups.*
- *European Working Time Directive - states the number of hours in a week and rest breaks that must be taken.*
- *Employment Relations Act, 1999 prevents part-time workers from being treated less favourably than full time employees.*
- *Employment Act, 2002 - gives employees the right to request flexible working time in the case of children under 6.*

Mark allocation
1 mark for Act.
1 mark for why.   **(1 + 1) x 3 (6 marks)**

(b) State and explain THREE benefits for Connahs Quay Antiques in having staff that are motivated. **(6 marks)**

Expected answers
- *Share the workload - the senior repair worker can not do all the work.*
- *Staff turnover - may leave the business and take skills elsewhere, perhaps to competitors.*
- *Cash flow reasons - the business must make the repairs quickly and sell products to recover expenditure.*
- *Prevent errors - can be costly and time consuming to put right.*

Mark allocation
1 mark for benefit.
1 mark for applied explanation.   **(1 + 1) x 3 (6 marks)**

13 Environmental issues

What are environmental issues?

The environment is the surroundings in which people live and in which businesses operate. As businesses manufacture goods or provide services they make use of the environment. Consider the manufacture of a piece of furniture as shown in Figure 1. It will move through a number of stages in production. At each stage the environment is likely to be affected by the activities of businesses involved in the production process.

Figure 1 *The production process for a piece of furniture*

Stages	Issues
Grow the trees	*What damage will be done to the woodland?*
Cut down the trees	*Will they be replaced?*
Transport the trees to a factory	*How much fuel will be used? What exhaust fumes will there be?*
Cut the wood	*What will happen to waste?*
Use other processes to make the furniture	*How many other resources will be used? Will the factory be an eyesore? Will fumes emit from the factory? What noise will there be?*
Transport the product to the retailer	*Will traffic congestion be caused?*
Sell the product	*Will out of town retailers be located on greenfield sites?*

The example in Figure 1 helps to illustrate some of the major environmental issues facing businesses. When businesses make goods or provide services they:

- use up resources;
- create waste;
- create pollution;
- affect the surrounding area in which they operate;
- create other problems such as warming of the atmosphere;
- create transport difficulties and congestion.

Society is becoming increasingly concerned with the impact of businesses on the environment. These environmental issues will affect businesses and their employees in different ways. In some cases government legislation exists which constrains business activities. Some pressure groups, as explained in section 14, are set up to promote the protection of the environment. In some cases businesses self-regulate their own activities as a result of their own business aims and environmental policies. Figure 2 shows some of the main environmental issues facing businesses.

Figure 2 *Environmental issues*

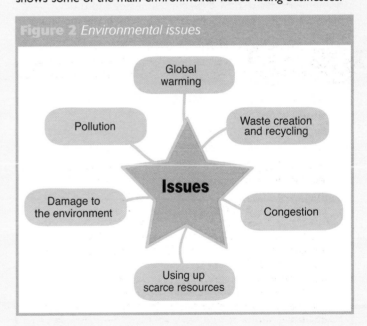

- Global warming
- Pollution
- Waste creation and recycling
- **Issues**
- Damage to the environment
- Congestion
- Using up scarce resources

Pollution

Pollution issues are about the contamination of the world's resources. Businesses may cause pollution by their activities in a number of ways.

Air pollution This is where business activities cause gases to be emitted into the atmosphere from machines, factories and vehicles. Examples of air pollution may be:

- a foundry producing smoke which is released into the air;
- the release of carbon dioxide into the air from the exhausts of lorries delivering materials;
- the release of nuclear energy due to safety failure in nuclear plants.

Water pollution This is the pollution of rivers, lakes and the sea as a result of business activity. Examples might be:

- pesticides used in agriculture passed into rivers or lakes;
- dumping of waste by factories near rivers, such as breweries;
- oil from cargo ships leaking into the sea, polluting water and fish and also damaging wildlife and the coast.

Noise pollution This is the creation of excessive noise levels in business activity which disturb society. Examples include:
- bars staying open late into the night with noisy customers;
- noise created by vehicles;
- noise from outside machinery used in road repair or building;
- late night flights.

A variety of pressure groups exist which attempt to put pressure on businesses to control pollution or on government to pass laws to limit or cut pollution levels. Examples in the UK include Friends of the Earth UK, Greenpeace UK and the National Society for Clean Air (NSCA).

Legislation to limit pollution in the UK includes:
- the **Environment Act, 1995** set up The Environment Agency to monitor pollution and set in place regulations on pollution issues such as air quality;
- EU **Air Quality Limit Regulations, 2003** set targets for EU countries to reduce ozone in the air.

Businesses that break legislation regarding pollution may be forced to pay compensation to those affected.

Some examples of how different businesses and their employees might react to limit or cut pollution are shown in Table 1.

Table 1 *How businesses and employees might be affected by pollution control*

Business Pollution Activity	Supermarkets Air Ensure refrigerators are checked and replaced with non-CFC units
Business Pollution Activity	Delivery business Air Change vehicles regularly, use diesel or lead free petrol
Business Pollution Activity	Clubs Noise Site away from residential areas
Business Pollution Activity	Farming Water Use natural pesticides
Business Pollution Activity	Chemical factory Air Use more efficient production methods, replace and maintain machines regularly.

Waste creation and recycling

Businesses create waste in the manufacture of goods and the provision of services. Waste is what is left over which is not required for production or not required by consumers who use the end product. Examples might include:
- waste metal left over when making car body parts;
- waste created in services such as hairdressing;
- equipment such as oil rigs or CNC machinery which are no

longer able to be used in production because they are worn out;
- packaging which is only needed to support or protect products, such as toy packaging or pizza delivery boxes.

Legislation exists in the UK to control the illegal dumping of waste. The **Environment Act, 1995**, for example, has regulations controlling the amount of waste business create. Businesses breaking legislation can be forced to pay compensation. The **Landfill Tax** is a tax on dumping of waste at waste disposal sites. The charge is designed to encourage businesses to reduce the waste they create. Pressure groups such as Waste Watch attempt to influence businesses to cut waste.

The recycling of waste is becoming increasingly popular by businesses. They may be able to reuse waste materials to create other products, which may cut cost or increase sales.

Some businesses have set up especially to make products from recycled materials. Some examples of products that may be created by recycling are shown in Figure 3. Other examples of how different businesses might react to reduce waste or make use of it are shown in Table 2.

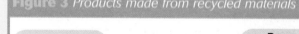

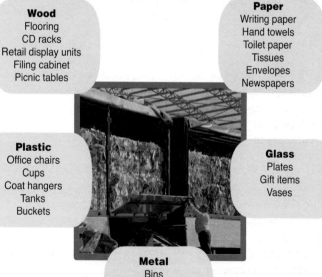

Figure 3 *Products made from recycled materials*

Wood
Flooring
CD racks
Retail display units
Filing cabinet
Picnic tables

Paper
Writing paper
Hand towels
Toilet paper
Tissues
Envelopes
Newspapers

Plastic
Office chairs
Cups
Coat hangers
Tanks
Buckets

Glass
Plates
Gift items
Vases

Metal
Bins
Storage containers
Paper clips

Table 2 *Methods to control waste*

Re-use e.g. toner cartridges for printers after being refilled.

Change production methods e.g. use more accurate measuring techniques and selection methods to reduce waste for example in food production.

Change designs and materials e.g. make smaller products which do the same job but do not require as many materials.

Disposable or reusable packaging e.g. reusable heated pizza bags.

Implications for businesses providing recycling services may include:
- training for employees;
- finding suitable supplies and suppliers;
- using suitable production techniques;
- finding appropriate customers who want to buy recycle products.

Implications for businesses wanting to recycle more may include:
- changing production methods;
- changing work practices, eg regular collections of materials to recycle, providing recycling collections or bins;
- buying materials that can be recycled for office use.

Global warming and the ozone layer

Global warming is a major environmental issue facing society. It is argued that the emission of 'greenhouse gases' into the atmosphere are causing a 'greenhouse effect' where the planet's atmosphere is warming up. The result could be the melting of polar ice caps and drastic changes in climate conditions.

A further problem is that the ozone layer around the earth which filters harmful radiation passing into the atmosphere and prevents it affecting us is being depleted by CFCs and other ozone depleting substances (ODS). This 'hole' in the ozone layer could result in harmful sun's rays passing unfiltered to the earth.

Many countries meet to agree targets to limit pollution which cause these effects. For example, the Kyoto Protocol limits greenhouse gas emissions by various countries, although not all countries sign up to the agreements. The Montreal Protocol limits ODS.

Steps that businesses and their employees may take to limit these effects by controlling the emission of gases into the atmosphere include using:
- efficient machinery which limits emissions;
- switching to pollution limiting production techniques;
- using smaller cars or train travel;
- changing product designs to reduce emissions.

Damage to the countryside

Business activity can cause damage to the surrounding area. Examples might be:
- open cast mining which often scars the land and leaves waste areas after mining ends;
- new factories or offices which can often not 'fit in' with the look of the landscape or the area in which they are built;
- road building to new premises which reduces green areas and the countryside ;
- airports which take up large areas of land and surrounding areas for access.

Businesses that take into account their effects on the landscape may consider a number of methods to limit any damage. They may fill in waste areas which are no longer required. They may ensure that designs are complementary to the surrounding buildings. They may also redesign landscapes so that they are aesthetically pleasing perhaps by adding grass or park areas.

Using scarce resources

Society is increasingly aware of the speed with which resources are being used up in production. Fuel sources such as coal and oil are becoming harder to find. Materials used in production leave fewer resources in the ground. Future generations may suffer as a result.

Businesses can follow a number of strategies to take these into account.
- Make use of alternative power sources, such as solar, wind power or hydro-electric to generate electricity.
- Find ways of conserving fuel, such as better insulation.
- Make use of renewable resources. For example, timber businesses may plant two new trees for every one cut down.
- Redesign products so that fewer resources are used.

Congestion

Road and traffic congestion is an issue facing society, particularly in a relatively small country such as the UK which has limited land space. Traffic congestion might be caused in a number of ways. Businesses might consider alternatives to solve these problems as shown in Table 3.

In the UK government has also introduced various schemes to reduce traffic on roads and in city centre areas. These include congestion charges for cars using inner London and Durham.

Effects on employees

Dealing with environmental issues can affect employees within a business in many ways. This will include managers making decisions and the job roles and operations of other employees.

Pollution Businesses concerned with pollution may:
- introduce no-smoking policies or have smoking areas and staff who want to smoke will have to take this into account in their work breaks;
- encourage high levels of testing of machinery by maintenance staff to prevent fumes;
- encourage staff to turn off mobile phones to stop noise pollution;
- ensure staff wear protective clothing;

Table 3 *Congestion*

Causes
Lorries delivering materials or components to factories.
Possible reactions by business
Use rail if possible. Deliver early in the morning or late at night or at weekends.

Causes
Vans delivering supplies to supermarkets.
Possible reactions by business
Deliver early in the morning or late at night or at weekends. Deliver more stock but less often.

Causes
Sales representatives using cars to visit city centres.
Possible reactions by business
Use email or conference calling for meetings if possible. Send samples by post.

- encourage managers to carry out regular audits to check waste disposal into water and the use of landfill sites.

Waste resources Businesses concerned with wasting resources may:

- introduce recycling policies where office staff are asked to save waste paper and place it in recycling bins;
- encourage managers to buy supplies from fuel-efficient suppliers or those which replace resources;
- train workers in recycling techniques;

- have targets for managers and employees to meet for recycling or reducing waste, with penalties or incentives if they are or are not met;
- ask staff to turn all power and lights off when not in use.

Congestion Businesses concerned about the impact on the environment of cars may:

- encourage train travel by their sales teams;
- have limited parking spaces;
- encourage shared rides to work with incentives.

Examination practice · EU pollution

In October 2004 The European Commission warned that a number of British businesses could face penalties for discharges into air and water. The European Pollutant Emission Register, based on data from members, highlighted pollution in EU countries. GlaxoSmithKline, for instance, was said to be responsible for 64.6% of the dichloromethane discharged directly into water in the EU via operations in Middlesex. The British arm of Huntsman Petrochemicals, the US group, was said to account for 19% of the benzene, toluene, ethylbenzene and xylenes pumped into water. BP Chemicals was said to be responsible for a further 11.6%.

American-owned Solutia in Newport and Runcorn was said to account for 29.2% of phenols discharged into water. Magnesium Elektron, based in Swinton was said to account for half the sulphurhexafluoride discharged into the air, while Ineos

Chlor, the chemicals company in Runcorn was said to account for 23% of dichlorethane discharged into the atmosphere.

An EU spokesperson warned that firms could fall foul of a 1996 EU directive. 'They might want to evaluate their potential for improving their environmental performance' she said.

Source: adapted from *The Guardian*, 9.10.2004.

(a) **Identify and explain TWO environmental issues facing the businesses in the article.** (4 marks)
(b) **Examine TWO reasons why the businesses may face problems as a result of these environmental issues.** (4 marks)
(c) **Explain THREE ways in which managers at the businesses should react to deal with these issues.** (6 marks)

Meeting the assessment criteria

The CK Group of companies are one of the fastest growing plastic recycling and waste management companies in the UK today. The business can call upon over 30 years of experience in plastic recycling, polymer compounding, film blowing, plastic trading, paper processing and waste management.

- CK Polymers plastics division buy and sell plastic waste, reground, recycled compounds and off-spec polymers. We also provide a range of plastic recycling and waste management services.
- The paper processing division SGS Paper Ltd are specialist converters and slitters of high quality (photographic grade) paper for a range of applications.
- CK Waste Solutions Ltd offer a fully outsourced recycling and waste management solution saving you time and money by giving you a single point of contact.

Source: adapted from www.ckpolymers.co.uk.

(a) Explain why this business is likely to take into account environmental issues. (2 marks)

Expected answers
- *It is recycling materials – it is taking into account that materials can be recycled into different forms and reused rather than disposing of them and creating waste and wasting resources.*
- *Has been in the business for 30 years – earns its income from recycling and waste.*

Mark allocation
1 mark for identifying recycling/waste management.
1 mark for why it is doing this. (2 marks)

(b) Identify and explain THREE ways in which the business's approach to the environment might affect its employees. (6 marks)

Expected answers
- *Training – employees will need to be trained on how to use recycling equipment and other processes involved in recycling.*
- *Finding suitable resources for recycling – staff will need to identify businesses that can provide materials/pick ups may be necessary.*
- *Need to wear protective clothing – materials may contain harmful chemicals.*

Mark allocation
1 mark for way.
1 mark for explaining the effect on employees. (1 + 1) x 3 (6 marks)

(c) Identify TWO possible environmental issues that this business may create as it carries out its work and explain how it can effectively minimise any problems caused. (6 marks)

Expected answers
- *Air pollution as it processes waste – maintain machinery, replace worn out machinery – less likelihood of escaping fumes, etc.*
- *Noise pollution from use of heavy machinery – site factory away from residential areas/ maintain machinery/monitor noise levels – fewer residents to be disturbed/less noise created.*
- *Congestion from deliveries of waste to factory – pick up at slower times of the day for traffic, don't make lots of journeys, effective load waste – will not have lorries on road at time of heavy traffic use.*

Mark allocation
1 mark for identifying issue.
1 mark for appropriate method of minimising issue.
1 mark for why this method will be effective.
(1 + 1 + 1) x 2 (6 marks)

14 Social and ethical issues

Social responsibilities and ethics

Businesses do not operate in isolation. They are affected by the societies in which they work and sell products. Their decisions can affect people in society and the decisions of people can affect them.

It is often argued that businesses have social responsibilities. Businesses obviously have to make a profit for their owners or they would go out of business. But they also need to take into account wider issues which society feels are important.

Ethics is about the 'right' or 'wrong' of any decision. Businesses often have to take into account what is morally or ethically right or wrong when making decisions. Some of these decisions are dictated by law, in which case the government has decided what is right or wrong and the law states what a business can or cannot do their own. In many other situations businesses have to make ethical decisions.

This section examines how taking into account the needs of society and making ethical decisions affect a business and the decisions of its managers and employees.

Business ethics

Ethics are about doing, morally, the right or wrong thing. Business ethics are therefore about making moral decisions in manufacturing and selling goods and providing services. There is likely to be some debate about ethically what is the right thing to do. People have different opinions and in some situations all people in business may not agree. Some ethical issues which affect businesses are shown in Figure 1.

Although there may be a debate about what might be the right or wrong decision, there is often a number of areas where people agree about the right thing to do. For example, most people in the UK might agree that a company should not use all employees' pension funds to stay in business or that widespread bribery should not take place to win road building contracts from government. Businesses that act ethically are often said to make these decisions. They take into account the needs of society and their social responsibility when making decisions.

Legislation can control and constrain businesses to act ethically. For example:

- the **Minimum Wage Act, 1998** ensures that employees cannot be paid lower than a certain wage per hour;
- the **Food Safety Act, 1990** makes it illegal to provide food which is unfit for human consumption;
- the **Environment Act, 1995** regulates air quality and waste.

Acting ethically might affect businesses, managers and employees in business in a number of ways. Table 1 shows how the decisions of people in a food business which has an ethical policy might be affected.

Codes of practice

Codes of practice are regulations drawn up which will affect how decisions are made by businesses. They tend to be voluntary agreements which businesses agree to conform. The regulations will usually include factors designed to increase the social responsibilities of business and promote ethical practices.

Figure 1 *Ethical issues*

Employee rights Examples of decisions which might be questioned in this area.
- Should a business pay very low wages to cut costs?
- Should a business use its employees' pension funds for its own means?
- Should all businesses have a workplace creche?

Animal rights Examples of decisions which might be questioned in this area.
- Should animals be experimented on to produce products which may benefit society's health?
- Should businesses make real fur coats?
- Should animals be forced fed to produce certain types of food?

The nature of products Examples of decisions which might be questioned in this area.
- Should a business sell toy guns to children?
- Should a business include lots of fat or salt in products to be tasty, but which might lead to obesity or health problems?

Trading policies Examples of decisions which might be questioned in this area.
- Should a business trade with a supplier from a country which abuses human rights?
- Should a business trade with a supplier which pays very low wages to workers in low income countries?
- Should a business sell arms to a country with a history of military action?
- Should a business use any means to compete, for example stealing classified information from other businesses?
- Should a bribe be offered to win an order?

The environment Examples of decisions which might be questioned in this area.
- Should a business pollute the environment to cut costs?
- Should a business dump waste in water?
This is dealt with in section 13.

Table 1 *How ethical policies might affect a food manufacturing business and its employees*

- Employees might be more motivated to work for the business rather than another which has poorer conditions of service and benefits.
- Managers might switch suppliers if they are found to be exploiting workers by paying them low wages.
- Employees might need to undergo training on how to ensure the highest quality standards.
- Managers might face higher costs by rejecting low price ingredients which do not conform to standards.
- Employees in product design departments might develop low fat alternatives to products.
- Employees must be careful when designing marketing campaigns so that customer sensibilities are not offended.
- Managers might not invest employees' pension funds in businesses which deal in arms.
- Managers and employees might face more work if customers respond positively to the image by buying more products. Profits might increase and so might rewards to employees.

Figure 2 *Ethical policies at the Co-operative Bank*

'To ensure that the bank's Ethical Policy is implemented effectively, Ethical Policy compliance systems are integrated into our everyday bank procedures. On applying for banking services with The Co-operative Bank, all business customers are required to complete an Ethical Policy questionnaire. These questionnaires are passed through to a Business Relationship Manager, and/or a member of the bank's New Business Centre, who undertakes an assessment of the proposal, against our Ethical Policy.'

'Only where no conflict with the policy is identified is a business offered banking facilities. This means that the bank will decline investment opportunities, regardless of any potential financial gain - the bottom line is ensuring that customers' expectations, as expressed through the Ethical Policy, are upheld. In line with this, in 2002, the bank declined 29% of businesses referred to its Ethical Policy Unit.'

Source: adapted from www.co-operativebank.co.uk.

Codes of practice may take a number of forms.
- They many be general codes of practice which can be tailored to individual needs. For example, the Institute of Business Ethics helps individual businesses devise codes.
- They maybe internal codes of practice produced by a business itself. Businesses such as Balfour Beatty, the buildings, rail and engineering group and Scottish Power, the provider of gas and electricity have codes of practice.
- Businesses in the industry might develop a code of practice. For example, the Association of the British Pharmaceutical Industry (ABPI) is the trade association for about a hundred companies in the UK producing prescription medicines. It produces a code of practice for all members.

Figure 3 shows how a leisure centre belonging to the Fitness Industry association might be affected by its code of practice.

Figure 3 *How FIA code of practice might affect a leisure centre*

FIA Code of Practice

2005 CODE OF PRACTICE Compliant

Are you thinking of joining a health club or leisure centre?

Click here for the ten essential questions you should ask before joining a fitness facility!

For further information on FIA member clubs, please contact info@fia.org.uk.

- Ensure staff training takes place for work tasks, e.g. spotting hazards, supervision of spa/pool hygiene, carrying out emergency procedures.
- Ensure documents that show emergency procedures, such as a fire evacuation, are in place.
- Ensure equipment is kept in a safe condition and inspected periodically.
- Carry out risk assessment.

Source: adapted from www.fia.org.uk.

Stakeholders

Businesses have a variety of stakeholders. These are groups with an interest in the decisions and activities of a business. Taking into account the needs of different stakeholders can affect the business itself and people who work in the business in many ways.

Owners The owners of the business will be different depending on the type of business organisation. Some businesses are owned by just one person, a sole trader. Some are owned by a few people in partnership and companies are owned by shareholders. All owners of the business are likely to expect the business to make a profit, so that it can continue trading and the owners will earn an income. In order to make a profit businesses must ensure that revenue from sales is maximised and costs are minimised. It will be one of the roles of employees and managers in the business to organise the business so that this is achieved.

Employees Businesses must also take into account the needs of their employees. These may include:

- being motivated;
- feeling valued at work;
- feeling safe;
- having equal and fair opportunities;
- being well and fairly rewarded.

How businesses do this and the effects on businesses and their employees is dealt with in sections 8, 12 and 15.

Customers and consumers Customers are people or organisations who buy the products of businesses and consumers are users of the end product. They have a wide variety of needs including:

- having a choice of products;
- buying safe products;
- buying products which are highly valued or are value for money;
- not being deceived regarding the nature of the product.

Legislation in the UK protects consumers. The effects on businesses and their employees is dealt with in section 15.

Suppliers Suppliers are other businesses that provide businesses with products, components or materials. Meeting the needs of suppliers will affect different businesses in different ways. Some examples are given in Table 2.

Table 2 *Meeting suppliers' needs*

Supplier	Possible effect on business
Supplier of parts from the US.	To allow time for delivery. To make payment in dollars.
Small supplier of food ingredients.	To make prompt payment to prevent cash flow problems.
Large supplier of food products to supermarkets.	Have storage and shelf space available. Make large regular orders.

Figure 4 *Tesco computers for schools*

Tesco computers for schools is a company initiative designed to reward customer loyalty and strengthen community relationships. The programme involves an annual voucher redemption promotion to help local schools obtain free computers and other information and communication technology (ICT) equipment. During a promotional period, customers were given 1 voucher for a certain amount spent in a store. Schools could then collect these tokens and redeem them for computers and ICT related equipment from a catalogue of equipment.

Source: adapted from www.bitc.org.uk and www.computersforschools.co.uk.

Figure 5 *Pressure groups and their possible effects on businesses*

Name Action on Smoking and Health (ASH).
Aim To reduce and eliminate health problems caused by tobacco.
Possible effect on business Reduced cigarette sales and advertising, changes in packaging to include warnings.

Name The Vegetarian Society.
Aim The promotion of vegetarian lifestyles.
Possible effect on business Changing ingredients for food manufacturers to non-meat alternatives.

Name London Cycling Campaign.
Aim To make London a world class cycling city and promote cycling.
Possible effect on business Increased demand for cycles and cycle accessories.

Name Society for the Protection of Ancient Buildings.
Aim To save old buildings from decay, demolition and damage.
Possible effect on business Employment and training for traditional skills, change projects from demolition to renovation for construction businesses.

Name Noise Abatement Society.
Aim To promote the control of noise levels.
Possible effect on business Reduce noise levels in the design of aircraft or car engines, location of 'noisy' premises such as clubs away from residential areas.

Name Greenpeace.
Aim To combat threats to the world's biodiversity and environment.
Possible effect on business These are dealt with in section 13.

Government The government earns money from businesses that sell products and make profits. Businesses pay Value Added Tax (VAT) on the sale of some goods. They pay National Insurance contributions on their employees. Companies pay Corporation Tax on profits. Government spends this money on a variety of activities including defence, social services and education. To satisfy government needs employers need to have effective systems for recording, collecting and paying revenue to government.

Financiers These are organisations such as banks, which provide businesses with funds. They require businesses to make regular repayments on time and keep records of payments.

Community Section 13 explained how businesses have a social responsibility. They affect and are affected by the communities in which they operate. Businesses that take into account the needs of communities provide services such as:
- training or play schools for children;
- road building and landscaping of the environment;
- support for education or social services.

An example is shown in Figure 4.

Pressure groups

Pressure groups are groups of people with similar interests that try to influence the decisions of government and businesses. Interests that people may have vary from the protection of animal rights or the environment, to the promotion of interests that they think should be highlighted like nuclear energy, to the support of particular products, industries and occupations. They use various methods to attract attention to their causes such as:
- rallies and marches;
- advertising on posters, in magazines on the Internet or radio and television;
- gaining support from government ministers.

Some pressure groups are large and well organised and have funds to spend. Others are set up from 'one-off' causes and action, such as the diversion of a road around a village.

Examples of pressure groups in the UK and some possible effects on businesses and their employees are shown in Figure 5.

Meeting the assessment criteria

In 2005 Nike's corporate responsibility report acknowledged that the business had some of its products manufactured in foreign factories which made use of 'sweatshop labour'. The business had bowed to international pressure from a variety of sources. Previously the company had refused to disclose details of its 700+ factories. It also admitted that some factories had harassed workers and that many had been made to work overtime. Over half of the factories had working hours of over 60 hours a week. Almost one in ten workers outside the USA were below the 'Nike Standard' of 16 years of age for making equipment and 18 years of age for trainers. A number of the factories also had restricted access to toilets and water.

A spokesperson said that the company wanted to show that it realised there were problems and was trying to put them right.

Source: adapted from *The Daily Star*, 15.4.2005.

(a) Explain ONE way in which the business might not have been following its own code of conduct. **(2 marks)**

Expected answers
- *The Nike Standard, is to employ workers over 16 years old for making equipment and 18 years old for trainers – 10% of workers outside the USA were younger.*

Mark allocation
1 mark for code of conduct.
1 mark for explaining why it has not been followed. **(2 marks)**

(b) Identify THREE other ways in which employees at the business might have experienced problems. **(3 marks)**

Expected answers
- *Working week of over 60 hours causes tiredness and fatigue.*
- *Harassment might reduce motivation.*
- *Restrictions to water and toilets might delay production and lead to demotivation and affect productivity.*

Mark allocation
1 mark for each way. **(3 marks)**

(c) Suggest TWO ways in which the business might react and how this might affect:
(i) employees;
(ii) the business. **(6 marks)**

Expected answers
- *Reduce working week – more productive workers (employees), more employees – perhaps increased labour costs (business).*
- *Employ older workers – workers more suited to employment and paid higher wages (employees) – different recruitment policies (business).*
- *Improve conditions – motivation improved (employees) – increased costs (business).*
- *Reduce harassment – improve motivation (employees) – introduce rules on conduct (business).*

Mark allocation
1 mark for way it might react.
1 mark for effect on employee.
1 mark for effect on business. **(1 + 1 +1) x 2**
(6 marks)

Examination practice · Cadbury Schweppes

Cadbury Schweppes is an international confectionery and beverages company. It has a strong portfolio of brands sold in almost every country in the world. It has nearly 54,000 employees and products which fall into two main categories:
- confectionery
- beverages.

Brands include Schweppes, Dr Pepper, Orangina, Trebor, Bournvita and Cadbury itself.

The core purpose of Cadbury Schweppes is 'working together to create brands people love'. It aims to be judged as a company that is among the very best in the business world - successful, significant and admired. The company has set five goals to achieve this. One relates to Corporate Social Responsibility. It aims to be 'admired as a great company to work for and one that is socially responsible to its communities and consumers across the globe'. This goal clearly states Cadbury Schweppes' responsibilities and recognises that what it does as a business impacts on communities and the lives of consumers.

Cadbury Schweppes takes its corporate social responsibility agenda seriously. It is a member of organisations like Business in the Community, International Business Leaders Forum and the Institute of Business Ethics. These organisations seek to improve the impact companies have on society.

A key part of the Cadbury Schweppes approach to business lies in its ethical behaviour and close relationship with its stakeholder groups. It believes that 'Respecting human rights and trading ethically is fundamental to the way we work, not just within our owned and operated businesses but also in how we interact with our wider value chain.'

The original Cadbury company was influenced by the Quaker values of the Cadbury family who started the chocolate business. They promoted justice, equality and social reform. The business argues that it continues to follow these principles today. It has always treated employees with respect and cared for their welfare. The company's site at Bournville, near Birmingham, is more than a factory with extensive amenities such as housing, sports facilities and parks all being part of the original complex.

Source: adapted from www.thetimes100.co.uk.

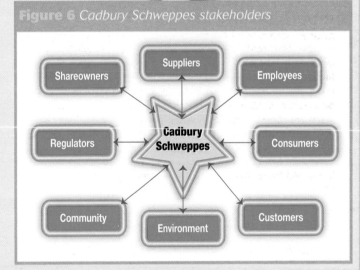

Figure 6 *Cadbury Schweppes stakeholders*

(a) Identify FIVE ways in which Cadbury Schweppes responds to the needs of its stakeholders. **(5 marks)**

(b) Identify and explain THREE ways in which the business and its employees might react to a pressure group aiming to improve the nation's health. **(6 marks)**

(c) Evaluate to what extent the business is an ethical company. **(5 marks)**

Constraints

Constraints on businesses are the restrictions placed on their activities. Restrictions on a business will limit how employees who work for the organisation operate.

Sections 8 and 12 explained how employees' well-being and motivation can be affected by their conditions of work and their equality of treatment. These are internal issues which affect employees and managers. This section examines external issues which limit and constrain how businesses act and affect people who work in them.

Legislation Some of these constraints are legal constraints imposed on the business. If businesses break legislation and are taken to court they can face fines under criminal law or a consumer might sue the business under civil law.

Self regulation Not all constraints are imposed. Some are self regulatory constraints. These are decisions by a business to limit its activities for its own reason, perhaps due to the nature of the industry in which the business competes.

Competition law

Businesses are in competition with each other for the custom of people who buy goods or services. Businesses use a variety of strategies and tactics to compete with each other. Many of these are within the law. However, the government has decided that some practices must be restricted.

Legislation often takes place when government decides that one or more businesses have an extremely unfair advantage compared to others and this advantage is often gained by unfair means. Competition law will affect both employees and managers within a business.

Competition may be constrained for two reasons.

- There is a monopoly. This is where one business controls a market. In practice this is very rare today, so it usually means that a business has over 25% of a market. Monopolies are often created by mergers, the joining together of two or more businesses.
- There is collusion between businesses. This where a few businesses work together to benefit at the expense of other businesses. They often use restrictive practices to restrict trade.

Legislation can take a number of forms.

The Competition Commission (CC) This is an independent organisation that investigates mergers. The **Enterprise Act, 2002** gave the CC the power to investigate mergers and anti-competitive practices. If competition is reduced it can stop the merger or prevent the anti-competitive practices.

Office of Fair Trading (OFT) The OFT:

- enforces legislation such as the **Competition Act, 1998** which prevents businesses from taking part in activities that prevent competition and businesses abusing a dominant

position. It refers business to the CC;
- enforces consumer legislation, for example taking action against unfair traders;
- investigates markets and may recommend stronger legislation.

The European Commission (EC) The EC can investigate anti-competitive practices in EU countries, for example the setting of prices across all EU countries.

Regulatory watchdogs These are organisations set up to constrain the activities mainly of former government owned monopolies such as water and gas as shown in Figure 1. They have the power to;

- set prices;
- help introduce competition.

Figure 2 shows how the actions of Ofwat might have affected employees and managers at a business.

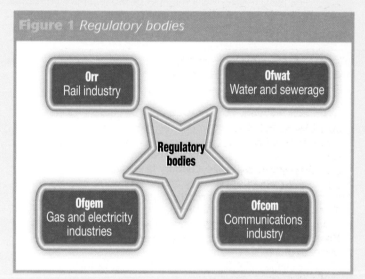

Figure 1 *Regulatory bodies*

- **Orr** Rail industry
- **Ofwat** Water and sewerage
- **Regulatory bodies**
- **Ofgem** Gas and electricity industries
- **Ofcom** Communications industry

Figure 2 *Effects of Ofwat on Pennon*

In 2004 Pennon, the water and waste recycling group, said that it would not contest Ofwat's decision to cap its price increase for South West Water customers at 25% above the rate of inflation for the next five years.

It announced that about 100 jobs would have to go as part of its drive to meet the demands placed on it by the industry regulator's review.

Ofwat's price review meant that South West Water customers would pay an average of £444 a year by 2009-10 for water and sewerage, the highest in Britain.

Source: adapted from *The Guardian*, 10.12.2004.

Consumer protection

Consumers are the users of the end product. They might be a person:

- eating a tin of baked beans;
- using a washing machine at home;
- travelling by airline;
- buying insurance;
- having their hair cut.

It is sometimes argued that consumers must be protected from the activities of business. Without constraints from legislation they would exploit consumers to gain greatest profit. The phrase *caveat emptor*, meaning 'let the buyer beware' is often used when referring to how businesses might operate without legal constraints.

A wide variety of legislation exists to protect the consumer. Different pieces of legislation affect employees within businesses in different ways. Some of these are shown in Table 1.

Table 1 *Examples of consumer legislation and how it affects managers and employees*

Act Weights and Measures Acts 1951, 1963, 1985.
Constraint Prevent underweight products.
Possible effects Managers must design quality checks and employees must constantly check quality.

Act Trade Descriptions Act, 1968.
Constraint Prevent misleading descriptions.
Possible effects Employees must be careful when writing product descriptions.

Act Unsolicited Goods and Services Act, 1971
Constraint Prevents sale of goods which have not been ordered.
Possible effects Managers must update consumer lists. Employees must deliver and supply to correct consumers.

Act Consumer Credit Act, 1974.
Constraint Protects consumers buying goods on credit.
Possible effects Employees must ensure payments are taken correctly.

Act Consumer Safety Act, 1978.
Constraint Prevents the sale of harmful goods.
Possible effects Ensure toys are designed with safety in mind.

Act Consumer Protection Act, 1987.
Constraint Makes firms liable for any damage that goods might cause.
Possible effects Ensure goods are tested widely before sale.

Act Food Safety Act, 1990.
Constraint Ensures food is safe.
Possible effects Managers must provide clean and safe conditions for work. Employees must prepare and cook food in a clean and safe way.

Act Financial Services and Markets Act, 2000.
Constraint Prevents crime and protects consumers in financial markets.
Possible effects Managers and employees must ensure consumer confidentiality.

Employment protection

Employment protection refers to legislation and self-regulation that looks after the interests of employees. Many of the laws affecting business and employees were covered in sections 8, 12 and 15, which give details of how legislation affects the motivation and well-being of employees. Legislation can affect employees in a business in a variety of ways.

Equal opportunities Equal opportunities legislation protects employees against unlawful and unfair discrimination at work in a number of areas.

- Pay. It is unlawful to pay two people different wages for doing the same job or work that is valued the same.
- Sex discrimination. It is unlawful to reject one person for a job rather than another simply because they are male or female.
- Race relations. It is unlawful to reject one person for a job rather than another simply because of their colour, race, nationality or ethnic background.
- Disability. It can be unlawful to reject one person for a job simply because they are in a wheelchair unless substantial changes are required.
- Age. After 2006 in the UK it may be unlawful to refuse to employ a person because they are over a certain age.
- Sexual preference. It can be unlawful to reject one person for a job simply because of their sexual preference.

Appointment, terms and conditions When employees are first appointed they are given a contract of employment. This states the terms and conditions under which they will work. Legislation protects these terms and conditions in a number of areas.

- Hours of work. There is a limit on the amount of time employees can work in a week and continuously work without a break.
- Leave. Employees are entitled to leave and absences for sickness with pay.
- Minimum wages. Employees of certain ages must be guaranteed a minimum wage.
- Flexibility. Employees are entitled in certain circumstances to work flexibly.

Redundancy, dismissal, grievances and discipline Legislation affects business in a variety of situations, including situations where employees:

- are made redundant and must be paid;
- are dismissed for breaking their terms and conditions;
- have a complaint against a business;
- must be given warnings regarding their behaviour.

Figure 3 *Benefits of flexible practices*

P&O Ferries

'We have 60 staff members, including officers, working part-time in the fleet who would probably have left if we had been inflexible. There is a lot of expertise to lose and we have incurred considerable costs in recruiting and retraining replacements.'

Source: adapted from www.dti.gov.uk.

Table 2 *How legislation and self-regulation can affect managers and employees in a business*

Organising work time	Managers might need to build leave into human resources plans. Employees can take time to look after family members.
Recruitment	Advertisements must be carefully worded by managers. Disabled employees can expect adjustments to help them work.
Selection	Managers must use tests that do not discriminate. Employees are given equal chances of promotion.
Costs	Managers can not simply sack staff to reduce costs. Younger employees have to be paid a minimum wage.

Self regulation also takes place in some businesses. For example, banks such as Barclays and HSBC pay more than the minimum wage. Figure 3 shows an example of flexible practices and their effects. Legislation and self-regulation can affect managers and employees in a business in a number of ways as shown in Table 2.

Health and safety

The health and safety of employees at work is protected by a wide variety of legislation. The main Act in the UK which affects businesses is the **Health and Safety at Work Act, 1974**. Under this Act, government can set regulations in place which affect how businesses operate and the activities of managers and employees.

The Act states that businesses have a duty to ensure the health and safety of staff so far as is reasonably practical. Managers and employees might be affected in a number of ways.

* There must be a written policy on health and safety on public display to all workers.
* Managers and employees must comply with this policy.
* Managers must give employees training, information and supervision on health and safety issues.
* Safety representatives must be appointed.
* Safety equipment and clothing must be provided free.

Different businesses are likely to have different risks. Some of these are shown in Figure 4. Businesses must have checklists of risks that must be prevented. It is vital that businesses assess risks regularly and take steps to prevent accidents.

The Health and Safety Executive and Health and Safety Commission are responsible for ensuring that the Act is carried out. Inspectors have the power to visit businesses and investigate. Businesses that do not comply with the law can be taken to court and fined.

Preventing accidents at work can benefit employees and managers. It can:

* improve motivation;
* reduce accidents;
* reduce absences or loss of work due to injury;
* reduce insurance claims and claims against the business;
* prevent errors.

Figure 4 *Risks and checklists in different businesses*

Construction company
Equipment is safe
Materials can be carried safely
Hard hats are worn
First aid training given
Scaffolding provided
Regular breaks
Number known for emergencies

Call centre
Regular breaks given
Correct posture training given
Not too close to screen
Screen glare prevented
Regular eye check ups
Phones and computers are safe

Trade union work

Trade unions are organisations set up to protect and promote the interests of employees who are their members. They have a variety of objectives as shown in Figure 5. If they are successful in achieving these objectives then managers in business and employees will be affected, as shown in Figure 5.

Wage negotiations Trade unions negotiate with business owners over the pay and conditions of employees. Negotiating on behalf of all workers is known as collective bargaining. If unions are successful in improving the wages and other benefits of their members, then:

* the terms and conditions of employees will improve;
* higher wages are likely to increase the costs of employees to businesses. Managers may be asked to cut costs in other ways to pay for these higher wages. They may have to find cheaper supplies, find more efficient ways to work or make some workers redundant.

Trade unions may take industrial action to strengthen their position in wage negotiations. This is dealt with later.

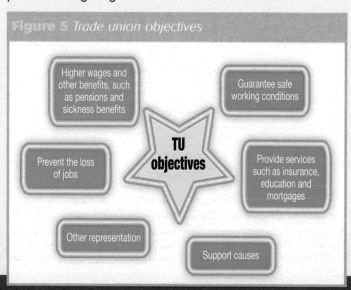

Figure 5 *Trade union objectives*

Higher wages and other benefits, such as pensions and sickness benefits

Guarantee safe working conditions

Prevent the loss of jobs

TU objectives

Provide services such as insurance, education and mortgages

Other representation

Support causes

Guaranteed safe working conditions Trade unions negotiate to improve the working conditions and safety of members. Improved safety conditions may lead to increased costs for managers as explained above. Employees who feel safe are likely to be more motivated and fewer accidents may mean less sickness leave.

Prevent the loss of jobs Trade unions often take action to prevent job losses or improve their position in wage negotiations. Action taken may involve:

- working to rule – so employees only carry out tasks in their job description;
- a go slow – where employees do their job but as slowly as possible;
- an overtime ban – a refusal to work any extra time;
- a strike – which can be all out strikes by all members for a long period, one day strikes or selective strikes in certain areas.

Owners and managers may react to strikes by:

- locking out employees;
- threatening to withdraw benefits which are not part of the contract of employment;
- threatening to make workers redundant.

Industrial action by trade unions can have a number of effects on employees and managers as shown in Table 3.

If disputes are not resolved, the Advisory, Conciliation and Arbitration Service (ACAS) may be asked to help with conciliation (help both sides find a solution) or arbitration (suggest a solution which both sides accept).

Providing services Trade unions often provide services for their members on other areas. These may include:

- providing insurance schemes or mortgages;
- setting up and running courses;
- discounts on travel;
- financial and legal advice;
- credit cards.

Support causes Trade unions support causes. These may include supporting a political party, a cause such as the campaign for nuclear disarmament or improvement in public sector transport. If successful, employees may benefit indirectly.

Working with business Trade unions are also increasingly becoming involved in business union partnerships and

Table 3 *Effects of industrial action*

- May improve conditions of employees if successful but raise costs for the business.
- Employees could face reduced earnings during action.
- The business's image may be harmed, leading to loss of sales and possible job losses in future.
- Bad feeling may develop during the action, which continues afterwards and working relationships may suffer.
- It may clear the air so that each side appreciates the others' concerns.
- Managers may need to reorganise work, use temporary employees or refuse to take on work during the action.

representing employees' views on European Works Councils.

Legislation A variety of legislation exists which controls the actions of employees and employers in industrial disputes and in other areas. Examples include:

- the **Employment Act, 1990** which made secondary picketing illegal. This is picketing outside premises by workers who are not employed at those premises.
- the **Trade Union Reform and Employment Rights Act, 1993** which states that strike action can only take place after a ballot and a majority vote for action.
- the **Employment Relations Act, 1999** which allows employees to vote for union recognition in certain cases;

Voluntary codes of practice

Some businesses have voluntary codes of practice which constrain their activities. They are regulations or conditions drawn up by businesses in a particular industry or by an organisation for business. They are not legal, but guide the activities of businesses. Examples are:

- Defra which has a Voluntary Code of Practice for the fast food industry to reduce the amount of fast food-related litter;
- the Advertising Standards Authority (ASA) which has a code of practice for advertising;
- a code of practice for commercial leases of property in England and Wales prepared by businesses in the property industry.

Examination practice · BT's services

BT allows other telecom businesses to make use of its telephone lines and other infrastructure. This is the wholesale part of BT's business. In February 2005 BT put forward proposals to re-organise its wholesale business in response to Ofcom's call for changes to increase competition for the UK's telecoms network infrastructure. The company voluntarily suggested creating a new access services division to provide clear and equal access to BT's local network for rival telecom providers.

Ofcom had warned that it could:

- deregulate the industry;
- impose regulations to create equal access;
- or force BT to split its business to offer access to other operators at a similar price to those supplied to BT's retail business (which provides telephone services to customers). BT also aimed to cut a range of its wholesale broadband prices and pledged to introduce faster services and reaffirm its

commitment to fair network access and a greater uptake of broadband.

Source: adapted from www.itweek.co.uk.

(a) Using examples from the telecom market, explain the difference between:
   (i) self regulation;
   (ii) regulation by Ofcom. **(4 marks)**
(b) Suggest TWO ways in which increasing competition might affect:
   (i) BT managers;
   (ii) BT employees. **(4 marks)**
(c) Examine TWO ways in which offering greater broadband access might affect employees at BT. **(4 marks)**
(d) Explain TWO ways in which the advertising of BT's broadband services might be affected by consumer legislation. **(4 marks)**

Meeting the assessment criteria

Dock workers in the UK were voting on industrial action in August 2004. It would be the first national strike since 1989.

Dockers, drivers and other workers at 20 ABP enterprises had rejected a 2.9 per cent pay offer and were voting on strike action. According to the company, only 300 of its 3,000 employees are covered by collective bargaining.

The Transport and General Workers' Union (T & G) was demanding a minimum wage of £7.50 an hour for all employees, a 5% rise for all rates over £7.50 and £10 an hour for drivers. It also wanted an hour off the 39-hour working week and other improvements to holidays, sick leave and parental leave. TGWU official Graham Stevenson argued 'If it takes a full national strike ballot to make progress so be it.'

Source: adapted from mua.org.au, 10.8.2004.

(a) Identify THREE objectives of the T & G.　　**(3 marks)**

Expected answers
* *Improved pay.*
* *Minimum wage.*
* *Shorter hours.*
* *Longer holidays.*
* *Sick pay.*
* *Parental leave.*

Mark allocation
1 mark for each objective.　　**(3 marks)**

(b) State FOUR features of a health and safety checklist for a dock worker.　　**(4 marks)**

Expected answers
* *Safe equipment in working order and maintained.*
* *Adequate training in the use of equipment.*
* *Provided with safety clothing.*
* *First aid equipment available.*
* *Safety office nominated.*
* *Adequate safety equipment and barriers.*

Mark allocation
1 mark for each answer feature.　　**(4 marks)**

(c) Explain TWO ways in which a strike might affect:
(i) employees;
(ii) managers;
at the business.　　**(4 marks)**

Expected answers
Employees
* *Reduced income - will not be working.*
* *Improved conditions if successful - strike is for lower hours.*
* *Conflict with employers could lead to poorer working relationships - strike is a major challenge.*

Managers
* *Many need to reorganise work - less staff available.*
* *May need to delay work - staff away, hopefully temporarily.*

Mark allocation
1 mark for each effect.
1 mark for why it comes from a strike.
　　(1 + 1) x 2
　　(4 marks)

(d) Evaluate the possible success of the strike action to benefit employees at the business.　　**(5 marks)**

Expected answers
For the action
* *Has a lot of support.*
* *Backed by a large trade union (T & G).*
* *legal if approved by a majority vote.*
* *Could gain in many areas.*

Against
* *Not a history of successful action for many years.*
* *Even if improvements agreed, few covered by collective agreement.*

Conclusion
* *Even if strike leads to some improvement in conditions and wages, not everyone will benefit.*

Mark allocation
1 mark for arguments for improvement (maximum 2 marks).
1 mark for arguments against (maximum 2 marks).
1 mark for conclusion.
　　(2 + 2 + 1)
　　(5 marks)

Setting up a business

Enterprise

People who set up businesses are called entreprenuers. They are the owners and without these types of people businesses would not exist in the private sector. The roles played by an entrepreneur in setting up and running a business are summarised in Figure 1.

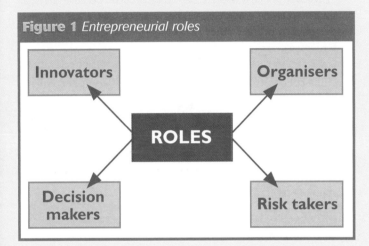

Figure 1 *Entrepreneurial roles*

- Entrepreneurs are innovators. This means that they provide the business idea. Innovation is discussed below.
- Organising involves buying or hiring resources, such as materials, labour and equipment. These are used to make a product or provide a service. Organising also involves giving instructions, making arrangements and setting up systems.
- Entrepreneurs have to make lots of business decisions. These might relate to product design, method of production, business location, price charged, who to recruit or what wages to pay.
- Entrepreneurs take risks. They have to pay money in advance for materials, labour and other resources. Some of this money is likely to be their own and if the business fails they could lose some or all of it. But if the business does get established it may make a profit. This belongs to the entrepreneur.

Who are entrepreneurs?

Not everyone has what it takes to become an entrepreneur. A wide range of skills is required to be successful. There is no strict list of characteristics but entrepreneurs do tend to be:
- hard working;
- ambitious;
- independent;
- highly motivated;
- creative;
- prepared to take a risk.

People set up businesses for a variety of reasons. They may:
- lose their job;
- be unhappy at work;
- not like working for someone else;
- develop an interest into a business;
- think they can make a lot of money;
- have a really new and innovative business idea.

Innovation

Innovation is to do with developing an idea into a product that is commercially viable. Entrepreneurs are innovators because they try to make money out of selling goods or services based on their business idea. Where do business ideas come from?

Exploiting a skill or interest A person may be very good at golf so they could start a business giving golf lessons.

Copying or adapting an existing idea Many businesses are set up by copying what another business does. A person may open an Italian restaurant in a different part of town to other restaurants. There may be slight differences in price, service and menu choice.

Spotting a gap in the market An entrepreneur might feel that a particular customer need is not being met in the market. For example, there might be a gap in the market for an express bus service between Cardiff and Liverpool.

New inventions Occasionally a business will emerge because a new product is invented. For example, Betfair, the UK betting exchange, was set up by Andrew Black when he introduced some revolutionary new computer software. Set up in 2000, Betfair had a turnover of £50m and won the Queens Award for Enterprise in 2004.

Market research Some business ideas come from analysing market research information. It may be simple research such as a questionnaire asking football supporters what sort of new magazines they would like to see. For example, according to Figure 2, there may be demand for a magazine based on European football.

Types of ownership

There are different legal forms which a business can take.

Sole trader Most businesses start out as sole traders. This is

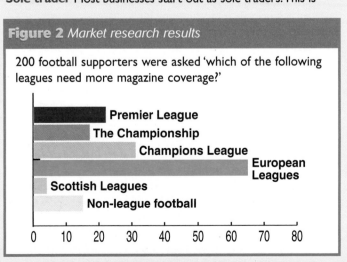

Figure 2 *Market research results*

200 football supporters were asked 'which of the following leagues need more magazine coverage?'

- Premier League
- The Championship
- Champions League
- European Leagues
- Scottish Leagues
- Non-league football

0   10   20   30   40   50   60   70   80

where the business is owned by a single person. That person is responsible for making all the decisions, organising all the resources and raising enough money to set the business up. If the business makes a profit, it all belongs to the sole trader. The advantages of this type of ownership is that there are no legal restrictions when setting up and it is the simplest and most common form of business. But owners have unlimited liability. Their personal assets can be taken to pay for business debts.

Partnership Some businesses are owned by two or a small group of people. This arrangement is called a partnership and the responsibility of running the business, generating the start-up capital and making decisions is shared between the partners. The profit or loss will also be shared. Unless a Deed of Partnership states otherwise, profits and losses are likely to be shared equally. The Deed of Partnership is a document which outlines the rights of partners. It is legally binding but does not have to be drawn up by law.

Private limited company Some businesses are set up by selling shares to a small group of people, perhaps a family. The money from the shares is used to set up the business and each shareholder is involved in decision making. The more shares a person has, the more control over decision making they enjoy. A lengthy legal process must be followed when forming a private limited company. Legal documents have to be drawn up and sent to the Registrar of Companies. There are also company laws which have to be followed. Shareholders have limited liability. They are only liable for the debts of the business. So they can only lose the money invested in the business, not their personal savings or possessions if there are debts.

Public limited company Some firms 'go public'. This means their shares are made available on the stock market where anyone can buy them. A lot more money can be raised this way but the company comes under closer legal scrutiny. Public limited companies have to follow the rules and regulations of the stock market in addition to the company laws mentioned above. It is expensive to become a public limited company and the process of 'going public' also takes a long time. Shareholders have limited liability.

Franchising Franchising is where the owner of a business idea (the franchisor) sells the rights to other businesses (franchisees) to sell its products or use its ideas. The franchisor may provide facilities and help, such as marketing, for a charge. It allows businesses to make use of a well known brand name, such as McDonald's.

Stakeholders

When setting up and running a business the owner will have to take into account the needs of other stakeholders. A stakeholder is someone who has an interest in a business. This means they might be affected by its activities in some way. Different stakeholders are likely to have different needs.

- Owners or shareholders have a financial stake in the business. They risked some of their money when it was set up. They are likely to want to make a profit and to see the company grow.
- Employees are hired to help make products or deliver services. They want fair wages, good working conditions, strong

leadership and to be valued.

- Managers are employed by the owners when a business grows. They are responsible for organising and making decisions. They have similar needs to other employees. But since they can influence the success of the business they tend to want more.
- Customers want businesses to provide good quality products at fair prices. They do not expect to be exploited and prefer businesses that offer good customer service, such as friendly and well trained staff.
- Suppliers want regular contracts with businesses, prompt payment and fair prices for their goods and services.
- The government wants businesses to prosper because they pay tax and provide employment. They enforce laws which are designed to protect other stakeholders from exploitation by businesses.
- Local communities rely on local businesses for training and employment. They may also provide local people with goods and services. Communities also want businesses to respect the local environment, keeping congestion down for example.
- Financial institutions and other financiers provide funds to allow businesses to set up or expand. They need businesses to be successful so funds can be repaid.

Legal implications

Owners have to be aware of certain laws and legal obligations when running their businesses.

Tax Sole traders and partners have to pay income tax on business profit. Limited companies have to pay corporation tax. Once turnover reaches a certain level businesses have to add VAT on to customer bills. Employers must also deduct income tax from their employees' wages.

National Insurance contributions Employers have to pay National Insurance contributions to the government. They also have to deduct these from employees' wages.

Licences Some types of business activity require a licence to operate. For example, a licence is needed to sell alcohol, fireworks and certain medicines. Licences are also needed to operate a bus or taxi service or to slaughter animals for meat processing. It is against the law to operate without such licences.

Consumer legislation There are many laws designed to protect

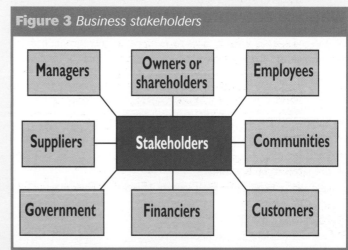

Figure 3 *Business stakeholders*

consumers from exploitation by businesses. For example, the **Trade Descriptions Act, 1968** prohibits businesses from making misleading or false statements about their products.

Employment legislation This is designed to protect employees from exploitation. For example, the **Employment Act, 2002** gives mothers and fathers of children under 6 the right to request flexible working hours.

Health and safety legislation This is also designed to protect employees. For example, the **Health and Safety at Work Act, 1974** requires firms to give health and safety training at work.

Environmental legislation This is designed to protect the environment. For example, the **Clean Air Act, 1993** limits emissions by businesses into the atmosphere.

Keeping records Businesses have to keep records of all their transactions. They are used to produce accounts which help show how the business is performing and may be required by the Inland Revenue to calculate tax.

Documents When trading businesses use documents. They provide evidence of transactions. Examples include, invoices, receipts, credit notes and delivery notes.

Insurance Businesses insure against theft, fire, damages and accidents to employees and the public.

Business advice

When setting up a business it is a good idea to get advice. For most entrepreneurs it will be the first time they have ever run a business. Good advice might improve the prospects of the business and help owners to avoid costly mistakes. Specialist advice is available from many different sources.

Individuals These include:
- friends and relatives who are already running businesses;
- accountants;
- solicitors.

Business Links These provide support, guidance and advice to firms that are about to start up. A number of areas are covered such as:
- business planning;
- raising finance;
- tax issues;
- legislation affecting business;
- business management.

Government agencies The Small Business Service runs a number of initiatives to help business start-ups and small businesses.
- Enterprise agencies help small and growing businesses. They offer free advice on business start-ups and training courses.
- Business Bridge organises forums where owners and managers can meet to exchange information and discuss problems.
- The Small Business Research Initiative encourages small firms to get involved in government research.
- Young Enterprise runs business education programmes for young people.
- Tendering for government contracts is a document which shows businesses how to bid for public sector work.
- Local Business Partnerships are used to help businesses and local authorities to streamline regulations together.
- The Ethnic Minority Business Forum advises ministers on helping ethnic minorities in business.

Banks Most commercial banks are happy to provide advice to entrepreneurs. They offer free consultations and provide information packs on setting up and running businesses. They are particularly good at helping with business plans, raising finance and other financial matters.

Others A wide range of other organisations can also offer help. These include the local Chambers of Commerce, Trade Associations, The Prince's Trust, Shell Live Wire, Business Clubs and the Federation of Small Businesses. Most of these have websites on the Internet or distribute free information using leaflets and documents.

Portfolio practice · Stonehaven

Stonehaven is a guest house run by Brenda and Ronnie Pimlott. They are equal partners in the business and share all of the responsibilities and work. They had always wanted to run a business together and decided to buy Stonehaven when Ronnie was made redundant from his sales job. Before they set up they got advice from their bank, a friend of Brenda's who is an accountant and the local tourist board in Devon. They also joined a local business club. Before opening they had to spend a lot of their own money refurbishing the rooms. They also had to get a fire certificate to comply with health and safety regulations. They now employ two part-time staff who help out at meal times and undertake various housekeeping duties. Most of their guests come at weekends. However, since Stonehaven was listed in a county accommodation guide, it has been getting busier during the week.

Source: adapted from author research.

(a) (i) **Identify FOUR stakeholders in Stonehaven.**
(ii) **What is the legal form of the business? Explain your answer.**
(b) (i) **Describe the needs of any two stakeholders.**
(ii) **Describe the advice that Ronnie and Brenda might have received before setting up.**
(c) **Analyse the legal implications of setting up the business.**

Visit the websites of some of the organisations that offer business advice OR obtain a business start-up pack from a bank.

- What types of advice do they give?
- What information is given about the types of skills and qualities that are needed to run a business?
- What information is given about the type of business you could set up?
- What financial information is given?
- What legal information is given?

Research task

Meeting the assessment criteria

For your chosen business you need to consider the factors that are important when setting up the business. You must investigate the motives for setting up, the type of ownership, the stakeholders, the legal implications and the advice the owner received.

Business example - Websters Tanning Salon

Websters is a tanning salon in Leeds. The main features of the business are:

- it is a sole trader owned by Angie Webster;
- £3,000 has been invested by Angie;
- there are two part-time staff employed;
- Angie got advice from her bank and her solicitor when setting up.

Source: adapted from company information.

Mark Band 1 *Provide basic knowledge and understanding of the key factors associated with starting a business, such as its legal form and stakeholders.*

Angie Webster set up a tanning salon in a Leeds suburb. She used £3,000 of her own money. The nearest one to where she lives is 12 miles away. She is going to operate as a sole trader which means she keeps all the profit. She is going to employ two students to help out at weekends. These staff are stakeholders. Angie is also a stakeholder and so are the customers and the local community. When setting up she got some legal advice from a solicitor about the use of sunbeds and the possible danger to customers. She also spoke to her bank.

Mark Band 2 *Provide sound knowledge and understanding of the key factors associated with starting a business, such as its legal form and stakeholders.*

Angie Webster is risking £3,000 of her own money to set up a tanning salon in a Leeds suburb. She thought it would do well because there was not another for 12 miles. She is going to operate as a sole trader which means she is the sole owner, makes all the decisions and keeps all the profit. She is going to employ two students to help out at weekends. These staff are stakeholders and Angie understands that she has to meet their needs. She pays them £1 above the national minimum wage and lets them have a break every two hours. She also paid for them to go on a customer services training day. Angie is also a stakeholder and so are the customers and the local community. When setting up she got some legal advice from a solicitor about the use of sunbeds and the possible danger to customers. She was advised to take out some insurance in case anyone made a claim against her. She also spoke to her bank. They gave her information on keeping a record of transactions and what documents would be necessary when trading.

Mark Band 3 *Provide comprehensive knowledge and understanding of the key factors associated with starting a business, such as its legal form and stakeholders.*

Angie Webster operates as a sole trader. She opened a tanning salon in Leeds using £3,000 of her own money. She spotted a gap in the local market for this service. The nearest salon was 12 miles away. As a sole trader she will be in complete control of the business. Angie will make all the decisions, organise other resources and keep the profit if the salon is successful. However, she is taking a risk. If the salon fails to attract enough customers the business could fail and Angie could lose her £3,000. Angie is a stakeholder because she has a financial stake in the business. Her customers will also be stakeholders and will want a good service with fair prices. In particular, they will want to be sure that the tanning machines are safe to use. Angie employs two part-time staff. These are also stakeholders and will want fair pay and good working conditions. Before opening the salon Angie took some advice. She spoke to her solicitor about what to do if a customer took out a claim against her for skin damage caused by a tanning machine. She was advised to take out some insurance. Angie also visited the bank manager to find out about VAT, keeping business records and the use of business documents. As a result she had some receipts printed.

Business planning

Why is planning important?

If an important event is going to be successful it has to be planned carefully. For example, how many people would go on holiday, move house, get married or throw a big party without planning it first? Without planning things might go wrong and the consequences can be very unpleasant. Setting up any business can be complex and time consuming. However, with careful planning the process is easier, less stressful and costly mistakes might be avoided.

Planning and resources

Business activity often uses lots of resources. For example, a small retailer selling gifts and souvenirs may have to:

- obtain a bank loan;
- find suitable premises;
- refurbish and fit the premises;
- arrange for utilities such as water, electricity, telephone and gas to be connected;
- buy in stocks of gifts and souvenirs;
- obtain a till and some printed till rolls;
- print some posters to promote the business;
- get some stationery and trading documents, such as receipts, printed;
- recruit some staff to help out.

In each of the above cases, gathering the resources takes time, organisation and planning. For example, when refurbishing the premises it may be necessary to draw up plans, get planning permission, get quotations from builders and decorators, choose fixtures, fittings, floorings and colour schemes, place orders and employ contractors, supervise the whole operation and deal with unexpected problems, such as builders failing to turn up. If an entrepreneur tries to set up a business without proper planning, many things can go wrong. The most common problems are that the opening of the business can be delayed and the start-up costs can be higher than anticipated.

Planning and monitoring performance

Once a business is set up the owners will want to monitor its progress and performance. Without proper planning it is difficult to do this. Unless specific plans are made it is difficult to know whether a business is living up to its expectations. Businesses might identify a number of key performance indicators. For example, Crown Cork & Seal, part of the US corporation Crown Holdings, makes a range of cans for food and drinks. It collects data to monitor its key performance indicators. These are summarised in Figure 1.

The company plans to reach a specified standard in each of these indicators. If the standard is not met an investigation is carried out to find out why. If a business does not plan to reach performance targets it is more difficult to judge whether the firm is doing well or not.

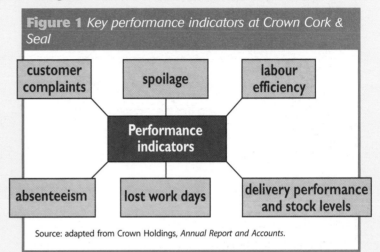

Figure 1 *Key performance indicators at Crown Cork & Seal*

Source: adapted from Crown Holdings, *Annual Report and Accounts.*

Planning, aims and objectives

The whole planning process is driven by the firm's aims and objectives as explained in section 1. When setting up a business it is much easier to make plans if the business has something specific to aim for. In the early stages of running a business the aims and objectives might be quite modest. For example, survival is likely to be a priority. A business might want to ensure that it is still trading in twelve months' time. Planning will also be easier if the objectives are SMART. Figure 2 outlines what this means.

Other examples of aims and objectives that a business might have when first setting up include:

- breaking even in the first year;
- reaching a specific sales target;
- achieving a specific market share;
- reaching a specific production target;
- making a specific amount of profit.

The particular aims and objectives a business chooses will influence the plans. For example, Sally Leibowitz set up a business selling luxury food hampers. She wanted to break even in the first year and worked out that she would have to sell 100 hampers to achieve this aim. Sally would have to make plans to ensure that she has all the resources to do this. If the business wanted to sell 150 hampers, however the plans would have been different. Sally would have needed to acquire more resources. She may have needed more money to set up, for example.

Once a business becomes established the aims and objectives might change. For example, a business may consider growth, profit maximisation, increasing shareholder value or social responsibility. Achieving these will need some strategic planning. This may involve introducing company-wide policies. For example, Tesco has developed its Tesco Express stores and has diversified into non-food products to achieve growth.

Figure 2 *SMART objectives*

Specific- stating exactly what should be achieved;

Measurable- able to be measured to decide if they have been achieved;

Agreed- everyone in the business understands and approves the aims;

Realistic- able to be achieved after taking into account resources, competition and market;

Time specific- state a time by which they should be achieved.

Key elements in business planning

There are certain key elements in business planning.

The market Once a business idea has been developed and objectives set, the next step is to look at the market. It would be very risky indeed to go ahead and set up a business without first analysing the market. This might involve:

- finding out the size of the market and whether or not it is growing;
- researching the main strengths and weaknesses of competitors. By doing this it may be possible to gain some advantage;
- constructing a customer profile. This involves identifying the characteristics of the people who are likely to buy the product. Customer profiles help businesses to target their products and marketing materials more accurately;
- deciding which marketing methods are appropriate and what prices to charge;
- organising a launch. For example, a new restaurant might invite potential customers, media and local dignitaries to a free evening on the first night. This will help to raise the profile of the business.

Although market research is expensive, it might help a new business avoid making some serious mistakes. Market research should also be ongoing. Consumer tastes can change quickly and it is important to keep in touch with market trends. Market research is explained in detail in sections 34 and 35.

Finance One of the most important tasks when setting up a business is raising finance. The objectives set at the beginning of the planning process will help determine how much is needed. It is normal for the owner to provide some of the finance needed but rarely is this enough. There is a number of different sources of finance, although many small businesses rely on bank loans. Other sources include the sale of shares for limited companies, venture

capitalists, business angels, government grants and loans, bank overdrafts, hire purchase and leasing. Once a business is established it can use retained profit as a source of finance. These different sources of finance are discussed in detail in section 18. When providing finance for business start-ups money lenders need to be convinced that the business is capable of repaying the loan. The chances of obtaining finance will be improved if business owners:

- provide a clear and realistic business plan;
- risk their own money;
- provide some collateral (some property or other assets to secure the loan);
- communicate their ideas effectively;
- produce some evidence of market research;
- demonstrate that they have the skills and commitment to make the business a success.

Production This aspect of planning is about choosing the methods of production and deciding which resources to use. However, most business ideas today involve providing a service, therefore, owners need to plan how the service will be delivered. Examples of tasks that might have to be planned include:

- finding a suitable location;
- determining what production methods will be used;
- deciding which resources will be needed;
- working the costs of the resources needed.

Personnel Human resource planning is an important activity in a large business. It involves forecasting the type and number of staff that will be required to meet the firm's objectives. When setting up a small business it is unlikely that large numbers of staff will be needed. However, assuming that some people will be employed, the owner will have to decide how many, what type, how they will be trained, how much they will be paid and what their roles will be in the organisation. Unit 1 looks at the importance of people at work in detail.

Cash flow One of the most important aspects of business planning is financial planning. It is common for business owners to overlook or misunderstand the importance of financial planning. This can lead to the business having financial difficulties. Owners must plan ahead so that they do not run out of cash. Without cash a business cannot trade. Constructing a cash flow forecast will help a business in the planning stages. This shows the expected monthly:

- cash inflows;
- cash outflows;
- net cash flow (cash inflow - cash outflow);
- closing cash balance (opening cash balance + net cash flow); over a future time period.

Once the planned closing balances have been calculated, owners can see, for example, whether or not they will need more cash in the future. Figure 3 shows the closing cash balances for Robert Henshaw's van delivery business in the first six months of trading. The graph, which is based on figures in his cash flow forecast, shows that the business will need some more cash in July.

The cash flow forecast can also be used to monitor the performance of the business. The planned cash balances can be compared with the actual cash balances. Cash flow forecasting is

Figure 3 *Expected closing cash balances for Robert Henshaw's business*

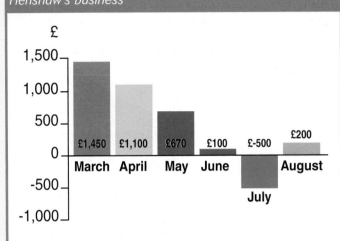

discussed in detail in section 22.

Profit Most businesses aim to make a profit at some stage. Expected profit can be calculated by subtracting the expected costs from the estimated revenue. At the end of the year a business will produce some financial statements which show how much profit has been made. These can be used to assess the performance of the business and help see whether objectives have been met. Profit is discussed in more detail in section 20.

Planning It is recommended that entrepreneurs should produce a comprehensive document outlining their plans in detail. This is called a business plan. Moneylenders or other investors will want to see this before providing funds.

Portfolio practice · The New Ale Co.

The New Ale Co is being set up in Birmingham by Ali Grant. After visiting Marble Beers, Manchester's only organic and vegan brewery, she decided that she could do the same in her home city. Ali was a vegan and knew that vegans could not drink real ale. This is because it contains a material called finings, a clearing agent made from fish bones. Yet real ale is a natural product and one that vegans might want to buy if there were no finings. Ali did some more market research. She used a vegan friend's website to post a questionnaire. Some of the results are shown in Figure 4. During the planning stage Ali spent a lot of time working out the costs of setting up. It would not be cheap, however, she planned to fund most of the set-up with £35,000 of her own money. She produced a cash flow forecast and wrote a comprehensive business plan.

She needed to borrow a further £10,000 from a bank and wanted to breakeven in the first year.

Source: adapted from company information

(a) (i) **Describe FOUR resources that Ali will need when setting up her small brewery.**
(ii) **What is likely to be Ali's aim when starting the New Ale Co?**
(b) (i) **Does Ali face much competition with her new product? Explain your answer.**
(ii) **What does the market research data say about Ali's business idea?**
(c) **Outline FOUR factors that Ali might include in her business plan.**

Figure 4 *Extracts from vegan questionnaire (1,300 responses from vegans)*

Obtain a copy of the *Yellow Pages* for your area.
- Find the restaurants section and record how many Italian, French, Indian, Thai, Chinese and Mexican restaurants there are in your area.
- Produce a graph or pie chart to show the data gathered above.
- If you were opening a restaurant, which would you choose? Give your reasons why.
- What other market information might you gather before opening a restaurant?

Research task

Meeting the assessment criteria

In your investigation you need to consider the factors that are important when setting up the business. You will be investigating the aims of the business, the importance of planning and the key elements in business planning. You will pay particular attention to market analysis.

Business example - Bean-there.com

Bean-there.com is an Internet café in Derry, Northern Ireland. It was set up by Aisling Collins who won the 2001 Entrepreneur of the Year Award. The main features of the business are:
- the idea came from a working holiday in Australia;
- it sells good quality Italian coffee, gourmet sandwiches, cakes and cookies;
- it is ideally located near to a major bus stop, tourist hostels, offices and shopping centre;
- it has modern décor – spiral staircase and bright colours;
- it charges £2.50 for half an hour or £4.50 per hour for Internet access.

Source: adapted from www.startups.co.uk.

Mark Band 1 *Provide basic knowledge and understanding of the key factors associated with starting a business such as planning and market analysis.*
Aisling Collins launched Bean-there.com in July 2000. Located in the diamond area of Derry city, this Internet café provides high speed Internet access for tourists, shoppers and local small businesses. During the planning stage she realised how important a good location was going to be. She managed to find a prime site that was currently empty. It was near to a bus stop, tourist hostels, offices and a shopping centre. During the planning stage Aisling also looked at the market. She noticed that the food provided by other cafés in the area was basic such as egg butties and watery tea. She decided that her café would sell more high quality food and drink.

Mark Band 2 *Provide sound knowledge and understanding of the key factors associated with starting a business such as planning and market analysis.*
Bean-there.com, located in the diamond area of Derry city, is an Internet café that provides high speed Internet access for tourists, shoppers and local small businesses. It was set up by Aisling Collins who won the Entrepreneur of the Year Award in 2001. Aisling understood the importance of thorough planning and spent quite a lot of time looking for the perfect site. She managed to find a prime location that was currently empty, although it took a while to track down the owner. It

was near to a large bus stop, tourist hostels, offices and a shopping centre. The Derry tour bus drops off passengers right opposite the café. During the planning stage Aisling also looked at the market. She discovered that there was not a single Internet café in the city. She also came to the conclusion that the food provided by other cafes was basic, lacking in choice and poor in quality, such as egg butties and watery tea. She decided that her café would sell more high quality food and drink.

Mark Band 3 *Provide comprehensive knowledge and understanding of the key factors associated with starting a business such as planning and market analysis, including a consideration of the pricing policy.*
After travelling around the world and working in San Francisco, where she learnt everything she needed to know about the Internet, Aisling Collins set up an Internet café. Bean-there.com, located in Derry City, provides high speed Internet access for tourists, shoppers and local small businesses. Aisling noticed the increasing numbers of tourists in the city since the Good Friday Peace Agreement, and set about creating a business that meets the new visitors' needs. Aisling linked up with local tour guides and proposed the café as a stop along the city's historical walking tour route. Tourists can now have a break, contact home, gather information on the area and even book visits to other attractions. The location of the café was a serious consideration in the planning stage. Aisling spent a long time searching for the prime location. She eventually found an empty site in the diamond district, but had to spend a further amount of time tracking down the owner.

Aisling also gave a lot of thought to the café menu. During the planning stage she undertook some market research. The was no other Internet café in Derry but plenty of conventional cafes. She visited them to see what they were offering. Generally, their menus were poor, offering things like fried egg butties and watery tea.

Bean-there.com has a modern design with seating capacity for 40 people. There is a spiral staircase and the café is decorated with bright colours. It boasts an extensive gourmet sandwich menu, including a wide range of speciality breads and wraps. Bean-there.com also supplies breakfast and lunch platters to local businesses.

During the planning stage, like many other start-up businesses, Aisling found it difficult to raise money. Banks would not take her seriously. Finally, since there was no other Internet café in Derry, she was able to charge premium prices for Internet access. She charged £4.50 per hour or £2.50 for half an hour.

Business resources

Managing business activities

Once a business plan has been finalised, the next stage in setting up is to gather the resources needed to run the business. Most owners will begin the process by organising the funding of the business. Until the business has finance it cannot acquire the other resources it needs. Business start-ups are usually funded by the owners. However, additional financial resources may be needed to meet the full cost of setting up and to help pay for the initial stages in trading. Once money has been raised the physical resources can be obtained. These include:

- premises;
- machinery;
- equipment;
- materials and stocks.

The types of physical resources needed will depend on the nature of the business. Before the business begins trading it may be necessary to recruit some staff to help out. Some very small businesses may need limited human resources to start with. However, if they are successful and start growing, it is likely that additional workers will be required. Once the business is up and running it will be important to monitor its progress and performance. This will help to ensure that the objectives are met.

Financial resources

Most businesses will have to obtain financial resources at some stage. There is a wide variety of different sources. But many small businesses can struggle to persuade lenders and investors to provide funding. Small businesses are often considered too risky by those providing funds.

Long term sources of finance

Figure 1 shows the different sources of long term funding available to businesses. Long term funding refers to money that is borrowed for and paid back over longer periods, such as five years or more. It is used to pay for resources that are likely to be used by the business for long periods of time. For example, a business might take out a 25 year loan to pay for its premises.

Share capital Limited companies can raise money by selling shares. Share capital is usually permanent capital. This means that share capital stays in the business for as long as it trades. Shareholders are entitled to dividends - a share of the profit made by the business. They may also be involved in decision making because shareholders are part-owners of a company. However, in public limited companies shareholders are only entitled to vote on who runs the company. An advantage of raising money by issuing shares is that large amounts can be raised because there are so many contributors. However, there are many administrative costs and the profit made by the business has to be spread more thinly.

Mortgage This is a long term loan that is secured on property.

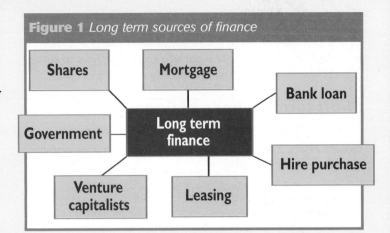

Figure 1 *Long term sources of finance*

Shares · Mortgage · Bank loan · Government · **Long term finance** · Hire purchase · Venture capitalists · Leasing

This means that if a business cannot keep up the loan and interest repayments, the lender is entitled to take ownership of the property. The interest rates paid on mortgages are relatively low and money can be borrowed for long periods such as 25 years.

Long term loans Financial institutions such as banks may provide loans. Most loans are **secured**. If a business does not repay the loan or make interest payments the bank can repossess assets, such as stock, machinery or money owed as debts. **Unsecured loans** are rare, as banks lose out. Interest rates on these loans tend to be higher to compensate for the risk.

Hire purchase (HP) Businesses can obtain machinery and equipment using hire purchase. Money is borrowed from a specialist called a finance house. For example, a business may buy a delivery van on HP. The finance house pays the supplier of the van and the business pays the finance house monthly instalments until the full cost plus interest has been met. The van will not belong to the business until the last instalment has been made. Until then the van legally belongs to the finance house. HP can be expensive because interest rates are high. However, it is relatively easy to get HP.

Leasing Leasing is the same as renting. Businesses can lease property, vehicles, machinery or equipment if they cannot afford to buy outright. It is a good way of acquiring such resources if they are only needed for a short period of time. The leasing company also meets the cost of repairs and maintenance. However, if resources are leased for a long period of time it may be an expensive form of finance.

Venture capitalists Many small businesses raise money from venture capitalists. These are businesses that specialise in providing 'risk capital' for young or fast growing companies. Some examples include Apax Partners, 3i and ECI. They raise their money from financial institutions and private investors. They may provide loans but are more likely to want a stake in the business. They often invest for between three and seven years. Some venture capitalists are individuals. They are called Business Angels and look to invest amounts ranging from £10,000 to around £100,000. They often have business experience and are prepared to take a risk.

Government Government funding is attractive because it is often cheap. For example, the Small Firms Loan Guarantee Scheme guarantees loans from financial institutions for small firms that have viable business proposals but which have tried and failed to get a conventional loan because of lack of security. Loans are available for periods of between two and ten years on sums from £5,000 to £100,000. There is a variety of other grants and loans available. But to qualify for financial help firms often have to set up in areas where unemployment is relatively high, for example.

Short term sources of finance

Short term finance is money that must be repaid within twelve months. Figure 2 shows the different short term sources available to businesses.

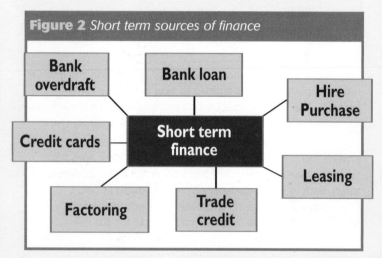

Figure 2 *Short term sources of finance*

Bank overdraft This is a common type of short term business finance. It involves a business spending more money than it has in its account. Businesses can use the bank's money to go overdrawn up to an agreed limit. Bank overdrafts are flexible and interest is only charged when the business is overdrawn. Interest rates are competitive but if a business exceeds its overdraft limit the rates can be very high.

Bank loan A business may take out a short term loan with a bank, for example. The amount, plus interest, must be repaid in regular monthly instalments, usually within a short period such as a year. This can be inflexible and the interest charged might be quite high.

Hire purchase (HP) HP can be used as a short term source of finance if a business buys some equipment, for example, and pays for it over a year in monthly instalments.

Leasing Leasing is also a short term source of finance if a resource is rented for twelve months or less. For example, a small construction business might lease a crane for two weeks.

Trade credit Sometimes a business can obtain goods and not have to pay for them straight away. Payment might be after 30, 60 or 90 days, for example. This is trade credit. It might appear to be a cheap way to borrow money. However, by delaying payment to suppliers businesses might be losing out on cash discounts if they had settled their bill immediately.

Factoring Factors are financial specialists that are often owned by financial institutions such as banks. They provide businesses with cash if they are owed money by their customers. Factors may take responsibility for the collection of debts. They may give a business between 80-90% of the value of an invoice when it is issued and then pass on the rest when the customer pays the bill. The factor charges a fee for this service.

Credit cards Credit cards can be used to obtain materials, services and fuel, for example. There is no exchange of cash when a credit card is used. Credit card users receive a statement at the end of the month listing all the transactions and showing the total amount owed. If users settle the bill within about 25 days there is no interest charge. However, if the bill is only paid in part, the interest charged on the outstanding amount is very high.

Retained profit

When a business makes a profit it is likely that some of it will be returned to the owners. However, the remainder will be retained and used to fund business activity. It might be used to boost working capital or it might be invested in a new venture, for example. The main advantage of using retained profit as a source of finance is that no interest has to be paid. It is also convenient because the money will already be in the bank account and there are no administration charges.

Physical resources

Businesses need a variety of physical resources to operate. When setting up some businesses will prefer to lease or rent resources. For example, retailers might lease shops and manufacturers might lease their factory units. It is also possible to lease plant, machinery and equipment. Leasing resources can help the cash flow of a business in its initial stages.

Premises One of the major resources of a business may be its premises. The type of premises needed will depend on the nature of the business. For example, a business that plans to sell clothes will need a shop in an appropriate location such as a shopping centreor high street. A manufacturer may look for an old disused factory or a new factory unit on an industrial estate. A solicitor setting up a new law practice will need an office. Estate agents will be able to provide information on the cost and availability of business premises.

Plant, machinery tools and equipment Nearly all new businesses will need to acquire a range of tools, equipment and machinery. Again, the type of resources needed will depend on the type of equipment. Some businesses need specialist equipment. For example, a dentist setting up a practice will need specialist dental tools and equipment that no other type of business would use. On the other hand, some equipment like vehicles, office furniture and computers, can be bought by a range of different businesses.

Materials and other physical resources Manufacturers need to buy raw materials and components. For example, a dressmaker will have to buy fabric, lace, ribbon, cotton, sequins, buttons and other materials. Office based businesses will have to buy stationery, toner for the photocopier and ink cartridges. Retailers will have to buy stock to resell. It will also be necessary to arrange for premises to be connected to water, gas, electricity and telephone. Other services, such as insurance, advertising and cleaning, will have to be organised. When buying resources like these there is often a choice of suppliers. Business owners must decide which suppliers to use. Their decision will be based on cost, quality, continuity of supply and reliability.

Human resources

Human resources are the people who work for the business. Various factors will affect the human resources of a business.

Staff quality Business will need to recruit staff. When first setting up staff may be limited. But as a business grows it will require a variety of employees with many skills. Business owners will want to recruit high quality staff. Generally, businesses will want to employ people who are:

- honest and trustworthy;
- reliable and punctual;
- flexible and cooperative;
- well motivated and willing to learn.

In some cases staff with particular skills, qualifications and experiences will be needed. For example, a small IT company might need to recruit staff with a degree in IT and some programming experience. Because a lot of new business activity involves providing services, it is often important to recruit staff with good people and communication skills. It may also be important to select staff who are good team workers because a lot of businesses organise their workforce into teams.

To help make sure that the best quality staff are appointed, businesses use references from previous employers to judge whether or not they are suitable. It might also be possible to test people before they are appointed. To improve the quality of the workforce a business might train their staff. If staff are well trained they will be able to do their job more effectively. They might also feel valued because the business has invested money in them, in which case they might be better motivated.

Cost and availability Businesses will want to recruit staff as cheaply as possible. However, if a business pays its staff poorly it might affect their motivation and productivity. Business owners have to pay staff at least the minimum legal wage. Generally, higher wages will attract better quality staff. In addition to wages businesses have to pay National Insurance contributions to the government. There is also the cost of training. Training is expensive and staff might leave soon after completing their training. This means that the money is wasted.

If a business needs to employ some specialist staff there may be availability problems. For example, if a local newspaper needs to recruit some reporters, there may not be any available in the town. This might mean that reporters have to be attracted from another area which could be expensive. When unemployment is low in the economy it becomes harder for businesses to attract and retain staff. The availability of workers might vary around the UK. Figure 3 shows that staff might be harder to recruit in the South because these regions are where unemployment is relatively low.

Figure 3 *Regional unemployment, Spring 2003*

SCOTLAND 5.7%

NORTHERN IRELAND 5.4%

NORTH EAST 6.6%

YORKSHIRE AND THE HUMBER 5.5%

NORTH WEST 5.1%

EAST MIDLANDS 4.3%

WEST MIDLANDS 5.9%

WALES 4.6%

EAST 4.2%

LONDON 7.1%

SOUTH EAST 3.9%

SOUTH WEST 3.9%

Source: adapted from *Regional Trends*, Office for National Statistics.

UK - 5.1%

A retailer requires some premises to lease for a clothes shop.

- Visit some local estate agents and compile a list of six suitable premises. The agent will possibly give you some written details.
- Draw up a table showing the location, size, rent, features and other details for each property.
- Write a recommendation suggesting which property would be the best.

Research task

Meeting the assessment criteria

In your investigation you need to identify the resources needed by the business. You will need to consider why particular resources are being used and how the business manages them to produce quality output.

Business example – Bennett's Fencing

Mike and Liam Bennett recently set up a small fencing business in Tamworth. They make a range of wooden fencing panels and supply local residents and two garden centres in the area. The business:

- leases a factory converted from a barn in a rural location about 8 miles from the centre of Tamworth;
- buys wood from suppliers in Scotland on 60 days trade credit;
- employs two full-time staff and four temporary staff. The temporary staff are laid off during the winter;
- leases most of its machinery, but purchased tools for £1,000;
- was set up using a £12,000 ten year bank loan and £18,000 of the owners' capital. A £5,000 bank overdraft was also agreed.

Source: adapted from company information.

Mark Band 1 *You need to provide a basic knowledge and understanding of managing resources in a business.*
Bennett's Fencing is located in a rural area. The isolated location was important so that people were not disturbed by the noisy electric saws used in production. The business was financed by a ten year £12,000 bank loan and a £5,000 overdraft. The owners also put some capital in and the main raw material is bought on trade credit. A lot of the start-up capital was used converting the barn into a factory. This meant that expensive machinery had to be leased. However, the leased machinery was very 'state-of-the-art' and efficient. The Bennetts employed two full time staff who are well paid. However, the temporary staff are unskilled and only get the minimum wage. Temporary staff were a problem because they keep leaving.

Mark Band 2 *You need to provide a sound knowledge and understanding of managing resources in a business.*
Once the funding for the new business was put in place, the Bennetts spent time finding suitable premises. It was important to locate the business away from residential areas because of the noise made by the electrical saws during production. The rural location was perfect. They also had a lot of space for storage, loading and unloading. The finance for the business was provided by a bank which allowed the brothers to borrow £12,000 over ten years. The bank also gave them a £5,000 overdraft. Another £18,000 was put in by the owners. Unfortunately most of the initial capital was used converting the barn and meeting health and safety regulations. This meant that the machinery had to be leased. However, leasing proved to be advantageous because the machines were new and their maintenance was the responsibility of the leasing company. The business did have one problem though. The Bennetts decided to rely quite heavily on temporary staff. This was because their demand was seasonal. However, the temporary staff proved to be unreliable and poorly motivated, probably because they were only being paid the minimum wage and were laid off in October.

Mark Band 3 *You need to provide a comprehensive knowledge and understanding of managing resources in a business and give reasons for their choice.*
Bennett's Fencing was funded from a variety of different sources. £18,000 capital was provided by the owners and a £12,000 ten year, long term bank loan was taken out. This was considered a suitable funding arrangement for this type of business because a lot of the start-up capital was spent on capital expenditure - converting the barn into a factory. One of the strengths of the business was its location. There was lots of open space and the noise from the factory did not disturb anyone in its rural location. Short term sources of funds included leasing, a bank overdraft and trade credit. The 60 day trade credit period for wood supplies was particularly helpful when the business first started trading. The Bennetts decided to lease their machinery. They wanted the best but could not afford to purchase it outright. Leasing gave them access to the best technology available. Leasing improved the cash flow of the business and the cost of repairs and maintenance was the responsibility of the leasing company. Human resources in the business were a bit of a problem. There were no real difficulties with full time staff. However, the decision to employ cheap, temporary staff during the busy summer months may have been a mistake. Staff turnover amongst the temporary workers was very high, probably because wages were set at the legal minimum. This resulted in production being disrupted, with customers receiving late deliveries. This was a problem that the Bennetts would have to address eventually.

Portfolio practice · Ma-Doner

Jo Dalton wanted to open a kebab shop in Ventnor on the Isle of Wight. She drew up her business plan and received £5,000 from The Prince's Trust to set up the business. However, she discovered that the money was not going to be enough to buy all the equipment she needed. Instead, she decided to use hire purchase. Jo priced up all the equipment she needed, including a fridge, cooker, chargrill, chiller cabinet, kebab burner and a carbon filter extraction fan.

Jo had problems finding a finance deal for the equipment, but persevered and found a local firm that sold catering equipment. They found a leasing deal to suit her and Ma-Doner is now paying for the equipment monthly. 'If I had had to pay upfront I probably wouldn't be here today' Jo said.

Buying the equipment on hire purchase has worked well for Ma-Doner. Jo managed to buy new equipment with guarantees, at only a slightly higher price than the reconditioned equipment that she had budgeted for. 'I have got peace of mind knowing that it is new and won't break down' she said.

Source: adapted from www.startups.co.uk.

(a) **State FOUR physical resources used by Ma-Doner.**
(b) (i) **How was the start-up funded?**
    (ii) **Discuss the advantages and disadvantages of using hire purchase to obtain equipment.**
(c) (i) **What human resources might Jo Dalton need if the business becomes a success?**
    (ii) **Discuss how the quality of staff might be improved by Jo.**

Monitoring quality and performance

Quality

Quality is vital for a business. Quality is a degree of 'excellence' achieved in business operations. A successful business must provide high quality products. These are products which meet standards and also the requirements of customers. For example, Figure 1 shows the features that may be considered important by a teenager when buying a computer. A business can sometimes gain quality standards for these features, such as:

- a Kite Mark for the quality of products such as crash helmets;
- a Wool Mark for the quality of woollen products;
- a Lion Mark for the quality of toys.

The quality of production processes is also vital. This might be the quality of manufacturing processes, such as the production of steel, textiles, printing or electronic components. It might also be the quality of a service such as transport, hotel hospitality, pest control or theme park entertainment.

The importance of monitoring quality

Businesses that achieve quality in production are likely to benefit. They might be able to:

- attract customers and increase sales;
- ensure waste is minimized and control costs;
- increase profits.

Business must ensure that quality is maintained at all times to achieve these benefits. This involves the use of various methods to ensure quality, including quality control, quality assurance and Total Quality Management (TQM).

The role of quality control

Traditionally the role of quality control was to inspect goods before they were dispatched to customers. However, although this prevented poor quality goods from reaching customers it did not prevent them from being made. Modern quality control attempts to prevent defective goods from being made. This is better because:

- customers never get to see a defective product;
- resources are not wasted in the production of a defective product that must be scrapped or reworked.

Modern quality control requires a commitment from every employee in an organisation to take responsibility for the quality of their own work. Businesses use a preventative approach to quality control where mistakes, errors and defects are prevented from happening in the first place.

Quality assurance

The aim of quality assurance is to develop an approach where quality is maintained throughout every stage in all processes used in the business. A business might identify certain quality standards at each stage in a process. These standards will satisfy or exceed customer expectations and staff will be committed to achieving them. If they are achieved, all of the time, then quality can be guaranteed or assured.

Some businesses try to achieve quality standards. These show that processes have been carried out to a high standard and to a stated specification. Once a business has been assessed and shown that it can reach and maintain these high standards, it will be accredited. For example, the International Standardisation Organisation (ISO) has standards which are recognized internationally. Many are highly specific and contain technical specifications or other criteria which must be met. A generic standard that can be gained by all businesses no matter what their product is the ISO 9000 accreditation. This shows standards that businesses achieve in managing their processes. It will help a business to:

- satisfy customers' quality requirements;
- comply with regulations;
- meet environmental objectives.

ISO 9000 accreditation is awarded by bodies such as the British

---

Figure 1 *Important features of a computer for a teenager*

Operation – does it have enough memory and speed?

Physical appearance – does it have a suitable style or design?

Reliability and durability – will it last?

Suitability – is it compact enough to fit in a small bedroom?

Guarantees – does the PC come with a guarantee that meets the cost of all parts and labour in the event of a breakdown?

After sales service – can it be delivered by the end of the week?

Image – is the brand name recognised?

Reputation – what do peers think of the business or product?

Standards Institution (BSI). Once a business has achieved accreditation, its processes are checked regularly to ensure that standards are being maintained. This approach to quality assurance will give customers confidence when buying products. Figure 2 shows the quality management principles for businesses wanting ISO 9000 accreditation.

Total quality management

Total Quality Management (TQM) adopts the modern approach to quality control. It is a philosophy which relies on a commitment to quality which is built into the system. It is a cultural approach and aims at preventing errors rather than identifying them.

Design TQM begins in the design stages of a product. For example, quality might be improved if certain materials are recommended or if a product can be made in such a way that errors do not occur.

Quality chains Every person working in a business is a link in a chain. They are both a customer and a supplier. For example, the work done by one employee at the start of a production line will affect those further down. The quality chain will break if poor work affects the next person down the line.

Total commitment TQM requires every single person in the business to be committed to high quality. This includes office staff, production workers, management and directors. Staff must take pride in their work and the people at the top of the organisation should lead by example.

Monitoring TQM relies heavily on monitoring a wide range of performance indicators to ensure that standards are being met. This involves gathering numerical information throughout the whole production process. The data must be analysed and if performance indicators do not reach specified standards there must be an investigation to find out why. This is called statistical process control.

Teamwork TQM requires the workforce to be organised into teams. This is the best way of solving problems because a team will have a greater range of skills, knowledge and experience than an individual. Teamwork also improves motivation because staff will support each other and communication will be better.

Customer focus TQM is customer driven. Businesses using TQM must focus on customers and be responsive to their needs and wants. Customers can help to set quality standards. For example, customer complaints can be analysed and used as a basis for product improvement.

Some benefits of TQM include:

* improved customer satisfaction;
* better quality right across the business;
* less waste and lower costs;
* improved communications;
* a foundation for further improvements.

However, TQM is expensive to implement because of high training costs. It also requires a lot of paper work and will only be successful if everyone is committed.

The importance of monitoring performance

Business owners have to monitor the performance of the business. This helps to:

* ensure that the objectives are met. Targets are usually set and unless checks are made there will be no way of knowing whether the business has met them;
* avoid trading difficulties. For example, by checking the cash position of a business regularly, it is less likely to run out of cash;
* identify times to take corrective action if the performance is not meeting objectives.

Solvency

One of the main aims of a business when it is first set up is to remain solvent. If a business becomes insolvent it has to cease trading. Insolvency occurs when a firm's liabilities (the amount it owes) are greater than the firm's assets (the value of resources owned). To remain solvent a business must avoid taking on too much debt and make sure it has sufficient cash to pay its immediate bills. One way of monitoring cash flow is to compare the planned cash position at the end of each month with the actual cash position. Figure 3 shows two bar charts for a new business. One is the planned cash position and the other is the actual cash position. The graphs show clearly that the actual cash position was worse than that planned after March. If this business had been monitoring its cash position on a regular basis, it may have avoided running out of cash in June.

A firm must also monitor its debt. It should compare regularly the amount it owes with the value of assets that are held. A business needs to ensure that the value of assets are greater than the value of liabilities. If the difference between the two is narrowing, this suggests that the business is losing money. It is also worth noting that a business can have cash but still be insolvent. For example, a business could borrow more cash to pay some bills but this would plunge the company further into debt.

Measuring profits

Owners will be particularly interested in the profit made by the

Figure 2 *ISO 9000 features*

Customer focus

Leadership

The involvement of people

A process approach

A system approach to management

Continual improvement

A factual approach to decision making

Mutually beneficial supplier relationship

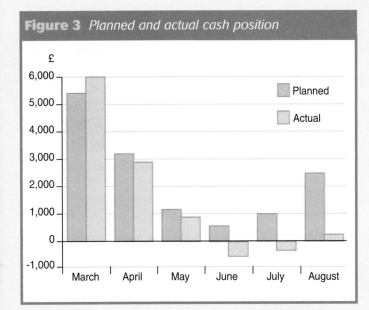

Figure 3 *Planned and actual cash position*

business. They will be interested in both profit levels and profit margins.

Profit levels Profit is the amount of money left over from sales revenue after all business costs have been met. A new business may not expect to make very much profit, if any, to start with. However, it must still monitor profit levels even if losses are made. A business might calculate the profit made each month and compare it with the planned profit figures. If the actual profit is below the planned profit, there may be a need for corrective action. For example, some more advertising might be needed to boost sales.

Profit margins Owners might also be interested in the profit margin. This is the amount of profit expressed as a percentage of sales revenue. For example, if a furniture manufacturer makes a table for £30 and sells if for £50, the profit made is £20. The profit margin is 40% (£20/£50 x 100). The higher the profit margin the better. Some owners may plan to achieve a target profit margin. Regular checks can be made to see if they are being achieved. Profit margins can be increased by raising prices or lowering costs. Profit margin calcualtions are dealt with in section 20.

Complying with laws

Businesses have to operate within the law. A number of laws have been passed which are aimed at businesses. These include:

* employment legislation;
* health and safety legislation;
* consumer legislation;
* environmental legislation;
* company laws.

If a business fails to comply with the law the consequences could be damaging and far reaching. For example, if a manufacturer infringes health and safety regulations at work, it may face problems. Failing to comply with legislation can incur legal costs and fines. It might also suffer a blow to its reputation. As a result it

may lose sales and potential employees may be discouraged from applying for posts.

Depending on the type of business activity, a firm will have to use systems to ensure that they comply with the law. For example, if a business discharges gases into the atmosphere as a result of a burning process, it will have to make regular checks to ensure that the discharges meet with environmental standards. Businesses that employ people must for example, provide contracts of employment, adequate working conditions, health and safety training and at least a minimum legal wage. It is the responsibility of any business to ensure that it complies with the law. It may be necessary to get legal advice if a business is unsure about its legal position. This is dealt with in sections 8, 12 and 15.

Identifying areas for improvement

Most businesses will want to improve performance even if their objectives have been met. This is because business is an ongoing activity and will be subject to external influences such as competition. To maintain or grow market share businesses have to be innovative and ever-improving. Areas for improvement can be identified by:

* monitoring and analysing quality data and financial information gathered during the normal course of trading;
* listening to customers, for example monitoring complaints or doing market research;
* listening to staff, for example at team meetings or through staff suggestion boxes;
* listening to advisors or specialists that might be employed.

Performance can be improved by:

* training staff to higher levels and in more tasks;
* modifying or launching new products to meet ever-changing customer needs;
* raising productivity, for example by introducing new technology or new working practices;
* raising quality, for example by using better materials or improved production techniques;
* enhancing customer services for example by acting on customer complaints.

Obtain a complaints form from a local business. Travel agents, train and bus companies or large retailers might have them.
* What questions do they ask?
* Who deals with complaints?
* How do you think the information is used by the organisation?

Research task

Portfolio practice · McGregor & Son

McGregor & Son set up a salmon farm in Scotland. Salmon production is carried out in two phases. The first is a fresh water stage where the ova are hatched and the young (smolts) reared in tanks or in cages in fresh water lochs. This takes around 10 - 15 months (although new technology enables fish to be put into the sea from 6-7 months now). The second phase involves growing the smolts in cages in sea water until they reach market size, which may take around 12 – 18 months. Most of their output is sold to processors or smokers in Scotland.

The business required a range of resources such as an on-shore base to service cages, store feed and other materials and an area for net washing and repairs. Unpolluted and sheltered water was needed to hold the salmon cages. Equipment such as vehicles, boats, moorings, cages, nets, feeders and accessories, net washer, harvest boxes, ice machine and a jetty crane were also required.

McGregor had to obtain a 15 year lease from Crown Estate Commission (CEC) for use of the sea bed. He also had to go on a training course to familiarise himself with the 10 different statutory bodies and more than 50 pieces of legislation that address salmon farming. The business had to register with the Scottish Office Agriculture Environment and Fisheries Department (SOAEFD) as required by the Diseases of Fish Act 1983. The farm is visited regularly by the SOAEFD.

Source: adapted from SAC Farm Diversification web site.

(a) McGregor & Son are not likely to make a profit in their first two years of trading. Explain why.
(b) (i) What might McGregor & Sons customers want in terms of quality?
(ii) What role might the SOAEFD play in quality control?
(c) How might McGregor & Son monitor the performance of the fish farm?

Meeting the assessment criteria

In your investigation you need to explain how a business manages its resources to provide quality output.

Business example – Friends Abroad Ltd

Friends Abroad Ltd was set up to provide holidays for single people. It organises special interest holidays for single people. The business:

- takes special care to ensure that each client is sold exactly the right sort of holiday by asking clients to complete detailed questionnaires;
- is customer focused and interviews all clients over the telephone after their holiday for valuable feedback;
- provides a wide range of special interest holidays, such as skiing, walking, camping, snorkelling and diving, sailing, golfing, and visiting historic sites;
- records and monitors all complaints;
- is a member of ABTA, an organisation which protects consumer rights and listens to complaints.

Source: adapted from company information.

Mark Band 1 *You need to provide a basic knowledge and understanding of business resources and quality issues.*
Friends Abroad understands the importance of satisfying customers and providing a quality service. It gathers lots of information about clients to make sure that they are sold the right sort of holiday. It monitors performance by interviewing clients over the telephone when they return. This will provide the business with feedback which can be used to improve the service in the future. The company is also a member of ABTA which gives consumers protection.

Mark Band 2 *You need to provide a sound knowledge and understanding of business resources and describe relevant quality issues.*
Friends Abroad Ltd is customer focused. This means that its activities are driven by customers. For example, it gathers a lot of information from clients before a particular holiday is sold. It matches the interests and needs of clients with specific holidays. This helps to guarantee quality. Friends Abroad attempts to improve the quality of its service by interviewing clients when they return. The information it gathers can be used to improve holidays in the future. The company also has a complaints procedure to help monitor quality and performance. The owner of the company deals with complaints in person. Sometimes clients are offered a free holiday if she thinks the case is a deserving one. Friends Abroad is a member of ABTA. This organisation protects consumer rights and listens to complaints.

Mark Band 3 *You need to provide a comprehensive knowledge and understanding of business resources and analyse the firm's approach to quality.*
Friends Abroad provides holidays for single people. This is a specialist area and the business needs to gather as much information as possible to ensure that customer needs are met. It does this by asking clients to complete detailed questionnaires. This information is used to make sure that clients are sold the most appropriate holiday. If their needs are perfectly matched by the holiday sold the consumer will be satisfied. Friends Abroad monitors quality and product performance in two ways. It records all customer complaints and deals with each case thoroughly. The owner takes responsibility for all complaints and deals with them personally. The company also telephones clients when they return. It has gathered a lot of useful information when doing this. It has been able to improve the quality of the service and products based on some of the telephone conversations. Finally, Friends Abroad is a member of ABTA. This organisation helps protect consumers. For example, they safeguard client's money when a holiday company collapses.

The profit and loss account

What are accounts?

Businesses must keep a record of their transactions with customers and suppliers. These are needed to produce financial statements, which can be used to help monitor the financial 'health' of the business. These financial statements are called accounts. Two key statements are produced.

- **The profit and loss account.** This contains information about the revenue, costs and profit that a business records during the year.
- **The balance sheet.** This contains information about the debts, capital and resources owned by the business.

Accounts are useful for different stakeholders in the business. Owners, customers, employees, the Inland Revenue, other competitors and banks that may provide loans can see how well the business is performing.

The importance of profitability and liquidity

In the long term businesses have to make a profit. This is because the owners want a financial return on the money they invested in the business. Although businesses might have other aims and objectives, it is still necessary for them to make a profit. Profit is the reward to entrepreneurs for taking risk. If they do not receive an adequate financial return they will withdraw their interest. This is likely to result in the business closing down.

The profit made by a business is usually an indication of how well it is doing. If profit increases over time this suggests that the business is improving. Figure 1 shows the profit made by Tesco over five years. During this time profit increased from £1,054m to £1,962m. This is a significant improvement and the shareholders are likely to be pleased with this performance. The increase suggests that Tesco is doing well.

In the short term, however, a business may be able survive without making a profit. For example, when a business first sets up many owners do not expect to make a profit for the first few months or even years. But a business cannot survive without cash. It is therefore important to make sure the business has enough liquid resources. Liquid resources include cash and those, such as stocks, that can be converted into cash within 12 months. Without cash, a business cannot trade. Cash is needed to pay immediate bills such as wages, telephone, electricity and raw materials. If these bills are not paid the services are likely to be withdrawn and the business could not operate. Monitoring the firm's cash position is a crucial management activity. The management of cash flow is discussed in more detail in section 20.

Assets, liabilities, expenses and revenue

The transactions recorded by a business are sorted by bookkeepers and placed into various categories.

- **Assets** are the resources that a business owns and uses. Examples include plant, machinery, equipment, vehicles, stocks and cash. Details of these are shown in the balance sheet and

Figure 1 *Tesco gross profit before tax 2001-2005*

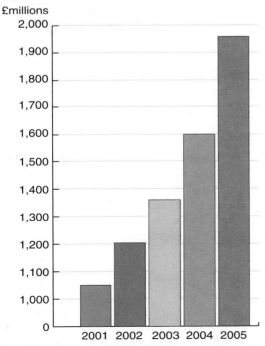

£millions

Source: adapted from Tesco, *Annual Report and Accounts.*

are explained in section 19.

- **Liabilities** are the debts of the business. The money owed to suppliers, bankers and other businesses for example. Details of these are also shown in the balance sheet and are explained in section 19.
- **Expenses** are the overheads of the business, such as rent, electricity and rates. Details of expenses are summarised in the profit and loss account.
- **Revenue** is the money that a business receives from selling its output. This is also shown in the profit and loss account.

Businesses will incur costs before they start trading, for example registering a company or converting premises. These may be called **start-up costs**. Once a business begins trading there will also be **running costs**, such as wages and heating.

The profit and loss account – sole traders

The amount of profit made by a business is calculated in the profit and loss account. The profit and loss account shows the income the business has received during a trading period. It also shows the expenditure on resources that have already been used and those that will be used within 12 months. Table 1 shows a profit and loss account for Manish Popat, a sole trader who set up an ice-cream parlour in Brighton in 2003. He has been trading for one year. What details does this profit and loss account show?

Turnover This is the revenue generated by Manish Popat's ice-cream parlour. In 2004 the business generated £67,500. This figure does not include VAT. This is because VAT does not belong to the business. It is sent to the government.

Cost of sales This is the cost associated with production. In this case it is likely to be the cost of buying in ice-cream and other stocks which are resold. For a manufacturer it could include the direct costs of labour, materials and other costs such as machinery maintenance.

Table 1 *Profit and loss account for Manish Popat*

Manish Popat Profit and loss account y/e 31.7.04	£	£
Turnover		67,500
Cost of sales		32,300
Gross profit		35,200
Less Expenses		
Wages	8,700	
Rent	10,200	
Heat & light	1,100	
Motor expenses	3,400	
Insurance	700	
Bank charges	550	
Other overheads	2,100	
		26,750
Net profit		8,450

Figure 2 *Cost of sales adjusted for stock*

	£
Opening stock	0
Add Purchases	34,400
	34,400
Less Closing stock	2,100
Cost of sales	32,300

The cost of sales has to be adjusted for stock. This is to take into account the stock the business had at the start of the year and how much was left over at the end of the year. Figure 2 shows the adjustments for Manish Popat's business.

In this case the opening stock is 0 because the business has just been set up. During the year Manish bought £34,400 of stock. Therefore the value of purchases for the year is £34,400 (£34,400 + 0). At the end of the year there was £2,100 left over. This is the closing stock and should be subtracted from the total above. The cost of sales is therefore £32,300.

Gross profit The gross profit for the business is found by subtracting cost of sales from the turnover. Gross profit is the profit made by the business before expenses have been subtracted. Manish Popat's business made a gross profit of £35,200. The top part of the account, where the gross profit is calculated, is known as the trading account.

Expenses These are sometimes called overheads. They are costs not associated with production. For example, Manish had motor expenses of £3,400. In total, the expenses for the year amounted to £26,750.

Net profit The amount of profit left over for the owner is called net profit. This is found by subtracting expenses from gross profit. Manish Popat's business made £8,450 in its first year of trading. Manish might decide to keep this or retain it in the business to provide extra funding.

Profit and loss account – limited companies

The accounts of limited companies are subject to some legal requirements and have slightly different features to those of sole traders. The profit and loss account for Moreton Ltd, a car maintenance and repair business, is shown in Table 2.

Limited companies have to publish their accounts by law. This means that anyone can see the accounts. It is usual for accounts to show two years' figures. This allows readers to make comparisons. The profit and loss account can be divided into three parts.

Table 2 *Profit and loss account for Moreton Ltd*

Moreton Ltd Profit and loss account y/e 31.12.04	2004 £000	2003 £000
Turnover	2,455	2,110
Cost of sales	1,430	1,270
Gross profit	1,025	840
Administrative expenses	820	710
Operating profit	205	130
Net interest payable	50	50
Profit on ordinary activities before tax	155	80
Taxation	40	20
Profit on ordinary activities after tax	115	60
Dividends	25	20
Retained profit	90	40

Trading account This is calculated by subtracting cost of sales from turnover, like a sole trader. It gives a figure for gross profit. Moreton Ltd made a gross profit of £1,025,000 in 2004.

The profit and loss account This is made up of a number of parts.

- Expenses are costs not linked to production, such as administration and distribution costs. They are totalled and entered as one figure to avoid cluttering up the account with detail. Moreton's expenses rose from £710,000 to £820,000 over the two years.
- Administrative expenses are subtracted from gross profit to show operating profit. This is net profit before tax and interest have been subtracted. Moreton's operating profit rose in 2004 from £130,000 to £205,000.
- Any interest paid or received has to be shown in the accounts of limited companies. Sometimes they are shown separately. However, in this case the net figure is shown (interest received – interest payable). In the Moreton account the net interest payable was £50,000 in both years.
- Interest is subtracted from operating profit to get the profit on ordinary activities before tax. For Moreton, net profit before tax has increased from £80,000 to £155,000.
- Limited companies have to pay corporation tax. This is subtracted to get net profit on ordinary activities after tax. Moreton's after tax profit rose from £60,000 to £115,000.

Appropriation account This shows what happens to profit which is earned. Some may be returned to shareholders as dividends, for example. This is subtracted from net profit to get retained profit. The dividend paid by Moreton rose by 25% to £25,000 in 2004. The retained profit will be used to buy new tools and equipment, for example.

Profit margins

Although the amount of profit made by a business helps to show how well a business is performing, a better indicator is the profit margin. This is the amount of profit a business makes in relation to its turnover.

Gross profit margin This is the gross profit expressed as a percentage of turnover. Figure 3 shows the formula to calculate the gross profit margin. Using this formula, the gross profit margin for Moreton Ltd in 2003 and 2004 were 39.8% and 41.8%. For example, in 2004 gross profit was £1,025,000 and turnover was £2,455,000, so the gross profit was £1,025,000 ÷ £2,455,000 x 100. The margins show a slight improvement. Whether a particular gross margin is good or not depends on the industry. Moreton would have to compare the 41.8% in 2004 with another car maintenance company.

Net profit margin The net profit margin helps to measure how well a business controls its overheads. If the difference between gross profit and net profit is small, this suggests that overheads are low. This is because net profit equals gross profit less overheads. The net profit margin is also expressed as percentage of the turnover and can be calculated using the formula in Figure 4. The net profit used in the formula is the profit before tax and interest, i.e. the operating profit. Moreton's net margins for 2003 and 2004 were 6.2% and 8.4%. For example, in 2004 net profit was calculated as £205,000 ÷ £2,455,000 x 100. Net profit margins have improved over the two years. Moreton would have to compare these with another company in the industry to judge whether the performance was good or not.

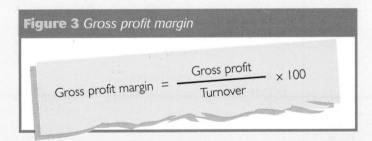

Figure 3 *Gross profit margin*

$$\text{Gross profit margin} = \frac{\text{Gross profit}}{\text{Turnover}} \times 100$$

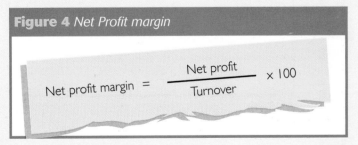

Figure 4 *Net Profit margin*

$$\text{Net profit margin} = \frac{\text{Net profit}}{\text{Turnover}} \times 100$$

- Choose three companies that trade in the same industry.
- Obtain annual reports from these companies. Alternatively visit their websites where profit and loss accounts can usually be accessed.
- Find the profit and loss accounts for these companies.
- Calculate the gross and net profit margins for each one.
- Explain which is the best performing company.

Research task

Portfolio practice · J Sainsbury plc

Table 3 *Profit and loss account for Sainsbury*

	2004 £m	2003 £m
Turnover	17,141	17,079
Cost of sales	15,658	15,688
Gross profit	1,483	1,391
Administrative expenses	827	717
Operating profit	656	674
Other income *	14	53
Profit on ordinary activities before interest	670	727
Net interest payable	60	60
Profit on ordinary activities before tax	610	667
Taxation	206	206
Profit on ordinary activities after tax	404	461
Dividends	309	305
Retained profit	95	156

* Includes profits on disposal of assets, profits from joint ventures and profit from the sale of property.

Source: adapted from J Sainsbury, *Annual Report and Accounts*.

J Sainsbury, the supermarket chain, is a public limited company. It has experienced strong competition in recent years due to the growth of Tesco, Asda and Morrisons. Table 3 shows the profit and loss account for Sainsbury in 2004.

(a) **Describe the running costs that Sainsbury incurs.**
(b) (i) **Explain how gross profit and net profit are calculated for Sainsbury.**
    (ii) **How might Sainsbury use the retained profit?**
(c) (i) **Evaluate the performance of Sainsbury during 2004 and (ii) discuss whether the shareholders should be concerned.**

Meeting the assessment criteria

For your chosen business you must identify and explain the start-up and running costs. You must also explain how the profit and loss account can be used to monitor the performance of the business.

Business example – Rejuvenations

Kelly Morrison practices aromatherapy, reflexology and stress management. Treatments range from a head and neck massage to a complete holistic consultation. Kelly spent £15,000 when setting up Rejuvenations. Most of the money was used to convert a shop into a treatment centre. The rest was spent furnishing the centre and buying essential equipment such as a treatment couch, computer, and treatment packs. In the first year of trading Kelly hoped to break even but exceeded her expectations. The profit and loss account is shown in Table 4.

Table 4 *Profit and loss account for Rejuvenations*

Rejuvenations Profit and loss account y/e 30.6.04	2004 £m	2003 £m
Turnover		71,600
Cost of sales		23,200
Gross profit		48,400
Less Expenses		
Wages	18,300	
Rent	12,000	
Heat & light	1,400	
Motor expenses	1,200	
Insurance	1,600	
Advertising	3,700	
Other overheads	5,200	
		43,400
Net profit		5,000

Source: adapted from company information.

Mark Band 1 *Provide a basic understanding of financial management by identifying some start-up and running costs and commenting generally on profit as a method of monitoring performance.*
Kelly Morrison started up by spending £15,000 converting a shop into a treatment centre and buying equipment such as a treatment couch. The money spent on decorating the premises and creating the right ambience was important for the type of business. Running costs can be seen in the profit and loss account. Examples include £18,300 paid in wages, £12,000 rent and £3,700 paid to advertise the company. In the first year of trading Kelly did well. She made a profit of exactly £5,000. This was better than she had planned.

Mark Band 2 *Provide a sound understanding of financial management by identifying some start-up and running costs and commenting generally on profit as a method of monitoring performance.*
When a business is first set up a lot of start-up costs are incurred. In this case, £15,000 was spent converting the premises into a suitable environment for a treatment centre. Money was used to decorate and furnish the centre to make sure that the ambience was appropriate for aromatherapy, reflexology, and stress management. Once a business starts to trade it incurs running costs. These are shown in the profit and loss account of Rejuvenations. Examples include cost of sales, such as oils and treatment materials, wages, rent, motor expenses and advertising. In the first year of trading Kelly hoped to break-even. However, according to the profit and loss account Rejuvenations made a £5,000 profit. This suggests that the business has performed well.

Mark Band 3 *Provide a comprehensive understanding of financial management by explaining the start-up costs and running costs and evaluating profit as a method of monitoring performance.*
Rejuvenations was set up by Kelly Morrison to provide treatment courses in reflexology aromatherapy and stress management. Treatments range from a head and neck massage to a complete holistic consultation. The start-up costs were about £15,000. Some of the money was used to convert a shop into a treatment centre. There were also decorating and furnishing costs. A number of assets were purchased such as a treatment couch, a computer and other equipment. Once the business started trading it had to meet a variety of running costs. The largest of these was the cost of sales. This is expenditure on materials such as oils and treatment packs. Other expenses which had to be met were wages, rent, heating, motor expenses and advertising. Despite these costs Kelly's business made a profit in the first year. She had hoped to break even but in fact Rejuvenations made £5,000. She planned to reinvest this in business. Finally, Kelly calculated the net profit margin. It was about 7%. She planned to increase this to 10% next year.

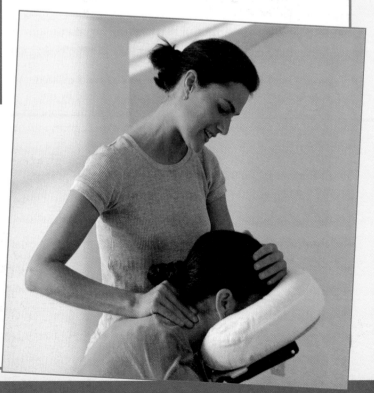

What does a balance sheet show?

The balance sheet shows the financial position of a business at a particular point in time. It provides information about the firm's assets, liabilities and capital.

Assets These are the resources that a business owns and uses. In the balance sheet they are divided into **current assets** and **fixed assets**. Fixed assets are those which the business buys to use over and over again for a long period of time. Examples include premises, plant, machinery, equipment and vehicles. Current assets are those that are used up in production such as stocks of raw materials and components and cash. Debtors, the money owed by customers, is also a current asset.

Liabilities These are the debts of the business. In the balance sheet liabilities are divided into **current liabilities** and **long term liabilities**. Current liabilities include money owed that must be repaid within twelve months. Examples would be money owed to suppliers and a bank overdraft. Any money owed for more than one year is a long term liability. Examples might include a mortgage or a five year bank loan.

Capital This is the money put into the business by the owners. For example, a limited company raises capital by selling shares. This is listed as share capital in the balance sheet. Capital is often used to fund the setting up of the business.

The accounting equation

The accounting equation shows a very important relationship that exists between the assets, capital and liabilities of a business. It states that the value of all the resources owned by a business, i.e. its assets, must equal the value of all the money introduced into and owed by the business, i.e. the capital and liabilities. This is shown in Figure 1.

The two sides of the equation must always be equal to each other. This is because the value of all the money raised by the business from owners and other creditors, must be the same as the value of all the resources bought using that money. For example, Sheila Timms used £6,000 of her own money and a £3,000 bank loan to set up a PC repair business. She bought a new computer for £2,000 and a vehicle for £4,500. She put the rest of the money in a business bank account. After these transactions the financial position of Sheila's business can be shown using the accounting equation in Figure 1.

Figure 1 *The accounting equation*

$$\boxed{\textbf{Assets}} = \boxed{\textbf{capital}} + \boxed{\textbf{liabilities}}$$

$$£2,000 + £4,500 + £2,500 = £6,000 + £3,000$$
$$£9,000 = £9,000$$

Sheila's business owns three assets, a computer (£2,000), a vehicle (£4,500) and cash in the bank (£2,500). The total value of these assets is £9,000. The value of capital put into the business by Sheila is £6,000 and the amount owed to creditors is £3,000. Therefore the value of capital and liabilities added together is £9,000 (£6,000 + £3,000). This means that the value of assets and the value of capital and liabilities added together are both the same at £9,000. This will always be the case for any business at any time.

Rearranging the accounting equation, as in Figure 2, can be useful to understand the structure of the balance sheet.

Figure 2 *Re-arranging the accounting equation*

$$\text{Assets} - \text{liabilities} = \text{capital}$$

The structure of the balance sheet

The financial information shown in a balance sheet is set out in a particular way. It is based on the rearranged accounting equation shown above. Table 1 shows the balance sheet for Brigitte Dauche's business, a patisserie.

Table 1 *Balance sheet for Brigitte Dauche's business*

Brigitte Dauche Balance sheet as at 31.12.04		
	£	£
Fixed assets		
Ovens		4,700
Equipment		4,000
Vehicle		3,000
		11,700
Current assets		
Stock	1,200	
Cash at bank	2,950	
Cash in hand	550	
	4,700	
Current liabilities		
Trade creditors	3,450	
Net current assets		1,250
Long term liabilities		
Bank loan		(4,000)
NET ASSETS		**8,950**
FINANCED BY:		
Capital		
Opening capital		7,500
Add Net profit		12,300
		19,800
Less Drawings		10,850
Closing capital		**8,950**

What does the balance sheet show? The top part represents the left-hand side of the accounting equation, assets–liabilities.

Fixed assets These are assets which are intended for repeated use. The business has three fixed assets, ovens, equipment and a vehicle. According to the balance sheet these are valued at £11,700.

Current assets These are assets which are likely to be changed into cash within one year. The current assets are stocks of raw materials, cash at bank and cash in hand. The total value of current assets is £4,700.

Current liabilities Current liabilities are monies owed which have to be repaid within one year. The patisserie has just one current liability. This is trade creditors. £3,450 is owed to suppliers.

Net current assets This is current assets - current liabilities. Net current assets shows the working capital of the business. This is the amount of liquid resources a business has to fund daily trading. In this case working capital is £1,250 (£4,700 - £3,450).

Long term liabilities These are monies owed which are not due to be repaid for at least a year. The patisserie owes £4,000 to a bank. It is shown in brackets because it is a minus figure.

Net assets This is the total in the top part of the balance sheet. Net assets is total assets less total liabilities. It is calculated in the balance sheet by adding net current assets to fixed assets and subtracting long term liabilities. The net assets for Brigitte's business is £8,950 (£11,700 + £1,250 - £4,000).

The bottom half of the balance sheet shows the capital of the business. It deals with the interests of the owner and represents the right-hand side of the accounting equation.

Opening capital This is the amount of money owed to the owner by the business at the beginning of the trading year. It is the same as the closing capital balance at the end of the previous year. The opening capital for the patisserie is £7,500.

The opening capital is added to the net profit for the year. This comes from the profit and loss account. Brigitte's patisserie made £12,300 net profit during the year. The balance of opening capital and profit is £19,800.

Drawings Drawings are money taken by the owner for personal use. Drawings are subtracted from opening capital and net profit to get the closing capital balance. Drawings is the money taken out of the business by Brigitte during the year for personal use. The closing capital for the patisserie is £8,950 (£19,800 - £10,850). This will be the opening capital balance for next year's balance sheet.

Closing capital The closing capital balance of £8,950 is exactly the same as net assets. This shows that the balance sheet balances and that assets - liabilities = capital.

Limited company balance sheets

The balance sheet shown in Table 1 is for a sole trader. Limited company balance sheets have slightly different features. Table 2 shows the balance sheet for Prince Ltd, a manufacturer of leather garments and goods.

The structure of a limited company balance sheet is the same as that of a sole trader. The top section shows assets - liabilities and the bottom section shows capital. However, there are some differences.

Table 2 *Balance sheet for Prince Ltd*

Prince Ltd Balance sheet as at 31.12.04		
	£000	£000
Fixed assets		
Tangible assets	2,100	1,950
Current assets		
Stocks	122	109
Debtors	255	208
Cash at bank and in hand	90	120
	467	437
Creditors: amounts falling due within one year	210	188
Net current assets	257	249
Creditors: amounts falling due after one year	(290)	(312)
Net assets	2,067	1,887
Capital and reserves		
Called up share capital	1,000	1,000
Other reserves	340	421
Profit and loss account	727	466
Shareholders funds	2,067	1,887

- Fixed assets include a total for tangible assets of £2,100,000 in 2004. Tangible assets are physical assets such as plant and machinery, vehicles, tools and equipment.
- Many businesses also have intangible assets (non-physical). These are not usually shown on the balance sheet unless they have been bought. One example is goodwill. This is the difference between the value of net assets and what might be paid for firm if it was sold. The amount paid is likely to be higher because the business has an established customer base.
- Current assets are listed in the same way as in a sole trader balance sheet. However, current liabilities are called creditors: amounts falling due within one year. The two terms mean exactly the same. Net current assets are calculated in the same way as in a sole trader balance sheet.
- Long term liabilities are called creditors: amounts falling due after one year in a limited company balance sheet. The two terms mean exactly the same and the amount is subtracted from the fixed assets and net current assets.
- The bottom half of the balance sheet shows the capital and reserves of the business. In a limited company account this is the money owed to the shareholders. Called up share capital of £1,000,000 is the money put into the business by shareholders.
- Reserves are shareholders' funds that have built up over the life of the company. One of the main ones is retained profit. This is listed as profit and loss account in the Prince Ltd balance sheet.
- The total amount owed to shareholders is £2,067,000 in 2004. This is exactly the same as net assets.

How might the balance sheet be used?

- It provides a summary of all assets, liabilities and capital.
- It shows the value of working capital. This is important because it is the amount of liquid resources a firm has to pay its bills. It is often said that if current assets are between one and a half and two times the size of current liabilities, the business has enough working capital, although it depends on the business. Supermarkets, for example, run on very low levels of working capital because they are paid mainly in cash.
- It shows the asset structure of the business. This is how the business has used all of the money raised. Prince Ltd has invested about 80% of its money in tangible assets. This means that the business owns a lot of plant, machinery and equipment.
- It shows the capital structure of the business. This shows the different sources of funds used by business.
- The net assets in the balance sheet provides a rough guide to the value of the business. Prince Ltd is worth roughly £2,067,000. Also, if net assets increase over time, this suggests the company is growing.

Limitations of the balance sheet

- The balance sheet does not list all of the assets. Unless intangible assets have been purchased they do not normally appear on the balance sheet. This means that the value of the company could be understated.
- The values of some assets may be inaccurate. For example, fixed assets are valued at cost less depreciation. Depreciation, which allows for the falling in value of fixed assets, as they are 'used up', has to be estimated by accountants. Therefore if the estimations are inaccurate the fixed asset values will also be inaccurate.
- The balance sheet reflects the financial position of the business for one day only. The values of assets, liabilities and capital are likely to change the next day when trading continues.

- Obtain two company balance sheets from annual reports or from the Internet. Choose two companies in the same industry.
- Compare the financial positions of the two businesses. Look at working capital, net assets, the amount of debt the business has, the asset structure, the capital structure and the cash position.
- Suggest which company is in the best financial position.

Research task

Portfolio practice · Pass & Go

Pass & Go, a driving school, was set up 12 months ago by Nathan Sharpe. He used £12,000 of his own savings and borrowed £6,000 from a bank. Nathan bought a dual control car and a computer and operated from his home in Devon. At the end of the year he felt that things had not gone too well. Some of the costs were a lot higher than he anticipated. A balance sheet is shown in Table 3.

(a) (i) **How much did Nathan take out of the business for his own personal use during the year?**
(ii) **What will be the value of opening capital in next year's balance sheet?**
(b) (i) **Explain TWO reasons why the business made a loss during the year.**
(ii) **Explain TWO limitations of a balance sheet as a means of financial management.**
(c) **Discuss the evidence in the balance sheet which might suggest that Pass & Go performed poorly in the first year.**

Table 3 *Balance sheet for Pass & Go*

Pass & Go
Balance sheet as at 30.6.04

	£	£
Fixed assets		
Car		12,600
Computer		1,000
		13,600
Current assets		
Debtors	500	
Cash	100	
	600	
Current liabilities		
Trade creditors	2,100	
Bank overdraft	1,900	
	4,000	
Net current assets		(3,400)
Long term liabilities		
Bank loan		(6,000)
NET ASSETS		**4,200**
FINANCED BY:		
Capital		
Opening capital		12,000
Less net loss		2,800
		9,200
Less Drawings		5,000
Closing capital		**4,200**

Meeting the assessment criteria

In your investigation you need to consider how a business will monitor its performance. You might explain how the balance sheet can be used to do this.

Business example – J & C Herbs

J & C Herbs, set up three years ago, produces culinary and medicinal herbs in the south of Scotland. The business rents twelve acres of land and a building (used for storage, processing and packaging). It was set up with a bank loan and £15,000 of owner's capital. This was used to buy irrigation and protection equipment, harvesting and drying equipment, seeds, fertilisers and sprays and packaging materials. The 2004 balance sheet for the business is shown in Table 4.

Mark Band 1 *Provide basic knowledge and understanding of financial management. Perhaps use a balance sheet to describe briefly the financial position of the business.*
J & C Herbs looks to be in a good financial position. It has quite a lot of working capital. This is because its current assets are much larger than its current liabilities. The business is also very solvent. It has over £12,000 of cash. During the year the owner took out £26,250. Since the profit for the year was £27,300, not very much was retained by the business.

Mark Band 2 *Provide sound knowledge and understanding of financial management. Perhaps use a balance sheet to analyse the financial position of the business.*
The balance sheet can be used to help monitor the performance of the business. In this case the balance sheet for J & C Herbs shows the business to be financially stable. Current assets are three times the size of current liabilities. This means the business has a good amount of working capital. The cash flow of the business appears to be good. The business has £12,200 of cash. This represents more than two thirds of the total for current assets and could easily pay off the current liabilities of £5,300. The balance sheet also shows that the business made £27,300 profit last year. Most of this was withdrawn from the business by the owner. This means that not much profit was retained by the business. This may not matter because J & C Herbs has a lot of cash in the bank.

Mark Band 3 *Provide comprehensive knowledge and understanding of financial management. Perhaps use a balance sheet to evaluate the financial position of the business.*
The balance sheet can be used in the financial management of a business. It provides some important information. For example, it shows how much working capital the business has. J & C Herbs has more than adequate working capital. Its current assets are three times the size of current liabilities. The business also has a good cash position. There is £12,200 in the business's bank account. This represents about two thirds of the firm's current assets. This will reassure the owner and perhaps encourage some investment in the future. J & C Herbs has also grown slightly over the two years. The value of closing capital is slightly higher than the opening capital. The firm also made a profit of £27,300 in 2004. Most of this was withdrawn by the owner. Finally, although the balance sheet is useful it has some limitations. For example, it does not include intangible assets. This means the value of the business might be understated. It is also a static document. This means that it will be out of date when trading continues the next day.

Table 4 *Balance sheet for J & C Herbs*

J & C Herbs Balance sheet as at 31.10.04	£	£
Fixed assets		
Equipment		6,700
Tools		2,300
		9,000
Current assets		
Stocks	3,500	
Debtors	2,100	
Cash	12,200	
	17,800	
Current liabilities		
Trade creditors	5,300	
Working capital		12,500
Long term liabilities		
Bank loan		(5,000)
Net assets		**16,500**
Capital		
Opening capital	15,450	
Add Profit	27,300	
	42,750	
Less Drawings	26,250	
Closing capital		**16,500**

Source: based on industry information - SAC Farm Diversification web site.

22 Cash flow forecasting

The purpose of cash flow forecasting

An important part of the planning process when setting up a business is cash flow forecasting. This involves:

- estimating the cash coming into the business each month;
- estimating the cash going out of the business each month;
- calculating the expected monthly cash balance.

Businesses produce **cash flow forecasts** to help control their cash flow. It is important to monitor cash flow because without cash a business cannot trade. It needs cash to pay bills such as wages and raw materials.

Cash flow forecasts are useful for businesses in a number of ways.

Planning They are part of the planning process when setting up and running a business. When constructing a cash flow forecast business owners and managers are forced to think about the future. This is because they have to estimate future costs and revenues. The forecast will show how much cash the business is likely to have at the end of each period, such as a month, in the future. This will help to show whether a business has enough cash to survive and meet other spending needs.

Loan applications When a business is setting up it may have to borrow money. Bank managers, for example, will need evidence to show that the business can repay a loan or overdraft. A cash flow forecast could be used to provide some of this evidence. The forecast will help show whether a business can afford the repayments in the future. It also shows that owners or managers have taken business planning seriously.

Monitoring cash flow During the year and at the end businesses can compare the cash balances in the forecast with those on their bank statement. The figures on the bank statement show the actual flows of cash and monthly balances. By doing this they can find out where problems have occurred. For example, why in a particular month was too much money spent? Constant monitoring in this way should improve cash control.

Constructing a cash flow forecast

A cash flow forecast is a financial document and is usually produced using a spreadsheet. It shows how cash is expected to flow into and out of a business during a future time period. The forecast shown in Table 1 is for Jenkins Ltd, a supplier of cakes and pies to shops in Cornwall. When constructing a cash flow forecast the figures are placed in columns which represent a particular period, in this case a month.

Receipts Receipts are the expected inflows of cash. In this case most of the cash is from sales of pies and cakes. However, in June, £1,500 is expected to be received from another source, a tax refund perhaps.

Payments Payments are the expected costs that the business will have to meet. These figures represent cash outflows. For

Table 1 *Cash flow forecast for Jenkins Ltd (£)*

	May	June	July
Receipts			
Sales	10,500	11,000	10,000
Other receipts	0	1,500	
Total receipts	10,500	12,500	10,000
Payments			
Wages	2,000	2,000	2,000
Raw materials	800	900	1,000
Rent	1,200	1,200	1,200
Other expenses	3,400	3,800	7,600
Total payments	7,400	7,900	11,800
Net cash flow	3,100	4,600	(1,800)
Opening balance	2,100	5,200	9,800
Closing balance	5,200	9,800	8,000

Brackets show negative amounts.

example, in May Jenkins Ltd expects to pay £2,000 in wages, £800 for raw materials, £1,200 in rent and £3,400 in other expenses. The expected total payments or cash outflows in May is £7,400.

Net cash flow Net cash flow is the difference between receipts and payments. If receipts are greater than payments net cash flow will be positive. If they are lower, net cash flow will be negative. The net cash flow for Jenkins Ltd is expected to be positive in May and June. For example, it is £4,600 (£12,500 - £7,900) in June. In July, however, it is negative at minus £1,800 (£10,000 - £11,800).

Opening balances The opening balance is how much cash the business is expected to have at the beginning of each month. For example, in July Jenkins Ltd expects to have £9,800.

Closing balances The closing balance shows how much cash is expected to be left after a month's trading. The closing balance is calculated by adding the net cash flow to the opening balance. For example, in May for Jenkins Ltd the opening balance is £2,100. The net cash flow is expected to be £3,100. Therefore, the closing balance is £5,200 (£3,100 + £2,100). In July the net cash flow is expected to be minus £1,800. This means that the closing balance will be lower at £8,000 (£9,800 - £1,800). The closing balance in each period becomes the opening balance in the next period.

Interpreting cash flow forecasts

Owners or managers have to interpret information shown in cash flow forecasts. A cash flow forecast is shown in Table 2 for Gurrinder Singh's photography studio which she plans to set up in April. What does it show?

- After a slow start sales are expected to rise steadily. They are expected to be relatively high near to Christmas.
- Gurrinder starts the business with £4,000 of her own money.
- Rent and advertising costs are expected to be stable each month.

Table 2 *Cash flow forecast for Gurrinder Singh's business (£)*

	Apr	May	Jun	Jul	Aug	Sep	Oct	Nov	Dec
Receipts									
Sales	500	1,000	1,500	2,000	2,500	3,000	3,000	4,500	6,000
Own capital	4,000								
Total receipts	4,500	1,000	1,500	2,000	2,500	3,000	3,000	4,500	6,000
Payments									
Rent	1,200	1,200	1,200	1,200	1,200	1,200	1,200	1,200	1,200
Equipment	3,500				2,000				
Advertising	500	500	500	500	500	500	500	500	500
Other expenses	300	300	600	300	300	1,000	300	300	1,000
Total payments	5,500	2,000	2,300	2,000	4,000	2,700	2,000	2,000	2,700
Net cash flow	(1,000)	(1,000)	(800)	0	(1,500)	300	1,000	2,500	3,300
Opening balance	0	(1,000)	(2,000)	(2,800)	(2,800)	(4,300)	(4,000)	(3,000)	(500)
Closing balance	(1,000)	(2,000)	(2,800)	(2,800)	(4,300)	(4,000)	(3,000)	(500)	2,800

Brackets show negative amounts.

- Large amounts are expected to be spent in April and August on equipment.
- Other expenses are expected to be higher than normal in June, September and December.
- Net cash flow is not expected to become positive until September. This is common for a new business.
- The closing balance starts as negative and get worse until August. The cash position improves at the end of the year and becomes positive in December. The business is going to be short of cash between April and November. This might be because insufficient funds were provided in the first place. Since the forecast shows that Gurrinder's business is going to be short of cash, she would have to take some action, as explained below.

Suggesting appropriate action

After analysing a cash flow statement it may be necessary for a business to take some action. If the forecast shows that a business has liquidity problems (i.e. is running out of cash, shown by negative closing and opening balances) the following action might be appropriate.

- Borrow some money.
- Postpone all unnecessary spending.
- Sell stock cheaply for cash.
- Collect debts more aggressively.
- Extend credit with suppliers.
- Sell some unwanted assets.
- Sell assets and lease them back.
- Reduce drawings.

In the case of Gurrinder's business, some action will have been necessary because the closing balance was expected to be negative for eight of the nine months, probably because she did not have enough start-up capital. Start-up capital would have helped to pay for the equipment and keep the business afloat while it became established. By December the business expected to have a positive closing balance. If the business finds that its closing balance is getting bigger and bigger, cash could be taken out by the owners or used for investment.

Benefits of cash flow forecasts

Cash flow forecasts have certain benefits for a business.

- They can show whether a business will have enough cash in the future. They also warn owners about possible cash shortages in the future.
- They force owners and managers to plan ahead. This should help to run the business more effectively.
- They can be used to provide evidence about the financial performance of the business when making applications for loans.
- When produced on a spreadsheet it is possible to show the effect of changes in payments and receipts on the closing balance instantly.

Limitations of cash flow statements

Cash flow forecasts also have some limitations.

- Much of the financial information in the forecast is estimated. If the estimates are inaccurate the closing balances will also be

Use the Internet or financial sections of newspapers to find a business that is experiencing cash flow problems.
Explain:
- why the business has cash flow problems;
- what measures have been taken to resolve the cash flow problems;
- whether you think the business will survive in the future.

Research task

inaccurate. This could result in owners drawing wrong conclusions and taking inappropriate action.
- Some owners might manipulate forecasts. They might overestimate cash inflows to make the expected cash position look better than it really is.

- External forces such as competition or economic factors could affect the actual cash flows. This will make the forecast less useful. One way to allow for unforeseen events is to build contingency funds into the forecast by making a monthly allowance for unforeseen spending.

Meeting the assessment criteria

In your investigation you need to consider how a business will monitor its performance. You can explain how cash flow forecasting can play a role in this task.

Business example - Alan Frank Sandwiches

Alan Frank sells sandwiches and other cold snacks from a kiosk he rents in Brighton town centre. He prepares a cash flow forecast every six months to help plan the running of the business and to monitor its performance. For example, he uses it to see whether he will have enough cash in the future. At the end of the six months he compares the estimated closing cash balances with the business bank statements to see how accurate his forecast was.

Mark Band 1 *Provide basic knowledge and understanding of financial management. Use cash flow forecasts to describe briefly the performance of the business.*
Alan understands the importance of firm financial management when running his business. He produces regular cash flow forecasts to aid planning and help monitor the performance. For example, he uses it to see whether he will have enough cash in the future. The forecast in Table 3 shows that sales are expected to rise as summer approaches. This is probably because the town is busier in the summer months. The cash position of the business is expected to be healthy and improve throughout the year. The closing cash balance is expected to rise every month. Over the period the closing cash balance is expected to rise from £1,100 to £4,800. At the end of the six months Alan will compare the estimated closing cash balances with the business bank statements. This will show him how accurate his cash forecasts were.

Mark Band 2 *Provide sound knowledge and understanding of financial management. Use cash flow forecasts to analyse the performance of the business.*
It is important for business owners to monitor the performance of their businesses. One way in which Alan Frank manages his finances is to construct cash flow forecasts. Businesses produce cash flow forecasts to help control their cash flow. It is important to predict cash flow because without cash a business cannot trade. It needs cash to pay bills such as wages

and raw materials. Alan's forecast in Table 3 shows clearly that the cash position of the business is expected to improve throughout the period. The closing cash balance is expected to rise from £1,100 in April to £4,800 in September. One reason for this is because sales are expected to increase during the summer months. The largest net cash flow is in April. This is because some new capital is expected to be introduced to boost the cash position. Without this fresh capital the closing balance would be just £100 in April. Raw materials costs are expected to rise throughout the year, but this is to be expected because sales also rise. Generally the business is expected to perform well over the future time period shown. Alan could take some cash out of the business later in the year when the balance is expected to rise above £3,000. However, this could depend on how much sales fall in the winter months.

Mark Band 3 *Provide sound knowledge and understanding of financial management. Use cash flow forecasts to evaluate the performance of the business. An intergrated approach might also be used by using break-even analysis for example.*
One way in which Alan Frank monitors the performance of his business is to construct cash flow forecasts. It is important to forecast the cash position carefully because without cash a business is not able to trade. Some cash is always needed to pay immediate bills. The forecast shows Alan what his expected closing cash balances will be for a six month period. He will also take the trouble to compare these closing balances with the balances on the bank statements each month. This will show how accurate his forecasts are.
The forecast in Table 3 shows that the business is expected to do well. The closing balances of the business are all

Table 3 *Cash flow forecast for Alan Frank's business (£)*

	Apr	May	Jun	Jul	Aug	Sep
Receipts						
Sales	2,000	2,500	3,000	2,900	3,000	2,100
Fresh capital	1,000					
Total receipts	3,000	2,500	3,000	2,900	3,000	2,100
Payments						
Rent	400	400	400	400	600	600
Raw materials	400	500	600	600	700	600
Other expenses	400	500	500	500	500	400
Drawings	400	400	400	400	400	400
Total payments	1,600	1,800	1,900	1,900	2,200	2,000
Net cash flow	1,400	700	1,100	1,000	800	100
Opening balance	(300)	1,100	1,800	2,900	3,900	4,700
Closing balance	1,100	1,800	2,900	3,900	4,700	4,800

expected to be positive and increase throughout the six month period. This is because sales are expected to rise and overheads are forecast to be be kept under control. The amount spent on raw materials is estimated to rise but this is to be expected if sales grew. By the end of the period the closing cash balance is predicted to rise from £1,100 to £4,800. Alan might decide to withdraw some of the cash for himself or invest it to improve the business.

Although cash flow forecasts are useful other methods of financial management might be helpful. For example, Alan might use break-even analysis to see if his business breaks even during the six months. To do this he would have to calculate costs and revenue for the period. If total costs are exactly equal to total revenue the business will break even. Finally, Alan would need to understand that cash flow forecasting has certain limitations. For example, much of the financial information in the forecast is estimated. If the estimates are inaccurate, the closing balances will also be inaccurate. This could result in Alan drawing incorrect conclusions and taking inappropriate action for the future period.

Portfolio practice · Shelly's Flower Shop

Shelly Simms plans to open a small flower shop in her home town of Worcester in March. She has found some premises which she can rent for just £400 a month. Shelly will put £1,000 of her own money into the business and borrow a further £1,000 from a bank in March. £900 of this money will be spent buying equipment and getting the shop ready for trading. Shelly expects running costs to be £100 a month except in August when she will have to pay an extra £1,000 for business rates. She plans not to take any money out of the business for personal use for three months. However, from June onwards she will pay herself £400 a month. She has estimated sales and stock purchases for a six month period. These are shown in Table 4.

(a) Using examples from the case study distinguish between start-up costs and running costs.
(b) Construct a six month cash flow forecast for Shelly's flower shop.
(c) Analyse the closing cash balances.
(d) Evaluate the options available to Shelly to deal with the cash position at the end of August.

Table 4 *Cash flow forecast, March-August, (£)*

	Mar	Apr	May	Jun	Jul	Aug
Sales	500	1,000	1,200	1,400	1,700	1,700
Stock (flowers & plants)	700	500	600	700	700	800

Budgets

A budget is a financial plan. It is often presented in a table or spreadsheet and shows how much money a business plans to spend or receive in a future time period. Budgets are usually produced for six or twelve monthly periods. Table 1 shows a cost budget for Intercafe, an Internet café. Each column represents monthly expenditure plans. For example, in January Intercafe plans to spend a total of £4,700. Some examples of planned spending in January include £1,000 for rent, £800 on wages, £500 on computer leasing and £500 on advertising. Over the six month period shown, Intercafe plans to spend between £4,450 and £5,090 per month. The pattern of planned spending is fairly steady. There are no sharp fluctuations.

Table 1 *Cost budget for Intercafe (£)*

	JAN	FEB	MAR	APR	MAY	JUN	Total
Rent	1,000	1,000	1,000	1,000	1,000	1,000	6,000
Wages	800	800	900	1,000	1,000	1,000	5,500
Computer leasing	500	500	500	500	500	500	3,000
Food purchases	700	800	900	900	1,000	1,100	5,400
Heating & lighting	900	900	800	700	400	400	4,100
Advertising	500	0	500	0	200	0	1,200
Other costs	300	450	490	500	600	600	2,940
Total	4,700	4,450	5,090	4,600	4,700	4,600	28,140

Types of budget

Businesses make use of different types of budgets.

Sales budgets The most important budget is probably the sales budget. This is because it affects all other budgets produced by a business. For example, if a business plans to increase sales during the year it will also have to produce more. This means that the production cost budget, the cash budget and the materials budget will all be affected. Sales budgets can show either the sales revenue planned by a business or the number of units it plans to sell. Table 2 shows the sales revenue budget for Aarzoo Kumar's business. Aarzoo supplies Indian foods to restaurants and other caterers in the West Midlands. The budget shows that sales revenue is planned

Table 2 *Sales revenue budget for Aarzoo Kumar's business (£)*

	APR	MAY	JUN	JUL	AUG	SEP	Total
Meat samosas	1,200	1,200	2,400	1,500	1,600	1,700	9,600
Veg. samosas	700	700	1,600	900	900	900	5,700
Shami kebabs	2,000	2,400	3,900	2,500	2,800	2,800	16,400
Sheek kebabs	1,000	900	2,100	900	1,000	1,100	7,000
Total	4,900	5,200	10,000	5,800	6,300	6,500	38,700

to increase over the time period. It also shows that sales are expected to be significantly higher in June than all other months. This is because Aarzoo has some contracts to supply food for a number of weddings in June.

Production budgets Production budgets are used to plan production levels. They are influenced by sales budgets and stock levels. Production budgets can show the number of units a business plans to produce or the costs of planned production. Table 3 shows the production budget for Aarzoo Kumar's business. Aarzoo does not keep any stocks since her products are perishable. The production budget shows how many units of each product must be made to generate the revenue plans shown in the sales budget. For example, in April, 6,000 meat samosas (which sell for 20p each) must be produced to generate the £1,200 sales revenue planned. Vegetable samosas sell for 10p, shami kebabs for 50p and sheek kebabs for 50p.

Table 3 *Production budget for Aarzoo Kumar's business*

	APR	MAY	JUN	JUL	AUG	SEP	Total
Meat samosas	6,000	6,000	12,000	7,500	8,000	8,500	48,000
Veg. samosas	7,000	7,000	16,000	9,000	9,000	9,000	57,000
Shami kebabs	4,000	4,800	7,900	5,000	5,600	5,600	32,900
Sheek kebabs	2,000	1,800	4,200	1,800	2,000	2,000	13,800

Purchases budgets These show the planned purchases of materials and other resources that a business needs. The purchases budget will have an important impact on cost budgets.

Labour budgets These can show the amount of money a business plans to spend on labour in a future period. Alternatively they could show the different types of labour a business plans to use, the number of workers needed or the number of labour hours planned.

Capital expenditure budgets These show the amount of money a business plans to spend on tools, machinery, plant and equipment.

Cash budgets These show how much cash a business plans to spend and receive. They are similar to cash flow forecasts explained in section 22.

Profit and loss budgets These show the amount of profit or loss a business plans to make. It will list all the costs and expenses that a business plans and the revenues it expects to generate.

Marketing budgets These show the amount a business plans to spend on promoting its products. It can include expenditure on advertising or other forms of promotion such as public relations.

Purpose of budgets

Budgets are used to help the financial control of businesses. For example, budgets can help a business avoid overspending. Managers use budgets for a number of reasons.

Controlling Budgets can be used by managers to control the level of spending in a business. Since budgets are plans they provide financial targets which staff are expected to meet. If the targets are met then spending will have been contained.

Reducing fraud Budgets can help to reduce fraud in a business. All spending has to be authorised by budget holders. This means that money cannot be spent unless the budget holder has granted permission. This stops staff from spending money on things for their own personal use.

Planning Budgets force a business to plan ahead. This means that managers are more likely to foresee problems before they occur. For example, they may avoid running out of cash by spreading expenditure on new machinery. If budgets were not used managers could be tempted to run businesses on a day-to-day basis. This could result in future problems being overlooked until too late.

Motivation Budgets can be used to motivate staff. If they meet the targets set by budgets they could be rewarded. For example, sales staff might be given bonuses for reaching sales revenue targets.

Budgetary control

Budgetary control is an ongoing process that involves making plans by setting financial targets, measuring the firm's performance and taking corrective action if targets are not met. The different stages in budgetary control are shown in Figure 1.

- Preparing budgets. The first step is to prepare the budgets. This involves the setting of financial targets. They are represented by the spending or revenue plans in the firm's budgets. Budgets themselves are influenced by the firm's business aims and objectives.
- Calculating variances. At the end of the budget period the performance is measured by calculating variances. A variance is the difference between a budgeted value and an actual value. Variances can be adverse or favourable. **Favourable variances** occur when the actual figures are 'better' than the budgeted figures. **Adverse variances** occur when budgeted figures are 'worse' than the actual figures. Table 4 shows some examples. For example, if total costs were planned to be £200,000 and actual costs were only £187,000, there would be a favourable variance of £13,000 (£200,000 - £187,000) because costs were lower than planned. If budgeted total revenue was £350,000 and actual revenue was only £310,000, there would be an adverse variance of £40,000 (£350,000 - £310,000) because revenue was lower then planned.
- Analysing variances. Variance analysis involves looking at the variances and trying to determine why they have occurred. For example, an adverse labour cost variance may have occurred because staff were working too slowly.
- Taking action. Once the reasons for particular variances have been established, managers must take action. This will help to improve future financial performance. In the above example, workers might need some extra incentive to ensure that they work more quickly. Even if variances are favourable, managers can take action. They can act positively if they discover reasons why actual figures are better than the budgeted figures.

Table 4 *Favourable and adverse variances*

Budgeted costs	Actual costs	Difference	Favourable or adverse
£200,000	£187,000	-£13,000	Favourable (as lower)
£200,000	£210,000	+£10,000	Adverse (as higher)
Budgeted revenue	Actual revenue	Difference	Favourable or adverse
£300,000	£330,000	+£30,000	Favourable (as higher)
£300,000	£280,000	-£20,000	Adverse (as lower)

Types of variance

Sales variance A sales variance is the difference between the budgeted sales revenue and the actual sales revenue. Sales variances will occur if either the volume of actual sales is different from the budgeted volume or if the budgeted price is different from the actual price. Sales variances might arise if:

- discounts are offered to customers;
- new competitors enter the market and drive the price down;
- there are shortages in the market and higher prices can be charged;
- there is a fall in demand due to a recession;
- there are changes in the quality of the product;
- changes in marketing activities affect demand.

Figure 1 *Stages in budgetary control*

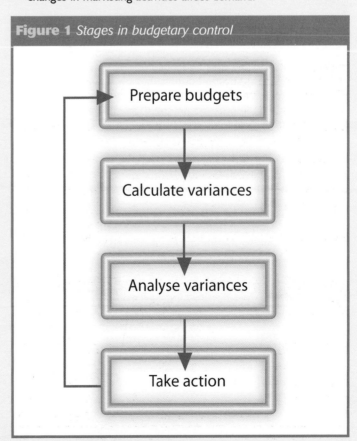

Prepare budgets

Calculate variances

Analyse variances

Take action

Materials variance A materials variance is the difference between the budgeted materials cost and the actual materials cost. Materials variances will occur if either the volume of actual materials is different from the budgeted volume or if the budgeted cost is different from the actual cost. Materials variances may arise if:

- materials are wasted in production;
- materials are bought from new suppliers at different prices;
- inflation causes the cost of materials to rise from suppliers;
- better quality or inferior materials are bought.

Labour variance A labour variance is the difference between the budgeted labour cost and the actual labour cost. Labour variances will occur if either the amount of actual labour is different from the budgeted amount or if the budgeted cost of labour is different from the actual cost. Labour variances may arise if:

- the productivity of labour changes;
- working practices change;
- workers are given better training or improved tools and machinery;
- wage rates change;
- the type of worker employed is changed.

Fixed overhead variance This is the difference between the budgeted fixed overhead and the actual fixed overhead. Fixed overhead variances might arise if:

- there are changes in overhead costs, such as rent, rates or insurance;
- efficiency is improved so that less factory space is needed for example.

Every year the government gives details of 'The Budget'. The Budget shows how much money the government plan to spend in the next financial year and where it is going to come from. Find out the following using either a publication such as the *Financial Times* from the library or placing 'The Budget' into a search engine on the Internet.

- How much does the government plan to spend in total?
- What are the main areas of government spending?
- Which is the highest item of government expenditure?
- How much is going to be spent on education?
- What are the different sources of government revenue?
- Which is the largest source of revenue?

Research task

Portfolio practice · Get Floored

Kerry Lau is a franchisee. She runs the Swallowfield branch of Get Floored which sells parquet blocks (herring bone and other patterns), plank and strip boards, skirting boards, architraves, stairs, boarders and matwells. The business also renovates and maintains existing wooden beams and staircases. She uses budgetary control to monitor the performance of the business. Table 5 shows budgeted overheads and actual overheads for the most recent six month trading period. During the year Kerry was ill for 6 weeks and was not able to work. Her assistant kept the shop open but was not able to carry out restoration work.

(a) **Using this case as an example, explain what is meant by budgetary control.**
(b) **Complete Table 5 by calculating the overheads variances.**
(c) **Explain the difference between a favourable and an adverse variance using examples from the case.**
(d) **Analyse the variances calculated in (b).**

Table 5 *Actual and budgeted overheads for a six month trading period for Get Floored*

	Budgeted	Actual	Variances
Rent	£9,000	£9,000	
Wages	£21,000	£27,000	
Heat & Light	£2,100	£2,300	
Insurance	£1,000	£1,000	
Motor expenses	£4,300	£3,800	
Other O'heads	£3,400	£3,600	
Total	£40,800	£46,700	

Meeting the assessment criteria

In your investigation you need to consider how a business will monitor its performance. You might explain how budgetary control can play a role in this task.

Business example - Liam's Gifts

Liam Johnson runs a small gift shop in Blackpool. After making a loss in the first year, his bank manager advised him to pay more attention to financial control. In 2004 he decided to set targets and use budgets. Table 6 shows the sales budget for Liam's business for the last six months of 2004. At the end of the year he calculated the monthly sales variances. These are also shown in Table 6.

Table 6 *Sales budget, actual sales figures and sales variances for Llam's gift shop, 2004 (£)*

	JUL	AUG	SEP	OCT	NOV	DEC	Total
Budgeted sales	13,000	15,000	14,000	10,000	8,000	5,000	65,000
Actual sales	15,000	18,500	14,000	9,500	7,000	4,000	68,000
Sales variance	2,000(F)	3,500(F)	0	500(A)	1,000(A)	1,000(A)	3,000(F)

Favourable variance (F)
Adverse variance (A)

Mark Band 1 *Provide basic knowledge and understanding of financial management. Perhaps use budgetary control to describe briefly the financial position of the business.*

After making a loss in the first year Liam followed the advice of his bank manager and paid more attention to financial control and monitoring. He decided to use budgetary control. This involves setting budgets, calculating variances by comparing budgeted figures with actual figures, analysing the variances and then taking corrective action. Liam decided to focus on sales revenue. In the last six months of 2004 actual sales were greater than budgeted sales. There was a favourable sales variance of £3,000 (£68,000 - £65,000). This means that sales for the budget period exceeded the target set by Liam. However, some months were better than others. Liam noticed that sales were better than planned in July and August but worse in October, November and December.

Mark Band 2 *Provide sound knowledge and understanding of financial management. Perhaps use budgetary control to analyse the financial position of the business.*

Liam wanted to improve the financial performance of his business and decided to follow the advice of his bank manager. Liam thought that if he set sales targets and monitored the monthly sales progress he would know what was going on and be able to respond to the information that he gathered. By setting targets for sales in budgets and analysing sales variances he might be able to improve sales levels in the future. In the last six months of 2004 there was a favourable sales variance of £3,000. However, some months were better than others. Liam thought that sales in July and August were higher than expected because the weather was generally good in those two months and there were more tourists in Blackpool. However, as winter approached sales figures did not meet

targets. For example, in December there was an adverse sales variance of £1,000. Liam thought that one of the reasons for this was that the shop was only open at weekends in December.

Mark Band 3 *Provide comprehensive knowledge and understanding of financial management. Perhaps use budgetary control to evaluate the financial position of the business.*

Budgetary control can be used by businesses to improve financial performance. It encourages business owners to set targets and monitor performance indicators such as sales and costs. Liam adopted this approach and produced a six month sales budget for his small gift shop. At the end of the budget period he calculated monthly variances and attempted to analyse them. The sales variance for the whole budget period was favourable. Actual sales exceeded budgeted sales by £3,000. However, the pattern of monthly sales variances threw up some interesting observations. The sales variances in July and August were both favourable. Liam thought that this was due to extra tourists in Blackpool attracted by the good weather. He also felt that sales could be higher if he extended opening hours in the summer, until 9.00pm instead of 6.00pm. However, in October, November and December sales variances were adverse. This was due to a lack of tourist customers in these months. It may also have partly been because he lost a bit of interest in the business and often shut the shop. For example, in December he only opened at weekends. Next year Liam decided to open all week. He also decided to raise prices a little. Liam felt that tourists would not really notice a 5% increase in the prices of gifts. This would help to raise sales revenue and in next year's sales budget he planned to raise total monthly sales revenue by around 10%.

Breaking even

Business owners often want to know how much they have to sell to break-even. The formula used to calculate break-even is shown in Figure 1.

Figure 1 *Calculating break-even*

A business will break-even where

total revenue = total costs

The **break-even point** of a business is where total revenue from sales is exactly the same as the total costs of producing a good or providing a service. The level of output where total costs and total revenue are the same is called the **break-even output**.

A business will need information about its costs and price to calculate the break-even output. For example, say that a business has total costs of £15,000 and charges £30 for its product. It will break-even at an output of 500 goods because £30 x 500 = £15,000. At this level of output the business neither makes a loss nor a profit. It simply breaks even.

The break-even point can be used to help monitor the performance of the business. For example, when setting up a new business an owner might aim to break-even in the first year of trading. If, by the end of the year, the business makes a small profit then the target has been exceeded. The break-even point is often crucial for owners. This is because they know that after the break-even point is reached, the sale of further units generates a profit. It can be an important 'milestone' for business owners.

Calculating break-even using contribution

One method used to calculate the break-even point is to use **contribution**. Contribution is the amount of money left over after variable cost is subtracted from the selling price of each unit of output.

Consider the example of Jack Bevan who plans to publish a lifestyle magazine called 'Highlife'. The magazine's fixed costs (FC) are £20,000 per month and its variable costs (VC) are £1 per copy. Jack plans to sell the magazine for £3.00. The contribution made by Highlife is calculated in Figure 2.

Figure 2 *Calculating contribution*

Contribution = selling price – variable cost

Contribution = £3 - £1 = £2

To calculate the number of copies needed to break-even a formula can be used. This is shown in Figure 3, which also calculates the number of copies Jack needs to produce and sell of the magazine to break-even.

Figure 3 *Calculating break-even using contribution*

$$\text{Break-even point} = \frac{\text{Fixed costs}}{\text{Contribution}}$$

$$= \frac{£20,000}{£2}$$

$$= 10,000 \text{ copies}$$

Jack Bevan's new magazine, Highlife, will break-even if 10,000 copies are sold. Total revenue will be £30,000 (£3 x 10,000) and total costs will also be £30,000 (£20,000 + [£1 x 10,000]).

Calculating the break-even point using costs and revenues

Another way of calculating the break-even point is to use total costs and total revenues. Jack Bevan's magazine will break-even if total cost is equal to total revenue. For Highlife fixed costs are £20,000 a month. Fixed costs are costs which do not vary with output. They might include the cost of a piece of machinery or buying a factory, for example. Variable costs increase as output increases, such as the costs of raw materials used in production.

Figure 4 *Calculating break-even using total costs and total revenues*

$$\text{Total cost} = \text{fixed cost} + \text{variable cost} \times \text{quantity sold}$$
$$TC = £20,000 + £1Q$$
$$\text{Total revenue} = \text{price} \times \text{quantity sold}$$
$$TR = £3Q$$

Break even is where:
$$TC = TR$$
$$£20,000 + £1Q = £3Q$$

To find Q:
$$20,000 = 3Q - 1Q$$
$$20,000 = 2Q$$
$$\frac{20,000}{2} = Q$$
$$10,000 = Q$$

Figure 5 *Break-even chart for Highlife*

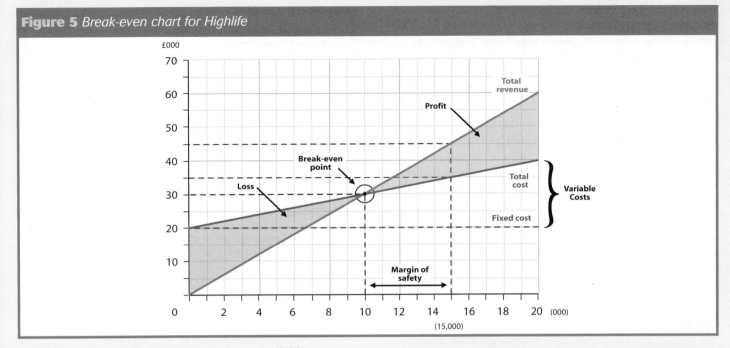

Variable costs are £1 per copy. The selling price is £3.00.

Figure 4 shows how the break-even output can be calculated. Note that this is the same output which was found using the contribution method of calculation.

Break-even charts

The break-even output for a business can be shown on a graph called a break-even chart. The break-even chart for Highlife is shown in Figure 5. The chart shows the total costs (TC), total revenue (TR) and fixed costs (FC) functions for the magazine. Output is measured on the horizontal axis and costs and revenue are shown on the vertical axis. What does the break-even chart show?

- The total revenue function shows the total revenue generated by different sales levels. For example, if 15,000 copies were sold, total revenue would be £45,000.
- The fixed cost function shows the level of fixed costs over a range of different production levels. Fixed costs do not change as output changes. In this case fixed costs are £20,000 at all production levels. It is not necessary to include the fixed cost function to show the break-even point.
- The total cost function shows the total cost of producing Highlife over a range of different production levels. For example, the total cost of producing 15,000 copies is £35,000. This is made up of fixed costs of £20,000 plus variable costs of £1 per magazine x 15,000 = £15,000.
- The **break-even point** is where total revenue equals total costs. In this case the **break-even level of output** is 10,000 copies of Highlife. Here both total revenue and total costs are £30,000.
- At levels of production above the break-even point **profits** are made. So, for example, if 15,000 magazines are produced and sold the business makes a profit of £10,000 (revenue of £45,000 - total costs of £35,000). The profit increases as more magazines are produced and sold.

- At levels of production below the break-even point **losses** are made. This is because total costs are greater than total revenues.
- The **margin of safety** shows the amount by which production can fall before the business breaks-even. So if 15,000 magazines are produced and sold the margin of safety is 5,000 (output of 15,000 - the break-even output of 10,000).

Constructing a break-even chart

The break-even chart for Highlife was constructed using the following steps

Calculate the break-even level of output This is shown above and is 10,000 copies.

Calculate points on the total revenue and total cost functions Both functions are straight lines so they can be drawn by joining two points that lie on each function. To plot the TR function we need to choose two levels of output and calculate the TR at each level. Any two levels of output could be chosen. However, construction will be simpler if 0 is chosen as one. It is also helpful to choose a second value which is twice the size of the break-even level of output. This would be 20,000 (2 x 10,000) in this case. Such a choice will ensure that the break-even point is in the centre of the chart. This will improve presentation. The value of TR at each output level is shown in Table 1.

Table 1 *Values of TR and TC at two levels of output for Highlife*

Q	Total revenue (TR)	Total cost (TC)
0	0 (0 x £3)	£20,000
20,000	£60,000 (20,000 x £3)	£40,000 (£20,000 + £1 x 20,000)

Plotting the TR function The TR function can now be plotted on a graph. The output axis should run from 0 to 20,000 copies and the vertical axis from 0 to £60,000. Using the information in Table 1, the two points, or coordinates, on the TR function are (0,0) and (20,000, £60,000). If these are plotted on the graph and joined up the TR function will appear as shown in Figure 5.

Plotting the TC function To plot the TC function we need to identify the total cost at two different levels of output. It is helpful to use the same values as those used for the TR function, i.e. 0 and 20,000. The total costs at each of these levels of output are shown in Table 1. The TC function can now be plotted on the graph. The two points which lie on the TC function are (0, £20,000) and (20,000, £40,000). If these are joined the TC function will appear as shown in Figure 5. Note that the TC function does not start at the origin like the TR function. This is because when output is zero fixed costs of £20,000 are still incurred.

The effect on break-even of changes in costs and price

The break-even chart can be used to show the effect on the break-even point of changes in fixed cost, variable cost and price.

Changes in fixed costs If fixed costs increase, a business will have to produce more to break-even. This is shown in Figure 6. When fixed costs rise both the fixed cost function and the total cost function shifts up. This means that the business will have to increase output from 20,000 to 30,000 to break-even. On the

other hand, if fixed costs were to fall the business will break-even at a lower level of output

Changes in variable costs If variable costs increase, the total cost function will be steeper because total costs will rise at every level of output. This means that the business will have to produce more to break-even. On the other hand, if variable costs fall the business will break-even at a lower level of output.

Changes in price If price increases the total revenue function will be steeper because revenue will be higher at every level of output. This means the business will break-even at a lower level of output. However, if the price is decreased the total revenue function becomes flatter and more will have to be produced to break-even.

Limitations of break-even analysis

Break-even analysis is sometimes thought to be a little simplistic. Some of its assumptions are also unrealistic.
- Break-even analysis assumes that all output is sold by the business. However, many firms are not able to sell everything they produce. Also, some firms deliberately hold stocks of finished goods to help cope with fluctuations in demand.
- The break-even chart is drawn for a given set of business conditions. It cannot deal with sudden changes in business variables, such as a sudden increase in rent and prices or changes in technology.
- The model relies heavily on the accuracy of cost and price data. If this financial information is inaccurate or out of date, the conclusions drawn on the basis of the data are flawed. For example, if the actual price charged is lower than that shown on the break-even chart, the business will not break-even at the level of output shown on the chart. It will be at a higher level.
- The break-even charts used here have linear (straight line) functions. In reality the shape of the total cost and total revenue functions are not likely to be linear.

Break-even analysis is not very helpful when businesses produce a wide range of different products. It is likely that each product will have different prices and different costs. One particular problem is dividing the fixed costs of the business between all the different products. There are methods, but each has its faults. Therefore, if the fixed cost incurred by each product is unknown or uncertain, break-even analysis is less useful.

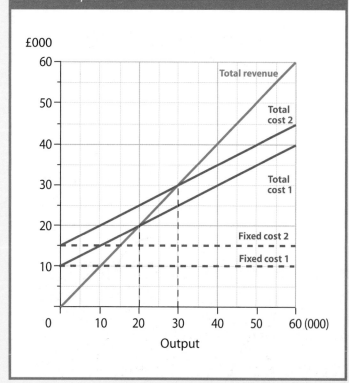

Figure 6 *The effect of an increase in fixed cost on the break-even point*

Meeting the assessment criteria

In your investigation you need to consider how a business will monitor its performance. You might explain how break-even analysis can play a role in this task. You will also need to understand the limitations of break-even analysis.

Business example - Webstart.com

Webstart.com, owned by Iqbal Khan, provides affordable website design without any need for technical know-how. You just point and click, and drag and drop, and the changes you make to your website are immediately live. Iqbal charges £15 for his online business service. Before starting, he did some research and checked out all the comparable products on the Internet. He found that most of them were American, too technical and too expensive. He paid £1,800 for a new laptop computer, so that he could be in touch with the business where-ever he was and spent a further £2,200 setting up the business. The variable costs were difficult to estimate, but he estimated that they were about £5 per customer. In the first year of trading Iqbal Khan hoped that he would get enough customers to break-even.

Source: adapted from company information.

Mark Band 1 *Provide basic knowledge and understanding of financial management. Perhaps use break-even analysis to describe briefly the financial position of the business.*
Iqbal Khan hoped to break-even in his first year of business. He wanted to recover the cost of his computer and other start-up costs. He had no experience of running a business and decided to carry on with his full-time job at a bank for the foreseeable future. His job would provide income to live off in the first year. If the business broke even he would not lose any money, but he would not make any profit either. Iqbal calculated that once his fixed costs had been covered, in the future, the contribution to profit would be £10 per customer.

Mark Band 2 *Provide sound knowledge and understanding of financial management. Perhaps analyse the financial position of the business using break-even.*
Iqbal Khan aimed to break-even in his first year of trading. He decided to use the information on costs and price to work out how many customers he would need to attract to break-even. He calculated the contribution each customer would make. It is:

$$\text{Contribution} = \text{selling price} - \text{variable cost}$$
$$= £15 - £5$$
$$= £10$$

This means that every sale made to a customer would contribute £10 to fixed costs or profit. The number of customers needed to break-even is:

$$\text{Break-even} = \frac{\text{Fixed costs}}{\text{Contribution}}$$
$$= \frac{£4,000}{£10}$$
$$= 400$$

Iqbal Khan now knows that if he attracts more than 400 customers in his first year of trading he will make a profit.

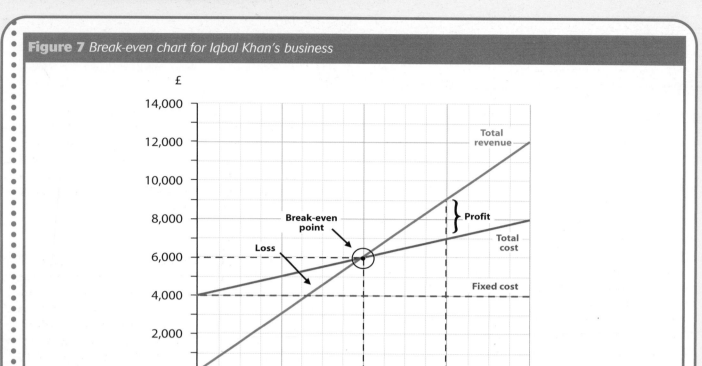

Figure 7 *Break-even chart for Iqbal Khan's business*

Mark Band 3 *Provide comprehensive knowledge and understanding of financial management. Perhaps evaluate the financial position of the business using break-even.*

After Iqbal Khan had decided to charge £15 for his websites he spent some time researching into the costs. He divided them into fixed costs and variable costs. Fixed costs were mainly the setting up costs, such as buying a new laptop computer. The variable costs, which were mainly administrative, were more difficult to establish. He estimated them to be £5 per customer. With this information he constructed the break-even chart shown in Figure 7. This shows that the business will break-even if he attracts 400 customers.

The chart helped Iqbal to analyse the financial position of the business. He can see how much profit or loss will be made depending on how many customers he attracts. For example, if he were to sell 600 websites he would make a profit of £2,000 (£9,000 - £7,000). However, he knew that break-even analysis had some limitations. If the variable costs were estimated incorrectly the break-even point would be different. For example, if he had underestimated the variable costs he would need to sell more websites to break-even. Iqbal Khan also knew that the break-even chart is drawn for a given set of business conditions and that it cannot deal with sudden changes in business variables, such as changes in costs and prices or changes in technology.

Portfolio practice · Mordue Records

Mordue Records is a small record company set up by Andrew Morgan providing an outlet for bands in the north east and Scotland. The label focuses on unusual and innovative styles of music and currently has about 12 bands signed up. It recently signed up a group called Abject Disorder and their first album, Distraction, was released as a CD two months ago. 2000 CDs were produced at a cost of £9,600. Mordue Records will sell the album to retailers and other outlets for £7 each. Variable costs are estimated to be £1 per album.

Source: adapted from company information.

(a) **Calculate the contribution made by each CD.**
(b) **Calculate the number of CDs that Mordue must sell to break-even.**

(c) **Construct a break-even chart to show the break-even point and the amount of profit made if all 2,000 CDs are sold.**
(d) **Evaluate the usefulness of break-even analysis to a company like Mordue Records.**

Spreadsheets, word processing and databases

The role of ICT in business

Most businesses today rely on Information and Communications Technology (ICT) to be efficient. ICT involves recording, storing, retrieving, manipulating and communicating information electronically. Computers are used to process information and transmit it to interested parties, both internally and externally. ICT has a wide range of applications in business, as explained in this section and section 26.

Administration Many routine tasks that involve 'paper work' can be carried out very quickly by computers. Examples might include the generation and posting of invoices and bills to customers, producing standard letters or memos, generating forms and other documents and storing huge amounts of information about customers, suppliers and staff. Computers can sort, store, manipulate, retrieve and transmit both written, numerical and visual information instantly.

Finance A lot of businesses use software to record their business transactions. Many of the systems used are integrated. For example, when a credit sale is made to a customer, the transaction is typed into the system once and is automatically entered into all the appropriate business accounts. The transaction will appear in the customer's own account, the firm's total sales list and the debtors list. Spreadsheets are also used a great deal in finance. They are very useful for presenting tables of financial information, such as budgets, cash flow forecasts and profit and loss accounts. Spreadsheets can perform calculations on tables of figures and produce graphs and charts.

Communications Developments in ICT means that information can be collected, sorted and sent electronically in a fraction of a second. Complex communications networks exist that are linked by computer and can be used to send instructions and information to people, departments and business sites all over the world. Mobile telephones, laptop computers, faxes and e-mail mean that people can work from a variety of locations. They can communicate with colleagues and access company information. The Internet provides wide ranging communication opportunities, including promotion, online selling and e-mailing.

Other applications ICT is used in production to feed information into computer numerically controlled (CNC) machines, to assist in stock control and to record and present production information, such as costs and performance indicators. It may be used in research and development (R & D) to carry out design work, tests and simulations. ICT is also used in personnel, security, marketing and many other areas of business.

Spreadsheets

Some types of information are best handled by spreadsheets. A spreadsheet allows a user to enter, store and present information in a grid on a computer screen. Most spreadsheets are used to manipulate numerical data. Table 1 shows that a grid is made up of a number of 'cells'. These cells are arranged in rows (information across the spreadsheet) and columns (information down the spreadsheet). Each cell is able to hold information which will fall into one of three categories.

- Numerical data. These are numbers which will be manipulated by the computer programme.
- Text. This refers to the words used in a spreadsheet, often headings.
- Formulae. These are the instructions given by the user which tell the computer how to manipulate the numerical data, for example add up a column of entries to give a total.

A spreadsheet is shown in Table 1. It is a sales revenue budget for Swaffham Motors. It contains information about the planned sales levels for each department over a six month period in 2005. Each column B to G shows the planned sales levels for each department each month. Each row shows the sales from a particular department over the entire six months. For example, row 3 shows the planned revenue from MOTs over the six months. Row 6 shows the total planned revenues for each month and Column H shows the planned total revenue from each department. Cell H6 shows the planned sales revenue for the whole period, i.e. £21,042,000. Totals can be calculated automatically in a spreadsheet. For example, the formula for cell B6 would be B2 + B3 + B4 + B5 or =SUM(B2:B5). If Swaffham Motors were to change any of the entries in the spreadsheet the totals will change automatically because of the formula.

Table 1 *A spreadsheet showing a six months sales budget for Swaffham Motors, 2005, (£000)*

	A	B	C	D	E	F	G	H
1	Department	JAN	FEB	MAR	APR	MAY	JUN	TOTAL
2	Repairs and maintenance	458	456	786	876	776	765	4,117
3	MOTs	110	98	97	89	103	130	627
4	Motor car sales	1,445	1,256	1,329	1,876	2,228	2,667	10,801
5	Parts and accessories sales	786	978	678	834	1,021	1,200	5,497
6	Total	2,799	2,788	2,890	3,675	4,128	4,762	21,042

Some spreadsheets are much larger than the computer screen with many columns and rows. The screen can only show part of the spreadsheet. However, scrolling enables the user to scan over the entire spreadsheet until the section required is shown on the screen.

Advantages of spreadsheets

There is a number of advantages of using spreadsheets.

- Numerical data is recorded and shown in a clear and ordered way.
- Editing allows numbers, text and formulae to be changed easily to correct mistakes or make changes to the data.
- It is easy to copy an entry or an entire series of entries from one part of the spreadsheet to another, or from one spreadsheet to another. This is particularly useful when one number has to be entered at the same point in every column.
- Numbers can be added, subtracted multiplied and divided anywhere on the spreadsheet.
- Spreadsheets calculate the effect of entry changes automatically. This is sometimes referred to as the 'what if' facility. For example, what would happen to cell X (total costs) if the entry in cell D (labour costs) increased by 10%? The answer can be calculated instantly.
- Many spreadsheets allow users to generate graphs and charts from the data.

Spreadsheets are used a lot to store and present financial information. They are used by management to aid decision making. One well known spreadsheet programme is Microsoft Excel. The budget in Table 1 was produced using Excel. Cash flow forecasts can also be produced using Excel. One of the problems when preparing cash flow forecasts is that if one of the entries needs to be changed, a lot of other numbers in the forecast, such as the closing balances, have to be changed as well. However, when an entry is changed in a spreadsheet any other cells linked by a formula will be changed automatically. This saves a lot of time and may prevent calculation errors providing entries are correct.

Break-even information can also be presented on a spreadsheet. Table 2 shows some break-even information. The fixed cost, variable cost, total cost, price and total revenue values are shown for a range of output 0 – 100 units. According to the table 50 units of output have to be sold to break-even. Both total cost and total revenue are £20,000 at this level of output. Again, the main advantage of using spreadsheets to present such information is the speed with which changes can be made to the figures if one entry has been amended.

Word processing

Word processing software, such as Microsoft Word, is likely to be used in all business departments. Documents such as letters, reports, forms and memos are likely to be used by a wide range of personnel. They can be produced, amended, updated and stored efficiently without generating huge amounts of paper that would have to be stored in a filing cabinet, for example. Using a computer for word processing has a number of advantages.

- Presentation can be of a high quality. All text is typed and users can choose from different font styles and sizes. Colour can be used and there is a choice of different presentation styles.
- Text documents can be drafted and 'polished' efficiently, by cutting and pasting and using a spell-checker. Word processing software applications can check grammar and punctuation to improve quality.
- Templates giving standard formats can be used for letters and forms. This saves time because much of the document will already be written. It might also help to build up a corporate image if standard documents contain the company logo, for example.
- Graphs, tables and clip art can be easily incorporated into text documents from spreadsheets and databases. It is also possible to merge documents.
- Documents can be sent to people as attachments using e-mail. This may avoid the need to print them out and save money on stationery and postage. This is particularly efficient if the same document has to be sent to a large number of recipients.

Databases

A database is really an electronic filing system. It allows huge quantities of data to be stored cheaply and efficiently. Every business which uses computers will compile and use databases. The information is stored so that it can be updated and recalled when needed. Table 3 shows part of a database for a furniture retailer. It gives details about the stock held by the business. The collection of common data is called a file. A file consists of a set of related records. In the database in Table 3 all the information on the Bathroom rails, for example, is a record. The information on each record is listed under headings known as fields, e.g. stock number, supplier, date delivered quantity and cost. A good database will have the following facilities.

- 'User-definable' record format, allowing the user to enter any chosen field on the record.
- File searching facility for finding specified information from a file, eg identifying all items of stock that were purchased before 31.5.04 in the file shown in Table 3. It is usually possible to search on more than one criterion, e.g. all stock purchased

Table 2 Break-even information in a spreadsheet

	A	B	C	D	E	F
1	Quantity	Fixed cost	Variable cost	Total cost	Price	Total revenue
2	0	5,000	0	5,000	400	0
3	10	5,000	3,000	8,000	400	4,000
4	20	5,000	6,000	11,000	400	8,000
5	30	5,000	9,000	14,000	400	12,000
6	40	5,000	12,000	17,000	400	16,000
7	50	5,000	15,000	20,000	400	20,000
8	60	5,000	18,000	23,000	400	24,000
9	70	5,000	21,000	26,000	400	28,000
10	80	5,000	24,000	29,000	400	32,000
11	90	5,000	27,000	32,000	400	36,000
12	100	5,000	30,000	35,000	400	40,000

Table 3 *An extract from a stock database*

Description	Stock no.	Supplier	Delivered	Quantity	Cost	Valuation
Bathroom rails	21-9911	A.G Fall	23.7.04	7	£32	£224
Bookcase	34-0011	Penrose	21.5.04	4	£56	£224
Dining table	13-3390	Simpsons Ltd	12.4.04	4	£200	£800
Dining chairs	13-3779	Simpsons Ltd	21.5.04	32	£20	£640
Hat stand	22-9871	IKEA	11.7.04	6	£7	£42
Settee (bed)	31-6620	Framping plc	4.7.04	7	£230	£1,610

before 31.5.04 that cost less than £150.
- File sorting facility for rearranging data in another order, e.g. arranging the file in Table 3 in order of age with the oldest stock at the top of the list.
- Calculations on fields within records for inclusion in reports. In this case the stock valuation is calculated by multiplying quantity and cost.

An example of a business using a database is shown in Figure 1.

How does computer software improve business efficiency?

Different computer software applications will aid businesses in different ways. For example, spreadsheets will help to speed up the construction of financial statements and word processing software will help produce standardised documents. However, business efficiency is improved due to some general features.

Speed Information can be processed much more quickly in computerised systems than manual systems. Therefore tasks can be completed more quickly, which will save time and money. Also, management can be supplied with up-to-date, accurate information more quickly, which will aid decision making.

Capacity Some businesses have huge numbers of customers and employees and conduct thousands or millions of transactions. They have to process vast quantities of information. Manual systems would require huge quantities of resources such as administration staff and storage space to store and process this information.

Data handling Computers allow information to be input and accessed from different locations around the country or even the world. For example, a customer database containing two hundred thousand entries could be accessed by any authorised employee anywhere in the organisation.

User friendly The design of most business software means that staff do not need any detailed knowledge of ICT to input and retrieve data. Consequently training costs could be lower and non-specialist staff might be employed in the business which will help keep labour costs down.

Accuracy Computerised systems are much more accurate than manual systems when processing data. Partly, this is because computers do not become distracted or tired when performing large numbers of routine operations. Also, managers will benefit from having more accurate information when making decisions. However, computers can only work with the information they are given. If data is entered incorrectly then the calculations from the computer are also likely to be incorrect.

Figure 1 *Boots' database*

The Boots Advantage Card was released in September 1997. When customers buy goods they are rewarded with points which can be exchanged for other goods. With the Advantage Card, Boots was able to gain information about customers.

- **Recency/Frequency/Value** - ultra frequent, very frequent, frequent, majority, occasional (own brand), occasional (proprietary), deal seekers, and large basket buyers.
- **Lifestyle/Lifestage** – customers were divided into two segments from age 16 to 65+/ Kids and No Kids.
- **Product Repertoire**.
- **Interests**.
- **Attitude/Needs**.
- **Shopping Mode**.
- **Demographics**.

This information is stored on a database and has been used in a number of ways, such as:
- customers were sent coupons based on their prior spending habits and encouraged to increase their average spending to earn the extra Advantage points;
- to introduce new products and services that data had indicated customers would welcome, such as the Mother and Baby at Home section.

Source: adapted from www.loyalty.vg.

Visit a local supermarket to find out about the ways in which ICT is used. You will be able see for yourself in the store how ICT is being used. However, with permission, you could use a short questionnaire to gather information from staff about how ICT makes their job easier. Use your findings to comment on how ICT helps:
- the business;
- employees;
- customers.

Research task

Portfolio practice · **Felham Industries**

Felham Industries makes hand crafted wooden products. Budgets are used to help the financial control of the business. Table 4 shows an incomplete production cost budget for the first six months of 2005. Fixed costs are £10,000, components are £20 per unit, labour costs are £50 per unit and other variable costs are £15 per unit. Felham Industries uses spreadsheets to produce nearly all of its financial statements. It also uses databases to store records such as customers, employees, suppliers, stock and fixed assets. All of Felham's employees undergo an ICT training course when they are inducted.

(a) Use a spreadsheet to complete the production cost budget for Felham Industries.

(b) Make the necessary adjustments to the budget if fixed costs fall to £9,000 and labour costs rise to £60 per unit.

(c) Explain the advantages to Felham Industries of using spreadsheets to produce budgets.

(d) Evaluate the affect that ICT will have on the efficiency of Felham Industries.

Table 4 *Production cost budget for Felham Industries (incomplete)*

	JAN	FEB	MAR	APR	MAY	JUN
Output (units)	100	150	150	200	300	350
Fixed costs						
Components						
Labour						
Other variable costs						
Total costs						

Meeting the assessment criteria

In your investigation you need to explain how software can support a business and help it operate more efficiently, make reference to the types of software used and how it is relevant to your chosen business.

Business example – Renita's Costumes

Renita Okon owns a busy costume hire business in West London. The business has a computer and Renita uses Microsoft Office to help run her business. She uses Excel to produce cash flow forecasts every four months. A forecast for a four month period in 2005 is shown in Table 5. Renita also has a database to keep a record of the stock of costumes and customer details. She uses the customer database to identify regular customers. Each month she prints off a report to identify such customers. If a customer spends more then £200 in a six month period she sends them a gift voucher for £20. The voucher is a standard document which Renita designed using a word processing

programme. The voucher can be personalised and has resulted in additional sales when used.

Mark Band 1 *Provide basic knowledge and understanding of business software. Identify and describe some software packages used by the business.*

Renita uses a computer to help run her business. In particular she uses spreadsheets, databases and word processing applications. She uses spreadsheets to produce cash flow forecasts. A spreadsheet allows a user to enter, store and present information in a grid on a computer screen. It can be programmed to calculate the receipts, total payments, net cash flow and closing balance automatically. Renita also uses a database to store customer information. A database is really an electronic filing system. It allows huge quantities of data to be stored cheaply and efficiently. Renita uses the database to identify customers who hire costumes regularly. She can do this because the database holds a record of every single customer

Meeting the assessment criteria

transaction. Renita also uses a word processor. She has designed a standard gift voucher that can be personalised. These are sent to reward regular customers and encourage them to remain loyal.

Mark Band 2 *Provide sound knowledge and understanding of business software. Identify and describe some software packages used by the business and explain how efficiency might be improved.*

Renita's Costumes is a busy business and benefits from the use of a computer. She uses a programme called Excel to produce cash flow forecasts. One of the problems when preparing cash flow forecasts is that if one of the entries needs to be changed, a lot of other numbers in the forecast, such as the closing balances, have to be changed as well. However, when using a spreadsheet, when an entry is changed any other numbers that are affected will be changed automatically. Renita also uses databases and word processing applications to improve the efficiency of the business. For example, by using standard documents, such as the personalised gift voucher, a lot of time is saved. Renita can also keep track of customer purchases on her database. For example, she can recall a customer's full details at the press of a button. Generally, the use of computer software speeds up administration tasks and the preparation of financial statements, improves access to data and saves space. Computers are also more accurate and the programmes employed by Renita are easy to use.

Mark Band 3 *Provide comprehensive knowledge and understanding of business software. Identify and analyse some software packages used by the business and discuss how efficiency is improved.*

As Renita's Costumes expanded Renita decided to invest £1,100 in a computer to cope with the growing workload. She also spent £199.99 on some software called Microsoft Office and attended an ICT course at her local technical college. Renita had never used a computer before and felt that the £300 cost of the ICT training would be a good investment. She found the programmes surprisingly easy to use and soon got to grips with spreadsheets, for example. She used Excel to produce cash flow forecasts and found that a lot of time was saved, particularly when changing entries in the forecast. For example, if the amount spent on costumes in April was changed to £4,600 on the spreadsheet, the total payments, net cash flow and closing balance for April would all change automatically. So would the opening and closing balances for May and June. Renita also uses databases and word processing applications to improve the efficiency of the business. By using standard documents, such as the personalised gift voucher, a lot of time is saved. She also used Microsoft Word to write letters, design leaflets and produce order forms. Databases are used to store customer records, stock lists, staff records and financial transactions. Renita suggests that her investment and training has paid dividends. Generally, the use of computer software speeds up administration tasks and the preparation of financial statements, improves access to data and saves space. Computers are also more accurate and the programmes employed by Renita are easy to use. Renita now has a lot more time to deal with the creative aspects of the business.

Table 5 *A four month cash flow forecast for Renita's Costumes*

	A	B	C	D	F
1		March	April	May	June
2	Receipts				
3	Cash sales	20,300	25,300	37,400	41,500
4	Total receipts	20,300	25,300	37,400	41,500
5	Payments				
6	Shop overheads	12,500	41,500	17,000	20,000
7	Casual labour	3,000	3,000	4,000	3,000
8	Drawings	3,000	3,000	3,000	3,000
9	New costumes		2,600		
10	Total payments	18,500	50,100	24,000	26,000
11	Net cash flow	1,800	-24,800	13,400	15,500
12	Opening balance	1,200	3,000	-21,800	-8,400
13	Closing balance	3,000	-21,800	-8,400	7,100

Types of specialist software

Many businesses use specialist software to help improve efficiency. It is possible to buy 'off the shelf' software packages which can be used by a wide variety of businesses. However, some businesses have to buy specialist software that is written and installed by an IT expert. This type of software will be tailored to the exact needs of the user.

Management Information Systems (MIS)

A MIS converts data from internal and external sources into information that can be used by managers to aid decision making. The diagram in Figure 1 shows how an MIS operates.

- Internal sources of data are generated by the business – staff time sheets and sales invoices, for example.
- External sources of information come from outside the business – bank statements and purchase invoices from suppliers, for example.
- This data is processed by the MIS to produce information that can be used to make decisions. For example, a business MIS is likely to have information about how much money each customer owes. From this information it would be possible to compile a list of customers that have owed money for more than three months. Managers might decide to target these customers for collection.

Generally, the bigger the business the greater need for a MIS. Each day a large corporation will process huge quantities of datawhich are then recorded, sorted, classified, summarised and stored. Quite often the data on one source document have to be recorded in many different files. For example, the data contained on a purchase invoice may have to be recorded in a supplier account, a creditors list, a purchases list, a VAT account and a stock list. A computerised MIS will do this automatically. A number of companies supply computerised MIS, such as Sage, Misys and Microsoft.

Accountancy software

Computerised accounts systems are very popular. They are used to record and store financial transactions and generate financial information such as creditors and debtors lists, profit and loss accounts and balance sheets. Many accountancy packages are integrated so that the different functions are linked. For example, if the details of a sales invoice are put into the system, both the customer account and the firm's sales ledger will be automatically updated. Then, when payment is made, the customer account, the sales ledger and the bank account will all be updated instantly. In financial accounting the most commonly used accounting applications include:

- invoicing;
- sales ledger with customer accounts;
- purchases ledger with supplier accounts;
- nominal ledger with sales;
- purchases, expenses and bank accounts;
- stock records;
- payroll records;
- profit and loss accounts;
- balance sheets.

Enterprise Resource Planning (ERP) software

ERP software helps a business to manage a number of activities, such as product planning, parts purchasing, maintaining stocks, communicating with suppliers, providing customer service and tracking orders. In recent years manufacturing companies in

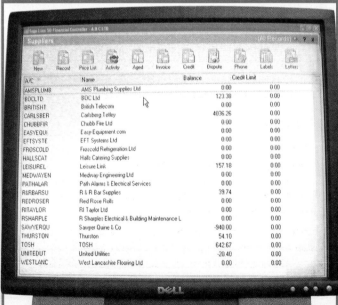

Figure 2 *A computerised purchases ledger*

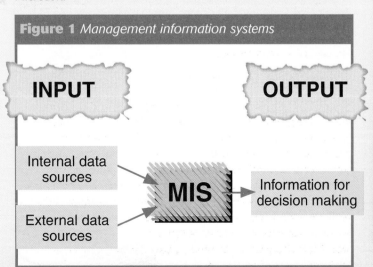

Figure 1 *Management information systems*

INPUT → MIS → OUTPUT

Internal data sources

External data sources

Information for decision making

Figure 3 *Benefits of computer aided design*

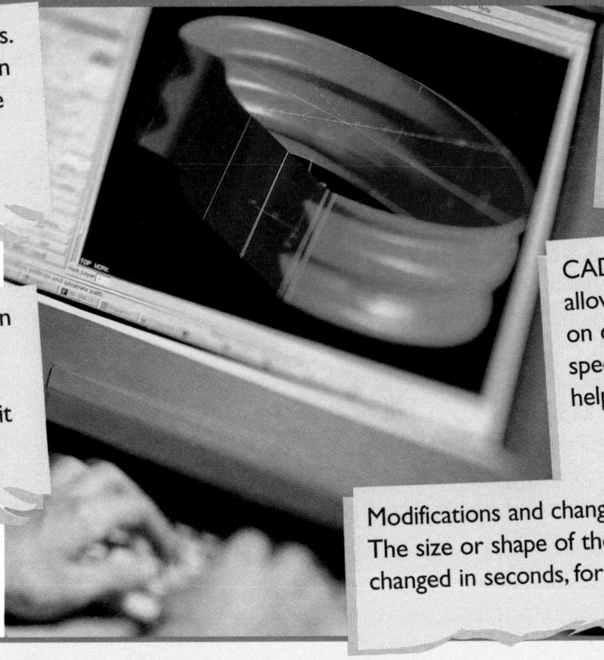

CAD has helped to reduce lead times. This means that businesses can design new products and get them onto the market more quickly. This can give them a competitive edge.

Problems are often more easily identified. This sometimes prevents the need for reworking later on. Also, the final design is more likely to be correct.

A wide range of designs can be shown on a computer screen. For example, two and three dimensional drawings, wire-framed models, electronic circuit board designs and architectural drawings can all be shown.

CAD systems handle repetitive work allowing the designer to concentrate on creative design work. The need for specialists may also be reduced, which helps to keep down costs.

Modifications and changes can be made easily. The size or shape of the design can be changed in seconds, for example.

industries ranging from aerospace to bicycle parts and circuit boards to boat docks have used ERP software to reduce costs, improve productivity, and enable new business strategies within their organizations. Many ERP systems are used to improve stock control. For example, Jerrard Bros plc, a lighting specialist, enjoyed stock savings in excess of 30% after implementing an ERP system. With space at a premium at its Croydon factory, efficient warehousing and stockholdings are extremely important and K3 Business Technology's ERP system reduced stock levels from £900,000 to £600,000. Since installing the system Jerrard's product lines expanded, but stock levels have remained constant. Without the extra products, stocks would have dropped even further to £500,000. Stock obsolescence and stock-outs have also dramatically reduced.

Computer Aided Design (CAD) software

CAD is an interactive computer system which is capable of generating, storing, and using geometric and computer graphics. It helps design engineers to solve design problems and is used in a wide variety of industries. Computer aided design has a number of benefits for a business. These are shown in Figure 3.

The Internet

The Internet provides a huge source of information and can be accessed using a computer and a modem. With the introduction of broadband, which has speeded up access to information, the use of the Internet has grown significantly. The Internet can be used by a business in a number of ways.

Accessing information Information can be accessed to help decision making. For example, a business could visit the websites of competitors to find out what products are being offered for sale and what prices are being charged. Businesses might also make use of economic, financial and news information. Some businesses are able to carry out market research using

information on the Internet. For example, they may be able to analyse 'hits' on their own web pages or search for information on industry trends.

Providing company information Most businesses have their own website which can be used to give information about the company to the outside world. Business websites contain corporate and financial information for investors, general information, such as the history of the company for the public, and information for customers, such as details about the company's product range. Business websites will contain links to other useful websites and a communication facility which allows people to contact the business by e-mail.

Offering services Some businesses advertise job vacancies on their websites and provide electronic application forms. People can apply for jobs online. This helps to speed up the recruitment process.

Marketing and sales Businesses are increasingly using websites for marketing purposes. Whole product ranges can be advertised and information given. Banner headings can be place on other websites to attract customers. Sales via the Internet are also increasing. This is dealt with later.

E-mail and intranets

E-mail is where people send text messages and other images to people using computers. It has helped to improve both internal and external communications in business. Businesses, other organisations and individuals have e-mail addresses. Information sent from one e-mail address, via a computer, modem and telephone, to another address is stored by a 'server', a computer dedicated to storage and network facilities. It stays in that address until it is accessed by the receiver. One of the main advantages of e-mail is that information can be sent instantly to anywhere in the world. It is also possible to send lengthy documents such as business plans and reports, drawings, photographs, spreadsheets and other images, as an attachment to the e-mail.

Some large businesses have an **intranet**. This is a company-wide computer network that links all staff in the organisation. This means that standard information, such as a daily news bulletin for example, could be distributed instantly to every single employee. This is a very efficient way of communicating relatively confidential business information.

E-commerce

An increasing number of businesses have e-commerce operations. This means that customers can buy products online. Examples include selling tickets for the theatre, cinema and sports fixtures, CDs and DVDs, books, tickets for coach, train and air travel, groceries, holidays, fast food such as pizzas, consumer durables and cars. In fact there are few products that cannot be purchased online now. Many people have Internet bank accounts and companies such as Telco, the telephone company, use online billing. The advantages of e-commerce are huge for both the business and customers.

Business benefits Benefits to a business may include:

- a retailer does not need shop space to sell products online which reduces costs and an airline can issue tickets electronically saving on staffing, stationery, postage and other costs;
- being able to offer products online 24 hours a day, 365 days a year;
- advertising products by sending direct mail, using 'pop-up' ads and their own websites, for example.

Customer benefits Customers might benefit from:

- lower prices;
- shopping without travel in the comfort of their own homes;
- placing orders at their convenience 24 hours a day, 365 days a year;
- access to 'electronic shops' all over the world.

Data protection

Many people have become concerned that personal details are stored on lots of computers and could be misused. However, the government has passed legislation to control the collection, storage, processing, and distribution of data. For example, the **Data Protection Act, 1998** specifies eight conditions with which users must comply. These are shown in Table 1. There is also legislation which aims to prevent the misuse of computers and makes it an offence to access certain unauthorised information. Finally, some EU legislation prevents the downloading of copyright music and outlaws the sending of junk e-mail known as spam by businesses.

Computers and health and safety at work

The increased use of computers in the work place has led to worries that employees may suffer physical harm as a result of spending too much time sat in front of a VDU. Some people, such as home workers and call centre staff, spend all day in front of a VDU. The effects associated with the use of computer equipment may include the following.

Table 1 *Conditions of the Data Protection Act*

- Personal data should be obtained fairly and lawfully.
- Personal data can only be held for specified and lawful purposes.
- Personal data cannot be used or disclosed in any manner which is incompatible with the purpose for which it was held.
- The amount of data held should be adequate, relevant and not excessive.
- Personal data should be accurate and kept up to date.
- Personal data should not be kept for longer than is necessary;
- An individual should be entitled to:
  (a) be informed by any data user if he or she is the subject of personal data and also have access to that data;
  (b) where appropriate, have data corrected or erased.
- Security measures must be taken by data users to prevent unlawful access, destruction, or loss of personal data.

Eye damage and defective vision According to IMPACT, the largest public sector trade union in the Republic of Ireland, although VDUs do not cause eye damage, they can highlight problems that are already there. And they can lead to eye strain and eye fatigue if you don't take the necessary precautions.

Muscle and skeleton problems These may be caused either by overexertion, known as Repetitive Strain Injury (RSI), or by static posture – sitting in the same position for a long period.

Operator stress Working in the same position at a work station for a long period can be stressful. It may also be a relatively tedious activity.

Health problems There maybe problems which might be related to radiation, such as miscarriages and birth defects and face rashes and reddening.

Guidelines exist for businesses that require staff to spend long periods sat in front of a screen. **The Health and Safety (Display Screen Equipment) Regulations 1992** requires companies to comply as follows.

- All VDU user workstations must meet the minimum requirements of the Regulations and BS/EU Regulations.
- All VDU user workstations are assessed in order to reduce the risks of the potential adverse health effects.
- The user's work routine allows breaks or changes of activity. Eye tests and remedial spectacles are provided, where prescribed, for users.
- VDU users are provided with adequate information and training on the adverse health effects and how to avoid them.

Confidentiality and security

The Data Protection Act requires businesses to store personal details safely and ensure that only authorised users have access to them. There are certain ways of protecting data stored by computers.

Computer passwords Access to personal information about customers and staff and other sensitive information, such as financial details, can be restricted. In these circumstances the data can only be accessed by authorised users. They usually require a password and a user name to be issued and recognised before anyone can gain access to the information.

Anti-virus software Computer viruses, which can damage both the information stored on computers and the software that operates them, are created by computer 'hackers'. Many viruses enter computer systems via e-mails. Viruses are attached to e-mails and sent to individuals and businesses. Once the e-mails are opened, viruses attack systems doing damage and spreading quickly. However, it is possible to buy anti-virus software which can detect and destroy viruses before they enter the system or repair files and systems if they are affected by a virus. The software must be updated regularly because new viruses are being created all of the time.

System back-ups Businesses should make back-up copies of all information stored on a computer to prevent losses. It is possible for computers to 'crash' due to technical problems or viruses. If data and programmes are not backed-up they may be lost completely.

Choose a well known business that sells products online and visit its website that sells products online. Identify information on the site that might be used by:
- customers;
- investors;
- employees;
- competitors.
Explain the advantages to the business of e-commerce.

Research task

Portfolio practice · **Wilky Group**

Wilky Group supplies bathroom fittings to major UK house builders. Wilky deals with a large number of sub-contractors which used to result in a huge mountain of paper and endless opportunities for mistakes. As the business expanded in recent years, so did the number of difficulties in the warehouse, such as picking errors, stock losses and warehouse congestion. According to IT and Logistics Director Dave Seagrove, 'Pick errors cost us a fortune. We had to pacify angry customers, arrange collection of the incorrect deliveries, raise all the necessary paperwork, put the items back in stock and either credit or re-deliver the right products'.

To resolve these problems Wilky installed an Enterprise Resource Planning (ERP) system. With this new stock control system, all products are scanned in as they are unloaded off the lorries and then stored in the warehouse. If a product is delivered without a barcode, the warehouse team simply print off a customised barcode sticker on a dedicated bar coding printer located in the goods-in area. Then, when the product is picked, it is scanned again ensuring that the right item is picked and the stock records are updated automatically.

The introduction of the ERP system has been a success. Wilky is now making record profits every month. The business has real time stock control, no bottlenecks in the warehouse operation, virtually error free picking, greatly reduced stock losses, greater visibility and above all, happy customers who get exactly what they want, when they want it.

Source: adapted from company information.

(a) **Describe briefly the purpose of an ERP package.**
(b) **Analyse the benefits to Wilky of using the ERP package.**
(c) **Discuss how Wilky might maintain confidentiality and security when holding information about customers on a computer.**

Meeting the assessment criteria

In your investigation you need to explain how software can support a business and help it operate more efficiently, make reference to the types of software used and how it is relevant to your chosen business.

Business example – Gerhards

Gerhards is a bespoke tailors located in Bristol. When Michael Fell joined the company as Accounts Manager an existing Sage accounting package was in use. However, the software was not being used to its full potential. The old manual system was still being used in its entirety, consisting of a typewriter, ledger cards and massive daybooks. The system needed five people to run it and took up a lot of valuable time.

Michael decided to use the software to its full capacity. When asked how Sage has benefited the company Michael argues that there was an immediate saving on audit fees which were halved. Also, it used to take auditors two weeks at the business to carry out the audit, but now one person could do it in three/four days. Michael also stated that customers of the business are mainly individuals and not companies. The business has a large database to store information about these customers. So sorting facilities are particularly important. The business often arranges customers by country of residence for mail shots and debt identification. The speed at which Sage can do this and then produce a report is far quicker than by hand and invoices can also be customised.

Source: adapted from www.sage.co.uk

Mark Band 1 *Provide basic knowledge and understanding of business software. Identify and describe some software packages used by the business.*
Gerhards uses specialist software in accounting. Such packages are used to record and store financial transactions and generate useful financial information such as creditors and debtors lists, profit and loss accounts and balance sheets. Many accountancy packages are integrated so that the different functions are linked. For example, if the details of a sales invoice are put into the system, both the customer account and the firm's sales ledger will be automatically updated. Then, when payment is made, the customer account, the sales ledger and the bank account will all be updated instantly. Gerhards uses a Sage accounting package. It is relevant because customers are individuals and not businesses. The software uses a large database and has an effective sorting facility. This enables the business to sort customers according to country of residence for mail shots and debt identification, for example.

Mark Band 2 *Provide sound knowledge and understanding of business software. Identify and describe some software packages used by the business and explain how efficiency might be improved.*
Like a growing number of firms, Gerhards uses specialist software packages to help run its business. Gerhards uses a Sage accounting package. When a new accounts manager was appointed the business was already using the package, but not to its full potential. The old manual system was still being used, which consisted of a typewriter, ledger cards and large daybooks. This system needed five people to run it and took up a lot of time. By making better use of the existing Sage system Gerhards was able to improve the efficiency of the business. For

example, auditing fees were reduced by one half and the amount of time it took for the accounts to be audited was reduced from two weeks to three/four days. Sage was also suitable for the type of customers served by the business. As a bespoke tailor Gerhards served individuals rather than companies. The Sage program provided a customer database which allowed Gerhards to sort customers

according to country of residence, which helped the business to target customers for mail shots and identify debtors more easily.

Mark Band 3 *Provide comprehensive knowledge and understanding of business software. Identify and analyse some software packages used by the business and discuss how efficiency is improved.*
Businesses use software packages for a range of activities such as design, stock control and internet selling. One common area of application is in finance and accounts. Accountancy packages are used to record and store financial transactions and produce financial information such as creditors and debtors lists, profit and loss accounts and balance sheets. Gerhards uses a Sage accountancy package. The system has been used for a while, but only when a new Accounts Manager was appointed was the system used to its full potential.

Before the appointment of Michael Fell, Gerhards used a combination of manual and computer systems. This was obviously inefficient. For example, the manual system consisted of a typewriter, ledger cards and massive daybooks. The system needed five people to run it and took up a lot of valuable time. It is possible that the people employed in the accounts department had not been trained properly to use the computer system.

Once the manual system was abandoned, efficiency improved. Gerhards benefited from lower auditing fees. Also, at one time it took the auditors two weeks on site to do their job, but now it only took one person three/four days. When questioned about the features of the Sage package which he finds useful Michael suggested that customers were individuals and not companies, so a large database was needed to store information. Sorting facilities were particularly important as the business often had to filter by country of residence for mail shots and debt identification. The speed at which Sage can do this and then produce a report was outstanding. The ability to customise statements and invoices also helped improve the efficiency of the system.

All this suggests that the software used by Gerhards is highly appropriate for the needs of the business.

Customers

Customers are individuals or organisations for which a product or service is provided. They have dealings with businesses and a variety of their stakeholders.

In personal terms, a customer is the person who asks for something. For example, if a teacher asks a student to write a report, the student will be the supplier and the teacher will be the customer. If a player is asked to play for a local team, the team manager and other team members are customers as the player is providing them with a service - the skills and willingness to play as part of the team.

In business terms, customers give others their business. Customers agree to buy or trade with others to provide them with an income. It is the customer that pays the money for the product or service that is provided.

Consumers

The consumer is the end user. Consumers are people or organisations at the 'end of the line'. Consumers use the product for its own sake, rather than just buying it as part of their own business activity. They may literally 'consume' the product if it is a food or drink. Or they might use it up as part of the production or development process for their own products, for example a raw material or a product from a service industry such as electrical power.

The consumer is not necessarily the person who purchases the product. For example, an adult may buy a toy in a shop, give it to a child who plays with the toy. In this example the adult is the **customer** of the shop, the child is the **consumer** of the entertainment and pleasure given by the toy.

A customer may also be the consumer, if they are dealt with directly and the product is a consumable item. For example, if instead of a toy the adult bought a ready to cook meal and ate it themselves, they would be both the customer of the shop and the consumer of the meal.

On a larger scale, a retail buyer may place orders and purchase goods in quantity and thus be the customer of the manufacturer or supplier. The retailer will then display the goods in its shop where they are bought by a shopper, the customer of the retailer, who may not be the consumer of the product from the point of view of the manufacturer. Their role as customer or consumer depends on what they do ultimately with what they buy. If the retail buyer in this example bought cleaning equipment from a cash and carry for use in the shop itself, then it would be both the customer (of the cash and carry) and the consumer, as the cleaning equipment is being used up by the retailer.

Internal customers

Internal customers are people who are provided with services within a business. For an employee they are likely to include the person to whom the employee reports directly, senior members of staff who ask the employee to do something, and members of the employee's immediate work team. Looking at other people in a business as customers can be very helpful for employees to establish standards of service, which may play an important part when it comes to performance reviews. Whilst internal customers may play an important role in the life of a member of a marketing team, the main focus of the work required for this unit is on external customers.

External customers

External customers are people or organisations (the buyers) outside of an organisation who are provided with products and services. They pay money for the products and services provided by a business or benefit from them in a material way. They include trade and retail buyers and consumers in some situations.

Why bother to understand customers?

For marketing planning purposes it is important to recognise the difference between the customer and the consumer. Having established who are the customers, the process of analysing and understanding their wants and needs can begin. Once this has been done, it is possible to identify where to aim the product and how to plan marketing activity effectively.

Customer needs

Customer needs are the basic requirements or desires at a given point in time that can be fulfilled by receiving or acquiring the right product. An example would be if you are thirsty you need a drink to satisfy your thirst. In a business context, if a shop has sold out of a particular line, it needs more stock to sell or will lose income.

It is often argued that satisfying customer needs is essentially a passive, quantitative activity, and that a pro-active marketing strategy, in a competitive market, should aim to meet customer wants in a qualitative way.

Customer wants

What a customer wants can be very broad and far-reaching. Wants are the customers' requirements in addition to just acquiring the product. They may include what the customer expects of a product and of the supplier in addition to just receiving the product itself. They are the reasons why a customer buys a particular product.

Using the example of thirst, a drink may satisfy the thirst (the need) but the customer may want the drink to have a nice taste, be cheap, be a well known brand, be packed in a can so that it can be drunk immediately and be stocked by many shops so that it can be bought easily.

In a business context, a shop may have sold out of a particular product. In addition to needing stock, its wants may include the product being at the right price, packed in the right quantity, delivered safely and on time, and a whole range of other customer service requirements.

Meeting customers' wants is sometimes referred to as adding value to a product. This is particularly important in competitive markets to make sure that that customers choose your product rather than those of competitors. It means that the customer is delighted rather than merely satisfied with your product.

A successful marketing strategy is based on meeting both the needs and the wants of your customers, in a profitable way. This means researching customers to identify the specific customer needs and wants that must be satisfied. If a business identifies needs and wants and decides which are the most important to the customer when making a buying decision, there is a good chance that customers will buy. Some examples of needs and wants for different products are shown in Table 1.

Table 1 *Needs and wants*	
Product	Nike trainers
Need	To support and protect feet
Additional wants	Fashionable, hard wearing
Product	Taxi ride
Need	Transport
Additional wants	Arrive on time, safe and pleasant journey
Product	D&G coat
Need	Keep warm and dry
Additional wants	Fashionable, exclusive, eye-catching design
Product	Shredies breakfast cereal
Need	Satisfy hunger
Additional wants	Available at many supermarkets, low fat, add fibre to diet

Source: adapted from National Readership Survey Open Access data.

How does a business attempt to understand its customers?

Depending on the product, customer profile and method of distribution, there is a number of simple ways that a business can gain an understanding of its customers.

Talk to customers This can be:
- formally through the use of marketing research interviews or questionnaires in a customer survey to collect data on their needs, wants, opinions and motivation;
- informally by asking for advice or opinion before launching a marketing plan.

Observe customers This can be done directly by literally watching them, for example watching the way shoppers walk around a supermarket. It can also be indirectly, by using film of customers in a buying situation or analysing appropriate secondary research on customer behaviour. A business will try to find out:

- what they do;
- how they behave;
- what they buy;
- how they buy.

Measure and analyse customers This can be done by using:
- own sales data;
- primary research that collects customer purchasing data or information on product usage;
- analysing secondary research based on customer purchasing or product usage.

Analysing customers The process of analysing customers will involve:
- segmentation;
- profiling;
- targeting.

Customer segmentation

This means dividing customers into identifiable groups, which share common characteristics. Segmentation is covered in more detail in section 33. There are many different ways of segmenting customers. The three main ways are shown in Figure 1.

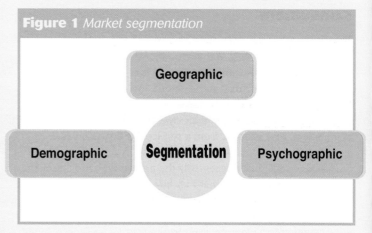

Figure 1 *Market segmentation*

Geographic

Demographic — Segmentation — Psychographic

Geographic This involves analysing customers and dividing them into groups based on geographic factors, such as where they are located, where they live, where they work and where they shop including which towns or shopping centres and postcodes.

Demographic This involves analysing customers and dividing them into groups based on demographic factors, such as age, sex, socio-economic group or household type.

Psychographic This involves analysing customers and dividing them into groups based on psychographic factors, such as lifestyle, interests, attitude, opinion, values.

These three ways work well when segmenting people as customers and consumers. But what if the customer is a business or industry rather than an individual?
- Geographic segmentation of businesses can be done, as it is still important to know where they are located, the region or area and how far from the production unit deliveries must be made.
- Demographic segmentation of businesses could include company size, based on financial measures, how many outlets they may have, how many people are employed, how big are the orders that they place and how much they buy in total.

Figure 2 *Profiting of Saga Holiday's customers*

The profile of customers for SAGA Holidays could be:
- over 50 years old;
- sufficient income to be able to pay for a package holiday and healthy enough to take a holiday;
- interested in travel;
- attracted by direct marketing;
- interested in value-for-money.

Source: adapted from www.saga.co.uk.

- Psychographic segmentation is not so relevant when dealing with businesses and organisations. But even they will have attitudes and methods of operating based on company ethos.

Other ways of segmenting businesses could include by industry, by market or by status, e.g. new customers or old customers.

Profiling

Having achieved segmentation, attention can be turned to profiling. This is the creation of a description or profile of the customer, based on features of the segmentation. An example is shown in Figure 2. Profiling is important for assessing market potential, developing a profile of the main customer types for the product and then predicting potential sales and for targeting customers.

Targeting

The aim of segmentation is to identify the most important groupings and use this to target and tailor marketing activity that is likely to be the most effective on that particular group. A business must decide whether to put resources into targeting consumers, (consumer marketing) or targeting buyers, (trade marketing).

Portfolio practice · **Merry Hill Retail Park**

Today, Merry Hill is one of the region's most successful shopping destinations, attracting over 21 million visits every year, with over 200 stores, 10,000 free parking spaces, offering a wealth of high quality services and facilities. Unlike other comparable sized shopping centres, Merry Hill is located at the heart of a densely populated urban conurbation, and this dramatically affects its customer base. Whilst Merry Hill has great regional appeal, particularly at key sales periods, over 70% of visits to Merry Hill come from within a ten mile radius of the site. A high percentage of them shop weekly or more frequently, using Merry Hill as they would a traditional town centre.

The Merry Hill Retail Park is located in the Midlands between Stourbridge and Dudley. Among its many attractions it lists the following.
- Customer Service Team - over 250 staff to ensure that Merry Hill is kept clean, safe and secure at all times.
- Customer Service Points – a number of information points on the malls, including a Central Information Point. The information point offers Merry Hill, local tourism, public transport information and gift cheques.
- Customer Service Rovers – a team of Customer Service Rovers can be found out and about on the malls to assist with queries. Unlike traditional Customer Service, the Rovers won't be behind a desk, making it easier for them to offer help when required.
- Customer Service Charter Mark – includes a 10 day exchange policy.
- Tourist Information - Merry Hill has a Heart of England Tourist Board registered Tourist Information Centre.
- Travel Shop - to make arrival and departure convenient and pleasant for visitors.

- Services for disabled shoppers - including courtesy wheelchairs and scooters and specific parking spaces for disabled shoppers in all car parks close to Merry Hill mall entrances.

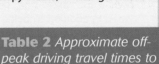

- A Bhs car park, a 5 storey award-winning car park which is well lit and has easy access via a bridge link to Next and TK Maxx as well as Bhs and the Tourist Information Centre.
- Child facilities including kiddy cars, a baby changing suite, buggy and wrist strap hire, parent and child parking spaces and Castle Hof play environment for children.
- Pamper Services including a therapy studio, wedding services and a hair salon.

Source: adapted from www.merryhill.co.uk.

(a) **Identify THREE examples of how Merry Hill meets customer needs.**
(b) **Identify THREE examples of how Merry Hill meets customer wants.**
(c) **Explain, using examples, how the management of Merry Hill could segment customers.**

Table 2 *Approximate off-peak driving travel times to Merry Hill*

Birmingham	30 minutes
Bridgnorth	30 minutes
Kidderminster	30 minutes
Redditch	30 minutes
Solihull	45 minutes
Sutton Coldfield	40 minutes
Walsall	30 minutes
Worcester	40 minutes
Merry Hill is also serviced by buses and trains	

For your chosen product, think about who are your customers.
- Make a list of the different types of customer, including family members, friends, teachers, other buyers and consumers.
- State what you provide and why they are your customers.

Consider situations where you are a customer.
- Make a list of each person or organisation which provides you with a product or service.
- State whether you are a customer, or a customer and consumer.
- Note what you think about the service that you receive. Is it what you want? Does it meet your needs? Could it be improved?

Considering your own needs and wants, identifying which are met and which are not, will help to identify the needs your own customers will be looking for.

Research task

Meeting the assessment criteria

You are required to produce an appropriate marketing mix for a new or existing product or service. Your work must include evidence of the identification of the wants and needs of customers and target markets.

Business example - Early Risers

The marketing mix for a 'wake-up' service, Early Risers, that will call mobile phones at times requested by subscribers as an alternative to using an alarm clock is being developed.

Oftel survey

According to the Oftel Residential Survey, 75 per cent of all adults in the United Kingdom owned or used a mobile phone in May 2003. Twenty one per cent used their mobile as their main method of telephony, with 8 per cent of homes only having a mobile, and no fixed line phone. Ownership of mobile phones varied with age. Nearly 90 per cent of people between the ages of 15 and 34 owned or used a mobile phone in February 2003. This proportion declined with age; less than a quarter of those aged 75 and over owned or used a mobile phone.

Source: adapted from *Social Trends*, Office for National Statistics.

Mark Band 1 *Description of the chosen product/service, basic description of the marketing objectives and the relevant segmentation and target market.*
From research, the basic need of customers was found to be the need to be woken from sleep each morning of the working week. In addition to being woken, potential customers had other wants, such as wake-up calls always being on time and that the calling should repeat until the phone is answered. The objective would be to provide a service that meets these needs and wants. The target market would be people who need to wake up early in the working week, who own mobile phones.

Mark Band 2 *Explanation of why the product/service has been chosen, what the marketing aims and objectives are and steps taken to identify the target market and segmentation.*
A survey was carried out to find the needs and wants of working people. A basic need to be woken on weekdays was found. But other wants, such as:
- calls on time;
- continuous ringing;
- a pleasant voice on the other end;

were identified. It was decided to have a marketing objective of providing this service. The target market would be mobile phone owners who worked in the week. Such people were interested in the service from the survey. Secondary research reports, such as those produced by Oftel, also backed this up. Mobile phone owners were continually seeking innovative uses for their phones, illustrated by the expanding market for new ringtones and the move to phones with built-in cameras.

Mark Band 3 *Comprehensive explanation illustrating depth of knowledge and understanding of the product/service, marketing aims and objectives, target market and segmentation.*
A survey was carried out to find the needs and wants of working people. A basic need to be woken on weekdays was found. But other wants were identified, such as calls being on time, continuous ringing, a pleasant voice on the other end and that it should cost no more than a basic call connection charge. It was decided to set a marketing objective of providing this service. Website research identified the main competitors for this service as O_2, Orange, T-Mobile, Tesco, Virgin and Vodafone.

The target market would be mobile phone owners who worked in the week. Such people were interested in the service from the survey. Secondary research reports, such as those produced by Oftel, also backed this up. But it was decided that not all owners of mobile phones would want this service, using data from the Oftel report. The most likely buyers and the target customers would be:
- males;
- aged 15-34;
- working;
- income in excess of £20,000 per annum;
- living in low-cost accommodation;
- owning a modern 'new generation' mobile phone;
- already subscribing to entertainment services on their mobile phone.

It was also decided that the service would be more successful in areas where ownership of mobile phones was highest, such as cities and large urban areas, rather than rural areas.

Before finalising the marketing mix, phone owners at a local college seen walking round the inside the canteen at lunchtimes were interviewed about the idea. Many thought an alarm clock would be far better. But it was concluded that most students surveyed were not in the target market, and although their opinions were valid, they should not be seen as a reason to deviate from the planned marketing mix.

28 Developing new products

What are new products?

'New products are the lifeblood of a business'. This is a cliché often repeated in business, but there is a lot of truth in this statement.

- Without new products a business will stagnate and be overtaken by competitors that have been developing and introducing new products.
- New products can give a boost and change the image from an old fashioned or slow-moving business to an innovator.
- New products can stimulate income and profit.
- New products can become the focus of activity, giving a sales team a good reason to talk to customers and a reason for customers to listen to the sales team.

A successful new product can rejuvenate a business and its workforce, moving the business forwards and overcoming competitors.

In reality very few genuine new products are ever introduced. There are few examples of a product that is so new that nothing like it ever existed before. Most 'new' products come about through ideas and innovation and are developments or changed versions of something that already exists. A product may be new:

- in the way it is presented, specified or used;
- in the way that it is perceived by customers and consumers;
- to a business or to a particular market.

Products which are totally and radically new however tend to be rare. Such new and original products are usually as a result of a new technological development, which consumers recognise as an advantage over old ways of doing something. Consumers are usually happy to adopt a new product based on new technology if it:

- allows them to do something quicker, easier or cheaper than before;
- allows them to do something they could not do;
- provides access to something they could not previously access.

New products fall into a number of different categories.

Genuine new products that did not exist before. It may be difficult to find examples, because as soon as they hit the market they are very quickly changed, modified and appear in different versions from other businesses. However, at the time of their introduction, it could be argued that products in this category were those shown in Table 1.

There have been many other examples and as breakthroughs take place, there are likely to be more in the future. The one feature that makes this category different is that the development and launch of such products is based entirely on risk. The risks are

Table 1 New products at time of introduction

Product	Reason
Televisions	Before the first television was developed nothing like it existed before. Televisions on sale today are in some way developments from the original concept.
Computers	Before computers analysis and computation was done by hand and brain power.
Digital technology	This is used for recording, photography, broadcasting, communication and other applications. It would have been genuinely new when it was introduced.
Genetically modified crops	Humans have selectively bred plants for centuries. But changing the genetic make-up of a plant and producing a plant that has characteristics deliberately added by a scientist was new.

Table 2 Product improvements

Product	Reason
Camera phones	Cameras and telephones existed before, but combining them into one unit created something new and different and changed the way that people communicate.
On-line ticketing agencies	Used for booking holidays, flights, theatres. The concept of booking agencies already existed. They were taken away from the high street and into the home through the use of the Internet.
Cars and road vehicles	New models are developed to bring improvements on past models by better performance, styling, comfort or safety. Improvements might include such things as new diesel engines and satellite tracking equipment.
Grocery deliveries	This service virtually ceased with the growth of supermarkets. In an attempt to improve their products and support websites, supermarkets have reintroduced home delivery after ordering on-line.
Washing powder	Most brands are re-launched regularly with new ingredients that claim to be an improvement over the old powders that are replaced.
Cat food in foil sachets	Instead of cat food sold in tins, the same brand and food is packed and sold in small, convenient foil sachets. Small sachets reduce the waste that occurs when a cat does not eat the full can.
Apple iPod and MP3 players	These use digital technology in a novel and effective way. It is a portable music player like a Sony Diskman, but stores thousands of tracks on a hard drive.

not only that the product is new, but that there may be no market for such a product, so the market may have to be created.

Product improvements This is the largest category of new products. These are improved or up-dated versions of existing products. It does not take a lot of changing for a business to bring about a small improvement in a product. Some examples are shown in Table 2.

A way of extending the life cycle of a product is to update constantly and bring out new improved versions of what is essentially the same product. This is dealt with later in this section.

New varieties of existing products This is also known as range extension. It is the introduction of additional flavours, colours, sizes of products that are currently in distribution and on sale. Some examples are shown in Table 3.

This approach to new product development is often used by a manufacturer to squeeze out competition, reducing the shelf-space in a shop that is available to competition by filling it with additional varieties of its own products.

Table 3 *New varieties of existing products*

Product	Reason
Emulsion paint	Manufacturers introduce new colours every year or season in an attempt to show consumers that they are up-to-date with current fashions. As far as consumers are concerned the paint remains the same.
Fruit drinks, ready meals and other food products	Manufacturers continuously introduce new flavours and withdraw flavours that do not sell well.
Deodorants	A brand may have a core range to which new fragrances are added every year.
Football replica kits	Details are changed each year and alternative versions are added to generate sales to fans, but the basic items that make up the kit remain the same.
Snack foods	The basic crisp remains the same, but the range of flavours grows. This form of product development can be seen in many food products.

Although not quite the same, this category could also include:
- promotional lines, such as multi-packs or larger sizes with a percentage extra free and products presented in other non-standard formats;
- me-too products, where businesses wait to see how a market develops before they introduce their own version of a product, usually when it is large enough. Examples are common in new or under-developed markets where risks are high. Small businesses often do the pioneering work to create a new market, then a large competitor enters with a similar product.

New uses for existing products Often marketing research will identify a gap in an existing market or a market that is not currently being supplied with a particular product. Sometimes it is the result of 'blue sky' thinking and consumer research that seeks

to identify potential new markets. Some examples are shown in Table 4.

This can be a difficult way to introduce new products. Consumers are naturally conservative in their buying and usage of products. To re-present a product that is recognised and accepted in one area of use, in a new and different area may take a lot of convincing promotion.

Table 4 *New uses for existing products*

Product	Reason
Chocolates	Consumer research identified that chocolates were never eaten after a meal. A marketing team and an advertising agency created a chocolate specifically for eating after a meal. The market was created by promoting the idea that it was sophisticated to eat chocolates after a meal. The market for this type of confectionery is now huge.
Yoghurt	Yoghurt was sold for many years as a dessert. Recently manufacturers have introduced biological yoghurt containing 'healthy bacteria' in small 'singe dose' sizes. These products are marketed as health food supplements. They do not make specific claims, but the promotion suggests that it will improve the general health.
Sport Utility Vehicles	These were originally built for off-road activities. They have become popular for family use. Many brands are now targeted at this market rather than the smaller sporting vehicles market.

The product life cycle

This is an important factor in marketing and product development. It is based on the observation that all products pass through a series of stages from initial concept and development through to the time when they are withdrawn from the market. The main stages of the product life cycle are shown in Figure 1.

Some products, such as those based on fads and fashions, or those based on technologies that are quickly superseded and replaced, will have a relatively short and fast life cycle. They reach maturity

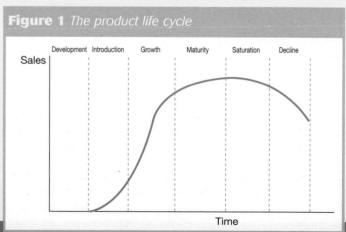

Figure 1 *The product life cycle*

Sales — Development | Introduction | Growth | Maturity | Saturation | Decline — Time

and peak quickly after launch and decline equally quickly. Others will have a long life cycle that extends the maturity stage through continuous marketing activity. This can maintain sales and keep a product profitable and prevent it from declining for many years. Examples of this are the Mars Bar and Coca-Cola. Both of these products receive regular marketing activity and both have enjoyed relatively long life cycles, which show no signs of declining. This illustrates that managing the life cycle of a product is an important skill in marketing.

Product re-launch

A relaunch is a way of taking an existing product, making any changes that are required to bring it up-to-date with the current market or customer expectations, and developing a new marketing plan that will promote it in the marketplace. The changes are likely to include:

- updating its specification, such as adding a 'magic ingredient' that can be used as the centrepiece of a new marketing campaign;
- changes to the design of the packaging, e.g. KitKat changed from paper and foil wrapper to a sealed wrapper;
- repackaging in a new style or format, e.g. Jif to Cif;
- producing new advertising and promotional material.

Re-launching is a relatively low cost way of creating interest around a product. A business may not face the high cost of developing a new product from scratch. It allows existing customers to look at a product in a new way and potential customers a reason to give the product a try.

The relaunch of a product is a useful way of extending the life cycle of a product if it is employed during the maturity-saturation stage, before it slips too far down the decline stage of its lifecycle. It is a technique that can be seen in regular use in highly competitive markets with strong brands, like confectionery, washing powders, magazines and newspapers. A relaunch can also be used if a product fails in a market. In this situation the product usually undergoes a radical change to overcome the reasons for its failure before it is re-launched.

Ansoff's product-market growth matrix

New product development is one of the options in Ansoff's product-market growth matrix. This is a tool that is used by businesses to identify which, of a number of options, a business could adopt to increase its sales. It is based on comparing the relative merits of selling existing products and new products in existing markets and new markets.

Depending on the aims and objectives of the business, and the strategy it wants to adopt, the Ansoff's matrix will suggest one of four options:

- **market penetration**, the safest option, based on selling more to existing customers, or taking sales from competition. It is the selling of existing products into existing markets.
- **market development**, seeking new channels of distribution or selling in different geographic areas, a slightly higher risk to the business. It is the selling of existing products into new markets.
- **product development**, selling new products into the existing market, with all of the risks associated with new products. It is

the selling of new products into existing markets.

- **diversification**, the highest area of risk - almost like starting a new business, based on developing new products for new markets.

Product failure

Badly managed new products can drain a business of resources. It can also create a poor image from which the business struggles to recover and may never overcome. Customers have long memories when products fail or do not live up to their reputation.

Despite the importance of the thousands of new products launched each year, the level of failure is reported to be around 80%-90% or even higher in some markets. This is not surprising. If all the new products launched were to succeed, there would be no room on the shelves in shops and the road would be clogged with new vehicles delivering all of the new products.

Why might a new product be said to have failed?

- It may simply be a product that does not meet the needs of customers and which they do not buy.
- Failure may be relative. It may be that the product has a particularly short life cycle and that launch and swift decline is the nature of that product.
- The failure may be that it just did not achieve the aims and objectives in the marketing plan. If re-launched with a different marketing mix it may achieve some success or at least last longer before it is again deemed to be a failure.
- The marketing policy of some businesses is to introduce many products through the year because it reinforces its image of innovation. It may be satisfied if just a few are successful, provided it makes an overall profit from all products launched.

Reducing the high failure rate

The high failure rate for new products should not be ignored and a business can take steps to reduce the chances of new product failure through the use of a comprehensive marketing research programme:

Internal assessment and audit of the business Before developing a new product a business must analyse itself. It might consider a number of factors.

- The current level of technology, manufacturing and distribution capabilities and capacity. A new product that increases utilisation of plant and equipment may be more attractive than a new product that requires new investment, for example.
- The perception of the business in the market place. Some products may be considered inappropriate by customers no matter how attractive the new market, for example a chemical company making soup.
- The attitude of senior management. For example, the marketing team of a charity may recommend that it becomes more commercial to raise funds. This may conflict with the original ethos of the organisation.

Technical research The business must make sure that the product does what it should do, that it performs as required and that it will not fail technically when used by consumers. In-house testing of a product before it reaches the marketplace can save time, resources and reputations.

Consumer research This can measure and confirm that a

market is worthwhile and to check that consumers actually want the new product proposed.

Customer research This can check that customers will buy a new product and take it into distribution. This usually needs to incorporate consumer research to provide potential customers with evidence that a market for the new product exists.

Product research This involves testing the concept and actual product with consumers to confirm that it meets their needs. If not, the business must identify what changes need to be made to the product.

Market testing This is the piloting of sales in a small, controlled number of distribution outlets or restricting sales to a small geographic area to test the marketing mix before committing resources to an expensive national launch.

Pick two businesses that you are familiar with, that operate in different markets.

- List the main products or product ranges from each business.
- Divide the lists of products into core products that each business has marketed from the start or for more than three years and new products that each business has introduced in the past three years.
- Compare the lists and assess which business has been most active in new product development and introduction. Consider the reasons why.

Research task

Portfolio practice · **Daily Bread**

Sharon Dewell started *Daily Bread* when she left college. *Daily Bread* provides a range of fresh sandwiches for sale, which Sharon makes herself, first-thing every day. She sells the sandwiches by taking them round local offices during the morning in the boot of her car. Customers can buy fresh sandwiches for their lunch directly from her during her visits. She has built up a good reputation and a regular, local customer base. When she started the business, Sharon put a lot of effort into making sure that the bread and fillings were of the highest quality and that they looked good. Customers can also ring her to request bespoke sandwiches at particular times of the day and pre-book their delivery time.

(a) **Explain TWO ways in which Daily Bread has improved the traditional sandwich sales service.**
(b) **Suggest ideas for:**
   (i) **new products;**
   (ii) **product development;**
   (iii) **diversification;**
   by the business.
(c) **Examine the possible risks involved and evaluate whether the business should attempt these.**

Meeting the assessment criteria

For a chosen product or service you must be able to identify and explain the different marketing strategies used by businesses to achieve their marketing objectives and meet the needs of their target markets. This will involve a consideration of the marketing activities used when developing new products of re-launching existing products.

Business example - Jane Haralambos Permanent Cosmetics

Jane Haralambos operated a beauty consultant and service, providing beauty care and advice to clients. After training in London in permanent cosmetic enhancement she changed the focus of the service she provides to permanent cosmetic enhancement. This is a revolutionary beauty treatment used to define eyes, brows, lips and cheeks, for example. It gives a soft, natural finish that imitates applied make-up. The effect is achieved by infusing hypoallergenic pigments into the dermal

layer of the skin where they remain, gradually fading over time. The results can be subtle or dramatic.

Jane offers a variety of other services from her own specialist treatment centre, which is part of a larger health and treatment centre in London. For example, she offers a tattoo removal service and the improvement of skin pigmentation. Jane has attracted a number of clients through word-of-mouth, people visiting the health centre and advertisements in specialist beauty magazines. She also hopes to gain more customers from her new website.

Source: company information, www.jane-permanent-cosmetics.co.uk

Mark Band 1 *Description of the chosen product/service, basic description of the marketing objectives and the relevant segmentation and target market.*

Jane Haralambos offers a revolutionary service to customers. Rather than simply applying make-up every time a person goes out or every day, a permanent, natural looking effect can be gained by treatment from Jane Haralambos Permanent Cosmetics. Other services include tattoo removal and skin pigmentation treatment. Jane changed her existing service to offer a specialist, different and targeted product. Her objective is to establish and then grow the business in the competitive beauty treatment market. Her target market is likely to be females looking for a permanently beautiful look or people looking for improvements in skin colour or tattoo removal.

Mark Band 2 *Explanation of why the product/service has been chosen, what the marketing aims and objectives are and steps taken to identify the target market and segmentation.*

Jane Haralambos's service was to provide beauty treatment such as make-up and beauty care. This is a competitive market with salons, home services and products that can be bought and used themselves by customers. Jane changed her service to offer a new, revolutionary service to customers. Rather than simply applying make-up every time a person goes out or every day, a permanent effect can be gained by treatment from Jane Haralambos Permanent Cosmetics. Other services, which are related, include tattoo removal and skin pigmentation treatment. This service is an improvement on existing beauty treatments. It saves time for people and gives a long lasting and visually appealing effect. Jane's objectives in launching this service would be to gain a market share in a competitive market and then grow the business by offering a specialist yet different product.

Her target market is likely to mainly be females looking for a more permanent look. It will also include males and females looking for improvements in skin colour and texture, plus those looking for tattoo removal. Jane researched the market before setting up. She chose a London base as more people in the capital could be looking for this service compared to, say, a rural location. She therefore stands a better chance of attracting her target market from a larger base of customers. Similar services are offered in the area, advertising in beauty magazines. But customers are attracted by quality products, standards and service. Jane trained with internationally recognised Dawn Cragg in Harley Street, London, which means that she is well qualified.

Mark Band 3 *Comprehensive explanation illustrating depth of knowledge and understanding of the product/service, marketing aims and objectives, target market and segmentation.*

Jane Haralambos's business offers a new, revolutionary service to customers. Beauty treatments are often time consuming. People pay large amounts for such treatment. It also takes up time to regularly apply make-up every time a person goes out or every day. Jane's business replaced her original beauty service. A permanent effect can be gained by treatment from Jane Haralambos Permanent Cosmetics, which specialises in providing permanent eyebrows, eyelines and lip enhancements, for example. Not only is time and money saved compared to non-permanent treatment, but it is more visually appealing. Other services, which are related, include tattoo removal and scar camouflage treatment.

Jane's objectives in launching this service would be to establish a market share in the competitive beauty market and then grow her customers. Offering a specialist product should help Jane's business to compete in the beauty treatment market, faced with the many salons, home services, tattoo parlors and products that can be bought and applied by customers themselves. Offering an additional range of services

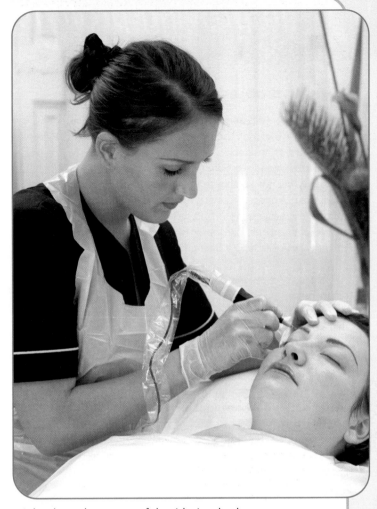

might also reduce some of the risks involved.

Jane carefully researched the market before setting up. Jane chose a London base as more people in the capital could be looking for this service compared to, say, a rural location. She therefore stands a better chance of attracting her target market from a larger base of potential customers. Similar services are offered in the area, advertising in beauty magazines. But customers are attracted by quality products, standards and service. Jane trained with internationally recognised Dawn Cragg at Harley Street in London, which means that she is well qualified. Her target market is likely to fall into a number of categories.

- Females in London looking for permanent eyeliner or lip colouring. This might be important for some clients in the capital, who eat out regularly or carry out functions. It might also appeal to actors or other people in the entertainment industry.
- Ageing men and women who want restore youth to their facial features. The UK has an ageing, yet active population. They have income to spend and may be attracted to such a service.
- People concerned about their appearance and who are looking to improve their skin's texture and colouring.
- Removing tattoos. Studies have suggested that they have a negative impact in interviews and other situations. People who had tattoos when they were younger may also be looking to remove them as they get older.

29 Improving profitability

Aims and objectives

There are many different marketing aims and objectives. Profitability is perhaps the most important for a business. Why? If a business is not profitable it will quickly run out of money to pay for materials, goods to sell or staff and other running costs. Further, it will not be able to build up retained profit for future investment. Profit is necessary for survival. Without profit the costs of the business will need to be paid from elsewhere, such as an overdraft, a bank loan, personal savings or investor's savings. Each of these will have a limit and will need to be repaid at some point.

Profitability is the measure of the level or proportion of profit compared to income from sales. It measures an organisation's ability to generate sales income in excess of the cost of producing that sales income.

Profitability alone is only useful as an indicator to the marketing and financial management teams in a business that the costing and pricing of a product is right. It can sometimes give an artificial indication that the marketing mix is right. But it is the actual profit generated that is important, as this will be real and can be banked or spent as required. The actual profit generated by an organisation will be the level of profitability multiplied by the rate of sales. It is no good having a high level of profitability if the product itself does not sell.

It is the responsibility of the marketing team to make sure that profitability is established, maintained and improved whenever possible.

What is profit?

The simple definition of profit is the excess of income over expenditure. Put even more simply, it is the money left from sales income after deducting the cost of producing the goods or services. Another way of calculating profit is the money added to the cost of goods or services to arrive at the selling price.

Profit can be expressed in absolute terms, such as an amount or a total cash figure, or in percentage terms, as a percentage of sales value or price.

Profit is sometimes referred to as a 'margin', as in 'a profit margin'. This is the same as expressing profit as a proportion of a sales value or price.

Profit is often calculated and measured in two basic ways - gross profit (GP) and net profit (NP). Examples are shown in Figures 1 and 2.

Gross profit

Gross profit is the basic raw measure of profit. It is the total sales value minus the cost of producing the good or providing the service. It does not take into account other overheads and operating costs such as tax, administration, distribution or marketing expenditure.

The gross profit is the money left from sales to cover the costs of marketing the product, operating the business and retaining some money in the business.

Gross profit can be calculated and expressed in two ways, as shown in Figure 1, which shows the gross profit of Alcom Ltd a manufacturer of buckets, and Hardware Stores, Lytham, a retailer.

Figure 1 *Gross profit of Alcom Ltd and Hardware Stores, Lytham*

Total amount

Gross profit = total sales value − production cost of goods

As percentage

$$\text{Gross profit margin} = \frac{\text{gross profit}}{\text{total sales value}} \times 100$$

EXAMPLE
A plastic bucket costs 10p to produce and is sold by Alcom Ltd to Hardware Stores, Lytham, for 50p.

The gross profit for Alcom Ltd

Gross profit = 50p − 10p = 40p per bucket

As a percentage

$$\text{Gross profit margin} = \frac{40p}{50p} \times 100 = 80\%$$

The bucket is sold by Hardware Stores, Lytham, to a consumer for £1.18.

The gross profit for Hardware Stores, Lytham,

Gross profit = 118p − 50p = 68p per bucket.
So, for example if 10,000 buckets were sold, Hardware Stores, Lytham, would make an overall gross profit of £6,800 (68p × 10,000).

As a percentage

$$\text{Gross profit margin} = \frac{68p}{118p} \times 100 = 57.6\%$$

Net profit

This is the money that is left after all costs have been added up and the total cost is deducted from the money that is coming into the business from sales.

Net profit **does** take into account all the expenses or operating costs of running the business. These include overheads and operating costs such as tax, administration, distribution or marketing costs. Net profit is sometimes referred to as **operating profit** or **profit on ordinary activities** for companies.

Net profit can be calculated and expressed in a number of ways, as shown in Figure 2, which shows the net profit of Alcom Ltd a

Figure 2 *Calculating net profit of Alcom Ltd and Hardware Stores, Lytham*

Total amount

Net profit = total sales value - cost of production - overhead costs

or

Net profit = gross profit - overhead costs

As a percentage

$$\text{Net profit margin} = \frac{\text{net profit}}{\text{total sales value}} \times 100$$

EXAMPLE

A plastic bucket costs 10p to produce and is sold by the manufacturer, Alcom Ltd, to a shop, Hardware Stores, Lytham, for 50p, which results in a 40p gross profit. Out of this 40p Alcom Ltd must pay (per bucket):

VAT	= 8.75p
Overheads	= 21.25p
Distribution costs	= 5.0p
Total	= 35p

The net profit for Alcom Ltd

Net profit = 40p - 35p = 5p per bucket.

As a percentage

$$\text{Net profit margin} = \frac{5p}{50p} \times 100 = 10\%$$

The bucket is sold by Hardware Stores, Lytham, to a consumer for £1.18. The plastic bucket costs 50p to buy and is sold to customers for £1.18 which results in a 68p gross profit. Out of this 68p Hardware Stores, Lytham must pay:

VAT	= 17.5p
Running costs	= 21.5p
Staff costs	= 10p
Advertising costs	= 5p
Total	= 54p

The net profit for Hardware Stores, Lytham

Net profit = 68p - 54p = 14p per bucket.
So, for example if 10,000 buckets were sold, Hardware Stores, Lytham would make an overall net profit of £1,400 (14p × 10,000).

As a percentage

$$\text{Net profit margin} = \frac{14p}{118p} \times 100 = 11.9\%$$

manufacturer of buckets, and Hardware Stores, Lytham, a retailer.

Improving profitability

One of the main objectives and responsibilities of the marketing team is to improve profitability. There can be three ways that the marketing team can improve profitability:
- raise prices;
- cut costs;
- change the product mix.

Before any improvement can be measured, the level of current profit needs to be confirmed by benchmarking, so that future levels of profit can be compared. Overall profit can be increased by selling more goods or services, but profitability is a function of the selling price and production cost.

Raising prices

Raising prices may be an option to increase profitability. Once the decision has been made to raise prices it should be done as quickly as possible to avoid losing income by selling at the old price. The only reasons to delay might be to inform customers and possibly to negotiate additional sales at the old price as a promotional incentive.

Market factors, such as competition, consumer expectations or willingness to pay raised prices, need to be investigated and taken into account before the price is actually raised. A rise may make a product uncompetitive and give competitors an advantage. Customers may have reached a limit for the price that they are prepared to pay and may buy a competitor's product as a lower price alternative if prices are raised. It is here that the strength of a brand and the strength of consumer loyalty become important.

Some businesses use **price leadership** as a factor in creating an identity for their brands. This is based on the idea that a most expensive brand is perceived to be the best and most desirable by some consumers. Certain products may have perceived 'price points', where retailers have an idea of where the price should be set for maximum consumer sales. However, retail price points can be moved and the retailer as well as the manufacturer can benefit from the increase in profitability produced by the price rise.

Financially, raising prices will also generate an increase in cash coming into the business so long as sales levels are maintained. Increased levels of cash are attractive to manufacturers, distributors and retailers.

Cutting costs

Cutting costs can be of great benefit to a manufacturer or supplier of the product. Any saving made would be 'invisible' to the distributors and retailers and, therefore, unlikely to be passed on.

Costs that might mostly easily be cut could be the production costs of the product. There are many areas where production costs may be cut to save money and thus increase profitability if the selling price is maintained. These include raw material costs, packaging costs, direct labour rates, machinery costs and other manufacturing costs.

Other than production costs, areas where costs could be cut may include distribution and transport. Also, there may be opportunities in the sales and marketing areas to cut costs that reduce the overheads in the business and thus improve profitability. These could include cutting staff or reducing wages and other employment costs. Care must be taken when considering the reduction of marketing budgets. Marketing expenditure is likely to come directly out of the profit generated by sales. If money is not spent on marketing it can be retained and contribute directly to the total profit that is made. However, cutting marketing expenditure may affect the organisation in other ways.

Profitability is the measure of the level or proportion of profit generated by sales compared to income from sales. On paper a product may appear to have a high level of profitability. But in absolute terms profitability is only useful if sales occur at a rate to generate sufficient income and total profit for the business, as set out in the business plan. Cutting marketing expenditure may result in consumer awareness and sales declining, competition getting ahead and distributors and retailers dropping the product because it is not being supported. It could result in a downward spiral from which sales never recover. Therefore it is no good having a product with high profitability that does not sell.

Changing the product mix

Changing the variables in the product mix can also lead to improvements in profitability. It is usually the responsibility of the marketing team to decide which products should be promoted and which customers should be targeted.

Products Having established the profitability of each product or product group within the current sales mix, the marketing team should be able to identify which product or group of products generate the highest level of profitability. If, overall, unit sales within a range of products remain stable, then selling more products with a higher percentage profit and fewer products with a lower percentage profit will improve the overall profitability of the business. The marketing team can do this through promotion, focusing on the products with the highest profitability at the expense of those with a lower level.

Customers Targeting the most profitable customers is another way of achieving improvement in profitability. Existing customers of a business will already know, buy and use the product. It will require relatively fewer resources, such as sales time and promotional spending, to service this group compared with trying to sell the same products to new customers. New customers are likely to require expensive promotion and incentives to convince them to buy a product. Thus profitability of sales to the new customers will be relatively lower. Similarly, it is likely to be more profitable to sell to local customers than to those in another country as sales, communication and transport costs are likely to be lower. In this situation profitability could be improved by focusing marketing activity on local customers.

The demographic profile of customers is another factor that may affect profitability. Branded goods manufacturers know that it is more profitable to market their products to higher income customers than those with relatively less to spend. Customers with more money are likely to buy higher cost items with a relatively higher level of profitability than consumers who, because they have a lower amount to spend, are forced to pay lower prices for products. The number of consumers is a factor that comes into this equation. A business may take a 'high value/low volume' or a 'low value/high volume' approach. Both can achieve a level of profitability. Which approach to take will be influenced by the overall aims and objectives of the business.

Make contact with the marketing team at a business that you are familiar with or where you have personal contacts. Explain that you are studying Applied Business and learning about profitability. Arrange to meet and interview a member of the marketing team and investigate:
- the main products or service that the business sells;
- how the business measures profitability;
- what targets are set for profitability;
- what are the main strategies used to maintain or improve its profitability;
- what changes have been made to the marketing mix to improve profitability.

This investigation should help increase the work relatedness of your learning.

Alternatively, use an Internet search engine to find news or financial reports on three businesses in different sectors that claim to have improved profitability. Analyse the reports and identify:
- the main products or service that each business sells;
- how each business measures profitability;
- what targets each business sets for profitability;
- the main strategies used by each business to maintain or improve its profitability;
- what changes each business has made to the marketing mix to improve profitability.

Compare your answers looking for common factors and try to explain any differences in approach to improving profitability.

Research task

Portfolio practice · Blacks Leisure Group plc

Blacks Leisure Group plc is a business that sells products to two specialist markets – outdoor wear and board wear. Its Blacks and Millets stores sell outdoor waterproof clothing and equipment for walking, hiking and camping. Its Free Spirit Boardwear stores sell clothing and equipment for skateboarding, surfing and skiboarding.

Table 1 *Gross and net profit, £000*

	2004	2003
Turnover	255,527	244,862
Gross profit	133,634	113,329
Net profit	16,070	13,108

Figure 3

'The mixed weather has held back sales of lightweight summer clothing … This weakness has, however, been more than offset by the very strong performance of outdoor clothing, which once again demonstrates the benefits of the Group's balanced portfolio of products and stores.'

'Millets is positioned as a mid-market, family orientated, value proposition aimed, primarily at the everyday consumer … Blacks is positioned as "The Outdoor Specialist", targeting the serious outdoor consumer … Free Spirit appeals to the young aspirational consumer who is fashion conscious and attracted to the lifestyle of the Boardwear offer.'

'Our most significant marketing initiative in the year was a national advertising campaign for Millets. This comprised regular insertions in the main national press titles … The aim is to attract new customers by emphasising what is different about Millets.'

'In developing new product ranges we have the benefit of our own exclusive brands which include Peter Storm … and Alpine. The Group also has the UK Distribution Rights for O'Neill, which is one of the leading brands in the boardwear market worldwide.'

Source: adapted from Blacks Leisure Group, *Annual Report and Financial Statement*, 2004.

(a) Identify (i) the products offered by Blacks Leisure Group plc and (ii) the target markets.

(b) Calculate the profitability of the business in 2003 and 2004.

(c) Explain the reasons why the profitability may have changed between 2003 and 2004.

Meeting the assessment criteria

For a chosen product or service you must be able to identify and explain the different marketing strategies used by businesses to achieve their marketing objectives and meet the needs of their target markets. This will involve a consideration of the marketing activities used to improve the profitability of the business.

Business example - Greg Northam window cleaning services

Greg Northam is setting up in a local area to provide a window cleaning service. He has estimated the costs and income the service he is offering.

Mark Band 1 *Description of the chosen product/service, basic description of the marketing objectives and the relevant segmentation and target market.*

Greg Northam will offer a window cleaning service to the local area. He has a new business and must make a profit over a period of time to survive. Greg has decided to target larger houses hoping to be profitable. He has estimated the costs and income of cleaning the windows of a three-bedroom semi-detached house with 8 windows. The total cost of providing the service for this type of house is £3.70. Overheads, such as payments on a loan for a van and ladders, buckets and cloths will be taken out of profit generated. Greg will charge £5.00 for the service. So the gross profit per house is £5.00 - £3.70 = £1.30. Profitability is (1.30 ÷ 5.00) = 26% This is low and may not generate sufficient profit to pay overheads and retain any profit. He may have to consider changing prices or costs to make a profit.

Mark Band 2 *Explanation of why the product/service has been chosen, what the marketing aims and objectives are and steps taken to identify the target market and segmentation.*

Greg Northam will offer a window cleaning service to the local area. He has a new business and must make a profit over a period of time to survive. He has found that there are few competitors in the area offering a regular service after talking to potential customers. Larger houses will be targeted. These have more windows to clean. Both of these factors mean that Jeff hopes to stand a greater chance of being profitable.

His costs include labour costs of £3.30 per house and materials costs of 40p. So the total cost for this type of house is £3.70. Gross profit is £1.30. The profitability of a three-bedroom semi-detached house with 8 windows is 26%. This is not sufficient profit. So his marketing objective is to increase profitability. One option is to raise price to these customers to £7.00 and hope his target market will pay this. This will produce a gross profit per house of £7.00 - £3.70 = £3.30. Profitability will then be 3.30 ÷ 5.00 = 66%. An alternative is to reduce costs perhaps using fewer materials. Cutting costs will mean that the total cost per house could fall to £3.00. Gross profit per house will then be £5.00 - £3.00 = £2.00 and profitability will be (2.00 ÷ 5.00) = 40%.

Mark Band 3 *Comprehensive explanation illustrating depth of knowledge and understanding of the product/service, marketing aims and objectives, target market and segmentation.*

Greg Northam will offer a window cleaning service to the local

area. Many new businesses fail within a short period of time. So Greg's main objective is to make a consistent and large enough retained profit to survive over a period of time to survive. Larger houses will be targeted. These have more windows to clean and he hopes to offer a high quality service geared to their needs, including cleaning conservatories and washing driveways. He has found that there are no competitors in the area offering such a unique service after talking to potential customers and looking at the operations of rivals. Both of these factors mean that Greg hopes to stand a greater chance of being profitable.

Initial costings have shown that profitability of a three-bedroom semi-detached house with 8 windows is 26%. This is based on a price of £5 and costs of £3.70, so gross profit is £1.30. This is not sufficient profit. So the marketing objective is to increase profitability without affecting the overall business in a negative way.

The business is considering two options to increase profitability. Option A is to raise the price to customer to £7.00 and hope that the target market will pay this. Option B is to reduce costs. Calculations show that raising price to customers to £7 will produce a gross profit per house of £7.00 - £3.70 = £3.30 and profitability will be 3.30 ÷ 5.00 = 66%. An alternative is to reduce costs. Cutting labour costs and reducing the amount of detergent will mean that the total costs per house will be cut to £3.00. Gross profit per house could then be £5.00 - £3.00 = £2.00 and profitability 2.00 ÷ 5.00 = 40%.

The results show that raising price will give the highest profitability. However, although Greg is offering a rather different service, competitors tend to charge no more than £6 for such houses. A small survey of customers said they would not pay £7 per house. Greg considered option B. He found that it would be relatively easy to cut his costs without reducing quality. He looked at ways in which work could be done more quickly so that his employees would not have to be paid overtime. Greg also looked at offering the same service to all houses. Smaller houses would use fewer materials, although there was a risk because they may not want the other services that Greg was offering and pay the price Greg needed to charge.

On reflection Greg decided that reducing costs would be the more effective option, even though profitability would not be as high as if prices were raised. Greg concluded that it is no use having high profitability if your service does not sell.

30 Improving market share

What is market share?

A business will use different marketing activities depending on the objectives it is aiming to achieve. One of these objectives is 'improving market share'. Market share is often used as an indicator of how well or not a business is doing. But it is not the figure itself that is important, but understanding what the figure means, how it is measured and how it is defined. A better understanding leads to the development and implementation of marketing plans that improve market share.

Market share is the proportion or part of a particular market that is accounted for by an organisation. Imagine the market as a round cake being cut into slices. The size of the slice will indicate the share of the market by a particular business. An example is shown in Figure 1.

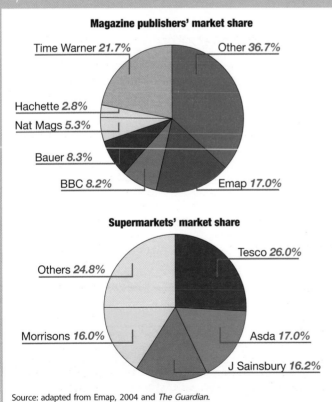

Figure 1 *Market shares of magazine publishers and supermarkets*

Magazine publishers' market share

Time Warner *21.7%*
Other *36.7%*
Hachette *2.8%*
Nat Mags *5.3%*
Bauer *8.3%*
BBC *8.2%*
Emap *17.0%*

Supermarkets' market share

Tesco *26.0%*
Others *24.8%*
Morrisons *16.0%*
Asda *17.0%*
J Sainsbury *16.2%*

Source: adapted from Emap, 2004 and *The Guardian*.

Calculating market share

Market share is usually measured as a percentage of a total market. This can be expressed in different ways. For example a business:
* may claim to have a 25% share of its market;
* say that its sales account for £1 in every £4 spent in that market.

Market share can be calculated from the formula:

Market share % = organisation's sales ÷ total market sales x 100

Market share is likely to be rising or falling according to trends, activity within the market and the general economic situation. So it is important for a business to keep track of the market size and market share on a regular basis. Market size and market share can change rapidly and a business may need tactical marketing plans to protect and maintain its share.

How is the market measured?

A business may be able to measure its own sales based on its own data, such as deliveries. But determining the size of the total market and measuring competitors' sales can be difficult. There are many independent marketing research organisations such as GfK Marketing Services and AC Nielsen that conduct primary research to measure and monitor the size of markets. Government statistical data on production will give total market size in terms of output, which can be compared with export figures and import figures to arrive at a figure for UK consumption. Other organisations like Euromonitor, the *Financial Times* and Mintel measure markets and produce regular reports that are available to purchase or to read in some libraries. Some examples are given in Table 1.

Table 1 *Estimated market sizes, UK*

Market	Size	Date	Source
Cinema box office	£143m	2003	Nielson EDI
Video games	£1,152m	2003	www.elspa.com
Soft drinks	£49.5bn	2003	Key Note
Sports clothing market	£3.25bn	2004	Key Note
Footwear market	£1.5bn	2004	Key Note

What is the size of the market?

Defining the market and what is being measured is important when interpreting, understanding and making claims for market share. The market may be defined and expressed in different ways, the most common being sales volume and sales value.
* **Sales volume.** This is the number of units sold or the number of individual items. For example the milk market could be measured by the number of litres sold or by the number of bottles sold.
* **Sales value.** This is the revenue generated by sales in the market.

Sales value can be measured as retail sales, retail selling price (RSP) or as trade sales, sometimes called manufacturer's selling price (MSP) or 'factory gate' prices. For example, the retail sales value of the market for milk is how much money is produced by sales from shops and home deliveries to consumers. Sales value (MSP) is how much money is generated when producers sell the milk to retailers and the food industry. The value of a market at RSP will always be greater than the value at MSP because of the retail mark-up.

The market itself may be viewed in total or it may be segmented - split into smaller sections.

The total market The total market for milk in the UK will include all types of milk. A supplier could express its market share as a percentage of the total market.

Product type The market can be segmented into basic types of milk that are on retail sale, such as whole milk, semi-skimmed milk, skimmed milk, flavoured or organic milk. Measuring market share of one of these types could give a higher market share depending on the segment and product type.

Distribution The market could be segmented in terms of distribution through supermarkets, independent shops, and doorstep deliveries. A milk supplier that does not sell into supermarkets, but only has doorstep deliveries, could choose to measure its market share against the 'doorstep delivery market', rather than the milk market as a whole.

Geographic segmentation Looking at smaller markets defined by geographic area or region can be another important way of looking at market share. For example, Roys of Wroxham describes itself as 'the largest village store in the world'. In Wroxham itself, a small village in Norfolk, the retail market is dominated by Roys of Wroxham. Within East Anglia, Roys remains an important retail force with stores in Norwich, North Walsham, East Dereham, Thetford, Sudbury and Bury St Edmunds. Outside of East Anglia Roys is virtually unknown, except by people who holiday in Norfolk, and will only hold a relatively small share of the overall retail market in the UK. But in Wroxham, Roys is the market leader.

Statements and claims for market share should not be taken at face value. It is important to investigate and clarify what market is being referred to, how it is defined and measured and how market share is being measured within the market. Table 2 shows an example.

Other ways of measuring a market and market share

Sales volume and sales value are the most common ways to measure markets and market share. But this is not the only way to measure a market or express market share. Other ways include:

- the number of customers;
- the number of visitors;
- the number of shops that stock a firm's products;
- the size of a target market in terms of the number of consumers;
- the share of airtime that is filled by advertising by a particular organisation;
- the share of press coverage of a particular story;
- the best selling books or recordings in the sales charts.

Each of these measures of the market will allow a business to calculate its market share by adding its own figures into the

formula. The aims and objectives of the organisation and how it wants to use market share information will determine how it chooses to measure the market, the units of measurement that are used, what is included and which segment is being measured. For example, Blackpool Pleasure Beach makes no claims for market share based on market value. But its website states that that Pleasure Beach, Blackpool is Britain's top tourist attraction with over 145 rides and attractions. This suggests that management has measured the market in terms of the number of tourist visitors, out of which it is the top attraction, the market leader. What is not clear is how 'tourist' is being defined. Is it all tourists making any visit in England? Tourists who visit seaside towns? Tourists who visit amusement parks? This illustrates why market share figures need to be examined carefully, so their meaning is clear.

Table 2 *Newspaper circulation (weekday)*	
Popular national newspapers	
The Sun	3,095,993
Daily Mirror	1,604,975
Daily Star	728,794
Middle market national newspapers	
The Daily Mail	2,285,137
Daily Express	896,455
Quality national newspapers	
The Daily Telegraph	864,285
The Times	641,661
The Guardian	327,527
The Independent	220,939
Financial Times	132,989
The Herald	79,078
The Scotsman	69,791
Total	10,947,624

Source: adapted from ABC.

The Guardian is published by Guardian Newspapers. Based on these figures, it could be said to have:

- 2.99% of the weekday market for newspapers (327,527 ÷ 10,947,624 × 100);
- 14% of the weekday market for quality newspapers (327,527 ÷ 2,336,270 ×100).

Brand share

This is a particular measure that is used, as the name suggests, to measure the share held by a named brand within a market. It is often used in competitive markets that are segmented by many brands owned by few manufacturers, where different marketing teams may manage different brands owned by the same organisation. A business can add together the brand shares held by each of its brands to arrive at an overall market share. An example of this is the washing powder market, which is dominated in the UK by Procter & Gamble and Unilever, each with a range of different brands that compete with each other.

The importance of market share

All organisations are interested in their 'market share' for a number of reasons.

- It is a good way of judging how well a business is doing compared with its competitors.
- It can help to compare the relative strengths of businesses that operate in that market.
- Market share can reassure management, show strength or dominance to stakeholders or to motivate a team by showing how much the business has to catch up to beat competition.

The same market share figure can be used in different ways depending on its intended audience. For example, a business with a 50% share of retail sales may promote this figure in the trade and to shareholders as an example of how well it is doing. Management may use this same figure to show how poorly it is doing and how much harder the business will have to work to grow to the 75% share that has been set as an objective.

Niche suppliers or larger suppliers with niche products may be satisfied with a small share of a large market. Mass-market suppliers will be looking for a large share or dominance of every market that they supply. These are covered in section 33.

Market share over time

A single measure of market share may be an interesting 'snapshot' at a point in time. But in a dynamic market it is important for a business to keep track of its market share and those of competitors because the market situation could change. A business needs to be up-to-date with the current market situation so that changes to the marketing mix can be made and tactical marketing plans can be implemented.

Measuring market size and market share over time is very important.

Trends It can show trends and highlight problems that may affect a business. The trend data can be reassuring and if it shows that a market has declined it can help explain why sales are lower for a given period. Equally, trend data can show up weaknesses in sales strategy if the market is growing faster than reported sales. For example, the management of a business may be quite pleased that its sales are growing at 10% each year. But it will be less pleased if the market is growing at 20% a year, double its own sales increase.

Prevents misleading figures A one-off figure can hide a slow decline in market share. A business could be losing 0.5% every 3 months. Each time the market share is reviewed management may

Figure 2 *Improving market share*

In 2003 marketing intelligence firm IDC reported that Apple Computers shipped 25% more Macs in the UK in the fourth quarter of 2003 than in the previous year. It was suggested that consumer interest in Apple's iPod portable music player helped to spotlight its Macintosh computer and benefited sales. For the full year, Apple had a 7.5% growth, giving the company a 2.3% market share overall in the UK. Desktop shipments declined 8% but notebook shipments of the PowerBook and iBook grew 40%.

think that the figure is satisfactory as it has only slipped a small amount. It is only by looking over time and making comparisons that large movements in market size and market share can be identified. If the business was declining at 0.5% every 3 months, this is still 2.0% a year. Over a five year period a business my have lost 10% and it may be too late to reverse the trend.

Improving market share

Improving market share is a common business objective. Management that sets the objective of improving market share is being positive and it is a good measure for the success, or not, of its marketing strategy. The variables of the marketing mix can be used and changed as part of the marketing strategy for improving

Figure 3 *Supermarket strategies to increase market share, 1995-2005*

- Wal-Mart entered the UK market by buying Asda in 1999. Its formula is based on low prices and selling non-food products.
- Supermarkets have responded to the increase in the number of people 'eating out' by increasing prepared foods, especially luxury own-brand ready meals. Some supermarkets are developing in-store juice and sushi bars. Sainsbury's has Starbucks coffee outlets in some stores.
- In September 2001, tesco.com announced it was on the verge of profitability. At the start of 2004, Tesco became the biggest online grocer worldwide, with sales of £500m worldwide.
- To challenge the potential threat from home shopping, shopping as an enjoyable leisure activity has been promoted. Asda has in-store chaplains, MP's surgeries, nail-polishing and pizza spinning. It has also hired trained actors to work as store greeters.
- Some supermarkets have introduced 'singles nights', such as Tesco in its city centre Metro stores, to attract single customers.

Source: adapted from www.corporatewatch.org.uk.

market share.

Product The product specification, features and benefits can be changed to provide added value to the customer and attract customers away from competitors. Market segmentation and the introduction of new products can also result in increased market share.

Price Price-cutting is a direct way of attracting customers away from competition, which could result in a short-term gain in market share.

Distribution Setting a target to increase the number of places

that stock a product will increase share of distribution and could result in increased market share if wider distribution leads to an increase in sales overall. Targeting a completely new channel of distribution to stock a product is another way of increasing market share.

Promotion Raising promotional activity and advertising expenditure can increase market share by increasing awareness and increasing demand.

Figures 2 and 3 show methods of improving market share in different markets.

Make contact with the marketing team at a business that you are familiar with or where you have personal contacts. Explain that you are studying Applied Business and learning about market share. Arrange to meet and interview a member of the marketing team and investigate:

- the market in which this business trades;
- how the business measures the market, including any primary research used;
- what units the business uses to measure the size of the market;
- how the business measures its market share;
- where this market share places the business in the market – market leader, in the middle, or only a small share;
- whether this share has changed and if so why;
- what has happened to make the market share change;
- what targets are set for improving market share;
- how the marketing mix is changed to help improve market share.

In addition to learning about improving market share, this investigation should help increase the work relatedness of your learning.

Alternatively, use reports in the business press or on

Internet websites to find examples of three different businesses, each trading in a different market and claiming market share. Analyse what you find and identify:

- the market in which this business trades;
- how the business measures the market, including any source of primary research used;
- what units the business uses to measure the size of the market;
- how the business measures its market share;
- where this market share places the business in the market – market leader, in the middle, or only a small share;
- any targets that have been set for improving market share;
- how the marketing mix has changed to help improve market share.

Compare your answers, looking for common factors and try to explain any differences in approach to improving market share.

Research task

Portfolio practice · **The UK broadband market**

On 7 April 2005 *Computing Magazine* reported data from a survey conducted by Forrester Research. It showed that UK households with broadband access had grown from 2.7million in 2003, to 5.9million in 2005, and was forecast to reach 11.4million by 2010 as in Figure 4.

(a) How is UK broadband market measured in this research?

(b) Which broadband provider is the market leader?

(c) Examine how the broadband providers might use their marketing mix to try to increase their market share.

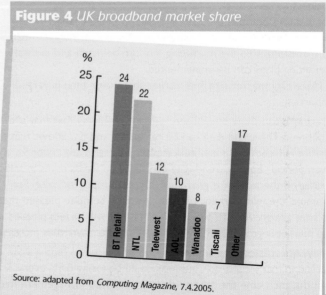

Figure 4 *UK broadband market share*

%

Provider	%
BT Retail	24
NTL	22
Telewest	12
AOL	10
Wanadoo	8
Tiscali	7
Other	17

Source: adapted from *Computing Magazine*, 7.4.2005.

Meeting the assessment criteria

For a chosen product or service you must be able to identify and explain the different marketing strategies used by businesses to achieve their marketing objectives and meet the needs of their target markets. This will involve a consideration of the marketing activities used to improve the market share of the business.

Business example - BlancDent

A new toothpaste is being launched called BlancDent. This toothpaste will aim to clean and whiten teeth at the same time. There is a certain amount of competition that already exists in this market from large companies with major brands. So it will be important to target an appropriate market in order to achieve market share.

Mark Band 1 *Description of the chosen product/service, basic description of the marketing objectives and the relevant segmentation and target market.*

The product launched by the business is BlancDent, a whitening toothpaste to be sold in the Republic of Ireland. The Irish market for toothpaste is worth an estimated €29 million. The main companies supplying this market are Colgate-Palmolive and GlaxoSmithKline. Colgate has 50.4% of the market. At present BlancDent could only gain 1.0% of the overall toothpaste market. But specialist whitening toothpaste holds about 10% of the overall market. So BlancDent could claim to hold 10% of the market for specialist whitening toothpaste, its target market. An objective is to double BlancDent's share of the overall market for toothpaste within the next year.

Mark Band 2 *Explanation of why the product/service has been chosen, what the marketing aims and objectives are and steps taken to identify the target market and segmentation.*

The product launched by the business is BlancDent, a whitening toothpaste to be sold in the Republic of Ireland. The overall market for toothpaste in Ireland is large at €29 million and Ireland's oral care market is valued at €48.8 million. It is also growing at 4% each year. Studies and figures from the industry have shown that growth is partly due to consumers trading-up to higher priced premium and specialist toothpaste such as whitening toothpaste. This is therefore the target market for the product. Competition is very strong between the two main suppliers, Colgate-Palmolive and GlaxoSmithKline. Colgate has 50.4% of the market. This has stimulated the growth in the whitening toothpaste segment. At present BlancDent could only gain 1.0% of the overall market, but 10% of the whitening market. Management's main objective is to achieve a 2% market share of the overall market and sales of €580,000 within a year. Growth in sales by the target market supports the choice of BlancDent whitening toothpaste as a dynamic product within a growing segment that is part of a large and well supported market.

Mark Band 3 *Comprehensive explanation illustrating depth of knowledge and understanding of the product/service, marketing aims and objectives, target market and segmentation.*

The product launched by the business is BlancDent a whitening toothpaste to be sold in the Republic of Ireland. The oral care market is worth €48.8 million and the toothpaste market an estimated €29 million. It is also growing at 4%. Studies and industry figures have shown that consumers have increasingly been 'trading-up' and buying specialist products, a major factor in increasing sales. The growth in the market for specialist whitening toothpaste suggests this to be a suitable target market. Market research conducted by BlancDent also shows that these consumers like the product and once they try it, they would continue to buy and use it.

Two large multinational companies dominate the market, Palmolive and GlaxoSmithKline. Colgate has 50.4% of the market and it has proved difficult for BlancDent to achieve distribution in the supermarkets where Colgate-Palmolive and GlaxoSmithKline are particularly strong. Both the leading suppliers have their own whitening toothpaste product, which competes directly with BlancDent.

At present BlancDent could only gain 1.0% of the overall market, but 10% of the whitening market. A major objective is therefore to achieve a 2% market share of the toothpaste market and sales of €580,000. To meet this objective of doubling market share in a year, BlancDent has produced marketing plans, which include:

- product – the introduction of a smaller 'trial' size;
- price – the smaller 'trial' size will be priced low enough to attract consumers, whilst still allowing retail customers to make sufficient return to stock the product;
- place – plans to boost distribution by targeting the sales force at independent pharmacies;
- promotion – plans for a new TV campaign and the use of outdoor media (posters) to promote the BlancDent brand.

The management of BlancDent plans to buy continuous retail audit data to monitor changes in the market for toothpaste and to keep track of the BlancDent market share to see if the marketing plans meet the objective of doubling market share.

Source: adapted from www.checkout.ie/marketprofile.asp?ID=140

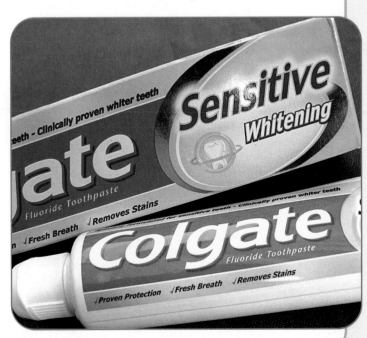

31 Diversification

What is diversification?

Diversification is where a business is prepared to change and move from its core market and enter totally new markets, with new products. The main objective of diversification is usually to expand the business in new and different markets without risking its core business. There are many examples of diversification in business.

Cafés that change to Internet cafés Here the core business has been based on selling food and drink. This market is crowded and sales are limited by the price of food available and the appetite of customers. Café businesses have diversified by moving into the communications market, providing Internet access for customers. The businesses are using established premises and services and adding a potential business for new customers who want to use the Internet. Internet access is charged by the length of time it is used. This produces sales in addition to income of food and drink.

Petrol stations that start selling groceries Here the core business is selling fuel and other goods associated with motor vehicles. Petrol stations have diversified into the retail food market with the addition of grocery products for sale. Businesses use their premises that are already paid for by sales of fuel to offer a new range of products to customers. Consumers who buy petrol may also buy grocery products rather than make another trip to a food shop. The reverse of this has also happened. Some food supermarkets have diversified into selling petrol from the same site as the food store.

Diversification in food supermarkets As food supermarkets groups grow and become increasingly competitive, they have used diversification to add to the portfolio of products in different markets that can be purchased under the name of the supermarket. Consumers can buy products from different markets under the same brand name under the same roof. Examples of this diversification has seen food supermarkets develop products for a range of different markets including clothing, pharmacy, dry cleaning, photo processing, banking, insurance and post office services. An example is shown in Figure 1.

The importance of a strong brand name

When diversifying, it helps a business to have a strong brand name that is recognised by consumers for:
- the image it projects;
- the generic qualities associated with its products and services.
It could be more difficult if the brand is linked exclusively to one product or market.

A good example of a brand that crosses markets and has enabled the business to diversify is Virgin. Originally a single independent music shop, then a music label and multiple retailer, Virgin has diversified over the years and brought new products bearing the Virgin name to many different markets, as shown in Figure 2. The Virgin business has kept music and entertainment at its core. But it has moved from market to market seeking potential for growth and development. Part of its success has been that it is willing to pull out of a market if it fails to meet its objectives and find another market which may be more successful.

There are other examples of how a strong brand name has enabled a business to diversify successfully, including Tesco, Sainsbury's and Nike.

Figure 1 Asda's George range

In 2004 it was reported that Britain's biggest clothing retailer was the UK supermarket Asda, owned by US firm Wal-Mart. The figures from retail market researcher Taylor Nelson Sofres underlined the growing power of supermarkets. For the 12 weeks to July 25, Asda raised its market share from 7.3% to 9.4%, compared with the same period last year. Asda's success has come on the back of its George range launched in 1990. The brand has five 'standalone' George stores in the UK. George at Asda is also sold in Wal-Mart stores in the US and Germany, helping to give it annual sales of more than £1bn.

Source: adapted from *The Guardian*, 23.8.2004.

Figure 2 Virgin diversification

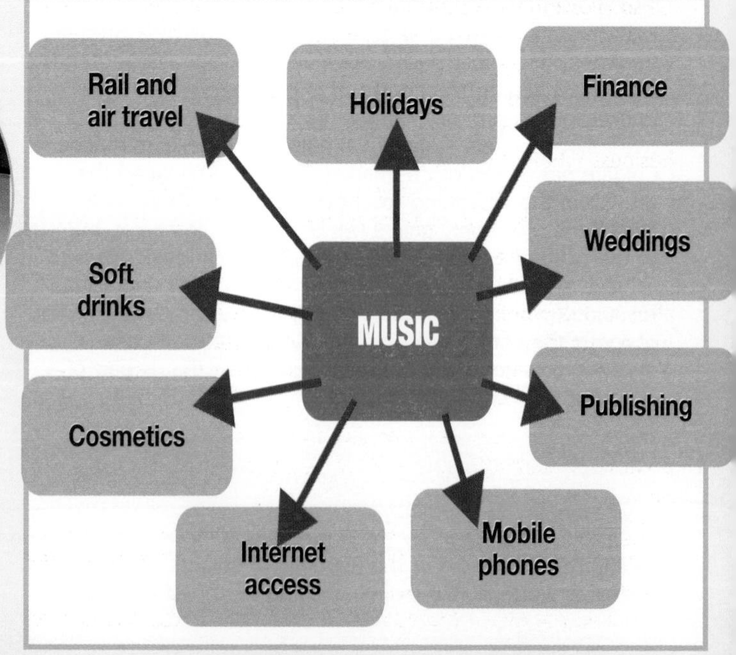

Rail and air travel — Holidays — Finance — Weddings — Soft drinks — MUSIC — Publishing — Cosmetics — Internet access — Mobile phones

Reasons for diversification

There is a number of reasons why diversification is a strategy that is attractive to businesses.

Not putting all your eggs in one basket A business can spread its risks across different markets. If one fails, the other markets in which it operates will hopefully protect the business from collapse. It reduces dependence on one product and one market.

Potentially high returns There may be large markets which offer huge opportunities and returns. It is attractive to expand the business by moving into these large potential markets.

Failure will not threaten the core business directly If sufficient resources are available, a business may be in a position to take a risk and try new products in new markets because failure will not affect its core business.

A business can use its skills and expertise in one market and apply them to another market If a business has been successful and has developed a model for success, this could be applied to another market.

It can give a new focus and direction to a business If a business has become stale and complacent, the challenge of entering a new market with a new product, may reinvigorate a business. It can also demonstrate to stakeholders that it is a business that has firm future plans and objectives.

It makes good use of resources by utilising them for new developments A business with an existing production facility or distribution network could use the strengths of these resources and maximise utilisation by making products for different markets or distributing new products to different markets.

Risks involved in diversification

Businesses need to be wary when pursuing diversification as an objective for a number of reasons.

- Entering the unknown is always risky.
- Diversification will require increased investment and resources. It can be expensive to develop new products and distribution systems for diversification.
- There is a risk that the business may find that new markets and new products do not operate in the same way as its core business where it has expertise.
- A business can lose sight of what is happening to its core business because it concentrates too much on diversification. This often occurs because the business is complacent about its core business and forgets that customers need to be looked after and competitors need to be monitored all the time to make sure that the core business is protected.
- It may become a drain on resources if the business does not set clear objectives for the point at which it will pull out of the new market or halt the diversification if it fails. There is little point in throwing good money away, just to try to save face and protect failed products.
- Failure creates a bad reputation for investors and consumers. Customers and the industry will be aware of diversification that a business is making. This will be watched carefully and examined critically if the business fails. There is also the danger

that the business may get a reputation for reckless diversification and failure. This could harm the core business, its reputation and its relationship with customers.

It may be possible to minimise these risks by:

- researching new markets before new products are launched;
- researching the needs of customers before new products are launched;
- test marketing products before they are launched;
- careful consideration of funds that are allocated;
- careful consideration of the effects of diversification and careful planning of its operation;
- contingency plans in case the diversification fails.

Diversification and growth

Diversification is one of the options in Ansoff's product-market growth matrix, covered in section 28. This is a tool that is used by businesses to identify which, of a number of options, a business could adopt to increase its sales. It is based on comparing the relative merits of selling existing products and new products in existing markets and new markets.

Depending on the aims and objectives of the business, and the strategy it wants to adopt, Ansoff's matrix will suggest one of four options.

Market penetration This the safest option, based on selling more to existing customers or taking sales from competition. It is the selling of existing products into existing markets.

Market development This is seeking new channels of distribution or selling in different geographic areas, a slightly higher risk to the business. It is the selling of existing products into new markets.

Product development This is selling new products into the existing markets, with all of the risks associated with new products. It is the selling of new products into existing markets.

Diversification This is the highest area of risk. It is almost like starting a new business, based on developing new products for new markets.

Visit a local garden centre.

- Note the time of the year and the market it appears to be trading in.
- List the main product groups that it sells and identify what would be considered to be its core business. You can do this by comparing the space devoted to different product groups.
- Identify any examples of diversification from its core business.
- Make contact with a senior member of the management team at the garden centre. Explain that you are studying Applied Business and learning about diversification. Interview the manager to investigate how its business changes each season and identify any diversification that occurs.

Research task

Portfolio practice · Milk Round, Wakefield

Geoff Coleman delivers milk door-to-door in a defined geographic area of roads and residential areas within Wakefield from a purpose-built milk delivery vehicle. Although Geoff is a self-employed sole trader, the business is a franchise in that it bears the brand name of a dairy, which supplies the milk and provides marketing support. The core market of the business is the supply and delivery of milk to consumer's homes. Although the supply of milk and branding is from the dairy franchise, Geoff is allowed to sell and market any other products that he feels are appropriate.

(a) Given this business:
   (i) identify THREE realistic ways that Geoff could diversify;
   (ii) suggest reasons why the business might diversify.
(b) Examine how Geoff could limit the risk of any diversification.

Meeting the assessment criteria

For a chosen product or service you must be able to identify and explain the different marketing strategies used by businesses to achieve their marketing objectives and meet the needs of their target markets. This will involve a consideration of the marketing activities used to achieve diversification.

Business example - Sports and Stars Bar

Café Life owns a number of number of cafés in the Tyne and Wear area of the North East. It had become aware in newspaper articles of two increasing trends in the area.
• People like to eat out and watch sports at the same time.
• There was an increase in the number of women parties and groups going out in the town areas.
It faced a considerable amount of competition in these areas from a variety of restaurants, bars and cafés. Its business plan identified that it needs to move into new areas to expand. It has decided to open a new establishment, The Sports and Stars Bar. The bar will be circular, with screens around the walls so customers can watch and eat. There will also be theme nights including, sports and fashion events and key episodes of 'soaps'.

Source: adapted from company information.

Mark Band 1 *Description of the chosen product/service, basic description of the marketing objectives and the relevant segmentation and target market.*
Café Life's core service is offering food and drinks for sale. To expand it needs to find new ways to meet customers' needs, given the strong competition it faces. So it has decided to diversify its core operation into the entertainment market. Customers can eat and view at the same time. Its main target markets will be sports fans, women's parties and television fans.

Mark Band 2 *Explanation of why the product/service has been chosen, what the marketing aims and objectives are and steps taken to identify the target market and segmentation.*
Café Life's core service is offering food and drinks for sale. The market was chosen because of the nightlife in cities like Newcastle and the culture of people 'going' out. There is also a large concentration of population. To expand it needs to find new ways to meet customers' needs, given the strong competition it faces. So it has decided to diversify its core operation into the entertainment market, so customers can eat and view at the same time. This market has been chosen because of the growing trends identified in newspapers and television about women's 'nights out' and also people going to the pub for a meal to watch football. A survey carried out by the business also confirmed this. The main target markets will be therefore be sports fans, women's parties and television fans.

Mark Band 3 *Comprehensive explanation illustrating depth of knowledge and understanding of the product/service, marketing aims and objectives, target market and segmentation.*
Café Life's core service is offering food and drinks for sale. The market was chosen because of the nightlife in cities like Newcastle and the culture of people 'going' out. There is also a large concentration of population. It faces a large amount of competition in the area. There is a variety of restaurants, cafés, pubs and other eating establishments. And there are also cinemas and theatres. But perhaps the combination of the two might give the business a unique selling point to customers. So to expand it needs to find new ways to meet these customer needs. The new Sports and Stars Bar is a diversification from its core market of food and drink sales into the entertainment market. Customers can eat and view at the same time. This market has been chosen because of the growing trends identified in newspapers and television about women's 'nights out' and also people going to the pub for a meal to watch football, confirmed by its own survey results. The main target markets have been identified for a number of reasons.
• Sports fans often like to watch the build up to the event. They may stay in the café for a long time both before and after a match, for example. So potentially earnings could be high.
• Women's parties are likely to have many customers at once, again increasing revenue.
• Television fans may want to eat out but not miss their favourite soap or other programme. They could record it for later, but there may be an incentive to watch with a group of friends. Again, many people may visit at once and may 'make a night of it'.

Brands

A brand is a set of criteria, features, specifications, attributes or values that:

- identify a product or product group; and
- differentiate it from competitors.

It is what makes the product different and identifiable in the eyes of customers. Examples might be the product name, design, term or any other feature of the product. The term 'brand' can also be applied to a trademark or logo that is used to identify a business.

A brand is a valuable commodity that reflects the perception that customers have about a business and its products. It can have a monetary value which represents its worth to the business and its stakeholders.

A brand can change a lower value product into something for which customers are prepared to pay a higher price. Also, a brand may become so strong that customers refuse to buy alternative products. Businesses, therefore, go to great lengths and great cost to create, maintain and protect the brand.

Brand image

Branding is about the creation and maintenance of an image that appeals to groups of customers. For example, petrol is a product which is technically similar wherever it is bought. However, some drivers will only buy Esso or BP petrol. Why, given that a car will work with petrol supplied by any company? Branding is likely to play a part in the decision of the customer. This situation can be analysed using the marketing mix, as in Table 1.

These variables will contribute to the images associated with different petrol suppliers. It is these images that customers relate to and will influence their choice of petrol. Psychologically, the choice of one brand of petrol rather than another will be affected by brand values and the image associated with a brand.

It is psychology and customer perception that help to explain the strength of branding in markets such as leisure clothing. Consider t-shirts made by different businesses. They may all be made from quality cotton, but the image associated with each t-shirt may be different. Figure 1 shows the images sometimes associated with different brands.

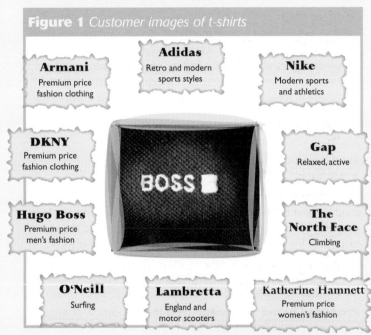

Figure 1 *Customer images of t-shirts*

Armani Premium price fashion clothing

Adidas Retro and modern sports styles

Nike Modern sports and athletics

DKNY Premium price fashion clothing

Gap Relaxed, active

BOSS

Hugo Boss Premium price men's fashion

The North Face Climbing

O'Neill Surfing

Lambretta England and motor scooters

Katherine Hamnett Premium price women's fashion

Table 1 *Branding of petrol using the marketing mix*

Product Petrol is basically the same raw material, but each business will have product features that appeal to different drivers.
- Petrol types – premium unleaded or superunleaded.
- Filling stations – style, layout of buildings, goods sold, lighting, signage, corporate colours.

Price The retail price of petrol is similar as most of the price is accounted for by tax and international oil markets set the raw material cost. Within the retail price there is some room for manoeuvre for businesses.
- Some try to be the cheapest in an area.
- Some maintain an image of 'quality' by being a little more expensive.

Place The location of a filling station will affect driver choice of which petrol to buy. Stations may be sited:
- on main roads;
- in housing estates;
- next to supermarkets;
- in out-of-town shopping centres;
- near to motorways.

Promotion Petrol companies do not want price wars. So they often use non-price competition in the form of promotion. This can include:
- sponsorship and advertising of motor sports and high performance of cars using their petrol;
- being associated with environmental issues to attract customers who share these values.

Brand awareness

Having or creating high brand awareness is an important objective in most marketing strategies. It is a key marketing objective, a target and a very important measure in marketing. High brand awareness means that an organisation or its products are recognised in the market. It is a strength that can be used to promote associated products with the same brand name. This will hopefully lead to high sales when the target market is ready to purchase.

A business may have the best technically performing product in the world. But if consumers are not aware of the brand, then they will not buy it given the many alternatives that are available. Brand awareness is the measure of what proportion of customers have heard of a brand or are conscious of its existence. It is created by a marketing team through promotion and application of the marketing mix.

Brand awareness is usually measured as a percentage of a given market, based on marketing research designed to measure awareness. A brand may have a high or low brand awareness. Decisions can then be made as to whether the level of brand awareness is acceptable or needs to be increased, as a marketing objective.

There are two ways of measuring and reporting brand awareness:
* un-prompted brand awareness;
* prompted brand awareness.

Un-prompted brand awareness This is the proportion of people in the target market that remember a brand without being given any clues. An example of measuring un-prompted brand awareness from market research in the paint industry is shown in Figure 2. Un-prompted brand awareness figures are often lower than expected as few people remember all the brand names of all the products that they buy or use.

Prompted brand awareness This is the proportion of people in the target market that say that they have heard of a brand when the name is mentioned. An example of measuring prompted brand awareness from market research in the paint industry is shown in Figure 2. Prompted brand awareness figures are usually high relative to un-prompted awareness figures, as people will often reply 'yes' to questions such as 'Have you heard of…?' because they do not want to look foolish for not having heard of the brand.

Despite this reservation prompted figures are considered realistic. This is because consumers are usually presented with a choice of brands when shopping and are likely to respond positively, i.e. buy a brand they have heard of and like rather than one they know little or nothing about.

The need to maintain brand awareness

Coca-Cola has one of the strongest brand names in the world. It is certainly one of the strongest brands in the beverages market. Yet it continues to spend many millions of pounds each year promoting its brand. Why? Coca-Cola recognises the strength of its brand and that it needs to be maintained and protected to ensure that in future it will generate sales and profits for the business. A strong brand name will help sell the current range of

Figure 2 *Un-promoted and promoted brand awareness for paint*

Un-prompted

EXAMPLE
'Please give me the name of a manufacturer of paint that you have heard of.'

RESPONSE
Crown 35%
Dulux 35%
Retailer brands 20%
Other makes 9%
Don't know any 1%

BRAND AWARENESS
High for two brands in particular

Prompted

EXAMPLE
'Have you heard of Dulux paint?'

RESPONSE
Yes 98%   No 2%

BRAND AWARENESS
High for Dulux

products and the reputation of the brand name will help when introducing new products.

The marketing world has a history of famous brand names that were strong in the past, but for a variety of reasons are virtually unknown today. Ratners, for example, was the leading chain of high street jewellery shops in Britain in the 1970s and 1980s. It enjoyed high brand awareness and had a brand image based on low prices and good value products. This led to mass-market appeal. A negative remark, made in 1991 by the owner of the Ratners chain about the quality of its goods, changed its image overnight. Its customers no longer wanted to be associated with the brand and its image collapsed, followed soon after by the business itself.

Brands can be 're-made' by changing their image and associations. For many years Lucozade, a fizzy drink, was bought as an aid to recovery from illness. Its brand image was based on this and as a consequence sales opportunities were limited. Today, Lucozade is marketed as a sports drink. It has an image associated with providing energy and high performance for people engaged in sporting activities. This change has been brought about through the creative use of the marketing mix.

Other reasons for increasing brand awareness

In addition to the reasons already given, other reasons for wanting a strong brand and high brand awareness include the following.

Competition Customer perceptions and understanding of one brand compared to another is an important factor in competitive markets. It can be the reason why consumers choose to buy one product rather than another that may be similar. The more competitive the market, the more important it is for organisations to establish a strong image for their product. There are many examples of this situation, including the washing powder market, pet foods and chocolate bars.

Segmentation Some organisations use the brand name to compete through segmentation. This is the dividing up of a market into groups or segments and the exploitation of gaps in a market as explained in section 33. The key is to develop a product for every segment or gap to keep out competition. This can be done effectively by using a strong brand name in each segment. Good examples of this approach can be seen in the retail industry where retailers use their own brand for segmentation. Baked beans in supermarkets is an example, as shown in Table 2.

Table 2 *Ways of segmenting the baked beans market*	
Manufacturers' brands	Heinz, HP,
Own brands	Tesco, Sainsbury, Morrisons
Own brand segmentation	
	Premium priced beans
	Value beans
	Organic beans
	Slimmers' beans

Launching new products It is easier to launch a new product with a brand name that customers and consumers have already heard of. If a new product can be associated with a brand that already has a strong name and reputation this can reduce the need to promote and explain the image and strengths of a product. A good example of this is the Sony brand name that can be applied to many new products. The high awareness and good reputation of the Sony brand means that customers who have a positive image of one Sony product are likely to try other Sony products when they are new to the market.

Entering new markets Trying to enter a new market with an unknown brand name is very difficult. Customers will have no reference points upon which to base their decision to buy. Faced with a choice between a familiar brand name and a brand that has never been heard of, most will buy the name they know, unless there is a strong reason to switch, such as low price. But any change in brand carries a risk that the new brand may not be as good as the familiar brand. Rather than take the risk, the familiar brand is the safe option. However, if a brand name is so strong and has such high awareness that it is known beyond its original market, then it can be used to help a business enter a new market. A good example of this is the Virgin brand name. Virgin has been applied to many different products in diverse markets, including music, rail and air travel and finance. The Virgin brand values are based on an image created and maintained by entrepreneur Richard Branson.

Investigate the brands which exist in the confectionery market by looking in a local store or supermarket.
- Which brands exist?
- Which companies produce these brands?
- What are likely to be the aims of the businesses in branding products?

Use a questionnaire to find out the level of brand awareness amongst people you know.

Research task

Portfolio practice · Dyson DC15 'The Ball'

In 2005 James Dyson, the inventor of the famous vacuum cleaner without a bag, combined this with another of his inventions. He had also invented 'The Ballbarrow', a wheelbarrow with a ball at the front to make steering easy. These two creations provided the inspiration for the launch in the latest in the line of innovative branded products.

The DC15 known as 'The Ball' went on sale in March 2005. It is a Dyson vacuum cleaner with a single large nylon ball at the front instead of wheels. It is designed to make steering easy, 'at the flick of a wrist', rather than the pushing and pulling of other vacuum cleaners.

It sells for around £320-£350, a relatively high price. But the business argues that there is more technology involved and that cleaning will be 30% quicker. James Dyson suggested that companies would try to produce their own versions of the 'The Ball' but would find it difficult because the product had 182 patents preventing the copying of designs.

The Dyson vacuum cleaner had become the market leader in the UK by 1995. By 2005 the business had 17.3% of the UK market by volume and 40% by value. In 2004, however, a Consumers' Association report suggested that the Dyson cleaner was less reliable than other branded products sold by Hoover, Panasonic and Electrolux. The business had also been criticised two years earlier for moving production to Malaysia, a low cost production area, making 500 staff redundant.

Source: adapted from *The Daily Mail*, 15.3.2005.

(a) Identify aspects of branding mentioned in the article.

(b) Explain how any of the variables in the marketing mix may have been affected by branding.

(c) Identify reasons why Dyson products need high brand awareness.

(d) Examine why consumer attitude to the Dyson brand is important.

(e) Discuss the importance of brands and branding in the market for electrical household goods.

Meeting the assessment criteria

For a chosen product or service you must be able to identify and explain the different marketing strategies used by businesses to achieve their marketing objectives and meet the needs of their target markets. This will involve a consideration of the activities used to achieve brand awareness.

Business example - Nestlé's KitKat

Nestlé is a multinational company that manufactures a range of products. These include breakfast cereals, ice cream, beverages, baby products and chocolate and confectionery. It has many branded products. These include the company name, Nestlé. But it also has branded products in the chocolate range such as Crunch, Smarties and KitKat.

Source: adapted from www.Nestle.com and www.confectionerynews.com.

Mark Band 1 *Description of the chosen product/service, basic description of the marketing objectives and the relevant segmentation and target market.*
The KitKat chocolate and wafer bar is manufactured by Nestlé. It is aimed at customers in confectionery markets. KitKat is one of the UK's best selling confectionery brands, with a very high brand awareness. The KitKat brand has been used since 1937. Over the years it has established a good reputation and an excellent brand image. Nestlé owns many famous brand names, but KitKat is likely to be one of the most famous, with the high level of brand awareness. One of Nestlé's marketing objectives is likely to be to maintain the position of KitKat in the highly competitive confectionery market. To do this it launches different versions for different market segments – people with different tastes. Each carries the Nestlé and KitKat brand names.

Mark Band 2 *Explanation of why the product/service has been chosen, what the marketing aims and objectives are and steps taken to identify the target market and segmentation.*
The UK has one of the largest confectionary markets in the world. According to a Euromonitor report the UK market

amounted to over £10 million per annum in the early 21st century. KitKat is one of the UK's best selling confectionery brands, with a well known and established brand name since 1937. There are many competitors in the confectionery market. Nestlés objective will be to maintain the market position of KitKat. The KitKat brand keeps competition at bay and the market interested by high levels of promotion and a continuous programme of new product introductions. The brand is advertised regularly on television, on posters and in other media, which help to maintain the high level of brand awareness. The Nestlé and KitKat brands are used to launch new products. Recent introductions have been flavoured KitKat such as plain chocolate, mint and orange. 2004 saw the launch of various KitKat limited editions, such as lemon & yoghurt, luscious lime, KitKat white (covered in white chocolate), KitKat dark (dark chocolate) and a Christmas Pudding flavour for Christmas. Each of these will be aimed at a different market segment. Each segment will have customers with particular tastes.

Mark Band 3 *Comprehensive explanation illustrating depth of knowledge and understanding of the product/service, marketing aims and objectives, target market and segmentation.*
The UK market for confectionery products has been estimated to be one of the largest in the world. In the early 21st century Euromonitor estimated that over £5.5 billion per annum was spent on confectionery. Other research suggests that each person eats around 14kg of confectionery per year. In this large market Nestlé's KitKat has become a well know established brand since its introduction in 1937. Brand awareness is high. However, competition from manufacturers such as Mars and Cadbury means that Nestlé's objective will be to ensure the strength of its brand is maintained. This will give it a competitive advantage over its rivals. Over the years the Nestlé and KitKat brand names have been used in a number of ways.

- Segmentation. KitKat is available in a range of sizes and packaging formats aimed at different segments of the market. Each segment is likely to have different tastes. The business has also launched limited editions such as lemon & yoghurt, luscious lime, KitKat white (covered in white chocolate), KitKat dark (dark chocolate) and a Christmas pudding flavour for Christmas.
- To launch new products. KitKat Chunky was launched in 1999, a large, single-finger version of the familiar chocolate and wafer finger bar. KitKat Low-Carb was launched in July 2004. It is the result of years of research and development. It meets the needs of people with a low carbohydrate lifestyle whilst keeping the look, taste, and reputation for quality associated with the classic KitKat product.
- To enter new markets. Nestlé launched KitKat Kubes, bite sized chunks packed loose in a bag. There is also a KitKat Easter egg for this seasonal market.

The KitKat website claims that there are at least 23 basic pack formats for KitKat. This demonstrates how Nestlé has the marketing objective to use the strength of the KitKat brand name to maintain its position at the top of the UK confectionery market. Nestlé aims to have a product for all the important segments and gaps in the market and to expand the business by using the KitKat brand name to enter new markets.

33 Market segmentation

What is market segmentation?

Market segmentation is the practice of dividing a market into discrete, identifiable groups of customers or consumers that have common characteristics and motivations. There are reasons why a business might segment its market.

- Each group can be treated independently and a business can tailor the marketing mix or develop products to meet the needs of each segment.
- Opportunities, such as niche markets, that have not yet been exploited and new product opportunities can be highlighted.
- It can show which segments are performing well and which segments need additional marketing support.
- Decisions can be made about which segments are likely to be profitable and worth pursuing and which segments should be ignored.

Segmenting a market

A business needs access to up-to-date market research data in order to segment a market. This may be from primary research conducted specifically to see how a market is segmented or from secondary research that has already been conducted. Segmentation can involve analysing marketing data and using different criteria to split the data in pre-determined groups. Another method of segmentation is to see which groupings form naturally within the data. Market segmentation will identify which segments of a market are large or small, strong or weak and already supplied with products or if there are gaps that are ready for product development and introduction.

The three main ways used to segment a market are shown in Figure 1.

Geographic segmentation

Geographic segmentation involves analysing markets and dividing them into groups based on geographic factors. These factors are usually physical, such as country region, but could include economic factors, such as population density. Some examples are shown in Table 1.

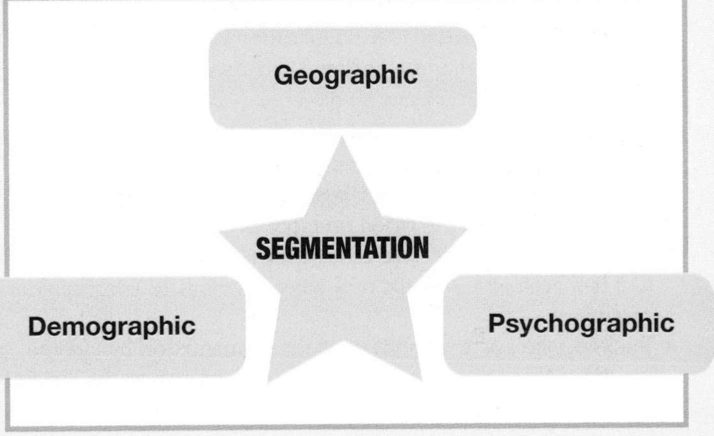

Table 1 *Examples of geographic segmentation*

Method By region.
Examples Regions such as Europe, Asia, North America, Africa, areas within a country, e.g. England, Scotland, Wales and Northern Ireland.
Method By country.
Examples Within national boundaries, e.g. UK, Republic of Ireland, France, China.
Method By local authority area within a country.
Examples Categorised by size, development or membership of geographic region, e.g. Department of Trade and Industry (DTI) regions.
Method City or town
Examples Population within ranges or above a certain level. e.g. towns with over 100,000 people.
Method By population density.
Examples High/low density, urban/suburban population, rural/semi-rural population.

Geographic segmentation means that each market can be treated individually, taking into account regional differences and requirements. This is useful for different types of business.

- Multi-national businesses can take into account the needs of different countries or regions in their overall marketing plans. An example is shown in Figure 2.
- National businesses can tailor the needs of particular areas

Figure 1 *Methods of market segmentation*

Geographic

SEGMENTATION

Demographic

Psychographic

Figure 2 *Geographic segmentation at McDonald's*

The McDonald's business is managed as distinct geographic segments: United States; Europe; Asia/Pacific, Middle East and Africa (APMEA); Latin America and Canada.

It also tailors its food to individual countries. For example, McDonald's India has developed a special menu with vegetarian selections to suit Indian tastes and preferences. McDonald's does not offer any beef or pork items in India. The business says that 'Only the freshest chicken, fish and vegetable products find their way into our Indian restaurants'.

Source: adapted from www.djia-valuation.com and www.mcdonaldsindia.com.

within a country in their plans.
- A small business may only advertise its products or services within a geographic area that it can reach effectively. A local Newcastle taxi service, for example, would not advertise in London.

Geographic segmentation and the marketing mix

The geographic segmentation of markets can affect the marketing mix of a business. Table 2 shows some examples.

Table 2 *Geographical segmentation and the marketing mix*

Part of mix	Effect	Example
Product	Nature of the product	Paint sold in Mediterranean markets needs to withstand sun and heat, but paint sold in Scandinavian markets needs to resist cold.
	Packaging	Some markets require full contents listed, others require nutritional information. Ready-to-drink coffee is available in cans in the Netherlands but not in the UK.
Price	Lower	Consumer goods sell at lower prices in Eastern European countries than they do in the West as incomes are lower.
	Higher	A UK manufacturer selling into the US will charge a higher price in the US than in the UK to cover transport costs.
Place	Availability	Products may not be sold in some countries due to regional differences, for example digital radios will not be sold in countries with only analogue wavelengths.
Promotion	Type of advertising	A small business such as a local car repair service can advertise in a local paper, use local radio and distribute leaflets in a local area using post codes.

Demographic segmentation

Demographic segmentation is where a market is analysed and divided into groups based on demographic factors. These factors relate to the economic and social features and characteristics of the market being segmented.

Age The UK Census 2001 provides broad examples of age groups. These are people aged 0 to 15, aged 16 to 74 and aged 75 and over. A more detailed breakdown may be 5 year age bands, e.g. ranges 0-4, 5-9, 10-14 up to 85-89, then 90 years and over. It may be more useful for a marketing plan to segment using larger age bands of say 10 years. Which bands are used will depend on the market and what the business wants to do with the different age segments.

Sex A market can be segmented into males and females. Many markets and products have a bias towards one sex or the other. This type of segmentation can be useful when the bias is extreme. For example, neck ties are worn almost exclusively by men, but bought by both men and women (as gifts). Segmentation will help plan promotion towards men (for wearing as well as buying) and women (for buying).

Socio-economic group Various methods are used to segment the market by socio-economic group. A widely used method in the media is shown in Table 3.

Table 3 *Social economic groups, National Readership Survey (NRS) social grade definitions (UK)*

Socio-economic grade	Social status	Occupation
A	upper middle class	higher managerial, administrative or professional
B	middle class	intermediate managerial, administrative or professional
C1	lower middle class	supervisory or clerical, junior managerial, administrative or professional
C2	skilled working class	skilled manual workers
D	working class	semi and unskilled manual workers
E	those at lowest level of subsistence	state pensioners or widows (no other earner), casual or lowest grade workers

Although still widely used, this classification can be unsophisticated and may not reflect modern society. Links between occupation and economic power are not so direct, so a number of other systems have been developed which reflect factors such as discretionary income, lifestage and working patterns.
- ACORN. This stands for 'A Classification Of Residential Neighbourhoods'. It is based on types of housing and the people that live there. This classification is linked to postcodes and is therefore a valuable tool when it comes to geographical targeting.
- Income. Like age, the bands used for segmentation by income can be tailored to meet the needs of the market or the current economic situation. Typical bands for annual income could be

under £10,000, £11,000 to £20,000, £21,000 to £30,000. Income bands are usually selected to be appropriate for the range of incomes in the market being segmented.

- Occupation. This segmentation assumes that different occupations have different levels of income which have an effect on the market. It can also be an indicator of social status or linked to behaviour factors which may be useful for marketing purposes.
- Marital status. The Census 2001 breaks down the population into single people (never married), married or re-married people, separated or divorced, and widowed.

Since 2001 the National Statistics Socio-economic Classification (NS-SEC) has been used for all official statistics and surveys in the UK as shown in Table 4. The Census 2001 website www.statistics.gov.uk/census2001 is a good source to see demographic segmentation in use.

Table 4 *The National Statistics Socio-economic Classification*

1	Higher managerial and professional occupations
	1.1 Large employers and higher managerial occupations
	1.2 Higher professional occupations
2	Lower managerial and professional occupations
3	Intermediate occupations
4	Small employers and own account workers
5	Lower supervisory and technical occupations
6	Semi-routine occupations
7	Routine occupations
8	Never worked and long-term unemployed

Demographic segmentation and the marketing mix

The demographic segmentation of markets can affect the market mix of a business. Table 5 shows some examples. Demographic segmentation is linked closely to branding, as explained in section 32. It is the use of different brand named products from the same organisation, each aimed at different demographic segments of the market.

Psychographic segmentation

Psychographic segmentation is where a market is analysed and divided into groups based on psychographic factors. These factors relate to subjective personality features, such as attitudes, ideas and opinions. Psychographic segmentation is particularly useful for identifying new or niche markets.

Lifestyle Lifestyles may fall into different categories. For example they may be:

- modern and trend-setting or traditional with few changes;
- expansive and willing to spend money in pursuit of pleasure or cautious with money and unwilling to spend more than is necessary.

Often, these segmentations are based as much on perception much as actual lifestyle differences.

Interests These would include sports, leisure activities and hobbies.

Table 5 *Demographic segmentation and the marketing mix*

Part of mix	Effect	Example
Product	Nature of the product	Deodorants have different scents whether aimed at men or women users, as different sexes associate different scents with personal hygiene.
	Packaging	Cans of soft drinks are sold singly for younger or unmarried consumers and in packs for consumers buying for a family.
	Branding	Higher priced brands of canned vegetables are stocked alongside supermarket own brand goods, segmented in premium, standard and budget brands, each priced at a different level for different income groups.
Price	Higher	Higher prices may be charged in food halls of Harrods or Harvey Nichols aimed at higher income groups and category ABC1 consumers.
	Lower	Lower prices may be charged by supermarkets such as Netto, Aldi and Lidl, aimed at lower income groups or categories C2, D and E.
Place	Availability	Some clothes and accessories are sold in high street designer shops such as Hugo Boss, Gucci and Vivienne Westwood in London or other cities aimed at higher income groups and ABC1s. Clothes aimed at lower income groups or categories C2, D and E may be found in markets.
Promotion	Types of advertising	PR campaigns can appeal to particular segments. Prada or Gucci advertising may take place in magazines aimed at ABC1s. A product aimed at young males, such as football boots, would not be advertised in a magazine that has a high readership of older married women, such as *Lancashire Life*.

Attitudes Markets can be analysed and segmented by attitude to politics, lifestyles, certain products. For example, some consumers will wear clothes that are made from real animal fur but others will not.

Opinions Groups with similar opinions of politics and social issues can be identified. Opinion polls are a widely used method of primary research to identify the mood or feelings within a target market. Products can be tailored to appeal to the attitudes of a segment. For example, the supermarket chain Iceland promotes the claim that none of the products that it stocks contain genetically modified (GM) ingredients.

Values These are often influenced by upbringing and family attitudes as well as social conditioning. Once formed, values are hard to change. Products can be changed and adapted to reflect the values of market segments. For example, the 'Fair Trade' product ranges for tea and coffee may appeal to ethical customers.

Taste People may see products as being in 'good or bad taste'. For example, some films have 'gross out' images and storylines and deliberate 'bad taste' designed to offend older people, but appeal to younger audiences where 'bad taste' is perceived as being amusing and entertaining.

Table 6 *Psychographic segmentation and the marketing mix*

Part of mix	Effect	Example
Product	Nature of the product	Magazines are geared towards different readerships, e.g. *Horse and Ride, FHM, Glamour, Hello, Kerrang, Men's Health* and *Art and Antiques* and niche markets can be targeted.
Price	Higher price	Crystal champagne sells for £100-£300 a bottle to consumers that embrace the hip hop lifestyle and to some star footballers. Tools and materials can sell for premium prices for some hobbies, e.g. carpentry.
Place	Availability	Retailers offer specialist products in particular shops geared to lifestyles, e.g. sports shops, 'new age' shops, American comic shops.
Promotion	Type of advertising	Some lifestyles might react better to visual advertisements such as fast cars. Radio and newspaper advertisements may be used for solicitors' services to appear 'serious and concerned'.

Psychographic segmentation and the marketing mix

The psychographic segmentation of markets can affect the marketing mix of a business. Some examples are shown in Table 6.

Other methods of segmentation

Sometimes businesses find that one method of segmenting markets is inflexible, not subtle enough or does not meet particular market situations. As a result, segmentation based on combinations of factors are used. For example, geo-economic segmentation that combines factors from both areas to identify, say, high-income families in a particular town or region can be used. ACORN, linked to postcode based marketing or promotional activity, can also be effective.

In some markets, such as trade or industrial markets, other ways of segmentation may be more appropriate. Examples could include segmentation by industry and by status, e.g. new customer/old customer.

Benefits and problems of segmentation

Market segmentation is a powerful tool in marketing. Each variable of the marketing mix can play a role in segmentation by tailoring products to meet the needs of each segment.
- New businesses can enter a market by targeting a particular segment.
- Established businesses can strengthen market share by producing new products to meet the needs of every segment.
- Niche markets can be identified and filled by existing or new products as appropriate.
- Competition can be kept out of a market by having a product for each segment and leaving no room for a competitor to enter.

However, there can be dangers associated with over-segmentation.
- Individual products can be picked off by competitors. If a market leader moves into smaller segments, a competitor that is particularly strong in one of those segments stands a better chance of beating the market leader as it knows the segment better and is already established.
- The finance department may argue that a highly segmented niche product may not be as profitable as it wants. But the marketing team may argue that it serves another purpose, such as keeping competitors out of a segment or showing that the business has a complete range or products.
- Range proliferation. Some businesses add products to a range for different segments just to keep competitors out of a market. This can have a negative effect on customers. They may become frustrated if all the available space is filled by products from one manufacturer.

Niche marketing

This is the development of a segmentation strategy. Niche marketing is based upon supplying a product that meets the needs of a small, discrete, specialist market or filling a small gap in the market.

Marketing research may identify a gap in the market or a group of consumers whose needs are not being met. The business must then decide whether it is worth specialising and concentrating marketing activity on the gap or the niche that has been identified. The niche must be large enough to be worth concentrating on based on the objectives of the business, such as profitability or the requirement to keep competition out of that niche.

A niche marketing strategy has a number of advantages for a business.

- Costs can be kept low.
- Relatively low sales can account for a big share of the market niche.
- A business can become a major player within the niche.
- Competition may be less. it could be ignored by mass marketing organisations.
- Customers can be satisfied by providing the product that is right for them.
- Marketing communication message can be focused.
- A business can become a specialist.
- A business can exploit specialism through higher prices which can increase profitability.

Large businesses can sometimes target niche markets. For example the UK paint market has both mass market products and highly specialised products aimed at niche markets. Smaller businesses can also successfully exploit niches. Some examples of niche providers are shown in Table 7.

Mass marketing

This is perhaps the opposite to niche marketing. A mass marketing strategy is based on providing a product that has wide appeal to a great number of consumers in a market that is very large in itself. There are many examples, including:

- vanilla ice cream, the most popular flavour within the large ice cream market;
- white paint, the top selling colour in the vast overall market;
- bedding plants in Spring will have mass market appeal as they will be the top selling plants in the garden plant market which is large.

Mass markets also have their own mass market brands, usually brands that have become household names or generic names. Some examples include;

- Hoover, a mass market brand of electrical household appliances that is associated with vacuum cleaners to the point that many people use Hoover to describe any brand of vacuum cleaner;
- Google has become the mass market brand name associated with Internet search engines to the point that it has become a verb and people talk about 'Googling' or say 'I will Google it.' when they mean search for it.

The attraction of mass markets to a business is that they are large, sell products in high volume and generate high levels of revenue and profit. Even a small share of a large market may be worth having. On the other hand there is a danger in achieving mass-market status. Consumers can be unpredictable and what is popular with the mass market this year may not be so next year.

Products for mass markets need a high level of marketing expenditure to enter the market and even more expenditure to remain in the market. Sometimes a short but profitable excursion into a mass market may be the objective a business has set. For example popular mass market ringtones can make a huge impact on the market, but have only a short product life cycle as there will be another popular ringtone along soon after. A mass market brand or product is also vulnerable to attack from smaller competitors that can pick-off small parts of the market with niche products.

Despite these reservations, many large organisations make high profits from being mass market providers.

Table 7 *Market niche providers*

Business	Niche
I Love Liquorice Ltd	An independent specialist retailer of traditional sweets.
Becker Underwood Ltd	Manufactures and markets a range of specialist niche products for the garden and horticulture markets.
Gecko Headgear	A specialist helmet manufacturer of lightweight headgear for extreme sports.
Artel Rubber	Manufactures high quality silicone rubber products for prestige motor vehicles.

Look in a copy of your local *Yellow Pages* directory. Identify three examples of:
- local businesses that have segmented their market geographically;
- national businesses that have segmented their market locally;
- businesses that have used demographic segmentation.

OR

Magazines often carry out surveys to find out more about their readers. Questions are asked to find out a variety of information about readers' characteristics. Find a magazine survey questionnaire from back issues of a magazine. Identify which questions in the survey are designed to find out about:
- geographic segmentation;
- demographic segmentation;
- psychographic segmentation.

Research task

Portfolio practice · Kuoni Group

One of the major businesses operating in the UK market for leisure travel is the international Kuoni Group. Its 2004 Annual Report stated that the Kuoni brand is 'positioned in the upper-to-middle pricing segments'. In the UK the business offers different holiday packages at different price bands under two different brand names.

Voyages Jules Verne Ltd. (VJV) 2005 brochures.
Country brochures include America Latina, China & Beyond, Travels in Italy and Dreaming of India.

Theme brochures include Journeys of Scientific Interest, World of Wonders, Le Weekend Extraordinaire, Travels through Ancient Lands, Great Journeys and Cruises of Discovery 2005.

Kuoni 2005 brochures.
Country brochures include Italy, Southern Africa, Australia, New Zealand & South Pacific, Morocco, Dubai, USA & Canada, India & Nepal, Swiss Winter and Swiss Summer.

Brochures based on 'what is important to you…' include Worldwide Our A to Z of long-haul travel covering 60 exotic countries, Family Worldwide 2005, World Class Luxury holidays from £2,500 per person, Selections Special Offers to Sri Lanka, the Maldives, Thailand and Indonesia in 2005, Limited Editions April to July Special Offers. Escorted Tours 2005/6, Sandals & Beaches, Weddings and Florida Sun.

Source: adapted from Kuoni, *Annual Report and Accounts, 2004* and author research.

(a) **Identify using examples THREE ways in which the business might segment the market.**
(b) **Using ONE of these methods, suggest how it might affect the marketing mix of the business.**
(c) **(i) Examine the reasons why Kuoni might segment its market and (ii) discuss whether the benefits will outweigh any problems.**

Meeting the assessment criteria

When producing the marketing mix for your product you need to have considered segmentation in your market and what this means to the marketing mix that you develop.

Business example - Great Windows Ltd

Made in Heaven is a made-to-measure curtain service, which is provided by Great Windows Ltd, a business that operates in the Harlow area of Essex.

A representative from the company measures a customer's windows and calculates how much fabric is required. The customer then chooses and buys the fabric they want and the team at Great Windows Ltd makes the curtains.

Table 8 shows a profile of all people planning to buy curtains in the next twelve months and a profile of those people who say that they will buy made-to-measure curtains. This is information downloaded from various sites on the Internet.

Mark Band 1 *Description of the chosen product/service, basic description of the marketing objectives and the relevant segmentation and target market.*
Great Windows Ltd is a business that operates in the Harlow area of Essex providing a made-to-measure curtain service. Its

objective is to target market segments that want this service to be successful. Geographically, it will operate only in the Harlow area. Using the information in Table 8, demographic segmentation suggests that the basic target market is women, aged 45-64, in the AB socio-economic group, who are married, working full-time and living in a home that they own. Psychographic segmentation suggests that only 5% of people planning to buy curtains in the next twelve months are likely to choose made-to-measure curtains. This suggests that made-to-measure curtains is a niche market.

Mark Band 2 *Explanation of why the product/service has been chosen, what the marketing aims and objectives are and steps taken to identify the target market and segmentation.*
Great Windows Ltd is a business that operates in the Harlow area of Essex providing a made-to-measure curtain service. Its objective is to target market segments who want this service to be successful. Searching the Internet did produce some data, as shown in Table 8. This suggests a niche market, sold in the local area, targeted at women aged 45-64, who are ABs, married, working full-time, who own their own home. But more information was needed before developing a marketing mix. Great Windows Ltd contacted a similar business in Scotland

Table 8 *Buyers of curtains*

All figures %	Total sample profile. All planning to buy curtains in next twelve months	Profile of people who say they will buy made-to-measure curtains
All buyers	100	5
Sex of buyer		
Male	48	44
Female	52	56
Age of buyer		
15-24	18	13
25.34	19	30
35-44	17	15
45-64	26	32
65+	19	10
Socio-economic classification		
AB	17	28
C1	25	23
C2	26	22
DE	32	27
Marital status		
Married	61	77
Single	24	13
Widowed, divorced or separated	15	10
Working status		
Full-time	37	45
Part-time	9	15
Not working	54	40
Household tenure		
Mortgage	44	65
Owned outright	23	17
Rented	33	18

that was not competing and was prepared to share customer information, as shown in Figure 3. This information reassured Great Windows Ltd that although only 5% of people planning to buy curtains in the next twelve months said they would buy made-to-measure, most of the money spent on curtains went to the independent specialist segment, businesses like Great Windows Ltd. Because of the profile of buyers of made-to-measure curtains, it is important that Great Windows Ltd presents the right image. It must appeal to the profile of customers targeted. The image must be of quality and reliability, which should appeal to the target market, women who are working full time. The business might also charge a premium price to demonstrate the value and quality of the service. Customers buy their own fabric so Great Windows will not need to carry stocks.

Mark Band 3 A comprehensive marketing mix which is clearly linked to the research and segmentation evidence and shows depth of knowledge and understanding of the relevant Ps.
Great Windows Ltd is a business that operates in the Harlow area of Essex, providing a made-to-measure curtain service. Its objective is to target market segments that want this service to be successful and grow in the long term. Searching the Internet produced some helpful data. This suggested a niche market, sold in the local area, targeted at women aged 45-64, who are

ABs, married, working full-time and who own their own home. Further information from a Scottish business about buyers confirms that although it is selling to a niche market, most people buy from independent businesses like Great Windows Ltd. In addition to targeting women aged 45-64, 32% of potential customers, it may also be worthwhile targeting women aged 25-34 as they represent 30% of target customers, another sizeable part of the market. The lifestyle and motivation of this latter group to buy made-to-measure curtains may be different to the older group, so the media used for promotion must be considered carefully.

The needs of the target groups must be taken into account in the marketing mix.

Product The business needs to make sure that the service is first class and appeals to women in the AB socio-economic group. For the same reasons, the quality of the finished curtains must be high. Added value features such as home delivery and curtain hanging in customers' windows might also be used.

Price Great Windows Ltd plans to adopt a premium pricing strategy. This should be in keeping with the expectations of the core socio-economic group.

Place There is little opportunity for varying the place element of the marketing mix as Great Windows Ltd only operates in the Harlow area of Essex. However, it may be useful to target the service at areas of the town where most of the houses are owner-occupied and lived in by people in the higher socio-economic groups.

Promotion The business is only operating in the Harlow area. So the media used for promotion must circulate, be read, and be listened to and watched by people in the local or nearby areas as some customers may be prepared to travel if the service is good enough. The following promotional strategy is suggested.

- Placement in the Harlow area *Yellow Pages* as it is used by all socio-economic groups to access local services.
- Press releases on a regular basis to the monthly Essex county magazine. This has an up-market readership profile that matches the profile of buyers of made-to-measure curtains. Consider advertising in the future if it proves to be worthwhile.
- Direct mail to owner-occupied households in higher socio-economic areas of the town and surrounding areas.

The following are not recommended.

- Local newspapers and free sheets - the readership profile means that there will be a lot of wastage as only a minority of the target market read these.
- Local radio and television as these have too wide a catchment area and could attract enquiries from a distance, which will be too far for Great Windows to service to the high standards set.

Figure 3 *Sales of curtains by outlet type, % share by value 2005*

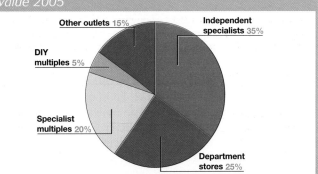

Other outlets 15%
DIY multiples 5%
Independent specialists 35%
Specialist multiples 20%
Department stores 25%

What is primary research?

Primary research is used to collect original data and information for the first time. This is known as primary data. It is 'raw' data as it has not yet been analysed or interpreted. Because it is new and original, primary research can be designed to meet the precise needs of a research project.

Primary research is sometimes called **field research** because the activity is conducted 'in the field' or the marketplace. It can be referred to as a **survey** when primary research is carried out to find data about a large number of people, known as a 'population'. All mean the same thing, that primary research is about collecting data, facts or opinions, direct from the original source of the information. People who take part in primary research and supply data are known as **respondents**.

Conducted properly, primary research should be able to provide data which can be interpreted to give answers to particular questions or to support plans, ideas or decision making.

Planning and organising primary research

Like all marketing activity, primary research needs to be planned to be effective. There is a number of steps that the researcher must take.

- Identify the problem and decide what they want to know, what to ask, what needs to be researched, when answers are needed and how much to spend (the budget for the project). A marketing research project needs objectives and a time plan or it could be a waste of resources and produce misleading information. A budget is important so that the cost does not increase out of proportion to the research.
- Decide how to collect the data in the most effective way. This involves choosing the most appropriate primary research method.
- Decide on the respondents to survey and the style and content of the questions.
- Decide how to analyse and present the findings, what the data means and what conclusions can be drawn. This information will form a basic marketing plan for the research.

Quantitative and qualitative data

Depending on the way it is conducted and what questions are asked, primary research can be designed to collect quantitative or qualitative data.

- **Quantitative data** is objective numbers, facts and figures such as how many, how much, how often;
- **Qualitative data** is subjective views, opinions, attitudes and motivations.

Quantitative data is usually produced by counting the number of times an answer is given, based on a set list of questions in a questionnaire or the number of times an observed action occurs. Quantitative data can be analysed statistically. Qualitative data is usually produced from open-ended questions, where the respondent is asked for their own words, description or opinion,

rather than answer from a set list. Focus groups, where respondents join in a discussion about an idea or topic, also produce qualitative data. This kind of data usually needs to be interpreted by an expert, such as a psychologist, rather than analysed statistically.

Uses of primary research

Primary research has many uses in business. These are shown in Figure 1.

Figure 1 *Uses of primary research*

Testing new ideas and opinions
- Who would buy a new product?
- Would people stop buying if a product changed?
- What do people think about a product or service?
- Do people think that the retail price is too high?

Facts about a market
- What is the target market?
- Who is buying most?
- What are the common characteristics of these people?
- How big is a market?
- How much do people spend?
- What share of the market do the main brands enjoy?

USES

Provide data on how often something happens
- How many people walk past a shop?
- How often do people use a supermarket?
- How many people enter the shop to buy something?
- How many products are returned to a manufacturer as faulty?
- How many people complain about the faulty product?

Marketing mix
- Primary research might help to:
- confirm what colour product or packaging style is preferred;
- suggest how much consumers are prepared to pay;
- show the type of shop where consumers would expect to buy a product.
- identify which magazines are read by the target market and are best for advertising a product.

How is primary research carried out?

There are many different primary research methods.

Observation Here data is collected by looking and recording findings rather than by asking questions. Observations can be open. For example, a respondent may be given a task such as following instructions on how to use a product. The researcher then watches and records how well they accomplish the task and what problems they find. Observation could also be used to count how many people visit a stand in an exhibition. Secret observation could be used to find out the way that most customers turn when they enter a shop. This will help the shop management plan the layout according to which way most people turn. A 'mystery shopper' is another common method of secret observational research. The behaviour of shoppers or shop staff is watched without them knowing and observations recorded.

Direct questioning Probably the most widely recognised method of primary research is the direct questioning of respondents in an interview situation, often with the aid of a questionnaire. A questionnaire helps to guide the flow of questions and records the answers from people being interviewed. Direct questioning can

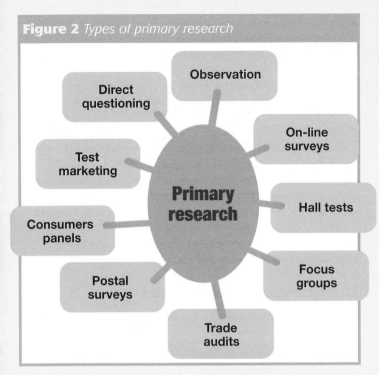

Figure 2 *Types of primary research*

Observation

Direct questioning

On-line surveys

Test marketing

Primary research

Hall tests

Consumers panels

Focus groups

Postal surveys

Trade audits

On-line surveys Increasingly, on-line resources are being used for marketing research. Although the method of delivery is different, on-line surveys are similar to postal surveys. Respondents are sent an e-mail to invite them to log on to the website of a research organisation. Using a discrete and secure website address, respondents are guided to an on-line questionnaire which is completed on screen and submitted directly upon completion. On-line surveys can range from straightforward reproductions of written questionnaires to surveys including photographs or moving images. A problem with on-line surveys is consumer mistrust of the Internet, particularly regarding security. People may also be concerned that completing an on-line survey will result in being bombarded with advertising and spam e-mails.

Hall test A hall test is an alternative to conducting street interviews. The research organisation books a hall or room to interview respondents rather than in the street. This has the advantage that respondents are more comfortable and secure and are more likely to provide better quality answers. As the environment is relatively confidential, respondents can be shown new products or advertisements or asked to sample new flavours and give their opinions.

Focus groups Focus groups are sometimes referred to as 'group discussion'. This is another form of direct questioning, but carried out with a number of respondents in a group, all being interviewed together. Focus groups are particularly useful for researching opinions and attitudes and uncovering ideas that the researcher may not have thought of in the first place. They usually take place in a quiet room in a hotel or a house and run for around 1-2 hours. The focus group is usually led by a trained psychologist. They aim to find out the feelings from the group that may not be expressed if interviewed one-to-one. Discussions will follow a 'pre-planned' route to make sure that the aim of the research is met.

Focus groups may be recorded on audio or video equipment, so that results can be analysed in great detail and individual quotes can be identified. To be effective, focus groups are usually 8-10 people. Any more and the group could become unmanageable and break up into several smaller groups. Any fewer and one person may become dominant, with others in the group not giving their opinions.

Focus groups are used widely to check current thinking and ideas, to monitor changes in social attitudes, to generate ideas for new product developments, to create stories for marketing, promotion and for public relations purposes. They are popular because they can be set-up quickly, results are generated immediately and they are relatively low cost to run.

Test marketing This is a form of primary research that is aimed at reproducing a national sales situation in a small controlled area before launching a product to the whole country. By selecting the right area for the test market, an organisation can test sales techniques, consumer purchases and acceptance of a new product, advertising styles and levels and other forms of promotion without the high cost of a full national launch. If a product is successful in a test market, marketing plans can be reproduced nationally. Conversely, if a test market is not successful, marketing plans can be changed and tested again, or the product may not be launched on a wider scale.

take place face-to-face, such as in the common street survey or one-to-one over the telephone (a telephone survey). Skilled interviewers can achieve high quality results from telephone surveys, which have the advantage that respondents are likely to be in the more relaxed surroundings of their own home. Against this, there can be a lot of wasted calls as respondents are not in when telephoned. Even when they are in, respondents may be distracted by what is going on in the home. Direct questioning is used for mass surveys, for example interviewing lots of people in the street or over the telephone and for individual in-depth interviews.

Another research method that uses direct questioning is omnibus surveys. These are surveys run on a regular basis, such as the first weekend of every month. A number of clients contribute questions to the overall survey and so the cost of setting up the research is shared.

Direct questioning has the advantage that if a respondent does not fully understand a question, it can be explained by the interviewer. There are likely to be fewer wasted questionnaires and the quality of the research is likely to be improved as a result.

Postal surveys This is an alternative to interviews. A self-completion questionnaire is prepared and mailed by the research organisation to respondents, together with a reply-paid envelope. A small incentive is often used to encourage respondents to complete the questionnaire and return it. Postal surveys have the advantage of being able to target households and respondents fairly precisely using postal code or to cover a wide geographic area. They can be based on mailing to an organisation's own database of customers or potential customers. They can also be longer than questionnaires used in face-to-face interviews as respondents are less likely to be under a time pressure to complete the questionnaire. Although the cost of printing and mailing postal questionnaires is relatively low on an individual basis, there is usually a high degree of wastage because questionnaires are not returned.

Consumer panels When research is required to measure changing attitudes or behaviour over a period of time researchers will often establish a consumer panel. This is a fixed group of respondents who are interviewed regularly. By recording any changes between each interview, researchers can see how attitudes or purchase levels have changed. These changes can be correlated against marketing campaigns to see what has been successful. Another way of using consumer panels is to establish a panel of experts or enthusiasts who will try out and test a product and report back to the business as part of a new product development programme. This method of using consumer panels is common with computer software and computer games designers.

Trade audits These are carried out with panels of shops or businesses in the same industry. Researchers will visit the premises of businesses on the trade audit panel regularly depending on the rate of sale of products in the market being audited. The researcher will measure stock levels and deliveries and from this calculate sales across the audit period. Trade audits are important for measuring market share or brand share and for showing seasonal trends. Trade audits can also show up long-term trends that are often missed by ad-hoc research surveys.

Who to survey – sampling and population

Having decided on the method of primary research that may be appropriate for meeting the objectives of the research, the researcher must decide who to survey, how to take a sample of people from the **population** and the **sample size**. This is known as the sampling plan. A **sample** of people to survey needs to be chosen. This is a number of people who are likely to be representative of the whole population. The population in a business survey might be every potential customer of the business or everyone in the market for its product.

For most primary research projects the total population that could be surveyed is likely to be large. It would be difficult and unnecessary to survey 100% of a population. Statistical evidence shows that it is only necessary to sample a percentage of a total population to get similar results to the total population to get similar results to the total population within acceptable levels of confidence.

The actual decision about how many people to include in the sample will depend on how much is in the budget to spend on the research, traded off against the level of accuracy required. In practice it is better to sample as many people as can be afforded. The higher the number, the more chance of the research being reliable. Whilst a low number will produce some data, the danger is that it will not be representative of the population. It might be suggested to survey at least 100 for a mini survey, up to 10% of a population or as many as can be afforded.

Questionnaires

A questionnaire is a structured document that contains all of the questions required to collect data. It is basically a list of questions that make up a survey. Although questionnaires are likely to be different for different surveys, some common features may include:

● an identification of what survey it relates to, a title or reference number;

● a control question to confirm if the respondent is suitable to interview, e.g. asking 'Have you taken a holiday outside of the UK in the past year?' (Yes = continue, No = end interview) may be used for a survey on foreign holidays;

● a means of classifying the respondent, usually based on basic demographic criteria such as age, gender, work status, income, socio-economic group;

● the questions themselves.

In addition it is important to include instructions on how the respondent should complete each question and how the interviewer should complete the questionnaire. Self-completion questionnaires will also need easy to understand introductions which explain the reasons for conducting the research, a sincere 'thank you' for completing the questionnaire and full details about how to return the questionnaire - address and 'when by' date. This should be supported by the self-addressed envelope.

The questions themselves

Certain basic types of question are commonly used in questionnaires.

Simple dichotomous questions These give the respondent a choice of two possible answers as in Figure 3.

Figure 3 *Simple dichotomous questions*

(a) Do you drink fruit juice? ☐ Yes   ☐ No

(b) Which of these two advertisements do you like the most?
☐ A   ☐ B

Multiple-choice questions These give the respondent a choice from a limited, pre-determined range as in Figure 4. An 'other' option is given in case a response that has not been considered proves to be the most popular answer. Sometimes a 'don't know' alternative is more appropriate. This enables respondents who genuinely have no opinion or cannot pick an answer from the given range to tick a box and complete the question. Without a 'don't know' option the survey would be incomplete, as this section of the population would not be represented. Multiple-choice questions enable the researcher to control the range of answers to a degree, which keeps the survey focused. This type of question is simple to ask, simple to answer and the answers will be relatively easy to analyse.

Open-ended questions These are designed to enable respondents to answer freely, without being restricted by the pre-determined choices of the researcher. Examples are questions (f) and (g) in Figure 5. Open-ended questions are very useful for assessing attitudes and opinions. But they can be more difficult to analyse because of the wide range of possible answers or because of the need to group similar answers so that conclusions can be drawn.

Scaling questions These questions are designed to measure the subjective attitude of a respondent to a given statement. There is

Figure 4 *Multiple-choice questions*

(c) Where did you take your last holiday of more than two nights away?

In the UK ☐
In Europe ☐
In the USA ☐
In the Far East ☐
Other (please state) _____

(d) What is your working situation?

Employed full-time ☐
Employed part-time ☐
Self-employed ☐
Not working ☐
Retired ☐
No job ☐
Full-time housekeeper ☐
Other (please write in) _____

(e) How many years should there be before a new edition of a travel book?

2 years ☐
3 years ☐
4 years ☐
5 years ☐
6 years ☐
Don't know ☐

a number of different ways that scaling questions can be constructed. One of the most commonly used is the Likert scale, which consists of five degrees of agreement, or not, with a statement. This is shown in question (h) in Figure 6. Another way of asking a scaling question is to use a semantic differential technique. In this type of question respondents given with a question and asked where along the scale their opinion would fit, as in question (i). The same question could be asked using a scale as in question (j). The point of a semantic differential scale is that it runs between two distinct alternatives, in this case very important or not very important. Scaling questions may also be presented in other ways.

Figure 5 *Open-ended questions*

(f) What do you think about being offered genetically modified (GM) foods to eat? (Write your answer here)

_____

(g) Why have you visited this town today? (Write your answer here)

_____

Figure 6 *Scaling questions*

(h) Fried egg sandwiches are a healthy alternative for breakfast (Please tick box that is closest to your opinion)

5 Agree strongly	4 Agree	3 Uncertain	2 Disagree	1 Disagree strongly

(i) Our sales assistants have been asked to smile when they serve customers. Do you think that this is: (Please tick box that is closest to your opinion)

Very important	Important	Somewhat important	Unimportant	Very unimportant

(j) Our sales assistants have been asked to smile when they serve customers. Do you think that this is: (Please tick box that is closest to your opinion)

Very important					Very unimportant

Planning the questionnaire

Although a questionnaire may appear to be just a list of questions, the order in which they are asked can make a big difference to the quality of the data produced. In general it is better to start with simple short questions, which are easy to answer, and follow a sensible and logical order. If any questions are likely to be personal, difficult or challenging they should be placed towards the end. Also, the questionnaire should not be too long. It could be tested first on a volunteer to see how long it is before they get bored. This will give an idea of the maximum length the questionnaire should be. It may be necessary to cut out some questions, but sticking to the most important questions should produce the required data. The recommended maximum length for:
- a face-to-face interview in the home is 45 minutes;
- a telephone interview is 20 minutes or less;
- a street an interview is 5 – 10 minutes.

These recommendations will limit the length of the questionnaire.

Piloting the questionnaire

Before finalising a questionnaire it is worth testing the questions by trying them out on a small number of people. In this way, any problems with the wording or the kind of answer you get for some questions can be checked. Any changes or improvements can be made before the survey goes into the field and it is too late to make any changes.

What to do with the findings

All of the examples of questions shown in this section are capable of producing quantitative data. This is data based on numbers that can be analysed statistically. Even the responses to the open-ended question can be grouped and counted as quantitative data. How much analysis is done will depend on what the research is designed to find out and the needs of the audience receiving the research. Marketing research professionals, especially statisticians, will demand higher levels of analysis than, say, a marketing manager who just wants a measure of market share, or a PR executive who wants a single fact upon which can develop a press release. The presentation of the results also depends on the audience. Computer spreadsheet programmes make the presentation of data easy to change to suit people's requirements.

Professional standards

Primary research is usually carried out by well-trained and often highly qualified experts in marketing research. They may be employed in this role within an organisation or they may operate as an independent agency that provides a specialist market research service. Market research should not be used as a guise for selling. This is considered to be very bad practice within the industry. Even inexperienced market researchers should follow professional standards for conducting research. All marketing research should be carried out within the professional and ethical standards and guidelines of the Market Research Society.

Write a questionnaire that will produce primary data about the soft drinks that people buy.
Typical questions may include the following:
● What type of drink do you prefer?
● Which brand(s) do you buy?
● Which flavour do you buy?
● Where do you buy your drinks?
● How often do you buy drinks?
In addition, you need to conduct local research in a range of shops to identify the selling price of drinks and any promotions that are running in-store.
Analyse the findings and draw some conclusions based on the aims of the research.
● What is the profile of people buying the drinks?
● How is the drinks market segmented?
● How can the marketing mix variables be applied to a new drink being launched?

Research task

Portfolio practice · Printview

Printview is a printer which provides local print services. These include leaflets for small businesses, small magazines advertising the services of local companies and business cards. It has been successful by targeting business customers in the local area. But it finds that paper printing is only a limited market. So it is considering offering a new bespoke service. It will scan in people's favourite pictures, such as their children, pets or holiday photos and print them onto personal items. Before it attempts to move into this new market it has decided to carry out some primary research. Table 1 shows the results of part of the primary research of 100 people surveyed.

(a) What does the information in Table 1 suggest to the business?
(b) What other types of questions should the business ask in the questionnaire?
(c) How might the information from these questions help the business to plan its marketing mix?

Table 1 *Survey results from the question 'What type of printing would you require?'*

T-shirts	37
Mugs and cups	18
Place mats	14
Key rings	7
Caps	24

Meeting the assessment criteria

For your chosen product or service you must identify and carry out appropriate marketing research and produce a marketing mix. When planning and using primary research you must consider the factors that will help ensure the primary research is relevant and appropriate. Once you have carried out the primary research you will need to analyse the results and use it to provide information that will help in the development of your marketing mix.

Business example - Cat Whisk

Cat whisk is a new cat food product. Primary research has been carried out by the manufacturer to consider the current market. The results are shown in Table 2. The data was found by interviewing 100 people who were cat owners.

Table 2 *Cat food survey results – age profile and income group*

Numbers of people surveyed =100	
Sex	
Males	38
Females	62
Age profile	
Under 15	0
16-19	12
20-29	20
30-44	36
45-59	22
60 and over	10
Socio-economic groups of cat owners	
AB	19
C1	23
C2	48
DE	10

Table 3 *Cat food survey results – type of product purchased*

What type of food do you feed your cat and in which form of packaging do you buy your cat food
Numbers of people surveyed = 100

	Cans	Pouches	Trays	Box	Bag
Wet	26	18	10	n/a	n/a
Dry	n/a	n/a	n/a	28	18

Which brand of cat food do you buy?
Numbers of people surveyed = 100

Whiskas	27
Felix	23
Friskies	14
Arthurs	12
Others	8
Shops own brand	16

Which flavour cat food do you buy?
Numbers of people surveyed = 100

Chicken	26
Beef	22
Rabbit	16
Fish	20
Others	16

Table 4 *Cat food survey results – place of purchase*

Where do you buy your cat food?
Numbers of people surveyed = 100

Supermarket	64
Pet shop	18
Garden centre	8
Other shops	8
The Internet	2

Table 5 *Selling prices and promotions in a local supermarket*

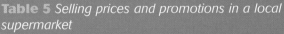

	Can	Pouch	Promotions
Whiskas	47p	29p	4 cans for the price of 3
Felix	47p	29p	15 pouches in special price pack
Friskies	38p	24p	None seen
Arthurs	40p	25p	None seen
Others	30p-49p	21p-30p	Prices cuts on some brands
Shop's own brand	45p	25p	Buy 4 get one free

Source: adapted from author research.

Mark Band 1 *Carry out and produce evidence of basic primary marketing research from a limited range of sources for your chosen product or service. There will be some attempt made at basic analysis of the information.*

Primary research from 100 cat owners has provided data in Table 2. More females in the survey own cats than males. The age group that owns most cats are people aged 30-44 who are neither teenagers nor very old people. The income group with the highest proportion of cats is people from the C2 band. The business might plan the marketing mix of Cat Whisk taking this data into account. It might advertise in magazines aimed at people older than teenagers or in women's magazines. Its price must not be too high as the C2 band is the second lowest income group.

Mark Band 2 *Carry out and produce evidence of sound primary market research, evidenced by a good range of relevant sources. There will be analysis of the primary research and extraction of the relevant information for your chosen product or service.*

Primary research from 100 cat owners has provided data in Tables 2-5. An analysis of the data in these tables could help the business to plan the marketing mix for Cat Whisk.

- Product. The survey results suggest that cat owners feed their pets a wide range of different products. Most people, 26%, bought chicken, although beef and fish were also bought by over 20% of people. 54% of people bought wet food and 46% dry food. This means that the business might need to offer Cat Whisk in different flavours and different packaging.
- Price. Only 19% of cat owners were in the highest income group, AB. The largest proportion was in income group C2. This might suggest that prices may need to be relatively low to be competitive.
- Promotion. Over half of all cats, 58%, were owned by people aged 30-59. This group of people are neither young nor very old. Promoting to magazines aimed at home owners might be useful. As more females own cats than males, promoting in magazines geared at females might also be a useful strategy.
- Place. Over half of all people buy pet food from supermarkets, 64%. This will be an important outlet for sales.

Mark Band 3 *There will be comprehensive primary research evidenced from a wide range of relevant sources, together with comprehensive original analysis.*

Primary research from 100 cat owners has provided data in Tables 2–5. An analysis of the data in these tables might help the business to plan a detailed marketing mix for Cat Whisk.

- Product. The survey results suggest that cat owners feed their pets a wide range of different products. Three flavours in particular, chicken beef and fish were also bought by over 20% or more people. 54% of people bough wet food and 46% dry food. The business is likely to face competition from four main brands in particular which account for 76% of the survey result. There will also be competition from own brands. This means that the business might need to offer Cat Whisk in different flavours and different packaging. Perhaps it might start by offering the three most popular flavours and then expanding its range.
- Price. Only 19% of cat owners were in the highest income group, AB. The largest proportion was in income group C2. ABC1s accounted for only 42% of cat owners. This might suggest that prices may need to be relatively low to be competitive, especially given the branded competition. The business might consider a price of say 38p per can to match Friskies, one of the cheaper brands.
- Promotion. 58% of cats were owned by people aged 30-59 and more cats were owned by females than males. Advertising in magazines geared at these target audiences might be a useful strategy. The business might attempt to establish a brand geared at this group by using a well known female aged around 30 to appear in advertising. However, the business must also consider promotions such as discounts offered by competitors. These often involve offering 'extra free' products with a certain quantity bought.
- Place. Over half of all people buy pet food from supermarkets, 64%. This is likely to be by far the most important outlet for sales. It may be worth concentrating on getting the product on sale in these outlets before moving into others.

The business must be wary about the extent to which this data is representative of the total population of cat owners. Comparisons must be made. Only 100 people were surveyed. National Statistics show that there are 7.5 million cat owners in the UK. So the business might conclude that the sample is not particularly representative. On the other hand a national survey suggested that 30% of cat owners in the UK are aged 35-44. So the business might argue that the survey might be a reasonable estimate for the age group.

Secondary research

What is secondary research?

Data that has been collected, analysed and presented for use in a project or report is called secondary data. It is any data that already exists and has been collected for another purpose. Investigating, analysing and using secondary data is known as secondary research. Secondary data may be **quantitative**, providing numbers, facts and figures. It may also be **qualitative**, providing views and opinions.

Sometimes secondary research is called **desk research** because the activity can be carried out at a desk or workstation as opposed to field research, which is the collection of primary data and usually takes place away from the desk.

Secondary research can be as important as primary research so long as the data is valid, is used in context and its limitations are understood.

Uses of secondary research

Secondary research has a number of uses.

Backgound It can be an important way of obtaining background information for a marketing project. For example, a market report might identify the growth in sales of mobile phones.

Issues It is often carried out at the start of a project to identify the main issues that need to be addressed. For example, a newspaper article might outline a growing awareness by customers of environmentally friendly products.

Evidence It can be useful for providing examples of statistics and supporting evidence in a report. For example, it might show trends that are taking place, such as growing sales of DVDs, or market shares of supermarkets.

Marketing mix It can be used to inform and to produce evidence for the marketing mix. For example, it might help:

- to influence the type of product, using information in journals about new technical innovations;
- to set the price of a product, using price lists in catalogues;
- to influence place, using information on the Internet about the growth of sales in different shops;
- to influence promotion, using data on advertising spending by businesses in reports.

The starting point for secondary research is the aims and objectives of the research. Questions such as 'Why am I doing it?' and 'What do I want to find out?' must be asked. Once aims and objectives have been set, the next questions are 'What sources of data are available?' and 'Where can they be found?'.

Sources of secondary data - internal

Secondary data can be found within an organisation itself. Most organisations will collect and hold a wide range of data, which is then analysed and presented to different teams or departments within the organisation.

Internal business data This could include sales records showing how much has been sold in a given period, how much these sales are worth and who has bought the goods. Sales may have been analysed by product, by area, by customer or by a member of a sales team. This data is likely to be used first by the senior management in an organisation and then stored for future use and analysis.

Accounts and financial reports Most internal business data will start with sales, particularly the value of revenue that these sales generate. The financial analysis of this data will result in one part of the business accounts. Other parts will include payments from customers, payments to suppliers, wages and other running costs.

Figure 1 *Secondary data*

Company annual reports show business performance and financial data

Trade journals can show market trends and competitors' product specifications

Most organisations will be able to use ICT resources to analyse and present financial data in a variety of ways to suit the needs of research users. The information can sometimes be found in company annual reports and accounts, as shown in Figure 1.

Customer data This could range from basic financial data, showing sales or deliveries to trade customers such as wholesalers or retailers, through to specific data about the buying habits of individual domestic customers and consumers. Data on trade customers will come directly from internal sales records. Information about consumers may have been collected from primary research, questioning consumers directly, or may be in a database produced from loyalty cards or credit card transactions.

Reports Over time most organisations will create a collection of research surveys and reports that were produced and used in the past for previous research projects. These can be a great source for secondary research, providing background against which to measure new findings or plan further research.

Sources of secondary data - external

Secondary data can also be found in material produced by other organisations.

Government published data Government departments and agencies collect a great deal of data. The information is sometimes referred to as 'official statistics' as it presents a picture of the country itself. This could include:

- population and demographic statistics (how many people);
- social statistics (what are the living conditions of the population);
- health statistics (what are the most common health problems);
- economic statistics (how much money is generated and where it is spent);
- industrial statistics (the structure and make-up of an industry).

To make this wealth of data easier to access, government statistics are usually grouped together and presented in easy to read reports. The 2001 Census, for example, contains demographic and geographic data about the entire UK population on a particular date in 2001. The data in the Census can be analysed for the entire population of the country, for a region, or to give a population breakdown for a specific town or district. There are many other ways in which government statistics are presented and reported. Most government statistics can be accessed at no charge, at libraries or from the Internet, although there may be a cost for individual reports if they are purchased outright. The Office for National Statistics (ONS) is the government agency responsible for collecting, analysing and disseminating UK statistics.

Commercial research reports These are produced independently by market research organisations and made available for sale. They cover a wide range of different products, markets and industries on a regular basis. They aim to provide a comprehensive background upon which business organisations can base their marketing plans. For example, a report on the ice cream market in the UK will include data such as the market size, value, main suppliers, main customers, a snapshot of the current situation in the marketplace, market trends from the past, and forecasts for the future. Organisations that publish such reports include the

Euromonitor, Key Note, the Financial Times and Mintel. Some manufacturers produce business reports containing secondary data about their trade sector for stakeholders or PR purposes. Industries also produce reports containing statistical data about their own industry, for example the Engineering Council and the Institute of Grocery Distribution.

Trade journals These provide a valuable source of secondary information on specific markets, industries or trade sectors. Trade journals often include reports on the state of the industry, supported by a wealth of data and research information as shown in Figure 1. This data may have been generated by the journal itself or may have been supplied by an organisation from within the industry or trade sector, such as a leading manufacturer.

Other media The business pages in national newspapers and business programmes on TV and radio will often include secondary research to support or illustrate a particular report that is being presented. Most libraries hold a wide range of secondary data in the reference and business sections. In some areas there will be a specialist business library that collects together a wide range of secondary data and may buy commercial reports or trade journals and make them available for public access. These libraries may also hold reports from manufacturers or industry groups. Some manufacturers or industry bodies provide their own reports.

The Internet Using the Internet and search engines is an easy way to start looking for secondary data. Examples of information that could be obtained include:

- British government statistics from National Statistics Online www.statistics.gov.uk;
- statistics and reports on EU members at www.europa.eu.int/comm/eurostat;
- foreign government websites provide data about a country, such as www.fedstats.gov and www.stat-usa.gov (USA), www.china.org.cn/english (People's Republic of China);
- commercial publishers provide limited access to their data, for example www.euromonitor.com, but access to all information may require a subscription;
- business sites such as www.virgin.com or www.boots.com will provide data about individual businesses.

Benefits of secondary research

Ease of access Access is quick as the collection of original data has already been done. It is usually easy to find because there can be many sources to choose from. Data may have been published, be in the public domain and be available in libraries, on the Internet or in the press. Data can also be easy to read, interpret or understand as it will have already been analysed and presented in a way that it is easily accessible for the original audience.

Relatively low cost The costs of collecting and analysing data will have been paid for by the organisation that commissioned the original primary research. This applies particularly to secondary research data that is already in the public domain, for example a survey in a newspaper article about the buying habits of people who are about to go on holiday. In contrast, research reports are produced and then sold by specialist publishers such as Mintel. To buy them direct from the publisher can cost many thousands of pounds. However, they can be available in business libraries where the cost is lower.

Flexibility Research can be done in your own time, as and when you can get to a library, Internet or other source.

Limitations of secondary research

Whilst secondary research may have been precisely right when it was carried out and used for its original purpose, certain limitations can reduce its usefulness in any current research project.

Relevance The data has already been collected and analysed for some other purpose. This means that it may not meet the precise needs of the current research project. This could limit its usefulness for the current project. For example, 2001 Census Key Statistics may provide total population data for a particular town. However, it may not say how many of the people in that town order take away pizzas on a regular basis because pizza consumption was not the original aim of the 2001 Census.

Bias The source of the data needs to be considered. Also, the reasons for collecting the data and presenting it in the way it appears must be taken into account. There can be bias. The originators of the research will have their own aims, objectives and motivation for conducting research and for interpreting and presenting it in a certain way. For example, a pro-smoking lobby group may publish research that shows that the majority of people they have polled do not object to smoking in restaurants. Before accepting this research, the secondary researcher must consider who the lobby group has polled (smokers or non-smokers), the size of the sample and the motivation for publishing the research (to show that anti-smoking legislation is not necessary). This is likely to be less of a problem for data from internal sources.

Age Secondary research may not be up-to-date as it will have been collected and used by its originator before it becomes available for wider access. For example, manufacturers and marketing organisations will often make their research findings available once the data is no longer commercially sensitive or confidential.

Comprehensive The data may be partial rather than comprehensive. It could also be data that is presented in such a way as to meet marketing aims or communicate a particular message. For example, for many years Pedigree Petfoods promoted the claim that '(in research) 9 out of 10 cats preferred Whiskas cat food to any other brand'. This marketing claim could have been backed up by research findings. However, it does not provide any information about how the research was conducted, how many cats or their owners were sampled, what else they liked to eat, and did not take into account the many cats that are fed other brands.

Portfolio practice · E-Shoes

The marketing team at E-Shoes, a manufacturer of trainers, has obtained a copy of the Executive Summary from the commercial research report, *Euromonitor Footwear in the UK*, 2004. Some of the information in the report is shown below.

(a) **State three pieces of information about the footwear market in the UK.**
(b) **Identify the largest target group of consumers in the market and how this is changing.**
(c) **Analyse (i) the level of competition and (ii) distribution in the market.**
(d) **Discuss other sources of secondary research that could help to research this market and how they would be useful.**

Table 1 *The UK footwear market*

MARKET SIZE. The UK market for footwear has grown by 1.9% since 2003 to reach a value of £5.1 bn in 2003.
MARKET SECTORS. Women's footwear was the largest sector of the UK market, with 47.7% of the market, representing a value of £2.4 bn in 2003.
SHARE OF MARKET. C&J Clark has remained the market leader with more than 12% of value sales due to its successful positioning and its high brand awareness.
MARKETING ACTIVITY. In 2003, the leading advertiser in the footwear market was Nike, with a total adspend of more than £6 m.
CORPORATE OVERVIEW. C&J Clark has remained market leader in 2003 with more than 12% of sales, combined with a strong three-year growth performance of 5.9%.
NIKE INC. Turnover increased by 8.1% in 2003 to reach US$10.7 bn.
MARKS & SPENCER PLC. Turnover decreased by 0.7% in 2003 to £8.1 bn.
C&J CLARK LTD. Turnover grew by 7% to £937 m in 2002 from £875 m in 2001.
STYLO PLC. Group turnover figures reached £232 m in 2003, up by 11.4% on the previous year.
DISTRIBUTION. Accounting for 39% of the market in value terms in 2003, specialist shoe shops remain the dominant retail channels in the UK footwear market.
CONSUMER PROFILE. The most popular type of shoes sold in the UK in 2003 were formal footwear, with 65% of all shoe sales.
MARKET FORECASTS. The market is forecast to grow by nearly 7.6% between the forecast period to reach a value of £5.5 bn in 2008.
SECTOR FORECASTS. The women's sector is forecast to continue dominating the market with a value share of 46.3% by 2008.

Source: adapted from *Euromonitor Footwear in the UK*, Euromonitor, June 2004.

Meeting the assessment criteria

For your chosen product or service you are required to identify and carry out appropriate market research to help produce an appropriate marketing mix. When selecting and using secondary research you will need to consider the guidance shown above, that will help to ensure that the secondary research you use is relevant, appropriate and as up-to-date as possible. Once you have found the secondary research you will need to analyse and use it to provide information that will help in the development of your marketing mix.

Business example - 'The Mirrors Live'

Four students at college have formed a band called 'The Mirrors'. They have a live recording from a gig that they want to sell in summer 2004 as a CD album. They have looked for secondary research data to help plan the marketing mix.

Table 2 *Value of music sales*, UK, (£000)*

Quarterly totals	April/June 03	April/June 04	%change
7" singles	166	307	+84.9
12" singles	2,709	2,876	+6.2
Cassette singles	268	-	-100
CD singles	9,751	10,541	+8.1
Total singles	**12,894**	**13,724**	**+6.4**
LP	1,606	1,175	-26.8
Cassette	721	417	-42.2
CD	200,568	208,516	+4.1
Total album	**202,568**	**210,108**	**+3.7**
Music DVD	6,419	7,103	+10.7
Total value	**221,881**	**230,935**	**+4.1**
Annual totals	**Year to June 03**	**Year to June 04**	**%change**
7" singles	544	924	+69.9
12" singles	12,477	11,186	10.3
Cassette singles	3,435	154	-95.5
CD singles	58,606	48,248	-17.7
Total singles	**75,062**	**60,512**	**-19.4**
LP	6,028	5,442	-9.7
Cassette	4,301	2,728	-36.6
CD	1,068,050	1,105,318	+3.5
Total album	**1,078,430**	**1,113,490**	**+3.3**
Music Video/DVD	28,734	48,591	+69.1
Total value	**1,182,226**	**1,222,593**	**+3.0**

* Shipments to all distributors and retailers from record companies.
Source: adapted from BPI website.

Mark Band 1 *Carry out and produce evidence from a limited range of sources and do a simple analysis of the information. Information from secondary data should give some market information about the chosen product.*
Annual totals show that the market for recordings is large, at £1,222 million for the year to June 2004. The market has grown +3.0%, from £1,182 million for the year to June 2003. The quarterly totals show that for the most recent quarter, April/June 2004, the total value of the market has grown at a greater rate, +4.1%, compared to the same quarter in 2003. Both sets of data suggest that the market for recordings is worth trying to enter to obtain a share in the form of sales of the live recording. The annual totals show that the product generating the greatest sales value is the CD album. So a CD album could be a suitable format for the recording.

Mark Band 2 *Use a combination of research to determine the characteristics of the target group or size of market or competition, with some indication as to the most relevant information. Draw some specific conclusion from the research.*
Annual totals show that single sales fell over two years. But they increased by 6.4% in April/June 2004 compared to 2003. So this may be a good time to release a single to help promote a CD album sold in summer 2004. A CD single would be an appropriate format. The type of single generating the most sales is the CD single. It had nearly 90% of the singles market in 2004. Although sales of 7" singles hold a small share of the market, 0.075% in the year to June 2004, this format has shown the greatest change in sales between June 2003-04, an increase of +69.9%. Quarterly totals show that the growth in the most recent quarter April/June 2004 has been even greater, at +84.9% and that the share of the market for 7" singles has nearly doubled to 0.13%. Although 7" remains a small part of the overall single market formats, it might also be a useful as an unusual 'novelty' format for promoting a live CD album.

Figure 2 *Products bought over the Internet, 12 months to July 2003, survey results and CD prices*

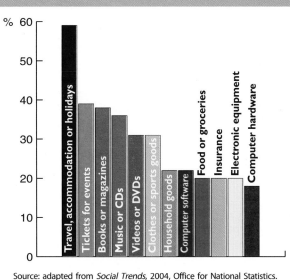

Source: adapted from *Social Trends*, 2004, Office for National Statistics.

Retail prices for CD albums, November 2004
HMV - 'chart' CDs £9.99
Tesco - most 'chart' CDs £8.39, reissues £4.97
Virgin Megastore - chart CDs £9.99, reissues £7.99
Woolworths - most 'chart' CDs £12.99, reissues £6.99
SPIN Compact Discs retail website - new releases £10.99-11.99, specialist reissues £7-8.99
Mute record label website - new releases £9.99-10.99

Mark Band 3 *Use a comprehensive range of secondary research from a wide range of relevant sources. There must be real application of the data to your chosen product, service or target group.*

The data in Table 2 and Figure 2 can help develop part of the marketing mix for the CD album. For example, the format of the product should be a CD. This has by far the largest sales in 2004 and was the only format showing an increase since 2003. Table 2 shows the extent of music sales through the retail trade. Sales through shops and to distributors are likely to be an effective way of distributing the CD. Figure 2 shows that in the 12 months to July 2003, 36% of people surveyed bought CDs over the Internet. So using the Internet could be another way of selling the CD, especially as downloading of music

increases. However, CD sales will face strong competition from spending on 'Tickets for events' and 'Books/magazines and e-learning/training material' which are purchased by a higher proportion of people than CDs. The list of retail prices gives a good indication of current retail selling prices in high street shops, from Internet retailers and direct from a record label itself. It may be better to sell the CD album at a low price such as £7.99. This might help to attract people to take a chance to listen to a new band that is only just starting out. However, the list only covers 6 of many outlets selling CDs. More secondary data may be needed on prices of CDs as this may not be representative. Also, CD prices fluctuate. So prices need to be checked regularly to keep up-to-date.

Use secondary data to research the price of DVDs.
- Think about the aims and objectives a business might have had when setting the price.
- Think about where the information can be found. Try to collect information from three sources.
- State how the prices of DVDs are different.
- Explain why these prices might be different.
- Suggest how these prices might affect the price of a new DVD being launched.

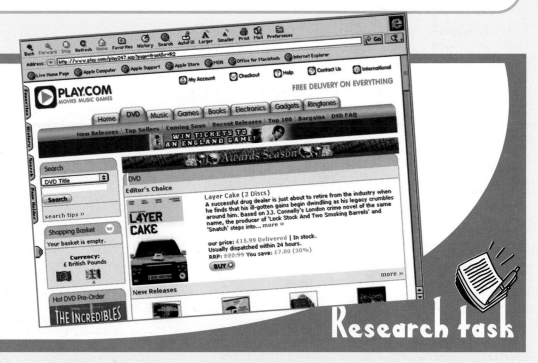

Research task

36 The marketing mix

What is the marketing mix?

The marketing mix is a term that is used a lot by individuals and businesses engaged in marketing activities. It refers to the combination of main variables that make up the marketing strategy and marketing plans. The main variables of the marketing mix are **product, price, place** and **promotion**, known as the 4Ps. Sometimes the marketing mix of services also includes the **people, processes** or activities and **physical evidence** or environment involved in delivering the service.

These variables can be viewed as decisions that must be made when bringing a product to market. The marketing mix is usually designed to achieve the marketing aims and objectives of the business, to meet or influence the needs and wants of customers and in most cases to attract customers to generate sales.

Product

This is the part of the marketing mix that specifies what it is that has to be marketed. A product can be either a physical good from manufacturers or a service from a provider. The way the product is defined may vary according to the resources available, the objectives of the business and the target market that the product is aimed at. Figure 1 shows important questions that a business must consider when deciding the nature of the product to be marketed. The marketing of a product is covered in section 37.

Price

This is the part of the marketing mix that establishes how much the product will sell for and as a result the potential income and profit from the product. Each of the questions in Figure 2 needs to be addressed before deciding on the pricing strategy and price structure of a product. The pricing of a product is covered in section 38.

Place

This is the part of the marketing mix that plans where and how the customer sees and buys the product. It is about how products are distributed to customers. The optimum 'place' for a product needs to be considered when developing a marketing mix. In the business world decisions about distribution can be outside the control of the manufacturer unless the manufacturer also sells directly to customers. Important place questions are considered in Figure 3. The distribution of a product is covered in section 39.

Promotion

This is the part of the marketing mix that creates awareness and desire for the product. Important promotion questions are considered in Figure 4. The promotion of a product is covered in section 40.

Figure 1 *Important product questions*

What is it? What do we call the product? How is it positioned?
Is it a good like a BMW car or a service like a taxi ride in London? Is it an Apple ipod or a Sony MP3 player? Is it a Christian Dior evening bag or an adidas sports bag?

How do customers experience the product?
Do they buy, use it and dispose of it, like a Duracell battery? Do they buy it, eat it and dispose of the packaging like a Domino's take-away pizza? Do they use it again and again like a Miele washing machine? Do they walk into it, look around and learn from their experience like a museum or art gallery?

How should it be packaged and presented to customers?
Should it be in a jar, bottle, bucket, plastic bag? If it's in a bottle, should the bottle be glass or PET? Should the bottle be clear, opaque or coloured? Should it be labelled or printed? Should the bottles be sold singly and/or packed in boxes of four, like Ribena light, or sixes like Tizer?

What shape, size, material, colour should be chosen?
Should it be a formal pin striped suit or a beige summer suit? Should a domestic iron be made from black plastic and chromed metal or in many different colours of plastic to match current decorative styles, with the metal coloured to co-ordinate with the overall design?

What do customers think that they are buying?
Are they buying a ticket to the theatre or are they buying an evening's entertainment? Is it a jar of honey or is it a healthy natural sweetener?

What materials or ingredients?
Should a unique flavour be used, such as Coca-Cola or Heinz baked beans, or should many flavours be offered such as Innocent smoothies? Should the basic raw material be used and the product changed to appeal to different customers or different markets, such as buttered popcorn or a salty, savoury popcorn?

What if it is a service?
How should it be recognised by potential customers as something that they want to buy? How should it be packaged and presented? For example, should a flight be off-peak air travel, business travel, long or short haul, early, last minute booking or stand-by?

Figure 2 *Important pricing questions*

What should it sell for?
Should it be a relatively high price like a Porsche car or a lower price like a Smart car? Can the price by set by the business like a can of paint or is it influenced by the market such as vegetable prices?

What pricing strategy?
Should the business lead on pricing like pharmaceuticals companies or mirror what competitors charge like magazines?

What is the price perception for this product within the target market?
Is this product thought to be a high price product like a Rolex watch or a low price product like Aldi margarine?

What price will cover costs and make the profit margin required by the manufacturer and all the links in the supply chain?
Does a high price need to be charged to cover higher costs of production like a gourmet meal? Can a relatively low price be set if average costs are reduced by producing large quantities like BIC pens?

How much to charge distributors?
Is it the same for a wholesaler or cash and carry customer like Costco as it would be for a major retailer like Tesco?

Will tax influence the price?
Will there be VAT like on CDs or no VAT like on children's clothes?

What does a low price say about a product?
Is it seen as a good value product like supermarket own brands or washing powders? Is it seen as a 'bargain' or is it seen as having low quality?

Who makes the choices and decisions about the marketing mix?

Depending on the size and structure of an organisation, different people or teams of people will be responsible for making decisions about elements of the marketing mix. For example, in a large organisation like Nike there may be a team of international marketing professionals that make up a marketing department, supported by extensive marketing research on the markets in which they trade. Individual markets, such as soccer or basketball, may have dedicated marketing teams, each responsible for making decisions that are right for that market or sector, within the overall aims of the company as a whole.

In contrast, in most small organisations marketing will be the responsibility of the owner or a director. In this type of organisation the marketing decisions are no less important. If you were to launch your own product, it is likely that you would have to make all of the decisions about the marketing mix yourself. There are organisations that will support companies that do not have sufficient marketing expertise in-house. These include marketing and market research agencies, some banks, trade and industry bodies and government organisations such as Business Link.

How are choices and decisions about the marketing mix made?

Decisions about elements of the marketing mix are most likely to be made from a combination of marketing research data and individual knowledge or expertise. The availability of resources is another important factor.

Decisions based on marketing research data are more likely to be objective and supported by information rather than opinion. However, subjective opinion based on personal knowledge or expertise built-up from real-life experience in the marketplace can also be important.

Each marketing decision must be viewed within the context of overall aims and objectives for the organisation. The appropriate ideas or supporting data should then be used to help make the decision.

Figure 3 *Important place questions*

What is the supply chain for the product?
Will it be sold via a retailer like Dixons selling electrical goods, a market stall like flowers, door-to-door like household goods sold through Lakeland catalogues, direct from an advertisement in a magazine like Saga holidays or direct off the screen from a website like Amazon selling books, CDs and DVDs?

Direct from the producer?
Is the producer equipped to sell and deliver direct to customers like take-aways or Dell computers? Do consumers expect to receive the product direct like hairdressing services?

Where do customers look for the product now and in the future?
Will traditional outlets be used like retailers or others like the Internet? Will there be a growth in out-of-town retail shopping centres at the expense of town centres? Where do they buy currently and is this changing like the growth of non-food products sold from supermarkets?

What influence can the manufacturer or service provider really have over how and where the product is placed in the market?
How can they maintain their place? What are the opportunities like the growth of town centre living, leading to high value shops and entertainment? What are the threats like the Internet leading to increasing sales from abroad? What factors are outside the control of the manufacturer or service provider like the ageing of the population?

What role can the Internet play in selling and distribution?
Is the product suitable for selling from a website like a book? Are target customers ready to buy from a website like the growth of downloading music or financial services from First Direct?

Indirect via wholesalers or retail distributors?
What is the role of wholesalers, cash & carry's, and retailers? How much influence does the manufacturer or service provider have over retailers?

Figure 4 *Important promotion questions*

Which promotional tools should be used?
What methods will be used? These include advertising like McDonald's 'I'm lovin' it', sales promotions, public relations, direct marketing or sponsorship like Virgin's sponsorship of the Formula 1 BMW team? Which are appropriate for the product and target market?

How much promotion?
Is there a large budget like Nestlé or a small budget like a local tanning centre? What is the competitive position of the business and its aims and objectives?

Which media to choose?
What media will be used? These could include newspapers used by insurance companies, magazines used by clothes or perfume companies, posters used by Nike, leaflets and magazines used by Orange, audio, such as radio and recordings used by solicitors, moving images including television and cinema advertisements, ambient media such as stickers or printed carrier bags with the Tesco name, branded display items like Nestlé chiller cabinets in shops or product placement in films and on television by Sony and new media, including texts, screen pop-ups, and other web-based opportunities used by Google.

How long should a promotional campaign run?
Is it long-term and strategic like Coca-Cola advertisements or is it tactical to meet a short-term objective like the launch of a new film?

The importance of resources

Resources can have a major influence on the choice of marketing mix. A large organisation with a significant marketing budget is in a position to spend considerably more on its marketing mix than a smaller organisation with only a small amount of money to spend.

There is a direct link between the size and scope of the marketing mix developed for a product and the size of the budget available, together with the willingness to spend that budget. An example is shown in Figure 5.

Watch an ad-break on a commercial television channel. Pick one of the products being advertised. Identify as much as you can of the marketing mix that has been created for that product.

- Note the product - what is it? What are the main features that make it a distinctive 'product'?
- Price – is price mentioned? If so how much? How does this compare with the price of similar, competitor products?
- Place – based on the information in the television commercial where can you buy the product? What are the different places you can buy the product? If 'place' is stated clearly consider why and what customers must do to buy the product.
- Promotion – you have seen the product being advertised on television. How frequently does the advertisement appear? How does this compare with other products being advertised during the ad-break? What, if any, other promotional activity is being applied to the product?
- What is the target market? Who is the product aimed at? Who is the advertising aimed at? Is there a difference? If so, why is there a difference?

Research task

Figure 5 *Marketing at Coca-Cola Enterprises Ltd. and Fentimans Ltd.*

Coca-Cola Enterprises Ltd. and Fentimans Ltd both produce high quality, sparkling beverages flavoured with cola. Both companies have products distributed in British supermarkets, and both compete for sales in the soft drinks market. Despite some apparent similarities of product and objectives, the marketing mix for Coca-Cola Enterprises Ltd. is far greater and more extensive than the marketing mix for Fentimans Ltd.

One of the main factors for this difference will be the size of the marketing budget. As part of one of the largest multinational food manufacturing organisations in the world, Coca-Cola Enterprises Ltd. has a very famous brand to support and some major international competitors. As a consequence its marketing budget is huge in comparison to Fentimans Ltd. and it is more likely that people will see Coca-Cola advertising than Fentiman's advertising. However, within its own budget constraints Fentimans Ltd. will have developed its own marketing mix which meets the objectives of the business, is right for its products and creates awareness amongst its target customers.

Portfolio practice · Ambrosia Devon Custard

Premier Foods plc is a UK manufacturer and marketer of shelf-stable (ambient) grocery products. The company manufactures and markets grocery products for the retail grocery and out-of-home markets … Branded products include Ambrosia (custard and milk puddings).

Source: adapted from http://today.reuters.co.uk/stocks/companyprofile.

Premier Foods, the maker of Branston pickle and Typhoo tea, said it hoped to pull free of tough trading conditions as winter creeps in and consumers turn to brands such as its Ambrosia custard. 'We're into the busy period now and goods like our custard and tea are biased towards the colder weather' said chief executive, Robert Schofield.

Source: adapted from The Guardian, 11.9.2004.

(a) **Using Figure 6, identify features of the marketing mix (price, promotion, product and place) of Ambrosia Devon Custard using examples.**
(b) **Examine ONE way in which each of the '4Ps' of the marketing mix for Ambrosia might be changed and how this might affect the product.**

Figure 6 Ambrosia Devon Custard advertisement

SAVE 50p
Ambrosia Rice Pudding/
Custard pots
4x135g
£1.49 99p

Meeting the assessment criteria

To meet the assessment objective for this unit you are required to produce an appropriate marketing mix for a new or existing product or service.

Business example - Beta Garden Tools Ltd

Beta Garden Tools Ltd is a business that manufactures plastic buckets. To use up scrap material it has designed and developed a lightweight hand-fork, made from recycled plastic, for weeding the garden. The company is based in Swansea and has received a Regional Innovation Grant of £25,000 to help market the new product. Although experienced in producing and selling plastic buckets to the packaging trade it has little experience of marketing consumer products. It needs advice on developing a marketing mix for the new fork. Some basic marketing research is available.

Selling prices for hand forks
Large DIY store: steel £6.58; stainless steel £7.98
Garden centre: steel £6.99; stainless steel £8.99

Table 1 Percentage of people who are interested in Gardening

Total		60%
Male		53%
Female		67%
Age group	15-24	30%
	25-34	47%
	35-54	64%
	55+	77%
Socio-economic group	AB	64%
	C1, C2	62%
	DE	54%

Source: adapted from RHS report, The Good Life Factor, April-May 2004.

Table 2 Gardening magazines

Readership of gardening magazines - 12 m to Sept 2004						
All figures %	Socio-economic group		Age		Gender	
Title	ABC1	C2DE	15-44	45+	Men	Women
Amateur Gardening	51.6	48.4	18.3	81.7	42.0	58.0
Garden News	49.5	50.5	16.2	83.8	50.8	49.2
BBC Gardeners World	64.5	35.5	28.7	71.3	36.8	63.2
Garden Answers	54.4	45.6	28.9	71.1	42.5	57.5

Source: adapted from National Readership Survey, Open Access data.

Mark Band 1 *Creation of a basic marketing mix for your specified product/service that covers all the relevant Ps.*

Based on the available market research, a basic marketing mix has been created.

Product A lightweight hand-fork for weeding the garden will be produced.

Price Local retail selling prices for metal hand-forks range from £6.58 to £8.99. Beta hand-fork could be priced within this range to be competitive.

Place Local research shows that hand forks are bought mainly from large DIY stores. This is an area of distribution that could be appropriate for the Beta hand-fork.

Promotion Females aged over 55 and in the ABC1 socio-economic group appear to be the largest groups of people interested in gardening in magazines. These could be target markets.

Mark Band 2 *Creation of a detailed marketing mix for your product/service, which shows a good understanding and knowledge of the relevant Ps.*

Product The product is a lightweight hand-fork for weeding the garden. But there are other aspects of the product that need to be considered. For example, the product will be manufactured in green to fit in with consumers' views of environmental products.

Price The local research on price is limited. Further research has shown that consumers may be willing to pay a premium for metal garden tools, but are reluctant to pay much for plastic tools. Given that plastic is the only material that Beta can use, it may be better to charge a lower price than the band range £6.58 to £8.99.

Place In conversation with family members it becomes clear that there are many other places where garden hand-forks can be purchased. The business might consider selling through large DIY stores and garden centres, for example.

Promotion The fork needs promotion in two areas:
- to the retail trade, in order to get the product into distribution;
- to consumers, to raise awareness. Females aged over 55 and in the ABC1 socio-economic group appear to be the largest groups of people interested in gardening. Advertisements in gardening magazines may be effective.

Mark Band 3 *Creation of a comprehensive marketing mix which is clearly linked to the research and segmentation evidence and shows depth of knowledge and understanding of the relevant Ps.*

Product The product is a lightweight hand-fork for weeding the garden. A different way of describing the product could be as follows.
- Function. The product could be marketed as 'an easy way to a weed-free garden without the effort of using traditionally heavy garden tools'.
- Colour. As the product is made from plastic it can be made in any colour. The business may choose a colour traditionally associated with the garden, such as green or black. It may also produce some in bright colours that will show up easily if laid on the ground.
- Packaging. The product could be sold simply with just a bar-coded label. However, given the profile of the target market value could be added by packing it in a card carton with a clear plastic window on the front to display the fork.

Price Local research reveals the following retail selling prices for hand forks.
- Large DIY store: steel £6.58; stainless steel £7.98.
- Garden centre: steel £6.99; stainless steel £8.99.

But local research is limited. Further research has shown that people may not be prepared to pay a high price. Given the product is made from plastic (a material perceived to be cheaper than metals) but is packed in a box (which should add value), Beta Garden Tools Ltd has decided the new fork will sell at £5.99. An investigation of costs has shown that this price is sufficient to generate profit for Beta Garden Tools Ltd and the retail distributors.

Place As a business Beta Garden Tools Ltd has only limited experience with supplying the retail trade. It needs to consider if selling through retailers, such as DIY and garden centres, is the best place for the new fork. It has also investigated selling:
- through independent garden centres via wholesalers;
- direct to gardeners via magazine advertisements;
- via an Internet site.

The business has decided that selling through retailers will reach a larger market, but it will also sell some directly as this will not increase costs too greatly.

Promotion The business will sell to both the retail trade and directly. Discounts and other 'bulk buy' deals will be offered to DIY shops and garden centres to help increase sales. When selling directly to gardeners via magazine advertisements Beta Garden Tools Ltd needs to decide which magazines to use for the advertising. Beta Garden Tools Ltd has compared the readership profiles of the magazines with the profile of their target market - females, aged over 55, in the ABC1 socio-economic group. It has decided that the profile of readers for BBC *Gardeners' World* magazine comes closest to the profile of the target market.

What is a product?

The term 'product' it can apply to:
- physical goods bought by customers and used by consumers;
- services that are bought, received or experienced by customers or consumers.

'Product' is often considered the most important of the four 'P's' as it is the product which defines and identifies what has to be sold - it is the one that will make money. Your 'product' is what you create, produce, manufacture or acquire to market and sell. Sections 28 and 31 look at the development of new products and diversification of businesses into other products.

Product specifications

Many people have bright ideas for products. Not all of these ideas are realistic or can be developed into something that sells and makes money. 'Product' in the marketing mix is about specifying and defining precisely what is for sale.

An example of a product specification for a shirt is shown in Figure 1. Similar information will be included in any product specification, whatever the product, although the materials used will vary according to the product itself. Services also need specifications, to make sure that nothing is missed and consumers know precisely what is being marketed and what service they will receive.

A product may be bought and used by consumers in a number of different forms. Most importantly, however, the customer must know precisely what it is that they are buying. If they are unsure, this could be a reason not to buy the product or to buy a competitor's product which may be clearer to understand and easier to identify.

A simple test to check if a product can be identified and understood clearly by potential customers is to:
- describe it in as few words as possible to someone who is not familiar with the product;
- confirm that they understand the product clearly by asking them to explain back what they think the product is all about.

In this way a business can make sure that customers recognise products for sale.

Product strategy

A business must plan its product strategy based on its overall aims and objectives. It may have narrow or wide product range or somewhere in between.

Narrow product range Some businesses are content to limit their products to a narrow product range that can be produced easily, to a good standard, and at a price that returns a satisfactory profit. Products may be aimed at a particular market or even a small niche market. Small businesses are often limited in their product ranges due to limited finance or the use of specialist skills.

Wide product range A business may be in markets that are growing, have many innovative competitors and survival depends on producing and launching a stream of new products to keep up with market developments. Businesses sometimes launch new products when some of their products are reaching the saturation stage of their product life cycle. This allows them to maintain revenue. As sales of some older products fall, they are replaced by sales of newer products.

Different businesses in different markets will need to adopt different product strategies that meet the needs of:
- the market;
- its own stakeholders;
- its own capacity.

Figures 2 and 3 show some examples.

Figure 1 *Examples of information that could be included in a product specification for a shirt*

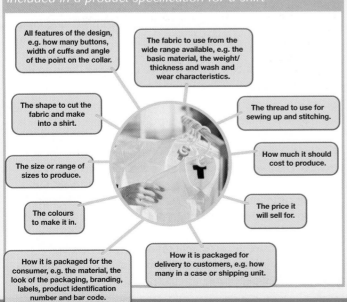

- All features of the design, e.g. how many buttons, width of cuffs and angle of the point on the collar.
- The fabric to use from the wide range available, e.g. the basic material, the weight/thickness and wash and wear characteristics.
- The shape to cut the fabric and make into a shirt.
- The thread to use for sewing up and stitching.
- The size or range of sizes to produce.
- How much it should cost to produce.
- The colours to make it in.
- The price it will sell for.
- How it is packaged for the consumer, e.g. the material, the look of the packaging, branding, labels, product identification number and bar code.
- How it is packaged for delivery to customers, e.g. how many in a case or shipping unit.

Figure 2 *Cellect Executive Chauffeurs (narrow product range)*

Cellect Executive Chauffeurs specialises in providing high quality private transportation services for business and leisure use in London and the surrounding areas. It includes chauffeuring to and from airports, seaports, helipads or train stations, sightseeing, shopping trips and dining and special events, such as Royal Ascot, The Wimbledon Tennis Championship, and Chelsea Flower Show. Services also include diplomatic and VIP services, anti-surveillance and protection and booking of accommodation, restaurants and theatres.

Source: adapted from www.cellect.net.

Figure 3 *Unilever's product range (wide product range)*

Unilever is one of the world's leading suppliers of fast-moving consumer goods. It has a number of product areas and many brands with variations.

Product areas	Examples
Cooking and eating	Colman's mustard
	Carte D'Or ice cream
	Birds Eye frozen foods
	Flora pro-active spread
	Boursin cheese
	PG Tips tea
	Cornetto ice cream
	Bertolli pasta
	Bovril drink
Beauty and style	Dove soap
	Lux soap
	Timoteo shampoo
	Vaseline products
	Lynx deodorant
Around the house	Domestos cleaner
	Persil washing powder
	Surf washing liquid
	Comfort washing conditioner

Source: adapted from www.unilever.co.uk/ourbrands.

Developing a product

There are various stages in the development of a product. They apply to the development of both goods and services.

Product brief In many businesses the starting point for a product will be a descriptive 'brief' from the marketing team. This will outline what they believe will have appeal and therefore sell in the market. This brief is likely to be based on marketing research or other data, such as sales information or customer requests. The product development brief will be more or less detailed depending on the business, but is likely to include some of the features in Figure 4.

Prototypes and samples It is usually the responsibility of a product development team working with members of the production team to produce a prototype or samples of the product. These early versions of a product can be used by the marketing team to check that they meet the product development brief.

Market research Prototypes and samples can also be used for marketing research. They allow a business to check that the product being developed meets the needs of customers and consumers.

Launch Once the marketing team has agreed that the sample product meets the needs of the market and that it will be a viable

Figure 4 *Product development brief*

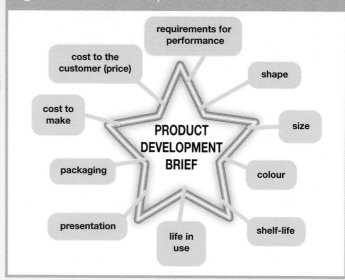

and profitable addition to the business, plans can be made for full production and its launch.

Customer driven and technology driven approaches

Businesses often take different approaches to the development of products.

Customer driven If the reason behind the development of a product is based on customer requests or meeting the needs of customers, as identified from marketing research, this is known as customer driven approach. It can also be referred to as being **market orientated** or having a **market oriented** approach as it takes into account the needs of customers in the market. It can be very successful, as meeting customer needs is key to the successful marketing of a product.

Technology driven Some businesses approach the market in a different way. They first develop and produce a product, often based on an idea or concept, and then they look for a market for the product. This is a way of working that is often adopted by businesses that are at the leading edge of technological development. It is a **product orientated/oriented approach**. This can be a risky strategy. It may turn out that there is only a small, limited market or even no market at all and the business will have already spent time and money on developing the product.

When developing a product it is easy for a business to get locked into what they can do from a technical or manufacturing point-of-view rather than what they should do because there is a viable market. Businesses therefore often use marketing research to identify a market or to confirm that a market exists for a product. Then, when the product has been developed, they use research to confirm that the product does actually meet the needs of customers and consumers. A business may develop the best product in the world, but if there is no market for it all the development work will have been a waste of resources. The business may have incurred unnecessary expenditure or investment which could have a disastrous effect on the business through over expenditure.

However, a technology driven approach is often used successfully in markets where the products are of a highly technical nature, such as pharmaceuticals or computer technology. New products may come about as a result of a technical development that could not have been foreseen by the marketing team or from marketing research.

Product management

It is the responsibility of the marketing team to manage the product. It must create a successful and profitable business out of selling the product and attracting customers to buy the product. This involves:

- managing a product and monitoring its sales and the marketplace through the use of research data;
- monitoring and adjusting costs and pricing to ensure profitability;
- creating the right marketing mix and implementing effective marketing plans to increase awareness of the product in the market so that it continues to generate sales;
- planning marketing research and product development to make sure that the product on sale remains right for the market.

Look for product specifications of two different goods and two different services. Depending on the product, you may find them in a number of different places. Look in instruction manuals, technical operating manuals, terms and conditions documents produced when setting up a business relationship and charter documents produced by service organisations. Specifications available for consumers are produced for many products, including pharmaceuticals, building products or motor vehicles.

Compare the product specifications that you find. Consider why some information is common to most of the specifications and why some pieces of information are exclusive to individual products or markets.

Alternatively, make contact with the marketing team at a business that you are familiar with or where you have personal contacts. Explain that you are studying Applied Business and learning about product management. Arrange to meet and interview a member of the marketing team who is responsible for product management and investigate:

- how they see their role in the business;
- their main responsibilities;
- their day-to-day activities;
- the main contribution that they make to the business.

Research task

Portfolio practice · Copella

Tropicana UK is a leading producer of fruit drinks, including the Copella juices range. The Copella range, is positioned at the top end of the market, usually at a premium price.

With its expertise and resources Tropicana UK could produce a huge range of juices with the Copella brand name, but limited the range to five. At some point a decision has been made about which flavours to choose and how it should it be packaged and presented to customers.

The Copella website stated on 20/06/2005:
'There have been many changes to Copella over the years, including new flavours such as Apple & Blackberry. Copella has just launched a new look with a bottle redesign and Copella Apple is now available in a new 330ml bottle. However, despite the changes, you can be assured the juice is as good as it's always been. Simple, natural, honest and true – Copella still reflects the timeless values of the Suffolk countryside.'

Source: adapted from www.copellafruitjuices.co.uk, on 20.06.2005

(a) **Identify THREE different decisions that may have been made about the packaging of Copella juices.**
(b) **Suggest reasons why Tropicana UK may have limited the Copella range to five flavours.**
(c) **Suggest ideas for primary market research that the business might carry out if it wanted to develop new products.**
(d) **Discuss to what extent the development of Copella was likely to have been customer or technology driven.**

Meeting the assessment criteria

You are required to produce an appropriate marketing mix for a new or existing product or service. You must justify all aspects of your devised marketing mix for your product or service.

This section, 37, deals with just one aspect of the marketing mix – Product. The suggestions below only cover the mark bands in terms of this aspect of the marketing mix. To cover the mark bands effectively you will need to take into account 'meeting the assessment criteria' in sections 36 to 40 which cover the marketing mix.

Business example - Helpcraft

Helpcraft manufactures products suitable for people with mobility difficulties. The product range is:
- rubber moulded grippers that can be pushed onto the ends of cutlery or tools;
- extended 'arms' with a moving grab mechanism to pick things up;
- plastic handles to attach to telephones.

It has decided to expand its product range into other areas. These include electronic moving chairs which help to lift people from the chair when they stand up.

Figures 5 and 6 show some information about this market.

Source: adapted from company information.

Figure 5 *UK population aged under 16 and over 65*

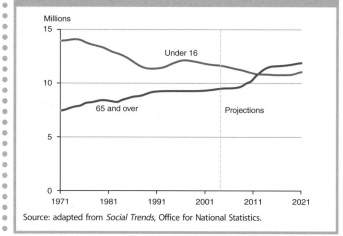

Source: adapted from *Social Trends*, Office for National Statistics.

Figure 6 *Great Britain population aged 90 and over*

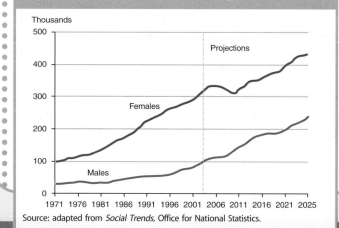

Source: adapted from *Social Trends*, Office for National Statistics.

Mark Band 1 *Creation of a simple marketing mix and a simple evaluation of the marketing mix and conclusions made without supporting evidence.*

Helpcraft makes products to help people with mobility difficulties. The product range includes rubber grips, extended plastic arms and plastic handles. It is a limited product range, geared at a particular market. The specifications are simple and the products are relatively easy to make, all from plastic. The target market is growing and likely to do so in future. So the choice of product in the marketing mix is a likely to be profitable for the business.

Mark Band 2 *Creation of a detailed mix showing an understanding of the 4Ps and a justification of the marketing mix, showing a range of supported evidence, arguments and conclusions.*

Products manufactured by Helpcraft are designed to help people with mobility difficulties. The product range is limited to simple designs and specifications that can be made from plastic, including rubber grips, extended plastic arms and plastic handles. The products are geared at a particular market – people who have mobility difficulties who are often elderly. The target market is growing and likely to do so in future. The UK has an ageing population. Figure 6 shows that the number of males and females aged over 90 is likely to rise. But perhaps also importantly, Figure 5 shows that the number of people over retirement age, 65+ is growing. So the choice of product in the range is a likely to prove profitable for the business. Costs must be controlled and sales should rise.

Mark Band 3 *Creation of a comprehensive mix linked to research and segmentation evidence and a comprehensive and fully justified account of all aspects of the marketing mix.*

The products manufactured by Helpcraft are designed to help people with a range of mobility difficulties. The product range is limited to simple designs and specifications that can be made from plastic. They include rubber grips, extended plastic arms and plastic handles. The products are geared at a particular market – people who have mobility difficulties - many who are often elderly. The target market is growing and likely to do so in future. The UK has an ageing population. Figure 6 shows that the number of males and females aged over 90 are likely to rise. But perhaps also importantly, Figure 5 shows that people over retirement age, 65+ are growing. There are also fewer younger people to look after them.

The choice of gerontic products in the marketing mix is a likely to be profitable for the business.
- Costs can be controlled due to the limited range produced and the simple yet standardised specifications.
- Sales should rise. The products only sells to a niche market. But it is one with particular needs which the products meet. The market is growing. The market for people aged 65+ is predicted to increase by around 50% in the next 15 years.

The expansion of the range could be a problem. Although they are related products, they may require different production techniques, different marketing and increased costs. Perhaps the business should find more simple ways to expand its product range, such as its range of plastic accessories.

38 Price

What is price?

Once consumers have seen a product, decided that it meets their needs and that they want it, the price is often the next thing they consider. Price is the charge made to purchasers of the product by a business or what customers have to pay to buy the product. This section considers where the price a business charges fits in the marketing mix, how a business determines the price of its products and the factors that go towards determining the price of a product.

Cost price

This is how much it costs a business to produce or acquire its product. Determining the cost price of a product is one of the most important management controls in marketing. Some businesses have specialist cost accountants that work with the product development and marketing teams so the cost of the product is measured and monitored at every stage in the development.

Knowing the cost price is important for the marketing team because any change in the cost price will directly affect the profitability of the product and will need to be addressed to protect profit margins. The most direct way of doing this is by reducing costs.

In every business, costs will be different. So depending on the product, different factors will be included in the cost price. In most businesses, the total cost price can be split into direct costs and indirect costs. Again, what is included in direct costs and indirect costs can vary depending on how a business wants to analyse its costs.

Direct costs These are all costs that can be related directly to the production of the product, such as:
- direct materials – the raw materials, bought-in components and packaging that are used to produce the product;
- direct labour – the wages and other costs of the workforce that is employed to make the product;
- direct production cost – the cost of the process, which may include energy, power and other fuel used directly in the manufacturing process.

Indirect costs Indirect costs, also called overheads, are the fixed costs that a business has to pay whether or not there is any production output, such as:
- indirect labour – the cost of employees not directly involved in the production process, including management, sales, marketing, quality assurance and other activities involved in the business;
- warehousing and distribution costs;
- rent, business rates, insurance and other business costs.

The total cost of these elements, added to the direct manufacturing costs, will give the total cost of the product. The total cost is usually divided by the quantity of products being produced to give the cost of a single product or unit of production, such as the cost per litre or kilo.

The cost price of a service can be calculated in much the same way, although the materials will be what are used in the provision of the service rather than in the production of goods.

Selling price

This is the price applied to the product when it is offered to the market. It is usually the price at which the business sells its products to distributors, such as wholesalers or retailers. It is sometimes known as the trade price. If a business deals directly with consumers, the selling price is what the consumers pay for the product.

The selling price has to meet the objectives of the business, including meeting sales and profit targets and allowing the product to perform in the market.

The difference between the total cost of the product and the selling price gives the business its gross profit margin. It is the gross profit that is retained by the business to:
- pay stakeholders;
- provide funds for investment in new machinery;
- pay for research and development;
- pay for advertising and promotions.

Gross profit will also be used to fund any discounting off the selling price or refunds that are given to trade customers. If the business sells the product for a figure below the total cost price it will make a loss.

How does a business decide what will be the selling price? It may take into account a number of factors.

Profit level This includes how much or what level of gross profit the business needs to survive and to pay for its planned investments. This is usually set as an objective by senior management within the business on advice from accountants.

Market place pricing This is how much similar products sell for - the price of competition.

Customer expectations Most customers will have an idea of the market price and what they are prepared to pay for a product. If a business charges too much, it may choose competition. If it charges too little it may raise questions over quality.

Distributor margins Each business in the supply chain (producers, wholesalers or retailers) will expect to make a margin when the product passes through their business. Distributor margins need to be considered in the costing equation because these additional costs to the cost price may raise the retail price beyond consumer and marketplace expectations.

Reducing costs

If the gross margin is not sufficient to meet the objectives or needs of the business, there are two ways that this can be addressed:
- raise the selling price;
- reduce costs.

Raising the selling price may not be an option because of market and competitor pressures. So the business may have to look carefully at reducing prices. There is a number of ways this can be done, but the most direct include:

- raw materials – buy cheaper, ask for a reduction from the supplier, find a new lower cost supplier or reduce the quantity used, as if less material is used then the cost price will fall;
- direct labour – cut wages or cut the number of employees engaged in production without reducing output;
- direct production cost – use the production equipment more efficiently to increase output within a given production time or use different equipment with a higher output and lower unit cost
- indirect costs – cut by buying services more cost effectively or cut the wage bill by reducing the number of employees not engaged in direct production.

Retail selling price (RSP)

This is the price paid at the end of the supply chain, usually by the consumer. If a business sells directly to consumers then the selling price and the retail price are the same. In this situation the producer has direct control over the retail price.

However, many businesses sell via a distributor, such as a retailer, that will set its own retail price for the product based on its own objectives. The producer may suggest what it believes is the optimum retail selling price for its product in the market. But it will have no direct control over the actual retail price that is charged.

Deciding on the retail selling price can be arrived at by taking into account factors such as:

- market place pricing – how much similar products sell for;
- customer/consumer expectations – what they expect to pay based on previous purchases and competitor pricing;
- distributor expectations – retailers will have their own objectives for gross profit on sales and this may be used to determine the retail selling price;
- profit at each point of distribution – as mentioned under selling price, each business in the supply chain will expect to make a

Table 1 *Women's perfume retail prices, 50ml bottles, Eau de Parfum*

Perfume	Price
Agent Provocateur	£36-37
Coty Exclamation	£5-£11
Dolce & Gabbana for Women	£18-£38
Burberry Touch for Women	£17
Vivienne Westwood Boudoir	£40-£42
Sisley Eau Du Soir	£55

Source: adapted from www.kelkoo.co.uk, 2005.

margin when the product passes through its business. Distributor margins need to be considered because they may raise the retail price beyond consumer and marketplace expectations or reduce the profit margin for the manufacturer;

- VAT – this is added at the current rate to most products sold in the UK and EU countries. Rates vary and some products may be zero-rated;
- marketing strategy – depending on its marketing objectives a business may adopt a particular pricing strategy for its retail selling price. The strategy may be to price low for market penetration, price high to skim the market or for price leadership, or to price in the same range as similar products, known as market-based competitive pricing.

Table 1 shows the prices of different women's perfumes.

Determining the optimum price

It is important that the selling price of a product is set within a range that is right for the market.

- Setting too low a price may not maximise the profit potential for the business.
- Setting too high a price may limit sales and could make competitor products appear more attractive to consumers.

If a price is set too high it can always be adjusted down until it is right for the market, using promotions, discounting or adding

Figure 1 *How the price of a product is made up*

Producer>wholesaler>retailer>consumer

Producer>retailer>consumer

Producer>consumer

Retail selling price
VAT
Retail margin
Wholesaler selling price
Wholesaler margin
Manufacturer selling price
Manufacturer gross margin
Indirect costs
Direct manufacturing costs

Retail selling price
VAT
Retail margin
Manufacturer selling price
Manufacturer gross margin
Indirect costs
Direct manufacturing costs

Retail selling price
VAT
Retail margin received directly by manufacturer as gross margin
Indirect costs
Direct manufacturing costs

Total costs {

value. But if a price is set too low it can lead quickly to losing money on a product as costs increase. Once set too low, it is very hard to raise the price because there will be resistance from customers and other market factors. However, no matter how low a price a business charges there will always be a competitor somewhere that will undercut this price to meet its own objectives.

Figure I shows how the price of a product, such as perfume, might be made up when sold using different distribution methods.

Supply and demand and the effect on price

Price is affected directly by levels of supply and demand. The supply and demand model of the economy describes how prices vary depending on the balance between:
- supply - the availability of product and;
- demand - how much the market wants to acquire of the product.

Demand If supply remains steady, then generally:
- the more that consumers demand of a product the higher the price that can be charged;
- the less consumers demand the lower the price that can be charged.

Various factors may affect demand by consumers including:
- incomes - the more people earn the more they are likely to buy;
- tastes - if something becomes fashionable people might buy it;
- other goods - if products become more expensive or less attractive consumers might switch to buy a different product;
- population - a rise in population might increase demand;
- advertising - promotion might encourage people to buy products;
- laws - legislation can encourage or discourage buying of certain products.

Supply If consumer demand remains steady, then generally:
- the more that businesses supply of a product the lower the price that can be charged;
- the less businesses supply the higher the price that can be charged.

If consumer demand for a product remains steady and more of the same product comes into the market than is being bought, then the price is likely to fall. Manufacturers may try to make it more attractive to consumers to buy, by lowering the price. Conversely, if less of the product is available than consumers want to buy, the price will increase as it becomes more scarce and consumers become willing to pay more to buy what they want. Figure 2 shows an example.

Figure 2 *The price of seasonal fruit*

Modern glasshouse growing and supermarket management techniques mean that tomatoes are generally available for 12 months of the year. In response consumer demand is now across 12 months. **Summer** During the summer, more tomatoes are produced because the outdoor crops enter the market. As a result, the price tends to fall as supply suddenly overtakes demand. Increased demand must be created to sell all of the tomatoes produced or risk losing them as wasted product, which would have no value to the producers. So prices are reduced. **Winter** During the winter tomato production is limited to glasshouses. This means that fewer are available. So the price tends to rise to capitalise on this reduced availability and to moderate demand to a level that can be met.

Identify a product that is sold to consumers:
- directly from the business;
- through retailers.

The product you choose should be the same brand in each supply chain. Examples could include CDs, computer games, confectionery, clothing.
- Identify the retail selling price in each supply chain.
- Consider reasons why the prices are the same or different when the product is retailed through the different supply chains

OR

Make contact with the marketing team at a business that you are familiar with or where you have personal contacts. Explain that you are studying Applied Business and learning about pricing. Arrange to meet and interview a member of the marketing team or an accountant who is responsible for pricing and investigate:
- how they cost their products;
- what they include in direct costs;
- what they include in indirect costs;
- how they set the selling price.

Research task

Portfolio practice · The price of shampoo

Figure 3 shows a basic costing sheet that has been produced by the accounts team at Extra Cosmetics Ltd. for a new shampoo product Shinee.

(a) (i) **Calculate the direct cost involved in the production of one 250ml bottle of Shinee.**
(ii) **Calculate the total cost for the production of one 250ml bottle of Shinee.**
(iii) **Calculate the selling price if Extra Cosmetics Ltd. wants to make 50% gross margin.**

(b) **Similar shampoo products have a retail selling price of £2.19 including VAT @ 17.5%. Suggest how Extra Cosmetics Ltd. could increase the profit that it makes on selling Shinee shampoo.**

Figure 3 *Costs for Shinee shampoo*

Raw materials
surfactant, colour, scent = £1.00 per litre

Packaging
1 x 250ml bottle 10p
1 bottle cap 2p
printed label 2p

Labour for running filling machine for Shinee bottles, £10.00 per hour. The machine fills 1,000 bottles each hour.

Factory overheads Estimated to be £1,000 per day, each day 10,000 bottles of Shinee can be filled.

Meeting the assessment criteria

You are required to produce an appropriate marketing mix for a new or existing product or service. You must justify all aspects of your devised marketing mix for your product or service.

This section, 38, deals with just one aspect of the marketing mix – Price. The suggestions below only cover the mark bands in terms of this aspect of the marketing mix. To cover the mark bands effectively you will need to take into account 'meeting the assessment criteria' in sections 36 to 40 which cover the marketing mix.

Business example - Concert tickets

In 2005 Cream, the rock supergroup of the 1960s featuring Eric Clapton, Jack Bruce and Ginger Baker, reformed for four shows at The Royal Albert Hall in London on May 2nd, 3rd, 5th, 6th 2005. Face value tickets for the concert were priced at £50, £75 and £125, although they were exchanging at many times that value on some Internet sites. *The Guardian* reported that 'The first live show for 36 years by Eric Clapton's blues/rock 'power trio' may have attracted the attentions of the media, but it has had difficulty snaring anyone under 40; young people are conspicuous by their absence from the bars and foyers of the Royal Albert Hall.'

Between 2-7 July 2005 Destiny's Child toured Great Britain, performing five dates, the first time since 2003. The face value of ticket prices at Earl's Court ranged from £27.50 to £40. Other venues included The Manchester MEN Arena.

Source: adapted from Guardian Unlimited, Ticketmaster, Albert Hall website.

Mark Band 1 *Creation of a simple marketing mix and a simple evaluation of the marketing mix and conclusions made without supporting evidence.*
Businesses involved in the pricing of concert tickets must decide what prices to charge. The prices must take into account certain factors. Prices must cover the direct and indirect costs involved in setting up the concert and the profit that the businesses involved want to make. But prices must also take into account the supply of tickets and the demand for the tickets. The prices

charged for Cream and Destiny's Child tickets are likely to be appropriate and effective prices. The prices are relatively high enough to cover costs. They also take into account that there is limited supply of tickets and high demand. This allows high prices to be charged.

Mark Band 2 *Creation of a detailed mix showing an understanding of the 4Ps and a justification of the marketing mix, showing a range of supported evidence, arguments and conclusions.*

Businesses involved in the pricing of concert tickets must decide what prices to charge. The prices must take into account certain factors. A low price will not cover costs, but a high price may deter customers. Prices must be high enough to cover the direct and indirect costs involved in setting up the concert, including wage costs, hire of equipment and transport and promotion costs. The price must also be high enough to make the profit that all businesses involved want to make. Prices must also take into account the supply of tickets and the demand for the tickets. The prices charged for Cream and Destiny's Child tickets are likely to be appropriate and effective prices. The prices are relatively high enough to cover costs. They also take into account the supply of tickets and the demand for tickets. Supply is limited to the number of seats in the theatres and the number of concerts. In both cases supply is relatively limited. Demand is likely to be very high. Cream have not toured for 37 years. Destiny's Child are popular current artists with a large younger fan base. High demand and limited supply will allow high prices to be charged.

Mark Band 3 *Creation of a comprehensive mix linked to research and segmentation evidence and a comprehensive and fully justified account of all aspects of the marketing mix.*

Businesses involved in the pricing of concert tickets must decide on an effective pricing strategy. The prices charged are likely to be influenced by a number of factors. If prices are set too low they will not cover costs. Setting too high a price will deter customers. The price of concert tickets must be high enough to cover the direct and indirect costs involved in setting up the concert, including wage costs, hire of equipment and transport and promotion costs. The price must also be high enough to make the profit that all businesses involved want to make. The relative prices charged are fairly high. These should be enough to cover the costs of venues, promoters and agents involved in the tour.

Prices must also take into account the supply of tickets and the demand for the tickets. Supply is limited to the number of seats in the theatres and the number of concerts. In both cases there are no more than 5 gigs. So supply is relatively limited. Demand is likely to be very high. Cream have not toured for 37 years. They have a large fan base over many years who will want to see concerts. Destiny's Child are popular current artists with a large younger fan base. The relative prices of Cream tickets are able to be set higher because fans are older and likely to have higher income to spend. They have also waited a long time to see the group and may be prepared to pay higher prices. Younger fans may not be able to afford relatively higher priced tickets. There may also be more seats available for Destiny's Child tickets so supply is higher.

High demand and limited supply means that charging high prices is likely to be effective for these concerts. The price charged for Cream tickets could have been higher.

What is place?

In the marketing mix 'place' refers to where a customer or consumer can buy or access the product. In practice this means the point of distribution, the end of the supply chain that is used to get the product from the producer to the consumer. Figure 1 shows some examples of the different methods of distribution which producers may use to get products to the consumer.

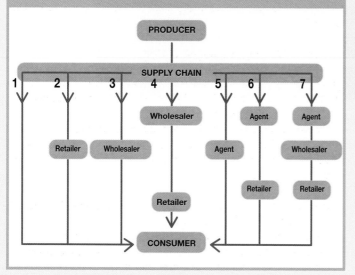

Figure 1 *Supply chains - methods used to get the product from producer to consumer*

Direct selling This is where the producer sells goods directly to consumers without the use of intermediaries or distributors, such as wholesalers or retailers. Services are often sold directly to consumers. This is method 1 in Figure 1. Direct selling can reduce costs and also be used to target customers. But it can be a limit on the coverage of the market.

Through wholesalers Wholesalers are businesses that 'break-bulk'. They buy large quantities from manufacturers and then sell to consumers via retailers or directly to consumers. Methods 3, 4 and 7 use wholesalers in Figure 1. Wholesalers take large quantities and can bargain for lower prices.

Through retailers There are many varieties of retail outlets in high street shops and shopping centres and on out-of-town shopping estates. They buy directly from producers or wholesalers and then sell to consumers. Methods 2, 4, 6 and 7 use retailers in Figure 1. Retailers can give a business a wide scope of distribution, but again may increase costs for a business. Businesses may also lose control of distribution, as explained later.

Through agents Agents are individuals or businesses that are often specialists in selling into particular markets. They can be effective if a business is selling to a specialist market or into an unknown market.

Some examples of these methods are shown in Table 1.

Table 1 *Distribution methods*

Method	Example
Direct selling	Pick your own strawberries at Garden Farm in Norwich. Avon Cosmetics Ltd sells products from its website and through party plans.
Wholesalers	Barnsley Footwear Distributors Ltd which deals in footwear brands such as Nike, Puma, Lacoste and Timberland selling to the trade only.
Retailer	Specsavers which sells Hugo Boss, Storm, Red or Dead and Monsoon frames.
Agents	Kinnersley Brothers Limited, an international importer / exporter and manufacturer's agent based in Bristol, UK, that specialises in fruit juices and oils & fats.

Using distribution methods

Using different distributions methods may require a different approach from producers or providers.

Direct selling A business may deal directly with consumers. This could include
- setting up it own retail outlets;
- using a mail-order catalogue;
- direct sell leaflets and advertisements;
- creating a website that consumers can buy from;
- selling door-to-door or running a party-plan scheme that brings together potential consumers to look at and try the product before their buy.

Any of these examples would be possible sales and marketing plans so long as the business has sufficient skills and resources to setup and run these schemes and resources to create awareness amongst consumers through promotion and advertising.

Retailers and wholesalers To meet place objectives when dealing with distributors and retailers, requires a different approach.

First, the business needs to research the market to establish how its product could be distributed by investigating similar and competitor products. This research should identify the most important distributors to target.

Next, the business will need to prepare a case to take to the target distributors to convince them that it is in their interests to stock and sell the product being marketed. This should be a combination of:
- product specification details, e.g. what it is, what it does, why it does it better than competitor products and the price;
- market research that supports the manufacturer's case, e.g. data on the size and dynamics of the market and market data that proves the product will be in demand;

- consumer research that shows that the product is right for consumers in the market;
- the package of promotional support that the product will receive to create awareness and demand which should help it sell.

The business will then need to maintain the distribution that it has gained. This will require constant monitoring through marketing research and a package of marketing plans and promotion to keep the product selling.

Control over distribution

'Place' in the marketing mix can be the factor that the producer has least control over. A producer or provider may set certain objectives for distribution and availability for consumers in most markets. But place is often controlled by retailers and other distributors that make decisions about whether or not to stock and sell a product. There are situations, however, where the producer may have some control over distribution.

Direct selling A producer may have control if it sells directly to consumers from its own outlets, its factory or via ordering on the Internet. Businesses selling services directly to consumers can have a great deal of control.

Branding and promotion If a brand is very strong or if there is heavy promotion, wholesalers and retailers may be 'forced' to stock the product. Also, consumers may expect certain top brands of beans or cereal to be stocked. Newly released DVDs and CDs are often heavily promoted and become ' must stock' items.

Consumer demand If demand is so strong, not stocking a product could put a business at a competitive disadvantage because the range it offers range is incomplete. For example, most consumers would consider that a newsagent would have an incomplete range if it did not sell most national daily newspapers.

Positioning Place can refer to precisely where the product is located within a retail store. This is something that the producer can advise on, but the decision will be up to retailers. This is dealt with later.

Even then, a powerful retailer may not stock or may withdraw a product because it has a disagreement with the producer over the cost, image or the level of marketing support given. Also, some retailers, particularly the food supermarket chains known as 'discounters', base their own brand image on the fact that they do not stock branded goods. Instead, they make up their complete product range from smaller, lesser-known or imported brands that can be sold at low prices compared with well known branded goods.

Place and consumers' tastes

During product development, businesses must carry out research to identify where consumers expect the product to be available and sold. If a product is in the wrong place or if consumers cannot find it easily, sales may suffer. Certain characteristics of consumers must be taken into account when setting place objectives.

Consumer behaviour can change Until recently grocery supermarket businesses traded exclusively from large retail outlets. Consumers had to visit the supermarket to buy what they wanted. The Internet and the worldwide web have changed all

that. Many supermarkets now have an on-line shopping website. Consumers with computers and Internet access expect to be able to buy groceries from a website as an option to visiting the supermarket itself.

Consumer expectations If a business launches and promotes a new product, consumers will expect it to be available where they normally buy similar, competitor products. For example, they will expect to find a new mobile phone in mobile phone shops, electrical stores and other places that sell mobile phones. If the new phone was only stocked in newsagents it would miss a huge section of the market looking in traditional outlets.

If a new national dry cleaning service is launched, sited on an industrial estate, consumers may look for it in the high street. Unless promotion is clear, they will not expect to have to visit industrial estates, where there may be plenty of properties at lower costs than in the high street. Even so, consumers may not be comfortable about visiting an industrial area to get their clothes cleaned.

Place within a retail outlet

Part of setting place objectives may include advising where the product should be located within the retail outlet to maximise sales. This could include recommending:

- the product is placed alongside those of competitors;
- the product is placed in a different product section, with non-competing but complementary products;
- the space required;
- the number of shelves;
- the height at which the product should be positioned in order to catch the eye of consumers;
- products are located at checkouts to create an impulse purchase, rather than tucked away on a shelf amongst other products competing for consumer attention.

Place and price

Marketing objectives for price may have a place element.

- If a business believes that its product should command a higher,

---

Figure 2 Dell distribution

Dell is one of the most successful suppliers of computers in the world and all of its business is conducted direct with its customers, consumers of the computer equipment. By not relying on retailers to stock, distribute and sell its goods, Dell can control the selling price, setting the price according to the competitive market and its own profit requirements. It sells its products directly in two ways;

- contacting the company directly;
- Internet sales.

Source: adapted from ww.dell.com.

premium price when sold it needs to target retailers that are less likely to discount the selling price.

- If the objective is to sell the product at a low, competitive price, then it would be no good targeting retailers that have an up-market image and try to sell goods at the maximum price their customers will stand.

But businesses that sell via distributors and retailers do not have the final say over the prices that are charged for their products. It is often the retailer's decision, based on its own objectives. Direct selling can bring control of 'place' and 'price' back to the manufacturer. An example is shown in Figure 2.

Place and promotion

Marketing objectives for promotion may also have a place element.

- Place can affect the decision about the geographical area where the advertisement is shown or distributed – national, regional, local.
- Place can affect the precise location for promotion, such as handing out leaflets outside a particular shopping centre or club, or showing the advertisement in a particular cinema, depending on the product, the target market and the marketing objectives.
- Place can affect the choice of promotional medium. For example, it is recognised in the magazine industry that an advertisement on a right-hand page has more impact than on a left-hand page and that the top of a page has more impact than the foot of the page. In television, advertisements placed between popular programmes will be seen by more viewers than if placed between less popular programmes.

Choose a popular product with a strong brand, such as Coca-Cola and a specialist market such as railway tickets.

- Identify how many different places these products are sold.
- Give as many reasons as you can why the products are sold at each place you have identified.

Then interview people in the street.

- Ask where they usually buy the popular product and where they usually buy the specialist product.
- Compare the answers you get from consumers with your own investigation into where each product is actually stocked.
- Draw conclusions from your findings. This should help you understand how businesses set objectives for place and how consumer expectations affect place.

Research task

Portfolio practice · BGO Records

Figure 3 shows a section from a full-page advertisement placed by BGO Records to promote its new releases.

(a) **Identify TWO 'places'/distribution methods that BGO Records may use for its new releases.**
(b) **Suggest ONE expectation that consumers may have about this product from Figure 3 and explain how it might affect distribution.**
(c) **(i) Explain which distribution method might allow the business to control its distribution better. (ii) Discuss whether this should be the only method the business should use.**

Figure 3 *BGO Records advertisement*

ginal master tapes nd additional sleeve notes

BGOCD651 • Ravi Shankar *Jazz Et Ragas*
BGOCD680 • Ian Matthews *Stealin' Home/Siamese Friends*
BGOCD671 • Mick Abrahams Band *At Last*
BGOCD668 • Otis Spann *The Blues Of/Cracked Spanner Head*
BGOCD673 • Cher *All I Really Want To Do/The Sonny Side Of Cher*
BGOCD670 • Shirley Bassey *Live At Carnegie Hall*
BGOCD641 • Merle Haggard *A Portrait Of/Keep Movin' On*
BGOCD644 • Spirit *Son Of Spirit/Farther Along*

All BGO new releases and catalogue available from good record shops everywhere or buy online at www.bgo-records.com

For a FREE 2005/06 BGO catalogue send a large (A4) sae to:
BGO Records, PO Box 22, Bury St. Edmunds, Suffolk IP28 6XQ

Meeting the assessment criteria

You are required to produce an appropriate marketing mix for a new or existing product or service. You must justify all aspects of your devised marketing mix for your product or service.

This section, 39, deals with just one aspect of the marketing mix – Place. The suggestions below only cover the mark bands in terms of this aspect of the marketing mix. To cover the mark bands effectively you will need to take into account 'meeting the assessment criteria' in sections 36 to 40 which cover the marketing mix.

Business example - Killer Kits/Model Mayhem

Killer Kits is a business that manufactures resin figure kits that can be made up into models of characters from sci-fi and horror films and television, such as Austin Powers, Batman and Basil Fawlty. It sells kits from its website www.killerkits.net and also at trade fairs, such collectors fairs at the NEC, in Birmingham. On 2 May 2005 it branched out by opening its own shop, Model Mayhem, in Liverpool. The shop is part of Gostens, a retail shopping centre in a converted warehouse on Hanover Street. Shoppers can buy the kits or arrange for them to be made up and painted.

Source: adapted from company information.

Mark Band 1 *Creation of a simple marketing mix and a simple evaluation of the marketing mix and conclusions made without supporting evidence.*
Killer Kits manufactures resin figure kits. It distributes them in three ways. One is directly to the public though trade fairs at centres such as the Birmingham NEC. Another is directly to the public through the use of the Internet website and online ordering. A further method is through its own retail shop in Liverpool. This is likely to be an effective distribution mix. A number of methods are being used and customers are likely to be more effectively targeted using these methods, particularly direct selling.

Mark Band 2 *Creation of a detailed mix showing an understanding of the 4Ps and a justification of the marketing mix, showing a range of supported evidence, arguments and conclusions.*
Killer Kits manufactures resin figure kits. It distributes them, the part of the marketing mix that deals with 'place', in three ways. One is directly to the public though trade fairs at centres such as the Birmingham NEC. This method is likely to be effective because it targets people who are interested in collectables. They can buy kits having viewed them at the trade fair. Another is directly to the public through the use of the Internet website and online ordering. Again this will be effective. People can see the products and read information by clicking on thumbnails. Products can then be delivered directly to homes. It is a relatively cheap way of reaching the target market. A further method is through its own retail shop in Liverpool. Running a shop will incur costs, although they have been minimised by being part of a complex. Stocks can be kept elsewhere and sent out as required. Using a variety of direct methods of distribution is likely to be effective for such a specialist market.

Mark Band 3 *Creation of a comprehensive mix linked to research and segmentation evidence and a comprehensive and fully justified account of all aspects of the marketing mix.*
Killer Kits manufactures resin figure kits. It distributes them, the part of the marketing mix that deals with 'place', in a number of ways. One is directly to the public though trade fairs at centres such as the Birmingham NEC. This method is likely to be effective to some extent. It targets people who are interested in collectables. They can buy kits having viewed them at the trade fair. However, there is the cost of getting to the event and hiring a stand. Also, it only takes place a few times a year. In itself, this method of distribution would not be sufficient.

Another is directly to the public through the use of the Internet website and online ordering. People can see the products and read information by clicking on thumbnails. Products can then be delivered directly to homes. It is a relatively cheap way of reaching the target market and proved effective in establishing the business.

A further method is through its own retail shop in Liverpool. Running a shop will incur costs. Choosing a site with relatively low overheads, which is part of a larger retail complex, will help. Stocks can be kept elsewhere and sent out as required. Choosing a city centre location such as Liverpool, with a large number of students and younger people, will also be effective for reaching the target market.

The distribution method used by the business allows targeted customers to be given information effectively and products delivered quickly. The business uses direct methods rather than selling to other retailers, such as comic shops, which may only want built models. Also they are likely to take part of the profit of the business. It may be possible to sell kits through other model shops, though they may not be specialists. In conclusion, it could be argued that using a variety of direct methods of distribution is likely to be effective for such a specialist market.

40 Promotion

What is promotion?

Promotion is how businesses make customers aware of their products or services. A variety of promotional methods can be used. They are designed to:

- attract new customers to buy new products of the business;
- ensure that existing customers keep buying the products of a business;
- attract customers away from buying the products of other businesses using comparisons;
- improve the image of products in the eyes of customers;
- attract customers to the business itself so that they buy other products;
- support customers that they have bought products.

Advertising

Advertising is a very popular method of promotion used by businesses. It is the use of paid-for space in the media to raise awareness of a product and communicate with a target market. Advertising is designed to sell or to carry a message to an audience. It is carried out in many highly creative ways, in a range of different media, as shown in Figure 1. Examples of advertising can be seen on television, in newspapers and magazines, in the street, in shops and in town centres, in fact anywhere where there is space to carry a message.

Decisions about which form of advertising to use in the marketing mix will depend on:

- what is appropriate for the product;
- the market it is aimed at;
- availability;
- access;
- the budget available.

Some examples of the most commonly used advertising media are shown in Table 1.

Before deciding which method of advertising to use, or whether to advertise at all, a business must set its marketing aims and objectives. Then it must make a decision, based on what advertising is appropriate and what is most likely to achieve the objectives set.

Another important factor in the decision making process is the budget available for advertising. Advertising space and time in different media cost different amounts, depending on the price of producing the advertisement and the size of the audience the medium will reach. The bigger the audience the more expensive the cost of advertising in that medium. For example, a page in *The Sun* newspaper, which has a huge circulation, is likely to cost more than a page in a newspaper with relatively fewer readers. Some specialist media which can reach a small but hard to contact group of consumers may also be expensive. For example, on a per reader basis it may cost more to advertise in a specialist magazine like *The Plantsman* than it does in a more general gardening title magazine which has a relatively large circulation and readership.

Sales promotion

This covers a range of methods and techniques that are used as an alternative to or in addition to advertising to persuade customers

Figure 1 Advertising media

Television | Radio

National & local newspapers | Internet | Magazines | Posters

Billboards | Cinema | Trade journals | Transport

Directories

Table 1 Advertising media

Media	Examples
Television	McDonald's 'I'm lovin' it' campaign with a catchy jingle to remember and images of youngsters enjoying themselves.
Radio	Paul Rooney solicitors, explaining verbally what services are offered.
National newspaper	The Travelodge national chain of hotels advertising in *The Guardian* national newspaper.
Local newspaper	Local Conlons opticians branches in Ormskirk, St Helens and Formby advertising in the *Ormskirk Champion*.
Internet	A banner headline for Orange mobile phones appearing on the *Yellow Pages* search engine to attract a large number of customers.
Magazines	A Cuprinol advert for treating fences appearing for target audiences in *The Gardener*.
Cinema	A Lord of the Rings trailer before other similar action/adventure films with the same age certificate.
Transport	Capital Gold London radio or Thomson directory adverts on London taxis.
Directories	The Barrowland theatre appearing in the Glasgow *Yellow Pages*.

and the target market to buy products. Commonly used and effective methods of sales promotion include those shown in Table 2.

Sales promotion often takes the form of an incentive that is offered to customers or consumers to buy the product. This is an inducement to try the product. It is usually only applied to the product for a limited time to act as a tactical marketing plan designed to:

- get consumers to try a new product;
- boost sales of a product when sales have slowed;
- clear stocks of a product that is over-stocked or out of date.

Just like advertising, before deciding on which method to use, or whether sales promotion is required at all, a business must set its marketing aims and objectives. Then it must decide what type of sales promotion is appropriate and what is most likely to achieve the objectives set.

It is important to consider aims and objectives carefully before deciding which method of sales promotion to choose. If the method chosen is not appropriate for the product and the market it could cost a lot of money and affect the reputation of the product. For example, a poorly chosen promotion by Hoover vacuum cleaners gave free flight vouchers to anyone buying a Hoover vacuum cleaner. The vouchers were worth more than the cost of the cleaners themselves and the business was inundated with consumers that bought the relatively low-cost cleaners and then demanded their holiday. This cost the business much more than it had budgeted. It also affected its reputation in the short term because of the poor publicity it received when it tried to limit the number of holiday vouchers claimed by consumers.

Public relations

This is the use of media and events to raise awareness of a product, to communicate a message or to change public opinion. The main difference between public relations and advertising is that, whilst advertising relies on communication through paid-for media space, public relations is based on the use of editorial space and broadcast time that is not paid for directly.

For example, when a business launches a new product it may send a press release about the product and a photograph to newspapers and news programmes on the radio and television. The media want the information provided by the business to report on the new product. The business will hope that reports in the media will generate awareness of the new product and encourage consumers to buy the new product.

The use of press releases is just one of the tools that public relations experts use to create awareness without it appearing to be explicit advertising. Public relations techniques can be used for all kinds of promotion and publicity and include press and customer receptions, open days and other publicity generating events. In addition to creating awareness, public relations can be used to change the image and perception of a product.

Figure 2 shows an example of public relations in action to generate publicity in the airline industry.

Direct mailing

This is the use of marketing media to communicate directly with customers and consumers. It may be in the form of leaflets and promotional material that is mailed directly to potential customers and consumers. Sometimes it is in the form of what appears to be a 'personal letter' direct from the business to the customer. Increasingly direct e-mail is also being used.

An important factor in direct mailing is the use of databases. They are used to manage information about customers, so that the direct mail can be sent to precisely the person who is in the market for the product at that time. Direct mail organisations

Figure 2 Airbus A380 superjumbo launch

In January 2005 Airbus threw a spectacular party for the A380 superjumbo, the largest civil airliner ever built. 5,000 guests including Eurpean Presidents, Chancellors and Prime Ministers watched a theatrical ceremony at the final assembly plant in Toulouse, France. Airbus chief Noel Forgeard predicted Airbus would sell 700 to 750 of the planes, which cost $260 million to buy and has a 15 per cent gain in costs per seat-mile compared to the Boeing 747-400. It already had 149 orders or commitments from 14 airlines. The A380 has room for 70 cars to park on its wings and looks similar to the Boeing 747, but with the top deck stretching all the way back to the tail.

This type of promotion is often used by airline manufacturers because:
- of the need for airline sales around the world;
- similar methods used by other airlines;
- to make an impact for a new product;
- the size and cost of the project.

Source: adapted from news.airwise.com.

Table 2 Sales promotion methods

Method	Examples
Coupons	Coupons given away by magazines to save up and exchange for products.
Loyalty cards	Boots Advantage Card which builds up points to exchange for goods.
Competitions	Travel companies hold competitions and give holidays as prizes.
Product endorsements	Samsung signed to sponsor Chelsea football club in 2005 for five years.
Special terms	Buy now pay later or interest free credit offered by DFS on sofas or Currys on electrical goods.
Product placing	Nokia mobile phones in Charlie's Angels films.
Free or value offers	'10% or 20% extra free' used on confectionery products or cereals.
Money off purchases	Buy One Get One Free offers (BOGOF) used by supermarkets.
Free gifts	CDs or DVDs given with the *News of the World* Sunday newspaper.

spend a lot of money on market research to build up databases that can be analysed and segmented to fit the target market as precisely as possible.

Sponsorship

This is when a business supports an event, an activity or an organisation, such as a sports team, in exchange for having its name or product brand name linked directly with the event, activity or the organisation being sponsored. Sponsorship is usually in the form of money, but it can also be in the form of donations of products, equipment or resources.

Examples of sponsorship can be seen by looking at the company and brand names on the shirts of many sports teams. Individual sportspeople often benefit from sponsorship and wear the sponsor's logo on their clothes when they are competing. Some television programmes also have sponsorship. This can be seen by watching television and looking for examples of brand names and logos that appear before the programme starts or between commercial breaks. Examples of this include The Simpsons on Sky One television being sponsored by Domino's Pizza and Coronation Street being sponsored by Cadbury.

Sponsorship can also be seen when businesses support major events. Examples could include the Glastonbury music festival, whose sponsors include mobile phone network Orange and Formula 1 motor racing, whose sponsors include high-tech sponsor LG Electronics.

Sponsorship can be a good way of increasing brand awareness with targeted groups, by linking the sponsor's name with the activity or event. It can also have positive benefits by creating an association in the audience's mind between the team or the event and the sponsor. For example, if fans of a particular team see that the team is being sponsored, they may have positive feelings towards the sponsor for also supporting their team. The sponsor will hope that the positive feelings translate into increased awareness, a positive image and increased sales.

However, sponsorship can sometimes work in reverse. Using the earlier example, consider what fans from an opposing team think about the business that sponsors their rivals. Their thoughts may not be positive and it could result in a section of the market boycotting the business that sponsors and supports their rivals. Similarly, if a business sponsors an event that receives poor publicity, this may reflect on the sponsor and its product sales.

Before a business decides to add sponsorship to its promotional plans it needs to think carefully and decide whether such sponsorship really helps the business to meet its marketing aims and objectives.

Factors influencing choice of promotion method

A business must ensure that it chooses promotion methods that are appropriate if promotion is to be successful. A number of factors might influence the choice of promotion method used by a business.

Objectives of the business The marketing mix of a business will be influenced by its overall corporate and marketing objectives. For example, a business that wants to expand sales quickly might use a method of promotion which has a large impact instantly, such as a national television campaign.

Market research Primary and secondary research by a business provides information about the market that might help a business decide the most suitable method of promotion. For example, an article in a trade journal might tell a manufacturer of golf equipment that exhibiting at trade fairs or golf competitions would be effective.

Nature of the business Some types of marketing might be more suitable to certain businesses. Trade journals are often valuable for technical products sold to other businesses, for example.

Target customers Certain types of promotion might be very effective in appealing to the target audience, whereas others might not. For example, if customers are not willing to travel far to use a service, then local promotion methods might be appropriate.

Size of the business Small businesses have limited budgets and markets. Larger businesses with larger markets may be able to spend a great deal more on promotion. For example, a local tanning salon might use a local newspaper to advertise its service but a chain of salons might use a cinema advertisement.

Nature of the product The type of product might affect promotion. For example, a product with moving parts might use a visual advertisement on television rather than on radio.

Competition Businesses in competitive markets often use similar promotion methods to their competitors. For example, large amounts are spent to launch new films, both in advertising, merchandising and other forms of promotion.

Impact Some promotions have greater impact than others. However, this does not mean that large, noisy promotions are most effective. It will depend on the target markets and the nature of the product.

Cost and budget Some promotions, such as television advertisements during peak time sporting events, can be extremely expensive. Others, such as leaflets, can be relatively cheap.

Law Legislation affects certain aspects of advertising, such as information that can be stated in adverts about products. This is dealt with in section 15.

External constraints Some pressure groups can constrain promotion. The Advertising Standards Authority, for example, is responsible for making sure that adverts are legal, decent, honest, truthful and responsible.

Select a large business and identify the methods of promotion that it uses. Compare these methods to promotion being carried out by a small business in your local area.

Use a search engine on the Internet, back issues of newspapers and magazines, and other media for your research. Identify the aims and objectives of the businesses that explain why each business has used particular promotional methods.

Research task

Portfolio practice · **Keys**

Vernon Keys runs a roofing and building business in Southport, Merseyside. He has built up contacts over the years both in the building trade and amongst customers. But he now wants to concentrate on interior renovation work. He has read reports in newspapers that the DIY boom was over in 2005. People who had previously thought about DIY, encouraged by makeover programmes, were now paying for work to be done.

Vernon decided to sell his specialist roofing equipment and scaffolding. He wanted to advertise his services within a 50 mile radius of Southport. He considered a number of alternatives to help him promote this change in business activity and decided on the following methods.

- To advertise in *The Southport Visitor*, a local newspaper.
- To place his name in the local *Yellow Pages*.
- To sponsor a local drama society where he had friends.
- To visit trade fairs in London each year to develop the prestige of his business.
- To place an advertisement on Capital Radio London. He could get this station on his DAB radio at home and thought that there would be many other people who would be attracted to such a popular station.
- To produce a glossy leaflet to distribute in the local area.

Source: adapted from company information.

(a) Examine the advantages and disadvantages of each method which Vernon is using to promote the new business.
(b) Using your analysis in (a), evaluate the likely success of Vernon's promotion methods.

Meeting the assessment criteria

You are required to produce an appropriate marketing mix for a new or existing product or service. You must justify all aspects of your devised marketing mix for your product or service.

This section, 40, deals with just one aspect of the marketing mix – Promotion. The suggestions below only cover the mark bands in terms of this aspect of the marketing mix. To cover the mark bands effectively you will need to take into account 'meeting the assessment criteria' in sections 36 to 40 which cover the marketing mix.

Business example - Blueyonder sponsorship of show on Virgin Radio

In 2002 Blueyonder, Telewest Broadband's high speed Internet service, signed a deal to sponsor the award-winning Pete & Geoff Show on Virgin Radio. It has a cult follolwing with a history of web links. Telewest would advertise on a banner campaign on the Virgin website. The Telewest Broadband service allowed people to surf the Internet ten times faster than a standard dial up modem. People can browse the web, download music and have video streaming and online gaming. The show would also include give-away prizes and promotional

trials and on-air credits for phone users.

On 1st May the company also launched a 3 month broadband taster campaign, aimed at homes with BT, AOL, Freeserve and other dial-up services. New customers paid £13.48 a month for their first 3 months of broadband, lower than the average cost of dial-up services in the UK. Customers could claim back the installation fee if they didn't want to continue with the service at the standard price.

Source: adapted from mediacentre.telewest.co.uk.

Mark Band 1 *Creation of a simple marketing mix and a simple evaluation of the marketing mix and conclusions made without supporting evidence.*

Promotion forms an important part of the marketing mix of a business such as Telewest Broadband. It used a number of methods to promote its fast broadband service. These included banner advertising on the Virgin website and the sponsorship of a radio programme on Virgin Radio. It also gave away free gifts and credits for phones and trials, forms of sale promotions. These methods are all likely to be effective in attracting customers. A large business in a competitive market such as mobile phones must have a number of promotions. It must also choose methods which attract its target market effectively, encourage people to buy the product and promote the name of the business and its products. The methods it has chosen are likely to do this.

Mark Band 2 *Creation of a detailed mix showing an understanding of the 4Ps and a justification of the marketing mix, showing a range of supported evidence, arguments and conclusions.*

Promotion forms an important part of the marketing mix of a business such as Telewest Broadband. The business used a number of methods to promote its fast broadband service. These included banner advertising on the Virgin website and sponsorship of the award winning Pete & Geoff Show on Virgin Radio, a form of public relations. The free gifts and credits for phones and trials are forms of sale promotions.

A large business in a competitive market such as mobile phones must have a number of promotions. It must also choose methods which attract its target market effectively, encourage people to buy the product and promote the name of the business and its products. The methods it has chosen are likely to do this for a number of reasons. The programme sponsored has a reputation and a following, particularly amongst those customers who are likely to want to buy broadband service and make use of its facilities, such as downloading music. So the market is being targeted effectively. Further, offering free trails is a useful way of attracting custom. It is perhaps more difficult to stop using a service once installed than it is not to use it in the first place.

Mark Band 3 *Creation of a comprehensive mix linked to research and segmentation evidence and a comprehensive and fully justified account of all aspects of the marketing mix.*

Promotion forms an important part of the marketing mix of a business such as Telewest Broadband. The business used a number of methods of promotion. These included:

- an advertising banner campaign on the Virgin Radio website;
- sponsorship of the award winning Pete & Geoff Show on Virgin Radio, a form of public relations;
- free gifts and credits for phones and trials, all sales promotions.

A large business in a competitive market such as mobile phones has to have a number of promotions. It will face competition from other broadband providers such as BT as well

as cable. They will make use of advertising media and other promotions which Telewest must combat.

It must also choose methods which attract its target market effectively, encourage people to buy the product and promote the name of the business and its products. The methods it has chosen are likely to do this. The programme sponsored has a reputation and a following, particularly amongst those customers who are likely to want to buy broadband service and make use of its facilities, such as downloading music. So the market is being targeted effectively.

Elizabeth Sheard the Sponsorship Manager at Virgin Radio said that Virgin Radio had over a million ABC1 adults between the ages of 25 & 44 tuning in each week and this is the key market for Blueyonder. She also said that Virgin was the most listened to online radio station in the world with the average online listener tuning in for approximately 20 minutes each session. This suggests that the choice of sponsorship and advertising will be very effective. John Orriss, head of marketing for Blueyonder said the campaign would enable the business to 'create further awareness within our key audience, of our broadband Internet service' and 'allow us to highlight the many benefits of high speed Internet access for music and film fans and anyone who uses the Internet at home'.

Offering free trails is a useful way of attracting custom. It is perhaps more difficult to stop using a service once installed than it is not to use it in the first place. Once the audience has been attracted by free trials, it may remain loyal.

Constraints

The marketing mix selected will be affected by both internal and external constraints. Constraints are like brakes being applied to marketing plans or to the business. They are limits that exist or parameters that are set, producing guidelines within which the plan has to operate. Constraints might:

- slow down a project;
- result in plans being changed;
- even lead to a plan being cancelled.

The marketing team may have some control or influence over some constraints. Other constraints are likely to be outside or beyond their control. But each may affect the marketing mix to some degree.

Some constraints can be avoided or reduced. Others may need to be overcome through the use of tactical plans to counter their effect. Although constraints may appear to be completely negative at first, they can result in a rethink that leads to a better marketing mix or a more creative, productive and profitable set of plans than originally thought.

Figure 1 *Internal constraints*

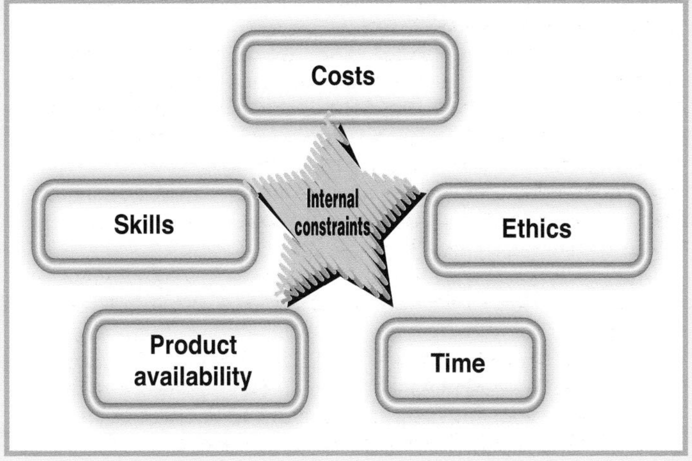

Internal constraints

These constraints exist within the structure and operating procedure of a business. They are likely to be set, applied and controlled by the senior management or influential stakeholders of the business.

Financial constraints These are perhaps the main internal constraint. They are usually set in the form of a budget. This is the amount of money that is allocated to a project. A budget can be based on real, market based costs required to be spent on a project, how much an organisation can afford to spend without hurting investors or damaging its viability, or an estimate of investment expenditure required for a forecast return on expenditure. Whichever way a budget is set, it will feel like a constraint on the marketing mix as there is always a reason to spend more money than the budget will allow.

Sometimes a financial constraint may be perceived to be external. For example, a supplier may raise its prices or the cost of a service may be higher than the budget allows. However, even though higher prices or costs may feel like the constraint is external, the real constraining factor is access to financial resources, the internally set budget.

Financial constraints can be changed or overcome by reassessing the situation and presenting the case for a change of budget, supported by marketing research, to senior management or the budget controller in the organisation.

Time Timing can affect marketing plans. For example, when a major new film is launched by Dreamworks or Warner Bros., it is preceded by trailers advertising the film for a certain period. Promoting too early or too late may lose impact on potential cinema goers.

Skills and expertise of staff Skills can affect marketing plans. For example, if a UK business is launching a new product abroad, such as in India, it may need to recruit an agent or a specialist marketing agency with knowledge of the market to promote, sell and distribute the product. Its current staff may lack this expertise.

Ethical standards These are the values and beliefs which influence a business. Ethical trading can mean taking into account social justice issues in business. Figure 2 shows how ethical standards can affect marketing decisions.

Product availability The availability of products can affect marketing plans. For example, car manufacturers often launch new models each year. They cannot be marketed until they are designed and manufactured.

External constraints

These are constraints that are usually beyond the direct control of an organisation, yet still affect the marketing plans. They may be set, applied and controlled by a range of organisations, such as the government, the European Union (EU), or a non-government organisation (NGO) such as a trade or industry association.

Political and economic factors

One of the main functions of government is to create and maintain economic conditions that allow the population to enjoy a

Figure 2 *Ethical standards at Ethical Wares*

Ethical Wares is an ethically-based mail order company run by vegans who seek to trade in a manner which does not exploit animals, humans or the wider environment. It states ' By the sale of these vegan products we hope to play our part in the promotion of a cruelty-free lifestyle'. Products include shoes, jewellery, bags, rugs and other accessories.

Source: adapted from www.ethicalwares.com.

Figure 3 *External constraints*

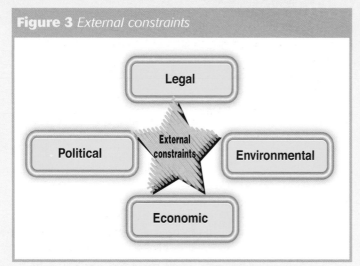

Table 1 *How economic factors might affect a business*

Factor	Effect
Rising inflation	Raise costs
Rising unemployment	Greater pool of labour
Trade restrictions	Fewer imports
Falling exchange rate	Exports cheaper and imports more expensive
Economic growth	More consumer spending

good and improving standard of living. Part of this includes protection from extremes or changes in the world economy that could affect the economic situation in a country. Governments also have a duty to protect consumers. This usually happens through changes in licensing or legislation. These factors will have an effect on marketing plans and can sometimes constrain marketing activity.

Political factors These are factors relating to government which affect businesses. An example of how political factors have affected the marketing mix is the way that the Sunday Trading Act 1994 has changed shopping patterns and marketing opportunities. The Act regulates opening by large shops on Sundays. Before the Act, large shops in England and Wales were required to give prior written notification to the local authority of their Sunday opening hours or changes in these hours. The retail industry lobbied government to deregulate Sunday opening to provide additional marketing opportunities, i.e. an additional day of the week for consumers to shop. Thus one constraint on retail marketing was removed, although it did introduce other constraints as it limited opening times to 6 continual hours between certain times.

Another way that political factors can affect the marketing mix can be seen in a run-up to a general election. Advertising media such as posters will be bought by political parties for promotion. This leaves fewer poster sites for advertising consumer products. The availability of poster sites could constrain where advertising occurs and the remaining poster sites will be priced at a premium, thus placing a financial constraint on potential advertisers.

Other political factors could include the effects of the Competition Commission rulings on marketing plans and the government establishment of regulatory bodies such as the Office of Water Services (Ofwat) which affect the marketing mix of suppliers of important public services. The Office of Communications (Ofcom) and the Advertising Standards Authority (ASA) can have a particular constraint on marketing plans as they control advertising and promotion in most media.

Economic factors These are factors relating to the operation of the economy. A variety of economic factors can affect businesses. Some are shown in Table 1. For example, interest rates may be lowered or raised to warm up or slow down the economy. As interest rates change, so does the amount of money available for investment in industry and for consumers to spend. If interest

rates are high, it will cost a business more to invest in a new production line. High interest rates mean that consumers have higher mortgage or loan repayments and less to spend on consumer goods and services. Conversely, low interest rates will encourage a 'feel good' factor among consumers. They will have relatively more income to spend, opening up marketing opportunities for suppliers of goods and services.

Legal factors

Legal constraints on the marketing mix and on marketing plans are the result of legislation. There is a great deal of legislation that could affect marketing plans. Most legislation affecting marketing has resulted from the objective of protecting consumers. The Trading Standards Central website www.tradingstandards.gov.uk is a good place to look to get some idea of just how much legislation exists to protect consumers.

There is no need to learn every part of every piece of legislation. But it is useful to understand how the principal pieces of consumer protection legislation can constrain the marketing mix. Some examples are shown in Figure 4. The Office of Fair Trading provides useful general advice on consumer rights in the UK. It also provides information relating to businesses and markets.

Before any marketing plans are put into practice it is always worth checking them against current legislation to make sure that no offences are likely to occur and no legislation is broken as a result of the plan. Once a potential constraint has been identified, steps can be taken and plans can be changed to avoid or reduce the effect of any constraint and reduce the chance of breaking the law.

Other legislation that could constrain and have an impact on the marketing mix include Sex, Race and Disability Discrimination and Equal Opportunities Acts. These are also dealt within sections 8 and 15.

Environmental and ecological factors

This is another group of external factors that could constrain marketing plans and activity. It could include environmental standards, environmental protection and voluntary codes and agreements that have been established to reduce the impact of commercial activity on the environment.

Examples of environmental standards include:
● the Montreal Protocol, concerned with substances that deplete the ozone layer, such as propellants and gases used in aerosols,

Figure 4 *Examples of legal constraints*

CONSUMER PROTECTION ACT 1987. Prohibits the supply of goods not in accordance with the general safety requirement or are unsafe and provides for the safety and protection of consumers by enabling regulations or orders to be made controlling consumer goods.

HEALTH AND SAFETY AT WORK ACT 1974. Controls the classification, packaging, labelling, carriage and storage of dangerous substances.

LEGAL CONSTRAINTS

TRADE DESCRIPTIONS ACT 1968. Prohibits the misdescription on the supply of goods and prohibits false claims for services, accommodation and facilities.

SUPPLY OF GOODS AND SERVICES ACT 1982. Details the rights of purchasers and the duties of suppliers of services.

SALE OF GOODS ACT 1979 and SALE AND SUPPLY OF GOODS 1994 and SALE OF GOODS (AMENDMENT) ACT 1995. Details the rights of purchasers and the duties of sellers in the sale of goods.

fire extinguishers, and refrigerators;

- the Kyoto Agreement, a framework laid down by 38 developed countries to reduce their emission of greenhouse gases to prevent global warming.

There are others and likely to be more in the future. The effect and constraint on the marketing mix may not be felt directly by every business. But all businesses will be affected indirectly as different industries have to find ways of reducing emissions. This in turn could affect the cost and supply of some materials used in production.

The environmental and ecological standards that are established by a business can also affect other businesses. Such standards are likely to affect the way that a business expects suppliers to operate. This could constrain some aspects of the marketing mix, particularly when it comes to the sourcing of raw materials and the use of renewable resources for production. A decision to reduce air pollution by airlines, might affect the marketing mix of airline manufacturers.

Other external constraints in this area would be voluntary and industry codes, competition, customer standards and requests. These are also dealt with in section 13.

Use newspaper articles to investigate how internal or external factors have affected the activities of a business over a period of time. Choose a well known business that is likely to have had a number of articles written about it, such as a car company, supermarket or a fashion clothing business. Identify the factors that have affected a business and how they have had an impact.

OR

Identify a business that could be affected by the ASA and legislation. Investigate how the ASA's activities and legislation could constrain the development of the marketing mix of this business.

OR

Design a questionnaire to identify and investigate the effects of both internal and external factors on a small business organisation.

Research task

Portfolio practice · Selling paint to B&Q

B&Q China in 2003 developed an educational promotion on water-based paints to inform its customers of the benefits. Operating companies will continue to be encouraged to give their customers the products and information to help enhance the quality of their home whilst making them more energy-efficient and environmentally sound. It is not our role to tell our customers how to live their lives, but as the debates around sustainable consumption and sustainable development evolve, we as a retailer need to be ready to respond through the products we offer and the information we provide.

Case study

Paint

Paint is core to home improvement. The story starts with its various raw materials, most of which are composed of hydrocarbons or titanium dioxide. Although these raw materials cause concern, the most significant issues surround product use. As paint dries, volatile organic compounds (VOCs) are emitted into the air, causing unpleasant smells and headaches. This is why B&Q UK has been reformulating paint to reduce its dependency on the solvents and VOCs. To help customer choice, the VOCs label was introduced in 1995. In 2004 this label will be reviewed to ensure compliance with the proposed EU paint directive, while the Asian businesses will look into rationalising the environmental labels on their paint ranges.

Source: adapted from *Growth, Returns ... and Responsibility*, Corporate social responsibility summary report from Kingfisher plc, 2003.

(i) **Identify the constraints placed on the marketing mix of a paint company wishing to sell its products in B&Q stores.**

(ii) **Examine how these constraints might affect the marketing mix of a paint company.**

Meeting the assessment criteria

You are required to produce an appropriate marketing mix for a new or existing product or service. Your work must include evidence on how the mix selected has been affected by both internal and external constraints.

Business example - CDRack

Students have chosen a vacuum formed CD holder as their product. The product, named the CDRack, will be produced in their D&T department.

Mark Band 1 *Basic evaluation of the marketing mix evidenced by conclusions made without supporting evidence or reasons.*
During the development stage it was decided that a simple design for the CDRack could be made without the need for additional equipment, which would prevent any extra cost. It was also decided to use a plastic that was suitable for vacuum forming and was within the agreed budget for the production cost of the CDRack. Looking around the town centre, the best places to achieve greatest sales for the CDRack were a local music shop and hardware stores. The best place to promote the CDRack would be in local media, such as newspapers. Economic conditions could affect price, so it would be best to keep it low.

Mark Band 2 *Justification of marketing mix showing a range of supported relevant evidence, arguments and conclusions.*
During development of the CDRack a simple prototype was made and shown to people. Some thought it was too big, but were told that the size was constrained by the size of the 'jewel case' used for CDs and to be worthwhile it had to hold ten CDs. A local supplier of plastic suitable for vacuum forming was found. A price was negotiated based on an initial forecast and a lower price for repeat sales if the product took off. This would improve profitability, as the retail selling price has an upper limit determined by the price of similar products. The best places to achieve greatest sales for the CDRack were a local music shop and hardware stores. They were close to the town centre. Selling further away might limit shoppers and sales. In addition, it was thought that the CDRack could be sold direct to consumers from a website. This was supported by a report on television, which said that increasing numbers of consumers were using the Internet for buying household goods. Special packaging for the mail order sales was needed. This was a constraint which was not costed into the original product, and could thus affect profitability. Packaging would be recyclable, which may help to take into account ethical considerations. The local newspaper would be a suitable media to advertise the CDRack. It was decided to spend most of the marketing budget on newspaper advertising, constraining other forms of promotion. This was justified as sales were likely to be in the local area. Prices were kept as low as possible as confidence in the economy had not recovered yet.

Mark Band 3 *Comprehensive and fully justified account of all aspects of the selected marketing mix showing originality of thought.*
During the development stage a simple prototype was designed. It was shown to two groups. Some consumers felt it was too big, but reducing size was rejected. Although this might save costs, the CDRack had to be large enough to hold ten CDs in a 'jewel case'. It was also shown to the local Trading Standards office which stated that the design chosen was suitable for sale to consumers and did not break any consumer protection legislation. The Trading Standards office also checked that wording used on the labelling was acceptable.

A local supplier was found to provide plastic suitable for vacuum forming. An initial price was agreed along with a reduced price for repeat sales which would improve profitability. An Internet survey was used to make sure this was the best price they could get, which it was. However, the supplier was also found to meet certain criteria laid down about ethical trading, such as good employee conditions and not buying materials from countries with oppressive political regimes.

Before the CDRack was launched the owner of a hardware store was interviewed to gauge her reaction and to check that the business had made the right conclusions about how suitable it was to sell in the shops in the town centre. She agreed that the town centre would be the most effective place to maximise sales. The positive comments on the product and location were used as part of their sales presentation to other shopkeepers. The business also decided to sell via the Internet. Television and newspaper reports, as well as surveys from the Office of National Statistics, indicated growing sales via the Internet by consumers.

Before committing to advertising in the local newspaper, the students sought opinion from the local shopkeepers about how effective this method of advertising was likely to be. After their comments confirmed this would be effective, most of the budget would be spent in local newspapers. However, another cost effective method was posters hung in shops that stocked the CDRack. The posters were carefully worded to comply with advertising legislation.

A local survey was carried out to check the retail selling prices of CD racks. Economic conditions were stable at the time. Inflation was low and interest rates had not been increased. But there was still a view that confidence had not yet recovered. Based on this, it was decided that keeping the selling price as low as possible was the correct strategy. It was also decided that, although special packaging was not included in the initial cost, it would be used. This is because it was recyclable and would appeal to ethical customers. Details of plastic waste disposal sites would be included on the packaging to fit in with the business's ethical stance.

42 What is electronic business?

The growth of electronic business

All businesses will have some aspect of electronic business (e-business). When they answer the phone, receive a fax or send an e-mail they are operating electronically. However, e-business generally refers to the use of electronic networks to carry out business functions, such as:

- an individual applying for a job over the Internet;
- individuals within an organisation exchanging e-mails and reports via their intranet system;
- the extension of an intranet network into an extranet to allow external users access to a company's systems, such as companies ordering goods from suppliers via intranet links, banks transferring money from one branch to another or individuals managing their bank accounts on-line.

E-business and e-commerce

E-business is using electronic networks to carry out business functions. **E-commerce** is defined in an Inland Revenue report as 'doing business electronically, whether communicating by PC, interactive television, console gaming machine or through high street kiosks'. In other words it is carrying out business transactions - the buying and selling of goods and services.

E-business began in the 1970s with the facility for banks to move money around using electronic record-keeping, followed in the 1980s by electronic mail and intranet facilities. Since the Internet came into wider use in the 1990s, opening up electronic business opportunities for anyone who had a computer, the growth seen in this type of business has been phenomenal. Data from the Office for National Statistics show UK Internet sales are doubling each year, totalling nearly £12bn in 2003.

Considering that radio took 38 years to reach 50 million people and television took 13 years, the growth of the Internet has been rapid. It took just four years to reach 50 million people and has created unprecedented business opportunities.

E-business is being carried on around the world, every second of the day and night, with no constraints concerning shop or bank opening hours or whether the office is staffed. Figure 1 illustrates how one simple transaction can generate several electronic transactions. But e-business does not only include business that most people are familiar with, such as a consumer purchasing from an on-line store like Amazon. There are many different types of e-business. Some examples are shown in Table 1.

Table 1 *Examples of electronic business*

Transaction	Examples
Consumer to business	Consumer to business shopping is generally referred to as on-line shopping. Examples include www.jessops.com for photograph prints or buying travel tickets on www.easyjet.co.uk. Many supermarkets now offer on-line shopping.
Consumer to consumer	The Internet now offers national and even global opportunities for individuals to exchange information and goods. Statistics on the eBay auction website show that in May 2005 there were 20 million listings. Opportunities to sell second-hand goods are provided through classified advertisement sites, in the style of 'small ads' in the local paper, such as www.findit.co.uk.
Business to business	Businesses can order goods and services, often through extranets. Prontaprint printing services franchises, for example, have the facility for regular customers to place their orders and re-order on line. Many businesses now carry out financial transactions on-line paying against invoices direct into a supplier's bank account.
Business to government	Businesses use electronic networks to provide a service to the government, such as filing their income tax returns to the Inland Revenue (www.inlandrevenue.gov.uk) or paying the London congestion charge (www.cclondon.com).
Consumer to government	Examples would include ordering a tax disc on line (www.dvla.gov.uk) or ordering road safety helmets from the County Council (www.hants.gov.uk).
Government to consumer	Examples would include Foreign Office travel advice (www.fco.gov.uk) and consumer advice (www.consumerdirect.gov.uk).
Government to government	Governments will exchange data and resources through the Internet, e-mail, intranets and extranets. This would not only include one country dealing with another country, or the EU with its member states, but also includes government organisations within a country exchanging data. For example, the DFES (www.dfes.gov.uk) gives schools the opportunity to download teaching resources.

Figure 1 *The effects of an electronic transaction*

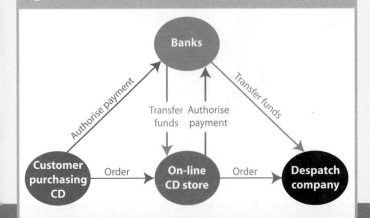

Why businesses trade electronically

It is likely that a business decision to set up an Internet presence will have been made as part of a programme to meet particular company objectives, such as increasing sales or reducing overheads, and so the main driving force behind establishing a website will differ from one company to another. This aspect of company objectives will be dealt with in more detail in section 43. However, general reasons for an on-line presence include those shown in Figure 2.

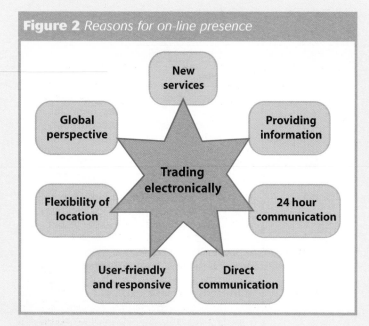

Figure 2 *Reasons for on-line presence*

The global perspective

A website presence opens up the potential for details of company products and services to be seen throughout the world. No accurate figures exist for the number of people who have regular access to the Internet, but estimates suggest it is between 600 and 800 million.

Providing information about the business

Many electronic businesses provide specialist services to other businesses - the individual consumer is unlikely to deal directly with them or even be aware of their existence. Examples of these types of business are:
- Thomsons Online Benefits (www.thomsonsonlinebenefits.com), a business which provides support to businesses in managing their benefit schemes, such as pensions, health care, discount shopping, company cars, fitness centre subscriptions;
- E-Merce Services (www.e-merce.co.uk), which provides IT solutions for business.

However such specialists can often find it difficult to establish contact with those who could best use their services. Establishing an Internet presence gives them the opportunity to provide extensive information on their services. Registering themselves with a search engine gives them the potential to reach a wide audience, most significantly those who are actively seeking the type of service they offer.

Direct communication

Advertisements on television, in a newspaper and other communications targeted at customers carry the risk that they may not reach the expected audience. By the very nature of the fact that potential customers have made their own way to the website, the business knows that they are communicating directly with those who have expressed an interest in the product or service on offer. Furthermore, the process of on-line shopping contributes towards the creation of databases which businesses can use for mail shots and customer profiling. Eurostar, the train service between UK and France and Belgium, for example, sends regular e-mails giving details of special offers, direct to previous customers.

24 hour communication

The Internet will give customers the opportunity to browse and shop at their convenience, accessing information and buying products and services from anywhere 24 hours a day, 7 days a week. This process does not depend on someone being at the other end of the line at that particular moment. On-line traders have no short-term worries if they want to shut the shop early or if someone rings in sick. And the global nature of the Internet means that someone in USA or the Far East can be buying goods from a business while its personnel are in bed, asleep. Figure 3 shows an example.

Figure 3 *Benefits of 24 hour communication*

Olga Knight is an artist who specialises in creating animal designs for greetings cards and prints. Olga does regular business with two companies in the USA, one of which is in Tennessee. She is able to exchange e-mails and business transactions with her customers via the Internet, www.olgaknightdesigns.com, without having to worry that the five-hour difference may mean that the business is not open or the office may not be staffed. They will simply read their e-mails during their own working hours and she will process their orders during her working hours.

Source: adapted from www.olganightdesigns.com.

Flexibility of location

The global nature of e-business has meant that a business can establish itself anywhere in the world, taking advantage of favourable overhead costs, being close to the source of supply, or simply making the decision to work in an environment that suits the owner's lifestyle. PFA Research of Bodmin, Cornwall, is a market research agency. The Internet and associated sophisticated communication systems, giving the ability to move datafiles across the world instantly, set up video conferences and send and receive information regardless of the time of day, creates a flexibility of location. This flexibility meant that Robert Rush, Managing Director of PFA was able to return to Cornwall, the area he was brought up in, to run his business. Not onlydoes his company enjoy the reduced operating costs of a location far from the capital, he is alsonear to family and friends.

Providing a user-friendly and responsive service

An on-line presence allows a business to be responsive to customer needs and to provide a user-friendly service. Some examples are shown in Table 2.

New services

The very existence of the Internet itself and the electronic transactions that it supports has spawned a new generation of products and services. E-businesses provide many services for other e-businesses. These include:
- website designers;
- information technology services;
- software development;
- payment systems (e.g. PayPal);
- database management.

Table 2 *How an on-line presence may allow a business to be responsive and user-friendly*

Feature	Benefits to customer/business
On-line ordering	Make immediate order Pay by credit or debit card Change order Confirm order When downloading, receive a product immediately
Track order	Check that order has been sent Check current situation
Contact the business	Request information Provide feedback
Personal accounts	Check outstanding orders Check amounts owing or paid Check history of orders

Golf Scotland (www.golfscotland.com) specialises in Scottish golfing holidays.
1. Visit the site of Golf Scotland and explain three factors that might have influenced Golf Scotland to have an Internet presence.
2. Identify and explain two features that are likely to make the website more attractive to potential customers than a brochure.

Research task

Portfolio practice · Football clubs

www.manutd.com
www.liverpoolfc.co.uk
www.bcfc.com
www.arsenal.com
www.whufc.com
The above football clubs have detailed websites providing a large amount of information. Contents include details of fixtures, results, the players, shopping opportunities, strip, supporters and statistics. All make extensive use of colour and carry news features.

(a) Identify the opportunities that e-commerce presents to these football clubs to reach new markets for their merchandise.

(b) Explain the advantages that their websites offer to raise awareness of both their performances on the football field and their other business activities, such as merchandising.

Meeting the assessment criteria

For your assessment you are required to identify and explain the purpose of an organisation establishing an on-line presence and discuss whether it meets the business' aims and objectives.

Business example - Giles and Gray

Giles & Gray are estate agents and surveyors. They deal in residential and commercial properties and have properties for sale or rent. They also offer a property management service. Another important aspect of their work is the professional services they offer which include surveys, valuations, arranging legal advice, homebuyers reports and arbitrating in rent disputes.

Mark Band 1 *Identification of the purpose of an on-line presence and a simplistic description of the content.*

Giles & Gray decided to set up a website to attract more people to look at the properties they have available. They intend to offer a user-friendly and responsive service for all customers, providing information directly. There are five pages on their website all designed in their corporate colours. Visitors to their website navigate by clicking on links entitled:

- Residential properties – visitors can look at the domestic properties available and will find details similar to those on the leaflets about houses that estate agents hand out, such as number of bedrooms and the price;
- Commercial properties – this shows availability of the types of properties that businesses would be looking for such as shops, lock up garages, offices and warehouses;
- Property management – their customers can see the services they provide, such as looking after properties when people are away, dealing with tenants of rented properties and property maintenance;
- About us – this page gives information about the qualifications and backgrounds of the three partners;
- Contact information.

Mark Band 2 *An explanation of the purpose of an on-line presence.*

Giles & Gray set up their website because they wanted to attract more people to look at the properties they had available. They intended to offer a user-friendly and responsive service for all customers, providing information directly. They had heard from other branches in their group that approximately 20% of people who request details have seen properties on the Internet. They felt that they could not afford to lose that opportunity to increase sales. A website offers them an additional media route for potential customers to access their services. They may also attract customers who were intending to visit the area in the future and wanted to carry out some preliminary research. Their website gives Giles & Gray the opportunity to establish communications with customers even before they have walked through the door of the shop, 24 hours a day. This is particularly important because of the fact that, as all the other estate agents in the area had a website, if they failed to do so they were losing the opportunity of raising awareness of their existence.

Mark Band 3 *Discuss whether the organisation meets its aims and objectives with an electronic presence.*

Giles and Gray want to attract customers, offering a user-friendly service which communicates information about the business directly. 45% of Giles & Gray's business is in residential properties - houses and flats. It is likely that many customers will be moving into the area from somewhere else. The Internet therefore would be a very useful tool for those people who might otherwise not bother to ring up or wait for details to come through the post because they can access the information from home or their office and can get instant feedback on what's available. This would meet their objective of attracting more people to look at their properties. It is also likely that people will look via the Internet at a much wider geographical area than they could possibly cover by actually travelling there, which raises the chances that Giles & Gray may increase their customer base by attracting people who would not originally have considered their area. The information would be available 24 hours a day,

On the other hand, Giles & Gray do not have the opportunity to gather data about the 'surfers' who are looking at their properties in the way that they can record details from people who call in at their office or telephone. Customers who do not find information that meets their particular requirements will simply surf away from their site. By relying heavily on their website, therefore, Giles & Gray may not be aware that there is a segment of the market whose needs they are not currently meeting and therefore lose the opportunity to gather data for increasing their customer database. Furthermore, while using the Internet will save postage and photocopying costs, the traditional process of sending out mailshots serves as a constant reminder of their existence and enables them to match properties to customers. These factors would suggest that the Internet is not the only means of achieving the objective of attracting people to look at their properties.

Giles & Gray need to ensure that the Internet complements their current information routes with their market and does not replace them.

Aims and objectives

Businesses set aims and objectives to give direction to the organisation and set out what it is trying to achieve. They are discussed in detail in section 1.

The aims of a business form the basis of decision making and strategic management. No major business decisions are likely to be made without referring to the aims that have been set for the business. A typical model around which discussions for achieving aims will focus is shown in Figure 1.

Figure 1 *Achieving business aims with an on-line presence*

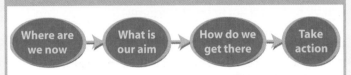

During the consultation process various strategies and tactics for achieving aims will be discussed and objectives set. The objective of establishing an on-line presence will have arisen from evidence that a website, and carrying out business electronically, will meet one or more of the aims the business has set itself. Examples of aims that may be met by creating a website are shown in Figure 2.

Figure 2 *Business aims and an on-line presence*

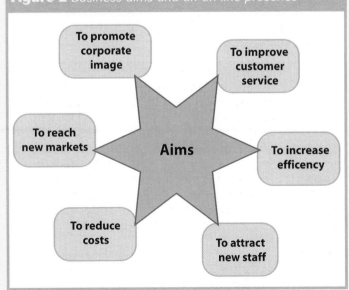

Promoting a corporate image

The Internet offers an additional media opportunity for a business to project its corporate image and promote its brands. Some businesses, for example, may attempt to establish their place in the customer's perception as innovative and modern. They may want to be seen as a leading-edge company in their industry. Swatch manufactures creative and innovative watches. It uses images, photographs and interactivity on its website which support its brand image of accessories for consumers with exciting and interesting lifestyles. Others may attempt to promote their image in a different way. Asda, for example, attempts to focus its advertising on establishing itself as a 'value for money' retail outlet and uses its website to reinforce this. This is shown in Figure 3.

Figure 3 *Asda website*

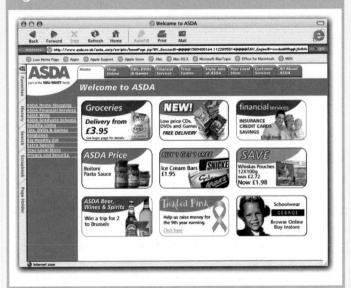

Reaching new markets and increasing sales

The introduction of on-line supermarket shopping has meant that businesses such as Sainsburys or Tesco can now target a new profile of customer – those who are restricted to the home. Providing an Internet shopping facility has opened up the potential customer base to those who find it difficult to visit the store in person. This new customer base not only includes customers within the immediate locality who find traditional shopping difficult because of physical disability, lack of transport or because they work anti-social hours. E-business presents opportunities for businesses to target potential customers nationwide or even worldwide as physical location is no longer a factor.

Section 42 explained the global opportunities to increase sales presented by carrying out business over the Internet. Before SDL Sheffield, (www.click2translate.com), a supplier of translation services, established an e-presence, its business was mainly from UK customers. It now reports that the majority of its business is from overseas, virtually all of its enquiries are via the Internet and its Internet business is doubling each year. Even smaller companies who twenty or thirty years ago would have been satisfied only with establishing a local reputation now have opportunities to extend their markets nationwide. An example is shown in Figure 4.

Figure 4 *Riverford Organic Vegetables Ltd*

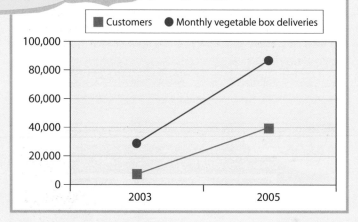

Riverford Organic Vegetables Ltd of Buckfastleigh, Devon started organic vegetable production in 1987, delivering to local shops. Since it began trading at www.riverford.co.uk it has become one of the largest independent growers of organic vegetables in the UK. Growth between 2003 and 2005 is shown below.

Source: adapted from company information.

Reducing costs

Many businesses, particularly those already established in the retail sector such as Sainsburys, Debenhams or HMV who have introduced on-line shopping, will continue to maintain their stores and may not therefore see many opportunities to reduce overheads. However, some businesses, particularly in the travel and leisure industries, offer discounts for purchasing on-line due to the considerable savings they have made in overheads. For traders who see e-business as their main activity there can be a significant reduction in costs compared with running a conventional office or shop. If nothing else, the business can dispense with the need to maintain stylish and expensive shop fittings to impress customers

Shifting the emphasis of a business from face-to-face customer service to e-business also provides opportunities to reduce running costs. Businesses that trade exclusively on-line can, for example, decide to run on very low stock, preferring to operate on lines similar to just-in-time stock control, ordering goods from their own suppliers as they are needed. This would dispense with much of the store room space and display areas, as well as the need to carry the high levels of stock seen in a conventional shop. Even when there is still a lot of stock, attractive display of the goods for browsing customers is not an issue – the goods can remain in packing cases in storage facilities rented in cheaper areas, rather than having to maintain an outlet in the High Street or a retail park. The stock control system itself and the fact that most e-businesses will be run through database systems can mean a huge reduction in time-consuming manual processing of data.

Staffing costs are another significant area that may see reductions, both in terms of number of staff needed and the skills,

expertise and flexibility, which can be expensive, required to run a traditional trading organisation. There are fewer time-consuming face-to-face encounters with customers, no training in handling customers and no short-term worries about shop opening hours and covering shifts, holidays and staff sickness. The time spent counting and banking money will be virtually eliminated as most transactions will be carried out digitally using credit and debit cards.

Attracting new staff

The *Charity Times* estimated that there were over 11 million on-line jobseekers in 2004, with the numbers growing rapidly, month by month. In addition, a study found that the Internet was the preferred choice for 45% of people looking for work. It concluded that no organisation, however small, can afford to ignore these figures.

The Internet is now well-established as a medium for job hunters. Any business seeking high-calibre, well-qualified and innovative staff will not ignore the opportunities that its own website provides for what is in effect a 'free' opportunity for advertising its vacancies. Examples of well known businesses which now routinely advertise job and career opportunities on their websites include:

- McDonalds (www.mcdonalds.co.uk);
- Shell (www.shell.com);
- The National Health Service (www.nhscareers.nhs.uk);
- Marks & Spencer (www.marksandspencer.com).

Figure 5 *On-line recruitment at Marks & Spencer*

Improving customer service

A company which has identified improved customer services as an aim is likely to feel that this can be achieved by the 24 hour availability of its service over the Internet, as explained in section 42. Its customers can choose a time to make purchases which is convenient to them and are not constrained by opening hours, accessibility of staff or where they live.

In addition, the process of buying and selling over the Internet enables e-businesses to build up huge databases which can be quizzed to identify trends in individual buying patterns and customer characteristics. Companies can then plan their product portfolios to match closely the profile of their customers, providing the products, services and on-line interface which will be most suitable for their market. Many e-businesses provide opportunities for receiving customer feedback which will identify further areas where refinements can be made to improve customer satisfaction.

Increasing efficiency

By its very nature, e-business makes extensive use of sophisticated and powerful software. This means that processing of orders and financial transactions are done through automated systems which generally will be many times more efficient than traditional methods. These systems can also provide detailed analyses of spending, identifying where savings could be made, and as discussed earlier, build up detailed customer profiles, giving the business confidence that their expenditure on advertising and promotion campaigns will be targeted through media appropriate for their market. As described earlier in this section, many e-businesses can streamline their stock control, not ordering stock until they in turn have received orders from their clients, which reduces the potential for waste or goods becoming out-of-date or damaged during storage.

Body Shop has a page on its website (www.uk.thebodyshop.com) entitled 'values'. Examine the page on the Internet.

1. Suggest the reasons why Body Shop may have decided to include a page outlining its values.
2. Discuss the benefits to Body Shop of displaying these values on its website.

Research task

Portfolio practice · Jarrang Ltd

Stafford Sumner owns Jarrang Ltd, an e-mail Marketing Communications Specialist. 'We offer a fully managed e-mail marketing service from conception to execution' says Stafford 'We plan, design, write, send, track and analyse e-mail campaigns on behalf of our clients. We manage e-mail campaigns for a wide range of businesses, both large and small, and covering sectors as diverse as leisure, education, and IT.

'In March 2003, around the same time as Jarrang was conceived, I took the decision to relocate back to the south-west. With a laptop, phone line and an air service linking Cornwall with London in just under an hour, I was pretty certain that my geographic location wouldn't hinder my business aspirations. It was the right decision and I now thoroughly enjoy the lifestyle that Cornwall has to offer, including a thriving business community, whilst making regular trips back to London for client meetings or just catching up with old friends.'

'When I am not working or networking, my current passion is learning how to sail at a local club on the Helford River in Cornwall. I am also an Advanced Driver and am currently an Observer for the Cornwall Advanced Motorists, which involves bringing drivers up to a high enough standard to pass the Advanced Driving test carried out by the Institute of Advanced Motorists (IAM). It's a great challenge and makes me feel as if I am doing something positive for the community.'

Source: adapted from company information and Profiles - www.ecademy.com.

(a) **Identify personal aims and objectives that Stafford may have and explain how e-business has enabled him to achieve these aims.**

(b) **Assess the impact that the location of Stafford's business may have on aims and objectives he may have in terms of:**

   (i) **customer service;**

   (ii) **costs;**

   (iii) **attracting staff.**

(c) **Suggest the aims and objectives that some businesses in the leisure, education and IT industries achieve by using Jarrang Ltd's services.**

Meeting the assessment criteria

For your assessment you are required to identify and explain the purpose of an organisation establishing an on-line presence and discuss whether it meets the business' aims and objectives.

Business example – Holiday Breaks

Holiday Breaks is a small business, offering a service for owners of self-catering holiday accommodation, houses, flats and caravans at coastal locations around the UK to advertise their properties.

Mark Band 1 *Show research of the factors influencing the establishment of an on-line presence.*

Holiday Breaks offers clients the opportunity to advertise their properties and target the right sector of the market. Potential holiday makers can see details of the accommodation on offer, lists of dates for availability and details for contacting the owners. Holiday Breaks wishes to increase the numbers of properties it has on its books. It interviewed 25 owners of holiday cottages which were advertised both on the Internet and in holiday magazines. It discovered that, on average, 65% of enquiries resulting in firm bookings came from the Internet. As a small business, Holiday Breaks wishes to take opportunities to keep overheads and running costs as low as possible. It has subscribed to a database list and has a list of 1,500 addresses of potentially interested customers to whom it planned to post a catalogue. It discovered that printing and postage of a good quality catalogue would cost £3,500.

Mark Band 2 *An explanation of the purpose of an on-line presence and how it meets its aims and objectives with an electronic presence on the Internet.*

The Internet is now established as a popular source of travel research and so travel businesses need to have a website in order to compete. Holiday Breaks now wishes to increase the number of properties it has on its books and feels this can be achieved by showing evidence that clients enjoy increased bookings through its advertising methods. The research with the 25 holiday home owners supported the decision to establish a web presence. Holiday Breaks also felt that the global nature of the Internet would mean that holiday home owners would be interested in advertising on its website service as it had the potential to target holiday makers from around the world.

Holiday Breaks has an aim of keeping costs low. A website would help achieve that aim. Taking account of the fact that existing personnel would have a change of job role, for example they would maintain the website instead of editing a catalogue,

the additional costs to the company of setting up and maintaining a simple website was estimated at £500 a year. This is in contrast to the £3,500 for distribution of a catalogue.

Mark Band 3 *Discuss whether this organisation meets its aims and objectives with an electronic presence.*

Running a website proved to be a much cheaper option for Holiday Breaks, which is aiming to keep costs low. Furthermore, the disadvantages identified for the catalogue proposal were not just the cost but the fact that a catalogue can get out of date quickly, if, for example, a property is no longer is available, whereas the website can be updated every day if necessary. This means Holiday Breaks can provide up-to-date information on the availability of the properties on its register, which is a very good customer service and is likely to be popular with existing and potential clients.

On the other hand, this immediacy means that Holiday Breaks needs to be constantly checking and can't afford to let too much time go by without up-dating. If it didn't do this holiday makers may not have confidence that the information they are looking at is correct and could stop using the site. This would conflict with the aim of increasing clientele as holiday home owners would soon become disenchanted with a service which lost them customers because it was not kept up to date. Furthermore the realisation amongst holiday makers that a catalogue cannot be kept up to date easily may encourage holiday makers to make telephone enquiries when the opportunity to offer alternatives can be given, which would have the potential to increase interest in properties and would be an argument against dispensing with the catalogue.

The competitive nature of the holiday business makes it essential that agencies such as Holiday Breaks see the Internet as part, although a very important part, of a complete range of promotion opportunities.

The impact on a business of its website

What is on a website?

The content of any website will be determined by the aims and objectives that the website is intending to achieve. For example, if the website is designed to increase sales, the likelihood is that there will be at least information about the products or services on offer. Depending on the type of business, other features of a website designed to increase sales may include:

- a facility for a potential customer to register an interest by supplying a telephone number or address for receiving further details;
- on-line catalogues, either to download or view;
- on-line shopping where the whole transaction from start to finish is completed on-line.

Table 1 looks at the aims in establishing a website that were identified in section 43 and suggests facilities that should be available on the website to help meet those aims.

Table 1 Business aims and websites

Aim	On-line facilities
To promote the company	Corporate colours, logo, company information, product information
To increase efficiency	On-line shopping, news pages, membership facility
To reduce costs	E-mail forms, product information in electronic format, on-line shopping
To reach new markets	Product information, on-line catalogue, on-line shopping, email forms for collecting customer information
To attract new staff	Job vacancies, corporate information, ethical policies
To improve customer service	Product information, contact details, help pages, Frequently Answered Questions (FAQ) pages, on-line shopping, links to complementary and supplementary product and service sites
To save money, e.g. by reducing stock control or printing and postage costs	News pages, corporate information, product information, on-line shopping, e-mail
To promote a corporate image	Use of logos, colour schemes, slogans and images, charity work, ethical policies

Further features on a business website may include:
- corporate information of interest to stakeholders, e.g. reports and accounts, mission statement, ethical policies, list of directors. Boots Plc, for example, has a section on its website entitled 'Welcome to Boots Group Plc' which includes an annual report and accounts, on-line voting for shareholders to cast their votes for the AGM, AGM minutes and the AGM agenda, as shown in Figure 1;
- news pages for new products and corporate information. Sony UK's Playstation website, for example, has a section entitled Latest.

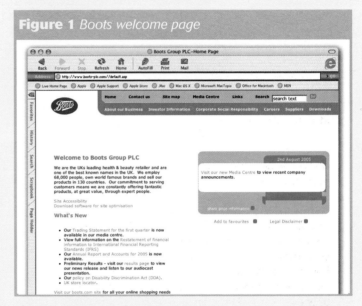

Figure 1 Boots welcome page

The effects on a business of its website

All business decisions will lead to both short and long term effects on the way a business operates. In that respect, e-business is no different. However the decision to extend into the world of e-business is likely to have a profound effect on the way a business operates, its costs and its personnel, particularly in the case of smaller businesses, where the experience may be unparalleled in their previous operations. Business activities that are likely to be affected by the introduction of an on-line presence are shown in Figure 2.

Communication

From the day that a business website is launched it has a new medium to which it can direct enquiries and from which enquiries will be generated. The business may start to receive fewer phone calls because customers can find the information they need on the website. Alternatively, it may start to see an increase in enquiries because it is reaching a much wider audience. The website will raise the awareness of the existence and purpose of the business, and reinforce its corporate image.

The introduction of e-mail alone will have an immediate effect on the speed of communication for the business, both internally and externally. An e-mail can reach its destination within seconds of it being sent and can be processed with equal speed. The growth of high-speed communications through the use of

Figure 2 *Business activities affected by an on-line presence*

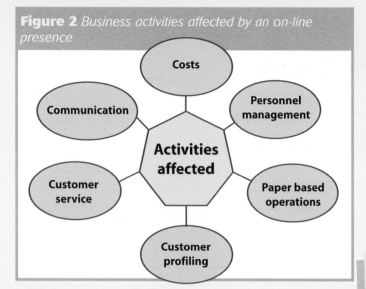

Figure 3 *Start-up costs*

In June 2005, Sally-Anne Baker set up Kitchen Goddess (www.kitchengoddess.co.uk), an e-business supplying household products. The prices she was quoted to build her website ranged from £1,000 upwards. She finally settled for a local company who were able to meet her needs in terms of how the website would look and function. For this they charged over £5,000. The cost of building the website and her stock were by far her largest start-up costs.

Source: adapted from company information.

broadband now enables movement of entire documents and images around the world within minutes. Decisions can be made safe in the knowledge that the latest business data has been made available.

Personnel can be contacted anywhere they have an Internet connection and can make decisions, receive updates, give business advice or exchange ideas, with quick and reliable access to the necessary data, through, for example, the company's extranet. Many of the examination papers set by the awarding body, Edexcel, are now marked on-line. Students' work is scanned into a secure website. The markers log onto an extranet, enter a secure area using their password and look at students' work from their computers at home.

Costs

Even the smallest of businesses will need to purchase equipment and software and seek technical advice to run a website. A small business may, for example, make the decision to lease equipment. This will have an impact on cash flow, taking account of the additional monthly outgoings.

A business embarking on e-business to improve internal communication or update systems, such as stock control or financial transactions, or in a more ambitious way by extending into e-commerce and inviting customers, clients and suppliers to trade with it on-line, is unlikely to have the technical skills and expertise necessary amongst its existing personnel. The business will need to have access to appropriately skilled personnel to set up and maintain the networks, and designers and managers for websites. This will be a large and expensive task. Whether the business decides to operate these services in-house, or, as is more likely to be the case with smaller businesses, to take out contracts with agencies and support services, this will incur significant short and long term costs. An example of the costs incurred by one small business in setting up an e-business is shown in Figure 3.

Whilst business may see a significant increase in costs in the short term, successful transition to e-business from the traditional method of making business transactions is likely in the long term to see, not an overall **increase** in costs, but a **change** in the way those costs are incurred. The most efficient of businesses will expect to see a

long term **reduction** in costs through increased efficiency savings and opportunities to downsize and reduce overheads, as discussed elsewhere in this unit. Furthermore, successful on-line purchasing opportunities should be expected to generate an increase in sales which will often lead to economies of scale.

Personnel management

The speed of communication discussed earlier raises expectations of speedy replies. Traditional paper-based transactions and filing systems will be replaced by the computer. Existing personnel will see their working methods and their job roles change almost overnight. There will be a need for training. There may be the need to re-structure. There may even be redundancies. For example, lead times may be reduced because the time taken to process an order could be significantly reduced. This will mean that less stock will need to be held at any one time and so the business may decide to reduce the size of the stock control team. The decision may be made to dispense with hard copy catalogues and price lists. The personnel involved in editing and processing those will no longer be needed.

All of these aspects have the potential to have a significant short and long term impact on staff management and motivation.

Customer profiling

The global nature of the Internet will see a gradual shift in the company's customer and contact base from local, to national and even international trade. This will result in the need for the business to review its marketing and communication strategies to take account of the different characteristics and needs of its customers, such as cultural, ethical and language differences.

The database structure that is essential for successful e-business enables the business to build up an accurate profile of its market. Many retail businesses offer membership services through which they collect consumer data. They have the ability to target groups of consumers who have expressed particular and specific interests. An example is shown in Figure 4.

Paper based operations

A move from conventional trading practices to electronic business represents a significant shift away from paper handling.

All transactions and monitoring will be carried out electronically. No more handling of cash or reconciliation of accounts at the end of the day. Some businesses may not even see the products they are dealing in. The shopper may have made the purchase through them but the business has simply, in its turn, lodged an order with another supplier, made arrangements with the despatch company, arranged the banking transfers and the item is shipped direct to the purchaser.

Customer service

Internet shopping has an impact on the customer services that a business provides. On-line supermarkets such as Tesco will not only need to include face-to-face communication and telephone in their customer services programme but now have to include an understanding of the impact on customers of having to use their shopping site, through guidance, tutorials and technical help and robust delivery, refund and replacement policies.

Stationers and newsagents such as WH Smith (www.whsmith.co.uk) and Empire Stores catalogues (www.empirestores.co.uk), for example, have very detailed help sections giving step by step guidance on the buying process. In order to retain customers the business has to maintain a user friendly interface with them and ensure that the website itself is speedy and efficient. Customer service is dealt with in detail in unit 5.

Short term and long term effects

Many of the effects of a website on a business explained above will be short term. They can be both beneficial and possibly problematic. For example, a successful website is likely to have short term benefits such as:
* an immediate increase in customers;
* an immediate increase in sales and turnover;
* improved communications with customers, such as feedback.

Possible negative short term effects might be:
* the increased costs of the hardware;
* the costs of running the website;
* the cost of training for staff;
* potential disruption resulting from changing work practices.

However, there are also long term implications. For example, a business may find that over time the number of responses to the website are greater and more cost effective than a leaflet mailing. It may therefore change its marketing strategy to take this into account. It may also find that suppliers or customers increasingly make use of the website to order or track supplies. The business may have to reorganise its stock control and ordering processes to take this into account.

Figure 4 *Confetti members' area*

Confetti provides products and services for weddings and special occasions. Examples of products include wedding planners, table decorations, wedding gifts and disposable cameras.

Members of the website need to be registered. The site says 'You need to be a registered user to access "my confetti", so that we can make sure your personal details are kept safe'. Members that sign up:

* get special offers tailored to suit them
* get access to personal planning tools
* can chat with other brides and grooms 24 hours a day
* get free advice from experts on anything they want to know about their big day.

The site also states:
why sign up?
* free newsletters by e-mail
* competitions and special offers
* your own FREE wedding website
* easy, secure shopping
* track all your orders
* and more.

Source: adapted from www.confetti.co.uk.

Effects of not updating

Websites must be maintained by businesses. Failure to update regularly can have implications for business.
* Failure to update software and ordering processes can result in technical difficulties and lost orders.
* Out of date information might be misleading for customers. Customer may place incorrect orders, resulting in returns.
* Out of date products may be listed. This may result in an increase in orders for products not for sale, leading to higher administration costs and wasted time, with no revenue.
* Out of date information presents a poor image to customers. They may decide to buy elsewhere.
* Updating is needed to prevent viruses.
* Failure to update may lead to problems with non-compliance of data protection legislation.
* Websites may look dated.

Identify a small business, club or voluntary group local to where you live, that does not have a website.
1. Interview a representative of that organisation and analyse the advantages of setting up a website to that organisation in particular.
2. Suggest the potential effects a website may have on the way it operates.

Research task

Portfolio practice · on-line counselling

Frances Mayo, who is based in Neath, runs a counselling service. In addition to offering traditional face-to-face counselling, Frances is using e-commerce to provide clients with an innovative on-line service. As Frances explained: 'This is ideal for folk who feel they cannot face anyone with their problem, and for folk who have illnesses, either physical or mental, and feel they cannot leave their home.' Frances regards her website as an important business asset since 'it gives people a choice of access and they can read my background and qualifications'. The site also provides information about fees and appointments, so that people do not need to telephone her for such information.

Source: adapted from E-Commerce – Inspiring Success, Opportunity, Wales and www.opportunitywales.co.uk.

(a) Identify and explain the opportunities that have opened up for Frances and her clients by her decision to provide on-line counselling.

(b) How might Frances' client profile have changed with her service now being available on-line?

(c) Assess how Frances' working day may have changed with the information on fees and appointments available on-line.

Meeting the assessment criteria

For your assessment you are required to identify the strengths and opportunities created by the Internet presence of a business, explain clearly the drawbacks and evaluate its website, making recommendations for its improvement in relation to its aims and objectives.

Business example - Domicil

Domicil is a multinational company selling a wide range of furniture and household goods. Its website gives details and images of its extensive furniture rage. It does not offer on-line shopping.

Mark Band 1 *Identify the strengths and opportunities created by an Internet presence.*

Domicil only has 12 stores throughout the UK which means that most people will be many miles from their nearest store. The effect that the website will have had on Domicil is that it now gives people from a much wider area the opportunity to browse through the products on offer. Some people who might not have bothered to make the long journey would now know it would be worth their while, as they will have seen products that would suit their needs. The website also has images and interactivity which display the products in realistic settings, such as children's picnic furniture in a pretty garden, which couldn't be shown in the shop.

Mark Band 2 *Identify the strengths and opportunities and explain clearly the drawbacks.*

The website can show the wide range of products available at Domicil. It also gives the opportunity to portray those products in a household setting by the use of photographic images and family models. This is an improvement on the way the products are displayed in the shop and may even lead to complementary sales. The use of colour and the company logo helps project the corporate image of the company, which features in its advertising campaigns. The effect of the website will be to increase consumer awareness of the products.

However, Domicil also offers a huge number of special bargains and little household gadgets that are interesting and fun to look at. It would be very difficult to show all of those on the website and so people looking at the website wouldn't know these products were on offer. It is difficult for a website to show the quality and feel of a product and some people may be put off visiting the store because an image of product has not given them the correct impression. Furthermore, furniture is strongly influenced by fashions, styles and colours and if efforts are not made to keep the website up to date, this could adversely affect customer interest.

Mark Band 3 *Evaluate the website of a business and make recommendations for its improvement in relation to achieving its aims and objectives.*

The business has decided to recommend that the site should offer on-line shopping. It already arranges deliveries throughout the UK for shoppers. So it would seem a sensible extension for it to enable consumers to purchase its products on-line. In this way the business would be increasing its market by opening it up to those who would consider the journey to the nearest store too great. Of course, Domicil would need to take account of the impact on the business of the financial and security costs involved in such a major decision.

Another recommendation to improve the website would be a feature where customers, before they visit the store, can find out if any item is in stock. This would improve customer service by saving those who had planned to go to the store a wasted journey. On the other hand, if a customer had actually been at the store when they discovered that the item was out of stock they may have chosen an alternative.

A third recommendation would be that the website has a registration section so that customers have to give their e-mail details when they start looking at what's on offer. In this way the store can build up a database for emailing special offers. The site could also then be personalised, so that when people log on next time it welcomes them by name. This would have the effect of improving customer service and establishing a database of genuinely interested consumers. However, some customers may object to giving their details and not go in to see what's on offer. They may even be suspicious of the store's motives in collecting the data, which would damage the store's image.

E-business and stakeholders

All business decisions have an impact on businesses and their stakeholders. The effects of e-business and the use of a website on the business itself has been covered in section 44. In the case of e-business in particular there are considerable implications for the way that the business itself and its customers and suppliers operate. There are also implications for competitors, as shown in Figure 1.

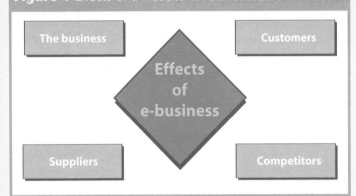

Figure 1 *Effects of a website on stakeholders*

The business

Customers

Effects of e-business

Suppliers

Competitors

Various aspects of this are dealt with throughout the whole of this chapter but the following issues have particular implications.

Impact on customers

E-business affects customers in a number of ways.

Customer power Businesses need to be aware of the fact that customers are becoming increasingly better informed and aware of the rival products that are available to them. Customers will have spent as much time viewing competitors' websites and will be aware of the choices that are available to them. This information and the ease of access to it, gives customers greater power over their buying decisions. Shopping around need no longer be the physical or time consuming activity it used to be, walking or driving from shop to shop to find the best deal in, say, electrical goods or computer software. Internet shoppers don't have to move away from their computers. They have a choice of goods from around the country, or, for many products and services, the whole world. Many of these websites will give detailed technical information and so customers can spend the time to become better informed and shop with greater confidence.

Intangible products In some cases the goods on offer may be an intangible product. This is something that cannot be physically handled. Computer software, e-books or music files, for example, will often be downloaded from a website or e-mailed to the purchaser without wrapping, packaging or postage. The purchase will be as instant as walking into a high street shop, more so in

fact as within a few minutes of paying for music download the Internet shopper can be relaxing listening to it in their own home.

Working harder Customers may have to work harder when Internet shopping. They have to browse through on-line catalogues and work their way through often complicated routes and drop-down menus to reach details of the product they are trying to buy and complete the purchase. There is no sales person there to take them straight to the product they are looking for, talk to them about it and carry it back to the checkout for them. Businesses, when designing a website, will make every effort to ensure that the shopping experience is as free from complexity and frustration as possible.

Trust Customers have to have trust in the company they are dealing with, which sometimes can be a difficult judgement to make. They can no longer touch or feel the product or assess the quality, although in this respect there is no difference between Internet shopping and catalogue or mail order shopping, which has been a significant source of retail business since the first mail order catalogues appeared over a hundred years ago in the late nineteenth century.

However, the global nature of Internet shopping makes this decision making more critical. Consumer rights legislation, for example, will vary from country to country. There is also growing concern about personal and financial information being exploited by unscrupulous organisations. Legislation which protects customers is explained in detail in sections 46 and 63.

Figure 2 *Searching for train times on-line*

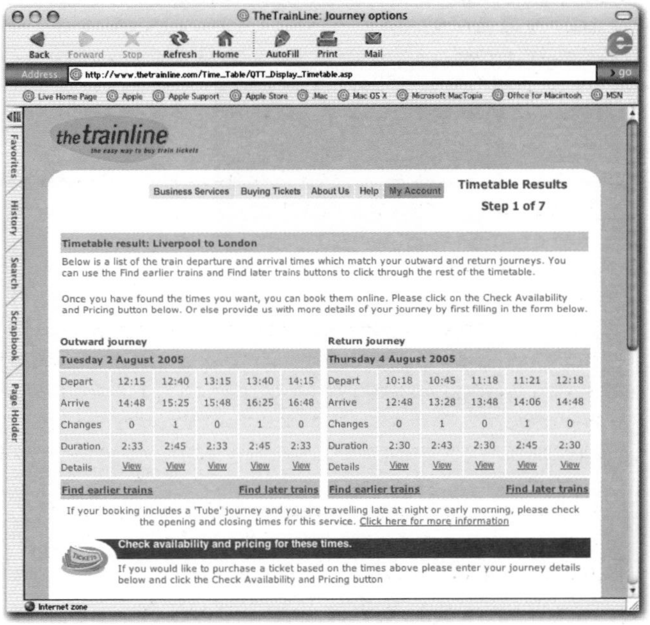

Personalised shopping Many customers will find that their shopping experience is personalised. A customer registering with www.Amazon.co.uk, for example, will find that next time they log on they will be welcomed by name. If they make a purchase, next time they will be offered a range of goods specifically targeted to them. Amazon do this by drawing up a list of goods in similar categories to those that went into your virtual shopping basket last time.

Registering with news groups means that news pages can be personalised to bring you news on topics in which you are particularly interested, whether they are politics, sport, travel, board games or health and beauty. Searching for travel times means that travellers can key in the times and dates they want to travel and they will be presented with a timetable suitable for them, rather than having to search through pages and pages of a paper timetable. An example is shown in Figure 2.

Pricing In some cases shoppers may find that the Internet is forcing businesses to be more price competitive. Consumers have the opportunity to be more informed and have a huge choice of websites to browse through. Furthermore, as costs are reduced for the business they are often passing that on in price reductions. Reportedly it costs 10 times more for a bank to service a customer who walks into a branch of the bank than one who uses the Internet. In some cases they pass these savings on to the customer by offering more favourable banking charges and interest rates to customers who carry out their transactions on-line. An example of the benefits of Internet banking is shown in Figure 3.

Impact on suppliers

The use of a website by a business will significantly affect the way the suppliers themselves operate. At the end of the line will be the customers who don't want undue delays in receiving their products and intense negotiations may have to take place between the Internet business and the supplier to improve delivery times. This process may be completed through an extranet, with the business having direct electronic access to the supplier's database of goods on offer, checking availability and making orders. The business is in effect doing its own on-line shopping.

The process will also work the other way. Suppliers may log into the system to see when invoices are likely to be processed or to check their customers' stock levels to estimate when the next order may be arriving.

Impact on competitors

Businesses watch very carefully the activities of their competitors. Petrol stations for example, will look at the prices of competitors in the locality when deciding how to set their prices. A competitor using a new marketing tool such as a website may pose a threat in that it may draw consumers' interest. If, in addition, the website offers on-line purchasing which the customer sees as an attractive and convenient option, rivals may start to see a fall in customers. Customers are often even prepared to pay increased prices for the convenience, such as delivery costs or losing the opportunity to shop around.

The response to an advertising campaign or promotion strategy by one company will often be the launch of another promotion or marketing activity by a competitor. A website is no different and businesses will be closely watching the Internet activities of competitors in terms of the customer interface, e.g. how vibrant and exciting it is, the market segment it may be targeting and of course the information that it provides and the products that are on offer.

Figure 3 *Egg on-line banking website*

One of the most successful banks to take the opportunity to offer on-line banking which went hand in hand with very favourable transaction rates was Egg. And the customers grabbed the opportunity. Egg achieved its five-year target of 500,000 customers within six months.

Source: adapted from bbc news website.

1. Carry out a survey of five people who use on-line supermarket shopping sites, such as Waitrose, Asda, Tesco or Sainsbury's, to identify:
   - the advantages to them of using this method of shopping;
   - the disadvantages to them of using this method of shopping;
   - aspects, if any, that they find difficult when navigating the site and ordering.
2. Using your survey findings, write a report on the impact of Internet shopping on customers.

Research task

Portfolio practice · Car manufacturers' websites

Review the UK websites of at least three car manufacturers. To help here are the website addresses of five car manufacturers:

www.bmw.co.uk
www.ford.co.uk
www.renault.co.uk
www.seat.co.uk
www.vw.co.uk

(a) **Suggest, giving your reasons, the market segments that these car manufacturers are most likely to be targeting. You may consider segments such as demographic, age, gender and lifestyle.**

(b) **For ONE of those websites identify ONE feature that you consider may make competitors feel they should make changes or additions to their own websites. Explain why you have selected that particular feature and suggest the likely additions or changes that the competitors may make.**

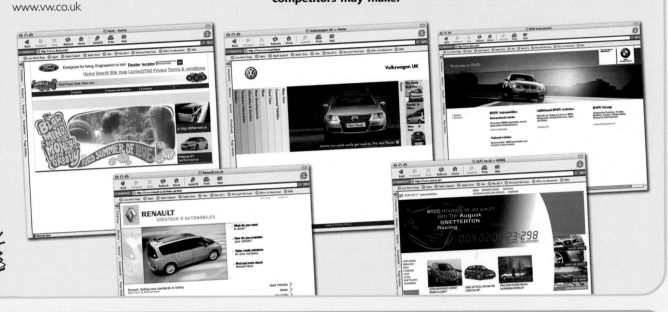

Meeting the assessment criteria

For your assessment you are required to show research of the factors influencing the establishment of an on-line presence, research and analyse the importance of factors influencing the establishment of an on-line presence and the potential opportunities and constraints of a business having a presence on the web.

Business example - Piggott & Henry and The Toby Jug Group

Piggott & Henry is a small shop in the Lake District selling hand-made soap which is produced on the premises. At present it does not use information technology in its business operations.

The Toby Jug Group is a small chain of 5-star hotels in the North West of England. It operates stock control through an EPOS system which will automatically raise orders and e-mail suppliers when stocks are running low. In accordance with its policy of supporting local industry, The Toby Jug Group has approached Piggott & Henry, asking it to be its supplier of soaps for its executive suites.

Mark Band 1 *Show research of the factors influencing the establishment of an on-line presence.*

At present Piggott & Henry's market consists of local people and tourists. The order from the Toby Jug Group will increase its annual sales of handmade soaps by 30%. It feels this is an offer it should not turn down. Not only will it generate significant additional business, but it will raise awareness of its products. Piggott & Henry has therefore decided to install a small computer system to receive e-mails. It is also considering establishing a website so that the business can put its website address on the soap packaging for the hotel suites and possibly provide an on-line ordering service.

Mark Band 2 *Research and analyse the importance of factors influencing the establishment of an on-line presence.*

If Piggott & Henry wants to accept the order from the Toby Jug Group, it will need access to the Internet to receive and process orders for soaps, as the Toby Jug Group will only issue orders via their EPOS email facility. Up until now, tourists buying its soaps who were then interested in further supplies had to write or telephone the business, which a lot of them may not bother to do. If people knew the business had a website and could order on-line, this may generate additional income. If Piggott & Henry accepts the order, the new type of clientele it will be marketing to, the guests in the executive suites of exclusive hotels, has the potential to increase its market, so that it will not just local people and tourists but wealthy business people and personalities who may be interested in further supplies.

Mark Band 3 *Research and analyse the potential opportunities and constraints of a business having a presence on the web.*

Using the Internet for the exchange of emails will present Piggott & Henry with the opportunity to increase its sales substantially and the website will also be an additional medium for promoting its products. The website will give it a modern image, which may appeal to the type of clientele who use the executive suites in the hotels. However, if one of Piggott & Henry's strengths is its traditional and old-fashioned image, having a website has the potential to damage that. It will need to use the website to enhance its traditional style by effective use of graphics, colour and design, while at the same time offering an up-to-date service.

Piggott & Henry could use the website to extend into on-line shopping which would provide an easy way for people to order its soaps, and would be very likely to increase sales. Many of the tourists and visitors to the exclusive hotels are likely to be from overseas and the worldwide nature of the web means that the business could be providing an information and ordering service for this group of consumers. However, it will also be important for Piggott & Henry to keep the website up-to-date in terms of the products and prices it has on offer.

One of the strengths of using electronic ordering from the point of view of Toby Jug Hotels is that it can carry much lower stocks than when ordering through traditional methods. This is because the faster processing, not relying on postal systems, means that the lead time can be reduced. This however, puts constraints on how Piggott & Henry operates, as it has to respond to orders quickly otherwise Toby Jug Hotels will run out of stock.

46 E-business, legislation and industry standards

Legislation

UK businesses operating over the Internet are subject to all UK laws in just the same way as any other trader. So, for example, they have to be aware of copyright issues when using graphics and music on their websites or registering domain names. Laws which are specifically designed to protect the consumer would still apply to those businesses which are operating on-line. These include the:
- **Competition Act, 1998**;
- **Consumer Credit Act, 1974**;
- **Enterprise Act, 2002**;
- **Unfair Terms in Consumer Contracts Regulations, 1999**;
- **Sale and Supply of Goods to Consumers Regulations, 2002**.

Consumer legislation is dealt with in general in section 63. In addition, businesses are required to meet their statutory obligations regarding consumer rights.

Consumer rights

When shopping on-line, consumers enjoy the same statutory consumer rights as when they are doing any other type of shopping whether in hypermarkets, department stores, high street stores or corner shops. The statutory rights which apply to any business sale of goods and services are as follows:

Goods must be:
- of satisfactory quality (free from faults);
- suitable for all the purposes intended;
- described correctly;
- safe and last a reasonable amount of time.

Services must be:
- carried out within a reasonable time, with reasonable care and skill;
- carried out at the price agreed in advance, or if not agreed in advanced at a reasonable price.

Shoppers who purchase goods or services from catalogues, by phone or over the Internet have **additional** rights, known as

Figure 1 *Distance Selling Regulations*

be given clear information

confirmation of the order and information in writing

Distance Selling Regulations
The shopper has the right to:

seven days in which to change their mind with full refund and protection from credit card fraud

have the contract be performed within 30 days, unless otherwise agreed. If the business is unable to complete within the 30 day or agreed period the customer must be informed and offered a full refund of all charges

Figure 2 *Virgin Wine Online and the Distance Selling Regulations*

In 2003 the OFT reported that Virgin Wine Online had revised its terms and conditions to give consumers a fairer deal following an approach by the OFT. The OFT had concerns that certain terms did not comply with the Distance Selling Regulations (DSRs) including those that:
- allowed delivery to be delayed for certain products beyond the statutory 30 days or the date agreed without refund;
- prevented reimbursement of delivery charges when a consumer cancelled. The DSRs state that the full sum paid must be refunded;
- prevented re-imbursement following cancellation until certain conditions had been met. The DSRs give consumers an unconditional right to a refund following cancellation;
- allowed cancellation to be made only by telephone or e-mail. The DSRs allow other methods too.

Source: adapted from www.oft.gov.uk.

Distance Selling Regulations. These are shown in Figure 1. Perishable goods, or goods made to order, are exempt from the Regulations. An example of a business which had terms and conditions with the potential of not complying with the Distance Selling Regulations is shown in Figure 2.

Data Protection Act, 1998

All businesses must adhere to the strict rules laid down by the eight principles of the **Data Protection Act, 1998 (DPA)** which was introduced to control the use of stored personal information. This places obligations on those who process information, while at the same time giving rights to those whose data is being processed. By the very way they operate, e-businesses necessarily have to collect data for delivery addresses and bank details for obtaining payment andstore it electronically.

In order to comply with the DPA the website must clearly inform the purchaser how the information is going to be used. If, for example, the business wishes to have the option to pass on details of its customers to other organisations, such as a subsidiary company or finance house, it is required to obtain specific permission from the customer for that process to take place. If the customer declines the offer, perhaps by ticking or unticking a box, under the requirements of the DPA it would then be illegal for the company still to pass their details on. Figure 3 shows the eight principles of the DPA.

Many e-businesses choose to declare privacy policies on their websites regarding confidentiality of personal data. The BBC website has a very detailed privacy policy (www.bbc.co.uk/privacy) which contains the two statements shown in Figure 4.

Figure 3 *The eight principles of the Data Protection Act, 1998*

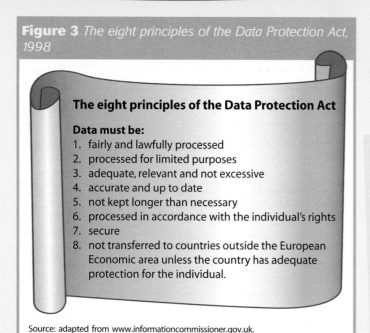

The eight principles of the Data Protection Act

Data must be:
1. fairly and lawfully processed
2. processed for limited purposes
3. adequate, relevant and not excessive
4. accurate and up to date
5. not kept longer than necessary
6. processed in accordance with the individual's rights
7. secure
8. not transferred to countries outside the European Economic area unless the country has adequate protection for the individual.

Source: adapted from www.informationcommissioner.gov.uk.

Figure 4 *BBC privacy policy*

We will hold your personal information on our systems for as long as you use the service you have requested, and remove it in the event that the purpose has been met We will ensure that all personal information supplied is held securely, in accordance with the Data Protection Act 1998.
Source: adapted from www.bbc.co.uk/privacy.

Other legislation

Other laws which control how an e-business may operate include the following.

Anti-discrimination laws Websites now face constraints under anti-discrimination legislation as regards their accessibility, for example the **Disability Discrimination Act 1995**, the **Disability Rights Commission Act ,1999**, and the **Special Educational Needs and Disability Act, 2001**.

The Electronic Commerce (EC Directive) Regulations, 2002 These ensure that the buying process is clear and the customer has plenty of opportunity to check and correct details before an order is placed.

The Control of Misleading Advertisements Regulations, 1988 These provide protection against misleading advertising inducing consumers to buy goods or services by deception, or by making unacceptable comparisons.

The Medicines (Advertising) Regulations, 1994 These prohibit unverifiable claims for pharmaceutical products.

The Trade Descriptions Act, 1968 This makes it an offence for a trader to apply a false description to goods or make reckless statements about certain aspects of services.

The Directive on Privacy and Electronic Communications A customer's e-mail address may only be included in e-mailshots if

he or she has consented to that. This consent would normally be given by the customer ticking a box on the on-line form. Figure 5 shows an example of a consent form on the www.multimap.co.uk website – an online provider of mapping services.

Figure 5 *Consent forms*

I would like to receive MyMultimap news and information

☐ By e-mail   ☐ On this phone

I would like to receive information and offers from Multimap's preferred partners

☐ By e-mail   ☐ On this phone

☐ Yes, e-mail me information on Multimap site upgrades, news and promotions.

Source: adapted from www.multimap.co.uk.

Codes of practice

Codes of practice are a form of self-regulation. They are a set of voluntary rules to which a company can subscribe, setting a framework for ethical behaviour. A code of practice may apply to how businesses treat their employees, the safety standards they adhere to in product development or perhaps a code of practice may cover environmental considerations such as how they dispose of waste. British Waterways, for example, which manages Britain's rivers and canals, has a code of practice aimed to ensure that its work enhances the natural environment.

One organisation which monitors business behaviour on the Internet is Safebuy (www.safebuy.org.uk). To qualify for membership of the Safebuy Scheme, Internet retailers are required to:

- adhere to the terms of the Sale of Goods Act, the EU Distance Selling Regulations and the EU Directive on Privacy and Electronic Communications;
- conform to the **Data Protection Act, 1998**;
- provide security for the processing of credit card transactions;
- include physical location and contact details for themselves on their website;
- display the total price consumers must pay for goods including delivery costs and provide a clear explanation of the delivery procedures;
- advise the consumer if 'cookies' are required for the processing of data;
- not use 'spam' for marketing purposes;
- avoid exploitation of children.

In 2005 members included Beauty for Nails (www.creativenailplace.com) which sells nail and beauty products, Britchops, a drum course (www.britchops.co.uk), and Camping and Camo which sells camping gear (www.campingandcamo.co.uk).

Table 1 *Organisations which lay down codes of practice*

WebTrader UK monitors business behaviour on the Internet via 'mystery shopping' exercises, monitoring of complaints, and customer feedback. 	Best Stuff (electrical goods) (www.beststuff.co.uk) Plates for You (find a personalised car number plate)(www.pl84u.co.uk).
Members of the Direct Marketing Association agree to adhere to its codes, including one that orders from children under the age of 16 will not be accepted without obtaining a parent/teacher's verifiable and explicit consent.	The Royal Mail (www.royalmail.co.uk) The British Heart Foundation (www.bhf.org.uk)

Table 1 shows examples of other organisations which lay down codes of practice, equally referred to as standards of conduct or codes of conduct. These organisations make particular reference to their standards for e-business. Two examples of companies who were members in 2005 with the right to display their logo on their website are shown in Column 2.

TrustUK operates an independent approval scheme (www.trustuk.org.uk). If an on-line shopper sees that the trade is displaying the TrustUK Hallmark, they know that the trade complies with a code of practice approved by TrustUK.

Source: adapted from www.trustuk.org.uk.

Investigate the Trust UK site.
1. Write a summary of the standards that TrustUK expects its members to maintain.
2. Identify the benefits to a business of seeking approval by TrustUK to gain the right to display its Hallmark.

Research task

Portfolio practice · **Charlie Crow, Costumes for Kids**

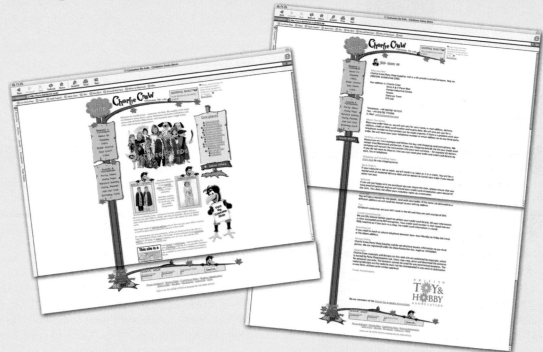

Charlie Crow (www.charliecrow.co.uk) provides children's fancy dress costumes, partyware, magic tricks, jokes and costume accessories.

Source: adapted from company information and www.charliecrow.co.uk.

(a) Explain, with examples applied in particular to Charlie Crow, the obligations that a business might have to its customers in terms of consumer rights and data protection. Access the website for further details to help with this activity.

Meeting the assessment criteria

For your assessment you are required to research factors influencing the establishment of an on-line presence, research and analyse the importance of factors influencing the establishment of an online presence, and research and analyse the potential opportunities and constraints of a business having a presence on the web.

Business example – Alipotteryimports.co.uk

When he was on holiday last year, Waqar Ali came across a pottery in a small village making very unusual dishes and jugs. He decided to sell them back home in the UK. He arranged a contract with the pottery to have 100 items delivered to him. Waqar set up a website and his new Internet business started trading right away.

Mark Band 1 *Show research of the factors influencing the establishment of an on-line presence.*

Waqar Ali knows that he would have a comparatively small target market. The Internet enabled him to reach a much wider audience than a small shop in one town would. As a new business, with a product that he has not had experience of marketing before, he decided selling on-line would run fewer financial risks than renting out retail premises and having to pay for shop fittings. He would also have to take steps to ensure he complies with legislation which affects on-line trading, such as protecting information.

Mark Band 2 *Research and analyse the importance of factors influencing the establishment of an on-line presence.*

It is important that Waqar Ali ensures that he complies with legislation that covers Internet trading. For example, if he is describing a dish as being oven proof, it must be. He also has to be aware of the additional consumer rights that customers have. If he decides to offer jugs and dishes for sale, he must make sure he can honour that order within 30 days and not expect, say, customers to wait until he makes his next trip abroad. Although Waqar sees a website as a cheaper option for advertising and distributing the pottery than setting up a retail outlet, he will still have costs in terms of the computer equipment and software and perhaps having to pay for technical advice.

Mark Band 3 *Research and analyse the potential opportunities and constraints of a business having a presence on the web.*

The financial risks that Waqar Ali took were fewer than if he had invested capital in opening a shop and traded by the traditional methods. He also is likely to experience fewer cash flow problems since he doesn't need to buy large quantities of dishes and jugs as he would have had to do at first if he had opened a shop.

However, there are still financial risks for Waqar. For example, Distance Selling Regulations affect the rights of customers trading on-line. Customers have seven days to change their mind. So if someone has purchased a jug and decides that it doesn't meet their needs, he could be faced with increased cash flow problems, especially if this is a frequent occurrence.

As customers will have to give their e-mail and postal addresses for the business to deliver the goods, Waqar can build up a database of interested people to whom he can send regular information about new products. He must ensure, however, that the website is secure, so that he complies with the conditions of the Data Protection Act. This means ensuring that customers' details are secure and cannot be accessed by other people.

47 Financial costs of a website

Website costs

The costs of creating and running a website can vary enormously depending on the level of expertise used to build and manage the site. Straightforward programs are available enabling anyone with basic IT skills to design a website. However, most businesses will want to employ a graphic designer to give a professional look and feel to the website and will consult experts on the management of the supply chain.

Furthermore, e-business websites will be run through databases which can be complex and require experts to set up and maintain them.

All of this type of support can run into many thousands of pounds. One way of cutting costs is to go to a DIY e-commerce service which supplies templates for simply filling with text and graphics relevant to the particular needs of the business. Many smaller businesses find this a favourable option, partly for ease of use and partly because it makes financial planning easier. The main problem of this approach, which could make it unattractive, particularly to larger organisations, is that it makes differentiation and branding through the design of the website more difficult.

Whichever route a business chooses, there are some costs which have to be met whatever the size and format of the site.

Hardware

There is a variety of hardware required to operate a website.

Computers Despite the advent of Internet connection via mobile phones and television anyone planning on running an on-line business will still need a speedy **computer** with the highest specification and memory practically available. The computer will need to work via a **modem** which provides the technical processes for connection to the Internet. One computer and one modem of course would only be sufficient for the smallest of businesses. Larger enterprises could be working through many hundreds if not thousands of computers, all networked via intranet and extranet links across the world.

Cables and wires In order to create **access** to the Internet, the computer and modem will need to link to the Internet via cables, telephone wires or wireless networks. It would be unrealistic for a business to expect to use the same telephone line on which it would normally receive and make its telephone calls so it would have to take account of the costs of setting up the link and maintaining the connection. Most businesses would expect to use broadband to be certain of enjoying speedy Internet connection.

Digital cameras It is likely that the business will wish to furnish the website with images of the products on offer. Larger businesses will already have a strategy in place for producing photographs or products for catalogues and other promotion and marketing purposes. But smaller businesses may need to consider the acquisition of a digital camera or a scanner to create images of the products that will be offered on the website and graphic design software such as Macromedia Flash or Adobe Photoshop.

Software

Most people who use the Internet regularly make use of **browsers**, such as Internet Explorer or Netscape Navigator and an e-mail program. E-business is no different and those basic software tools will still be required.

Figure 1 *Firewall protection*

A firewall is a security system intended to protect an organisation's network against external threats, such as hackers.

Figure 2 *Anti-virus protection*

A virus is a program or piece of code that loads itself onto the computer and replicates itself. A virus is dangerous because it can quickly use all available memory and bring the system to a halt.

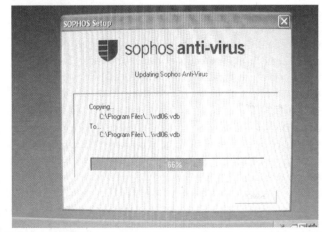

For the foreseeable future, security will always be a major issue in any Internet trading, both security of the business's own data as well as maintaining the confidentiality of customers' details. **Firewalls** and **anti-virus software** are a necessity. Some examples are shown in Figures 1 and 2. Businesses may also make use of systems to protect pop-up ads.

If a small business makes the decision to create its own designs and not use an outside agency, it will need **web authoring software**, such as Macromedia Dreamweaver or AdobeGoLive.

Specialist **e-commerce software** is a necessity for managing the 'shopping trolleys' and processing the orders. An example is shown in Figure 3. Keying in e-commerce software into a search engine provides a wealth of choice in software available. Table 1 shows the facilities that would be available on a typical piece of e-commerce software.

Other set up costs

A business setting up and operating a website will face a number of other costs.

Table 1 *E-commerce software*

The business interface	Add and edit company and contact details Create catalogue Add, delete, edit items in the shop Import images of items Arrange the look of the shop – colours, fonts, layout View orders and customers
The customer interface	Read about the company Contact the company View items on sale Search items by type or category Add items to the shopping trolley View the shopping trolley Proceed to checkout

Figure 3 *A shopping trolley at www.ekmpowershop.com*

Internet Service Provider The business will of course need to register with an Internet Service Provider (ISP) a company that provides Internet connection, such as Supanet or Telewest. Most of these service providers will also provide web space, the place where the site 'lives'. The costs of these vary hugely but a small business is likely to be able to find an ISP that will provide web space and support e-business for less than £200 per year.

Domain name It will be necessary to purchase a domain name which is the address of the site that visitors navigate to. www.ford.co.uk and www.britishairways.com are examples of domain names. Happy Harry's Fish Bar, for example, may decide to register the name happyharryfish.co.uk as a domain name. These are relatively cheap, sometimes as low as £10 a year. It is possible, of course, that the name the business wants to register will already have been purchased by someone else. In that case it

would have to decide whether to choose a different name or contact the owner of that name and negotiate a price for them to sell it. The website www.greatdomains.com has many interesting names for sale. At the time of writing, for example, the domain name tycoon.com was on sale for $350,000 (just over £200,000).

Design and construction costs These can be difficult to quantify because they will vary due to many factors, such as the size of the business, the product being marketed and the aspirations of the business in terms of the image it wishes to project. The business will need to shop around for the best deal and the cost of this facility will be determined by the budget and the business objectives.

Advertising An ambitious business will consider using an advertising agency (or use existing qualified personnel) to ensure that the wording, content and layout of the site are correctly constructed for the profile of its expected market.

Payment on-line Businesses wishing to sell goods or services through their websites will have to arrange a method of accepting credit or debit card payments. A small business might use PayPal, an international service whose fees in 2005 ranged from 1.95% to 3.4%, plus £0.20 per transaction, depending on the volume of transactions. Or it may also chose an e-commerce software provider such as BazaarBuilder (www.bazaarbuilder.com), which will offer shopping cart facilities for sale of up to 15 separate items for about £100 a year. Larger business may consider setting up an in-house system, using a merchant account provider such as WorldPay, which will offer unlimited selling and card processing facilities for about £300 per year.

Personnel

Once the website has been set up it needs to be maintained and kept up to date. A small company may only need a few people to do this. For example, Silly Jokes (www.sillyjokes.co.uk), East Midlands winner of the 2004 Department of Trade & Industry 'Recognising Business Excellence' awards, employs two people full time updating and managing its website. A large company could have an entire department devoted to maintenance of its website.

The department store, Debenhams, employs 28 people in its website division.

Apart from the costs of employing personnel, there will be an ongoing need for training due to:
- the unfamiliar software and processes at start-up;
- innovations constantly appearing on the market with the rapidly changing technological scene;

- upgrades to systems and introductions of new techniques;
- a new approach to customer service as outlined in section 44. Staff will need the skills to respond rapidly to electronic communications, make changes to the website interface or effect improvements to the supply chain where problems have been encountered.

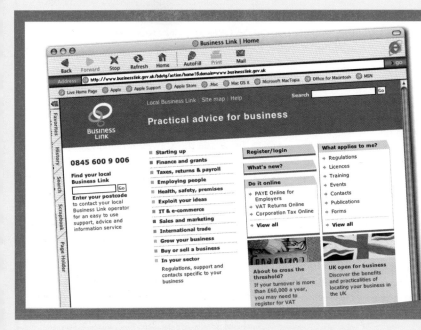

Business Link (www.businesslink.gov.uk) is a government funded website giving practical advice to business. The section entitled 'Get the Right Website for your business' is an interactive tool giving guidance for setting up a website.

For a small local business with which you are familiar, access www.businesslink.gov.uk, click on 'IT and e-commerce', then click on 'Find out which type of website is best for your business', then answer the questions when prompted.

Research task

Portfolio practice · Harveys Handmade Chocolates and cakes

Jo Basso runs Harveys Handmade Chocolates and cakes from her shop in a small village in Leicestershire. A significant amount of her business comes from her mail order service. She has now decided that she would like to increase her business by selling her products on-line. A friend is going to build and manage her website for her. Jo has asked you to find out the availability of a suitable domain name for her website, the cost of purchasing the domain name and hosting a website. Carry out the necessary research and prepare a report for Jo.

The following websites may be of help to you:

www.nominet.org.uk

www.uk2.net

www.streamlinenet.co.uk

www.websitehostdirectory.com

www.shopfitter.com

Meeting the assessment criteria

For your assessment you are required to show research of the factors influencing the establishment of an on-line presence, research and analyse the importance of factors influencing the establishment of an on-line presence and the potential opportunities and constraints of a business having a presence on the web.

Business example - www.dannys4snacks.co.uk

After a long period of time unsuccessfully looking for work, Dan Branch decided to start his own business. His stepfather, who worked in a small factory on a trading estate said that everyone kept complaining about the poor service and quality offered by the sandwich delivery company. He suggested that Dan set up his own business making and delivering snacks. Dan found he was eligible for a grant from the Prince's Trust and started planning his new business. He went round to see all the businesses on his stepfather's trading estate. His website www.dannys4snacks.co.uk had the facility for customers to order the sandwiches they wanted delivered the next day.

Mark Band 1 *Show research of the factors influencing the establishment of an on-line presence.*
The financial costs of setting up an e-business, particularly for a small business, can usually be considerably less than trading from shop premises. Dan may even be able to work from home if his kitchen met the environmental health regulations.

Dan would be able to offer facilities for customers to order the sandwiches on-line, which gave them another route in addition to telephoning orders or handing him a form when he made deliveries.

Mark Band 2 *Research and analyse the importance of factors influencing the establishment of an on-line presence.*
Finance will be a significant factor for Dan. He has been out of work for sometime so he is unlikely to have much money saved

and he would be unlikely to get a bank loan. The Prince's Trust grant would cover establishing an e-business but would not be enough to cover shop premises.

Dan was hoping that he could encourage people to use the on-line ordering facility. This meant he would not have to spend time listening to phone messages, or employ someone to answer the phone while he was making and delivering sandwiches, nor did he have to hang around at companies waiting for paper forms to be collected.

Mark Band 3 *Research and analyse the potential opportunities and constraints of a business having a presence on the web.*
Dan will still have to invest in computer equipment for keeping his records and, as he is planning on letting customers order through the website, he needs the software for handling that which can be expensive. He will probably have to spend money on training so that he, and anyone he employs, can learn the programs.

Dan, of course, still has to have somewhere to make his sandwiches and store his equipment, and he will also need a delivery van but he can look for smaller premises than he would have needed if he had opened a snack bar.

Dan has given himself the opportunity to run his own business. He probably could not have afforded to if he had decided to trade by traditional methods through a shop. The innovative nature of e-business gives him an additional challenge which he could find fulfilling. If Dan doesn't have good artistic skills he may have to pay someone to take photos of his sandwiches and design his website. However, for Dan's business, this aspect may be less important as he is likely to be working in a small geographical area. Much of his business is likely to come by word of mouth rather than from people browsing on the Internet and he will also have the opportunity to build up a face-to-face relationship with his clients, who will get to know the range of sandwiches he has to offer.

Opportunities

The decision to enter the world of e-trading is a major undertaking for any business, large or small and would be the subject of detailed assessments through decision making tools. Whichever decision making tools are used, such as SWOT analysis, explained in section 81, a feature of the analysis of the decision would be a close examination of the opportunities that e-trading would bring to the business.

Many of the opportunities that e-business offers will have arisen out of a need to meet the business aims and objectives described in section 43. Clearly, for some businesses there will be specific opportunities that present themselves for that business in particular. An example is shown in Figure 1.

This section outlines the generic benefits that e-businesses have identified.

Global markets

This is likely to be the driving force behind many companies' decisions to move into e-business. The Internet gives customers the opportunity to browse and shop at their convenience from wherever they are able to sit at a computer with an Internet link. They can access services 24 hours a day, 7 days a week. E-businesses have the capacity to reach people around the world, offering products and services to a global customer base. BBUK (www.bannerboxuk.com), for example, a small UK-based business which designs logos and banner advertisements, has 80% of its orders from the USA.

For many small businesses first setting up an e-presence, their objective is likely to be only to extend their reach across more than just the local area. This will help them to expand their market. An example is shown in Figure 2.

The Internet has grown to become a huge source of income for thousands of businesses. In 2005 the Interactive Media in Retail

Figure 1 *Photobox*

Photobox (www.photobox.co.uk), which was named Online Retailer of the Year 2005, provides real photoprints from its on-line lab. Customers can personalise them and share photos online. When Photobox launched its website in 2000 it had identified that at the time there were no other UK-based websites providing this service. So it took the opportunity to close a gap in the market, enjoying, for a time at least, the benefit of an exclusive market.

Photobox now claims to be the market leader in photo community websites with household names amongst its partners and clients. It has extended into offering a range of services on its website including printing photos onto gifts such as paperweights, bags, cushions and calendars. Photobox's affiliate programme gives owners of other websites the opportunity to earn commission by displaying its logo.

Source: adapted from www.photobox.co.uk.

Figure 2 *Electricshop website benefits*

Electricshop (www.electricshop.com), a family-run business, was established in 1972 as a supplier of high quality electrical household appliances. It started Internet trading in 2001. Although the nature of its business means there will be limitations on the extent to which Electricshop can tap into international markets, simply by using the Internet to target the whole of the UK market, Electricshop has increased turnover through its Internet trading from £1m to £10m in 5 years.

Source: adapted from www.electricshop.com.

Group (IMRG) reported that:
● over half of all holiday bookings are made over the Internet;
● in the first six months of 2005, over10 million tracks had been legally downloaded over the Internet by music lovers in the UK. This was almost twice the level for the whole of 2004, easily outstripping UK sales of physical CD singles.

Figure 3 shows the growth in UK Internet Christmas shopping from £1.4 billion in 2002 to £4 billion in 2004.

Figure 3 *Growth in UK Internet Shopping*

Source: adapted from Interactive Media in Retail Group research data.

Promoting a corporate image

Businesses can use their website as part of their marketing strategy to promote a corporate image. IKEA's website (www.ikea.com) in Figure 4, for example, shows a long list of the countries in which IKEA operates and then asks customers to select a location. This immediately identifies IKEA as a large, worldwide company and as such makes the customer feel that it is likely to have access to global styles offering unusual and interesting designs. It also suggests a very large company which would promote its concept of low price offers through its buying power.

Websites use the corporate design, display the logo and give information about the company. The interactivity and animation on websites such as McDonalds (www.mcdonalds.co.uk), Coca-Cola (www.cocacola.co.uk) and Barbie (www.barbie.com) reinforce each company's reputation as innovative, creative and appealing to young people.

Improved communication with customers, suppliers and employees

The data collection necessary in completing an on-line transaction gives companies a chance to maintain a database of customers they know are interested in their products to whom they can send promotional material. The technique of 'web-casting' enables businesses to receive valuable customer feeback. Customers, possibly from all over the world, can interact with their suppliers. The National Assembly of Wales (www.webcasting.wales.gov.uk), for example, promotes the work it does by enabling Internet users

Figure 4 *IKEA website*

to view its sessions live and then requesting viewers' comments. The technique of webcasting can be used to keep suppliers, employees and other branches informed of company developments. Webcasting is increasingly being used to broadcast Annual General Meetings over the Internet so that shareholders who are unable to attend in person can view the proceedings live.

Reduced costs

Banks, in particular, have embraced the e-business concept enthusiastically. The branch system, whereby customers physically walk into a branch of a bank and deal with a cashier over the counter, is very expensive. Figures suggest that the buildings, the people, and the equipment represent about 50% of a bank's operating expenses.

Investment in stock is also reduced. Many car dealers who trade on-line, for example, very often have significantly fewer, if any, cars ready for immediate sale. They take details of the customer's specifications and then search for the car to order, considerably reducing cash flow problems and the cost of premises.

The use of e-mail reduces costs in postage, telephone bills and fax. There is even evidence emerging that those companies who deal on-line are seeing fewer instances of staff stress as the reduction in face-to-face contact with customers gives greater control over time management.

Automated processes and staffing

Automation has allowed businesses to change the way in which they manage their human resources. A business, for example, having introduced on-line operations can:
● make staff available for other processes in the business;
● dispense with those staff altogether and perhaps downsize.

Elimination of a layer in the supply chain

Businesses distribute products to customers in many ways. This is explained in section 39. Some businesses use intermediaries in the supply chain. Others attempt to sell directly to customers with no intermediaries. On-line trading allows businesses to deal directly with customers. For example, Gear4Music (www.gear4music.com) is a retailer of musical instruments, music equipment and specialist audio/video computer systems. It uses the Internet to market its instruments direct to the public, bypassing traditional retail and distribution channels.

Shrinking the competition gap

Small businesses can compete on equal footing with much bigger companies by using on-line selling. Whether they are a large or small business and whether the company has invested thousands or just a few hundred pounds in their website, the medium and interface with the customer is exactly the same – a web page. In this respect, the small corner shop competes equally with a state-of-the-art department store.

Furthermore, small businesses can easily compete on quality and availability. They are no longer disadvantaged by the fact that they can't invest huge amounts of money in an advertising campaign or the need to carry large amounts of stock.

New profile of customers

E-business gives the opportunity to target new markets. A survey by NOP showed how more than 4 million children in the UK use the Internet, with many of them looking at adverts and shopping on-line. Tesco (www.tesco.com), for example, was the first on-line retailer to design a website which can be used by anyone with a sight problem.

Personalised marketing

Section 45 explained how customers can now experience a personalised shopping experience, being greeted by name and offered products that are likely to suit them. The technology involved with a website means that a business will carry detailed data of an individual customer's buying habits and can target individual customers with products that match or complement their previous purchases. Delivery and email addresses will all be on record to provide opportunities for accurate targeted marketing. An example of a personalised page is show in Figure 5.

Secure payment

Reports suggest that credit card fraud is on the rise, with fraud on the Internet rising dramatically. The options that are now open to businesses to accept payment on-line through secure routes help ensure that transactions are safe. Figure 6 shows the padlock icon displayed in Microsoft Windows which indicates a secure payment connection.

A small business is likely to use a payment processing agency, such as Paypal, while large businesses may opt for setting up their own in-house systems using a merchant account provider which offers credit card processing services, such as WorldPay. The knowledge that a business uses a trusted and secure payment processing method will create consumer confidence and attract customers. Payment costs are discussed in section 47.

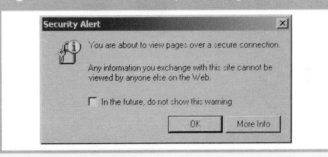

Figure 6 *Microsoft Windows padlock logo*

On-line ordering

On-line ordering both by the customer and by the business itself processing customer orders and ordering their own stock from suppliers, leads to greater efficiency. The stock control software that businesses will need to manage large amounts of stock and processing orders over the Internet gives the advantage of always having up-to-date and accurate information on stock levels. Most systems will alert the business, or even the suppliers directly, when stocks are running low. The reduction in paperwork and the automation of the process will lead to reduced staff costs and greater accuracy.

Visual Planet (www.visualplanet.biz) was established in 2001, born out of the frustration of being unable to access information after closing hours in a high street, waiting around business reception areas and the inability to access key information on the business being visited. Visual Planet provides interactive holographic displays, electronic display panels and electronic touch panel posters of the type that you might see at exhibitions or in a shop window. Branches of HSBC use its display screens to raise brand awareness and Goldsmith Jewellers use Visual Planet screens to advertise their products.

1. In your local area, identify one business which could effectively use a Visual Planet plasma display screen to:
   - attract new staff;
   - improve communications with customers.
2. Explain how the use of the plasma display screen may achieve those objectives.

Research task

Figure 5 *Personalised shopping page*

mothercare

your pregnancy	preparing for baby	new baby 0-3 months

Hi J an, welcome back.
If you're not J an click here

Portfolio practice · Lush Longboards

Lush Longboards (www.lushlongboards.com) is a supplier of longboards and accessories along with power kites, mountain boards and grassboards. It is successfully taking a niche product to a wide audience by introducing a website into its business strategy.

Source: adapted from E-Commerce 2004 Awards.

(a) Explain what is meant by a 'niche product'.
(b) Describe the particular opportunities that having a website offer to a company which targets a niche market.
(c) Analyse features from the website which can help Lush Longboards:
  (i) develop products which meet its customers' needs;
  (ii) promote the sports for which it provides accessories;
  (iii) enhance its customer service programme.

Meeting the assessment criteria

For your assessment you are required to show research of the factors influencing the establishment of an on-line presence, research and analyse the importance of factors influencing the establishment of an on-line presence and the potential opportunities and constraints of a business having a presence on the web.

Business example - www.conventiondays.co.uk

Nic has always liked music, television and films. When a friend, Tim, suggested they started their own convention business, he thought it was a brilliant idea. Themes might include sci-fi, memorabilia, antiques, television or film conventions. Nic and Tim invested £2,500 in sound and video equipment and advertised in local newspapers and shop windows. Their service includes organising the convention, including merchandise for sale, and activities such as celebrity signings. Their website details all the services they offer and shows picture of recent conventions. They also have a 'bulletin board' where people who have been at one of their conventions can give feedback.

Mark Band 1 *Show research of the factors influencing the establishment of an on-line presence.*
Nic and Tim knew that there would be limited demand for their service in their town alone and were planning on targeting a wide geographical area, across three counties. They also felt that the cost of a website was significantly less than the costs of advertising in newspapers or the local radio over the geographical area they were targeting.

Mark Band 2 *Research and analyse the importance of factors influencing the establishment of an on-line presence.*
Advertising in newspapers and shop windows for all those areas would be very expensive, whereas there are no geographical restrictions on the Internet. Their business is new and so they would have limited funds. Having a website gave them the opportunity to invest their funds in the best quality equipment

rather than on expensive advertising. Nic and Tim were able to show pictures of the conventions and people enjoying themselves. This gave the opportunity to establish their style in a way that an advertisement could not.

Mark Band 3 *Research and analyse the potential opportunities and constraints of a business having a presence on the web.*
The bulletin board proved to be an excellent opportunity to raise awareness of their service and create good communication links with their customers. Once people had posted a message they told all their friends to have a look at it which had the effect of promoting their product. However, due to the global nature of the Internet, they have to ensure information is protected. They found that they needed to spend time monitoring the bulletin board to make sure that the messages were genuine, data was protected and the business complied with all legislation.

It is important that the website is updated regularly, particularly if they advertise that there will be pictures of recent parties on the website. This could be time that they may feel was more efficiently spent in researching new market opportunities.

The website offered good promotion opportunities. It was able to show photos of the range of conventions and activities they organised. However, they were aware that the website ran the danger of giving ideas to competitors, who could then copy an idea and take away their customers.

Threats

Section 48 looked at the opportunities that businesses would have identified when making the decision to develop an on-line presence. This section looks at the threats, or potential dangers, to a business of an on-line presence. Some of these are shown in Figure 1.

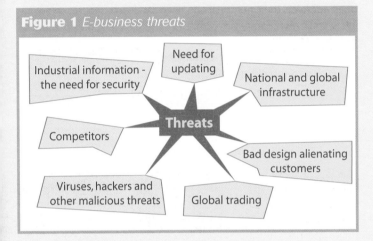

Figure 1 E-business threats

Competitors

Competition is a threat to a business in any form of trading, whether it is an e-businesses or a traditional business. However, the ability to update websites instantly and respond quickly to changes in the market means that the Internet is particularly competitive. It is no longer necessary to wait until an advertising campaign can be developed or to devise methods to raise customer awareness of a new product or service. It can be announced on the website and promoted through e-mails. So any business that has made an investment in an innovative idea or marketing strategy may find that its competitors respond within a very short time.

The sheer size of the Internet makes it difficult to establish a unique selling point (USP) or to stand out as different from competitors. A shop in a town centre which specialises in book-binding is unlikely to have many competitors in the locality. A search in most *Yellow Pages* directories would reveal two or three bookbinders at the most. A search on 'bookbinding services' in the Google search engine presents ten pages of websites to browse through. The size of the Internet also makes it harder for potential customers to navigate to the website. Section 51 deals with strategies to reduce the threat of the website sitting on the Internet with no-one ever reaching it.

Global trading

Any form of global trading, whether conventional importing and exporting of goods or services across the Internet, runs risks when taking account of the global aspect. If a business is targeting the global market, it has to take account of certain factors, such as:
- cultural, religious and social differences when designing websites and determining product lines;
- ensuring that the products it is supplying comply with local regulations and laws. Laws covering consumer protection, for example, vary from country to country, particularly outside the EU.

Businesses which rely on overseas trade will also need to take account of the impact of fluctuating exchange rates. For example, when the pound is strong UK products or services will become uncompetitive on price when compared with those of their foreign rivals.

National and global infrastructure

Effective e-business in goods is highly dependent upon 'robust' and effective delivery services. Products have to be physically moved around without damage. Also, to be competitive with traditional shopping methods, e-business must be prepared to meet customer expectations that they will receive almost as quick a service as they would if they had made a trip to the shops.

A business could face problems if it does not ensure that orders reach customers in the shortest possible time. In November 2004, for example, the Royal Mail warned that a lack of sophisticated infrastructure and delivery channels meant retailers could miss out on the multi-million pound shopping opportunities at Christmas. The decision on how goods are to be transported and delivered is even more crucial if the intention is to trade in overseas markets.

Viruses, hackers and other malicious threats

The malicious threats that the Internet presents have a language of their own. Some of the terminology is shown in Figure 2.

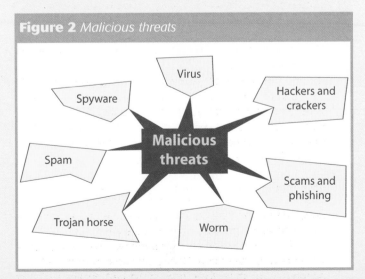

Figure 2 Malicious threats

Hackers and crackers The term 'hacker' in the world of computers means someone who is an expert in discovering the finer details of a program. Legitimate hackers are employed to help a colleague enter a system when a password has been lost or forgotten, debug a copyright software program, or test a system's security. However, some hackers have malicious or even criminal motives. They can cause huge damage to systems by violating the security.

The term 'cracker' is increasingly being used to distinguish illegal hackers from hackers who are working legitimately. This criminal activity causes systems to malfunction, losing huge amounts of data, and can download financial and personal details about the company and its suppliers and customers.

Scams and phishing These refer to activities of fraudsters who send out emails claiming to be from a reputable company, often banks or payment agencies. The message requests the recipient to click on a link to update their personal profile or carry out some transaction. The link takes the victim to a fake website designed to look like the real thing. However, any personal or financial information entered is routed directly to the scammer. If a business learns that its customers are being targeted in this way they will need to act quickly to warn customers and be prepared to provide regular information, contact details and support. An example is shown in Figure 3.

Spam This is unsolicited bulk or junk e-mail. Receipt of bulk e-mail can clog up a business system and take up staff time. Bad experiences with spam may result in receivers routinely deleting mailshot-style e-mails which means that a genuine communication between businesses and other businesses or customers may inadvertently be lost. Larger businesses have spam detector software which will divert suspected spam e-mail. This could result in an e-mail that has been incorrectly identified as spam, at best, being delayed, or at worst, being deleted.

Spyware This is a software that surreptitiously monitors computer activity.

Trojan horse This is a malicious code hiding behind a legitimate program waiting for a certain time to release itself.

Virus A virus is a program or piece of code that loads itself onto the computer and replicates itself.

Worm This is a program which copies itself to other systems over a network.

Figure 3 *'World Cup' virus*

In 2005 Windows users were being warned not to open a virus that posed as a message from football body Fifa. Some of the messages sent by the virus said that users had won tickets to the World Cup football tournament in 2006. The variant seems to have caught a lot of people out because its release coincided with a mail out by Fifa telling fans about tickets.

Source: adapted from www.bbc.co.uk/news, 4.5.2005.

Unless an organisation's computer systems are adequately protected against viruses and other malicious threats it may find that its e-mail systems are infected, resulting, in some cases, in:
- receiving and sending unwanted e-mails;
- disruption and damage to their systems;
- invaders stealing valuable information, including customer details.

If anti-virus software or firewalls are not installed and regularly updated, these threats can result in problems, such as the cost of rectifying the damage. A business may even have to cease trading temporarily. This is not only damaging to the business' own financial situation, but is likely to harm consumer confidence. Customers will not return to an e-business which they believe does not keep their personal and financial details secure, could infect their own computer with a virus or simply appears to be inefficient.

Figure 4 describes how e-commerce has become particularly vulnerable to malicious attacks.

Figure 4 *Bot networks*

In September 2004 research by Symantec reported in *Computer World* stated that the number of computer systems hijacked by hackers implanting malicious remote control software, known as bot networks, increased dramatically over the past six months. Bot networks allow hackers to take control of networks of infected machines. The number of systems infected by bots rose from under 2,000 a day to over 30,000 systems a day over the first six months of the year.

Bot networks pose a risk to businesses because they allow hackers to exploit new vulnerabilities more quickly and effectively than other techniques, such as creating malicious worms. The research revealed that hackers are increasingly turning their attention to e-commerce sites, which are dependent on Internet for their financial survival. E-commerce was the most highly targeted industry sector during the first half of 2004. Small businesses also bore the brunt of a growing number of attacks.

Source: adapted from *Computer World*, 20.9.2004 www.computerworld.com.

The need for updating

An effective website cannot just be created and then forgotten about, as explained in section 44. It needs to be kept up-to-date, not just by ensuring that publications and news reports are recent, but with an interface that stays modern and fresh looking.

Tastes in website design change in just the same way as tastes in fashion and music change and a 'dated' look to a website will be off-putting to potential customers and may not promote the image that a company seeks.

Poor design which alienates customers

In the same way as an advertising campaign can misfire, so can website design. If trading is to be carried out through the website, poor design can have a potentially more damaging effect on the business. Not only is this expensive, time-consuming and achieves the wrong customer perception, but is very likely to result in loss of customers. Figure 5 suggests some design issues which may lead to the loss of customers.

Figure 5 *Features of poor website design*

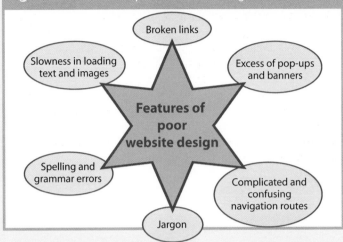

- Broken links
- Slowness in loading text and images
- Excess of pop-ups and banners
- Features of poor website design
- Spelling and grammar errors
- Complicated and confusing navigation routes
- Jargon

Industrial information – the need for security

Many websites contain a wealth of information about companies' activities. Some organisations will use their intranet and extranet facilities to exchange data between departments, suppliers and partner organisations. Any breach in the security processes can give competitors damaging information, harm consumer confidence or generate bad publicity. An example is given in Figure 6. And of course the business may well find itself facing action under the law, for example the Data Protection Act. Usually businesses ensure security of data through password-protected networks.

Figure 6 *Website security problems*

In September 2000, Barclays Bank suffered a security breach. Following a software upgrade, four of the bank's customers reported that they were able to see other customers' account details. Despite the fact that no customers lost money and the system was repaired within a few hours, it was suggested that this resulted in a loss of trust in the security of on-line banking.

Source: adapted from www.vnunet.com and news.bbc.co.uk.

Using a search engine, navigate to the website of any large company that would be regarded as a household name. Browse through the pages.
1. Identify features that have the potential to cause the company some degree of loss if the company has not taken the appropriate safeguards. The losses you consider may be in terms of financial losses or loss of goodwill or reputation.
2. Explain why these features have the potential to cause loss, using examples particularly relevant to the business you have chosen.
3. Suggest some safeguards or procedures that the company is likely to have put in place to minimise such losses.

Research task

Portfolio practice · Sam's Boutique

Sam's Boutique sells a wide range of women's clothing. Sam's most popular ranges are the slightly used garments. Her customers know that she only has clothes which are in tip-top condition, but as they are second-hand the prices are kept low. She advertises them as being 'gently worn'. Many of her second-hand clothes are designer lines. This side of her business is so successful that she is thinking of setting up a website and e-trading. She intends to use the website not only to sell clothes, but to advertise the fact that she buys good quality used clothing.

(a) **Investigate the threats that Sam's business could face if she decides to start trading through the Internet.**
(b) **Discuss whether Sam should launch the website given these threats.**

Meeting the assessment criteria

For your assessment you are required to show research of the factors influencing the establishment of an on-line presence, research and analyse the importance of factors influencing the establishment of an on-line presence and the potential opportunities and constraints of a business having a presence on the web.

Business example - Flying High

Flying High offers hot air balloon flight across the Midlands. There is not a great deal of competition in this type of business so the company receives a lot of enquiries from a wide area. It has recently established a website and now takes bookings over the Internet.

Mark Band 1 *Show research of the factors influencing the establishment of an on-line presence.*
The most significant factor in Flying High establishing a website was that it would be a medium for giving potential customers information. For most people a balloon flight is a new experience and they have little knowledge of what is involved such as times of the year that they fly, the time of day, the length of the flight and the cost. It was also felt that a website presence was necessary for a company that perceived itself as modern and innovative, offering new and adventurous experiences

Mark Band 2 *Research and analyse the importance of factors influencing the establishment of an on-line presence.*
Time spent dealing with telephone enquiries had become a serious issue. A survey of telephone calls established that only one in five calls resulted in a sale. The telephone calls were time consuming and staff found the repetition of the same information time and time again tedious. The website was able to project the image that the company was wishing to create for itself. It showed colourful pictures of beautiful scenery with images conveying the peaceful experience of a balloon flight. The business also felt that the market segment who were its most likely customers, the adventurous and affluent, were most likely to be Internet users seeking product information through websites and being willing to make bookings on-line.

Mark Band 3 *Research and analyse the potential opportunities and constraints of a business having a presence on the web.*
The website was a form of informative advertising and was able to answer enquirers' basic questions. The reduction in the number of telephone enquiries offers the potential for staff to be released for more challenging, interesting and cost effective activities. A further opportunity that the website presented was that a growth in sales may be generated. The staff could be re-directed to deal with the additional workload involved. However, one drawback was the loss of personal contact and the persuasive effect of dealing with the enquiry on a one-to-one basis.

Flying High has to be aware of the potential malicious threats that will exist for any business trading on-line. It needs to install

virus checkers and firewalls and ensure that it has a secure payment system when customers book on-line. Flying High is in the entertainment industry, a luxury, and if customers are concerned about security of their personal and financial details they will simply go elsewhere. Flying High itself could be in danger of losing valuable information or disruption to its systems if it does not protect its system and make back-ups. For a business where adherence to safety is a major issue breaches of security could be disastrous. It may, for example, lose records of equipment tests, maintenance or training records. It may even be vulnerable to malicious attack with the target of deliberately sabotaging its systems.

A further constraint is that it is essential Flying High keeps the website up-to-date. Old price lists and event details will cause irritation to customers and may even lose those who would be concerned that a business of that type should be vigilant about paying attention to detail.

50 Effective websites

What makes an effective website?

Asking what makes an effective website is a bit like asking what makes a good painting, piece of music or a car. It depends on what the aims and objectives were in creating or obtaining it in the first place. In the case of a car, the main criteria for deciding if it meets someone's needs may focus on whether it can be piled high with shopping twice a week, or driven long distances on motorways every day, or taken on off-road rallies or whether it establishes the owner's wealth and status. A website is similar. If it meets the company's aims and objectives of, for example, recruiting staff, or defining its corporate image, it is likely to be effective.

Most efficient business organisations will have set performance targets for assessing the success of the website against other targets they have set, such as a percentage increase in sales or a reduction in costs. A website that is not effective can be disastrous for a business. This is not simply because the business won't have met its aims and objectives. A poor website can damage consumer confidence in its efficiency and reputation for customer care.

Although it is difficult to lay down precise parameters for measuring the effectiveness of a website, there are certain characteristics that feature in most good websites and that good web designers would need to take account of. These are shown in Figure 1.

Figure 1 *Features of a good website*

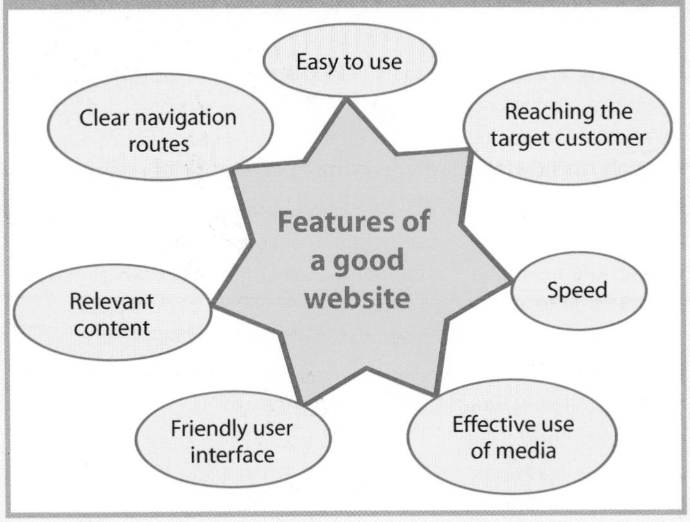

Speed

How would customers feel if they went into a store to rent a DVD, asked if it had the latest releases and the shop assistant disappeared into the storeroom without saying anything, leaving them to wait, not knowing what was happening? Businesses are unlikely to tolerate this behaviour from staff. In the same way they would aim to avoid their website treating customers in this way.

The Internet has a wealth of choice. So if customers find they are kept waiting too long for pages to load, there is usually somewhere else they can go to get the information or the product they want. If there really isn't an alternative and they have to just sit and wait they will be very frustrated and dissatisfied customers. Sometimes speed will be to do with the Internet Service Provider (ISP) provider. This is an area that should be investigated if the business frequently receives complaints about speed. The most common reason why slow downloads occur is because the site carries too many graphics or the graphics have not been optimised for the web.

Navigation routes

Easy and understandable navigation routes would quickly guide the customer through what the business wants them to do. This could be, for example, filling a shopping trolley and going to the checkout. In the same way that an itinerary would be planned for a journey that had several stops and changes, routes through a website need to be mapped out and planned carefully. This will allow the user to reach the targets that the menus suggest and ensure they don't get 'lost'. As in a supermarket, if customers cannot find the products they are looking for, they won't return.

Some sites provide a **site map**. This acts like a store guide in a department store. It helps the user to see all the pages available if they haven't been able to arrive at a page by browsing around. Site maps also serve as a monitoring tool for those responsible in the organisation for passing information on to the website manager.

Figure 2 *Site map for the eBay website*

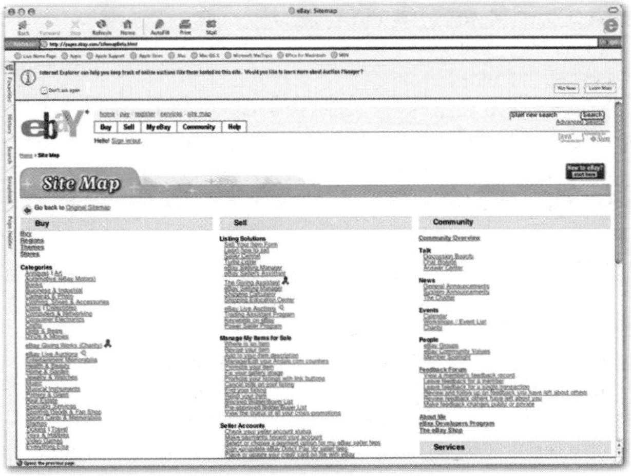

eBay is the on-line market place where customers can buy and sell locally, nationally or globally. There are many different categories of products to buy and sell. To navigate through the site customers can use the site map.

Source: adapted from http://pages.ebay.com/sitemapBeta.html.

They can glance at the site map from time to time to check that there aren't pages that have been left at the end of a route for months or even years, as can happen with very large websites, and are long out of date. An example is shown in Figure 2.

Easy to use

Once the navigation routes are planned the method of moving through those routes needs to be clear to the user. The standard that is often discussed is 'three clicks'. No information should be more than three clicks away from anywhere else on the site.

Apart from standard hyperlinks, the most common methods for inviting Internet shoppers to move to the next page or stage are the use of check buttons, drop down menus or icons. Users would also expect to see a search tool to seek out information or products which may not be easily identified from menus, as shown in Figure 3.

Figure 3 *Navigation through the Ocean site*

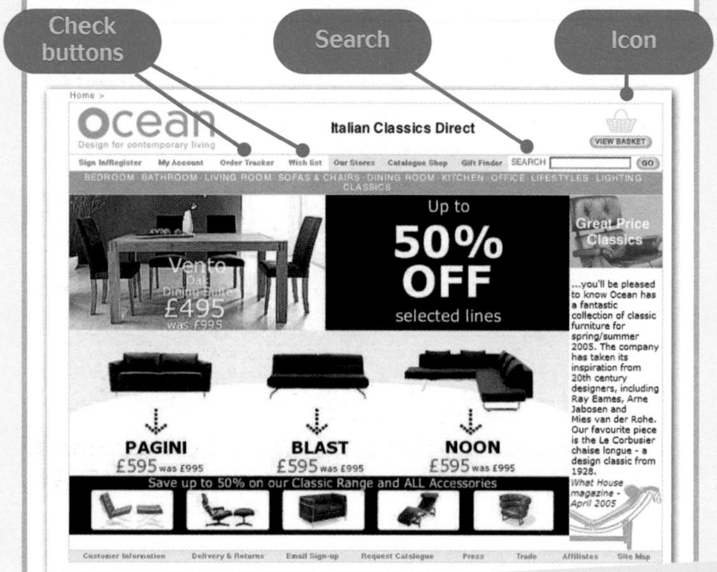

Check buttons

Search

Icon

Ocean sells designer Italian furniture through its stores and directly to customers through its website.

Source: adapted from www.oceanuk.com.

Use of media

The dilemma always exists about how much interactivity and visual 'busy-ness' there should be on a site. As a general rule, it is recommended that too many media effects, such as music, animation and graphics, should be avoided. They slow the site down and get in the way of what the user actually wants to do which is obtain the information about the company it needs and perhaps spend money.

However, some companies may feel that use of multimedia is integral to establishing the position of the business. Disney On-Line (www.disney.com), for example, as an entertainment company, is likely to feel it necessary for its website to have some element

of entertainment in it. Those companies who have successfully developed websites with a high level of multimedia, such as Disney or Pepsi-Cola (www.pepsi.com) will almost certainly have invested many thousands, if not tens of thousands, of dollars in the software and personnel skills to develop and maintain it.

User interface

Routes and hyperlinks need to be accessible on the immediate page without significant scrolling up and down the page or movement of the mouse backwards and forwards across the page. It is also recommended that the whole site has a corporate 'feel', perhaps by the use of colour or logo positioning or layout. In this way the user will not feel at any stage that they have inadvertently moved off the site. On every page there needs to be a route back to a menu or the home page so that the user can easily start again if they have not achieved what they set out to achieve.

It is as of much importance as layout and design to make sure that rigorous checking takes place. The site should be free from spelling or grammar errors, all information needs to be carefully checked for accuracy and all links must be tested to make sure the user doesn't reach a dead end, or worse still, 'Page not Found'.

Content

The content of the website will, of course, vary depending on the purpose.

Contact Most websites include contact details, even if it is just a simple e-mail form. Businesses will want to make themselves available to:

* customers who may wish to obtain further information or who have an issue with a product or service;
* other businesses that may have interesting services to offer them.

Shopping If the website is for shopping there obviously will be an on-line catalogue and buying forms. But these websites should also have at least the terms and conditions, contact details and tutorials on 'how to shop' and what to do in case of complaint.

Information If the purpose of the website is to provide corporate information it might contain company accounts, details of how to contact the head office, a mission statement, environmental policies or industrial relations information. These will be of interest to suppliers, investors, employees and job applicants.

Promotion Other companies may choose to promote their corporate policies and standards. Body Shop (www.bodyshop.co.uk) for example, has links to their policies on community trade, animal testing, human rights and the planet prominent on their first page. This is shown in Figure 4.

Figure 4 *Body shop links*

Figure 5 *The Ted Baker and TVV Productions websites*

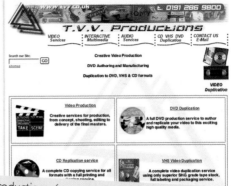

The Ted Baker (www.tedbaker.co.uk) website makes use of music, animation and cartoon characters with catalogues displayed in a fun way. It is an entertaining experience, aimed to appeal to the age group at which it targets its clothes and accessories. Young people are likely to return to it as searching through the on-line catalogue is exciting as well as being informative and giving shopping opportunities. The website complements the retail outlet activity of the business.

TVV Productions (www.tvv.co.uk), a business which offers video and DVD production for production companies, industry and education, is likely to be targeting its website at other businesses. It gets over 90% of new leads from the site. The site has minimal animation, but is packed with detailed information of the service it offers and its prices.

Business customers using this site are unlikely to be attracted by animation. They want to be able to access information as quickly as possible. They are looking for a company that will take their business seriously. TVV Productions, therefore, is meeting the needs of target customers effectively with its website.

Source: adapted from company information.

Reaching target customers

Targeting the correct segment of the market is as important for a website as it is for any other form of marketing. Section 51 discusses how awareness of the existence of the website and what it has to offer can be raised.

However, once the customer has arrived at the website the interface must be appropriate to the market segment the business is targeting and be engaging. A website is a form of communication and effective communication requires understanding the needs of the audience in the way communication is conveyed. The characteristics of the audience are likely to have significant influence over the design of a website.

Figure 5 shows examples of how reaching target customers is carried out effectively in two business websites in two different ways.

Portfolio practice · E-banking

Figure 6 *E-banking homepage*

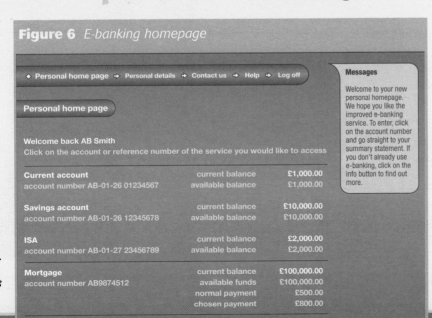

Figure 6 shows the homepage of an e-bank account of AB Smith who now almost exclusively uses e-banking and rarely visits his local branch.

(a) **Suggest the advantages to a bank of offering on-line banking.**
(b) **Evaluate the effectiveness of this page in terms of content, giving appropriate information to customers and ease of use. Alternatively, if you use an on-line banking or savings facility, you may prefer to evaluate the pages of your own on-line bank. Make two recommendations for improvements, giving your reasons.**

1. Ask at least ten people who have used the Internet to make a purchase to score the following features on a 1-5 scale of importance to them in making their shopping easy and pleasurable:
    * speed;
    * clear navigation routes;
    * animation and graphics.

2. Making reference to the data you have collected, review the websites of three well-known companies who provide Internet shopping opportunities.

Research task

Meeting the assessment criteria

For your assessment you are required to show research of the factors influencing the establishment of an online presence, research and analyse the importance of factors influencing the establishment of an online presence and the potential opportunities and constraints of a business having a presence on the web.

Business example - Lucy's cards

Lucy works at home making greetings cards and gift tags. Up until now she has sold them to friends and family and she has also been very successful with her displays at local hairdressers, florists and craft fairs. She has decided that she would now like to sell her cards over the Internet.

Mark Band 1 *Show research of the factors influencing the establishment of an on-line presence.*
By creating a website Lucy will increase the number of people who will learn about her product. She will be able to show her complete range without having to make sure there is always one of every type in her physical displays. Lucy had also thought that the only other alternative if she wanted to expand her services was to open up a retail outlet and that would be very expensive.

Mark Band 2 *Research and analyse the importance of factors influencing the establishment of an on-line presence.*
It is likely that Lucy has saturated her existing market. Simply selling to friends, family and other local clientele gives her little opportunity for growth. Working from home, as at the moment, she has very low overheads. Although creating a website will involve purchase and maintenance of computer equipment and appropriate software which will increase her overheads, this increase will be minimal in comparison with running a retail outlet.

Mark Band 3 *Research and analyse the potential opportunities and constraints of a business having a presence on the web.*
The website will give Lucy the opportunity to extend her market, potentially nationally or even internationally. It gives her opportunity for growth with a low increase in overheads. She will be able to design an interface to her website that reflects the style of her cards, so this would be seen as an additional promotion tool.

If Lucy fails to get the right support and expertise in creating her site, her project could fail. If, say, her site did not look professional or was not easy to navigate, her customers might not be willing to return. It is also important that the design of her website, while reflecting the style of her cards, is also appropriate to the market she is targeting and her product. Her cards are expensive, ranging from £2.50 to £5, so she is unlikely to be selling to children. It would be recommended that the design of the website should reflect the sophistication seen in her cards and her target clientele.

Source: adapted from company information.

Setting up a site

In any business function the process will involve setting objectives, taking action and review and evaluation. A company's website will be no different. Figure 1 shows one model for the major decisions that have to be made in establishing a website.

This section examines the practicalities involved in establishing a website. It also acts as a summary of many of the issues raised in sections 42-50 concerning e-business, websites and on-line activities.

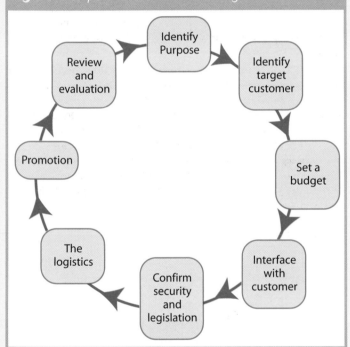

Figure 1 *Steps involved in establishing a website*

Identifying purpose

Table 1 suggests typical reasons, with examples, why a business may decide to set up its own website.

Many websites of course will have more than one purpose. For example, www.channel4.com and www.bcc.co.uk could be classed as covering all of the categories in Table 1. However, these enormous websites, while maintaining an underlying corporate feel, will be designed with individual pages and sections. These individual pages will take account of the audience which they are targeting and the proposed content, whether it is information about schedules, educational resources or games for example.

Section 43 looked at some of the aims and objectives that might have led to a business deciding that a website would meet its needs. The reasoning behind the website must be clear and defined otherwise the website will lose direction. If the website is intended to help boost sales, how is that going to be achieved?

Table 1 *Reasons for setting up a website*

Purpose	Example
Educational	www.samlearning.com – exam revision course.
Promotional	www.london2012.org – London 2012 Olympic Games.
Informative	www.dti.gov.uk – Department of Trade and Industry, offers guidance and advice for businesses and consumers.
Commercial	www.bol.com – Books on Line.
Recreational	www.virgin.net - music downloads.

Will it be by:
- providing on-line shopping facilities; or
- improving the amount of technical information to which potential clients have access?

E-business must be business-driven and not IT driven. The fact that the Internet can allow customers to process orders on-line doesn't mean that the business must offer them the facility to do so. The business must have identified that this will meet a business aim or objective. In this case an aim might have been to improve customer service.

Identifying target customers

A priority for any business establishing an e-business must be to work out who is the target market. The sheer size of the Internet market can make it difficult to decide exactly who is likely to be interested in your particular business. However, planning a website is no different from designing leaflets, brochures and manuals. The business needs to determine who is likely to be reading the website and their technical competence, expectations and needs. For example, a business expecting to attract overseas trade may decide to display its prices in dollars and euros as well as pounds or have a link to a currency converter site.

Figure 2 shows the results of research that suggests that the format of a website should be different depending on whether the website is targeted predominantly at males or females.

Setting a budget

Any business project will have constraints in terms of budget. Section 47 looks at the financial costs of a website and the budget will determine how ambitious the website will be. Decisions about:
- the interface;
- the size of the site;
- the management of the site;
- the content of the site;

Figure 2 *Targeting websites at males and females*

Should a website that is targeting a female market use a different online approach to a website that is targeting a male market? Absolutely yes. Like most things in life, when it comes to online behaviour, men really are from Mars and women are from Venus.

If your target market is predominantly female, you need to prioritise the following factors when putting together your online strategy.

- Entertainment value.
- Security and Privacy.
- Convenience.

However if your target market is mostly male, you should be focusing on the following factors to maximise the effectiveness of your online strategy.

- Previous online purchasing experience.
- Information and organisation.
- Repeat purchase incentives.

Source: adapted from Free Style Media - www.freestylemedia.com.au/article25.asp.

will all depend on the budget that has been set as will considerations of whether the work should be done in-house or through the use of external consultants and agencies.

Many small businesses are unlikely to have the necessary expertise within the organisation. They will need the support of a consultant for both the IT aspects and the design of the site itself.

Interface with customers – web authoring tools

Although it is possible to create a website in common word processing packages such as Microsoft Word, most businesses will use software specifically designed for the purpose such as Macromedia Dreamweaver, Adobe GoLive or ColdFusion. This is particularly the case if they are intending to combine the website with database applications or an intranet for creating on-line catalogues, collating customer information or exchanging data with staff and suppliers.

If a high level of interactivity or animation is to be used on the

website developers may turn to graphics packages such as Macromedia Flash, FreeHand or Adobe Photoshop and Image Ready.

Interface with customers – design, colour, image, font, media mix

Many businesses will take the opportunity to extend their corporate image into their websites, through the use of colour, fonts and logos. The Royal Mail website (www.royalmail.co.uk), for example, has its headings and links in its traditional pillar box red. Research has been carried out into the readability of websites with regard to colour mixes and design and its impact on the psychology of the audience. Red, for example, is perceived as being associated with feelings that are energetic, exciting, passionate or erotic. Most colours carry both positive and negative implications. The downside of red evokes aggressive feelings, suggesting anger or violence. Table 2 shows some more examples.

Table 2 *The impact of colour on websites*

Colour	Positive associations	Negative associations
Orange	Flesh, the friendly warmth of the hearth fire, approachability.	Lack of discrimination or quality.
Yellow	Color of sunshine. optimistic, upbeat, modern	Overwhelming.
Green	Nature (plant life, forests), life, stability, restfulness, naturalness.	Decay, fungus, mould, toxicity, artificiality.
Blue	Coolness, spirituality, reserved elegance, sophistication.	Sadness, passivity, alienation or depression.

Source: adapated from paper on Art, Design and Visual Thinking, Charlotte Jirousek, Cornell University.

In any aspect of design, whether it is, say, art, clothing, or publishing, colours and styles are subject to fashion. Websites are no different. A website using a particular combination of colours and fonts can quickly become old-fashioned. Not only is it important to keep the content of the website up-to-date but the website designers will constantly be reviewing the layout and appearance to maximise customer satisfaction.

The amount of interactivity and inclusion of images will depend on the target customer, the image that the company wishes to project and the purpose of the website. The Nike website (www.nike.com), for example, has a high level of interactivity, animation and sporting, attractive images. In comparison, the Office of National Statistics (www.ons.gov.uk), whose visitors will be sourcing information for academic, business and personal research, has little animation and is packed with text and links.

Confirming security and legislation

The Internet offers opportunities to find masses of information and buy products from around the world without moving from the office or homes as explained in section 45. Section 49 details some of the threats of the Internet. Many of these are associated with ensuring security and complying with legislation.

Software protection Businesses must make sure they have appropriate firewalls and virus checkers in place to protect their systems and confidential information.

Virus protection Businesses must ensure that they are not responsible for spreading viruses to customers and suppliers.

Legislation Businesses must protect the confidentiality of their customer information. This is a legal obligation under the Data Protection Act. Any business which does not enjoy customer confidence in its ability to handle customers' personal data will quickly find itself in difficulties. Section 46 details other Acts and legislation which may be applicable to particular industries.

Warnings Some businesses, whose own systems may be very secure, may have to warn customers against fraudulent attacks. As part of their customer service, most banks warn customers against divulging their log-in, password and account details to anyone. They also make clear their policy of never sending a request by email for a customer to reply with their account details in order to 'check their systems'.

Payments Some small businesses with websites still expect payment by cheque through the post or by electronic transfer of funds through on-line or telephone banking systems. They may not anticipate sufficient on-line custom to justify the cost of an on-line payment system or may have concerns about security. However, most businesses who offer Internet shopping will provide opportunities to pay on-line through credit or debit cards. Sections 47 and 48 discuss secure payment methods.

The logistics

No website can be set up until a domain name has been registered and an Internet Service Provider (ISP) established. Section 47 gives more information on these aspects. At an early stage decisions will have had to be made as to how the orders are going to be processed and how they are going to be stored, packaged and delivered. Negotiations will have taken place with suppliers to confirm continued availability. Appropriate stock control software needs to have been sourced. Section 47 gives some detail on e-commerce software.

Promotion

How can a business raise awareness that it has an Internet presence? A large organisation will incorporate its website details in all its promotional activities. The BBC television and radio channels, for example, always include website addresses when encouraging viewers and listeners to seek further information about a programme. However, there are strategies available on the Internet itself that are accessible to all businesses. Some are shown in Figure 3.

Figure 3 *Raising awareness of e-presence*

Search engines In the head of a website, there is the option to include key words in the Meta Tag instructions. The Football Association (www.thefa.com), for example, includes the words grassroots and three lions in its Meta Tags. Key 'grassroots' into the Google UK Search engine and one of the options takes you to the FA Grassroots soccer development programme. Keying in 'three lions' also gives the FA site in the list. Websites can also be **registered** with search engines and directories such as Yahoo! who will require keywords and descriptions to be submitted

Bookmarks A notice is placed on the website saying 'Bookmark this Site' to encourage visitors to the site to return at a later date.

Links with other sites For example, in 2005 Transport for London was carrying a link to the 'Back the London Bid' campaign for the 2012 Olympics. Sites often carry links to related sites. For example, music sites often carry links to CD sales sites.

Banners and pop-ups Businesses can arrange for a banner with your logo to appear on someone else's site, perhaps by a reciprocal arrangement, or some agencies will arrange, for a fee, for your banner or pop-up to appear on sites that are likely to pick up new customers for you.

E-mail this page to a friend Placing a notice on your site suggesting 'E-mail this page to a friend' has the potential to generate new traffic.

E-mail lists Many sites will require registration before some of the details can be viewed, and internet shopping sites will usually request an email address for confirmation of orders. These e-mail details may be used to send an e-mail shot about special offers and new developments.

Review and evaluation

All business processes and functions will be subject to review and evaluation and websites are no exception. A business will have set targets and criteria for evaluating the success of its website and will have put in place processes for measuring that success.

An essential aspect of the review process will cover topicality of the website - how up-to-date and relevant it is. If the first page that is presented to the visitor has a notice dated two or three years earlier, the visitor immediately lacks confidence that the whole website has been updated recently. Imagine how customers would feel if they went to a website to discover, when an order was placed, that the prices were out of date, the products were no longer on offer or the technical specifications given were for discontinued items.

Visit the following websites:
BMW — www.bmw.co.uk
BP - www.bp.com
Cadburys - www.cadbury.co.uk
Kelloggs www.kelloggs.com
Royal Bank of Scotland - www.rbs.co.uk
Explain how they use their website design and content to reinforce their corporate image and brand.

Research task

Portfolio practice · **Tuesday**

Tuesday is a weekly magazine. It has some features and stories but 75% of its readers purchase the magazine for the travel and holiday classified advertisement section. Although it has a very old-fashioned image it is still a popular choice for people who want to arrange their own holidays by booking the accommodation and travel separately. Consequently, it is also one of the first choices for people who want to advertise their holiday accommodation to let.

Tuesday has only just entered the e-commerce world by setting up a website. The website gives information on how to subscribe to the magazine, the costs of advertising and also has downloads of articles from past editions. None of Tuesday's classified advertising is shown on the website, although it is possible for an advertiser to submit a classified advertisement via the website. However, as Tuesday does not accept credit card payments, those submitting the classified advertisement still have to follow it up with a letter and a cheque.

(a) Suggest why *Tuesday* may have decided against accepting credit card payments.

(b) Suggest and explain the impact that setting up the website may have had on the way that *Tuesday* operates.

(c) Recommend two additional features that *Tuesday* may include on its website and assess the impact that they will have on *Tuesday*.

Meeting the assessment criteria

For this assessment you are required to draw up an outline plan showing initial thoughts for the construction of a basic website for a business that does not currently have a presence on the web, present a design brief for the proposed new website and construct the new website which is appropriate to the selected business.

Business example - Hazelwood Rovers

Hazelwood Rovers amateur football team have just finished a particularly successful season. They have decided that they should take advantage of this success and seek sponsorship. You have been asked to design a website for them to which they can direct potential sponsors to learn about the club. The manager is also concerned that two of her best players have been approached to join a semi-professional club, so she is hopeful that the website will attract new members.

Mark Band 1 *Draw up an outline plan showing initial thoughts for the construction of a basic website for a business.*

The plan for the website

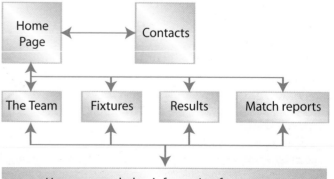

Sourcing information: contact manager, trainers, players and supporters to obtain the relevant data, e.g. fixture list, photos of players.

Timeline – arrange ISP, web space, investigate and register domain name; obtain software; design basic layout and seek ideas and approval; re-drafting; all materials to be collated six weeks prior to launch.

Mark Band 2 *Present a design brief for the proposed new website.*

Hazelwood Rovers Website – Design Brief

Objectives of the website

- To raise the public profile of Hazelwood Rovers.
- To provide a medium for sponsors to promote themselves.
- To improve communication between players, management and supporters.

Audience

- General public.
- Players.
- Management.
- Supporters.
- Sponsors.

Design specification

Site to include the following.

- Photographs of the team.
- Kit details.
- Sponsors' logos and links to sponsors' websites.
- Results page.
- Fixtures page.
- Match reports to be supplied by the players.
- Email and telephone contact details and postal address.

Functionality

- Colour scheme to match team colours.
- Design to be vibrant with an exciting sporty feel.
- Some use of flash animation.
- Clear navigable routes (see plan above) with every page linking back to the home page.
- All pages to have a similar texture and colour scheme to give corporate feel.

Budget

- Total budget - £2,000.

Timing

A critical path analysis will be drawn up. Completion by the start of the next season.

Mark Band 3 *Construct the new website which is appropriate to the selected business.*

To obtain the marks in Mark Band 3 for this case study, the website should show that it has the potential to meet the stated objectives. The student would be expected to use the appropriate web authoring software such as Dreamweaver or ColdFusion to design a website which reflects the plan and design brief they had indicated. To obtain these marks the student would have to show evidence that he/she had taken account of the target audience that had been identified in terms of design, language and content and that the routes through the site are clear and navigable. The website and its functions should be a realistic representation of what could be achieved with a budget of £2,000.

What is customer service?

The phrase 'the customer is always right' is frequently quoted when management is training staff in good customer service. In reality a customer is often wrong. However, if a business wants to keep its customers it needs to behave as though the customer is the most important element of its business and then cater for what the customer wants, needs and expects.

Most people think of customer service as something that is provided by staff selling goods or services to members of the public. In reality it has a very much wider meaning, which includes the following situations.

- An assistant packing a customer's bags in a supermarket.
- A travel agent sending out a copy of its new brochures to its regular customers.
- A bank manager visiting a business customer to discuss a loan.
- The finance department of a business making certain that its staff are paid correctly and on time.

A **customer** is any individual or organisation which has dealings with a business as shown in Figure 1. Customers are individuals or organisations for whom a good or service is provided. **Customer service** is therefore about providing the customers with what they want, need or expect.

Figure 1 Customers

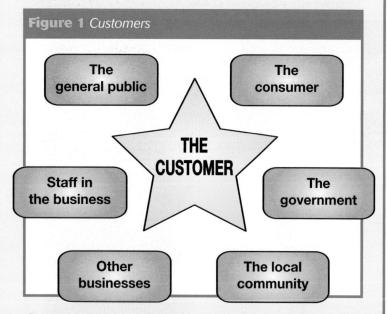

- The general public
- The consumer
- Staff in the business
- THE CUSTOMER
- The government
- Other businesses
- The local community

Figure 2 Customers and consumers

Farmer employs farm labourers to produce grain for a miller.

Internal customers
Farm labourers
Mill operators
Bakery staff
Shelf stackers
Till operators
Supervisors

Miller uses mill operators to produce flour for a baker.

Business customers
Miller
Baker
Supermarket

Baker employs bakery staff to make bread for a supermarket.

Consumers
Shoppers

Supermarket employs shelf stackers, till operators and supervisors to help sell bread to a shopper.

Customers and consumers

It is important to understand the difference between the terms customer and consumer. A **consumer** is someone who buys or receives the **final product** (good or service) for their own personal use and could include:

- a parent buying shoes for his or her children;
- a couple borrowing money from a bank to buy their house;
- a private individual putting a bet on a horse race;
- an old age pensioner receiving treatment in the local hospital;
- a family sitting at home watching television.

All consumers are customers, but a **customer** is often not a consumer. An example is given in Figure 2.

Why is the customer so important?

Many goods and services today are **market orientated**. This means that they need to be made so that they match what the customer wants. For these products customers will also expect and even demand good customer service. Examples of market orientated products tend to be those which have a high level of competition, such as food, clothes and cars.

Some goods and services are so brilliant, unique or necessary that customers will always want to purchase them. These are known as **product orientated** goods and services. With these kinds of products, good customer service is not absolutely necessary because customers will buy them anyway. Examples of product orientated goods and services in the past were very common, with major domestic services such as gas, electricity, water, telephones provided by only one state owned supplier. Today they are rarer, but they would include a local bus service with no competition and many popular bands whose fans will buy their CDs almost whatever they produce.

In some cases it is possible to find market orientation and product orientation for the same product. When this happens, the level of basic customer service is often very different for the two groups. For example, commuters travelling into London by train pay high prices and often have to stand because there are not enough seats. People going up for the day and arriving after the rush hour or at weekends, usually have plenty of space and are charged much lower fares.

Where internal customers are concerned, these will be the staff who are working together to produce the goods or services provided by the business. If the staff are not happy with the service that the business or their colleagues are providing, they will not be motivated and they will not perform as efficiently as they could. In extreme circumstances they may go on strike or even leave the business.

The effects of good and poor customer service

Even apparently minor comments can show a business in a bad light. In contrast, the recognition of excellent customer service can give a business the opportunity to make the most of its reputation. Figure 3 shows examples of different levels of customer service.

Old and new customers

Providing good customer service is important for both existing customers and new customers. Businesses do, sometimes, treat the two types of customers differently. In March 2002, for example, the *Guardian* reported that the Halifax Building Society was ordered to pay £7 million to 10,000 existing mortgage holders because it had offered new borrowers cut price loans but had not reduced the interest rates for existing borrowers. Existing customers received £350, on average, and additional compensation for the inconvenience, of £150. Nationwide and Abbey National had already been ordered by the Financial Ombudsman to make similar repayments to their existing customers.

The reasons why old and new customers may be treated differently include the following.

- Long standing customers are familiar with the business and what it provides and may not change even with poorer customer service.
- New customers do not know the business and may need extra care and attention to get them to try it out.
- Long standing customers may be entitled to additional loyalty benefits, such as higher discounts, store vouchers, even air miles.

The difference in treatment also applies to staff working for businesses.

- New staff may need to be attracted when there are shortages by offering them a higher starting salary, sometimes called a 'golden hello'.
- Loyal staff may receive higher rates of pay, longer holidays, larger pensions and better promotion prospects.
- In many businesses age can determine how much people are paid, especially those in their teens.

Figure 3 *Levels of customer service*

Which? Magazine visited six chain stores across the UK and in 75 fittings for bras they found that in 59 cases poorly fitting bras were recommended by the staff.

A third were not comfortable, in some cases the cups were too small, the wrong back size was provided and wires were the wrong shapes. In one store a researcher in her eighties was recommended a 'push 'em up, stick 'em out' moulded bra where the underband was too loose, the underwiring was the wrong shape, and the effect was to make her breasts spill out at the front and the sides. *Which?* concluded that it could not recommend any of the six chains that were visited.

Source: adapted from *Which? Report Samples – Health & Beauty*.

We're taking the chance to gloat and let you know about all the awards we've won - we're a great place to work and bank:

- awarded 'best overall customer service' for the second year running, 'best credit card' and 'best ISA provider' at The Guardian Consumer Finance Awards 2004 (September 2004)
- voted 'best Internet banking provider 2004' at the Your Money Direct Awards 2004;
- voted 'best online bank' by readers of *Personal Finance Magazine* (May 2004);
- voted 'the best current account in Britain' by Moneywise (March 2004);
- awarded 'Best Online Bank and Building Society Website' at the Online Finance Awards 2003;
- voted top in the UK's league table for electronic banking customer satisfaction (Virtual Surveys - May 2003, July 2003 and again in October 2003).

Source: adapted from The Smile website.

On the Trafford Centre website at www.traffordcentre.co.uk select the 'customer services' option, which will take you to their customer service page. Look at the range of customer service facilities that are on offer.

1. Make a list of the features that will help consumers and those that would help the businesses with stores, restaurants, etc, in the Centre.
2. Explain why each of these features are important for the success of the Trafford Centre.

Alternatively, search the Internet for another out of town shopping centre and carry out the same activity.

Research task

Portfolio practice · Midland Mainline 'No services'

> Midland Mainline's real time train information is temporarily unavailable, due to the withdrawal of all services today, Sunday 12 December.
>
> Please accept our apologies for the inconvenience.

This message greeted passengers who tried to find on-line information about Midland Mainline's travel arrangements for December the 12th 2004. For many passengers this meant that they could not travel, or needed to take lengthy, time-consuming alternative methods.

Why did it happen? There was a dispute between the managers of Midland Mainline and the staff, represented by Aslef (the rail union), over pay. But there were additional complications.

- Aslef had warned members that they should not refuse to work as it might contravene their agreed contracts.
- Sunday was chosen because the train drivers had a contract that said that working Sundays was voluntary.
- The withdrawal of staff came on the day new rail timetables were introduced nationwide as part of a major shake-up.

Source: adapted from www.midlandmainline.com.

(a) **Identify all of the customers involved in this dispute classifying them as:**
    (i) buying customers, staff or other parties;
    (ii) customers or consumers.
(b) **State what each of the different customers listed for question (a) would want as a result of this dispute.**
(c) **Explain how each of the customers identified in question (a) is likely to have:**
    (i) been affected by the action of the drivers;
    (ii) been affected by Midland Mainline's message.

Meeting the assessment criteria

This is covered in section 53.

53 Internal and external customers

Who are the internal and external customers?

A successful business has to think about the needs of both its customers outside of the business itself, such as consumers, and those who form part of the business, such as its employees. This section distinguishes between internal and external customers and how their needs, wants and expectations differ. It also considers how these differences will affect what the business must provide for effective customer service.

Internal customers

An internal customer is a person or part of the business which, through its involvement, directly contributes to the production of that business. Internal customers will include all of the examples in Figure 1.

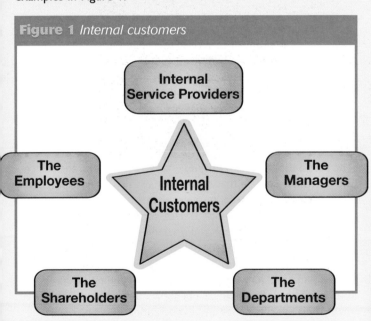

Figure 1 *Internal customers*

Internal Service Providers

The Employees

Internal Customers

The Managers

The Shareholders

The Departments

For each of the internal customers shown in Figure 1, the business will need to consider:
- their needs, wants and expectations and how these differ for different types of business;
- the impact that they could have on the business if these needs are not met;
- how the business can best provide customer service for these internal customers.

Why are internal customers so important?

Internal customers are the people who make the business work. If they are not treated properly they will start to withdraw from the business. When this happens the business will not be able to provide the expected service to the external customers. This withdrawal may be extreme, as when staff leave the business. It could also be less extreme but potentially just as damaging, as when staff are de-motivated and cannot be bothered to treat external customers with the care and respect that they expect.

Employees

Employees or staff produce the goods and services of a business. Many are in direct contact with external customers. When they work efficiently the business is likely to do well. When they feel that they are not being treated properly they may work below their potential. In extreme cases they may leave, go on strike and even dissuade external customers from using the business.

Employees will have all of the following basic needs and expectations and the business should consider carefully how they can be met.
- Fair payment for the job and payment on time.
- Good physical working conditions including facilities to use when not working, such as a canteen, gym, etc.
- An attractive package of benefits such as reasonable holidays, discounts, occupational pensions.
- Good promotion prospects.
- A sympathetic ear to listen to and deal with any complaints.

An example is shown in Figure 2.

Figure 2 *Marks & Spencer staff benefits*

In the first week of December 2004 the 67,000 staff at Marks & Spencer were given an unexpected Christmas bonus in the form of massive discounts on M&S products.

Customers shopping in M&S had already been offered sale prices of 20%. Staff were then offered, for the first time ever, an additional 40% off products.

Source; adapted from www.ft.com.

The needs and expectations of employees will vary from business to business. Table 1 shows some fairly typical needs and expectations for staff working in particular jobs. Figure 3 shows how the Royal Navy tries to meet possible expectations of new recruits.

Table 1 *Needs and expectations of different staff*

Job	Needs and expectations
Teacher	Free teaching resources - to ensure up-to-date and accurate teaching. An occupational pension - to provide a good pension and compensation for relatively low rates of pay.
Customer Service Advisor in a bank	Comfortable chairs - much of the advice is given to customers sitting down. Cheap loans - this is a major part of banks' business and staff expect special treatment.
Waitress in a restaurant	Free meals - food is being cooked on the premises, so free meals are easy to supply. Tips - this is a standard way for waiting staff to earn extra payments for providing good service.
Welder in a car plant	Protective clothing - the work may cause sparks so protection is needed. Overtime - pay may not be very high, so employees may want the opportunity of earning more money.
Computer Programmer	Free eye tests - working in front of a monitor can strain the eyes. Flexible hours - individual parts of programming often need to be completed by a certain time and not during specific hours of work.

Managers

Managers are the main decision makers of a business. They should ensure that the objectives of the business are being met. Poor management is often the major cause of a business doing badly. Managers therefore need their expectations to be met so that they can operate effectively. Their needs and expectations include:

Figure 3 *Pay and benefits for Royal Navy Ratings*

From April 2004:
- Entry Pay, £11,432
- Additional pay for service at sea (after 18 months), £4.18 to £10.65/day
- Variety of employment, with a change of job every 3 to 4 years
- Training for the Navy and for jobs when leaving the Navy
- Free access to high quality sports facilities
- Free medical and dental care
- 30 days paid leave plus bank holidays
- Free accommodation at sea and subsidised accommodation on land
- A resettlement package on leaving of 11 weeks paid leave and a grant of up to £3,000
- A generous Navy pension and a lump sum payment of three times the annual pension figure.

- a good rate of pay and benefits that reflect the added responsibilities that they have, and their positions in the business;
- the authority to make decisions and the backing needed to ensure that staff will carry out their decisions;
- respect from the staff whom they manage.

As with other employees, the needs and expectations of managers will vary depending on the type of business they are in and the type of manager they are.

Owners of businesses and shareholders

The responsibility that a business has to its owners, and hence the customer service that it provides, usually varies considerably depending on the type of business that it is. With sole traders, partnerships and many small private companies, the owners are fully involved with the day to day running of the business and are essentially the managers.

With public companies, shareholders generally only hold shares and have very little to do with the running of the business. These shareholders need a customer service that will meet their specific needs and expectations.
- A good return on the money invested.
- An efficiently run business that will protect their investment and increase its capital value in the future.
- Involvement in really important decisions.

If the business does not meet these expectations potential shareholders will not invest and existing shareholders may sell their shares, or even cause the business to be closed. For example, it was reported in the media that in November 2003, investors holding 35% of the shares in the new ITV company being created through the merger of Carlton and Granada managed to stop Michael Green being installed as chairman.

Departments

Most businesses, unless they are very small, are divided up into departments, each with a distinct set of functions. These

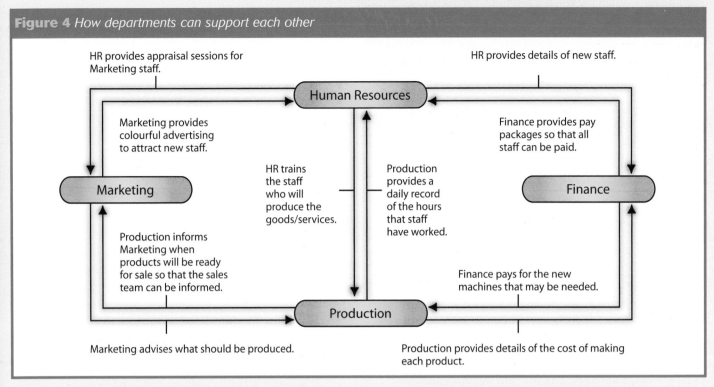

Figure 4 *How departments can support each other*

HR provides appraisal sessions for Marketing staff.

HR provides details of new staff.

Marketing provides colourful advertising to attract new staff.

Finance provides pay packages so that all staff can be paid.

HR trains the staff who will produce the goods/services.

Production provides a daily record of the hours that staff have worked.

Human Resources

Marketing

Finance

Production informs Marketing when products will be ready for sale so that the sales team can be informed.

Finance pays for the new machines that may be needed.

Production

Marketing advises what should be produced.

Production provides details of the cost of making each product.

departments do not, however, operate in isolation and the activities of one department will have direct effects on what happens in other departments. Departments rely upon each other and it is vital that the service that they provide for other departments is supportive and efficient. If it is not, the business is unlikely to produce as effectively as it might and it is also likely to cause friction between departments.

There is a huge number of connections between departments and most decisions within one department will affect one or more other departments. If the Marketing Department decided to run an advertising campaign then the Finance Department would need to pay for this, Human Resources might need to provide extra staff, and Administration might need to make contact with the newspapers, television companies, etc. Figure 4 shows how departments might be connected. This shows only four main departments and only one customer service flowing from each department to each other department.

Figure 4 shows an example of the links between all of the departments except Marketing and Finance. The business might also want to consider 'How could Marketing help Finance in deciding what price to sell products for?' or 'How could Finance support Marketing when Marketing wants to trial a new product?'

Internal service providers

Internal service providers are staff or departments that provide services to other parts of the business. Their main role is to supply employees, departments and the business with services as though they were customers.

In the past the Administration Department was a major internal service provider, providing services for all of the other departments. These services included:
- running reception;

- providing communication links with external customers through a centralised telephone and postal system;
- managing the security of the buildings;
- ensuring that rooms and corridors are regularly cleaned;
- providing a canteen for staff.

Today, with the prominence of ICT, the ICT Department usually provides services to the whole business by:
- providing an internal Local Area Network;
- maintaining working external connections for e-mailing and access to the Internet;
- ensuring that all ICT facilities are working properly;
- repairing and replacing hardware;
- ordering and supplying consumables such as paper, printer cartridges, CDs and DVDs;
- training staff on the use of software programmes.

An example is shown in Figure 5.

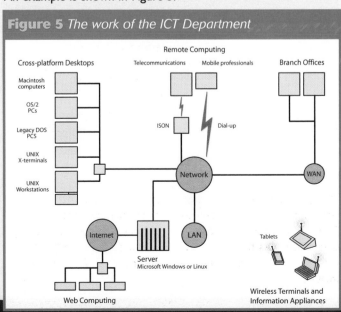

Figure 5 *The work of the ICT Department*

Figure 6 *British Forces Post Office (BFPO) as a service provider*

The British Forces Post Office (BFPO) Agency provides mail and Post Office counter services to Forces personnel, their dependants and authorised civilians whilst serving outside Great Britain, and a secure service for protectively marked material for the MOD, other Government departments and Defence related Organisations in the United Kingdom (UK). A service for official mail is also provided through a network of Defence Mail Centres (DMCs) and Ministry of Defence locations within the UK via a comprehensive network overseas.

Source: adapted from www.bfpo.org.uk.

Different types of business activity will need different internal service provision. Banks and insurance companies often have call centres which will deal with simple inquiries only passing on more complex or individual issues to local branches. Hospitals will have a centralised unit which buys and stores all of the medical equipment and day to day medical supplies. Figure 6 shows an example of providing different services to different internal customers and catering for external customers.

External customers

External customers are people or organisations which are outside the business. The range of external customers can be very wide and includes the examples in Figure 7.

Generally the external customer is the person or organisation for whom the business is providing its goods or services, i.e. the buyer. However, there are also customer services that a business needs to supply to suppliers and society as a whole.

Good external customer service is vital for a business. Studies indicate that an unhappy customer will not only take his or her business elsewhere, he or she will tell between 12 and 20 people about that single poor service experience.

Figure 7 *External customers*

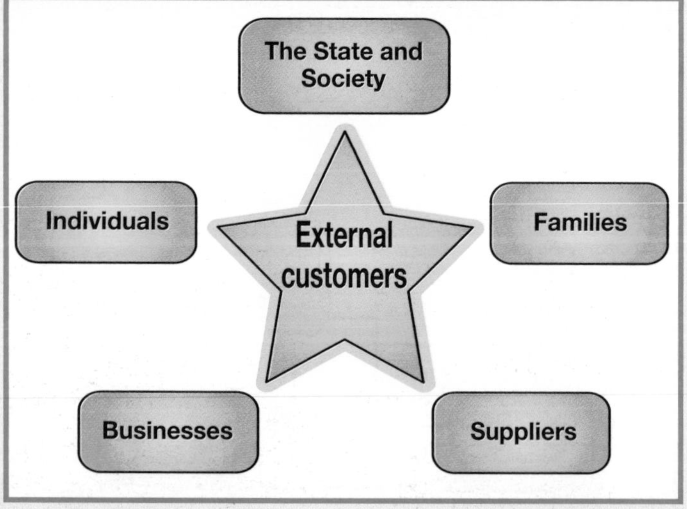

Buying customers

Most of the external customers who are buying the goods or services will share some basic needs, wants and expectations. These include the following.

- Value for money.
- Reliable goods and services, including guarantees.
- Easy access to staff who can deal with their specific needs.
- Accurate and truthful details about the products, their benefits and faults.
- Provision for special needs such as disability, payment over time and language difficulties.
- Friendly, punctual and well presented staff.

Consumers

Consumers want finished goods and services for their own use. Their needs and requirements will depend heavily upon their own personal circumstances, such as age, gender, ethnic background, and whether they are individuals, couples or families. These are considered in section 54.

Business customers

These customers will have slightly different needs because they are buying goods and services so that they can run their businesses efficiently and, usually, make profit. For businesses the following kinds of customer service are often vital.

- Prompt delivery of products, as delays may prevent them from carrying on the business.
- Quality goods and services that meet their specific business needs.
- Discounts for buying in bulk.
- Recognition, and possibly discounts, for being regular repeat customers.
- A reasonable period of credit, so that they can produce and sell their products before they have to pay their suppliers.
- Separate figures for VAT, because they are likely to be claiming that back.
- Support services to rapidly deal with any problems that occur with the goods or services.

An example is shown in Figure 8.

The influence that business customers have over the customer service that their suppliers provide for them usually depends on:

- how important they are as customers;
- whether or not there are other suppliers who can supply them with the same products.

Suppliers

For many businesses it is vital that they provide good customer service to their suppliers. Otherwise the suppliers may refuse to continue to deal with them. Obvious examples of important customer service would be:

- paying any money owing on time;
- staying loyal to one supplier rather than simply looking for the best deal;
- not taking advantage of the fact that one's business is large and the supplier's business is small;

Figure 8 *Screwfix*

Screwfix Direct is the UK's largest direct and online supplier of trade tools and hardware products. It has been supplying the trade for over 30 years and offers customers all of the following benefits.

- Trade prices, stated with and without VAT.
- 10,000+ stock lines.
- Alphabetical index of all items plus search engine for their web site.
- Next day delivery.
- Discounts ranging from 6% when £100 is spent to 10% on all purchases over £1,000.
- A credit account with payment at the end of the month.
- Free ordering on-line, by fax, post or telephone.
- Money back guarantee on all items returned unused within 30 days.
- Free on-line or paper copy of catalogue.
- Refund of money lost if fraudulent use is made of credit card details.
- Message boards so that customers can talk to each other, exchange views and opinions and help each other out on topics related to the trade.

Source: adapted from www.screwfix.com

- dealing with any queries as quickly as possible.

There are also more personal customer services that businesses can provide for their suppliers, such as:

- ensuring that each supplier has a specific named contact within the business;
- paying suppliers in the way that is most convenient for them, e.g. cash, cheque, BACS;
- recommending them to other business colleagues in the same industry;
- arranging joint social events through which the staff in the two businesses can get to know each other.

The State and society

The State, sometimes incorrectly thought of as just the government, is a major customer of business. It collects taxes, but it also requires businesses to implement a huge range of laws from the minimum wage to health and safety and equal opportunities legislation.

Society is really just another word for the state because we, the people, are the state, and businesses have responsibilities to society in general and not just the government.

Businesses are as much a part of the state and society as we, as individual citizens, are and businesses have a duty to behave appropriately and support the state. The kind of customer services that a business should provide to the state and society are:

- keeping accurate tax records and paying taxes on time;
- obeying the laws that protect customers, employees and the environment;
- providing open records of what it does so that everyone knows whether or not it is taking advantage of them and using unethical practices;
- supporting the local community in which it is located;
- using local and national resources and employees rather than simply looking for the cheapest factors so that it can make as much profit as possible;
- supporting worthwhile causes.

Sainsbury lists five management roles in its recruitment section at www.sainsbury.co.uk/recruitment.

- **Department Manager** in charge of a separate in-store department, e.g. frozen foods, electrical and clothing.
- **Convenience Operations Manager** acting as a Deputy Manager to the Store Manager and ensuring that the store operates efficiently.
- **Duty Manager** ensuring that the Department Managers are doing their jobs correctly on a day-to-day basis.
- **Store Manager** taking overall responsibility for an individual store and ensuring that the store is well run and meets its targets.
- **Regional Business Manager** responsible for a number of stores in a region and their success in terms of targets set by head office.

1. Using either the basic descriptions given above or, preferably, by researching the Sainsbury recruitment website, list the different needs that each manager would have in terms of the support they would need from other staff and the information that they would need before they could do their jobs efficiently.
2. What would be the effect on Sainsbury if these managers could not carry out each role effectively?

Research task

Portfolio practice · Bunzl

Bunzl plc is a specialist distribution group which provides goods and services in a number of areas. These include catering equipment (kitchen utensils, china), cleaning, plastic and paper packaging, healthcare (gowns, face masks, bandages) and vending machines. The business has a corporate social responsibility policy. The overall policy is made up of seven underlying policies covering standards of business conduct (code of ethics), health and safety, employees, customers, environment, suppliers and community.

Ethics The code of ethics of the business sets out standards of behaviour for Bunzl employees. It covers conflicts of interest, compliance with laws, rules and regulations, dealing in Bunzl shares, protection of confidential information, protection and proper use of company assets, relationships with customers, suppliers and employees, compliance with the code and reporting of unethical behaviour.

Health and safety The Group Health and Safety Committee comprises representatives from each business area. In 2004 the business had a number of objectives including a reduction in accident rates and an increase in the ownership of personal safety. Methods used to increase ownership included improved induction training, refresher training on safety matters for warehouse managers and a variety of face-to-face and DVD/CD Rom training. Figure 9 shows the change in accidents/incidents.

Employees The business has management development programmes, specific skills training, performance management processes, and offers challenging and responsible roles. It strives to promote from within whenever appropriate. It also carries out attitude surveys and publishes the *Bunzl World* magazine to keep staff informed.

Customers Every employee is responsible for ensuring that any contact with customers and the public at large reflects professionalism, efficiency and honesty. The business carries out customer service surveys. Over 50% of staff have attained ISO 9001:2000 accreditation and the business has won a number of awards for service.

Environment The business works to implement environmental management systems compatible with the ISO 14001 environment standard. Figure 10 shows how this has been implemented in the business.

Suppliers Bunzl works with suppliers to ensure the welfare of workers and that supplies meet or exceed recognised standards.

Community The business sponsors projects such as cancer research and local charitable initiatives.

Source: adapted from www.bunzl.com.

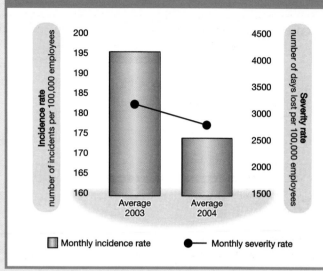

Figure 9 *Accident/incident rates 2003/2004*

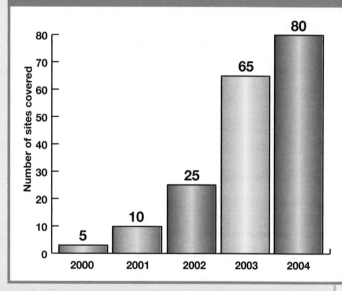

Figure 10 *Sites achieving ISO 14001*

(a) **Identify the (i) internal and (ii) external customers of Bunzl.**
(b) **Explain the likely expectations of these customers, using examples.**
(c) **Explain how Bunzl's corporate social responsibility policy is meeting the needs of its customers.**

Meeting the assessment criteria

For your chosen organisations you will need to identify and describe all of the major internal and external customers, explain their expectations and evaluate how well the organisations meet their customers' needs and expectations. Below is an example related to internal customers. An example related to external customers is in section 54.

Business example - JJB Sports plc

JJB Sports plc is the UK's leading sports retailer with around 430 stores in the UK. It provides high quality, branded sports and leisure products. In-store employment opportunities include:

Area Managers   Store Managers
Assistant Managers   Golf/Bike Managers
Cycle & Golf Supervisors   Supervisors
Head Cashiers

As part of its employment policy the business is fully committed to all Equal Opportunity legislation and also freedom to join a trade union, payment of the minimum wage and only voluntary overtime. There is also a commitment to on-going training. Training programmes include the Modern Apprenticeship Programmes for 16-24 year olds. This is available for employees working more than 20 hours and not in full-time education. Most training is in the workplace and leads to NVQs in Customer Service or Retail Operations, and Key Skills. Training is free and requires no formal entry qualifications.

Source; adapted from ww.jjb.co.uk.

Mark Band 1 *Identification and description of the internal customers and their needs and expectations.*

Each of the listed employment roles could be identified and described. Here, as an example, the job roles for employees on the Modern Apprenticeship Programme are likely to be Sales Assistants and Supervisors. Descriptions would include their job roles, age (between 16 & 20), how many hours they worked (over 20 hour/week) how long they had worked there, current qualifications, etc.

Mark Band 2 *Explanation of their expectations using relevant illustrations.*

This should come from a survey of actual staff who are wanting to join, or who are on, the Modern Apprenticeship Programme. Likely expectations would include:
- gaining valuable qualifications;
- recognition for the work they are already carrying out;
- improved promotion prospects;
- increase in rates of pay after gaining qualification.

Mark Band 3 *Detailed explanation of how far these expectation have been meet by the organisation.*

For each of the expectations identified in Mark Band 2 you will need to evaluate how well they have been met, considering such questions as:
- How valuable are these qualifications?
- Do they improve job prospect within and outside JJB Sports?
- Does promotion normally depend on getting these qualifications?
- Is there an automatic pay rise with these qualifications?

Customer characteristics

Section 53 looked at the different types of customers that a business has and the general needs and wants of these groups. This section deals with more specific characteristics that customers have because of their family status, income, age and lifestyle. The potential range of characteristics that a business needs to take into account when providing customer service is very wide indeed, as shown in Figure 1.

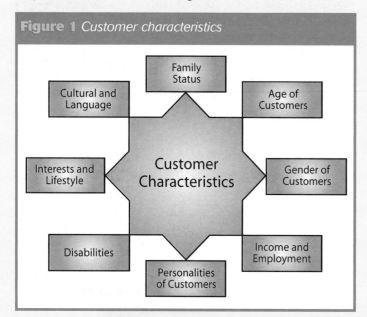

Figure 1 *Customer characteristics*

These characteristics generally relate to people not businesses. They could be either external, e.g. consumers or people in other businesses, or internal, e.g. employees or other colleagues. For each of the characteristics explained in this section, private external customers will be the main focus, but internal customers and business customers will also be considered for some characteristics.

Family status

A person's situation in relation to the family is very important in terms of the needs and wants that they have. Some of these relate to age. These are dealt with later in this section.

Individuals These will be people living on their own. They tend to buy just for themselves and may need and expect the following kind of special customer service.

- Smaller portions in supermarkets.
- Flats rather than houses.
- Individualised training programmes in a gym.
- Not to have to share tables in a restaurant.
- Holidays which bring people together with other individuals.

In the workplace, internal customers who are individuals may expect to be treated as such and not just as 'another employee'. Often businesses provide couples and family members with additional perks that do not benefit individuals, e.g. providing private medical cover, such as BUPA, to the whole family.

Couples Some people will have specific expectations because they are couples. Often they are both working (known as DINKs – Dual Incomes No Kids) and this also affects what they expect. Couples' expectations may include the following.

- To have meals for two provided by supermarkets.
- Hotel accommodation with double beds.
- To be able to sit next to each other on public transport.
- Quality products because they can afford them.
- Separate or joint demands on businesses, e.g. banks, because they both have their own incomes.

One half of a couple at work may expect additional perks, such as BUPA to cover their partners. They may also expect to be allowed to take their holidays when it is convenient for their partners, have their partners invited to the office parties and have their partners receive a company pension if they die.

Families Where children are still at home, or at least where the parents are still providing for them, there will be distinct expectations, such as:

- facilities for children in hotels;
- smaller portions, and reduced prices, for kids in restaurants;
- discounts for family tickets to theme parks, to swimming pools and on family holidays;
- baby changing facilities in both Ladies and Gents toilets;
- a wide range of items in supermarkets that will appeal to each member of the family.

Members of families who are working and who have young children at school will expect to be allowed to take holidays during the school holiday period. The law now gives mothers and fathers the right to take time off when a baby is born. But they would also expect time off when a family member is ill. Many businesses provide crèche facilities for parents with young children and that is now becoming a more common expectation.

Age and gender (sex)

Age Age is a major factor when it comes to providing appropriate customer service because people of differing ages have widely differing needs and expectations. Table 1 shows how these needs and expectations may change with age, taking the situation of a supermarket.

Age is also an important factor in terms of how a business should deal with its internal customers. Younger employees may lack experience and need more training, more advice and support. Employees approaching retirement age may need support and guidance in terms of what they will do after retirement and how to manage on a pension that is much lower than their weekly wage.

Gender (sex) Gender is important in terms of the types of products offered, especially in terms of clothes, cosmetics and some parts of services such as in medical treatment. In addition,

Table 1 *Expectations of different age groups using a supermarket*

Age	Customer needs and service
0-2	Most children will simply be accompanying a parent as he or she buys goods. Trolleys with baby seats provide safety and allow the parent to concentrate on shopping.
3-5	Toddlers may want to walk around the shop, pick up goods and wander off. Crèches may be provided, breakable and easily opened items moved to high shelves and a tannoy system used for returning lost children.
6-12	These children have some independence and may be allowed to make some buying decisions. On likely products, clear and simple labelling should be used and less healthy products could be stocked away from places where children might find them.
Young teens	These customers may have their own spending money and they value their independence. Inappropriate goods or goods with a legal age limit should be sold at separate counters or by checkouts. On the other hand, staff need to treat these customers as just as important as any others.
Students, unemployed pensioners	Many of these people may have lower incomes and supermarkets need to provide cheap ranges of products, but ones which still provide good quality.
18-65 workers	People in this age bracket will have many different needs and expectations, but these will tend to depend on the levels of their incomes, their interests and their family commitments. These are dealt with elsewhere, although age does form a major part in many of their buying decisions.
OAPs	Old age pensioners may have low incomes. But as they become much older they are often living on their own and may be frail and have special dietary requirements. Supermarkets can respond to these needs with value products, single portions and facilities such as home delivery.

businesses should be providing some specific customer services that are different for men and for women. Examples include:

- separate toilets at railway stations;
- separate changing rooms at swimming pools or in clothes shops;
- priority calls outs for women on their own when cars break down;
- ensuring that both male and female employees are available should a customer need to discuss delicate matters;
- providing catalogues that separate items for men, women and both.

In the workplace there are many pieces of legislation that specifically state that men and women must be treated in the same way and that certain facilities must be provided so that neither is disadvantaged. Examples of these are shown in section 8.

Disability

The law dictates that there must be a specific basic level of customer service provided to disabled people. For employees this was covered in section 8. Figure 2 shows an example.

The law only sets down the minimum requirements for the services that must be provided. Many businesses exceed these requirements and they have good reason to do this. The Disability Rights Commission has pointed out that 'There are some 8.6 million people in the UK with some form of disability

– a recent estimate puts their collective spending power at more than £50 billion a year'.

Disabilities run from the minor to the severe. Businesses need to be aware of these if they are going to provide customers

Figure 2 *How legislation affects businesses with disabled employees*

Small businesses across the UK are facing one of the biggest legal upheavals since the introduction of the minimum wage - the extension of the Disability Discrimination Act. Until now, companies employing fewer than 15 people have been exempt from the law, which aims to protect the rights of both disabled employees and customers. But from Friday, 1 October, small firms will have to fulfil the same requirements as bigger companies.

This means small businesses will have to make 'reasonable adjustments' for disabled staff, such as fitting a disabled toilet and ensuring that the company's services are usable by disabled customers, by, for example, providing any necessary documentation in large print. Where necessary, small firms will also have to install ramps or wheelchair lifts to overcome 'access barriers' such as a flight of stairs.

Source: adapted from BBC News, Sept 2004.

Table 2 *Services for disabled people*

Disability	Customer needs and service
Unable to walk and in a wheelchair	• Easy access for the wheelchair. • Shelves at an appropriate height. • Lifts to different floors.
Blind customers	• Shop well laid out with few obstructions. • Staff available to talk to and to serve customers. • Braille versions of instructions and information.
Customers with dyslexia	• Pictures to provide instructions and information. • Short written words. • Staff available to talk to customers.
Inability to turn taps or knobs.	• Taps operated with the arms or elbows in disabled toilets. • Doors that can be pushed open and closed. • Bottles with simple levers that open and close them.

with good customer service. Table 2 shows examples of disabilities and the kind of service that would be expected and should be provided.

Culture and language

The UK has a multicultural society with people of different races, religions and cultures and good customer service needs to take this into account. The **Race Relations Act, 1976** makes discrimination on the grounds of race, colour, nationality, ethnic and national origin illegal in England, Scotland and Wales and very similar legislation relates to Northern Ireland.

Good customer service will, however, go beyond ensuring that there is no obvious unlawful discrimination and will cater for the needs of people with different cultural needs. Some examples include the following.

• Printing information, instruction, advice, menus in different languages.
• Explaining clearly and taking time with customers whose first language is not English.
• Making certain that people cannot jump queues and annoy other customers, as in many cultures queuing is not usual.
• Ensuring that food is prepared in staff canteens in such a way that all employees can find something appropriate to eat irrespective of the restrictions of their religions.
• Understanding how foreign business customers expect to be treated when they come to discuss buying or selling of products.

Figure 3 shows an example.

When analysing what customers want from businesses in terms of customer service and how that varies with different

Figure 3 *How culture can affect customer service*

In business matters the Arabian culture is a non-confrontational one which seeks the least conflict possible. Pressure sales tactics are considered as a sign of a bad deal because they cause discomfort and might lead you to be thought of as a person whose presence is considered unpleasant. For the Arab businessperson, there is no separation between you as a person and the business you represent.

cultures the following criteria have been found to be important.

Authenticity In some cultures customers expect that what they are being told is the truth. In the UK people tend to take much of what we are told as simply marketing hype, even the parting comment of 'have a nice day'.

Caring Some cultures believe that one should provide the best for others and that should be extended to business situations. Staff should want to provide what is best for their customer.

Control In some situations customers want control, as with choosing what they want to drink. In other situations, as in a hospital, they might want others to take control.

Courtesy In many cultures it is expected that the staff in a business are there to serve the customers so they should be courteous.

Formality vs friendliness Many cultures expect a formal relationship between staff and customer and one that should not be over friendly. Others expect a close and friendly service.

Promptness In the UK, with fast food and rushed lives, many people expect prompt and fast service. But for some cultures buying and selling is a social activity in which hurrying is considered impolite.

Income and employment

Income The level of income that people have is likely to affect the type and level of service that they expect. People on low incomes are more likely to want cheap basic products that are value-for-money. They may shop around for bargains and may be attracted by such additional services as free delivery, incentives such as 'buy-one-get-one-free' and the provision of reduced prices as products reach their sell-by dates.

People on higher incomes may be less concerned by these factors and may want higher quality which they are prepared to pay for. Some people see their wealth as a reason why they should be treated as someone of 'particular importance' and may expect priority service.

It is important for good customer service that all customers, irrespective of their income or how much they are going to spend, are treated the same.

Most businesses cater for different incomes by providing a range of products at different prices. Table 3 shows the price range for some of the 47 different types of toilet tissue on offer at Sainsbury.

Table 3 *Toilet tissue at Sainsbury (Price per 100 sheets)*

Type	Quality	Price
Andrex Moist	40 sheets	£3.92
Sainsbury's Perform & Protect Moist	40 sheets	£1.88
Charmin Double Regular	4 rolls	46p
Quilted Velvet	4 rolls	23p
Andrex Soft	9 rolls	16p
Sainsbury's Supersoft	18 rolls	14p
Sainsbury's Revive	12 rolls	11p
Sainsbury's Basic	9 rolls	5p

Source: author research.

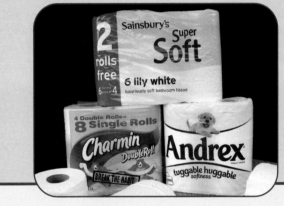

Table 4 *Customer expectations when buying a guitar*

Customer	Customer expectations
Buying first guitar still learning	• A relatively cheap guitar. • Advice on best model. • Part exchange if it is going to be upgraded later.
Moving from acoustic to electric	• Advice on a suitable model. • The opportunity to play models through a good amp. • Advice on suitable amps, leads and the best pick ups.
Experienced rock guitarist in a band looking for a suitable replacement	• The opportunity to try out many guitars in the shop. • A hard case supplied with the guitar. • A robust guitar that will deal with heavy playing on stage.

Type of employment In many cases the type of employment that one has is closely linked to the level of income that one has. Hospital surgeons are paid considerably more than nurses or porters. Sometimes, however, the nature of the job can affect the type of customer service that the individual expects. People in authority, such as teachers, police and senior managers will expect respect, and even obedience, from people for whom they are responsible. These people may also expect a similar respect when they are buying goods and services.

Interests, lifestyle and personality

In the final analysis all customers are slightly different and that is mainly because they all have different personality and interests. Good customer service should recognise these features and treat people as individuals.

Personality In terms of personality, there will be people who are confident or shy, easy-going or up-tight, friendly or stand-offish, trusting or suspicious, argumentative or accommodating. Customers will also be affected by the mood they are in. They may be happy, angry, impatient, thoughtful, frightened, bored, worried or relaxed.

For each personality and each mood staff need to be able to identify it and treat the customer in the appropriate way.

Interests It is also important that customers' interests are taken into consideration as this is very likely to affect the level of customer service that the customer expects. If customers are going into a music shop to buy a guitar, their expectations will

be closely linked to what they want the guitar for, as shown in Table 4.

Many businesses deal with both the general public and people from other businesses. It is important that the staff identify which is which because the interests in the product are likely to be different, and the level of help, advice and services, such as delivery, guarantees and returns policies may also be different. Some examples include the following.

- Is the customer in a garden centre an amateur or professional gardener?
- Is the customer in a wine shop a restaurant owner needing a dozen or two dozen bottles of quality wine for the restaurant or an individual wanting a nice wine for dinner?
- Is the customer in a bank running a business and needing to be advised on a £500,000 loan for expansion or a private customer wanting to know why they cannot get money out of the 'hole in the wall'?

Lifestyle This is also important in customer service as the following examples should show.

- Office workers with pressurised business lifestyles may want fast food, sandwich bars, convenience foods and all night supermarkets.
- Teenagers and 'early twenties' out for the night may want a lively atmosphere, tolerant staff and drinks that are not over-priced.
- A retired couple with time and money to go on holiday two or three times a year may want comfort rather than excitements, good accommodation and food and convenient travel.
- Keen sportspeople may want their local sport centre to provide a range of sporting activities, to arrange competitions, have good changing and washing facilities and a shop where equipment can be bought.

Portfolio practice · Unilever

Unilever is an international manufacturer of leading brands in foods, home care and personal care. Its brands fall into three areas – foods, home care and personal care. Table 5 shows products offered by the business.

Source: adapted from www.unilever.com.

(a) (i) Using Table 5, identify which Unilever products are likely to be specifically aimed at the types of customer listed below.
(ii) Justify your answers explaining how the products meet these needs.
- **Customers who worry about how much they spend.**
- **Customers who are health conscious.**
- **Customers with young children.**
- **Customers who care what they look like.**
(b) Describe the characteristics of customers who would be attracted to the following products.

- **Bertolli**
- **Knorr**
(c) Unilever also produces Birds Eye Wall's ice cream and Viennetta. Write a short description that would sum up each of these products in the same way as has been done for the products in Table 5.

Table 5 *Unilever brands*

Brand	Examples of product	Comment on website
Food products		
Bertolli	Pasta	It you're looking to lead a healthy Mediterranean lifestyle, Bertolli is there to lend a hand.
Heartbrand	Ice cream	Our Heart ice cream range aims to inspire people of all ages to taste the fun side of life.
Birds Eye, Findus	Frozen foods	Fresh freezing is the most natural way to preserve food and lock in all the taste and goodness as nature intended.
Lipton	Teas	Making a big splash in the global beverages market.
Becel, Flora	Margarine	If you want products that are good for your heart, the choice is obvious.
Blue Band, Rama	Margarine	Try our healthy, affordable and convenient range of margarine products.
Knorr	Soups	At Knorr we are passionate about good food. Our products help people make every meal a little more special.
Slim-Fast	Weight loss products	Millions of people over the world have lost weight and improved their lives with Slim Fast.
Personal care products		
Axe	Deodorant	Helping males keep a step ahead in the mating game.
Lux	Soap	Everything about Lux is a delight to the senses.
Rexona	Deodorant	Releasing extra protection as you need it, ensuring your deodorant won't let you down.
Sunsilk	Hair care products	Providing solutions to everyday hair needs.
Dove	Soap	Celebrating beauty's diversity.
Pond's	Soap	Helping to keep your skin looking and feeling naturally beautiful.
Signal	Toothpaste	Helping you to taste life to the full by protecting and enhancing your oral health 24 hours a day.
Home care		
Cif	Cleaning products	The power to deal with even the toughest dirt, every day.
Domestos	Cleaning products	Experts in killing germs. With Domestos you can be absolutely certain the job is done.
Radiant	Washing powder	No other brand knows more about delivering superior whiteness than Radiant.
Comfort	Washing powder	The best care for your clothes, yourself and your family.
Omo	Washing powder	Giving your kids the freedom to get dirty, safe in the knowledge that Omo will remove those awkward stains.
Surf	Washing powder	Surf is great at cleaning and leaves a little extra change in your pocket.

Holidays show a huge variety of different customer needs and expectation and simply looking through a single holiday brochure, available in travel agent outlets, will allow you to identify different types of customers and the kinds of holiday that they provide to meet these needs.

Alternatively you can check the kind of holidays available on-line at a travel agent's website, for example www.thompson-travel.com, www.thomascook.com, www.goingplaces.co.uk, www.firstchoice.co.uk, www.lastminute.com and www.expedia.co.uk.

1. Collect a brochure from your local travel agent which shows a range of different holidays on offer. Alternatively access one of the websites listed above.

2. From the brochure or website identify the different types of customer being offered holidays, e.g.
   - family status: with children, singles or couples, age ranges.
   - different interests: adventure, historic, sun, clubbing.

- different income levels and lifestyles.
- any other specialist holidays available.

3. For each of the types of customers outline the services being provided for them, e.g. parents with young children being offered crèche facilities, children's portions, family rooms, etc.

4. Consider all the possible needs and expectations of each type of customer and then check to see if this has been provided, e.g. will the busy executive who needs to take holidays at the weekends be able to?

5. Make certain that you consider all of the customers' needs for each type of customer, including, for example, insurance, methods of payment, when they can travel, expected levels of comfort, how delays will be dealt with and how accessible the agents are if customers have queries.

Research task

Meeting the assessment criteria

For your chosen organisations you will need to identify and describe all of the major internal and external customers, explain their expectations and evaluate how well the organisations meet their customers' needs and expectations. This will involve a consideration of the needs of different customers.

Business example - Central Library at Croydon

Mark Band 1 *Identification and description of the external customers and their needs and expectations.*

All details relate to disabled customers. Different types of disability are considered:
1. Those in wheelchairs.
2. Those finding it difficult to climb stairs
3. The blind and partially sighted.

Descriptions of their needs and expectations would relate to the specific disability and the fact that this is a public library. It should also be remembered that people without disabilities will be using the library and will have their own expectations.

Mark Band 2 *Explanation of their expectations using relevant illustrations.*

For the disabled the explanations of their likely expectations should be given in terms of the disability and the fact that this is a library, e.g. a blind person would expect to find a book that is either written in braille or is a spoken book. All identified disabilities should be considered and the expectations should also be explained in terms of what the law requires. Again, there are customers without disabilities who need to be considered.

Mark Band 3 *Detailed explanation of how far these expectations have been met by the organisation.*

For each of the expectations identified in Mark Band 2 you will need to evaluate how well they have been met. The list of features includes both positive and negative elements so comments can be made on what improvements could be made. The requirements of the law should also be considered to check that this business meets with those requirements. Again, consider the customers without disabilities.

Table 6 *Access*

Outside Access	Inside Access
• The street lighting on approach to the building is moderate.	• The ground floor area is level.
• There is no level access into the building	• The main area is well lit.
• There is/are 12 step(s).	• This venue does not play background music.
• The steps are well lit.	• The floors which are accessible by lifts are 1-4.
• The steps are medium height.	• Staff do not need to be notified to use the lift.
• The steps do have handrails.	• The lift is well lit.
• The handrails are on both side(s) going up.	• The lift does not have an audible announcer.
• There is a ramp.	• The lift does not have Braille markings.
• The ramp is fixed.	• Adapted toilets are available.
• The ramp is located at the front entrance.	• There is level access to the standard toilets.
• The gradient of the ramp is moderate.	• The toilets are well lit.
• There is no alternative entrance for mobility impaired patrons.	• The library does not house books in Braille.
• There is no bell at the entrance for wheelchair users.	• The library does house books in large print.
• The main doors open automatically.	• The library does house books on tape.
• There are 6 accessible parking bays 50 metres from main entrance.	• There is not a smoking area in the venue.
	• Registered assistance dogs are welcomed.
	• On level 1 of the library there is a Kurzweil machine which will read text.
	• The library also has a machine to enlarge text.
	• Books in braille can be ordered.

Source: adapted from the DisabledGo website (www.disabledgo.info) which provides details about access to a very wide range of organisations.

The degree of customer service expected

Customer expectations

The level of customer service in a particular business will depend not only on the type of good or service being provided, but also on how important it is to the customer. Customers' expectations about the service that will be provided change depending on a range of factors.

- How much was paid for it.
- Where the product was bought.
- How essential it is in the eyes of the customer.
- The complexity of the product.
- How long it is expected to last.
- Whether the customer service is being provided before, during or after the product is bought.

Most of the examples in this section focus on the external customer. A short section at the end relates each of these factors to internal customers, mainly employees.

The price

Generally, as products become more expensive, customers will expect more and improved customer service. Customers buying a postage stamp over the counter in a newsagent are likely to expect prompt and polite service, a stamp of the right value which will stick to the envelop and the correct change. Customers buying an expensive diamond ring from a jewellers are likely to expect that:

- the business will guarantee it is genuine;
- cheques, debit or credit cards can be used for payment;
- it is properly adjusted to fit the wearer's finger;
- it will be packaged in a strong quality case;
- it will be gift wrapped if requested;
- that it would be replaced free of charge if any fault was found with it.

The most expensive items that people buy tend to be houses, holidays, cars and pensions. For each of these customers expect a high level of customer service from the business that is selling it, as shown in Table 1.

When businesses buy products from other businesses they often buy more than one item, so even though the individual item price may be small the total bill may be large. The business customers may then expect:

- a discount for bulk buying;
- free delivery;
- credit facilities so that payment can be made later;
- sale or return facilities;
- to be placed on a mailing list to be informed about new products and special offers;
- a named contact in case something goes wrong or additional orders are made.

Where the product is sold

If people buy a Playstation Portable at a 'knock down price' from a travelling sales van, they may not expect to find very

Table 1 *Customer expectations when buying expensive products*

Product	Typical specific expectations
Holiday bought through a travel agent	• Brochures in the shop to help decide on the best holiday. • Cheap holidays out of season. • Packages that include travel, accommodation and insurance. • That all holidays sold are backed by ABTA. • That holidays can be cancelled in emergencies without too much loss. • That booking and confirmation are carried out by the agent. • That a wide range of payment methods is available.
House bought through an estate agent	• Information on houses with full details of room sizes and size of garden. • Viewing of houses that are of interest when it is convenient to the buyer. • The results of searches provided by the seller. • Clear and accurate communication with the seller so that no delays are caused. • Recommendations of mortgage providers and solicitors if the buyer has not made their own arrangements.
Car bought from a car sales showroom	• Clear and accurate details about performance and reliability. • The opportunity of a test drive. • A warranty for major parts for at least a year. • The opportunity to pay for it over a period of time. • Clear instructions on when it should be serviced. • The opportunity to part exchange their current car. • To have the car cleaned inside and out before it is collected or delivered. • A full tank of petrol. • A year's road fund license.
Pension bought through a pensions broker	• The offer of different pension packages. • Advice on the most suitable package for the individual who is buying it. • Regular check ups from the broker to see if any additional services are needed. • Selection of pension providers who are covered by the industry's guarantee system. • Details of any agreement sent to the individual's bank so that monthly payments can be made by direct debit.

good after sales service if something goes wrong with it. On the other hand, if they buy it from a major retail chain they would expect to receive a guarantee, money back or a replacement if it goes wrong, information on games, the ability to pay with a credit card and delivery to any UK address if required.

If goods are bought through the Internet then expectations are again likely to be different. Most customers would expect that:

- the good would be cheaper than buying it in a shop;
- a full and accurate on-line description is given;
- the good would be delivered, with or without extra cost;
- the good would be properly packaged for delivery so that it is not damaged;
- the good could be returned if it was faulty and that full postage/delivery costs could be reclaimed;
- payment will have to be made before the good is sent;
- any private details, especially payment details, will be kept secure by the business.

Many of these expectations now have to be met by law, as explained in the **Consumer Protection (Distance Selling) Regulations, 2000** in section 46.

In reality there are a great many different places where

Table 2 *Customer expectations when buying fresh fruit and vegetables*

Where sold	Expectations and level of service
Pick-your-own	<ul><li>Free car parking.</li><li>Punnets or bags provided for collecting the fruit and vegetables.</li><li>Payment by cash or cheque only.</li><li>Types of produce limited to what is in season.</li></ul>
On-line	<ul><li>Clear and accurate details of what is on offer.</li><li>Delivery when needed, even same day.</li><li>Items to be delivered fresh and properly packaged.</li></ul>
Market stall	<ul><li>Cheap fruit and vegetables.</li><li>Rapid service.</li><li>Reduced prices at the end of the day.</li></ul>
Farmers' market	<ul><li>Fairly high prices, but also high quality.</li><li>Organic products available</li><li>Specialist items, e.g. many different varieties of potatoes and apples.</li><li>Produce coming from local farms.</li></ul>
Supermarket	<ul><li>A wide range of home produced and foreign goods.</li><li>Loose and pre-packaged items.</li><li>All items listed to be in stock.</li></ul>

products are sold. Each of these will have different customer expectations and levels of customer service. An example for fresh fruit and vegetables is shown in Table 2.

How essential is the product

If customers consider that a product is essential they may have high expectations about it and the customer service that goes with it. Where a product is of little importance to customers they are usually less concerned about the customer service. What customers view as essential or of little importance will depend on what they need the product for. An example is shown in Figure 1.

Figure 1 *Customer service at Wimbledon*

For Facilities Management Catering Ltd (FMC), the Official Caterer to the Wimbledon Tennis Championships, obtaining high quality strawberries is vital because customers at Wimbledon now expect them to be available and will pay well for them. FMC expects the highest quality, usually Grade 1 from Kent, and it also expects the strawberries to be picked the day before, with the stalk attached and delivered fresh, with no bruises to Wimbledon at 5.30 a.m.

Source: adapted from www.fmccatering.co.uk.

Private customers thinking about buying strawberries from a supermarket as dessert for the family supper are likely to consider mainly the price and what they look like. There will be many other products that could be bought instead and because strawberries are not that important to them they will not be thinking about how or where they were grown, nor what time they arrived in the morning.

Table 3 shows products that most people would consider are particularly important and the kind of customer service that they might expect.

The complexity of the product

Some products are easy to understand and use and customers do not need much additional customer service. Other products are very complex and a high level of customer service is needed if the customers are to get effective use of the product.

Examples of complex products and the kind of specialist customer service needed are shown in Table 4. All would require expert advice about which to choose and how they would be operated.

With simple products, customers do not normally expect particularly high levels of service. When buying a half pound of butter customers will expect it to be fresh, packaged and have basic details such as sell-by-date and fat contents, but they will not expect instructions on use or even storage.

How long the product is expected to last

The longer a product is expected to last, the more customer service may be expected. Most people's weekly groceries will be consumed within a week or in some cases a month or so. Where products are expected to last for years, as with a house or a car, then additional customer service might be expected,

Table 3 *Customer expectations when buying essential products*

Product	Customer service expected
Hospital treatment	• High quality medical treatment. • Friendly and informative doctors and nurses. • Short waiting time before being seen. • Hygienic wards and operating theatres. • A quiet environment. • Good aftercare.
Garage providing brake linings for the car	• Quality product that will safely stop the car. • Correctly fitted by the garage. • Rapid fitting when needed. • A durable product which will not need to be replaced too frequently. • Checks at each service and MOT. • Public liability insurance in case something does go wrong.
A pair of glasses	• The eye defect is carefully assessed by a qualified optician or member of staff to give the right prescription. • Tints, lens protection, different thickness of glass or plastic are offered. • Help is provided in choosing the right frames. • Guarantees. • Customers are notified of the next checkup.

Table 4 *Customer expectations when buying complex items*

Product	Customer service expected
Computers	• Hardware and software that matches the customer's needs without unnecessary extras. • Pre-loaded software. • Manual and instructions. • Protection against viruses and electrical surges as standard. • A 24 hour help line to sort out problems. • On-site or return to base facility when major problems occur.
Modern cars fitted with many electronics	• Clear instructions on what any fault lights indicate. • A warranty on all major parts. • Clear instruction on what parts need to be checked or replace at each service. • Support and training offered to any garage that services that type of car so that faults can be detected and repaired.
Stair lifts for the elderly	• Correctly fitted. • Simple instructions for their use. • A repair service that will come out immediately to deal with faults. • A durable product that will last.
Fighter planes for the military	• Clear outline of the training needs for pilots. • Reliability in battle conditions. • Immediate replacement of faulty parts. • Planes constructed to the specification provided by the military.
Some mortgage schemes with changing rates of payment	• The payment structure explained in clear and simple terms. • Comparison of the specific mortgage being offered to other mortgages on the market. • Early repayment of the mortgage being allowed without a substantial penalty. • Support and help if the customer finds difficulties with payments.

such as the ability to pay for it over a three year period, or with a house, a twenty five year period. With long lasting products the following kind of additional services may well be expected.
• Longer time to pay for it.
• A warranty or guarantee that will cover the product over a number of years.
• Continued support in terms of advice, parts, repairs, and help lines.
• With some products, e.g. cars, the possibility of selling it or part exchanging it before the end of its useful life.

With products that are not going to last for a long time some important customer service might still be expected.
• Recycling facilities for bottles and cans.
• The same products being stocked so that replacements can be bought.
• Proper storage facilities in store so that perishable items will last as long as possible when they are taken home.
• Sensible amounts of packaging so that the home is not filled with unnecessary waste products.

Before, during or after a product is bought

Different types of customer service will be expected before, during and after a product is bought. Some of these services will apply to most products, others will vary depending on the type of product being bought.

Before Before products are bought customers will expect the following customer services.

- Information on what products are for sale and where and when they will be available.
- Some details about the price and any special offers.
- Staff from the business to be available if further details about the product are wanted.
- The quality of the product is being protected through proper transport and storage.
- The opportunity to pay in advance, e.g. with concert tickets and deposits on holiday bookings.

During During the buying of products customers will expect that:

- staff treat them courteously, provide them with honest information and advice and serve them promptly but do not pressurise them;
- where products involve electrics, mechanical parts, equipment and clothes they can be tried out or tried on to see that they work effectively;
- stores, showrooms or websites laid out so that it is easy to browse and find the products that are wanted;
- stock is available and will be provided when needed;
- a range of payment methods will be available.

After After the product has been bought the customer may expect:

- protective wrapping or packaging;
- delivery if requested;
- a warranty or guarantee;
- information about new products such as upgrades;
- servicing and repair of durable goods such as cameras.

Internal customer service

The level of customer service expected, and provided by businesses, also depends on similar factors to those shown above.

How much was paid for staff The reality is that employees on higher levels of pay expect, and receive, higher levels of customer service. Perks, such as share options, free medical cover, even the canteen in which staff eat, are determined by one's position (and hence, usually, pay) in the business.

Where the staff are recruited from There are many employees in the UK who come from other countries and sometimes they are not treated in the same way as employees with British nationality.

Some businesses will also treat people from different educational backgrounds differently. Graduates from Oxford or Cambridge still gain jobs with higher pay, better promotion prospects, and even incentives to join the business (golden hallos), which are simply not offered to other graduates.

How essential the staff are in the eyes of the business Essential staff generally receive better customer service than non-essential staff. Low paid staff, with poor working conditions, tend to be staff that could easily be replaced. When staff are essential businesses will try to ensure that they are happy and will remain with the business, by offering higher wages, additional perks and promotion prospects.

The complexity of the job Generally the more difficult or challenging the job is the more pay and perks the person will be offered. There is often an important bonus for the skilled worker in that they will be given more independence, additional resources and greater recognition.

How long the staff have been working for the business In many jobs the level of pay is related to how long an employee has been working for the business. Other factors that typically depend on length of service are the position reached in the business, pension rights and the level of redundancy pay.

Select a contrasting pair of shops that sell clothes, for example a major chain such as Next or River Island and a Charity shop such as Scope or Help the Aged. Think about the following questions and visit the shops before writing up the answers.

1. Describe the kind of customers who might typically visit each of the two outlets.
2. Explain what their expectations are likely to be and justify why they are likely to have those expectations.
3. Compare the basic customer service offered by each of the two outlets, for example:
- range of products offered;
- number of staff dedicated to displaying, advising on and selling clothes;
- what customer services are offered before, during and after the sale.
- what customer services they have on the premises, e.g. changing rooms, mirror, chair and display racks.
4. Consider how well each outlet met the needs of the customer through the customer service it provided.

Research task

Portfolio practice · easyJet

easyJet is a budget airline which has 217 routes across 65 European destinations. It also offers a variety of other travel related services such as car rental, currency exchange, travel insurance, airport transfer and hotel bookings. The business offers what some people call a 'no-frills-service'. This can mean that little, other than the essential service of flights is offered, but at very competitive prices.

On the flight there is an easyJet magazine and an easyKiosk lunch and refreshment service, where people pay for their meals. There are some self-service check in kiosks at certain airports such as Nottingham East Midlands, Geneva and Berlin, which save time. Customers can book online, ringing or through a travel agent.

In 2004 a Guardian and Observer survey into customers' views about travel companies placed easyJet 18th out of 29 companies in the category of short haul flights, behind Finnair, JMC and British Airways, but ahead of Ryanair, Air France and Air 2000. It was voted 5th best in the online booking category out of 22 businesses.

A Consumers' Association *Holiday Which?* survey of about 20,000 readers in 2003 found that 54% of customers would endorse the airline. This was behind Singapore Airlines (80%) but ahead of competitors such as bmibaby (50%) and far ahead of other airlines such as JMC at 8% and My Travel at 14%. Holiday Which? editor Patricia Yates said 'No-frills airlines have changed the way many of us think about travel. Special deals for peanuts mean weekends in Europe can be a spontaneous purchase, in addition to our main break.'

Source: adapted from www.easyjet.com, *The Guardian*, 11.3.2003, 11.5.2004.

(a) **Identify TWO expectations that customer might have of an airline such as easyJet:**
    (i) **before the flight;**
    (ii) **during the flight;**
    (iii) **after the flight.**
(b) **Explain how far easyJet might meet the expectations of its customers.**

Meeting the assessment criteria

For your chosen organisations you will need to identify and describe all of the major internal and external customers, explain their expectations and evaluate how well the organisations meet their customers' needs and expectations. This will involve a consideration of the degree of customer service expected by customers.

Business example - Hillarys' made-to-measure home service

Hillarys is the UK's leading made-to-measure blinds specialist with a turnover of more than £85million a year and a 23% share of the domestic made-to-measure blinds market. It has 14 shops throughout England and Wales and also provides a national network of advisors who will visit people's homes and help with the choice of blinds. If customers want a visit from an advisor the following steps take place.

Step 1 Telephone a central free number to arrange a visit to the customer's home.

Step 2 Arrange a visit at a time to suit the customer.

Step 3 When the advisor arrives the customer can check through the range available and discuss ideas and any issues.

Step 4 The advisor will measure the windows.

Step 5 The customer will be provided with a no-obligation quote.

Step 6 A deposit can be taken and work will begin on making the blinds.

Step 7 Once made, the advisor will return to fit the blinds for the customer.

In 2004 Hillarys was named 'Sales Operation of the Year' at the National Business Awards. In part this award was given because of its expanded contact centre which helps to ensure that customers can have blinds measured, made and fitted when the customers want and within two weeks.

Source: adapted from www.hillarys.co.uk.

Mark Band 1 *Identification and description of the external customers and their needs and expectations.*

Customers are private individuals buying fitted blinds from advisors visiting their homes. Expectations may include the following.

1. Visit from advisors when convenient.
2. No pressure to buy.
3. Blinds fitted by an experienced fitter.
4. Work completed within two weeks if required.
5. High quality product.

Mark Band 2 *Explanation of their expectations using relevant illustrations.*

Customer's expectations about how the service provides visits, advice and fitting come from advertisements that explain these services to the customer. Expectations about quality may come from the fact that this is a well known national company and it has won awards for its service. Expectations may also arise because of the pride people take in their own homes, the fact that they may be too busy to visit the shops, and that these are made to measure blinds so price may not be a major concern.

Mark Band 3 *Detailed explanation of how far these expectation have been met by the organisation.*

Hillarys gets 8,500 of orders a week which suggests customers are satisfied and that the quality is good. It has over 800 advisors, so customers should have visits and fittings made when they want. The Awards have been received for fast and effective customer service. All blinds are made to the customers' specifications and fitted professionally so quality should be high and the price is likely to reflect that.

The importance of staff

In most businesses it is the staff that customers first come into contact with. Staff can create a good or bad first impression of the business. It is, therefore, vital for good customer service that staff are properly trained and can provide what customers expect.

Appearance

Customers expect that staff will be dressed appropriately for the job they are carrying out and for the type of good or service that they are supplying. They also generally expect them to be tidy. When dealing with food or personal contact with customers, as in the case of a dentist, customers expect staff to have high standards of personal hygiene.

Clothes In businesses with many outlets it is common for staff to be required to wear a uniform. This helps to improve customer service in a number of ways, as shown in Figure 1.

For many businesses smart clothes, rather than a uniform, are demanded. People working in the service industry are often expected to wear suits or neat clothes that will present a professional image to their customers.

There will, of course, be many places where smart clothes might seem inappropriate, as with staff in a specialist guitar shop mainly dealing with people between the ages of 10 and 30 or bricklayers working on a home extension.

Tidiness Customers do not just expect staff to be wearing smart or appropriate clothes. They may also expect that staff will look tidy. This helps to create a feeling that the staff have made a special effort just for them. Tidiness would include the following basic outward appearance.
- Clean clothes, with no obvious stains.

Table 1 *Personal hygiene*

Catering staff serving food to students in a school.	Hair tied back, wearing a net or cap, hands washed.
Nurses in a hospital taking blood samples.	Clean uniform, hands washed and disinfected between each patient.
Staff sharing a small office together.	Deodorants used, clothes changed daily.
A dentist examining a patient.	Clean hands, disposable gloves, clean teeth, wearing a face mask.

- Hair cut neatly and brushed, faces shaved or facial hair trimmed.
- Ties, if worn, properly done up.
- Any additional items, such as name badges, correctly displayed, straight and in sight.

The level of tidiness that customers might expect will depend on the good or service that is being provided. Most bank customers expect staff to have a very tidy appearance. However, customers buying fruit and vegetables from market stalls might not expect to be served by people in suits or a female with a name tag saying 'you are being served by Sally'.

Hygiene In many situations the personal hygiene of staff is a major consideration in the minds of customers. Customers having their ears pierced will expect the needle or gun to be sterilised. However, they also expect that the member of staff will have clean hands, will have nothing under the fingernails and will not be breathing germs on them.

The level of personal hygiene will depend on the goods or

Figure 1 *Staff uniforms*

Staff will all wear similar styles of clothes, which gives a professional look to the business.

In retail outlets when staff in different branches wear the same clothes this creates a corporate image which can put customers at ease when they are away from their usual branch.

Customers can easily identify staff, which makes asking for help easier.

Appropriate clothes can be supplied which help staff to carry out their jobs, e.g. protective clothing for staff in garden centres so they can carrry sharp or dirty items to customers' cars.

Differences in clothes can help customers to distinguish the job or position of the person they are dealing with.

services being provided. Table 1 shows some examples where personal hygiene is particularly important and the action by staff that might be expected from their customers.

Timekeeping

External customers expect shops, offices and factories to be open when they are scheduled to be open. They also expect that staff will deal with their individual needs speedily and efficiently.

Punctuality Most staff work set times and both the business and the customers expect staff to be where they should at the right time. If they are not, the following effects may occur.

- The premises may not be opened on time and customers may be annoyed and possibly lost.
- Customers who have appointments may become angry or leave.
- Deliveries may not be made.
- Other staff may have to do additional work to cover for the person who is late.

Prompt service Customers hate to be kept waiting around, especially when there appears to be no good reason. Good customer service will ensure that customers are dealt with as soon as possible. Where there are delays, customers must be kept informed about the cause and how long the delay is likely to be.

At the same time it is important that customers do not feel that they are being rushed. The best customer service strikes a balance between fast, efficient service and making the customer feel special.

Product knowledge

If customers knew exactly what they wanted they would simply research what was available and then order it. Many customers need advice from experts about what to buy and how to use products. They expect the people selling the goods or providing the services to have a sound and reliable knowledge of the products.

In some situations customers rely heavily on the product knowledge of staff. This would generally be the case in the following situations.

Figure 2 *Product knowledge about a computer*

Can you help me? What do all of these features do and do I need them for e-mailing my grandson?

Operating system: Microsoft Windows XP Media Centre
Processor Class: Pentium M
Processor Speed: 1.7GHz
RAM: 1024 MB
Hard Drive Capacity: 80 GB
Hard Drive Speed: 5400rpm
Wireless: 802.11g
Screen Size: 15 inches
Primary Optical Drive: DVD+/-RW
System Weight: 7.8lbs
Type: Desktop Replacement, High-end Multimedia Media Centre, Multimedia

- A patient visiting the doctor.
- A student attending college.
- A tourist on a guided tour.
- A householder requesting the most suitable shower unit for their bathroom.

Figure 2 shows some information which staff might be asked by a customer buying a computer.

In most situations customers expect staff to have good basic product knowledge and to be able to answer the following sorts of questions.

- Are these shoes made of leather?
- Will this software work on my computer?
- Are there any nuts in this pastry?
- Does my insurance policy cover me for skiing accidents?

Inter-personal skills

People in the workplace usually need to communicate with many other people, e.g. other staff, managers, customers and suppliers. It is, therefore, very important that they have the right inter-personal skills to ensure that all of these other people are comfortable with them and are provided with what they need.

Communication Effective communication, as part of customer service, is covered in section 58. Here we are looking at the characteristics staff need in order to provide that effective communication.

Where customers are concerned it is vital that staff both listen to what is wanted and respond with clear and focused information. This requires the following.

- The ability to listen to customers and work out what they really need.
- Answering customers' questions effectively. 'Effectively' here means that answers are accurate, made within a reasonable time and using language that is easy for the customer to understand.
- Asking the right questions when it is not clear what customers want and doing this so that it does not make the customer feel inferior.
- Providing customers with all the information that they need to make the right choice, use the product as it should be used and give them effective support.

Attitude Customers want and usually expect to be treated as the most important part of any business transaction. It is, therefore, important that staff have the right attitude towards their customers. The characteristics of an effective staff attitude are shown in Figure 3.

Handling difficult customers and complaints The most challenging aspect of customer service comes when staff have to deal with a difficult customer. This often occurs when customers have found something wrong with a good or service they have purchased, but it can occur from the moment customers first come into a shop or office, or ring up.

Good customer service will require staff to listen carefully to the requests, complaints or awkward requirements of customers and then deal with the situation without upsetting them. There is, however, a point at which difficult customers become impossible. They may then start to affect other customers. Staff will need to identify what behaviour is completely unreasonable and will need to know how to handle the situation so it does not adversely affect other customers or the business.

Figure 3 *Effective staff attitudes*

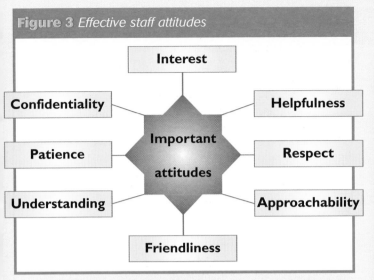

- Interest
- Confidentiality
- Helpfulness

Important attitudes

- Patience
- Respect
- Understanding
- Approachability
- Friendliness

Where there is a complaint about goods or services that have been provided, staff must listen to the complaint sympathetically and record details of the complaint. They must then ensure that customers are provided with a solution or reassured that their complaint will be dealt with urgently. For example, a refund or replacement may be given or the complaint could be referred to colleagues to improve the product or service. In some cases compensation may be offered.

Teamwork

For effective customer service it is sometimes vital for staff to work as a team. It is then important that each team member not only provides the best service possible to the customer, but also provides efficient service to other team members. Table 2 illustrates some examples of teamwork.

Training

Some people have an instinctive feel for how to treat customers. However, for many staff specific training is needed.

Even where staff have good customer service skills it will be necessary from time to time to provide additional training, for example when new products are being introduced for sale.

The next time you go out shopping, or go with someone else who is shopping, carry out the following tasks.
1. In advance write out a list of your (or their) specific needs and expectations as a customer.
2. In the store, observe how staff behave when serving you (or them) and note the good and bad elements of customer service the staff provide. Do not write this out at the time because this may offend the staff and the store and it may change the way that the staff behave.
3. Evaluate how well your (or their) needs were met by the person who was serving, writing out clear explanations of why the person did nor did not meet the needs and expectations.
4. Write a short outline of how the service could have been improved explaining why your recommendations would improve the service. It is very easy to conclude that the service received is good, or very good, but it is rare that there is no room for improvement.

Research task

Table 2 *Examples of teamwork*

Situation	Team members' roles	Possible consequences if not carried out effectively
A customer in a supermarket wants to buy alcohol but the checkout person is under 18.	Checkout staff need to scan the customer's purchase and ring for help. The checkout supervisor needs to respond to the bell or flashing light and find out what the problem is before taking action, for example authorising sale by an over-18 year old.	Delays can be caused and this may mean that not only the customer but anyone queuing behind is kept waiting.
A customer orders a new washing machine and asks for it to be installed on a specific day.	Sales assistants will show the customer a range of washing machines, take the order and discuss the need to take out insurance cover. Administration staff will process the order, arrange delivery and send the insurance request to the insurance company. The installer who collects the machine delivers it to the customer on the agreed day and installs it. The insurance company's administration staff record the cover ready for any claim.	If the details of the machine, customers' addresses or delivery dates are not correctly passed on, the customer may get the wrong machine delivered to the wrong address on the wrong day. This will annoy the customer and waste the time of everyone involved. If the insurance is not passed on the customer may not be insured if something goes wrong with the machine.
A customer books a holiday for two weeks for a family in Portugal.	The travel agency assistant will discuss the customer's needs, check availability, take the booking and deposit, and record all the details. Administration staff send out the tickets and ask for the final payment.	If the wrong details are recorded the customer may get the tickets on the wrong day or for a different holiday and it may be too late to do anything about it.

Meeting the assessment criteria

For your chosen organisation you must consider how effectively staff provide customer service. You will need to consider all of the elements that help to ensure staff are providing this service, from their personal appearance to the training that the organisation you are studying provides.

Business example - Lidl

Lidl's mission statement
It's about simplicity
We buy and sell - pure retail.
We are totally focused on one aim - to offer our customers everyday top quality products at the best possible prices.

Lidl is a German supermarket chain with branches across the UK. Staff roles for each store include:
• Store Manager;
• Shelf stacking;
• Checkout operation.

Lidl provides a good range of basic grocery products, but with limited frills and a simple layout of aisles with items stacked, or on shelves, on either side. Typical customers' expectations that relate to staffing are:
• a good range of basic products;
• very competitive prices;
• normal shopping hours;
• prompt resolution of complaints;
• clear labelling and display of goods on offer;
• all products available on the shelves;
• a fast and efficient checkout system;
• help in terms of where products are to be found.

Source: adapted from www.lidl.co.uk and author research.

Mark Band 1 *Basic evaluation of customer service activities with basic recommendations.*

This basic evaluation should list the major elements of the staff's customer service and state how good they are or not, for example, how often the shelves are re-stocked, how fast goods are scanned at the tills and how many staff are available to provide advice. Where customer service is observed that could be improved, basic recommendations should be made that would improve them. This should include details of any important services that seem to be missing.

Mark Band 2 *Sound evaluation of customer service activities with thought about which are the most important customer services for this business and recommendations for improvements with clear reasons for each.*

Decisions will need to be made about which customer services are most important. For example, do customers want fast checkout service, a good range of products or value for money most? To establish this, it would be useful to get details from customers. It would then be necessary to check how well these services are being provided. Lidl has a good reputation and is well known for the speed that staff pass items through the checkout. But an evaluation will need to be made about how important customers feel this is and which services of the business are most important. Where recommendations for improvements are being made, there must be justified reasons given. For example, if it was recommended that a greater range should be stocked, there must be evidence that customers feel more variety is important.

Mark Band 3 *Detailed evaluation with clear judgments, fully supported conclusions and appropriate recommendations.*

Evaluation must be in depth, considering a wide range of customer services provided by staff and supported with clear evidence. For example, customers may have listed rapid checkout processes as a major priority. If the results of a questionnaire showed that 8 out of 10 customers were satisfied, this would support the conclusion that this element was being met. Further details may also be needed. This might include, for example, a calculation of the number of people that built up in a queue before a new till was opened. Recommendations should be based on the information gathered. One recommendation might be that a certain number of staff should be available and given the task of opening other tills very quickly, when necessary, to prevent any delays when people are queuing. The number of people that build up in a queue before this happens might be suggested. A comparison might also be made with other supermarkets. This might show, for example, that service is faster at Lidl.

Portfolio practice · MDI Ltd

MDI Ltd is a wholesale importer of cycle parts from countries such as Italy and France selling into the UK market. 95% of its goods are sold to cycle shops. Price lists are sent out once a year, showing the latest prices and styles. The shops want the latest designs as soon as they are available, especially in the main racing season between February and June. They need to know the exact specification of any new design so that they can match their customers' needs.

Orders are mainly taken by MDI Ltd over the phone during office hours between 9.00 am and 16.00 pm. MDI Ltd also calls shops regularly each week with details of the latest products available. Deliveries are made each day and promised within 48 hours of an order. Each member of staff has their own client list for which they are responsible. Figure 4 shows the results of a survey carried out by the business with 100 of its business customers.

Source: adapted from company information.

Figure 4 *What are the most important services?*

Service	
Delivery on time	
Availability of stock	
Attitude of staff	
Product knowledge	
Teamwork	
Appearance of staff	

0   20   40   60   80   100

(a) **List the customer services which are provided by the staff.**

(b) **(i) Explain why product knowledge is so important to the customers.**

(ii) **Identify the type of product knowledge customers would expect staff to have.**

(c) **Using Figure 4, assess how well MDI Ltd is meeting the expectations of its business customers.**

Premises

Section 56 dealt with how effective customer service could be delivered through factors that related to the staff. This section will consider how the premises and the product itself affect customer service. It will also consider the importance of providing a quality product or service.

There are two main aspects of the premises of a business that are likely to be of particular concern to customers. These are:

● where the store, office, factory is located;
● how the store, office, factory is laid out.

Location of premises

The location of a business will be important to both internal and external customers.

For staff Staff will need to get to work and probably travel during the rush hour. Generally the time and cost of getting to work is not paid for so if businesses are located in awkward locations this could make staff think twice about working there. It may also be the case that the business premises are not located near any shops or cafés so staff will not be able to go out at lunchtime to get food.

Where businesses are located in difficult places, they could think about providing the following customer services for their staff.

● Paying a travel allowance.
● Re-location payments so that staff can move closer to their work.
● Transport for their staff, either to and from home or to and from major transport centres.
● Taxis if staff have to work late.
● Staff car parking.
● A company car, especially if public transport does not go near the premises.
● Facilities, even baths and showers, so that staff can refresh themselves after their travel.
● A subsidised canteen so staff can get meals whilst at work.

For external customers Their main concerns will also be how easy it is to get to the business and if there is parking provided, but also if it is near other businesses that they want to visit. Many retail businesses have decided to move their premises from 'high street' locations to 'out-of-town' locations. This has helped customers who are buying large quantities of goods, or bulky goods and can now drive their cars and park close to the stores.

Some retail businesses have premises both in the centres of towns and cities and also on the outskirts. Tesco supermarket chain, for example, has five different types of outlet designed to cater for the different needs of a wide range of customers, as shown in Table 1.

For many shoppers what attracts them to stores is finding a wide variety of different types of shop all in the same location. Figure 1 shows an example. This is one reason why shopping

Table 1 *Tesco stores*

Tesco Express	A convenience store serving local neighbourhoods.
Tesco Metro	Compact stores located in busy areas.
Tesco Superstore	Our most frequent layout, with groceries and non-food items.
Tesco Extra	A hypermarket, with a wide range of non-food goods.
Home Shopping	These stores operate Tesco.com grocery home shopping.

Source: adapted from www.tesco.com/storelocator.

precincts, malls and even dedicated shopping and leisure complexes are popular. For many of the well known retail stores, such as Next, WH Smith and Game, and service providers such as NatWest, Costa Coffee and McDonald's, their customers expect to find outlets in these places and the businesses need to ensure that they have a branch located there. Some premises are sited away from rivals, so they can differentiate from other businesses.

Figure 1 *Trafford Centre*

The Trafford centre in Manchester has many shops under one roof, including JJB Sports, Selfridges, HMV, Boots and Dixons. It also has a food mall with many different restaurants and cafes.

Source: adapted from www.traffordcentre.co.uk.

When evaluating how effective the location of the business premises are the following sorts of questions need to be considered.

● How convenient is the location for the external, and the internal, customers?
● On what basis was the location chosen, and how does that match the needs of the customers?

- How close are the businesses to centres of population?
- Are there any special features provided for the customers that help them reach the location or use the location, e.g. special buses, maps showing the location, and delivery of purchased goods?
- What additional features could be included that would improve the level of customer service provided?

Layout of premises

The layout of most businesses can have a major effect on the service provided to customers. This is most easily seen in shops where customers expect to have easy access to the goods and be able to find their way around the shop without have to ask for help. Layout is also important for staff.

For staff. In many jobs staff are moving about and need easy access to where they need to go. Obvious examples include:

- shelf stackers in a supermarket who may need to move large trolleys up and down aisles;
- assistants in a clothes shop having to hang clothes back on the rails after customers have tried them on;
- an administrative assistant delivering post to staff in a four storey office block;
- Teachers and students having to move from room to room for different periods during the school day.

Where staff are working in one main part of the premises the layout and working environment need to be set up so that staff are comfortable and safe. This would include ensuring that staff are protected from dangerous machinery and substances and have access to fire exits, but also that the noise level, temperature and lighting are acceptable. An example is shown in Figure 2.

Figure 2 *Effective workspace layout in an office*

For customers in shops. The layout is important for both customers and the business. In a supermarket the standard layout is to have long aisles, with shelves on either side, and signs hanging from the ceiling to show where particular types of product are. For the customer this layout is now familiar and as long as the supermarket does not change the layout customers soon know where the goods that they want are. For the

business the main advantage is that many goods can be stocked and easily seen by the customers. There is the added advantage that customers need to pass other goods as they go to the shelf with the item they really want and, frequently, they will be tempted to pick up other goods on the way.

In other types of business premises the layout will reflect the type of good or service being sold. Some examples are shown in Table 2.

Accessibility is particularly important for disabled customers. This is covered in section 54.

When evaluating how effective the layout of the business premises is the following sorts of questions need to be considered.

- Who are the customers? Staff, shoppers, people using public transport?
- What are their needs in terms of how the premises are laid out?
- What are the special needs that customers and the business will have because of the type of good or service being sold?
- How does the layout affect customers?
- Are there constraints in terms of the size of the premises, the need for features such as display units, changing rooms and the likely number of people on the premises during peak periods?

Table 2 *Customer expectations of premises*

Business	What customers may want
Banks	Confidential meetings so it is important that there are places where conversations will not be overheard, possibly a separate office.
In a betting office	To read the list of riders and tips from the newspapers. These are displayed on the walls so desks and seats are needed in front of them.
In a fast food restaurant	To sit down so tables and chairs are needed, but also space to queue to order food, bins placed conveniently to get rid of packaging, cups and plates.
In a travel agents	To look at brochures displayed in racks on the wall, but when they inquire about holidays they need seats set opposite staff who are sitting with computers and checking availability.
Self-service greengrocers	Fruit and vegetables well displayed, space to walk around and pick up items, weighing machines to check how much they are buying and the till placed near the exit so that they can buy everything they want before paying and leaving.

Quality products

For most customers the quality of the product is a major factor in terms of what they want from a business. The measure of quality may be similar for goods and services, as with value for money, or it may be more specific and related to the particular good or service being provided. Figure 3 shows some of the main features that customers might expect from quality products.

Figure 3 *Features of quality products*

Value for money When customers buy a product they expect its quality to reflect how much was paid for it. Customers buying fireworks for Guy Fawkes night will expect a much bigger and brighter display from a 21 multi-shot Armageddon costing £47 than from a pack of 10 indoor sparklers costing £1.

For many people the price is seen as the main measure of quality, but at the same time customers want a bargain. That is why sales are so successful, especially when the goods or services had an originally high price and are now being sold at half, or less, of the original price.

At the same time customers do expect value, even from the cheapest of products. When people buy a stamp to send a birthday card to a relative it may only cost 21p or 30p but they expect the card to be delivered safely, to the right house and preferably next day. Most products are advertised to perform a particular function and if the price is acceptable to the customers and it does perform that function effectively they will feel that they are getting value for money.

Performing its function The functions that different products have cover a huge range. Some examples are given in Table 3. There will be some general characteristics that customers expect, such as reliability, ease of use and safety and some that will apply to particular products, such as durability.

When evaluating how well a business provides customer service in terms of quality it is vital to work out exactly what the main functions of the product are. The main function of a thermos flask, for example, is to help keep a liquid warm, but this needs to be done safely so that the person does not get burnt. Quality will therefore be measured in terms of its ability to take boiling water without breaking or leaking and to avoid

Table 3 *Examples of expected functions*

Business	What customers may want
Bread knife	Cuts or saws through all types of bread and will last for years.
TV dinner	Easy to cook, tasty, served on disposable packaging.
Walkman	Light to carry, anti-jog, plays CDs and MP3, quality sound.
Anti-dandruff shampoo	Will get rid of dandruff, safe to use on scalp and near eyes.
Pension	Easy to pay into, provides sufficient funds to live off when retired.
Meal in a quality restaurant	High quality ingredients, prepared by a renowned chef, produced and served on time.
Police answering a burglary call	Swift response, thorough investigation, catching the burglar, return of stolen property.
Examiner marking a student's paper	Accurate and fair marking, completed on time.

hot materials such as metal coming into contact with a person's skin. It also needs to retain heat, so that the liquid is still hot hours later.

With retailing both the quality of the product being sold and the quality of the actual service of selling need to be evaluated. So when dealing with a retail outlet, such as a clothes shop, the basic functions of the clothes need to be established, for example to keep people warm, provide attractive fashion, keep their shape when cleaned and last for months or even years. Then, the basic functions of selling need to be evaluated, for example, helpfulness of the staff, changing facilities, ease of payment, and after sales services.

Safety and security For most products safety is a concern. For some products this becomes one of the major tests of quality. Where children are involved this is particularly important. When buying toys for children, customers want to know that the toy is safe for that age group and where babies are involved most of the products bought, such as food, clothes, nappies, creams, prams and cots, will be bought with safety at the top of the list of concerns.

It is not just goods that parents want to know that there children are safe with but also services. Are they being properly supervised at primary school, is the swimming instructor fully qualified, and will the corkscrew ride at the theme park hold them securely as they flip over and over?

Many products for adults will also have safety as a main feature of quality, as with bikes and cars, electric drills, fireworks, journeys on public transport, watching major sporting events in crowded stadiums and saving money in a bank.

Figure 4 *Jester Events*

Jester Events is a professional Corporate Hospitality & Venue Finding Company. It lists the following skills as highly important for the work that it does for its clients.

- An in-depth knowledge of many venues.
- Up-to-date knowledge about the venues and their staff.
- Brochures based on recent visits to the venues to check the physical conditions and staff performance.
- The ability to answer in-depth questions about the venues.
- Knowledge about the potentially confusing law of contract.

Source: adapted from www.jesterevents.co.uk.

Many of these safety issues are now covered by legislation, as explained in section 64.

Good product knowledge

Section 55 looked at the effect that the complexity of a product has on the need for specialist information, advice and instruction. This can be provided through clear written instructions but in many cases customers want help and advice from the member of staff who is selling them the product. For staff to able to do this they need good product knowledge and the ability to match particular types of products to the needs and want of the customer. An example is shown in Figure 4.

The starting point must be find out exactly what the customer's needs and wants are. That sounds fairly easy, but some customers are reluctant to give too much detail, especially about sensitive and private matters and some customers simply do not know exactly what they want. The skill, in both cases, is to find out as much as possible without annoying the customer. It is also important not to force products onto customers simply because the business wants the product sold. Often that leads to a dissatisfied customer in the long run.

In many businesses staff need to know about a wide range of products before they can match the most suitable to the customer's needs. Dixons stocks a huge range of audio, video, games and camera equipment, as shown in Figure 5.

When evaluating how effective the staff product knowledge is, the following sorts of questions need to be considered.

- How important is product knowledge for the product being sold?
- What details do the customers need about the products?
- How wide and deep is the staff's knowledge of the products they are selling?
- What supporting information is available, in manuals and instructions?

Figure 5 *Examples of Dixons' electronic equipment*

In most of Dixons' stores the staff will specialise in particular types of products, for example cameras and camcorders. This allows them to learn the main features of all of the products in their section so that they can provide professional advice.

Source: adapted from www.dixons.co.uk.

- 66 Digital Camera
- 9 SLR cameras
- 3 disposable cameras
- 8 compact cameras
- 36 Digital Camcorders
- 1 analogue Camcorder
- 58 MP3 and Digital Audio Players
- 66 Apple iPod
- 8 Napster Compatible Digital Audio Players
- 31 Personal CD Players
- 41 Portable CD Stereos

Source: adapted from www.dixons.co.uk.

Select any business (other than a public library) that you have good access to and carry out the following tasks.

Table 4 *Andover library*

Tasks	Examples from Andover Library
1. Describe the purpose the business.	Lending books and music to the general public. Allowing customers to use the reference section. Providing introductory courses for adults and events for children.
2. Draw the layout of the business's premises.	This should be done by visiting the premises and noting down all of the main features such as shelving, displays, counters and specialist rooms.
3. List the different types of customers.	(a) Borrowers for recreational reading, but also for research. (b) The staff. (c) The government which pays for the service and expects access for all.
4. Describe what is important to them in terms of layout.	(a) Well laid out shelves, clearly labelled so they can find books, etc. on the topics they are particularly interested in. (b) Need to be able to check books in and out which is well located in Andover at the entrance, but have private areas for breaks. (c) Government will expect layout to meet legal requirements. There is a lift for the disabled, wide access.
5. Evaluate how well these needs are being met.	(a) The public uses the library regularly and finds the layout clear and helpful. The tables available for people who want to research are occasionally crowded. (b) Staff can move easily throughout the library as it is spacious and can therefore carry out all of their duties efficiently. (c) Access into and around the library is good but books are stacked on shelves some of which are out of reach of someone in a wheelchair.

Source: author research.

Research task

Meeting the assessment criteria

For your chosen organisation you will need to consider how effectively businesses provide customer service. You will need to consider all of the elements that help to ensure that efffective service is being provided. This will involve a consideration of the layout of premises and the quality of the products and services provided by the businesses.

Business example - Dyson

Figure 6 shows the efficiency of the Dyson Dual Cyclone vacuum cleaner and the Dyson Root Cyclone vacuum cleaner compared to conventional bag and bagless vacuum cleaners. The Dual Cyclone has been taken as the standard measure and the other vacuum cleaners compared to that.

The laboratory tests showed that both Dyson products lost no suction power as they collected more and more dust. The performance of the bag and bagless standard vacuum cleaners lost suction as soon as they started to collect dust and by the time they had collected 250 grammes of dust their suction performance was cut to 40% or less of that of the Dyson products.

Source: adapted from www.dyson.co.uk.

Figure 6 *Suction measured in air watts compared to the Dyson Dual Cyclone*

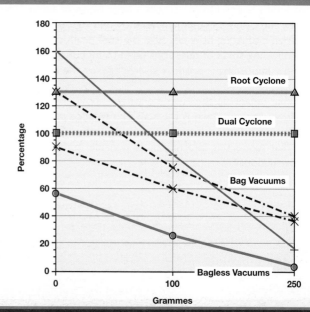

Mark Band 1 *Basic evaluation of the product quality with basic recommendations.*

This would use the laboratory research to state the clear conclusion that Dyson's products are ahead of the field by the suction measure. Further research on the Dyson products would show how this was achieved, noting the difference in technology between the Dual Cyclone and the Root Cyclone. Consideration should be given to the needs of the customers and the importance to them of having very high performance in terms of removing dust. At this stage all of the features of products should be considered including the different nozzles, the weight, the durability, ease of cleaning it and the manoeuvrability. Where there are any concerns about the quality, basic recommendation should be made as to how this could be improved.

Mark Band 2 *Sound evaluation of the product quality with showing judgement in what data is selected and presented and with conclusion supported and some recommendations.*

At this level different sources of information should be used and not just that of the company. Users could be interviewed, press reports checked and websites such as www.vacuumcleanerexpert.com looked at. The evaluation should then be two sided and conclusions about the strengths and weaknesses of the products supported by sound reasoning, such

as competitors products were also tested but performed significantly worse as the dust clogged up the filters. Dyson's products do not have this problem because they have no filters and the dust is forced to the bottom of the collection unit by the cyclical motion of the air. Negative critical reviews of the product also need to be evaluated.

Mark Band 3 *Detailed evaluation of the product quality with clear judgements, fully supported conclusions and appropriate recommendations.*

The evaluation is about a specific business so all of its products should be included and assessed in terms of quality. At this level additional criteria need to be introduced, such as does the quality justify the relatively high price, how easy is it to get replacement parts, can it clean right up to the edge of the room without using the attachments? The conclusions should also be fully justified, for example noting that laboratory tests was done using an industry standard IEC 60312 DMT Type 8 dust composition test. Recommendations also need to fully justified, for example, giving well researched and argued reasons why Dyson should move to the Root Cyclone technology and how much of the business should be centred on the new 2 drum washing machine technology.

Portfolio practice · Jevons Design and Print

Jevons Design and Print is a designer and printer of leaflets. It has a small design studio next to a print shop located next to a motorway junction. It has an excellent local reputation for design and is often innovative, producing designs which are then imitated by competitors. Nearly all of its customers come from the North West area. Many customers prefer to pick up the their leaflets themselves after printing.

The five designers at the business work on G5 Apple Macintosh computers with 20 inch screens, each located at a workstation on their own desk. When a job comes in it is placed into an inbox located on a central desk in the studio. Each station also has stacked shelving with intrays and outtrays for jobs which are allocated and storage areas for other materials, such as reference material or CD Roms. The transfer of materials from one intray to another can sometimes be a problem unless the customer has clearly labelled all materials. Even then, artwork can sometimes get lost if a particular job is shared amongst a number of staff. Scanning of photographs is done

away from the design area. There is a large area of the studio which is not used.

The print area has two large presses. These take up much of the space on the print floor. The rest of the area is used for storage of materials and finished products. The three production staff often find it difficult to negotiate their way between presses. This can sometimes delay jobs.

Table 5 shows the relative prices and turnaround times for printing a 10,000, full colour leaflet job of a number of printers, including the design element.

(a) List the (i) strengths and (ii) weaknesses of Jevons.
(b) Evaluate the position of Jevons in relation to its competitors.
(c) (i) Evaluate the efficiency of the service that Jevons is providing for its internal and external customers and (ii) recommend changes it might make to improve its service.

Table 5 *Printer comparison*

Printer	Location	Price	Turnaround
Jevons	North West	£2,200	7 days
Printer A	London	£3,000	5 days
Printer B	Spain	£2,000	3 weeks
Printer C	Manchester	£5,000	3 days

Source: adapted from company information.

Communication and customer service

Customer service in business is often poor because there is a problem with communication somewhere in the organisation. When, for example, free delivery is offered to customers but the goods are delivered to the wrong house because the sales staff took the address down incorrectly, that is likely to make the benefit of free delivery considerably less attractive in the eyes of the customer. Similarly, when a customer in a restaurant spends fifteen minutes studying the menu before choosing the Duck a la Bordelaise he or she does not want to be told 'Sorry, duck is off' and then have to choose all over again. Good customer service would have been to change the menu and tell customers about the changes.

For communication to be effective it is important that the message that is intended to be sent actually gets across and is understood.

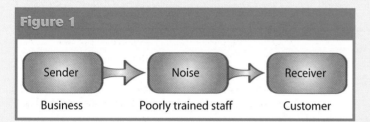

Figure 1

Sender → Noise → Receiver

Business — Poorly trained staff — Customer

The sender needs to think carefully about what the main message is and what will be the best way to get the message across. There are many reasons why the wrong message may be received including:

- not enough care was taken in preparing it;
- the wrong method of communication was chosen;
- something happened as it was sent which either stopped the message getting through or distorted it - known as noise, as shown in Figure 1;
- the receiver did something to stop the message getting through, for example throwing mail in the bin without reading it.

The way in which a message needs to be constructed and sent in order to be effective will depend very heavily on what the message is and who the sender and receiver are. The apparently simple message from staff to customers that they are there to help is conveyed in all of the following ways.

- A sales assistant in a shoe store asking customers 'Can I help you' as they enter the store.
- Sales staff manning the Customer Service Desk in a supermarket.
- A buzzer at the side of a patient's bed in hospital.
- A notice on the bottom of a flyer giving a telephone number and saying 'Please ring for further information'.
- The tannoy on a ferry being used to announce that the information desk is on level three.

It is also important for a business to know that its message has been received and understood by its customers. It therefore

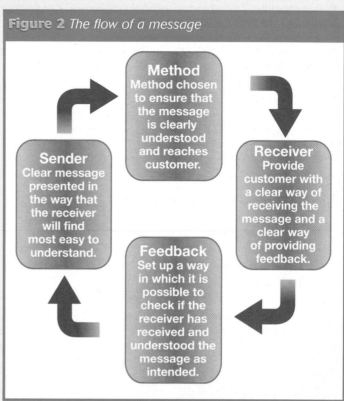

Figure 2 *The flow of a message*

Sender
Clear message presented in the way that the receiver will find most easy to understand.

Method
Method chosen to ensure that the message is clearly understood and reaches customer.

Receiver
Provide customer with a clear way of receiving the message and a clear way of providing feedback.

Feedback
Set up a way in which it is possible to check if the receiver has received and understood the message as intended.

needs to ensure that it receives feedback from the customer. The normal flow of a message should be as shown in Figure 2.

When evaluating the effectiveness of different methods of communication the primary questions that need to be asked are, did the message get through to the customer as intended, and if not what changes should be made in the future to ensure that it does? These questions apply to all methods of communication. Further questions should be asked to evaluate the effectiveness of specific methods of communication and these are listed after each method below.

Methods of communication

There are many different methods of communication. This section will look at the most common in business. It will also look at ones that are particularly appropriate for

Table 1 *Communication methods*

Spoken	Written
• Meetings.	• Memos.
• Speeches.	• Letters.
• Interviews.	• Reports.
• Talking to staff or customers.	• Notices.

Visual	Electronic
• Sign language.	• E-mail.
• Body language.	• Television.
• Posters.	• EPOS.
• Photographs.	• Surveillance cameras.

communications to external customers and those that are appropriate for internal customers. It will consider the questions that should be asked when evaluating the effect of the communication on customer service.

The main ways of communication are **spoken**, **written**, **visual**, and **electronic**. Common examples are shown in Table 1.

Face to face communication

Face-to-face is still the most common method of communication, although the growth of e-commerce through the Internet is beginning to change that. Face-to-face does not just include people talking to each other. It is important that staff realise that messages are being conveyed in other ways as well, for example through a handshake, pointing, facial expressions and body language. Some common examples of face-to-face communications are shown in Figure 3.

Figure 3 *Face-to-face communication in business*

When external customers visit stores, offices and other places where goods are being sold or services offered.

Internal customers on a day-to-day basis as staff talk to each other and in appraisal meetings, departmental meetings and interviews.

When evaluating the effectiveness of face-to-face communicating the following sort of questions should be considered.
- Was the member of staff's body language positive?
- Did the member of staff listen to the customer carefully?
- Was any written record kept?
- How were confidential matters dealt with?
- Was it useful to show the customer something, for example how to use the product correctly?
- Was the customer, internal or external, put at their ease when being interviewed?

Written communications

The potential range of written communication is huge, from writing down an address so that a customer can write to head office, to a 500 page report on a new marketing plan so that the Directors can decide whether or not to spend the businesses capital on developing a new product. Below are three examples of written communication which show this difference.

A legal contract A contract between one business and another, or being provided by a solicitor for a customer selling their house, needs to be very detailed and specific. The detail will be very thorough and the language very technical. The reason for this is that if there was any dispute between the buyer and the seller it may have to be settled in court and the lawyers and judge will decide which side will win on the basis of what was actually written in the contract.

Contracts are, therefore, very formal, as are most business letters, notices about health and safety regulations and job application forms. For these types of communication precise and accurate information is vital.

Memorandums and post-it notes These are short reminders and will use few words to convey the basic message. E-mails are also usually short. These types of communication need to be very precise because there are so few words to refer to and having to go back to the person who wrote them is often a major waste of time.

Financial documents Business accounts, invoices and purchase orders above all need to be accurate. They are usually set out in a very structured way so that customers know exactly what they are communicating. Even a fairly simple financial document such as a receipt has a wide range of details on it and is laid out so that the customer knows where to find each part.

When evaluating the effectiveness of written communications the following sort of questions should be considered.
- How clear is the writing, printing and language because the sender may not be available to explain?
- Does the message need to be kept, if so, is it on something that can be easily kept?
- Does it contain all the needed information?
- Are long documents well laid out so that it is easy to find the part that is needed?
- How confidential is the message?
- How quickly does it need to be communicated?
- Does the message need to given to many people at the same time?

Visual communications

These are in addition to the face-to-face communications from staff to customers. They include all of the following.
- **Signage** showing customers where to go inside shops and offices, as with signs showing what is in each aisle in a supermarket. Signage would include pointing out fire exits. These need to be clear, short and visible.
- **Advertisements, posters and billboards**. These need to be attractive and eye catching, but also persuasive and informative.
- **Television, film, video, DVD and presentations on OHP and PowerPoint**. These use images to get the message over so careful design, editing and presentation are important. They also need equipment or space for viewing and the business must ensure that the customers have access to these.
- **Staff** in terms of what they wear, how they behave, how smart they are, all create an image of the business.
- **The premises** also create an image of the business and customers will notice if it is dirty, there is rubbish about,

there are cracks in the walls and the paint is peeling.

- **The product** should also be displayed so that it looks important and attractive, is well packaged, and suggests quality.

When evaluating the effectiveness of visual communications the following sort of questions should be considered.

- Would the use of colour make the message more clearly understood?
- Is the visual message being displayed in the right place?
- Is the time length of the visual image correct? If it is too long customers may lose interest.
- Is the balance between persuasion and information right?

Electronic communications

As new technologies develop more and more of the messages that a business sends to its customer, and the other way round, are electronic. These include all of the methods shown in Figure 4.

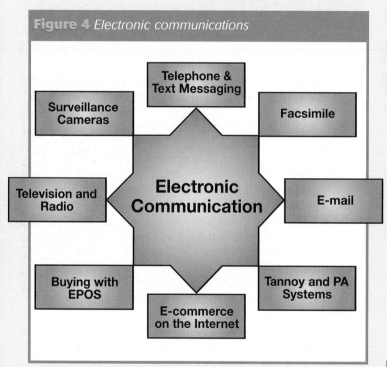

Figure 4 *Electronic communications*

Some of these electronic methods are two way, as with a telephone or video conferencing and it is possible for the people involved to talk to each other, ask questions and check if the message is understood. Video conferencing allows the people to see each other as well so it is possible to observe body language.

Other methods simply send a message which it may or may not be able to respond to using the same method. Texting and e-mails can be replied to fairly easily, but the messages sent by television, radio or public address system and collected by a surveillance camera are only one way, and a different method is needed for further communication. This means that the message needs to be very clear because it is not easy to check what it

means if there is any confusion.

The major benefits of electronic communications are that they can be very quick, can be used over long distances and usually provide an automatic way of storing the message. With Electronic Point of Sale (EPOS) data is taken automatically when a customer uses a debit or credit card and, if they have a loyalty card as well, all of the information about how much has been spent, what was bought and how often is matched to a profile of the customer.

Today e-commerce, buying and selling through the Internet, is growing rapidly. That means that businesses need to consider how to provide the best customer service possible through their website. Easy navigation, wide choice, easy and secure payment methods, clear instructions on how to buy, providing a way to contact the business for further information, all have to be thought about.

Customers also now expect to have an electronic method of communication with the business, such as home shopping facilities on the Internet, on-line banking, on-line betting, 24-hour news programmes, and digital interactive television. However, care needs to be taken with these communication methods, as shown in Figure 5.

When evaluating the effectiveness of electronic communications the following sort of questions should be considered.

- Does the customer have the right technology to receive and send messages?
- Is there another method of communication easily available if the technology breaks down?
- How secure is the data that is passed electronically, especially confidential financial information such as credit card numbers?
- How easy is it to make the messages personal so that customers feel important?
- Can the customer choose whether or not to receive the message?
- Where the message is only one way how can the sender check that it has been received?

Figure 5 *On-line communication and security*

In July 2005 a man was sentenced to six years in prison for stealing up to £6.5 million, through gaining and using customers' account details on-line. In the same month a survey of 1,500 people was published which showed that 13% of e-banking customers had stopped banking on-line, and 12% of people buying goods on-line had stopped shopping on-line. The main reason given was that they did not trust the security.

Source: adapted from www.bbc.co.uk.

Use one of the following sources to provide the information for this portfolio practice.
- Your school or college.
- The place where you work if you have a part-time job.
- Where you have been at work experience.
- A business that you visit regularly.
1. Make a list of all of the different customers, both internal and external, that the business has. This may require additional research if you do not have direct knowledge of these.
2. Outline the types of messages that need to be communicated to and from each of these customers, and the basic purpose of the messages.
3. Identify the methods of communication that are used for these messages and evaluate how effective they are.
4. Consider how the communications in the business could be improved and provide justifications for any suggested improvements.

Research task

Meeting the assessment criteria

For your chosen organisation you will need to consider how effectively businesses provide customer service. You will need to consider all of the elements that help to ensure that effective service is being provided. This will involve a consideration of the importance of communication in providing an effective service and in presenting the right image to customers.

Business example - Body Shop

Figure 6 shows the homepage of Body Shop UK's website for August 2005. In evaluating the effectiveness of this website as a method of communication, it would be important to check both what was on this home page and what was on the other link pages. Even on this front page there is a great number of different messages being sent. The comments made below about the website in terms of meeting the Mark Band criteria will use both this page and the other links..

Mark Band 1 *Basic evaluation of communications with a description of the various methods used.*
This would identify the web base for the communication but also refer to the use of text and pictures and links to other pages. It would note the feature such as a search facility and named other pages at the top of page or through the drop down menu. The basic evaluation could be made on ease of use, clarity of instructions, attractiveness of the pages and the facilities being offered such as the store locator and the very wide database of products. Basic weaknesses might list the lack of prices, the fact that you cannot locate stores by clicking on the UK map, etc.

Mark Band 2 *Sound evaluation of communications with thought about which are the most important ones for the business and recommendations for improvements with clear reasons for each.*
At Mark Band 2 clear reasons should be given for why the communications are good or bad. Thought needs to be given to what message each part of the website is trying to get across and to whom. There are many different customers catered for here from shoppers to people seeking employment and students studying the business. Does the web site deal effectively with each of these groups? For this assessment band there should also

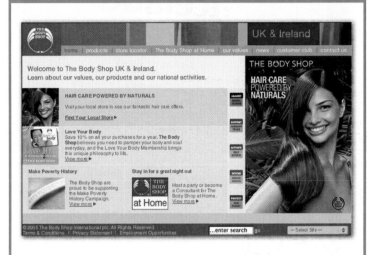

Figure 6 *Body Shop website*

Source: www.uk.thebodyshop.com/web/tbsuk.

be recommendations for improvements which could include changing the way the website communicates, or recommending better ways of communicating the messages.

Mark Band 3 *Detailed evaluation of communications with clear judgements, fully supported conclusions and appropriate recommendations.*
For Mark Band 3 the evaluation must be in depth, considering the wide range of communication that is provided and matching these to the needs of the different customers. The facilities should be looked at in detail and positive and negative conclusions supported with evidence and justifications. For example, if 'cats' is typed into the search facility the only result is about 'cuts'. On the other hand if students are looking for details and examples of the Body Shop's approach to environmental and social issues there are many pages of information and links to policy statements and a library of references. Recommendation for improvements need to be based on careful research and full justifications.

Portfolio practice · Iceland

Iceland is a retailer of frozen food products. Figures 7 to 11 show four methods of communication used by the business to convey information to customers.

Source: adapted from *The Guardian*, 18.12.2004.

(a) **Identify the information that is being communicated in each medium.**
(b) **Explain the strengths and weaknesses of each communication medium.**
(c) **Iceland has over 700 UK stores. 250 of these sell home appliances. For all the possible media available to Iceland, evaluate the most effective for communicating this information to customers.**

Figure 9

Figure 7

Iceland

Iceland Foods Limited

98 Queensmead
Farnborough
Store Tel: 01252 520851
Showroom: 01252 370249
Your Store Manager is
Tony
You were served today by
ADAM

```
                                    £
0036913 Kumala Chardonnay WI  3.99
0036913 Kumala Chardonnay WI  3.99
0036913 Kumala Chardonnay WI  3.99
                             -1.97
   *        **MULTISAVE**

****                        BAL 10.00
```

Figure 10

Figure 8

Iceland Home Home delivery Store locator Appliances Contact us

Welcome to Iceland.co.uk

Home Delivery
Why struggle with heavy bags? We'll deliver them FREE* direct to your door!
Find out more ▶

Store Locator
Looking for your nearest Iceland store? Let us help you.
Take a look ▶

Appliances
Deal of the Week! Save £130
Buy online ▶

Millions of entry and discount tickets to be won
Choose from 5 of the UK's top attractions.
▶

Job opportunities
Take a look at our latest vacancies.
▶

About Iceland
We offer great products at clear-cut prices.
▶

© Iceland Foods Ltd 2005

Figure 11

At Christmas 2004 Iceland advertised its products on television showing a family skating and arranging a whopping banquet, with numerous processed meats and snacks.

Balancing the needs of the customers and the organisation

Section 52 looked at the importance of customer service in general terms. Sections 53-58 considered how the individual needs of customers affect the type of customer service that should be provided. This section looks at how customer service affects the organisation itself.

All stakeholders in a business have their own wants and needs, including the business itself, represented by the shareholders and owners. Sometimes the needs of different stakeholders will be the same, as should occur in a school or college, where parents, students, teachers, senior management, support staff and the government are all working to provide high quality education for the students. But in many situations the wants of the different stakeholders actually conflict.

Figure 1 shows typical demands placed on the money that a commercial business makes. Generally if one customer benefits in terms of pay, profits, taxes or prices, the other customers will lose out.

For the business, in the end, there is also a specific objective, such as making high profits for the shareholders, or raising funds for charities, or providing the highest education possible on a limited budget. The business needs to ensure that in meeting the needs of the various customers, it does not finish up failing to meet its basic objective.

Many successful businesses have managed to balance the needs of most, and occasionally all, of their customers. Some supermarkets, for example, are able to keep prices low for buying customers, offer staff competitive rates of pay, earn very attractive profits for their shareholders and raise very significant levels of taxation for the state. However, suppliers may complain that the supermarket is heavy handed and forces them to take lower payments for their goods than they feel they should be receiving. Meeting the customers' demands for a wide variety of fresh fruit and vegetables all year round often means very high food miles and the use of lorries, ships and planes that pollute the atmosphere.

Balancing the needs of different customers

It is unusual for all customers' needs to be met all of the time. When the needs of different customers conflict the business will have to decide which needs will or will not be met, and, when certain needs are not going to met, how to still keep the customers happy with the business. Table 1 shows some conflict situations and how the business might reduce any negative effects of them.

Table 1 shows examples of potentially major areas of conflict. But for businesses there are likely to be more individual situations.

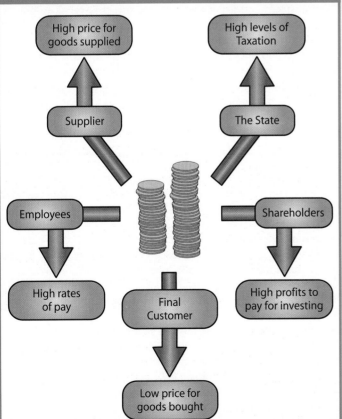

Figure 1 Demands on the organisation

Table 1 Conflict situations

Situation	Possible solutions
Employees feel that they are not getting enough pay whilst profits are very high.	• Offer other benefits such as discounts on the firm's products. • Provide a high quality work environment. • Reward employees with shares in the business so that they can share in the profits.
Suppliers feel they are being exploited and paid less than they should be.	• Offer long term contracts so suppliers can feel secure about the future. • Give bonuses to the suppliers if their products sell particularly well. • Treat each supplier as an equal when discussing prices, for example.
Local residents complain that traffic to and from the business at rush hour is causing noise pollution and congestion.	• Consider changing the shifts in the business so that they do not coincide with the rush hour. • Put pressure on the local council to improve road layouts near the business. • Organise events, provide sponsorship for local interest groups so that the community feels more a part of the business.

- Which member of staff will be offered promotion when a senior job becomes free?
- How will a restaurant cater for smoking and non-smoking customers?
- How will a supermarket cater for customers with just a few items and not upset those with a trolley load?
- How should a business with limited car parking distribute these spaces between staff and other customers?
- Should a hospital allow visitors at any time or only when it is convenient for staff?

When evaluating the effectiveness of the way in which a business copes with the conflicting needs of different customers the following steps need to be considered.

- Identify clearly what the needs of each customer are and how they conflict.
- Decide, giving justifications, which are the most important needs and whether one customer's needs are more important than the others'.
- Describe how the business is meeting the needs and which needs are not being meet.
- Identify any ways in which the business provides different services for customers whose main needs are not being met.
- Evaluate how well all services that are being provided meet the main, or secondary, needs of the customers.

Customer lifetime value

Businesses also need to think carefully about what will happen if they do not treat customers correctly and they decide to go to another business. With most products customers will either repeat buy, as with grocery shopping or going to the dentist, or they will up-grade as with buying computers or cars. In both cases the business wants to ensure that the service provided for the first purchase is so good that it persuades the customer to come back again and again.

Many businesses now think about their customers in terms of what they could, or will, spend over their lifetime of dealing with the business. This is known as **customer lifetime value**.

Customer lifetime value is not just the total money that will be spent with the business that is important in working out what this value is. The business will need to consider various costs and benefits of keeping, or losing a customer. These include:

- the cost of attracting the customers to the business in the first place;
- the cost of retaining them with targeted offers;
- the cost of getting them back if for any reason they leave;
- any negative comments made to other potential or actual customers if customers leave because they are dissatisfied;
- the total likely amount spent whilst the customers are with the business;
- the positive publicity that satisfied customers will give to friends and acquaintances;
- the longer the customers are with the business the more information it should have on them so that it can effectively target promotions or special offers.

Mission statements, customer charters and pledges

Most businesses recognise the importance of not only meeting customers' needs but being seen to meet them. They, therefore, publish statements of intent about how they will meet the needs of their customers and this gives a basis on which their customer service can be evaluated.

Mission statements A mission statement is a basic statement of the fundamental purpose of a business. It is what the business is trying to achieve. It can be very short and general as with Walt Disney's statement 'To make people happy.' The Courtyard Theatre Training Company has a much more detailed mission statement, as shown in Figure 2.

Figure 2 *Courtyard Theatre Training Company mission statement*

The underpinning philosophy of the company is that the best training for a life in the theatre is to work in the theatre. Guided and stretched by experienced professional practitioners, you are part of a company learning your craft by active involvement in every aspect of theatre.
You will be exposed to all pressures of professional life therefore learning accordingly. The Company has established a fine reputation for the continuing quality of its work, which is a tribute to the training methods used.
You train as you work - a genuine 'hands-on' programme of productions with a professional paying audience. Courtyard is production orientated with training integrated thematically around the productions.

Source: adapted from www.thecourtyard.org.uk/mission.htm.

Mission statements are always made so that they relate to one or more of the business's customers. Frequently they are fairly general and, because they are intended for publication, they tend to make claims about how good the business is and what positive objectives it has for its customers. Generally businesses do not state that they are in business to make profits. But in reality most commercial businesses do have high profits as a major mission for their shareholders and owners.

Mission statements vary considerably from one business to another and it is sometimes quite difficult to work out exactly what the mission is. Some businesses make statements about what they do rather than what their mission is. Some businesses also make mission statements as part of their statements on corporate responsibility.

Examples of mission statements for well known UK organisations are shown in Table 2.

When evaluating the effectiveness of a business in terms of what its mission statement states, the following questions need to be considered.

- What is the mission statement actually claiming is the purpose of the business?
- Which customers is the mission statement aimed at?
- Are there other business objectives that are just as important, such as making profits for the shareholders, that have not been put into the mission statement?
- How well does the business meet the objectives stated in the mission statement?

Table 2 *Mission statements*

Business	Mission statement
Superdrug Stores (retail chemists)	Our mission is to be the customer's favourite, up-to-the-minute health and beauty shop, loved for its value, choice, friendliness and fun.
Metropolitan Police	To make places safer. To cut crime and the fear of crime. To uphold the law.
Scottish & Newcastle (Brewer)	Our mission is backed by four strategic objectives. - Brand growth. - Total innovation. - Most efficient operations. - The best team.
Oxfam (Charity)	Oxfam works with others to overcome poverty and suffering.
Dixons	In a rapidly growing business, it is important to remember our shared purpose. '**Being the Best**' sets out for the Group how we want to do business. That means: - operating with integrity; - giving outstanding service to customers; - respecting our colleagues; - continually seeking ways to improve performance; - and, of course, working together to beat the competition.

Source: adapted from company websites.

Customer charters

A mission statement makes a statement of intent, but it does not provide any provision for the customer if that intent is not met. Businesses have, therefore, created charters which clearly set out a list of specific objectives that the business agrees to be judged by, and a list of actions or remedies that the customer is entitled to if the stated objectives are not met. An example is shown in Figure 3.

Figure 3 *Customer charter of British Waterways*

British Waterways

Customer Charter

Charter Mark
British Waterways holds the Charter Mark, a recognition awarded by the government to public sector organisations that have excelled in terms of customer service.

The Charter Mark scheme aims to help organisations make real improvements in the delivery of services. The benefits to the Charter Mark holder are not just the satisfaction of offering an improved service, but also the feedback and recognition that guides development and boosts staff morale.

Our commitments under our Customer Charter
We work hard to meet the rising expectations of our customers, and to help us meet those expectations we carry out a regular programme of surveys of our [...] results have told us that 95% of boaters rated the [...] very good and 95% of towpath visitors said they [...] enjoyment of their visit. However, we [...] for further improvements.

Figure 4 *Customer charter of Cardiff Local Authority Building Control Section*

- The right to expect a polite, friendly, courteous and helpful service from staff.
- Forms, information and guidance leaflets that are clear, unambiguous and easy to follow and complete.
- A letter acknowledging the receipt of your application sent within 3 working days of receipt.
- All plans checked within a target of ten working days.
- An enforceable right to expect a decision within 5 weeks of submission.
- To answer all calls within 5 rings.
- If an inspection is asked for before 10:00 a.m. we guarantee to come and see you the same day.
- Response to all reported dangerous structures within 1 hour if there is an immediate danger to members of the public and within 24 hours in all other cases.

If any part of the service has not reached the standards outlined customers are invited to contact the Building Control Manager.

Cardiff Local Authority has a customer charter for its Building Control Section, dealing with public buildings in the authority. It contains the provisions shown in Figure 4.

When evaluating the effectiveness of a business in terms of what its customer charter states the following steps should be taken.
- Note carefully what the charter states about the business and what the minimum customer service will be.
- Evaluate the business's customer service against these minimum standards.

Other pledges

Some businesses make their commitments to their customers in the form of a pledge. These may be mission statements or even parts of a customer charter. There are also pledges that are too specific or short term to put into either a mission statement or a customer charter. Examples would include:
- Esso's price watch pledge to at least match the prices in local petrol stations;
- The Officers Club mid-season sale with fashion shirts at £3 and fashion trousers at £4, while stocks last;
- United Co-operatives' pledge to donate £100,000, the equivalent of a day's profit, to the relief effort following the Tsunami disaster.

The impact of effective and ineffective customer service on the organisation

This has been briefly covered in section 52 and details about keeping records and improving customer service will be covered in the sections that follow.

The major effects of poor customer service are likely to be the loss of customers and poor publicity, both of which are likely to lead to lower sales and the loss of market share and profits. An example is shown in Figure 5.

In contrast the positive publicity of consistently good customer

Figure 5 *NTL*

In 2001 Ciao, the on-line community that critically reviews and rates millions of products and services for the benefit of other consumers, asked its members to review NTL, the communications business. Members graded it fourth out of 11 landline companies but when it came to customer service the comments were very negative and included 'Their customer service is terrible', 'Long queues when contacting customer services' and 'Customer service is appalling, once you actually get through, (usually about 20 mins), they promise you the earth and deliver nothing.'

The BBC Watchdog programme reported in February 2005 on the hundreds of viewers who had written in to complain about the service provided by NTL. Watchdog then highlighted three examples of very poor service. NTL apologised unreservedly and aimed to improve in future, but the damage of the negative publicity was arguably already done.

Source: adapted from watchdog and www.ciao.co.uk.

Table 3 *Customer Service Team of the Year finalists, 2005*

Team or location	Business
Customer Care	Clarks International
Customer Care Department	Iceland Foods
Normanby	Ladbrokes Ltd
South Ruislip	Sainsbury's Supermarkets

service will encourage customers to use the service. Publicity would include word-of-mouth comments by customers, news reports, and awards such as the National Customer Service Awards. The award for the Customer Service Team of the Year in retailing is given for a team that demonstrate commitment to high standards of customer service in their organisation, both through personal dealings with customers and by contributing to the overall customer care policy by their involvement in communications, problem solving and innovation. The finalists for 2005 are shown in Table 3.

1. Using businesses' websites, advertisements in flyers, newspapers, magazines or on the television, or visits to business outlets, identify one pledge from six different businesses.
2. For each pledge identify how that pledge will benefit the customer and what conflict that might create for the business and for other customers of the business.

For example, Specsavers' customer promise from its website states 'We want you to be completely happy with your purchase at Specsavers Opticians. If you have any concerns within six months of the date of purchase, we will put it right. No quibble, no fuss.' This give buyers the chance to have any concerns put right up to six months from purchase and if there is to be no quibble and no fuss that should be done free of charge and should allow dissatisfied customers to return goods. Staff must also respond positively to any concern however silly it seems. For Specsavers this could be expensive and it could waste valuable staff time if concerns include complaints that glasses keep getting dirty. This could also put added stress on staff.

Research task

Portfolio practice · Abbey National Restructuring

As part of its Corporate Responsibility statement on the Workplace, Abbey National stated 'Our aim is to make Abbey a place people want to join, give their best, love to stay and are proud to be part of.'

Following the takeover of Abbey National by Spain's Banco Santander Central Hispano (BSCH) in November 2004, there was a drive to reduce costs by £150 million by the end of 2005. In order to achieve this, a total of 4,000 jobs will be cut, or about one sixth of the total workforce. Major cuts will come from its IT division in Milton Keynes with a loss of 200 jobs although 50 staff are being offered redeployment at BSCH's IT subsidiary Isban, also located at Milton Keynes.

By June 2005 Abbey had already reduced the workforce by 3,000 and cut costs by £101 mil. This has helped profits for the sixth months to June 2005 to stay much the same at £294 mil even though total revenue fell by £59 mil. Market share has risen from 8.2% to 9.2% with improvements in revenues from bank accounts, credit cards, unsecured loans

and investment products.

Source: adapted from media news and company reports.

(a) Identify the internal and external customers referred to in the data.
(b) For each type of customer identified describe the effect that the changes announced by BSCH will have upon them.
(c) Evaluate how well BSCH has balanced the needs of the customers and the organisation.
(d) Suggest, and justify, any other actions that BSCH might have taken to ensure effective customer service.

Meeting the assessment criteria

For your chosen organisation you will need to consider how effectively businesses provide customer service. You will need to consider all of the elements that help to ensure that effective service is being provided. This will involve a consideration of how a business meets the needs of its customers without compromising its own needs. It also involves considering the impact of ineffective customer service.

Business example - Translink's Passenger Charter

Northern Ireland's Translink is a brand name introduced in late 1996 to cover the integrated services of Ulsterbus, Citybus (now Metro) and Northern Ireland Railways (NIR). Translink, a state owned company, has been given a specific objective to reposition the railway as an attractive and viable travel option and to meet the growth targets of the Regional Transportation Strategy. To achieve this, all aspects of service must be transformed to attract greater passenger numbers. Translink has therefore published a Passenger Charter. Full details are available from www.nirailways.co.uk/peoplescharter.asp. As part of this charter Translink is committed to the following performance targets shown in Table 4.

Table 4 *Performance targets of Translink*

- 99.2% of all buses and trains will run as planned.
- 99.5% of trains on the Dublin line will run as planned.
- 95% of all buses will arrive no more than seven minutes late.
- 95% of trains on the Bangor line, Portadown line and Larne line will arrive no more than five minutes late, and 85% will arrive on time.
- 90% of trains on the Dublin line, Londonderry line and Portrush line will arrive no more than 10 minutes late.
- When planned essential engineering work is required, we will give you at least 28 days' notice of possible delays and diversions caused by this work.

Source: adapted from Translink Passenger Charter at www.nirailways.co.uk/peoplescharter.asp.

Table 5 *General Consumer Council for Northern Ireland, performance of Translink*

	Charter target	Citybus	Ulsterbus	NIR
Reliability	99.2	99.0	99.6	99.4
Punctuality				
Buses (% of buses no more than 7 minutes late)	95%	90%	93%	-
NIR Dublin/Londonderry Lines (% of trains arriving within 10 minutes of published time)	90%	-	-	94%
NIR Bangor, Portadown & Larne Lines (% of trains arriving within 5 minutes of published time)	95%	-	-	88%

In April 2005 the General Consumer Council for Northern Ireland published the following findings on the performance of Translink, as shown in Table 5.

When passengers were asked to rate punctuality of services 53 per cent of Citybus passengers, 54 per cent of NIR passengers and 78 per cent of Ulsterbus passengers said that they believed punctuality to be good.

Source: adapted from General Consumer Council for Northern Ireland report at www.gccni.org.uk/press/article/id/247.

Mark Band 1 *Basic evaluation of meeting the needs of the customer and how this affects the organisation with basic recommendations.*
To meet the basic evaluation the declared performance targets should be compared to the General Consumer Council's data, stressing those targets which were met and those which were not.

There should also be a basic recognition of the nature of the organisation, which is state owned, and the overall objective of making rail and bus transport an effective alternative to the car.

Basic recommendation should then be focused on which parts of the service need to be improved to meet the targets and, as this is state owned, what Translink, or the government should do about the shortfalls.

Mark Band 2 *Sound evaluation of meeting the needs of the customer and how this affects the organisation showing judgement in the selection and presentation of findings with supported conclusions and recommendations.*
This should take into consideration all of the data shown. Comments would be expected on how close to the targets the services were, the relatively low levels of customers who rated punctuality as good and the targets not commented on by the General Consumer Council.

At Mark Band 2 it would be expected that other sources would be accessed such as press reports. For example it might be noted that Translink has, for the fifth year in a row, been short-listed for the prestigious UK bus 'Oscar' in the annual Bus Industry Awards.

Recommendations need to be justified, for example, the NIR Bangor, Portadown & Larne Lines clearly need major improvments because they are 7% points below target. Specific recommendation should be being made on the basis of study that indicates why this figure is so low.

Mark Band 3 *Detailed evaluation of meeting the needs of the customer and how this affects the organisation with clear judgements, fully supported conclusions and appropriate recommendations.*
At Mark Band 3 there needs to a more investigative approach that begins to assess why targets have not been met. It should also consider the role of the Northern Ireland Government in this, including the requirements laid down and the amount of money that was made available to implement the improvements in service.

Additional research should also show what actions are planned to correct the shortfalls on the targets, for example, the likely effects of the delivery of 23 new trainsets from Spain which are expected to be in service by the end of 2005.

It would also be expected that other elements of the Passenger Charter, not just performance, were assessed and commented on, as well as assessing the success of the basic overall objective of getting more people to move from using their cars to using public transport.

Why measuring is important

Before the quality of a business's customer service can be evaluated it needs to be measured. That may seem like a simple thing to do but it is often quite complex, as will be shown in this section and section 61.

Good customer service is often the main factor that distinguishes a business from its competitors. It is, therefore, vital for the business to know just how good its customer service is and if it can be improved. In order to check the current level of customer service and any improvements over time, there must be an accurate way of measuring it.

Measuring customer service will allow the business to:
* identify what is important to the customer;
* set minimum acceptable standards of service and then check if these are being met;
* identify specific areas where standards are not at an acceptable level and put in place procedures to correct this, such as staff training programmes;
* set targets for the future, which may also act as an incentive for staff.

Where there is no real measurement in a business it is quite possible that the business will have little idea of what is really important to customers and how well its expectations are being met. Often relatively minor changes that could be made to improve services are missed and the services continue to be poor.

Section 61 deals with common methods of collecting and analysing data. This section shows the basic ways of measuring customer service.

How is quality measured?

How customer service is measured will depend on what service is being provided. As there is a huge range of different customer services the basic ways of deciding on a suitable measure will be shown with examples, but the process will be the same for most, if not all, services.
* Identify what is involved in providing the service
* Check that this is really what the customer wants
* Decide on how the service will be measured
* Set up ways of in which the service can be regularly checked.

These steps are shown in Figure 1 for staff punctuality in a clothes store.

Before even this relatively simple measure for punctuality is set up and used, management would need to consider how long it takes staff to get ready after they have arrived and before they are in the store ready to serve customers. They also need to consider if this is paid working time and if it is not whether that is affecting the customer service that is provided to their employees.

In many cases what seems to be a simple customer service to measure is in fact very complex. Table 1 shows some of the factors that need to be considered when a business offers customers a delivery service.

Figure 1 *Setting up a measure for punctuality*

Punctuality means that staff arrive on time and are available to serve customers at the time agreed with their managers.

Customers want the store to open on time and for staff to be available to serve them when they are in the store.

Punctuality will be measured by when staff arrive against the time when they were supposed to arrive.

Staff will clock in. Punctuality will be checked every week by the manager.

Table 1 *Measuring customer service for deliveries*

Factor	Possible basis of measurement
Time of delivery	• Hours when delivery is possible. • How convenient is this for the customer on a scale of 1 to 10? • If late, how many minutes, hours, days?
Speed of delivery	• Hours, days between definite order, or buying, and delivery. • Time between loading and delivery in say, minutes per mile.
Area of delivery	• Districts or towns where delivery is free. • Radius for free delivery from the store. • Areas for which there is a charge. • Areas where delivery is not offered.
Safety of the product during delivery	• Number of complaints about damaged goods. • Checks made by staff before loading, on unloading and on unpacking.
Where delivery was not possible	• Number of non-deliveries. • Number of return trips. • Calls to customers to re-arrange delivery logged.

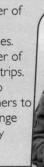

Figure 1 *UK Delivery Charges for 'tennisnuts.com'*

1. FREE delivery on all orders over £70. Charge of £5 for all orders under £70.
2. UK delivery will normally be within 2 to 4 working days from receipt of order.
3. UK 24 Hour (UK Mainland only) delivery is £5 EXTRA (ie £10 for orders under £70 and £5 for orders over £70. (NB 24 HR delivery will NOT be possible for goods ordered on Fridays).

If you need delivery on Saturdays, you need to ring 01923-827637 to arrange this.

Also ... 24 hr delivery MAY NOT be possible if goods are ordered after 1 pm on any given day.

Overseas Delivery Charges (excludes table tennis tables) (weight limit of 2 kg)
Northern Ireland, Republic of Ireland, Isles of Man, Scilly & White, Channel Islands (£8)
All European countries (£20)
USA and CANADA (£25)
Far East & Japan, Australia & Rest of the World (£40)

Source: adapted from www.tennisnuts.com/ishop/677/shopscr455.html.

Table 1 shows measurement of customer service for the external customers. There will also be customer service for internal customers such as other departments. These would include checking the delivery schedules, making certain that external customers signed the delivery note, collecting receipts for any petrol or diesel bought, recording times and destinations of journeys. Customer service for these would be measured by how often and how thoroughly these tasks were carried out.

When deciding on a basis for measurement it is important that it is something that is definite, easily measured and easily understood. Where services are similar then similar measures should be used as this will allow comparisons. It must also be fair and recognise that different situations may need different standards. If a supermarket has set a minimum number of items that must on average be scanned by staff at the checkout in a minute, it would be unfair to have the same minimum for a trainee.

Examples of how different customer services could be measured are shown below. For each measure there will be some agreed minimum standard that provides a **benchmark** against which the actual customer service will be measured.

Staff
• Appearance – comparison with an agreed standard of dress.
• Prompt service – time taken to greet customer, answer phones or check if items are in stock.
• Helpfulness – monitor entries on comment cards, create a list of what are helpful actions and record how often these are carried out.
• Reliability – number of repeat customers, periodic tests on product knowledge.

Premises
• Tidiness – quantity of litter, frequency of cleaning, frequency of inspections
• Accessibility – width of aisles, opening hours, number of lifts
• Well stocked – number of different products, number of items out of stock, number of items on shelves.

Quality of products
• Quality of goods – number of returns, sales figures
• Quality of services – number of complaints, sales figures
• Value for money – prices compared to competitors, repeat purchases, returns where there are no faults.

What needs to be measured will also depend on what type of business is making the checks on its customer service. Typical measures are shown for three different types of business below. For each, just one aspect of the business is considered.
In order to provide a detailed review and analysis of the quality of the customer service being provided by a business the starting point must be 'What measure was being used and was this the right measure for that particular customer service?'

Table 2 *Specific measurements in different businesses*

Business	Required measurements
Checkouts in a supermarket	• Speed of scanning items. • Length of queues. • Supply of bags and wine carriers. • How quickly supervisors respond to checkout staff's queries. • How closely the cash in the till matches the EPOS record. • Are staff being replaced on time?
Help line for computer business	• How quickly calls are answered. • Percentage of positive solutions over the phone. • How clearly instructions are given to the customer. • The accuracy of recording the customer's details and concerns and how the problems were resolved. • How frequently staff are being trained on new computers and new versions of software.
The egg packaging section of a major egg producer	• Accuracy of matching sizes of eggs to size indicated on the boxes. • Number of eggs that are cracked or broken. • Accuracy of labelling in terms of size and type of egg, best and sell by date.

Using either your school or college or where you work or go for recreation, carry out the following tasks.
1. Write down how you think the organisation will test how clean the premises are kept and state what the minimum standards should be.
2. Work out a scale that would show just how good or bad the cleanliness was.
3. Check the premises to see if it comes up to the standards that you have set and measure it on the scale you have created.
4. Discuss with the supervisor in charge of cleanliness how it is actually checked and what measures are used.
5. Compare the organisation's methods and standards to yours.

Research task

Portfolio practice · Customer service in the hotel industry

Table 3 shows the results of a survey carried out by the marketing information business Taylor Nelson Sofres into the service provided to customers in UK, French, Dutch and Belgian hotels. 2,500 mystery customer visits were used for the research.

(a) **Rank the questions in the order that you think would be most important for customers staying in a hotel.**
(b) **Explain how effective each of these measures is likely to be in terms of what the customers feel is important when staying at a hotel.**
(c) **Which country provided the best overall service? Justify your answer.**

Table 3 *Service provided by hotel staff in different EU countries*

	UK	France	Holland/Belgium
Did the waiter offer the wine of the month?	42%	19%	20%
Were you offered tea/coffee?	75%	47%	56%
In the restaurant, were you offered a drink before your meal?	73%	65%	72%
On checking out, were you asked if you had enjoyed your stay?	56%	41%	39%
Was the service efficient and professional?	85%	82%	78%
Were you acknowledged with a warm and friendly greeting?	88%	91%	9%
Were the reception staff clean and well presented?	98%	99%	100%
Were the toilets clean and well maintained?	94%	93%	83%
Was the bedroom clean and tidy?	96%	100%	93%
On arrival at breakfast, were you greeted in a warm and friendly fashion?	88%	76%	77%

Source: adapted from Taylor Nelson Sofres at www.hospitalitynet.org.

Meeting the assessment criteria

For your chosen organisations you will need to understand the importance of maintaining and improving the quality of customer service. This will involve a consideration of the techniques used to measure the quality of customer service.

Business example - Marks & Spencer

Table 4 shows Marks & Spencer's record on pesticide. Based on this table it could be argued that it was relatively poor. Since then it has made major changes in policy and is now rated by Friends of the Earth as the one of the two leading supermarkets in terms of dealing with pesticides.

Table 4 *Pesticide residues in supermarket food, 1998-2003*

Supermarket	Percentage of fruit and veg with residues	Number
Marks & Spencer	47	225
Safeway	43	674
Sainsbury's	42	1,217
Asda	42	884
Co-op	42	206
Tesco	42	1,493
Somerfield	41	241
Waitrose	41	210
Morrisons	39	325
Total	42	5,475

M&S has prohibited the use by its suppliers of 60 pesticides. Although some of these are banned in the UK already, the M&S prohibition will apply globally. 19 other pesticides can be used on a restricted basis only. M&S has committed to phasing out any pesticides which may pose health or environmental risks before they are officially banned. It has set targets for residue reduction in fresh produce and is aiming for zero residues in the long term.

Source: adapted from Friends of the Earth Briefing, Pesticides in Supermarket Foods, July 2004.

Leading the way on pesticides

At Marks & Spencer we try to limit the amount of pesticides we use, while maintaining a high quality of fresh produce. Pesticides are chemicals, man-made or naturally occurring, used to destroy pests and diseases that damage our crops. Without them, we risk losing 30-40% of our food supply.

We carry out regular pesticide tests and if there's more than the recommended level we will not sell the crop. Our growers and suppliers, the government, and independent laboratories also check pesticide residue levels.

It's important to remember we test our food for pesticide residues using highly accurate measurements - the equivalent of finding a grain of salt in a swimming pool. So any traces we do find are usually very small. We have set a long term goal to eliminate all pesticide residues from fruit, vegetables and salads as well as prohibiting the use of potentially harmful pesticide chemicals.

Source: adapted from www.marksandspencer.com.

Table 5 *Marks & Spencer pesticide residues (at or below 0.04 parts per million) – targets and performance*

	2004 Sample size	2004 % residue-free	2003 % residue-free	Ongoing target residue-free
Vegetables	95	88	90	90
Potatoes	61	75	71	80
Salads	17	94	76	80
Fruit	79	37	39	60
Organics	35	94	96	100
Other foods	61	77	72	
Totals	348	73	72	

Source: adapted from Your M&S - Corporate Social Responsibility Report at www2.marksandspencer.com.

Mark Band 1 *Explanation of how the organisation maintains, monitors and improves customer service quality. Relevant up to date information, a range of sources. Supported conclusions.*

For Mark Band 1 it would be necessary to have one major source and that could be M&S's own website or the Corporate Social Responsibility report. This shows the choice of measurement at or below 0.04 parts per million and the targets set in terms of the percentages in which that measurement should not be exceeded.

Basic analysis should stress that there are some improvements from 2003 to 2004 and that some of the targets are being met, but others, e.g. fruit, are being badly missed.

Mark Band 2 *Sound evaluation of the product quality with showing judgement in what data is selected and presented and with conclusion supported and some recommendations.*

All parts of the data should be used to show the improvement from the situation in Table 4. This provides an independent source that confirms the movement from being the worst supermarket to being named as one of the two market leaders in terms of pesticides.

The analysis should, however, acknowledge the shortfalls and how far away M&S is from the intended long-term goal of having no pesticide residues.

Mark Band 3 *Detailed review and analysis of the quality of customer service and how the organisation maintains, monitors and improves customer service quality. A wide range of sources. Full analysis.*

This should include details of the need for this kind of monitoring, and a survey of customers opinions would be a useful addition.

Detailed analysis of how the measuring is carried out (in this case independently), how often (carried out and published monthly) and of the progress towards a 100% residue-free target.

More references to independent comments would also be expected such as, for example, Friends of the Earth's comment that M&S worry too much about the look of the fruit and vegetables.

61 Monitoring methods

Monitoring customer service

The first step in monitoring the level of customer service provided by an organisation is to work out how it will be measured and then to set benchmarks or minimum standards against which the actual service can be checked. Choosing a suitable basis for measuring was dealt with in section 60. This section will look at the wide variety of methods that are available for organisations to collect data. Section 62 considers how the data can be effectively analysed and how improvements can be made to customer service.

The methods of collection and the analysis are likely to be different for internal and external customers but they will cover three main points.

- How the data can be collected.
- How it can be analysed and presented.
- How the results can be used to improve customer service.

Methods for internal customers

The methods of collecting data to assess how effective the provision of customer service is for internal customers will generally be the same for staff, managers and departments. Shareholders will need a different approach and that is considered at the end of this first section. Figure 1 shows many of the important methods used to collect data from staff.

Appraisal Staff appraisal systems are primarily designed to assess how well members of staff are carrying out their job roles. In many businesses the appraisal process takes the form of a discussion between the members of staff and their line managers. During this discussion many issues may be raised including how the members of staff feel they are being treated, any concerns about pay, working conditions, promotion

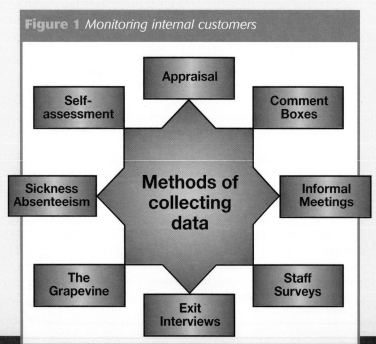

Figure 1 *Monitoring internal customers*

Appraisal

Self-assessment

Comment Boxes

Sickness Absenteeism

Methods of collecting data

Informal Meetings

The Grapevine

Exit Interviews

Staff Surveys

prospects and any additional training they feel they need. All of this provides the line manager with data about how well the business is providing customer service for the staff.

Where the relationship between the member of staff and the line manager is good, this will be an effective way of collecting data. However, because the line manager is in a position of authority staff may not say what they really feel.

Staff surveys Sometimes concerns about the customer service being supplied to staff may be more general. Businesses might then carry out a wider staff survey to try to appreciate how the majority of staff feel about a particular issue. An example is given for the National Staff Survey in Redditch and Bromsgrove Primary Care Trust at the end of this section.

Staff turnover and exit interviews If there is a high turnover of staff, this may indicate that there is something wrong with the way staff are being treated. This may be poor working conditions, low pay, poor management, unfriendly staff or the attractions of a different job. The staff turnover figures may indicate that there is a problem but in order to find out what it is, management will need to talk to the leavers.

An exit interview provides an opportunity for the staff who are leaving to explain why they are going. This will be effective where the leaver is encouraged to say what they want, although some leavers will want to get out as quickly as possible and may refuse the interview or lie in it.

Sickness, absenteeism and punctuality If staff are absent or late for work this can also indicate lack of motivation which may be caused by the way they are being treated at work. Collecting data on this will not identify the cause but it might indicate that there is a problem. Where staff are persistently late or absent there should then be a meeting with that member of staff to try to find out the reason.

Self-assessment Usually the person who has the best understanding of the customer service being provided to staff is the member of staff themselves. Self-assessment allows staff to consider what is important for them. This can form part of an appraisal process but a common way of ensuring that the self-assessment is focused is to create a self-assessment questionnaire.

The questionnaire should see the member of staff as the centre of research and common questions would include how they feel they are performing, what training and support they need and what targets they feel are appropriate for their future performance. If the questions are carefully phrased this can be a very effective method of assessing how staff feel about the customer service they are receiving.

Comment boxes Some businesses provide their staff with comment or suggestion boxes where they can post comments. One major advantage of this is that comments can be made anonymously and this often means that the members of staff will be more honest in their comments. The main drawback, if the comments are anonymous, is that it is then difficult to follow up any comments with a discussion.

Figure 2 *Comment boxes and informal meetings of staff*

Informal meetings These would include day to day conversations with staff and social events. Where discussions are informal staff are often more relaxed and willing to say things that they might not have said in a formal meeting. Barriers can be broken down, at which point staff may feel that they can make critical comments without offending anyone.

It also allows management to get to know their staff better and through this they may find ways of supporting staff and improving customer service which they had not been aware of before. They may, for example, find that a member of staff has an elderly relative who needs to be made comfortable for the day before they leave for work. Knowing this, they may be able to change the work rota so that the member of staff can start work later.

The grapevine Often information about particular members of staff does not come from direct contact with them. Instead it comes from colleagues and managers making comments about them. The main potential drawback with this is that what managers are being told may not always be correct. It is, therefore, important that follow up discussions take place with

the actual members of staff to find out what is or is not true.

Feedback from shareholders The most common ways of receiving comments from shareholders are through letters received by management and through the Annual General Meeting (AGM). When shareholders are particularly unhappy about the way the business is being run, they are likely to raise their concerns with the management or the directors in writing.

In addition there will be an AGM which all shareholders will be entitled to attend and at which they should be able to express their views. Sometimes shareholders will band together to put pressure on directors and managers if they feel very strongly about the way the business is being run, as shown in Figure 3. In extreme cases directors may even resign if pressure is very great.

Figure 3 *Shareholder views*

In May 2005 about a quarter of the shareholders in the mining business Xstrata PLC voted against the proposed payments of £2.2 million in special bonuses to two top executives - the Chief Executive and the Finance Director. The voting was 160 million against to 358 million in favour, so the payment, almost double their pay packets in 2003, was carried but under heated protest.

Source: adapted from press reports.

Methods for external customers

The main details given below relate to how a business can gain information about the customer service being provided to the end customer. It is also important that the business is aware of the service being provided to its other external customers, its suppliers, the government and society. Some of the methods covered below will be suitable for this but other more direct methods may also be required.

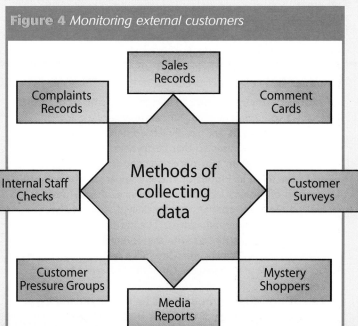

Figure 4 *Monitoring external customers*

Methods of collecting data
- Sales Records
- Comment Cards
- Customer Surveys
- Mystery Shoppers
- Media Reports
- Customer Pressure Groups
- Internal Staff Checks
- Complaints Records

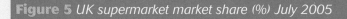

Figure 5 *UK supermarket market share (%) July 2005*

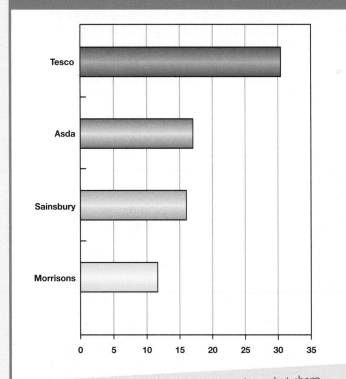

Continuing high sales figures have taken Tesco's market share from 28.1% to 30.4% in the last year. This shows that the company is getting many things right as far as their customers are concerned.

Source: adapted from Taylor Nelson Sofres (TNS) Monthly Report.

Sales records Generally it is true that if customer service is very bad customers will go elsewhere to buy their products. Sales records should, therefore, help to identify if there is a problem with the service or the product itself. If sales are falling, or one branch is particularly poor when compared to the others, this can indicate a customer service problem. Whilst this will suggest a problem, identifying the actual cause is likely to require an additional method of research. If sales records show improvements or high market share, this may indicate good customer service, as in Figure 5.

Customer surveys These can take many forms, from formal interviews to comment cards and even observation.

- **Comment cards** are usually left somewhere prominent in the business premises so that customers can pick them up and either fill them out there and then or take them home and post them in. Hotels or travel companies often use this method of monitoring customer service. Usually there is limited space for comments, especially if space is also provided for name and address. The cards also tend to have very general questions as with the comment card for the National Trust's Winchester City Mill which simply asks 'What do you think of Winchester City Mill? We welcome your comments.'
- **Customer questionnaires** will be longer and more structured with a set of questions that often cover a range of

services and or products provided by the business. These have the benefit of gathering more data but if they are too time consuming customers may simply not bother filling them in.

- **Customer interviews** tend to be more formal with customers invited in to discuss specific issues with staff in the business. This does allow for more developed answers and the interviewer can ask additional questions and gain fuller answers about problem areas.
- **Focus groups** can also be used for this kind of feedback. Usually focus groups, as the name suggests, will be concentrating on just one or two major issues related to the product or the customer service being provided. For many people this is less intimidating than a more formal one-to-one interview and it also helps to build up a general feeling about any problem issues. The danger is that one or two dominant members may create a biased view of what the whole panel actually feels.
- **Observation** of customers can often give clear indications that something is wrong as when customers walk into a store glance around and walk quickly out again. Many customers will show exactly what they are feeling through their body language and their facial expressions. However, it can be dangerous drawing too many conclusions just from observation. The customer who walked in and out of the shop so quickly may simply have gone into the wrong shop or have been late for a bus.

Complaints records Each time there is a complaint about some aspect of the business this should be recorded. Checking the records of complaints should identify particular issues that the business needs to address. It may also identify particular staff who are causing problems for good customer service and for them appropriate training is also likely to be hinted at.

Most customers will only complain if there is a serious issue involved so this tends to be a fairly effective way of monitoring customer service. Unfortunately there are some customers who will complain about almost anything and often without good grounds. Records from these customers need to be identified and put to one side.

Customer pressure groups In some industries customers have formed their own pressure groups in order to make comments about the way that businesses in that industry run their business. These groups can provide valuable feedback on how well a business is delivering its customer service. An example is shown in Figure 6.

External regulatory bodies As well as groups that are set up by consumers to raise issues about the service being provided in certain industries, the Government has also set up specific bodies to regulate certain industries and has appointed **ombudsmen** whose role is to act on behalf of the general public when issues arise in particular industries.

In the UK there are nearly 90 regulator bodies, which include the following.

- The Advertising Standards Authority.
- The National Lottery Commission.
- Strategic Rail Authority.
- Financial Ombudsman.
- General Medical Council.
- Health and Safety Executive.
- The Office of Fair Trading.

Figure 6 *Rail Passengers Council*

The new Rail Passengers Council was formed in July 2005 to act as the official, independent voice of rail passengers. It is a single GB-wide organisation which replaces the previous council and regional committees. It has the following main functions:

- to act as the rail passenger consumer champion that secures improvements to services. The RPC will provide passengers with help and advice on how to get the best from the national rail network, explain their rights and help them when things go wrong
- to help shape the development of the main policies, procedures and regulation of passenger issues
- to act as a national campaigning and lobbying organisation. There will be a strong emphasis on passenger research, publications and effective communications.

Source: adapted from www.railpassengers.org.uk.

- Public Services Ombudsman for Wales.
- Ofgem – Office of Gas and Electricity Markets.
- Ofwat – Office of Water Services.
- Postwatch - the watchdog for postal services.

Each of these authorities has a role which includes ensuring a appropriate standard of service for the external customers and they will provide regular feedback to businesses in their industry on how they are performing.

Media reports Media reports can be both positive and negative. They will be found in general media forums such as national newspapers, specific consumer forums such as Watchdog on television and *Which?* magazine, specific trade publications such as *The Grocer* or in a specialist research publication such as Mintel.

Many of the reports are made after careful investigation of an industry, specific business or specific product. Most of these

Table 1 *Typical methods of checking specific customer service functions*

Factor	Method used
Speed of checkout staff in a supermarket	Staff sign on with a code then speed is recorded using the EPOS system which records each item scanned and the time.
Politeness and accuracy of staff in a call centre	Calls are recorded and supervisors can then listen to the conversations and assess how well staff have performed against an agreed standard.
The cleanliness of customer toilets	Hourly inspections with suitable actions taken if not clean and each inspection signed on a chart on the wall.
The quality of teaching in a school	Lesson observation by a teacher's line manager.
The popularity of a website	The number of hits received each day recorded as customers log on.
Value for money on a fruit and vegetable store in a market	Visual check of the prices of the competition in other parts of the market and in local greengrocers and supermarket outlets.

reports are available to the general public and it is therefore a very important source of information for a business about its products and service. Most people believe what they are told by the media and if negative points are being made they need to be acted upon as quickly as possible.

Internal staff and product checks In addition to listening to what external customers and other commentators have to say about the customer service being received, it is also vital that business makes its own regular checks of the service being provided. The methods chosen for these checks will depend on what part of the service is being checked. Table 1 shows some examples for different customer services.

Mystery shoppers Some of the internal checks will be made with the member of staff knowing this is happening. A mystery shopper is someone whom the staff do not know who will visit the premises to buy something or make inquiries. As they do this they are mentally noting how they have been served against a list of criteria that they were given beforehand. On leaving the business they then write out details of their visit and how staff dealt with them and feed this back to the business.

Mystery shoppers are trained at their job and so the business should receive accurate information of how staff are actually treating their customers. Although the term mystery shopper is used this method of research is used in many different businesses. Catering 4 Success, based in Lancaster, offers restaurant owners the services of a mystery diner.

Portfolio practice • Royal Mail Quality of Service

In June and July 2004 a survey was carried out for Royal Mail, Postwatch and PostComm.

- Royal Mail Group plc is a public limited company wholly owned by the Government. Royal Mail collects and delivers letters and packages, promotes excellence in direct mail as the mainstay of the advertiser's marketing mix and designs and produces the UK's stamps and philatelic products.
- Postwatch is an independent organisation set up to ensure that post offices, Parcelforce, Royal Mail and any competing postal providers, give the best service possible to you, their customer.
- Postcomm - the Postal Services Commission - is the independent regulator of the postal market and it is our job to make sure postal operators, including Royal Mail, meet the needs of their customers throughout the UK.

The main objective of the survey was to ensure that the new Royal Mail Quality of service targets, to take effect from April 2006, reflect customer expectations and requirements. Data was collected from four main groups of customers; domestic, small business, medium business and the top 500 business customers. Data was collected using the following methods.

- Focus Groups – Domestic and Small Business Customers with a pre-meeting set of questions on how often they used the postal system using a diary for 7 days.
- In-depth Interviews – Medium and the Top 500 Business Customers conducted in a 40 minute interview by telephone.
- Telephone Interviews – Domestic and Small Business Customers. 2,300 interviews were conducted using a questionnaire which took about 13 minutes to answer.
- Online Interviews – Medium and the Top 500 Business Customers. 705 interviews were conducted using a questionnaire.

Source: adapted from the Royal Mail Quality of Service survey.

(a) **Explain the different interests that the Royal Mail, Postwatch and PostComm are likely to have in terms of the customer service provided to business and the general public sending mail.**

(b) **Explain why it was important to divide the customers into four main groups for the survey.**

(c) **(i) Explain why each method used to obtain data would be effective for working out what customers expected.**
(ii) Explain why each method was likely to be the best for the particular groups targeted.

1. In your local area visit a range of different businesses such as banks, fast food restaurants, clothes or shoe shops, general retail stores, such as Woolworths or WHSmith.
2. Collect copies of comment cards, complaint forms and customer questionnaires. These may be on display or you may need to ask for them.
3. For each method of collecting information compare how they differ for the different businesses, noting down:
   (a) what information is being asked for and why this might be different for the different businesses;
   (b) how the method will help the business collect data to monitor and improve its customer service.
   (c) Suggest any improvements that might be made to the comment cards, complaint forms and customer questionnaires that you have collected.

Note: if many students are collecting the same data the businesses may not be prepared to provide data in such large quantities. If this is happening, split up the businesses you are going to visit and share the items that you have collected.

Research task

Meeting the assessment criteria

For your chosen organisations you will need to understand the importance of maintaining and improving the quality of customer service. This will involve a consideration of the techniques used to monitor the level of service provided to customers.

Business example - Redditch and Bromsgrove Primary Care Trust

In 2004/5 the Redditch and Bromsgrove Primary Care Trust took part in a national staff survey. For larger trusts a sample of staff was used. The survey had 224 questions created for the whole country. The questionnaires were delivered to each authority and then distributed by internal post. Staff sent their completed questionnaires using a pre-paid envelope. If they did not send back the questionnaire, two reminders were sent. For the Redditch and Bromsgrove PCT 310 completed questionnaires were returned out of a sample of 505.

The results of the survey showed many of the monitoring methods used by the Redditch and Bromsgrove PCT had positive results for their staff, including:

- two-thirds of staff could talk openly to their line manager about flexible working;
- a clear majority of staff felt their appraisal was useful in improving the way in which they did their job and left them feeling their work was valued.

On the negative side, results of the survey pointed out:

- 3 out of 10 of those staff members who conduct appraisals said they had not received training from the Trust during the last 5 years;
- around a third of the staff said they did not have an Individual Performance Review (IPR) in the last 12 months;
- 3 out of 10 staff said their team did not meet regularly to discuss its effectiveness or potential improvements;
- more than 1 in 4 staff said they were not satisfied with the employer's valuation of their work;
- over 4 out of 10 staff said they did not get clear feedback about their work and almost 3 in 10 said they did not get clear feedback specifically from their supervisor.

Source: adapted from Worcestershire Health Authority Report at www.worcestershirehealth.nhs.uk.

Mark Band 1 *Description of the methods used to monitor customer service quality.*

This would outline basic details of the methods used by the Trust, noting the staff survey itself, communications between staff and their managers and the existence of an appraisal and Individual Performance Review. The methods should be explained and put into the context of the staff at the hospitals.

Details of how these methods are carried out should be provided, noting such details as the sampling process.

Details of problems would summarise the negative points listed in the data and from any other research.

Mark Band 2 *Explanation of how the organisation monitors customer service quality using relevant and up-to-date information.*

This section should identify the basic purposes of the methods shown and provide details of any commitments made by the business to staff, for example, the Education, Training and Employment Development Policy for the Trust states ' Every member of staff must be provided with the opportunity to meet with their immediate line manager or supervisor, at least once per year, to discuss their development needs'.

For the methods, explanations of how they work and monitor customer service should be given, for example, the way the staff survey was conducted, where it came from and the sampling process.

Mark Band 3 *Detailed review of the methods of monitoring customer service and how effective these are likely to be in providing the organisation with the data that it needs.*

In terms of the methods there should be a critical evaluation of how they are operated and how effective they are likely to be in terms of identifying and hence improving customer service for the staff.

It should note that the staff survey is only a sample, that not all questionnaires were returned, and assess the effects these factors will have on providing accurate data. The levels of dissatisfaction with appraisal and IPRs should be noted and assessed in terms of how effective the methods will be. Reasons for shortfall should also be explained, e.g. for the poor response for the staff survey such details as some of the staff addresses were wrong.

Any suggested changes in practice should be explained and justified, e.g. immediate action to ensure annual appraisals and IPRs take place for all staff in order to guarantee that the stated policy commitment is met.

Analysing the data

Deciding on a way of measuring customer service and deciding on a method of collecting the data is only part of the picture in terms of maintaining and improving customer service. Once the data has been collected the following steps are also needed.

- The data must be analysed so that it is easy to understand.
- The data must be measured against an agreed standard to find out how good or bad the customer service is.
- the cause of any problems must be identified.
- actions need to be taken to correct any problems.

When the data is collected it can be in many different forms, from a recorded telephone conversation or a written customer complaint sheet to a formal interview or numbers showing how fast a job is being done. Analysing the data is the process of changing the raw data into a form that can be easily understood and used.

With some data this may be a relatively easy task as with recording when staff arrive for work. In other cases what seems easy to analyse may actually be fairly complex and will require many factors to be taken into account before valid conclusions can be drawn. For example, checking the speed of checkout staff in a supermarket in order to find out who is not scanning at least 30 items a minute seems straightforward but in reality all of the following questions need to be considered.

- When does the scanning start? Is it when the customer places the items on the conveyor system, when staff pick up the first item or when the first item is scanned?
- Is any account taken of how big the items are, labels that will not scan and need to be typed in, or items that do not have a bar code?
- What happens if the customer asks a question and staff have to stop scanning in order to answer it?
- When does the scanning stop? Is it when all items have been scanned or when the customer has paid?
- If staff have to ring for assistance will that be taken into account?
- Will the time of day be taken into account and how long the member of staff has been working?
- Will the experience of the member of staff be taken into account?

Data collected through consumer panels, interviews and one-to-one discussions can be particularly difficult to analyse. A great deal may be said, some of which is important and some of which is not. One problem is that what was said may not have been written down, so the first step must be to record all the main points. If many people are being surveyed there will be the additional problem that they may all express similar points in different ways. To create a meaningful and useful final set of data the business must decide how to categorise these different answers, perhaps with a scale. For example, when asking customers what they thought about the helpfulness of staff the scale might be as shown in Figure 1.

Figure 1 *Scale for categorising customer responses*

Very Helpful	Helpful	No opinion	Unhelpful	Very Unhelpful

Ticks or tallies could be used to make it easier to quantify how good or bad a situation might be. On the other hand the interviewees might have explained why they thought the service was good or bad and that might be just as important to record.

Analysing data and putting it into a meaningful and easy to understand form is vital for monitoring customer service. How well this is done will be a major factor in determining if a business can effectively monitor, maintain and improve its customer service.

Benchmarking

Once the data has been analysed and presented in an appropriate form it needs to be evaluated to find out just how bad, or good, the customer service in the organisation is. For this to happen, clear benchmarks need to be set against which the actual service can be measured.

The selection of an appropriate benchmark will depend on two main factors:

- The type of customer service
- What should be considered an acceptable minimum standard.

The type of customer service Benchmarking for services that have specific measures should be fairly straightforward, as shown in Table 1.

Table 1 *Examples of specific benchmarks*

Customer service	Possible benchmark
The speed of answering a phone.	Before the 5th ring.
When staff arrive for work.	15 minutes before the store opens.
How often supermarket shelves are checked and filled.	Once every hour.
The price of goods compared to competitors.	At least matching prices.
The number of staff appraisals provided each year.	A minimum of two appraisals each year.
The minimum level of payment for staff.	10% above the National Minimum Wage.

For other customer services benchmarking is much more difficult because it is difficult to measure the service in the first place. For example, it is difficult enough to give an exact measure for staff's attitude to customers and that makes setting a minimum acceptable standard for attitude even more difficult. In the end it may have to come down to the number of **customer complaints** about a particular member of staff. The benchmark would then be some specific number of complaints, hopefully with a target of zero.

A survey by CRL Solutions of 545 businesses found that the most frequently identified method of checking the business's customer service was to use data generated from customers' complaints and from enquiries by customers. The survey also found that the main reason for carrying out research, just above improving the customer service (54%), was to quantify customer service levels (55%). To do this the data, and the benchmarking, need to be given a numerical value.

This is rather like the driving test where there are certain mistakes, 'majors', that are considered so serious that the person fails, and 'minors' which, in themselves, are not too serious but if there are too many the person can still fail. The benchmark is 1 major or 15 minors.

Some failures of customer service will be so serious that immediate action needs to be taken and there will be others that need to be addressed if they become persistent and/or too widespread. The benchmark should again be something clearly measurable.

The minimum acceptable standard The final benchmark chosen needs to reflect what the business thinks is the absolute minimum standard for itself. It may be based on any of the following standards set:
- by the business with no reference to other businesses;
- by the business when comparing performance in one store/region/country with that in others;
- matched to those of its immediate competitors;
- as the accepted norm for the industry;
- as dictated by government or a public regulator;
- with the agreement of its customers, following discussions.

Published standards

Section 59 looked at mission statements, customer charters and pledges. These also set benchmarks and statements of intention in terms of the customer service that the business will provide. Sometimes these are stated as very clear commitments for the business in the form of a code of practice. Sometimes they are more general and will be found in mission statements or statements of corporate social responsibility. Some may be created by the business itself, some are recommended by the industry and some are dictated by legislation or regulators.

Corporate social responsibility (CSR)

Businesses recognise that they have responsibilities to all of their stakeholders including the community as a whole. The specific responsibilities that a particular business is committed to taking on will be given in a statement of corporate social responsibility (CSR). This will include details of how it will deal with its customers, both internal and external. But it will also give details of its responsibilities in terms of the wider community, the environment and social factors such as

supporting education and charities. These wider commitments are now seen by businesses as part of good customer service and form part of the monitoring, maintaining and improving process.

CSR commitments are very varied as is shown in Table 2.

Business	CSR commitment
Barclays Bank	Together with our partners, the Football Foundation and Groundwork, we're creating over 300 new spaces for sports over the next three years by transforming neglected land into new sporting facilities.
Vodafone	Our Content Standards are designed to protect users – particularly children – from inappropriate content, contact and commercialism.
Rolls-Royce	Reduce the amount of energy consumed by 9 per cent by the end of 2006, relative to 2003 Levels.
John Lewis Partnership	No supplier will recruit or employ children under the age of 15 unless International Labour Organisation (ILO) developing country exemptions apply.
Tesco	Age Concern has been chosen as Tesco Charity of the Year 2005. We are working together to raise more than £2 million to combat isolation and poverty for older people.

Table 2 *The range of CSR commitments*

Source: adapted from company websites.

Codes of practice

Some businesses lay down their own codes of practice, many others adopt industry codes of practice which set down minimum standards for the industry as a whole. Codes of practice cover many different businesses, as the examples below show.

A code of practice for commercial leases in England and Wales This was created by the major bodies involved in commercial leasing, for example, the Association of British Insurers, the British Retail Consortium, and the Law Society. The code contains recommendations for landlords and tenants when they negotiate new leases of business premises and when they deal with each other's businesses during the term of a lease.

British Code of Advertising, Sales Promotion and Direct Marketing The Committee of Advertising Practice (CAP) is the self-regulatory body that creates, revises and enforces the Code. The Code sets a standard against which marketing communications are assessed and applies to:
- advertisements in newspapers, magazines, brochures, leaflets, circulars, mailings, e-mails, text transmissions, fax

transmissions, catalogues, follow-up literature and other electronic and printed material;
- posters and other promotional media in public places, including moving images;
- cinema and video commercials;
- advertisements in non-broadcast electronic media, including online advertisements in paid-for space (e.g. banner and pop-up advertisements);
- viewdata services;
- marketing databases containing consumers' personal information;
- sales promotions;
- advertisement promotions.

Farm Assured British Pigs (FABPigs) The scheme is aimed at the whole UK industry. It aims to attract producers willing to adhere to high standards of production which are then independently audited to ensure that they are maintained. It aims to provide a high level of confidence to both the retailer and the public as to the quality of the product both from a health viewpoint and the ethical standards of the methods of production. The Scheme covers a wide range of aspects of production as well as transportation, slaughter and processing.

Legislation Many codes of practice are now laid down by law and business must follow them. There are also other laws which set minimum standards for businesses when dealing with customers. These are covered in sections 63 and 64.

Improving customer service

The whole objective of benchmarking, measuring and monitoring levels of customer service, and of setting out mission statements, codes of practice and pledges is to work towards improving the standards of customer service provided by a business.

Reviewing and recommending changes Once the data on the actual customer service performance has been collected and analysed it needs to be compared to the benchmarks, codes of practice and any other standards that have been set down. A judgment will have to be made which considers the following questions.
- How serious are any problems with the customer service?
- If there is more than one problem, which is the most important?
- What steps need to be taken to correct the problem?
- If changes are made what effects will they have on all of the customers, external and internal?
- Are new benchmarks or codes of practice needed?

One possible example is shown in Figure 2.

The changes that will be needed will depend on what part of the customer service provision was found to be below standard. It may be a specific element, such as prices being

higher than competitors' prices or staff arriving late for work. In such cases the business will need to work out how it can lower prices without damaging profits too much, or how it can ensure staff are at work on time which may require replacing them. Alternatively, it may be a more general problem as when staff have a negative attitude or a series of bad press reports come out. Then more extensive solutions may be needed.

Training needs In many cases of poor customer service it is the staff who are underperforming in some way. When this happens it is usually necessary to implement some form of additional training.

The choice of training provided will need to consider various points, including:
- A clear assessment of what staff problems there are and, hence, what training is needed.
- A decision on which staff need training and possibly which staff need replacing.
- Planning on the timing of the training so that this does not further reduce the service offered to customers as the training takes place. Figure 3 shows an example of training times at a library.
- A decision on who should carry out the training as previous training has clearly not been effective.

Types of training have been covered in unit 1.

New services To improve customer service provision it is not enough for businesses simply to look at what they already have in place and try to improve this. There may also be important services that they do not provide at all, but ones that customers would like and may expect. Figure 4 shows an example.

Customer expectations are changing all the time. The sort of services that many businesses are having to consider now include:
- the offer of home deliveries;
- on-line shopping;
- loyalty schemes such as club cards and discounts;
- the latest methods of payments and credit facilities
- for staff, the provision of more flexible working arrangements;
- for staff, more secure pension provisions.

It is also generally acknowledged by business experts that the level and type of service that customers receive has in very many cases become more important than price for the customer.

Figure 2 *The 80/20 rule*

When surveyed customers will identify only some of a business's products or services as providing them with most of their value, as a general rule 20% of the products provide 80% of the value in customers' eyes. The business should, therefore focus its time and energy on those critical 20% services and spend less time on the trivial 80% of services.

Figure 3 *Notice from York Central Library*

Notice

York Central Library will be closed for staff training from 9.00am - 1.00pm on the first Thursday of each month, starting on 7 April 2005. The training days are:

7 April 2005	5 May 2005	2 June 2005
7 July 2005	4 Aug. 2005	1 Sept. 2005

Figure 4

Research by *Which?* has found that one in seven mobile phone handsets develops faults within the first year. That is more than two million customers suffering. Motorola, Sony and Ericsson handsets were identified as the worst offenders.

When customers complain to the retail store that sold them they are often told they cannot deal with any faults on phones not covered by insurance if the problem is reported to them more than 28 days after purchase. This is a rule that the shops have come up with and could contravene the Sale of Goods Act, 1979 which requires the provision of goods of satisfactory quality.

Mr Tynan, the author of the report added that customers should never accept being passed on to the manufacturer to complain. 'The retailer has to sort out the problem: not the manufacturer, not the insurer and not the network. I can't see any circumstances why the customer would be passed on to a manufacturer.'

Source: adapted from *The Scotsman*, Aug 2005.

For any business that you are familiar with obtain a copy of its Customer Charter, Code of Practice or corporate Social Responsibility statement. These should be available on the business's website or may be available at a branch of the business. Note that some businesses do not have these.
1. Select a part of the document that relates to something that you know about the business and evaluate how well the business is meeting its commitments.
2. (i) If there are shortfalls, suggest suitable actions the business should take to correct these.

(ii) If there are no obvious shortfalls suggest actions that the business could take to make the customer service even better.
3. Check through the main sections of the documents and note down any important commitments that you feel have been left out. Justify why they should be included.

Research task

Portfolio practice · Industry Benchmarking Results for Woolworths Group plc

The Customer Support department this year participated in a Benchmarking exercise carried out by Call Centre Focus (a publication specialising in the Call Centre Industry, to which many contact centres and retailers subscribe). The benchmarking exercise was carried out across 25 national contact centres, marking them on set criteria and ranking them within the group of 25.

There were four main areas measured (each with further criteria) which followed the 'customer journey'.

- **Quality of welcome** This measures warmth of the opening welcome, rapport, pace, enthusiasm, personalisation with the adviser's name and genuine interest and is classed as the most important phase of a call.
- **Handling of the enquiry** This measures the adviser's ability to identify the customer's needs through questioning, listening skills and active responses and the overall control of the call.
- **Response to the enquiry** The assessment here is about the strength of company knowledge, the quality of the information supplied versus the customer's needs and any 'added value ingredients' i.e. did the adviser offer over and above what the customer originally enquired about and express interest in the future progress of the query.
- **Relationship and close of the call** Areas taken into account here are those that leave a lasting impression i.e. empathy, degree of trust or confidence built, the quality of the attention received and the overall impression left by the adviser.

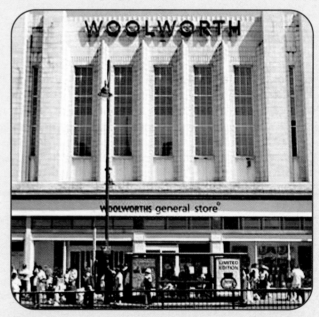

(a) **Explain the benefits to Woolworths Group of taking part in a benchmarking exercise with 24 other businesses.**
(b) **Why are the four main areas described as the 'customer journey'?**
(c) **How easy or difficult would it be to measure each of these four main areas?**
(d) **Explain why this execise should lead to improvements in Woolworths Group's customer service provision.**

Source: adapted from Woolworths Group plc – Corporate Responsibility Report 2005 at www.woolworthsgroupplc.com.

Meeting the assessment criteria

For your chosen organisations you will need to understand the importance of maintaining and improving the quality of customer service. This will involve a consideration of the techniques used to maintain and improve the level of service provided to customers.

Business example - P&O Ferries Survey - Three elements of customer service

The Call Centre
Training at the call centre takes 3 weeks. During this time, you sit with a 'buddy' and help by keying in information while they talk on the 'phone. You watch what they do and, when you feel ready, you make your first call.

The call system is based on 5 main points of quality service:
- tone of voice
- personality
- courtesy
- accuracy in recording information
- good product knowledge

Trainee telephonists are monitored once a week, in order to check the quality of their customer service. This means that at least 15 trainees are being listened to every week by customer service management.

When dealing with rude customers, the policy is that it's always best to explain what went wrong and not to dismiss the complaint straight away. Every complaint is viewed as an opportunity to retain customers and full refunds are always considered under reasonable circumstances. When dealing with angry customers, the policy is to take down the facts and promise to call them back with a full explanation. This gives the customers time to calm down and behave rationally.

Dealing with written correspondence
Grammar, spelling and clarity are the three most important points to be aware of. P&O Ferries receives about 2000 letters a month. The figure is high because letters come from customers using all three ferry routes. All letters are dealt with using the corporate standards used by most large businesses, known as ISO 9000 Standards, which specify that:
- a complaint must be answered in 2 days;
- any other correspondence must be answered in 5 days.

These standards are regularly audited, every three months. The company has strayed from them only twice, even though there has been 200% more work this year. All post is stamped on arrival, and every letter gets two signatures from the two customer service managers. The measurement of success is based on the amount of further correspondence the company receives, after dealing with queries and complaints from customers (i.e. less correspondence = more satisfied customers).

Dealing with special needs
Some correspondence has to be dealt with in other languages (this also applies to phone calls), in order to give the best customer service to non-English speakers. P&O encourages this by paying an extra £1,078 p.a. to staff who speak another language. All announcements over the loudspeaker are intended to be clear and fluent and, in order to get this effect, staff are trained to read out information phonetically.

P&O Ferries prides itself on the facilities it offers to the disabled. These include:
- free travel for guide dogs and carers accompanying blind and deaf people;
- special cabins that cater for the disabled person's needs;
- lifts to the Club Lounge (on the top deck) on all new ships;
- lifts to other parts of the ship;
- identification badges;
- a special procedure to help safe embarkation.

When a disabled person arrives to collect his/her ticket, the ticket office telephones the staff responsible for loading vehicles to inform them that a disabled person is about to come on board. The passenger is told to put on hazard lights and is then directed to the lift nearest to his/her door so he/she can get out easily.

Source: author research.

Mark Band 1 *Description of how the organisation maintains, monitors and improves customer service quality.*
Three examples of P&O Ferries methods and standards are shown in the data. The details should be used to show how standards are set, how staff are brought up to or maintained at the standard and how the services are monitored.

The likely effectiveness of the standards and the basic service should be considered, especially in terms of maintaining the standard already achieved and in terms of improving it for the future.

Mark Band 2 *Explanation of how the organisation maintains, monitors and improves customer service quality using relevant and up-to-date information from a range of sources with analysis of the information.*
In Mark Band 2 there should be an explanation of how the measures indicated in the data ensure that there is effective customer service through its standards and its monitoring procedures.

A range of sources should be used for this including P&O Ferries' own Customer Support programme and other up-to-date studies and press reports. For example a case study 'Virtual European call centre for ferry operator' by BT, published in 2005, could be used to show how P&O Ferries is improving its call centre facilities.

A full study should also examine the service for internal customers.

Mark Band 3 *Detailed review of the quality of the customer service in an organisation and its maintaining monitoring and improving methods and techniques using information from a wide range of sources and full analysis.*
In Mark Band 3 there should be critical evaluation of the service being provided. For example, although complaint letters are dealt with very promptly, there are 2000 a month. Additional research would highlight the fact that many of these complaints are about such things as delayed crossings which are generally out of P&O's control because of poor weather.

There should also be critical evaluation of the methods being used. Should the trainee or supervisors decide when a person is ready to start taking calls? Is monitoring of calls once a week too little, enough or excessive and what effect will it have on staff?

Again other sources should be used as for example with the problems for staff when P&O announced job cuts, which was widely reported in the press and by BBC News.

Legislation, regulation and working procedures

The supply of goods and services to customers and customer service in the UK are influenced by a variety of factors.

- Legislation - United Kingdom (UK) laws and European Union (EU) directives which become UK laws set out the legal rights of customers when buying goods or services and the legal operations of businesses in relation to customers.
- Regulations which might be set in place by legislation or by independent or government bodies which oversee the industries in which the business operates.
- Working procedures set up by the business itself or the standards which businesses must maintain to be competitive within the industry.

These constraints will affect the level of customer service offered by a business. They aim to improve the standard of service from a customer's point of view. However, they will also have a major impact on the business.

Legislation, regulation and working procedures may affect many areas of customer service. These are shown in Figure 1. This section looks at the impact and effect on customer services. Section 64 examines how the safety of personnel, customers and visitors is affected.

Nature and standards of products offered to customers

Legislation will influence the nature and standard of the good or service that a business can sell to customers. It can affect the:

- type of product which is offered for sale;
- the ingredients or materials used in the product;
- the product design;
- the quantities in which the product is sold.

Some of the ways in which customer service is affected as a result of complying with legislation are shown in Table 1. The nature and standards of products can have a direct effect on the safety of customers. This is dealt with in section 64. Some industries have their own organisations which regulate standards of the products offered to customers, such as:

- the Federation of the Electronics Industry (FEI) which is the trade association for companies in the IT, communications and electronics industries;
- the Association of British Travel Agents (ABTA) which regulates the travel industry.

Some businesses regulate themselves. For example, an ethical business may not buy its supplies from manufacturers using cheap labour. Other ethical businesses refuse to produce certain products or products tested on animals.

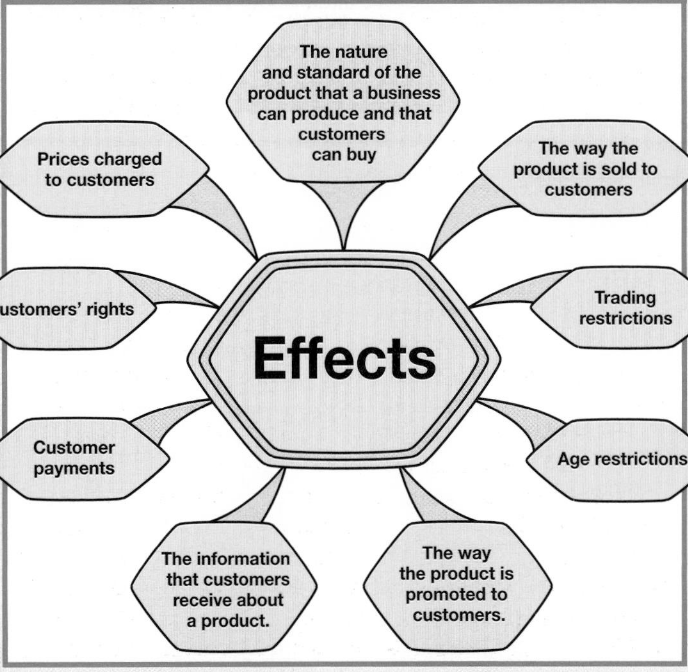

The way in which products are sold

The different ways in which products are sold to customers is also influenced by legislation and regulation. Legislation can influence:

Figure 1 *Effects of legislation, regulation and working procedures on customer service*

The nature and standard of the product that a business can produce and that customers can buy

Prices charged to customers

The way the product is sold to customers

Customers' rights

Trading restrictions

Effects

Customer payments

Age restrictions

The information that customers receive about a product.

The way the product is promoted to customers.

Table 1 *Effects on customer service of regulating the nature and standards of products*

Sale of Goods Act, 1979
Effect - products sold must be of merchantable quality and fit for the purpose.
Example - customers cannot be sold a tent which has tears or bottles which have leaks.

Supply of Goods and Services Act, 1982
Effect - Services must be of merchantable quality and at reasonable rates.
Example - tourists cannot be booked into a two star hotel when they have bought a holiday in a five star hotel.

Food Safety Act, 1990
Effect - Food must comply with standards.
Example - customers cannot be sold fruit which is decayed or food which has passed its 'sell-by' date.

Weights and Measures Act, 1985
Effect - products must not be sold in deficient quantities.
Example - customers cannot be sold a 500gms bag of tea which only contains 400gms.

Road Traffic Acts, 1988 and 1991
Effect - prevents the sale of unroadworthy vehicles.
Example - customers cannot be sold a car which would not pass an MOT.

Source: adapted from www.tradingstandards.gov.uk

- selling in shops;
- doorstep selling – selling at the door, at home or in the place of work;
- distance selling – all forms of contract concluded where both parties do not meet face to face, including press adverts with order forms, a catalogue, telephone, teleshopping and the use of the Internet (e-commerce);
- timeshare sales of holiday properties.

For example the **EU Directive 2005/29/EC on Unfair Commercial Practices** prohibits pressure selling and aims to outlaw 'sharp practices' in selling to customers. The **Unsolicited Goods and Services Act 1971** makes it an offence to demand payment for goods sent to customers that have not been ordered. In 2001 electronic documents were added. The **Consumer Protection (Distance Selling) Regulations, 2000** set out regulations for Internet, digital television, fax or phone selling. For example:

- the customer must be given clear information about the goods or services offered;
- there is a 28 day period of response in regard to the product;
- after making a purchase the customer must be sent confirmation;
- customer has a cooling-off period of 7 working days.

Internet legislation, regulations and working practices are covered in section 46.

Age restrictions

Various legislation restricts sales on products to children. Examples include:

- the **Protection of Children (Tobacco) Act, 1986** and The **Children and Young Persons (Tobacco) Act, 1991** which prevents sales of cigarettes and tobacco to children and controls the siting of vending machines;
- the **Licensing (Young Persons) Act, 2000** which prevents sales of alcohol to children;
- the **National Lottery Act, 1993** which prevents sales of Lottery tickets to anyone under the age of 16.

Figure 2 shows products with age restrictions in the UK.

The way that products are advertised and promoted

Legislation and regulations affect the way in which products are advertised or promoted to customers. For example, the **Food Safety Act, 1990** regulates the descriptions used in the advertising of food and the labelling of food on packaging. A food manufacturer cannot describe food in a way that is misleading on the labelling. Businesses therefore need to think carefully about the wording and images which they use on labels and packages.

A business must also be careful about the wording and images used when advertising its products in the media. The **Advertising Standards Authority (ASA)** is an independent body which regulates and controls advertising in the UK. Each year it investigates over 10,000 claims against advertisements and promotions to make sure that they conform to the British Code of Advertising, Sales Promotion and Direct Marketing, known as the CAP code. This code states that advertisements must be :

- legal, decent, honest and truthful;
- prepared with a sense of responsibility to customers and society;
- in line with fair competition principles.

The ASA does not have the power to force a business to remove an advertisement. In practice it often works with businesses to rework advertisements that it feels breach the code. In some cases it may put a great deal of pressure on the business to remove the advertisement. Figure 3 shows an example of how the promotion by a business was affected by the ASA.

Providing information

Many laws influence the information that businesses provide to customers about their products. As explained earlier, statements made on labelling and in advertisements are affected by legislation and regulation. Other examples are shown in Table 2.

Finance and payments

Legislation and regulation will influence how businesses collect customer payments and also retain financial information about

---

Figure 2 *Age restricted sales*

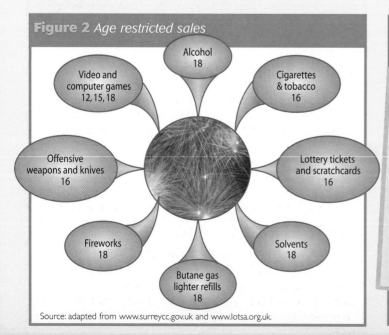

Alcohol 18

Cigarettes & tobacco 16

Video and computer games 12, 15, 18

Offensive weapons and knives 16

Lottery tickets and scratchcards 16

Fireworks 18

Solvents 18

Butane gas lighter refills 18

Source: adapted from www.surreycc.gov.uk and www.lotsa.org.uk.

Figure 3 *An example of the work of the ASA*

In 2005 the Advertising Standards Authority (ASA) ruled that a drink advertisement which led to complaints because it showed people spitting should not be shown before 9pm. The ASA received 272 complaints about the Fanta Z advert, calling it 'disgusting'. The advertisement showed people spitting out Fanta Light, which a voice-over explains does not taste as good as the new Fanta Z. The ASA said it was concerned young children would see the spitting as fun and easy to copy.

Coca-Cola, which makes Fanta Z, said the advert was not meant to be offensive. It agreed to amend the 40-second commercial's media scheduling to comply with the ASA's ruling.

Source: adapted from news.bbc.co.uk and www.asa.org.uk.

Table 2 *Legislation and information*

Development of Tourism Act, 1969
Effect - prices must be displayed in hotels.
Example - customers know that a room will cost £100 a night and cannot be misled on prices.

Trade Descriptions Act, 1968
Effect - prevents false or misleading information.
Example - a specialist activity centre cannot say that it offers climbing tuition if it does not have the facilities or staff to provide the service.

Sale of Goods Act, 1979
Effect – a product must correspond with the description, be of satisfactory quality and be fit for the purpose
Example - a waterproof jacket must keep out the rain.

Trade Marks Act, 1994
Effect - places control on the fraudulent use of a trademark.
Example - a t-shirt manufacturer cannot sell its own shirts with a Nike, Ellesse or Armani trade name, mark or logo.

Source: adapted from www.tradingstandards.gov.uk.

customers. For example, the **Consumer Credit Act, 1974** provides safeguards for consumers buying goods on credit. It also controls formats for indicating credit charges and documentation used by customers. The **Estate Agents Act, 1979** provides protection for clients' money when buying and selling property.

The financial services market is regulated by the **Financial Services Authority (FSA)**. It was set up by the **Financial Services and Markets Act, 2000** to prevent fraud and protect customers. Businesses can only operate in financial markets if they meet certain criteria.

Pricing

The control of pricing is an important part of legislation designed to protect customers' interests. Raising prices is one way in which businesses can make profit. If they are in a dominant position they may be able to 'exploit' customers by raising prices to very high levels. In other cases they may change prices as part of their pricing strategies. Legislation and regulations restrict the extent to which businesses can alter or set prices in a number of cases.

Price displays The **Prices Act 1974** and **1975** control and regulate price displays. They require prices to be indicated on goods or services offered by retailers.

Misleading pricing The **Consumer Protection Act, 1987** outlaws misleading pricing by businesses. It attempts to ensure that prices charged to customers are accurate and prevent exaggerated claims. So, for example, a business which claims to be charging 50% less than a year ago for a CD player but in fact charges the same price is likely to be contravening the Act.

Public utility prices The prices of utilities used by customers are regulated by a number of bodies in the UK.
- Ofwat (the Office of Water Services) - the water industry.
- Orr (the Office of the Rail Regulator) – rail industry.
- Ofgem (the Office of Gas and Electricity Markets) – the gas and electricity industries.
- Oftel (the Office of Telecommunications) – the telecommunications industry.

Businesses in these industries are often large. Some were former state run monopolies which were the only provider of the service. In many cases they still have dominant positions and limited competition, although the government is trying to introduce competition in these markets. One of the main roles of these bodies is to set limits on the prices charged by businesses providing public utilities. An example is shown in Figure 4.

Figure 4 *Ofgem price restrictions*

In November 2004 Ofgem, the regulator of the gas and electricity industries, announced a five-year price control to come into effect in April 2005. Companies will be able to spend £5.7 billion in strengthening and developing their networks and will be required to improve quality of service.

The proposals will result initially in an average increase of 1% on distribution charges in real terms, or about 6% on the average domestic customer's monthly bill. For the remaining four years of the price control period, prices will rise on average by no more than the rate of inflation.

Source: adapted from tdworld.com.

Customers' rights

Customers have a number of other rights under legislation. Some examples are shown in Table 3.

Table 3 *Customers' rights*

The Sale and Supply of Goods to Consumers Regulations, 2002
Effect - provide minimum rights on faulty goods and the right for returns, replacements and compensation.
Example - a faulty microwave must be replaced with the same model.

Sale and Supply of Goods Act, 1994
Effect - partial rejection.
Example - customers can reject two items of confectionery in a multi-pack that do not meet the description of the goods.

Directive 1999/44/EC on Sale of Consumer Goods and Guarantees
Effect - ensures guarantees and warranties.
Example - a business has to guarantee the conformity of the goods with the contract for a period of two years after delivery. If the goods do not conform, consumers can ask for the goods to be repaired, replaced, reduced in price or for the contract to be rescinded.

Unfair Contract Terms Directive 93/13/EEC
Effect - prevents an imbalance in the rights of the parties (the business and the customer) in the sale of products.
Example - a contract for the sale of machinery must be in clearly written terms and not have conditions which favour the seller.

Trading restrictions

Some large businesses or businesses which dominate a market because there are few sellers may be in a position to exploit customers. Legislation in the UK and EU aims to restrict activities which may be against the customers' interests. Such activities may include the following.

- Abusing a dominant position in the market, for example by raising or fixing prices. This may be the case if a merger between two business takes place or a business is in a monopoly position. Businesses in the UK with over a 25% market share are known as legal monopolies.
- Operating as an agreement, cartel or restrictive practice, for example by agreeing to restrict supply, rig bids to tenders for work, divide up sales in a market or refuse to sell to a business to force it out of the market.

The **Competition Act, 1998** prohibits these activities.

The Office of Fair Trading (OFT) and the Competition Commission (CC) have the power to investigate activities which restrict competition in any of these ways. Under the **Enterprise Act, 2002** the CC has the power to take action to remedy restrictions which may affect customer service.

Effects on businesses of compliance

How might complying with legislation, regulations and other restrictions affect a business? Table 4 shows some examples.

Table 4 *Effects on businesses and customer service*

Effect	Example
Costs	A business may have to change its advertising, food ingredients or labelling to meet regulations.
Training	Staff may need to be trained to prevent breaking legislation in the way products are sold or to take into account age restrictions.
Pricing	Energy businesses must operate within price restrictions. Information about sales and discounts needs to be checked to ensure that it is not misleading.
Product	R&D must take into account safety standards when designing products.
Production	Stocks must take into account the need for replacement of faulty goods.
Work practices	Returns policies must be put in place. Wording of contracts must be checked against legislation.
Strategy	Mergers which might be investigated may be stopped voluntarily.

The implications of non-compliance

Businesses that do not comply with legislation, regulation and working procedures may be affected in a number of ways. There are certain negative effects that the business may face.

Criminal law Some legislation is under criminal law. The activities of businesses which break these laws are a criminal offences. In these cases, businesses can be:

- prosecuted;
- fined;
- in some cases those responsible may even be imprisoned.

Some of the main criminal laws in the UK include the **Trade Descriptions Act, 1968**, the **Consumer Protection Act, 1987**, the **Food Safety Act, 1990** and the **Trade Marks Act, 1994**.

Civil law Under civil law customers must sue a business and take it to court. If the court rules that a business has broken the law, businesses may be ordered to pay customers compensation. Some of the main civil laws in the UK include the **Sale of Goods Act, 1979**, the **Supply of Goods and Services Act, 1982** and the **Sale and Supply of Goods Act, 1994**.

Other effects There is a number of other effects that non-compliance may have on a business.

- Products may be seized by courts.
- Business activity may be restricted in future, for example a product may no longer be able to be sold.
- The image of the business may be damaged in the eyes of customers. This may result in custom being lost to competitors.
- Directors may be disqualified.

However, in some cases businesses may risk non-compliance. They may feel that the costs of compliance outweigh the potential costs of non-compliance. A small business for instance, may be prepared to take the risk of breaking legislation because the costs involved in the 'red tape' of meeting the legislation are too great and may force it out of business. On the other hand a large business may feel that the costs of fines, for example, are relatively small and worth paying rather than meeting all legislation.

Select a business that can be influenced not only by legislation, but also by a well known controlling organisation. Examples might include:

- an energy company influenced by Ofgem;
- a telecommunications company influenced by Ofwat;
- a travel agent influenced by ABTA;
- a large business with advertising that may be investigated by the ASA.

1. Make a list of the areas of the business that could be affected by legislation and the actions of the organisation.
2. Explain how compliance might affect the business.
3. Explain the effects of non-compliance and discuss the implications for the business.

Research task

Meeting the assessment criteria

For one chosen organisation you are required to include evidence of the impact and effects of legislation, regulations and working practices on the customer service offered by the organisation.

Business example - Orange

Orange is a mobile phone operator which offers a variety of telephone services including sending phone, photo, video and text messages. Services offered include pay-as-you-go and monthly payments. The company was launched in the UK on the 28th April 1994. In 2005 it operated in 18 countries and had 50 million customers worldwide. Orange promotes its products in a number of ways. For example, its TV advertising produced to support the launches has embraced the cultures of the countries in which it operates.

In 2004 mobile companies in the UK, including Orange, developed a Code of Practice. One part of this is that some commercial content will be classified as unsuitable for those under the age of 18. They will be placed behind counters and only available to those who can verify their age.

As part of the telecommunications industry the price of Orange's services is regulated by Oftel, the industry watchdog. In 2001 for example, Orange criticised Oftel's plans to cut the price of mobile calls by inflation minus 12% (i.e. if inflation rose by 5%, prices would fall by 7%).

Source: adapted from www.orange.co.uk, www.theregister.co.uk, www.mda-mobiledata.org.

Mark Band 1 *Identification of key UK and EU legislation, regulations and working practices in relation to the products or services offered by an organisation.*
This requires an identification of the key legislation, regulations and working practices in the UK and EU that apply to Orange.
This could include:
- laws relating to the nature of products offered by Orange such as the **Sale of Goods Act, 1979**;
- laws relating to the way in which products are sold such as the **Consumer Protection (Distance Selling) Regulations, 2000**;
- controls relating to age restrictions;
- controls by independent bodies such as the ASA;
- controls by other organisations such as Oftel.

Mark Band 2 *Explanation of key UK and EU legislation, regulations and working practices in relation to the products or services offered by an organisation.*
This requires an explanation of the key legislation, regulations and working practices in the UK and EU that apply to Orange.
This could include:
- how the **Sale of Goods Act, 1979** might affect the nature of the products offered by Orange;
- how the **Consumer Protection (Distance Selling) Regulations, 2000** might affect the way in which products are sold over the Internet, such as the rights of customers;
- how working practices have affected age restrictions on products sold;
- how controls by the ASA might affect the promotion and advertising by Orange;
- how controls by oftel might affect the prices charged by Orange to customers.

Mark Band 3 *Explanation of key UK and EU legislation, regulations and working practices in relation to the products or services offered by an organisation, applying findings to particular products or services with realistic examples.*
This requires an explanation of the key legislation, regulations and working practices in the UK and EU that apply to Orange using realistic examples.
This could include the following.
- How the **Sale of Goods Act, 1979** affects the nature of the products offered by Orange. So if it offers pay-as-you-go service this must allow customers to top up as they make phone calls.
- How the **Consumer Protection (Distance Selling) Regulations, 2000** affects the way in which products are sold over the Internet. So customers buying phones sold on the website must have guarantees and returns procedures.
- How working practices such as the developed Code of Practice have affected the age of customers.
- How controls by the ASA affect the type of content used in advertising by Orange.
- How Oftel controls the prices charged by Orange to customers. For example, in 2001 it regulated prices by RPI minus 12%.

Portfolio practice · Specialist cake making

Carl Millwest runs a small business which manufactures specialist cakes and sells them from a store which is part of the bakery. One of the attractions to customers is to see their products being made through a glass partition into the bakery. Potential customers can also see the products being made before they order. Cakes can be ordered with specialist designs. For example, a customer can bring along a photo of a person and their face can be 'sculpted in ice' onto a birthday cake.

The business has found that sales tend to drop off in summer. It is considering two promotional strategies. One is to lower the price of the product and advertise it as 20% cheaper for the summer. The second is an advertising campaign in the local area. It wants to make an impact and is considering using 'shock tactics' in the adverts, such as people gorging out on cake and looking extremely satisfied.

Source: adapted from company information.

(a) Identify THREE laws that might affect the activities of this business.
(b) Explain (i) how each might affect the business and (ii) how the business might set in place practices to comply.
(c) Explain how non-compliance might affect the business.

Safe working

Business must operate in a safe and secure working environment. Section 63 explained that various laws, regulations and working practices affect the supply of goods and services to customers. These constraints also affect the working environment of businesses. Business must put in place policies to ensure that different aspects of work are safe and secure. These are shown in Figure 1.

Figure 1 *Areas that require protection in business*

Safety of customers

Security procedures

Areas that require protection in business

Safety of visitors

Safety of personnel

Safety of customers

Ensuring customer safety can take a variety of forms for businesses.

Products Businesses must ensure that the products they sell to customers are safe. Legislation is designed to protect customers from harmful products. Businesses that sell unsafe products may face fines or other penalties. Trading standards officers investigate businesses to ensure that they are complying with laws.

Table 1 shows some examples of how complying with legislation to produce safe products might affect the procedures and practices of a business. All products require safety standards. Table 2 shows processes that might be used to check the safety of certain products.

There are also independent organisations which exist that attempt to ensure safety of products. For example:
* the British Toy and Hobby Association (BTHA) developed the Lion Mark as a symbol of safety when displayed on toy packaging. All toys sold in the EU are required to meet the requirements of the **Toys (Safety) Regulations, 1995**;
* the British Standards Institution (BSI) issues the BSI kitemark

Table 1 *Complying with legislation to ensure safe products*

Motor Vehicles (Safety Equipment for Children) Act 1991
Requirements of Act - regulates shape, construction and quality of restraining devices for young children.
Example - simulate movements of young child when car is mobile, crash test.

Video Recording Acts, 1984 and 1993
Requirements of Act - the classification of videos/DVDs.
Example - check against classifications.

Food Safety Act, 1990
Requirements of Act - the safety of all food products.
Example - check all ingredients and test food products before they are sold.

Table 2 *Products where safety is particularly important*

Product	Safety requirements
Toys	Ensure safe to put into mouths. Ensure no harmful metal pieces.
Food products	Ensure fresh and non-contaminated ingredients. Ensure hygiene in production.
Transport	Ensure safety equipment which works (seat belts, impact resistance bags). Ensure safe working of parts and steering.
Safety helmets	Test for impact. Ensure cushioning is effective.
Electrical goods	Ensure no electrical faults.
Machinery	Ensure safety equipment is fitted and operates. Ensure no mechanical or electrical faults.

to a variety of products that conform to safety standards and ISO 9000 quality assurance standards;
* the British Electrotechnical Approvals Board (BEAB) inspects domestic appliances.

To be able to gain approval to use such quality marks businesses must submit products for approval and testing to show that they meet standards. These standards must then be maintained.

Figure 2 shows an example of how procedures must meet

Figure 2 Kitemarking for Christmas lighting products

Noma Lights Ltd sells Christmas lighting and decorations. It states that 'Any product which is certified under the Kitemark Scheme and which claims compliance with a British or European Standard undergoes thorough testing prior to acceptance under the scheme. Once accepted, all production is subject to the most stringent tests at all stages of production. Kitemark factories are visited regularly and all procedures evaluated, checked and approved by BSI's team of roving inspectors. Additionally, product is purchased in the open market and checked by BSI's technicians at Hemel Hempstead for continued compliance. Noma is proud to have an unblemished record of Kitemark production and is (we believe) the only importer offering Kitemarked Christmas lighting sets.'

Source: adapted from www.noma.co.uk.

Table 3 Products where safety is particularly important

Service	Policies and procedures
Taxi service	Check the qualifications and skills of drivers. Ensure drivers have a clean licence and a knowledge of the local area.
Child care	Ensure staff have qualifications, experience and temperament. Ensure 'police checks' are made.
Hairdressing	Ensure staff have qualifications and experience. Ensure equipment is working and materials are safe and not out of date.
Restaurant	Ensure staff are skilled and experienced. Ensure products are safe.
Leisure centre	Ensure safe facilities and staff are trained.

safety award standard requirements.

Services Businesses must also have policies and procedures to ensure their services are safe for customers and comply with legislation. For example, the **Supply of Goods and Services Act, 1982** requires services to be of 'merchantable quality' and at 'reasonable rates'. If services are not of merchantable quality the safety of customers may be compromised. Examples may include the safety of:

- a boat trip on a lake;
- a ride on a fairground;
- customers in a hotel.

Providers of services will also have to comply with specific health and safety legislation. For example, businesses which offer hair or beauty services must comply with the **Control of Substances Hazardous to Health (COSHH) Regulations, 2002** which deal with materials that might be used in beauty treatments. In some cases, local authorities require services providers to be registered and comply with standards of service. They are inspected by trading standards officers to ensure they comply with standards.

Some examples of specific services and the safety policies that might be required are shown in Table 3.

The **Financial Services and Markets Act, 2000** regulates the activities of many businesses providing services in financial and exchange markets, including banks, building societies, insurance companies and pensions companies. These businesses must have policies to comply with this Act which include activities such as dealing in shares, making investments and advising on life policies. The **Financial Services Authority (FSA)** will only allow businesses to trade in financial services if they comply with legislation. This should ensure that only reputable and experienced businesses handle people's money, which should help to protect investments and prevent theft.

Payments Ensuring the security of people's money is vital when receiving payments for goods or services. Many people are now using credit cards to pay for products. Businesses must have secure payment systems to accept customer payments, such as the use of PIN numbers. They must all have procedures

to ensure that payments are made correctly and money is taken from an account correctly. Many retailers today ask customers using credit or debit cards to insert their personal numbers out of sight from a viewer. This can be a relatively secure method of payment.

Secure payment methods are particularly important when selling products over the Internet. Customers need to set up passwords and identification numbers for their accounts. Website trading must be safe, with secure, non-accessible pages for payments. This is covered in section 46.

Customer information

Businesses must ensure the safety of customer information. The **Data Protection Act, 1998** protects the collection, storage, processing and distribution of information kept about customers and employees by businesses. It has eight conditions with which businesses must comply, as shown in Figure 3.

In order to achieve these a business may :

- provide customers with ID numbers and passwords;
- install software to protect computer files;
- only allow approved staff to access information;
- provide training in data handling and protection to staff;
- update information regularly and accurately;
- only request information from customers, on application forms or orders forms, that is essential;
- make information available and in an accessible form for customers on request.

Safety of customers and visitors

Customers and other visitors need protection from a variety of other risks when visiting premises, such as shops, factories or businesses. Businesses can put in place a number of procedures and security measures to ensure their protection.

ID and security checks As explained above in relation to

Figure 3 Procedures to comply with the Data Protection Act

Good information handling principles

- Processed fairly and lawfully
- Processed only for limited purposes
- Adequate, relevant and not excessive
- Accurate
- Not transferred to countries outside EU without adequate protection
- Processed in accordance with individuals' rights
- Kept secure
- Not kept longer than necessary

payments and data, ensuring that a person is who they say they are can ensure customer safety. It might prevent fraudulent use of credit cards, for example. Security checks may prevent unauthorised people entering a factory or unauthorised parts of an office or retail establishment.

Drills and evacuation procedures Carrying out regular drills for evacuation in case of fire or any other risk in offices, stores and other business facilities is vital for the safety of customers and visitors. This is true for all businesses, but may be especially important for large operations, such as sports events or airports.

Training Training staff in emergency procedures, evacuation procedures, how to administer first aid and other safety measures will improve safety for visitors and other staff.

Other checks A variety of other checks may be necessary for the safety of visitors and staff. These should include:
- checking fire escapes are clear;
- checking windows are locked when required, for example to prevent theft of customers' belongings;
- checking safety barriers are in place and working;
- maintaining the standard of the building;

- ensuring that production methods comply with legislation, such as the **Clean Air Act, 1993**, to ensure the safety of visitors to factories;
- ensuring fire escapes are clearly marked and visible.

Public liability In the UK, it is estimated that up to one million public liability insurance claims are made each year and the trend is growing rapidly as more people become aware of their right to seek compensation. A business can take out public liability insurance which covers it in the event of injury, illness or disease to any member of the public and loss of or damage to their property. Insurance cover is often as much as £5m or £10m.

Safety of personnel

The safety of personnel in a business is vital. Staff who are injured or ill at work may:
- take time off;
- have to be covered by other workers whilst they are absent;
- become less motivated as they are working in an unsafe environment;
- return and be less productive;
- leave altogether;
- sue the business and claim compensation.

Injuries to staff can also affect the customer service provided by the business. For example, if an experienced member of staff is absent or demotivated then the advice given by a temporary employee or a less than enthusiastic worker may not be as helpful to customers. Customers may buy goods they don't want. They may decide to shop elsewhere. The image of the business may suffer.

In the UK the main legislation which protects employees is the **Health and Safety at Work Act, 1974**. This places certain legal obligations on businesses as shown in Figure 4. The Heath and Safety Commission (HSC) and the Health and Safety Executive (HSE) are responsible for ensuring the Act is carried out. The Act allows regulations to be brought in when required to protect employees. Some examples include:
- the **Manual Handling Regulations, 1992** which relate to the handling of loads;
- the **Control of Substances Hazardous to Health Regulations, 2002**, which relate to the control of substances in production which could be hazardous to health, such as nuclear fuel or chemicals.

Figure 4 shows a variety of procedures that businesses may introduce to comply with legislation and to ensure the safety of employees.

Select an organisation where the health and safety of customers, visitors and employees might be particularly important.
For example, it could be:
- a local supermarket;
- a manufacturer of safety equipment, such as a child's seat in a car or a cycle helmet;
- a construction business.
1. Identify the possible areas of activity in the business where the safety of customers, visitors or employees

might be affected.
2. Identify and explain legislation that might affect business operations. You can find information on legislation from the DTI or from local authority trading standards.
3. Explain how businesses might put in place policies to ensure that they comply with legislation.

Research task

Figure 4 *Procedures to comply with legislation and regulations to ensure safe working practices*

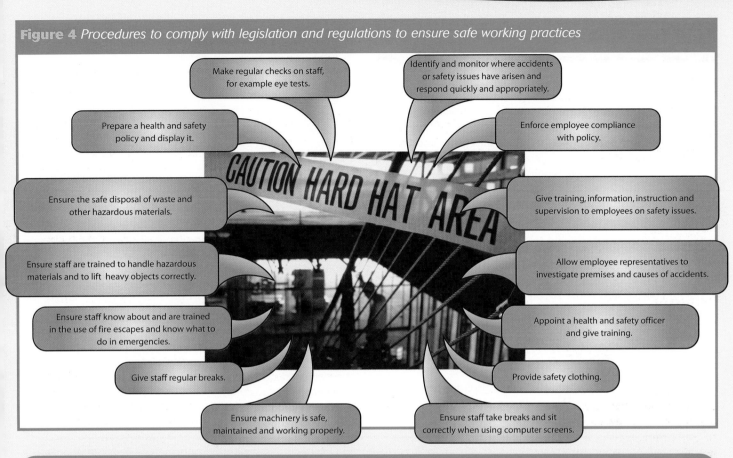

- Make regular checks on staff, for example eye tests.
- Identify and monitor where accidents or safety issues have arisen and respond quickly and appropriately.
- Prepare a health and safety policy and display it.
- Enforce employee compliance with policy.
- Ensure the safe disposal of waste and other hazardous materials.
- Give training, information, instruction and supervision to employees on safety issues.
- Ensure staff are trained to handle hazardous materials and to lift heavy objects correctly.
- Allow employee representatives to investigate premises and causes of accidents.
- Ensure staff know about and are trained in the use of fire escapes and know what to do in emergencies.
- Appoint a health and safety officer and give training.
- Give staff regular breaks.
- Provide safety clothing.
- Ensure machinery is safe, maintained and working properly.
- Ensure staff take breaks and sit correctly when using computer screens.

Meeting the assessment criteria

For the chosen organisation you are required to include evidence of the impact and effects of legislation, regulations and working practices on the customer service offered by the organisation. The evidence must consider the impact on the health and safety of customers, visitors and personnel and the policies and procedures that the organisation puts in place to ensure that it complies with these safety and security measures.

Business example - Carnworld Leisure Centre

Carnworld Leisure Centre is a popular leisure centre with over 1,000 members, who pay annual or monthly fees, which vary based on age. For example, the fee for two adults is £800 a year. Children under 5 with an adult use the facilities free. There are 32 staff. They include managers, administration staff, exercise supervisors, tutors and café staff.

It has five main areas:
- an exercise room – classes, including pilates and yoga, are held at different times of the day by trained tutors;
- a gym – with rowing, cycling, cross trainers, weights and running equipment;
- a swimming pool and sauna – classes such as aqua aerobics and swimming lessons are held as well as general use;
- treatment areas – offering treatments such as facial care, massage and sports injury treatment;
- an entrance hall with a small café and a relaxation area.

Members are given access cards which they swipe on entry to confirm their identity. All members are given an induction into the gym and have an exercise programme devised for their needs. Customers must book in advance for exercise classes. Treatments are at extra cost to the annual fee.

Source: adapted from company information.

Mark Band 1 *Identification of key UK and EU legislation, regulations and working practices in relation to the products or services offered by an organisation.*
This requires an identification of the activities in the leisure centre

which could affect the security and safety of:

- customers;
- visitors;
- employees.

The key legislation, regulations and working practices in the UK and EU that apply to these areas would then be identified. This could be general service provision legislation such as the **Supply of Goods and Services Act, 1982** and the **Health and Safety at Work Act 1974** or specific legislation such as the **Adventure Activities Licensing Regulations, 2004**.

Mark Band 2 *Explanation of key UK and EU legislation, regulations and working practices in relation to the products or services offered by an organisation.*

This would explain how the key legislation, regulations and working practices in the UK and EU would apply to the activities of the leisure centre. It would consider:

- legislation, such as the **Supply of Goods and Services Act, 1982**;
- regulations, such as the **Control of Substances Hazardous to Health (COSHH) Regulations, 2002** or registering with trading standards;
- general good working practices.

It would explain how legislation could affect the services offered by the business. This would consider how all legislation could affect many areas of the business including:

- the quality of service offered;
- the security of customers and data;
- protection of customers' details;
- the safety of staff employed by the business.

Mark Band 3 *Explanation of key UK and EU legislation, regulations and working practices in relation to the products or services offered by an organisation, applying findings to particular products or services with realistic examples.*

This would explain how the key legislation, regulations and working practices in the UK and EU would apply to the activities of the leisure centre, but apply legislation to particular aspects of the business with examples.

This would include a consideration of all areas of the business and how policies have been introduced to ensure safety and security in areas such as:

- the quality of service offered - whether the standard of pool facilities meets trading standards;
- whether safety marks are included on equipment, such as kitemarks;
- whether adequate safety procedures are in place to protect customer data, such as registration cards;
- whether adequate training has been given to staff to consider emergency procedures;
- whether products used in treatments comply with COSHH Regulations.

Portfolio practice · Fisher Scientific, UK

Fisher Scientific UK manufactures a range of products in specialist ranges, serving specific markets including Apparatus, Chemicals, Chromatography, Life Science, Microbiology, Drug Discovery, Chemicals, Safety and Education. Extracts from some of its policies are shown below.

Health and safety policy

The maintenance of high standards of Health and Safety for all employees, customers and the public is a subject to which Fisher Scientific UK Ltd attaches particular importance. It is Fisher Scientific's policy to promote continuous improvement in the health, safety and welfare of its employees insofar as is reasonably practicable, by:

- the provision and maintenance of plant, systems and working environments that are safe, without risks to health and adequate with regard to facilities and arrangements for the welfare of employees at work;
- making arrangements for ensuring safety and absence of risk to health in connection with the use, handling, storage and transport of equipment and materials;
- the provision of the appropriate information, instruction, training and competent supervision;
- the internal publication of performance measures;
- the conduct of operations in such a way as to ensure that the surrounding population and visitors to the site are not exposed to health or safety risks;
- ensuring joint consultation with employees in the achievement of the aims of this policy;
- contributing towards the formation of and observing all relevant codes of practice;

- monitoring the effectiveness of such an overall policy through the EHS Committee;
- developing an annual plan which highlights key tasks for the organisation;
- auditing systems to maintain high standards of compliance; This policy will be regularly reviewed and revised as necessary.

Privacy policy

At Fisher Scientific UK Ltd we are committed to safeguarding your privacy. We believe that the best way to protect the privacy of our customers and suppliers is to tell you what information we gather and ensure that you understand and consent to our uses of such information.

We may ask you for certain information such as contact information, telephone numbers, fax numbers, your email address, your location and the name of your organisation. This information is stored on our databases. The databases enable the business to collect personal information from you, to do business with you and respond to your queries.

Source: adapted from www.fisher.co.uk.

(a) **Identify THREE possible UK laws which might affect the activities of the business.**
(b) **Explain how these laws might affect the business.**
(c) **Explain policies that the business could or may have introduced to ensure the safety of:**
  (i) **customers;**
  (ii) **visitors;**
  (iii) **employees.**

How promotion is used by businesses

Promotion and consumers' wants and needs

Promotion is an important part of the marketing mix explained in section 36. It is the part of the marketing mix that is designed to influence and change customer buying plans. It can:

- affect customers' wants and needs that can be fulfilled by buying the right product;
- reinforce or change customers' wants and needs in addition to just acquiring the product.

Promotion can influence the reasons why a customer buys, or does not buy, a particular product. A successful marketing strategy is therefore based on meeting both the needs and wants of customers, in a profitable way.

Successful promotion

Successful promotion must inform, raise awareness and create desire about products in a way that meets the aims and objectives of the business, within constraints. For example, if a business aims to achieve 10,000 sales a year of a new product, it may have to create an anticipation amongst customers about the new product. It might choose to use a large amount from its promotional budget to make a great impact. An example is shown in Figure 1.

Figure 1 *Coca-Cola's launch of C2*

In 2004 Coca-Cola launched C2, a new drink with half the sugar, carbohydrates and calories of regular colas. The new product was introduced first in Japan and then in the United States in summer. It used a two-stage advertising campaign and made sure advertising reached all outlets (television, radio, billboards and the Internet). The first advertisements aimed to generate awareness. The second focused on stressing lower sugar and fewer carbohydrates. Advertisements were placed at the same time on all major television networks the night before the launch. On the day of the launch, consumers could access clips of the television commercials on the Internet. More than 10 million bottles were given out as samples at special events.

Source: adapted from http://executiveeducation.wharton.upenn.edu and www.carbwire.com.

Successful promotion must also be appropriate for the product, the market place and customers. This can be achieved by:

- researching customers and the market place;
- using creative input to make the promotion distinctive and effective in a competitive market where many promotions are being run to attract and influence customers;
- using experience and common sense to make sure that any promotion is appropriate.

When investigating promotion a business will need to answer certain questions, as outlined in Figure 2.

Figure 2 *Important promotion questions*

- What is it and how is it communicated?
- How is it implemented and how does it operate?
- What is the scale or extent of the promotion?
- Who will benefit from the promotion?
- **Investigating promotion**
- Who is the promotion aimed at?
- What is the extent of promotion and how long does it run?
- Who is the promoter?
- Whose promotional message is being communicated?
- What are the aims and the objectives of the promotion?

Table 1 *Reasons for promotion*

Aggressive reasons

- Creating awareness of a business, its products or a particular issue.
- Increasing sales volume or sales value.
- Launching a new product by raising awareness and attracting new customers.
- Increasing the number of customers by attracting customers of competitors' products.
- Increasing market share.
- Creating, enhancing or changing the image of a business or its products.

Defensive reasons

- Protecting a business from competition.
- Protecting a product from competitive pressure, such as a new, alternative, product or a competitor's marketing activities.
- Making a product viable and helping it to justify its continued inclusion in a product range in terms of sales, income and profit generated.
- Business survival against market forces.
- Protection from bad publicity that could affect the image of the business or its products.

Reasons for promotion

Promotion may be used by a business for aggressive or defensive reasons. These are shown in Table 1. Whatever its specific reason, promotion is carried out to affect customer behaviour in some way.

Promotional tools

Promotional tools are a collection of techniques that a business can use in its promotional plans. The main tools used by businesses are shown in Figure 3. There are other promotional tools that may be used, but these are the most common. They are explained in detail in sections 66-70.

Figure 3 Promotional tools

Sales promotions – promotions when products are bought, such as price reductions or free offers.

Public relations – the use of editorial space and broadcast time that is not paid for directly like advertising, such as media announcements.

Advertising – carrying a message using media such as television, radio, cinema, newspapers, magazines and the Internet.

Promotional tools

Direct marketing – communicating directly with customers and consumers in the target market.

Sponsorship – supporting an event, an activity or an organisation in exchange for having its name or product brand name linked directly with whatever is being sponsored.

Meeting the assessment criteria

In 2005 the MG Rover Group, manufacturer of motor cars, was subject to criticism in the media as a result of the collapse of the business and indecision over its future. It was suggested that creditors could expect 'nil or negligible returns on debts' and that anyone seeking to take over the business would 'encounter significant problems.'

Source: adapted from *The Guardian*, 11.6.2005.

(a) Suggest ONE way that the business could use an appropriate promotional technique to help overcome this problem. Justify your answer. **(2 marks)**

Expected answers
- *Use public relations/PR techniques to change consumer perception/image of business – this could result in positive stories about the quality of the cars/designs/engineering to rebuild status/reputation of business.*
- *Reduce price of cars – this would generate goodwill amongst buyers who will be pleased to get a good quality car for a lower price.*
- *Add value through offering an incentive gift to buyers – this will help overcome negative feelings of potential buyers as they will be pleased to be getting something for nothing.*

Mark allocation
1 mark for example of appropriate promotional technique.
1 mark for justification. **(2 marks)**

Examination practice · Keira Evers, Abstract Artist

Keira Evers is an artist who lives in Carlisle. She specialises in 'abstract' art based on the landscape of the Lake District. She has noticed that a number of shops have opened recently in the area selling prints of the Lake District and offering framing services.

Keira has decided that she needs to increase her promotion. She feels that the service she offers is unique in the area. She is also considering a 'tailored' service, where people can describe the picture they want and she will paint it.

Source: adapted from company information.

(a) Identify (i) ONE aggressive reason and (ii) ONE defensive reason Keira might have for the promotion and state why each is necessary. **(4 marks)**

(b) Give TWO promotional techniques that Keira might use in the local area to increase her sales and explain why each example is appropriate. **(6 marks)**

Sales promotion

What is sales promotion?

A well known saying is that 'There is no such thing as a free lunch'. This means that however attractive something may appear, it is likely that there will be 'strings' attached. There may be a hidden agenda or an ulterior motive, or a favour may be asked in return.

This can be applied to sales promotion. No matter how attractive the promotion may appear to the customer, it will need to do something that is to the advantage of the business making the promotional offer. If customers want to benefit from the sales promotion offer, they need to buy the product being promoted. It is this sale, the acquisition of customers' money and the profit generated which is the advantage to the business making the sales promotion offer.

Sales promotion methods involve offering customers some **incentive** to buy a product. Different types of sales promotions are used in different ways, depending on the aims and objectives of the business. Most sales promotions will have a primary aim. But they will also have secondary aims or benefits for the business as a result of running the sales promotion. Some of the reasons for running a sales promotion are shown in Figure 1.

Types of sales promotion

Sales promotions are presented in lots of different ways. Some are highly creative. But however they are perceived by the market, there will be a marketing strategy behind them all. The most common types of sales promotion are shown in Figure 2.

Price reduction

Price reduction can take many forms as shown in Table 1. Price

Figure 1 *Reasons for sales promotion*

- Investigating promotion
  - A combination of reasons/primary objectives plus additional benefits
  - As a incentive to try/buy/stock
  - As a reward to regular customers
  - To attract new customers
  - To appear cheaper/better value than competitors
  - To increase customers' overall spending/to increase income
  - To reinforce a marketing strategy
  - To increase market share/brand share
  - To sell more product

reduction tends to be used to meet short term, tactical marketing objectives for products or product ranges.

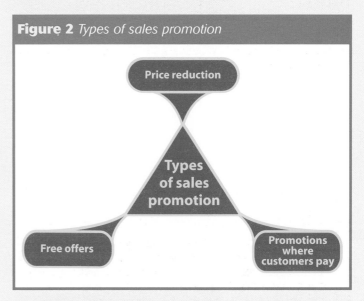

Figure 2 *Types of sales promotion*

Types of sales promotion
- Price reduction
- Free offers
- Promotions where customers pay

A feature of all price reduction schemes is the use of a 'close out' or date when the promotion finishes, after which the discount no longer applies. This is important for a business. Without a finishing date the price reduction could run continuously and customers would always be able to claim a price reduction. This could have a major effect on profitability and money would need to be set aside in the event, however unlikely, that all discount vouchers issued were claimed and needed to be honoured.

Some loyalty cards do not exchange points for vouchers, but offer a straight cash discount based on the value of points redeemed, or even gifts. Certain businesses use the term 'everyday low prices' or similar. This may be an attempt to position the business as a value supplier. But competitive pressures mean that as soon as customers get used to the 'everyday low prices' the business will need to use other promotions to remain competitive.

Extra product free Examples might be 25% more breakfast cereal packed in a box selling for the same price as the normal size box, or 33% extra free Vimto, a 2 litre bottle for the usual price of a 1.5 litre bottle. This type of promotion appears in many forms, but all result in a reduction in the price to the customer for a given unit of the product.

Buy one get one free (BOGOF) This gives the customer a second product, halving the retail price for a single product. It may increase the volume of sales, but it does not increase the retail value of sales. The objective may be to:
- encourage customers to switch to the brand being promoted from another brand;
- make customers think that they are getting a good deal if they shop at the retailer that is running the promotion.

Table 1 *Price reduction methods*

Method	Example
Straight price reduction	Product X usually sells for £1.00, but for a limited period it will be on sale for 80p.
Percentage price reduction	All furniture will be 50% off until the end of the month.
Vouchers	Vouchers with a monetary value are deducted from the selling price at point of purchase, if used by a certain date.
Unit price reduction	BOGOF, 3 for 2, multi-packs.
Loyalty cards	Collected points that can be exchanged for money off vouchers.
Annual or seasonal sale	For a short period all products on sale will be reduced in price.
Discount vouchers	Used to continuously reward shoppers for their loyalty, to promote new products or to give a boost to seasonal lines.

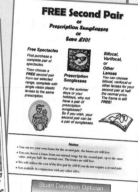

Three for the price of two This encourages customers to spend more than they may have planned to spend on just buying the one product they need, as they feel that they are making a saving. Total spending is greater and this increases income for the seller, usually the retailer, which can be used to pay running costs or generate interest from the bank.

Multi-packs Product X may sell at 50p for one. Six products taped together or in a single pack may be sold for £2.50. This is an example of a multi-pack promotion. By buying the multi-pack the customer is spending more on the total purchase. But the unit price of a single product is reduced and thus a cost saving is perceived by the customer. Multi-packs are often used for low value, everyday purchases, such as chocolate snack bars, paper tissues and soap.

Multi-pack promotions attempt to persuade a customer to switch from a competitor brand to the product that is promoted. The objective may be to increase the sales value by incentivising the customer to spend £2.50. The customer will be making a saving and the retail profit margin per item may be reduced. But the customer has been encouraged to spend more than the 50p that he or she would have spent just buying the one product actually needed at that time.

Other effects of this type of promotion are to:
- put pressure on competitors - while the customer is using all the extra products bought in the multi-pack he or she is not buying a competitor's brand;
- increase consumption - the customer has more product and as

a result he or she is often more generous or extravagant with the way the product is used;
- increase volume through the factory, as each purchase is of three packs rather than just one;
- clear excess stock that has resulted from the product not selling at the rate forecast;
- clear seasonal stock to make way for stock for the new season.

Although these types of promotion can have a dramatic short term effect on sales volume, a downside is that the consumer is 'taken out of the market' for as long as it takes to use all of the product. This means that the cycle of:

'buying > consuming > buying more'

is disrupted. In medium term repeat purchases will be reduced.

Free offers

At its simplest this type of promotion says 'buy this, get this free'. Free offers can take many different forms. However, the main condition is that the consumer pays for the product being promoted **before** they are rewarded for the purchase with the free item.

Free gifts Some retail loyalty cards offer to exchange points collected for free gifts. This is an alternative to loyalty schemes that offer discounts in the form of cash or vouchers. Free gifts for points schemes encourage customers to spend more in the shop and build up points for gifts that are displayed in mail order type catalogues. This type of loyalty scheme is popular with promoters as customers' perceived value of gifts is often much greater than the cost of the actual gift, at trade prices, to the promoter.

Competitions Another common way that free offers are presented is in the form of competitions. Rather than give every purchaser a low value free gift, a competition offers a limited number of purchasers the chance to win a high value free gift, such as a holiday, a car or a large sum of money. There is perhaps little to differentiate between a competition, which requires some skill and judgement to enter, and a lottery, which does not require any skill or judgement.

Free offer promotions, with prizes including competitions, prize draws and instant win offers, are subject to legal restrictions. Promoters must avoid running illegal lotteries and are advised to check with the **Committee of Advertising Practice**, or to take specialist legal advice. To avoid any problems, promoters will usually include an element of skill and judgement in the competition. To achieve this a tie-breaker will often be used, such as 'In 15 words tell us why you want to win this competition…' to identify the winners. A free entry 'no purchase necessary' statement is sometimes made to avoid creating an illegal lottery if entry in a chance-based prize promotion depends on buying the product.

Samples Giving customers a free sample of a product being promoted for them to try is an effective way of introducing a new product or overcoming resistance to buying something unfamiliar. Sometimes samples are distributed unsolicited, door-to-door in a mass campaign, in the same way as leaflets. These tend to be small, low value samples. More targeted sampling occurs when a business has a database of customers that are likely to buy the product if they know about it. Free samples can create this awareness. Some examples are shown in Figure 3.

A possible danger of free offers is that it can be wasteful and therefore unnecessarily costly to give incentives to consumers that might have bought the product anyway. An example of this is shown in Figure 4.

Promotions where consumers pay

This type of promotion is known as a **self-liquidator**. In addition to meeting the promotional aims, the promotion is designed to be self-funding, i.e. to be both attractive to customers and to pay for itself. Customers are given access to a special offer for a low or

Figure 3 *Samples*

- Motor car manufacturers often use the offer of a test drive. This is the 'free' use of a car for a period of time, giving customers a chance to sample a make of car they may have never tried.
- Sampling is sometimes done by demonstrators who put on a show of handing out samples of a product for people to try. This can often be seen in large retailers, shopping centres or supermarkets, where the product being sampled is on sale.

Figure 4 *Free newspaper offers*

Newspapers give away free CDs or DVDs to appear to be more attractive than rival newspapers. Regular buyers of the newspaper would buy it anyway, free gift or not. So the incentive may be wasted on these buyers. It may attract some new customers who are just buying the newspaper to get the CD or DVD, but the loyalty of these customers may only be short term, for one issue only just to get the free gift.

Despite this:
- the newspaper may achieve its objective of diverting buyers from rival newspapers in the short term;
- it may meet the objectives of its advertisers by boosting circulation and readership for a short period;
- it may even gain some new readers that try the newspaper to get the free gift, like it, and become regular readers until a competitor makes a better offer.

subsidised payment if a purchase is made of the product being promoted.

For example, coffee manufacturers sometimes offer consumers the chance to buy a coffee mug at a price that is lower than the price of similar mugs bought in a shop. It is likely that in a promotion like this the mug would be branded with the name of the coffee. This acts as a long term advertisement for the coffee. It reinforces the brand each time the mug is used.

Planning sales promotion

There is a number of considerations when planning a sales promotion.

Aims and objectives It is important to have a clear view of the aims and objectives when running a sales promotion. A promotion must fit in with the overall marketing plans and marketing mix or there is no point in running it. The marketing team should be able to forecast what is likely to result from the promotion. This may be increased sales, wider distribution or greater market share.

Cost A sales promotion needs to be costed carefully. It must be cost effective and achieve its marketing objectives or an alternative marketing plan should be considered. It needs tight control on the budget to make sure that it does not become more expensive than forecast. This can be achieved by setting a maximum budget, capping expenditure and setting a closing date after which the promotion will stop. Without controls like this the cost of a sales promotion can quickly get out of control.

Resources A sales promotion may be created and implemented by the business itself. If it lacks the resources, it can be carried out by a specialist sales promotion agency that has the necessary skills, expertise and resources to run the promotion on behalf of the client business.

Timing The launch of a sales promotion must be timed to maximise its full potential. There is little point in a manufacturer of decorative lights trying to launch a new sales promotion in December. By then it will be too late to be effective. Retail stores will already have stocks of decorative lights that they want to sell before January. It may, however, be appropriate for a retailer of decorative lights to promote in December when it wants to clear the lights from its store.

Equally important is the start date and the finish or closing date for a promotion. They must be clear to avoid overruns on the budget and claims or competition entries being made long after the promotion should have finished. Like other production processes, sales promotion will be subject to **lead times**. This is the time it takes to produce the different materials required, to launch it to a sales team and to introduce the promotion into the trade ahead of a launch date for a product. The lead time must be built into the marketing plan.

Table 1 *Appropriate methods off sales promotion*

Method	Example
BOGOF	May be appropriate for bottles of dish washing liquid, but not an appropriate sales promotion for a motor car.
Discount vouchers	May be appropriate for grocery items but not for designer jewellery.
A competition aimed at promoting a new soft drink aimed at young people with a prize holiday to Skegness	May not be as attractive as a prize holiday to Ibiza, no matter how charming Skegness may be.

Appropriateness It important to consider whether the sales promotion method is appropriate. Some examples are shown in Table 2. A business must think about how the sales promotion will be perceived by customers and conduct market research if necessary to find out.

Codes of practice All sales promotions, broadcast advertisements, direct marketing communications and other marketing communications concerned with promotion in the UK are subject to the **British Code of Advertising, Sales Promotion and Direct Marketing**. This Code is like a rule book for the industry and for any business that is involved in promotion. The Code is revised and enforced by a self-regulatory industry body the Committee of Advertising Practice (CAP) (see www.cap.org.uk).

Meeting the assessment criteria

A major chain of chemist shops has told a manufacturer of self-tanning spray that it wants to feature a promotion on its best-selling 125ml size during the summer months.

The chemist shops want a cash discount from the manufacturer that will reduce the selling price by 33.45% from £8.49 to £5.65.

(a) State ONE reason why the chain of chemist shops is likely to want this promotion. **(1 mark)**

Expected answers
* *To increase sales volume/to clear stock.*
* *To appear attractive to customers.*
* *To compete/because retailing is very competitive.*
* *To promote stores as places where shoppers get good value/bargains.*

Mark allocation
1 mark for reason. **(1 mark)**

(b) Apart from the direct cost, explain why the manufacturer is likely to be reluctant to agree to this promotion.

(3 marks)

Expected answers
* *Retailer wants discount in the form of cash - £2.84 per spray is likely to reduce manufacturing profit considerably - may not consider promotion worth running.*
* *Low price devalues brand – promotion is only about price - once*

lowered, consumers will expect low prices in the future.

Mark allocation
1 mark for reason why manufacturer reluctant.
1 mark for explanation
1 mark if reason applied to this promotion. **(3 marks)**

(c) Describe an alternative type of sales promotion that the manufacturer could offer that will not cost as much as the discount offer. Justify why this would be a suitable alternative to discount for the chemist shops. **(4 marks)**

Expected answers
* *Self-liquidating offer on associated beach product – consumer funds promotion rather than manufacturer – maintains full selling price/profit levels/perception of quality – at the same time is seen by consumers as an attractive offer and relevant to purchase/use of tanning spray.*
* *Holiday competition – chance to win a high value/luxury holiday with purchase of tanning spray – value of prize much higher than 33.45% discount – consumers like the chance to win something big and will think that the chemist shop is more interesting/attractive/has a better image than by just cutting prices, which can be seen as lowering standards/image/quality.*

Mark allocation
1 mark for basic alternative promotion.
1 mark for description of promotion.
1 mark for why suitable alternative.
1 mark if applied to chemist shops. **(4 marks)**

ʟxamination practice · **High street bank attractions**

High street banks are particularly interested in the custom of students and are keen to sign them up when they first attend university. In 2004 the high street banks were lining up a 'tasty range' of offers to tempt the new university intake. Most banks offered a free £1,000 overdraft as standard, but they also had a tempting range of other promotions. Some interesting promotions are shown in Table 3. Students should also consider the interest rate they will be charged if they go over their agreed limit. It is worth asking how such incidents would be treated before an account is opened. For example, in 2004 HSBC said it wouldn't add extra charges to students who went over their limit.

(a) (i) Based on the information, identify the customers that banks are targeting and (ii) explain ONE reason why they are keen to attract these customers.
(4 marks)

(b) Give TWO reasons why the promotions in Table 3 are appropriate for the customers the bank is targeting.
(2 marks)

(c) Discuss whether sales promotions are likely to be the most important factor in attracting customers.
(4 marks)

Table 3 *Bank promotions*

Bank	Offer
Lloyds TSB	Six '2 for 1' meals at Twice the Spice and Frydays restaurants. 10% off products at Blackwells bookshop.
NatWest and HSBC	A five-year young person's railcard, worth around £100 which gives a third off all rail travel in the UK.
HSBC	A free BSM driving lesson, annual student insurance from £24, and 20% off any purchases of Lonely Planet guidebooks.
The Royal Bank of Scotland	A 25% discount on selected concert tickets in the UK. A tie up with Vodafone which gives students a 40% discount on pay-as-you-talk handsets, up to a maximum of £120. Discounted nightclub entry and 20% off some CDs and books.
Barclays	A £20 Waterstone's/HMV voucher when students pay in £500 and a 15% discount on vouchers at both stores.

Source: adapted from *The Guardian*, 10.6.2004.

Advertising

What is advertising?

Advertising is a very popular method of promotion. Advertising refers to the use of any paid-for space or time in the media that is used to meet the aims and objectives of a business. Advertising can be used to achieve a range of objectives as shown in Figure 1.

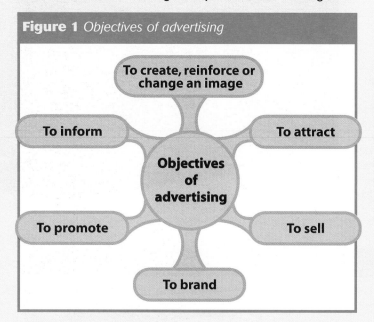

Figure 1 *Objectives of advertising*

- To create, reinforce or change an image
- To inform
- To attract
- **Objectives of advertising**
- To promote
- To sell
- To brand

Advertising is designed to sell or to carry a message to an audience. It can be presented in many highly creative ways and can be seen in a range of different media. Examples of advertising can be found all around:
- on television;
- in newspapers and magazines;
- in the street;
- in shops and town centres;

in fact anywhere that there is space to carry a message. Few advertisements are designed to have a single message. Different types of advertising are used in different ways, depending on the aims and objectives of the business. Most advertising will have a primary message, but will also have secondary aims or benefits for the business as a result of running the advertisement.

Reasons for advertising

As outlined in Figure 1, advertising is used to achieve a range of business objectives.

To sell The main objective of the majority of advertising is to sell something. It shows the product, then creates the desire, or vice versa depending on the advertising and communications strategy adopted by the business for the product. Advertising to sell is not just used by manufacturers or service providers. It is also used by retail organisations that want to move products off their shelves and generate income from the products that they stock and distribute.

Direct sell advertisements are used by businesses that have decided the best way of distributing products is to sell directly to consumers, cutting out other distributors such as wholesalers and retailers. Direct sell advertisements have to deliver a powerful message for two main reasons.
- They have to present and explain the product being sold.
- They must also be convincing enough to motivate the reader of the advertisement to make contact with the supplier and convince them to buy the product there and then.

Examples of direct sell advertisements are shown in Table 1.

Table 1 *Direct sell advertisements*

Place	Examples of products
Magazine supplements with Sunday newspapers.	Clothing, gifts and furniture.
Cable and satellite television channels.	Entertainment products such as DVD sets or magazine subscriptions.
E-tailing websites on the Internet.	Games, software, music downloads and ring tones.

To inform This is when the objective of an advertisement is to convey facts or information to the audience. Examples can be seen in public service advertisements run by government departments to announce a new benefit or to remind taxpayers of the deadline for completing and submitting income tax return forms. Businesses also need to inform, such as warning when a fault is discovered in a product or a bank or building society informing customers about interest rates. An example is shown in Figure 2.

Figure 2 *Informative advertising*

To attract Most clubs, theatres, cinemas, museums and other entertainment or tourism venues want to attract more visitors. So they need to advertise. An example is shown in Figure 3. By attracting visitors they are will attract income if the visitors have to pay for access. Museums and other places that have free entrance may need to attract a certain number of visitors to prove to their stakeholders that they are meeting a need. Schools and colleges also advertise to attract students and to attract staff to teach the students. In these examples the objective of advertising these products is to attract customers. Sometimes advertising is used to attract support in the form of financial donations, such as advertising done by charities.

Figure 3 *Attracting customers*

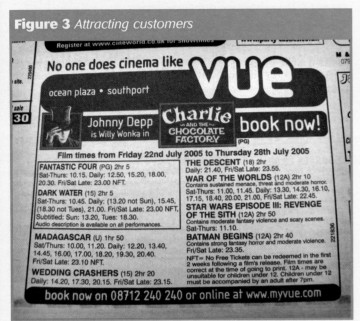

Figure 4 *Promoting*

To promote This is similar to the 'to sell' objective. It would include promoting or publicising an event, such as a dance or concert. Also, it means that an advertisement may be used to communicate a sales promotion. In this case the advertisement would communicate the offer, either a discount or competition or whatever form the sales promotion takes and the product or business being promoted. Retailers often use advertising to promote themselves, to publicise events and to promote sales or special discounts as shown in Figure 4.

To brand Brands feature in advertising in a number of ways. Some examples are shown in Table 2.

To create, reinforce or change an image Depending on the choice of media and the way that the medium is used, advertising can be an effective way of creating, reinforcing or changing an image. Creating an image is one of the objectives of advertising when a new product or business is launched. The computer games industry, for example, uses advertising to create an image that appeals totally to its target audience. It uses images, sound and graphics to exclude anyone outside this target audience. Once a business has an image that it is satisfied with and meets its marketing objectives by appealing to its target audience, advertising is used to maintain and reinforce the image it has created. Examples of this can be seen by looking at the way that well known brands such as Gucci or Coca-Cola reinforce their image

Table 2 *Brand advertising*

Method	Example
To create and support a brand in a specific way	Nike, Audi, Gap and others rely on brand image to add value to the product range and attract customers that are already committed buyers of the brand.
To support the brand by association with flagship products	Sony and other companies have a range of technical products. The business will select a limited number of products from its range, advertise them extensively, and the audience will start to associate the technical innovation with the brand name. When customers are looking to buy another technical product, they are more likely to choose one that bears the brand they have seen advertised. There is an association between the brand and the innovation displayed by the flagship product.
As an endorsement of quality and reputation	Tesco, Marks & Spencer, Procter & Gamble and other businesses that are in highly competitive markets use this method of advertising. In this situation, the advertising concentrates on the product features and the brand is used as a final endorsement of the product.

through repeat advertising. Advertising to change an image often occurs when a product is being relaunched, or when an image is perceived to be tired and outdated and no longer appealing to the target market.

Advertising media

Decisions on which form of advertising to use in the marketing mix will depend on what is appropriate for the product, the market it is aimed at, availability and access, and the budget available. Advertising makes use of many types of media. The main types of media available to most marketing teams can be grouped as:

- print, such as newspapers, magazines and posters;
- audio, such as radio and recordings;
- moving image, including television and cinema;
- ambient media, a wide range of non-traditional media and branding opportunities
- new media, includes texts, SMS, screen pop-ups, and other web-based opportunities

Each of these main types of media is explained and developed in sections 71-75.

Before deciding on which method of advertising to use, or whether advertising is required at all, a business must set its marketing aims and objectives. It must then make the decision, based on what is appropriate and what is most likely to achieve the aims and objectives set.

Another important factor in the decision making process is what budget is available. Advertising space and time in different media will cost different amounts, depending on the price of producing the advertisement in the first place and the size of the audience the medium will reach. The bigger the audience, the more expensive the cost of advertising in that medium. For example, a full-page advertisement in a national daily newspaper which has huge circulation is likely to cost more than a page in a local newspaper which has a much smaller circulation and relatively fewer readers.

However, depending on the business or product being advertised, it may be more appropriate to choose to advertise in a local newspaper rather than a national newspaper. For example, a local flower shop would not advertise in a national newspaper as it would be very difficult to service any orders that it receives from outside its immediate, local operating area. Conversely, a washing powder manufacturer that wanted to launch a new product with national advertising coverage would waste money if it decided to advertise in every local newspaper in the country. It could be more cost effective to advertise in a national newspaper, which could achieve national coverage with just one issue.

Factors to consider when planning advertising

A business must consider many factors when planning its advertising.

Media profile This is a description of the reading, viewing or listening market for a particular medium. The description will take the form of a geographic, demographic and psychographic segmentation (see section 33). When planning advertising for a

product it is important to match the profile of advertising media used as closely as possible to the profile of the target market for the product. If the profiles match, advertising is more likely to be successful. If the profiles do not match, the advertising may not achieve the marketing objectives. There will be a lot of wastage and expense as a result of advertising to people that are not in the market for the product. For example, if a new computer game is advertised in a gamer's magazine the profiles of the readers of the magazine and buyers of the game will be very close. If that same new game was advertised in a national daily newspaper, it may have the same number of games buyers among its readers, but the advertisement could be wasted on the majority of readers who are not in the market for computer games.

Coverage This is the percentage of the target audience that will be reached by a particular advertisement. Coverage can be increased by repeat advertising because each time an advertisement is shown the individuals within the percentage that are exposed to the advertisement will be different. Another way of increasing coverage is to advertise across a mix of different media. For example, a business may use television advertising to reach a mass audience and support the television advertising with posters. This mix will increase the exposure to heavy television viewers and also pick off the part of the target audience that does not watch much television.

Frequency This refers to how often an advertisement appears. It may be once a month or once a week in newspapers and magazines or, in the case of television and radio advertising, the number of times during a day the advertisement is broadcast. It can also be used to describe how often an individual in the target audience is likely to see a particular advertisement during an advertising campaign. Advertising plans often compare the likely effects of short, high frequency campaigns with longer, low frequency advertising. The decision about which to choose will be a balance of the cost and the impact of both campaigns against the objectives for advertising in the first place.

Timing A business needs to consider when advertising will be launched to make sure that it makes a big impact and maximises its potential. When planning the advertising of a product that has a definite start date, such as the opening of a new film, the timing of the advertising is vital. Starting too soon could mean that the target audience may be stimulated, but frustrated that it has to wait before the film is launched. Starting too late could mean the advertising may not have sufficient time to achieve full coverage of the target audience and will be wasted. It is important to plan the timing of advertising at the same time as other marketing plans to make sure that they co-ordinate and support each other. Equally, it is important to have a cut off date in advertising plans, to decide when not to advertise. Reasons for stopping advertising may depend on:

- the budget;
- the overall marketing plans, aims and objectives;
- the product life cycle;
- seasonal factors.

For example, it would be a waste of money to continue advertising an old product that has been replaced by a newer version. Like production processes, advertising will be subject to lead times, the time it takes to produce the advertisement and book it into media ahead of a start date. The lead time must be built into the marketing plan.

Appropriateness It is also important to consider how appropriate a particular medium is for the product being advertised. A particular medium may appear to match the profile of the target market. It may also appear to be cost effective. However, if it is not appropriate the image and reputation of the product may be affected. A small classified advertisement in a magazine, that has the right profile for car buyers, may not be as appropriate for a new model as full-page advertisement in the same magazine, for example. It is also important to consider what the audience can do as a result of seeing the advertisement. It would be no good advertising a direct sell product in a cinema where the audience will find it difficult to use their mobile telephones to call and buy the product. In this case it would be better to advertise to people in their homes. Here they will have access to the telephone, light to see to dial and are less likely to disturb the rest of the audience.

Cost All advertising costs money. Advertisers are likely to have a limited budget to spend on advertising. Balancing the two to get the most effective advertising out of a given budget is an important part of planning promotional activity. The cost of advertising can be divided into two different areas.

- The cost of production. This is how much it costs to create and put together an advertisement before it can be used. At the one extreme is the cost of producing a television advertisement, which is likely to be many tens of thousands of pounds. This will include not just the creation of the ideas and concepts for the advertisement, but the writing of the script, the hiring of actors, production crew, the film studio and the skilled technicians that make the film. During an evening's viewing of any commercial television channel there are many advertisements that vary in the cost of production, from lavish mini films with actors, through animated commercials to simple commercials that just show products on a simple set. The production of advertisements for other media is relatively less expensive as they require less resources for production.
- The cost of media space. This is how much it costs to actually show the advertisement to the target audience. Like production

cost the cost of media space varies according to how many people will see the advertisement, the proportion of the target audience that is reached and the impact it makes. The cost of media space is also affected by its own market and competitive forces. Newspapers and magazines compete with each other for advertisers as much as they compete for readers. As a result, they will use promotional tactics to attract advertisers, price being one of the most common. There is similar competition for advertisers between commercial television channels and commercial radio stations. Media space is also subject to supply and demand. This means that when demand is high the price of advertising space rises, for example at the time of important sports events. When demand falls, the cost of advertising will fall to attract advertisers back into the market.

Business objectives The most important consideration when planning any advertising is 'Will this advertising help meet the aims and objectives for this product or for the business in a cost-effective way?' If the answer is yes, then advertising is a marketing plan to consider. If not, then another marketing strategy may need to be found.

Advertising controls All advertisements should be legal, decent, honest and truthful. In addition to the terms and conditions laid down by individual media owners, all broadcast advertisements, sales promotions, direct marketing communications and other marketing communications concerned with promotion in the UK are subject to the British Code of Advertising, Sales Promotion and Direct Marketing. This Code is like a rule book for the industry and for any business that is involved in promotion. The Code is revised and enforced by a self-regulatory industry body, The Committee of Advertising Practice (CAP) (see www.cap.org.uk). The rules of the CAP Code apply not only to the advertisements in newspapers, magazines and on posters, but to many other methods by which companies communicate with consumers, including direct mail, emails and text messages, cinema commercials, special offers and prize promotions. Some examples of controls are shown in Table 3.

Advertising is also subject to consumer protection legislation, the most important being the **Trade Descriptions Act, 1968** which protects the customer against false claims, as explained in section 63.

Table 3 *Advertising controls*

Control	Effect
The BCAP Radio Advertising Standards Code	Sets out the rules that govern advertisements on any radio station licensed by Ofcom.
The BCAP Television Advertising Standards Code	Sets out the rules that govern advertisements on any television channel licensed by Ofcom.
The Advertising Standards Authority (ASA)	The independent body that endorses and administers the CAP Code. It is also responsible for investigating and adjudicating on complaints about advertisements by enforcing the BCAP code. (www.asa.org.uk).
Ofcom	The UK's communications industry regulator with wide ranging responsibilities across the UK's communications markets. At the end of 2003 Ofcom inherited the duties of the five existing regulators it replaced - the Broadcasting Standards Commission, the Independent Television Commission, Oftel, the Radio Authority and the Radiocommunications Agency.

Meeting the assessment criteria

Look at the advertisement in Figure 5 from a *Yellow Pages* directory.

(a) Identify ONE example of branding that is shown in this advertisement. **(1 mark)**

Expected answers
* *ABC.*
* *The ABC Garage Door Systems lettering/logo.*
* *The RGI symbol.*

Mark allocation
1 mark for example of branding. **(1 mark)**

(b) Explain why each of the following elements are included in this advertisement.
(i) The list of different manufacturers of garage doors, e.g. Cardale and Hormann. **(3 marks)**
(ii) The offer of free quotations. **(3 marks)**

Expected answers
List of different manufacturers
* *To show that the business offers a variety of garage doors - which offers choice to the customer - which should make ABC more attractive to customers.*
Offer of free quotations
* *To attract customers into buying the product/service - customers are attracted by perceiving that they get 'something for nothing' - free offers are a powerful incentive for most customers.*

Mark allocation
3 marks for each element. **(6 marks)**

Figure 5 *Yellow Pages advertisement*

Examination practice · BT and iTunes

In 2005 it was announced that BT had invested £6m in a new advertising campaign to promote a tie-up with Apple's iTunes digital music download service. The campaign, devised by advertising agency Abbot Mead Vickers, will run with the strap line 'collect the soundtrack to your life with Broadband from BT'. It will include a TV campaign which would run from 8th July to the end of September, supported by extensive press, online and direct marketing activity.

A BT spokesperson said the campaign is designed to bring to life the 'soundtrack to your life' theme with images and music from UK artists such as Supergrass and KT Tunstall.

The campaign promotes a new deal with iTunes, which offers new customers up to 40 free music tracks of their choice when they sign up to a BT Broadband or BT Yahoo! Broadband package. New customers will also receive a £15 discount on the purchase of an iPod. The offer will run until 23 October.

As part of the deal, iTunes will accept BTclick&buy, BT's online payment system, as payment for iTunes purchases.

Source: adapted from www.nma.co.uk.

(a) **From the information, state TWO reasons for the BT advertising campaign.** **(2 marks)**
(b) **Identify TWO factors which may have influenced decisions about the campaign and explain how each factor might have been of influence.** **(6 marks)**

Public relations

What is public relations?

Public relations, also referred to in its abbreviated form PR, is a promotional tool that, like advertising, uses media and events to achieve a range of business objectives. These include:

* to sell;
* to inform;
* to attract;
* to promote;
* to brand;
* to create, reinforce or change an image or public opinion.

Although PR may have similar objectives to advertising, it works in a different way. The main difference is that, whilst advertising relies on communication through paid-for media space, PR is based on the use of editorial space and broadcast time that is not paid for directly like advertising. For example, when a business launches a new product it may send a press release about the product and a photograph to newspapers and news programmes on the radio and television. The news media want to use the information provided by the business to report on the new product. The business hopes that it will generate awareness of the new product in a way that is not obviously advertising and ultimately that consumers will buy the new product.

The use of press releases is just one of the tools that PR experts can use to create awareness without it appearing to be explicit advertising. PR techniques can be used for all kinds of promotion and publicity and include press and customer receptions, open days and other publicity generating events. In addition to creating awareness, public relations can be used to change the image and perception of a product.

Like advertising and other promotional tools, PR must be planned to be effective. Different PR techniques are used, depending on the aims and objectives of the business. Most PR plans will have a primary aim, but may also have secondary aims or benefits for the business as a result of running the promotion.

PR can be used and presented in lots of different ways. Some are highly creative, but however they are perceived by the market there will be a marketing strategy behind them all. The most common methods of PR are shown in Figure 1.

Media relations

Public relations experts will offer to represent a business in the media. They will:

* generate positive publicity for the business;
* manage the calls and enquiries from the media to enable the business to concentrate on what it does best, i.e. run the business;
* protect the business from negative publicity or at least reduce its impact on the business, should it occur.

In practice media relations means keeping the news media and trade press up-to-date with news of the business, its products and any statements made by management. It will also handle the promotion of products in the media through the use of press releases, product features, news briefings and other events. Most articles in consumer magazines that describe new products will be as a result of placement activity by a PR expert. Many journalists rely on PR releases to help them keep up-to-date with new products, using stories and photographs provided by PR agencies. PR can work across all media. So in addition to traditional 'press' releases, the PR industry uses e-mail and other technology to spread the message on behalf of clients. An example is shown in Figure 2.

Figure 1 PR methods

Types of PR

* Creating, reinforcing or changing image or public opinion
* Spin
* Media relations
* Reporting on research findings
* Product launches and events
* Lobbying

Figure 2 Virgin press releases

Source: adapted from www.virgin-atlantic.com.

Product launches and events

The launch of a new product, or an important announcement about a business, will often be based on a PR event. These events are often linked to other marketing activities, such as the start of an advertising campaign or attendance at a trade exhibition. Sending a press release may be limited to a few pages and a photograph. A new product launch, however, is often important enough to invite journalists to a venue, a hotel, or conference centre. Sometimes the venue may be a room at the business itself, if appropriate, so that journalists can look around the business. Sometimes members of the press may even be invited on trips abroad.

There is also the opportunity of being briefed by a senior representative of the business, such as the managing director or sales director. This gives journalists the opportunity to question the business direct and is likely to result in more publicity than a simple press release. At such an event the product will be presented and journalists may be given samples or the opportunity to use the product and report on it objectively.

To attract busy journalists the choice of venue is crucial. It must be interesting enough to attract them and convenient for access. However, the launch itself must be worthwhile or it could be perceived by the journalists as being a waste of time and not generate the good publicity that was the original objective of the event. Product launches are often extravagant affairs that generate a lot of publicity. This is likely to be one of the main objectives. Television news programmes often have reports of new product launches that make the headlines. Other PR events, such as press conferences or a range of publicity 'stunts', are designed to generate news and publicity for an organisation, a cause or a movement. An example is shown in Figure 3.

Figure 3 *Publicity for an organisation*

In recent years the Fathers4Justice organisation has staged a number of audacious publicity stunts when members dressed as comic book superheroes appear on public buildings. The resultant publicity surrounding the event and the removal of the superhero-clad protester raises awareness of their cause.

Reporting on research findings

The use of marketing research findings is a common but effective way that PR can be used to generate publicity. The Consumer's Association, the consumer support organisation, is particularly effective in the use of research to generate publicity. The reports in each issue of its *Which?* magazines are based on independent research. To support the publication of each issue *Which?* sends out news stories based on the headline reports from the research in its magazine. Many of these are picked up by the news media and turned into news stories, that credit *Which?* as the source for the research. This is a powerful way of promoting subscriptions to its magazines.

Other examples can be seen in the news media. They usually start with '… business X reports that in its research 9 out of 10 people believe that …'. Using research can generate PR coverage, but it needs to be interesting, relevant and honest, otherwise it could be turned around and generate bad publicity.

Lobbying

This is the use of PR to try to influence 'policymakers' in favour of a particular cause. A business example would be if a company wanted to expand the size of its manufacturing capacity with the building of a new factory and it faced resistance from the local authority. A PR campaign based on lobbying would focus on explaining the benefits of such an expansion to all the influential stakeholders in the local authority. It would aim to put pressure on the local authority itself to change its mind.

Lobbying is also carried out effectively by community groups that state their case to bring about changes or improvements they want. PR is used to communicate with the policymakers to win their support and make the changes required by the lobby group. Examples include lobbying for cycle lanes or community transport for elderly people.

Creating, reinforcing or changing image or public opinion

This is an important role of PR. It is important for a business to have an image that is right for its target market. Once established, this image must be maintained and reinforced to make sure that the business and its products continue to appeal to the target market.

Through the use of publicity and promotional events, PR can create an **image** and protect that image over time. The image of a business is its 'public face'. It needs to be as attractive to target customers as possible. If not, the business could suffer as the market is attracted to competitors who may have more appeal. The image is created by a combination of the use of media, the products it produces, the cultural references it is associated with and the way it conducts itself ethically. Supermarkets, for example, have many similarities, although each has a slightly different image. Image is created through the use of products, colour, logos and photographs which all contribute to how the businesses are perceived.

Public opinion is closely related to image and perception. A business may have its own view of how the public perceives it. But

Figure 4 *Gap image*

In December 2004 it was reported in the media that Gap, the San Francisco based retailer, was looking to change its image in a number of ways.

- It wanted to shift customer perception that Gap brands have jeans and T-shirts not only for a morning walk or an evening stroll but also casual wear for a range of occasions like brunch, casual parties, a casual workplace or an evening get-together.
- It planned to change the images of its stores to make them more attractive to children and mothers. Examples included placing designs such as footprints painted on the floor to help kids figure out shoe size and story book readings to create a 'community of mums'.
- Its Old Navy stores offered gifts for the holiday season, like faux fur-trim jackets paired with neon striped scarves or cable-knit ponchos and fair isle sweaters.
- It was planning to change its collections according to the varying taste of customers of different countries. For example, European men are more daring with clothes. Consumers in Europe are more into heavy wear with lots of embroidery and embellishments.

Source: adapted from www.apparelresources.com.

this may be different from how it is actually perceived. The main way to measure this is through marketing research. Once the research has been done, a view can be taken and the changes made to the public image, if necessary. PR can help bring about this change by the use of publicity and promotion that makes the right connection with the public. For example, if a business is perceived to sell low quality products, this can be addressed by improving the actual quality, but it will need to be supported by PR that demonstrates that the quality has actually improved or to encourage news reports that support this position.

Figure 4 shows an example of how the image of a business may be changed to meet its target customers' perceptions.

Spin

Spin refers to the use of PR to put an interpretation or explanation on a piece of news or an event that is different from the way it is perceived by the majority of the audience. For example, a news story from an independent reporter, such as the BBC or a programme such as Watchdog, may be different from the same piece of news given by the business that is the subject of the news report. Politicians are often accused of spin, placing their own interpretation on something that they could not possibly have had anything to do with.

In business spin is used to avoid or deflect bad publicity. An example would be when a business has a programme of redundancies. The news media may focus on the number of people that will lose their jobs. The business or its PR representatives will spin the story to focus on the opportunities for the remaining workforce that will keep their jobs as a result of improving the prospects of the business through the redundancies.

Factors to consider when planning PR

Aims and objectives It is important to have a clear view of the aims and objectives of the business when running a PR campaign. It must fit in with the overall marketing plans that result from the marketing mix or there is a danger that it will be misinterpreted or waste money.

Cost A PR event or campaign needs to be costed carefully. It must be affordable, as well as being cost effective in the way that it achieves the marketing aims and objectives. If not, an alternative marketing plan should be considered.

Resource A PR event or campaign may be created and implemented by the business itself. However, coming up with creative and original ideas, writing press releases that are not just descriptive but are interesting enough to be published, and convincing media to publish the press releases and any photographs require special skills. Usually, a business will employ a PR expert or use the services of a specialist PR agency that has the necessary skills and resources to run the event or campaign on behalf of the client business.

Timing A business must consider when a PR event is held, when a campaign will start and when it will finish. Alternatively a PR plan may be expected to run over a long period, drip feeding stories and information into the media. PR events are often timed to coincide with and reinforce product launches and new advertising campaigns, to gain maximum media coverage and impact. PR can also be opportunistic in the way that it picks up current news stories and uses them to the advantage of the business. An example of this would be a business that supplies waste recycling industry, sending round a news release to promote its products following news headlines about the need for UK industry to be better at recycling waste. By doing this, the business is hoping to pick up publicity and sales for itself, from the larger, more general story that has made the headlines.

Timing in PR is also important when it comes to damage limitation. The speedy use of PR can deflect bad publicity. Examples of this crop up all of the time, especially when a well-known celebrity is in the news headlines as a result of breaking the law or an embarrassing event. This situation can be applied to a business that receives bad publicity for a product that is faulty or has other problems.

Appropriateness Like advertising and sales promotion it is important to consider appropriateness when planning PR events or campaigns. An event that is inappropriate can backfire and generate negative publicity quickly. Negative publicity can take a long time and often a lot of financial investment to overcome. For example, it could be embarrassing for an organisation promoting organic food to hold a PR event at a venue that does not itself serve organic food. Journalists may expose this kind of error quickly and report it in the media.

Meeting the assessment criteria

Choose Shoos Ltd imports footwear that is designed in Italy and manufactured in the Far East. The range was launched at the Footwear UK show (part of the larger Moda fashion exhibition) at the National Exhibition Centre (NEC) Birmingham in February, taking orders for stock for the following Winter.

The exhibition organisers have provided a press office and arranged a press briefing event on the opening day of the exhibition.

(a) Explain ONE other way that public relations (PR) could play a part in the promotion of the new range. **(3 marks)**

Expected answers
- *Produce a press release/photographs and mail it to editors of trade press – will reach/create awareness of new range for editors that do not attend exhibition - this information will hopefully be published.*
- *Run own press/publicity event on stand - invite key editors/journalists to see new range first hand - let them try/sample the shoes.*
- *Contact local radio/TV stations - ask if there is any opportunity of taking part in news programmes/fashion oriented chat shows/daytime shows to introduce new range - use the opportunity to generate awareness as well as sell shoes.*

Mark allocation
1 mark for PR method.
1 mark if applied to promotion of new range.
1 mark for explanation.   **(3 marks)**

Examination practice · Apple press announcement

At its Worldwide Developer Conference in San Francisco on June 6, 2005, Apple, the computer manufacturer, announced plans to deliver models of its Macintosh computers using Intel microprocessors by June 2006 and a transition of all its Macs to using Intel microprocessors by the end of 2007. Steve Jobs, Apple's CEO, said 'Our goal is to provide our customers with the best personal computers in the world, and looking ahead Intel has the strongest processor roadmap by far'. 'We are thrilled to have the world's most innovative personal computer company as a customer' said Paul Otellini, president and CEO of Intel. 'Apple helped found the PC industry and throughout the years has been known for fresh ideas and new approaches. We look forward to providing advanced chip technologies, and to collaborating on new initiatives, to help Apple continue to deliver innovative products for years to come.'

Source: adapted from www.apple.com.

(a) From the information, identify the role of PR used by Apple and Intel. **(1 mark)**
(b) Identify TWO factors which may have affected the decision to use this type of PR and explain how each might have affected the decision. **(6 marks)**
(c) Evaluate this method of PR to Apple and Intel. **(4 marks)**

Direct marketing

What is direct marketing?

Most marketing and promotional plans are designed to raise awareness and communicate with as much of the target market as possible and as effectively as possible. Using traditional media will mean that there is likely to be a percentage of wastage. This is because the message being communicated is received by people outside the target market, who make up the wider audience for all media.

The effectiveness of marketing and promotional activity can be increased through the use of media to communicate directly with customers and consumers in the target market. This is known as direct marketing.

Direct marketing was once looked upon as a fringe activity to support other marketing plans. But it has grown in importance in recent years. Research in 2005, carried out by the Future Foundation for the Direct Marketing Association (DMA), stated that UK companies are spending £14.1bn annually on direct marketing budgets. As a result, direct marketing is said to be generating around 9% of all consumer sales, which means that it is an important promotional tool for many businesses.

Reasons to use direct marketing

There are many advantages to businesses in using direct marketing. Some are shown in Table 1.

A key feature of direct marketing is the use of databases to manage the information about customers. They allow marketing communication to be directed precisely at the person who is in the market for the product at that moment in time. Direct marketing organisations spend a lot of money on market research to build databases that can be analysed and segmented to fit the target market as precisely as possible. This is sometimes known as 'database mining' because of the way that the information in the database is subjected to detailed scrutiny and analysis in order to identify the precise target group. Once the data has been collected

and analysed, the list must be kept up-to-date. This is done by 'cleaning' the database, checking that the information is still current by contacting the individuals on the database and asking them to confirm that the data is correct.

Direct marketing can take many different forms. Some of the most popular are shown in Figure 1.

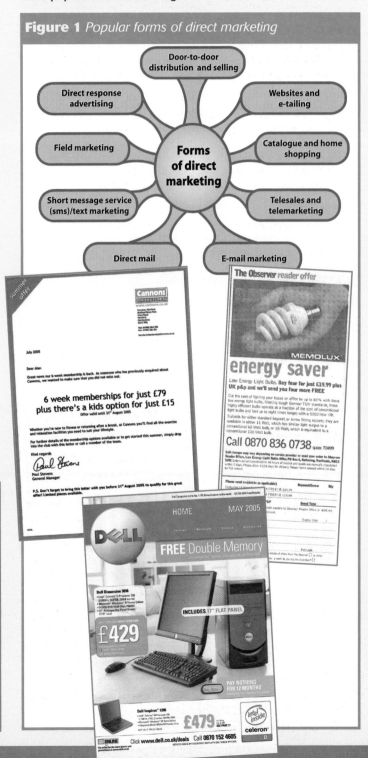

Figure 1 *Popular forms of direct marketing*

Forms of direct marketing

- Door-to-door distribution and selling
- Direct response advertising
- Websites and e-tailing
- Field marketing
- Catalogue and home shopping
- Short message service (sms)/text marketing
- Telesales and telemarketing
- Direct mail
- E-mail marketing

Table 1 *Reasons for direct marketing*

- The ability to target customers more precisely.
- The ability to communicate directly with the target market.
- It can reduce the wastage factor, advertising to people that are not in the target market. This can be especially important if a business operates in a limited geographic area.
- Its precision means that it is relatively cost effective for each sale achieved.
- By selling direct it avoids the need to establish distribution though the retail sector and gives the supplier the retail margin.
- Many customers are pleased to be dealing direct with the supplier rather than through an intermediary.
- Customers think that they are getting something special, that is not generally available.

Database marketing and the use of direct mail

This is the use of information in a database for direct marketing. In this situation direct marketing can take many different forms. The most common is the use of leaflets and promotional material that are mailed directly to potential customers and consumers. Most homes will receive some direct mail. The range of material sent to homes is likely to include a wide range of leaflets and promotional material. This shows the range of businesses that use direct mail.

Direct mail is sometimes referred to as 'junk mail'. This is a result of direct mail not being targeted precisely enough and being sent to someone who is outside the target market. If the person is in the target market then the direct mailing will not be perceived as junk mail, but as something useful and interesting that may prompt them to buy the product. Sometimes direct mailing is in the form of a 'personal letter' direct from the business to the customer. This is a common approach used by businesses in finance or insurance. Increasingly, direct e-mail is also being used.

The use of door-to-door leaflet drops is closely related to the use of direct mail. In this situation a geographic area is segmented and targeted for distribution of promotional leaflets based on criteria set by the business whose leaflets are being distributed. The targeting tends to be less precise as it is unlikely that the business delivering the leaflets will know the names of individuals within a household. But it can be a very effective way of raising awareness in a local area. Door-to-door leaflets are a favourite of local businesses shown in Table 2.

Table 2 Local businesses using door-to-door leaflets

- Restaurants.
- Estate agents.
- Take-aways.
- Tree management and felling.
- Window cleaning.
- Car washing and valeting.
- Gardeners.
- Painters.
- Decorators.
- House cleaners.
- Plumbers.

FREE ADVICE AND ESTIMATES

Specialists In Garden Design, Construction and Maintenance
Tree and Shrub Pruning
Paving and Driveways
Fully Qualified Tradesmen - 25 years experience (Kew Cert.)

Powerwashing for Drives and Patios

Clovelly Landscapes

Prop: T.A. Trafford

12 Moorhey Crescent
Penwortham
Preston PR1 0ST

Tel: (01772) 746772
Mobile: 0777 9486 935

M. A. MOXHAM
*Painter and Decorator
of Penwortham*

Introducing
EMMA COOK
Specialist Paint Finishes

46, Shaftesbury Avenue,
Penwortham, Preston, PR1 0EL
Telephone: (01772) 745806 & 816680

Catalogue and home shopping

Mail order shopping has always been popular in the UK. Research published by Euromonitor estimates that the UK market for mail order and home shopping continues to grow. In 2002 it reached a value of nearly £11.758 bn, making it a very important retail sector. In the past the business was dominated by a small number of large catalogues that offered a wide range of goods, including clothing, home and leisure goods from Littlewoods, Kays and GUS (Great Universal Stores). Catalogues offered a wide choice and the

convenience of home delivery. Another attraction was the credit terms offered. The full price was often divided into a number of small payments that were collected by a local agent once a week or monthly. The growth in consumer use of credit cards has changed this aspect of the appeal of mail order catalogues. Now, the focus is much more on offering good value, good quality products combined with the benefits of being able to choose in the comfort of the home and have the goods delivered to the door.

Another change in mail order has been the growth of specialist catalogues focused on niche markets. Many hobby and leisure interests have a specialist mail order catalogue. The success of these small specialist catalogues has been based on combining the general appeal of mail order shopping with the opportunity to buy specialist items that are not available in shops. Catalogue providers use database marketing to promote their catalogues to consumers that have the profile to match the goods being offered. Some examples are shown in Table 3. There are many more specialist catalogues. What they all have in common is the use of database marketing which provides the opportunity to sell direct to the target market.

Table 3 Specialist catalogues

Business	Products
Lakeland	Kitchenware, cooking and household goods.
Viking	A business-to-business stationery catalogue.
Screwfix	DIY tools and fixings.
Lands' End	Clothing and products for the home.

One further change in catalogue and home shopping has been the method of communication. Mail order via post remains the most common method of delivery of goods to the home. But there has been a growth in mail order via telephone ordering and also in mail order via the Internet, the fastest growing sector. Most mail order catalogues now have an 'on-line' version. Many of the major high street retailers have also introduced an on-line shopping option. In addition, many new retail ventures have decided to set up as on-line e-tailers as an alternative to either traditional shop premises or even mail order catalogues. This is yet another example of how the large markets are being segmented into niches and each niche is attracting suppliers of specialist goods to meet the needs of customers.

Information about the use of catalogue and home shopping can be found at www.britishcatalogues.co.uk. It shows a cross section of major mail order catalogues that are operating today, as well as a history of catalogue shopping in Britain.

Door-to-door distribution and selling

Perhaps the most direct selling method is a sales person turning up on the doorstep with a range of products to sell. This has been a sales method traditionally associated with household goods. Businesses such as Betterware, a direct seller of houseware, and Avon cosmetics have made a great success of this method. The business usually supports the door-to-door direct sales team with a product catalogue that is left with customers. The order is collected at the next visit. These businesses used no other method of distribution in the past. However, many door-to-door sales businesses have adapted to modern ways of selling and buying. They now offer customers the opportunity to buy their products from catalogues, by telephone or over the Internet, as well as from representatives that call at the door.

Milk and dairy products also have a tradition of door-to-door delivery. This industry has seen a decline in trade as more customers shop at large grocery supermarkets and add milk and dairy products to the normal weekly shopping. As a result, dairy deliveries have had to look at ways of improving their business. Some examples are shown in Table 4.

> **Table 4** *Methods of improving dairy businesses*
>
> - Adding to the product range associated goods, such as organic vegetables and food products.
> - Targeting older customers who do not have access to large grocery supermarkets.
> - Offering a leaflet and magazine delivery service that can take place during a milk delivery round.

Telesales and telemarketing

This is the communication of sales and marketing information via the telephone. For many small businesses, particularly those offering **business to business** (B2B) products or services, this is how they start to communicate with customers. It often involves 'cold calling' - telephoning without any previous contact. Some businesses rely totally on telesales for business and employ specialist telesales organisations to generate sales leads which can then be followed up by their own specialist or technical sales representatives.

Telesales has earned a bad reputation as a result of indiscriminate calling and pressure selling of household goods, such as double glazing and fitted kitchens. However, used in the right way and carried out by well-trained telesales staff, it can be of benefit to a business and its customers. A regular call to check on stock levels and to take orders as required can be a valuable service to small businesses that may not have the resources to do this themselves. In this situation telesales can help them avoid the problems of going out of stock of a particular item, with a resulting loss of sales and reputation.

E-mail marketing

Although disregarded by many e-mail users as unwanted 'spam', there is a place for direct e-mails in the marketing plans of many specialised businesses. Some businesses go to great lengths to collect e-mail addresses of people that may be interested in their products, offering incentives for e-mail addresses, such as running competitions. The names and addresses they collect may not be customers today, but could be in future.

Businesses like ticket agencies, hotel groups and travel companies use direct e-mails effectively. They record what customers buy and then e-mail them with news of availability of similar items. The idea is that if customers have bought once, there is a high likelihood that they will buy again.

The use of targeted e-mails is also being employed effectively by music groups that have a small but dedicated cult following. Such groups may not have widespread distribution through traditional music retail outlets, but they can e-mail each of their fans directly to inform them of new releases. There are advantages for both the group and its fans.

- The group reaches the target market very cheaply.
- The target market is pleased to get the news direct from the band.
- The target market is likely to buy direct, as it will be buying something that is not generally available.

Short message service(sms)/text marketing

The widespread distribution of mobile phones, combined with the high use of text messages, means that this has become an important communications medium for marketing purposes. The effective targeting of text messages relies on a business having an accurate and up-to-date database to identify customers that are in the target market. From this database the business can then launch its campaign.

Text marketing is being used to communicate new product news and promotional offers. New technology, such as Bluetooth, will enable text marketing to become even more targeted in the future as mobile phone messages are linked to retail sites and even promotional displays within a retail outlet. Customers walking by will be sent a message from the shop or display to attract them into the shop, to create awareness of the promotion and encourage them to buy.

Field marketing

This is a group of activities within direct marketing. Examples are shown in Figure 2. These activities are considered to be 'direct marketing' activities because they all involve face-to-face contact with customers and consumers.

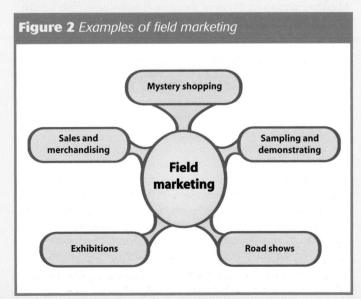

> **Figure 2** *Examples of field marketing*

Sales and merchandising Many businesses still rely on a team of sales representatives to communicate news of new products or promotional deals to business-to-business (B2B) customers. An extension of this is **field merchandising**. It is the use of a team that visits retail sites on behalf of a manufacturer to make sure that its products are being displayed in the optimum way and that promotional material is in place. Merchandisers have also become businesses in themselves. For example, many products placed in shops to generate 'impulse sales' are owned and maintained by merchandising organisations. The retailer takes a percentage of the sales in exchange for the use of the space in its shop for the rack of products. Examples include racks of hair and beauty accessories, CDs, greetings cards and paperback books.

Demonstrations The use of demonstrators, or people giving out samples of new products, can be seen in many large retail outlets, such as supermarkets and shopping malls. This is a popular way of generating interest in a product or getting consumers to try a new product, such as a food or drink, that they would not normally buy.

Road shows On a larger scale, simple product demonstrations can develop into a 'road show'. This is direct marketing from a mobile vehicle, such as a caravan, which is effectively a mobile exhibition or product display. If customers cannot get to see a product, the business takes the product to them. Road shows are often located in town centres, shopping malls, railway stations or other areas where a large number of people pass by.

Exhibitions Exhibitions and trade shows are a more formal, static version of the road show. A business will buy space in an event that is organised to attract customers to a central venue where they can see products and meet representatives from a number of businesses. Having bought the space in the exhibition it is up to the business how it uses the space to attract attention and present its products. Exhibitions are a valuable and important way of launching new products.

Exhibitions take place in many areas of the UK. Figure 3 shows two examples of large centres although there are many smaller centres locally. The advantages of exhibitions are shown in Table 5.

Mystery shopping Mystery shopping is when researchers pose as customers and record how they are dealt with by staff in shops that are being researched. Mystery shoppers can be used to

Figure 3 *UK exhibition centres*

The National Exhibition Centre near Birmingham. www.necgroup.co.uk gives information about what is on.

Earls Court and Olympia in London. www.eco.co.uk gives information about what is on.

promote products by rewarding retailers that offer a particular brand when the mystery shopper asks for a generic product. They can also be used to monitor the quality of customer service or security in a business, by reporting the good and bad points of how they were treated. An example is shown in Figure 4.

Table 5 *Advantages of exhibitions*

- They attract large numbers of potential customers, often far more than could be contacted by calling or visiting to present the products.
- The products themselves will be on show so that customers can see them, handle them, use them and then draw their own conclusions.
- Exhibitions and trade shows are run throughout the year at venues large and small for business to use.
- Some exhibitions are very specialised and aimed at a particular target market. Others are more general and will feature products and exhibitors from different trade sectors.

Figure 4 *Use of mystery shoppers*

Guardian Newspapers Limited (GNL) is comprised of the *Guardian, The Observer, Guardian Unlimited, Guardian Weekly* and *Money Observer*. In 2004 it was planning to recruit a team of mystery shoppers (target 47) from retired Guardian personnel who will be reporting back each month on all aspects of the reader offers service.

Source: adapted from www.guardian.co.uk.

Direct response advertising

This is an advertising campaign run via press, television or radio, which includes a direct invitation for a customer to telephone for further information or to purchase the goods or services. Usually a business will employ the services of a bureau or call centre to act on its behalf to run the direct response campaign. They will receive telephone calls and fulfil the customer request for further information to be given or sent, or to take orders for the goods or services offered. Examples of direct response advertising can be found in many media, as shown in Table 6.

Table 6 *Direct response advertising*

Media	Effects
Magazines and newspapers	Range from full-page glossy advertisements to smaller 'offers' that are presented as being exclusive to readers of that particular magazine.
Radio	Direct response not only has to present the product and attract customers. It also relies on the listener taking down details of how to make contact, such as telephone number or web address.
Television	It is sometimes seen within normal advertising breaks between programmes. But it is not common because of the cost and the need to explain not just the product, but also the means of ordering and payment. Products being advertised tend to be aimed at the mass market. Direct response advertising has evolved into specialist shopping channels such as QVC and Ideal World. They present products and generate direct response sales.

The most important factors about direct response advertising are:
- to make it easy for customers to make contact – a clear and bold telephone number or web address for example;
- to make it easy for customers to pay – usually via credit card.

Websites and e-tailing

The growth of computers with Internet access in homes has led to a massive growth in web-based businesses. Many businesses have a website from which they seek to sell direct to customers, as explained in unit 4. For some businesses this is the only way that they trade. For others, such as the major high street retailers, it is just another way of communicating and distributing to their customers.

If a business wants to trade successfully from a website, it is important to let customers know that it has a website. Competition on the Internet means that it is rarely enough to rely on customers using search engines to find a website. The site itself will need to be marketed to potential customers, just like any other product.

Factors to consider when planning direct marketing

Aims and objectives It is important to have a clear view of the aims and objectives of a business when running a direct marketing campaign. It must fit in with the overall marketing plans that result from the marketing mix or there is a danger that it will be misinterpreted or waste money.

Cost Direct marketing needs to be costed carefully. It must be affordable, as well as being cost effective in the way that it achieves the marketing objectives. If not, an alternative marketing plan should be considered.

Response rate Response rates, a forecast of how many responses, how many enquiries or sales are likely from direct marketing, are available for most media. The **Direct Marketing Association** (www.dma.org.uk) monitors response rates and provides information and advice for businesses planning direct marketing activity. In its 2003 report, the **Direct Mail Information Service** (www.dmis.co.uk) noted an average response rate across three thousand direct mail campaigns of nearly 11%. Just like any other business promotions, this rate will vary widely depending on the market, the design of the mailing and other variable factors. Many businesses experience response rates of just low, single figures. This indicates a huge wastage. Careful targeting, and improvements to the design of the mailing and the promotional offer can improve the response rate.

Resources A direct marketing campaign may be created and implemented by the business itself. However, it may be more effective to employ the services of a specialist organisation to deal with direct marketing activity and to handle responses. This will free the business to concentrate its own resources on the core business.

Timing Like any other marketing plans, a business must consider when a direct marketing campaign is run, when it starts and when it should end. It must also consider when the target market will be open to direct marketing, when it is likely to generate the best response, and how to avoid times when the target market is likely to be distracted or not accessible, such as during summer holiday periods.

Appropriateness As well as timing, it is important to consider appropriateness when planning direct marketing activity. For example:
- some products can be sold effectively by telesales;
- some require visual or practical demonstration;
- some are more suited to direct response advertising than others;
- some may demonstrate well, but others are best sold in boxed form.

A campaign that is not appropriate can generate negative publicity quickly.

A business must also consider how the target market will respond to the direct marketing campaign. Conducting marketing research by piloting the campaign in a small test area before launching is a good way of testing what will work well and what may need changing or improving to make the campaign more effective.

Meeting the assessment criteria

The marketing team at Seeford College is considering using direct mail to promote new evening classes in leisure subjects.

(a) State what is meant by direct mail and give ONE example that you have seen to support your statement. **(2 marks)**

Expected answers
* *Marketing/promotional communication that is sent/mailed direct to target market.*
* *Marketing material that is mailed to homes/businesses.*

Examples
* *Mail shot promoting local theatre.*
* *Menu from local restaurant posted to homes in catchment area.*
* *Double glazing leaflets mailed to people's homes.*
* *Mail order stationery catalogue sent to business customers.*
* *Fashion brochure with mail order sale offers sent to customers.*

Mark allocation
1 mark for statement.
1 mark for example. **(2 marks)**

(b) The marketing team plans to send a covering letter and an information sheet about the courses in each mailing. Explain the function of each item in the mailing. **(6 marks)**

Expected answers
Covering letter
* *Introduces college.*
* *Explains why mailing is sent.*
* *Lists/explains content of each item in mailing.*
* *Notes address/phone/number/contact details.*
* *Notes important facts such as start date/end date/cost/how many classes.*
* *Provides contact name for further information - so that recipient can*
find out further information if required - creates personal contact with organisation.

Information sheet
* *Lists subjects/classes.*
* *Explains the content/coverage of each course.*
* *States how many/how long for each class/course.*
* *Gives details of teaching staff/names/credentials.*
* *States location of each course.*
* *Gives details of outcome of course - gives details of any qualification/certification likely to be obtained as a result of course - provides references for person receiving letter.*

Mark allocation
1 mark for each point of explanation
or
1 mark for point of explanation + 1 mark application
+ 1 mark for development. **(6 marks)**

(c) Describe how the college can create or obtain an address list for this mailing. **(2 marks)**

Expected answers
* *Use database of names/addresses on file – use names of people that have previously takes leisure courses/expressed interest in the past.*
* *Use electoral role – select households in areas that match target market.*
* *Buy a mailing list from a list broker of people that match target profile of customers – someone else has already done the work of profiling/selecting names within target market.*
* *Advertise in local newspapers – ask people who are interested in leisure courses to provide names and addresses.*

Mark allocation
1 mark for how list obtained or created.
1 mark for developed answer. **(2 marks)**

Examination practice · Lands' End

Lands' End is a direct merchant of traditionally-styled clothing for the family, soft luggage and products for the home. It works directly with mills and manufacturers, cutting out intermediaries and passing on savings to customers in lower prices. An essential part of its promotion is the 250 million plus catalogues a year that it sends to customers' homes. These include:
* The Lands' End Catalogue - casual clothing for men and women;
* Lands' End Kids - clothing for children from newborns to pre-teens;
* Lands' End for School - uniforms and school-appropriate clothing, designed to meet dress-code requirements in sizes for children and adults;
* Lands' End Home - products for the home with a focus on 'honest value'.

Also, www.landsend.com is the world's largest (in business volume) apparel website. It aims to foster 'one-on-one relationships' with its customers. For example, customers can create a 3D model of themselves from their measurements and then try on an item. Customers can also subscribe to a newsletter which is sent directly to their e-mail address.

Source: adapted from www.landsend.com.

(a) (i) From the information, identify TWO different methods of direct marketing used by Lands' End. (2 marks)
(ii) Give TWO benefits for the business of using each method. (4 marks)
(b) Explain TWO effects on the business of using the promotion described. (6 marks)
(c) Evaluate the importance of market segmentation to Lands' End. (4 marks)

Sponsorship

What is sponsorship?

Sponsorship is when a business supports an event, an activity or an organisation in exchange for having its name or product brand linked directly with the event, activity or the organisation being sponsored. The main aim of sponsorship is to raise awareness of the business through its association with whatever it is sponsoring. Sponsorship is usually in the form of money. But it can also be expressed by donations of products, equipment or resources.

A business may want to attract sponsors itself, to support its own activities with money or resources. This is a situation for many sports clubs or small organisations that do not have sufficient resources. Examples of sponsorship can be found in many ways in many industries. Some examples are shown in Table 1.

Reasons why a business may choose sponsorship

There is a number of reasons why a business may choose sponsorship. These are shown in Figure 1.

To create awareness The sponsor associates its name or logo with something that is seen by its target market, using the awareness created by the person, organisation or event being sponsored. Having created the awareness, the sponsor will hope that this translates into its overall marketing aims and objectives, such as increasing sales or attracting investors.

Figure 1 *Reasons for sponsorship*

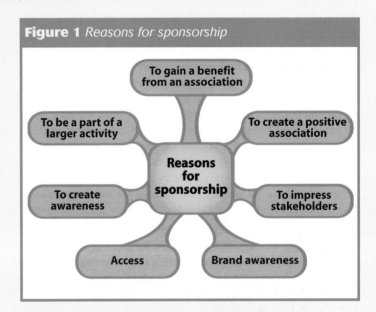

To gain a benefit from an association

To be a part of a larger activity

To create a positive association

Reasons for sponsorship

To create awareness

To impress stakeholders

Access

Brand awareness

To create a positive association with the person, organisation or event being sponsored A business many want to demonstrate to the target audience that it supports the local community by paying for a piece of new equipment at a local hospital, for example. Another example would be a manufacturer that sponsors a famous football team to gain positive association from its fans and good publicity if the team is doing well. The downside is that this may put off customers who are fans of an

Table 1 *Sponsorship of sports activities, television and events*

Activity	Examples
Sports	• Sports teams with the name or logo of a sponsor on its shirts and around the ground where it plays. • Individual competitors or players often benefit from sponsorship and wear the sponsor's logo on their clothes when they are competing. • Racing cars painted with the name of a sponsor.
Television	• Some television programmes on commercial channels state '… brought to you by …' and the name of the sponsor at the start and finish and in commercial breaks. Examples include The Simpsons on Sky One television sponsored by Domino's Pizza and Coronation Street on ITV sponsored by Cadbury.
Events	• The name of a sponsor printed on posters and programmes for a music concert. • The Glastonbury music festival, whose sponsors include mobile phone network Orange, and Formula 1 motor racing, whose sponsors include the high-tech company LG Electronics.

opposing team. Also, if the team does badly, then there is a risk of being associated with 'losers'.

To gain a benefit from the association with the sponsored person, organisation or event This may be in the form of publicity, fame and access to tickets or corporate hospitality.

To impress stakeholders, such as customers and the trade Many sponsors think that sponsoring something famous or with a high profile will impress customers and key stakeholders such as trade buyers or investors. Examples can be seen when organisations with traditional images, such as banks, sponsor youth events like music festivals. This may be the case, but research must be carried out to confirm that positive associations will be created by sponsorship. It must then be monitored because tastes and attitudes change over time and the benefits of sponsorship may decline or become negative. To reinforce its image a business may continue to sponsor the same event over a long period of time. A danger is that the market may take the sponsorship for granted and it will no longer attract any publicity or have positive benefits.

To be part of a larger activity A business may gain by being part of a larger activity which receives more publicity than it could afford itself. Sponsorship can help make a small marketing budget go further, by buying into a large event and using the publicity and promotion created by the event to promote the sponsoring business. An example would be a small manufacturer that could not afford its own television advertising, but could sponsor the driver of a sports car in a race with television coverage. As a result, the business could get promotion when its name and logo appears on the driver on television. The business could gain additional promotion by contacting its customers and suggesting that they may like to watch the race on television. Alternatively it could take customers along to the race for some corporate hospitality.

Access A business may sponsor a sporting or entertainment event to gain access to seats and corporate hospitality facilities. These can be used as incentives for its workforce or as a promotional activity for its customers and the trade.

Brand awareness Sponsorship can be a way of increasing brand awareness with targeted groups, by linking the sponsor's brand with the activity or event. It can also have positive benefits by creating an association in the audience's mind between the team or the event and the sponsor. For example, if fans of a particular team see that the team is being sponsored, they are likely to have positive feelings towards the sponsor for also supporting their team. The sponsor will hope that the positive feelings lead to

Figure 2 *Television sponsorship*

In 2004 a variety of television and radio programmes were being sponsored.

Sponsor	Programme
Cadbury	Heartbeat
Prudential	Michael Parkinson's chat show
Cif	How clean is your house?
Mr Muscle	Moving day
Nokia	X-Factor
Heinz	Emmerdale

Source: adapted from www.cocojambo.com.

increased awareness, a positive image and increased sales. Examples of well known sponsors in 2004 and 2005 are shown in Figure 2 and Table 2.

Reasons why a business may want to be sponsored

Another aspect of sponsorship is being sponsored. Rather than sponsoring something outside of the business, a business may want to attract its own sponsorship to the business. There is a number of reasons for wanting to attract sponsors. These are shown in Figure 3.

Figure 3 *Reasons for attracting sponsorship*

Table 2 *Sponsorship in 2005*

Sponsor	Organisation, event or product
Cheltenham and Gloucester (C&G) building society	Royal Shakespeare Company
BMW	*Fleet News* awards
Nokia	Live 8
Coca-cola	Football League
HSBC	Cereals 2005
BT, 3i and Capgemini	Microsoft Imagine Cup UK Software Design Challenge
Orange	2005 National Business Awards

Source: adapted from company websites, 2005.

Financial support If a business is small and does not have sufficient financial resources to fund research, development or promotion it may consider sponsorship as a way of attracting finance. In this situation, the business will need to prepare a strong marketing plan that explains the benefits for sponsorship to potential sponsors, such as:
- positive publicity;
- an association with an innovative new development;
- demonstrating to stakeholders a commitment to helping the industry and smaller developing businesses.

Promotional support If a business does not have the expertise or resources for its promotion, attracting sponsors is something that it could consider. It could offer sponsors the opportunity to have their name or logo on promotional material in exchange for helping to fund its activities. For example, some local newspapers produce posters for local events, overprinting details of the event onto blank posters, headed with the name of the newspaper.

Personal support This may be in the form of skills and expertise that may not be available within the business. This personal sponsorship is sometimes called **mentoring**. It is where a business seeks support from an individual or organisation that has the required skills or expertise and is willing to share this. The benefit for the sponsor or mentor is that they may be perceived to be helpful, which could be of positive benefit to them and part of their own aims or objectives.

Positive association Success breeds success. To be associated with, supported by or sponsored by a successful organisation will generate positive associations and a 'halo effect' from the sponsor.

Dangers associated with sponsorship

Whilst it can be of great benefit to business, there are dangers associated with sponsorship that should be considered before committing.

Negative association and bad publicity If the organisation, person or event that is being sponsored attracts bad publicity for any reason, the sponsors are likely to suffer from associating with the bad publicity. Using an earlier example, consider what fans from an opposing team might think about the business that sponsors their rivals. They might boycott the business that sponsors and supports their rivals. A similar problem could arise if a business chose to sponsor a particular popular performer to become its spokesperson and then this person received bad publicity. In this situation, the sponsor would be in great danger of becoming associated with this negative publicity.

Not achieving aims and objectives The event being sponsored may not achieve the aims and objectives set when sponsorship was agreed. This situation can arise when representatives of the event being sponsored over-forecast the size of the audience or the amount of publicity the event will attract. Promises of 'television coverage' sound great. But if it fails to materialise, sponsors are likely to feel that they have been misled. Similarly, if an event is billed as the biggest, best or fastest and it fails to live up to the claims, the sponsor will again be let down.

Appropriateness The sponsored person, organisation or event may not be appropriate for the sponsor. This happens when a business fails to match what it sponsors to its target market. Examples may include:
- a low priced, mass-market brand that sponsors a minority, up-market event like an opera;
- an exclusive brand could miss its target market if it sponsored an event with wide popular appeal.

If the target market cannot relate to the person, organisation or event being sponsored then the sponsorship needs to be reconsidered in the light of the aims and objectives of the marketing plan. It may be that the sponsorship is not designed to appeal to the customers but to investors, a completely different market. This is why it is important to consider sponsorship within the aims and objectives of the business. The sponsorship may also become generic, taken for granted. As a result the sponsor ceases to gain any direct benefit.

Ending sponsorship A sponsor may feel that it cannot stop sponsorship because of the negative publicity that this will attract. This happens when sponsors try to end long term associations with a sponsored event. Competitors and the trade may conclude that the business must have 'financial problems' because it is ceasing sponsorship. If the business was successful, why would it stop the sponsorship? This can be overcome through the use of PR. However, it is important to plan an exit strategy for ending sponsorship before the sponsorship starts to avoid this potential problem in the first place.

Demands The organisation doing the sponsoring and providing the money may make demands on the business being sponsored that it cannot or does not want to meet. The threat of refusal could result in the cancellation of sponsorship and the loss of money.

Factors to consider when planning sponsorship

Aims and objectives It is important to have a clear view of the aims and objectives for sponsorship. It must fit in with the overall marketing plans that result from the marketing mix. If not, there is a danger that it will be inappropriate and a waste of money. However interesting or exciting a sponsorship deal may sound, a business must decide what it wants to get out of it. It must consider 'Why should we spend money sponsoring?'

Cost Sponsorship can become costly. The cost may be in the form of a one-off payment or paying a certain amount over a period of time. This will set the length of time for the sponsorship. There is a temptation when sponsoring a regular, ongoing event or organisation, such as a sports team, to continue the sponsorship payments year after year. A moral pressure may be applied by the organisation being sponsored, threatening that if sponsorship ceased it would not be able to continue. This may be true, but should not be confused with the business reasons for sponsorship. To overcome this problem, a business must set a budget before deciding on sponsorship. This can be used to cap the maximum spending on sponsorship and to measure the cost-effectiveness of sponsorship against other forms of promotion. It must be affordable, as well as being cost effective in the way that it achieves the marketing objectives. If not, an alternative marketing plan should be considered.

Resources Depending on the organisation or event being sponsored, a business may deal with the organisation itself or with an agent of the organisation whose job it is to raise income through sponsorship. The main resource sought is likely to be money. But sometimes sponsorship may take the form of materials or goods. For example:

- a manufacturer of energy drinks could sponsor a marathon race by providing quantities of its drink for the competitors;
- a paint manufacturer could sponsor a new youth club by the provision of paint and decorating materials.

Providing materials rather than cash is often more cost effective for a business. Production costs will be considerably lower than the perceived value of the goods, which will be at its retail price, and the business will still gain benefit by the sponsorship.

Timing Is the sponsorship going to be a one-off or is it ongoing? This is a decision that may have to be made. Also, does the timing fit in with other marketing plans? It could be a waste of money sponsoring an event during the summer if the main period of sales and marketing activity is at the beginning of the year. Another aspect of timing is to consider how long the effect of sponsorship is likely to last.

Appropriateness Like advertising and sales promotion, it is important to consider appropriateness when planning sponsorship. Sponsoring a person, organisation or event that is appropriate can benefit both businesses greatly.

Meeting the assessment criteria

Keep Fit Supplies (KFS) is a shop that sells sports clothing, footwear and equipment. The manager of KFS has been asked by a local basketball team if the shop will sponsor the team next season.

(a) Give TWO reasons why KFS might want to sponsor the local basketball team. **(2 marks)**

Expected answers
- *To raise awareness of the shop with basketball players/friends or family of players/audience at local basketball games.*
- *To sell sports gear to basketball players/friends or family of players/audience at local basketball games.*
- *To demonstrate support for the local community.*
- *To gain positive publicity for the shop by association with team wins/success.*

Mark allocation
1 mark for each reason. **(2 marks)**

(b) Recommend TWO appropriate ways that KFS could sponsor the team and justify each of your recommendations. **(4 marks)**

Expected answers
- *Donate kits with shop name/logo on it – name/logo will be displayed during matches and will create awareness amongst audience watching match.*
- *Give them cash in exchange for renaming team after KFS/displaying shop name at games – creates awareness/demonstrates support for team.*

Mark allocation
1 mark for each appropriate way.
1 mark for justification. **(1 + 1) x 2 (4 marks)**

Examination practice · Virgin and MTV

MTV UK and Ireland's music show, Total Request Live (TRL), secured a one year sponsorship package with Virgin Mobile in 2005. The £450,000 deal would give Virgin branded credits throughout the show and a new content area of the MTV website. Virgin Mobile users will also be offered TRL content, such as interviews, competitions and videos, via their handsets. The TRL show was launched at the end of January with a focus on producing content from the UK and Ireland. Dan Salem, commercial director for Viacom Brand Solutions, said: 'The partnership between TRL and Virgin Mobile is a perfect fit from an audience and brand point of view. MTV's vast insight into entertainment, celebrity, youth and music will undoubtedly sit well beside Virgin Mobile's brand culture, helping to deliver a highly effective solution'. James Kydd, brand director at Virgin Mobile, said: 'We chose TRL as it shares many of the same brand values as Virgin Mobile – music, celebrity and sometimes irreverent humour! We are looking forward to getting our customers into the studio to enjoy the fun.'

Source: adapted from www.mediaweek.co.uk.

(a) From the information, give ONE reason why:
(i) Virgin might want to sponsor MTV's Total Request Live; **(1 mark)**
(ii) Total Request Live might want sponsorship from Virgin. **(1 mark)**
(b) Evaluate how appropriate it would be for Virgin to sponsor MTV's Total Request Live. **(4 marks)**
(c) Discuss why the business may have decided that the sponsorship should be limited to a one year deal. **(4 marks)**

Investigating promotional media

There is a wide variety of media used for promotion. The main media used in marketing plans are shown in Figure 1.

Figure 1 *Promotional media*

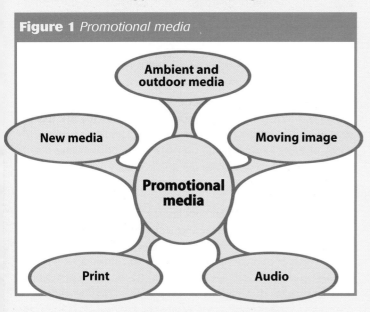

Businesses must compare different media to analyse and evaluate how successful they might be. This may appear difficult at first. How is it possible to compare a bright, colourful, larger-than-life advertisement in the cinema, with a small advertisement in a specialist magazine? The basic tools for this kind of comparison are outlined in sections 71-75.

Print media products

In the broadest terms, print media products are anything that is printed and designed to be looked at and read. Examples are shown in Figure 2.

Figure 1 *Print media*

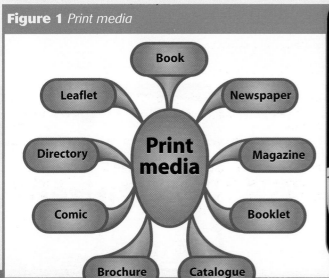

A wide range of print media can be investigated by visiting a library, newsagent or other retail shop. This will show that the print media market is very wide snd very competitive. For example, newspapers and magazines:

- are available in many different shapes and sizes;
- are aimed at different readers with different interests;
- are published at different frequencies and sold at different prices, each targeting a different segment of the market.

The print media industry in the UK is extremely dynamic, with new titles appearing virtually every week.

Consider print media that one person might buy and read compared to those that they do not. What might be the difference? Considering this will help to understand how different print media have different target markets and appeal to different audiences. This is important when planning a campaign using print media.

Why use print media?

What are some of the positive attributes of print media?

Range A quick glance in any newsagent shows that there is an incredibly wide range of print media products available on the market. In addition, there will be a wide range of trade media and specialist media that are circulated to interested readers by direct mail and subscriptions. These print products will not always be found in a retail newsagent. The wide range is designed by the publishers that supply the market to provide a product to suit readers with every taste and interest.

From an advertising point of view, this also means that there will be a print product to match just about every consumer profile. If required, promotional activity can be targeted at a very precise group of consumers. The wide range of available print media has also resulted from the intense competition between publishers. In any of the mass markets, such as daily newspapers, gardening magazines or magazines aimed at females or males, there will be a

number of competing publications that readers can choose to read, depending on the particular editorial approach and style that appeals to them. Table 1 shows an example of the different magazines available to people interested in different styles of music.

For an idea of just how many print media products are available for advertising in the UK look at a copy of the *brad* media directory. This lists every available print advertising product in the UK and gives details of circulation, readership numbers and readership profile. It is used by advertising agencies to plan campaigns (www.intellagencia.com/bradsamplepages). There are also websites on the Internet that provide similar sources of data.

Flexibility Print media is available in many different forms that have different frequencies of distribution, such as daily, weekly, monthly, annually and variations in between. There is likely to be a print media product that has the right frequency to meet the marketing objectives for the business. There is also a flexibility in the size of the advertisement. Depending on its aims, objectives and budget, an advertiser can choose the size of the advertisement placed in print media. It could be a large 'double page spread', a single advertisement across two facing pages, a full page or any division of that page that is acceptable to the medium.

Most print media also carry small 'classified' advertisements at the back of the publication. These are usually short, simple advertisements, but they can be very effective if they are appropriate for what is being advertised, such as a low cost personal or specialist product from a private advertiser.

Precise targeting In addition to the mass circulation print products, which are useful for raising a general awareness, there appears to be a magazine for just about every subject to meet the needs of every interest group, no matter how small. It may only be a newsletter circulated within the group, but it provides a print media opportunity to get a promotional message to that small group.

Print media also offers an opportunity for relatively precise targeting based on geographic segmentation (see section 33). For example, an advertiser that only trades in one town, or has a defined area of operation, should be able to choose a local print product, such as a local newspaper, that also circulates in a similar area. This means that advertising will not be wasted by being distributed in geographic areas where the business does not trade.

Regional and national media are options for advertisers that want to reach consumers in a wider geographic area. This geographic flexibility makes print media ideal for testing advertising or piloting the sales of a product in a small area before rolling-out to national sales and advertising. Table 2 shows examples of regional newspapers in the UK. Some target a city and its surrounding area or part of a city, some towns and some counties.

Print media will also include directories such as *Yellow Pages* for the promotion of consumer services, and trade directories, which collect together suppliers to different trades and industries. Directories usually circulate in a defined area or industry and can be very useful for precision promotion.

Table 1 *UK music magazines*

Name	Market/music
Kerrang	Heavy metal
NME	Rock
Mixmag	Trans, house, electro
Mojo	Alternative rock
Smash hits	Pop
Billboard	USA charts
fRoots	Roots, folk and world music
Country Music People	Country
Vibe	Rap, R&B, Hip Hop
B&S	Blues, soul
Gramophone	Classical

Table 2 *Local newspapers*

Name	Geographical area
Ormskirk Champion	Area around Ormskirk in West Lancashire.
Liverpool Echo	Merseyside.
Dunmow and Braintree Times	Area around Great Dunmow and Braintree in Essex.
Evening Standard	London.
Cornish Guardian	Cornwall.
Cambridge Evening News	Cambridge.
Huddersfield Daily Examiner	Huddersfield in Yorkshire.
Trafford Messenger	Trafford in Manchester.
Lancashire Evening Post	Preston to Lancaster.

Table 3 *Trade media*

Name	Industry
The Grocer	The retail industry.
Packaging Today and Packaging News	The packaging industry and all users of packaging materials.
Draper's Record	The fashion industry.
Campaign, Marketing Week and Media Week.	The marketing industry.
World Leather	Leather related products.

Trade media readily available Unlike just about all other promotional media, print media offers direct access to the trade through trade magazines. These are specialist publications that are produced for and read by people engaged in the commercial, technical, distribution and trade side of an industry as opposed to most other media that are aimed at consumers. Using trade magazines means that a business can promote its products direct to retail buyers, trade customers, distributors and owners of businesses that would normally be very difficult to contact.

Most industries and markets will have specialist trade media aimed at a particular industry. Trade magazines also fulfil an important role in being a major source for job advertisements in particular industries. There are hundreds of trade magazines, one or more for each segment of industry. Table 3 shows some examples.

Relatively low cost Print media is a relatively low cost method of promotion, at least compared with television advertising. Like any market, the cost of print media advertising is subject to a number of variable factors. They include:

- production costs, which will vary according to the cost of designers and photographers employed to produce the advertisement. A famous named designer or photographer will cost more than buying these services locally;
- the location of any photography. A photo shoot in the Caribbean is likely to be more expensive than a photo shoot in a local studio;
- technical costs. The production process for a colour advertisement is likely to be more expensive than for a black and white advertisement;
- circulation and readership. The greater the circulation, the more people are likely to see the advertisement, then the more the advertising space in that medium will cost;
- competition. In a market where a number of print products are competing, such as the market for celebrity magazines, most publishers will be offering promotions and incentives like price reductions, to attract new advertisers away from competitor magazines.

Why not use print media products?

What are some of the considerations for not using this media?

Limited life The cliché that today's newspapers will be tomorrow's waste paper is often the case. The life of an advertisement in a print product will be affected by the frequency of the publication. Advertising in a daily newspaper will be gone by the next day. An advertisement in a monthly magazine will have a life of at least a month or longer if it is passed on to other readers, for example in a doctor's waiting room. But whatever the print product, it will have a finite life before it becomes outdated and discarded, along with all of the advertisements it contains. This means that advertisements in print media product need to work hard in order to make an impact during the life of the product.

Non-intrusive Most people buy print media to read the information it contains. This means that advertisements in print media are easily ignored by the reader as they move from article to article. The reader can simply turn the page and miss the advertisement.

There are exceptions to this. Some magazines and newspapers are bought specifically because they contain advertisements that the reader wants to look at, such as job advertisements, used cars, holidays or estate agents' advertisements for homes. Some magazines like *Exchange & Mart* and *Daltons Weekly* only carry advertisements. Consumers buy these magazines purely to search the advertisements, like a database, for products they are looking to buy.

High wastage At any given time, only a proportion of readers of any print media product will be in the market for the goods being advertised. As a result, the advertisement is wasted on all of the other readers, unless it is memorable enough for them to retain information until they are in the market for those goods. A way around this is to plan a long term 'drip-feed' campaign that becomes a constant reminder to readers.

Wastage is also a factor if an advertiser has a particular defined target market, such as a niche product. Within the readership of any mass market publication there will be a number that fits the target market. But the advertisement will be wasted on the rest of the readers. In this situation it may be more appropriate to choose a print media product that matches the niche target market more precisely. This is less of a problem for advertisers of mass market products that can choose an appropriate mass medium to reach their market.

Meeting the assessment criteria

Sugargoods is a major manufacturer of confectionery products that have wide distribution in supermarkets, newsagents and convenience stores in the UK. The marketing team is developing a marketing plan to launch a new range of cough sweets, 'Soothies', that are designed to relieve the symptoms of a sore throat. They are aimed at adults aged 18 years and over. Sugargoods usually uses television advertising for new product launches, but this time the advertising agency is recommending the use of print media for the launch promotion.

(a) Give TWO reasons why print media should be considered for the launch promotion. **(2 marks)**

Expected answers
- *Wide range of print media to choose from.*
- *Production cost low relative to television.*
- *Promotional budget will go further as media cost is relatively lower than television.*
- *Could select print media that is read by target market.*
- *Less wastage than television advertising.*
- *May be seen by some people that are not regular/heavy television viewers.*

Mark allocation
1 mark for each reason. **(2 marks)**

(b) Explain how print media could play a part in promoting 'Soothies' to supermarket managers and shopkeepers. **(4 marks)**

Expected answers
- *Print media includes trade press – trade press aimed at/read by shop mangers/shopkeepers.*
- *Could print insert to be distributed in trade press – inserts fall out and likely to be looked at before they are discarded which will create awareness.*
- *Trade press likely to have specialist media for different types of customer – could try different advertising/promotion in different media to see which works best.*

Mark allocation
1 mark for how print media could play a part (maximum 2 marks).
1 mark for applying to situation (maximum 2 marks). **(4 marks)**

Examination practice · Mieka Designs

Mieka Sherry designs women's clothes. She is particularly interested in designing clothing which can be worn in the day, but quickly adapted for visiting restaurants or clubs in the evening. Her designs mean that wearers do not need to change clothing. She feels that her clothing has two main markets:
- young professionals, who do not want to go home from work to change;
- young women with children who may have little time to change before going out at night.

Mieka's business needs to expand. She has been very successful at selling to clients in the local area by word of mouth recommendation. But now she wants to sell to retail clothing chains and also offer a 'tailored' service, where people can select their own designs, which can be charged at a premium price. She is considering which print media to use from the variety available.

Source: adapted from company information.

(a) **Give Mieka THREE general features of print media.** **(3 marks)**

(b) **Give TWO examples of print media that would help Mieka to achieve her aim of retail distribution. Justify each example.** **(4 marks)**

(c) **Describe ONE way that Mieka could use print media to achieve her aims in the consumer market.** **(4 marks)**

72 *Audio media*

What is audio media?

In the context of media used for promotion, audio media refers mainly to radio advertising. However, it may also include recorded promotional inserts in CDs, tapes and any other music reproduction media. Less mainstream methods could include public address announcements in shops or shopping centres that promote products, special offers or encourage customers to buy, as shown in Figure 1.

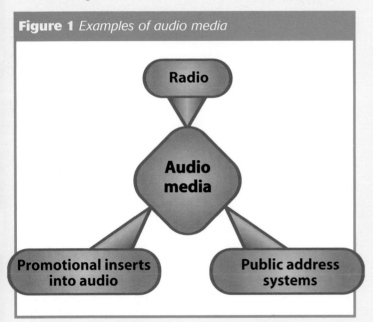

Figure 1 *Examples of audio media*

Listening to any commercial radio station will give a flavour of the way that audio media is used for promotion. Like television advertising, radio commercials tend to be inserted into the normal format of the programme being broadcast, at the beginning, end or between segments in the show. The frequency of advertising breaks in radio will be determined by demand for advertising space.

Different stations will attract different styles of advertisement. This will depend on:
- the nature of the product;
- the style/image of the station itself;
- target market for the product being promoted.

With no pictures to sell the product, audio media has to be particularly creative in its approach.

Customers now have greater access to a larger number of stations through:
- DAB (digital audio broadcast) radio;
- Sky Digital;
- the Internet.

This has increased the scope of audio advertising. Some examples are given in Table 1. The *brad* media directory gives details of commercial radio stations in the UK.

Why use audio media products?

What are some of the positive reasons for advertising using this media?

Creative opportunities The use of audio recording techniques provides a great opportunity for creativity. Words, music and sound effects can all be used to produce advertisements that are creative, memorable and actually work for selling products and services and providing information.

Relatively low production costs This is certainly the case compared to the cost of producing commercials for television. Production is often done by the radio station itself as it has all the equipment and technical staff on site to run the station.

Flexibility The relatively low production cost means that an advertisement can be changed or updated frequently, if required.

Relatively low media cost This is the case compared with television. However, the cost of radio advertising time is subject to the same supply and demand laws as other media cost and to get a true comparison it is best to use a 'cost per thousand' measure (see section 78).

Table 1 *Radio advertising*

Radio station	Description	Possible advertiser/product
Radio City 96.7	Liverpool-based music station	Local Merseyside businesses
Classic FM	Classical music station	Classical CDs, financial products
Kiss 100 FM	London dance station	'Youth'-related products
talkSPORT	Sports and discussion station	Sports products
Oneword Radio	Plays, books, comedy and reviews	Books, theatre, concerts
Virgin Radio (FM)	National Rock/pop station	Entertainment and lifestyle products
Sunrise Radio 1458 AM	Asian music, news and culture	Travel, specialist food suppliers

Loyal audience Listeners take personal 'ownership' of their favourite radio programmes and presenters and listen to them on a regular basis. This is particularly true with local radio stations, which focus on their communities. This means that once established the audience can be clearly defined, profiled and segmented if required. It is also likely to be relatively stable and regular, which means that targeting and media planning can be done effectively.

Perfect for associated products What better medium to advertise music products, as well as fashion and lifestyle products, than during a music programme on commercial radio when the target market is listening? A positive association can be created by radio advertising. Advertising on a fashionable station can mean that many listeners will associate the product being advertised with the station. This can create a 'halo effect', with the 'trendyness' of the radio station rubbing off on the product and giving it some credibility to the audience.

Can reach 'difficult' markets Young people who have jobs are often difficult to reach with advertising. They may be working during the day and unlikely to have access to traditional broadcast media. During the evening they are likely to be out, enjoying themselves. Radio broadcasts can be targeted at 'drive time', the time when people commute to work and back in their cars, or listen to portable radios when on public transport. 'Drive time' is usually considered to be between 7:00 am to 9:00 am and between 3:00 pm to 6:00 pm.

Targeting Radio advertising can also be targeted at other precise times when the target audience is likely to be tuning in and listening, such as when they get up, when they get back from work, when they get back from the evening's entertainment. Whatever the time, there will be a radio audience. It all depends on how much market research is available to enable media planners, the people who decide when is the best time to advertise, to produce an effective media plan to reach these audiences with advertising.

Why not use audio media products?

Why might a business decide not to use this media?

Coverage The proportion of the target audience that can receive the radio advertising may be limited. This is not such a problem for local or regional advertisers as there are many local and regional commercial radio stations. However, for national advertisers it can be more difficult and coverage may need to be created by using more than just one radio station. Classic FM has virtual national coverage, but the audience is clearly defined and biased to the music that it plays. Virgin Radio, Capital Radio and

Figure 2 *Ofcom and advertising*

In 2005 The Advertising Standards Authority (ASA) banned radio advertising for MasterCard and Travelocity.co.uk for running the risk of encouraging people to inhale helium. The Travelocity.co.uk commercial featured Alan Whicker, the former television presenter, sounding like he had inhaled helium so he could talk more quickly. The radio advertisement for MasterCard featured a man on the telephone singing to his girlfriend in a high-pitched voice, with a voiceover that said, 'A mobile top-up card and two helium balloons: £17. Making your girlfriend laugh, however far away she is: priceless'. The ASA agreed with two complainants that it was harmful to inhale helium and that the advertisement might encourage people to copy the idea.

Source: adapted from *The Guardian*, 29.6.2005.

Sunrise Radio have regional strengths and continue to expand their coverage. The opportunity for national commercial radio is changing as more listeners access radio stations via digital audio broadcasts (DAB) that are carried by cable and satellite television companies or buy a DAB radio. This means that the radio station can be accessed by anyone wherever they live – so long as they subscribe to the cable or satellite provider or own a DAB radio.

Creative challenge With no pictures, words or telephone numbers on display, just sound, radio advertising can be a challenge to the creative team that writes and produces advertising. Radio advertising relies on the audience listening, remembering and then bothering to do something about what they hear. To make them work, many radio advertisements rely on repetition. This can work, but it can also lead to annoying advertisements that can put off the audience, even creating negative feelings towards the product being advertised. There may also be other problems. An example is shown in Figure 2.

Appropriateness Radio may not be appropriate for certain products or the radio media available may not be appropriate. For example, if the only commercial radio station in an area plays 'Top 10' music, and has a young audience, then it may be great for music, night clubs and fashion products. However, it may not be appropriate if the product has a target market with an older profile, such as pension products or retirement homes.

Meeting the assessment criteria

LancSounds is a local commercial radio station in the North West of England where it competes with Dune FM, Radio City and around 30 other stations. Its marketing team is trying to come up with ideas for attracting more advertisers to the station.

(a) Give TWO reasons why a commercial radio station like LancSounds needs to continually attract more advertisers.
(2 marks)

Expected answers
- *To maintain income/profit.*
- *To stay in business.*
- *Because it is operating in a competitive market.*
- *Because there will be a natural turnover of advertisers as some stop advertising for their own business reasons.*
- *Level of advertising revenue likely to be seasonal so station needs to maintain a regular flow of advertisers to help cash flow.*

Mark allocation
1 mark for each reason.
(2 marks)

(b) Explain the benefits of using local commercial radio that could be used to attract potential advertisers.
(4 marks)

Expected answers
- *Loyal audience – which means that coverage could be built up through regular advertising.*
- *Relatively low production costs – which means that there will be more of budget left for airtime/more advertising spots.*
- *Radio is a creative medium – which means that radio ads will also be creative, which will help attract listeners/make ads memorable/help sell more products.*
- *Can reach markets that are difficult with other media – which makes radio perfect if advertising products for difficult target markets.*

Mark allocation
1 mark for each reason (maximum 2 marks) + 1 mark for explanation (maximum 2 marks)
or
1 mark for reason + 1 mark for explanation + 2 marks for development.
(4 marks)

Examination practice · Polo radio promotion

In 2004, Polo, the sweet sold using the slogan 'the mint with the hole' abandoned visual media. It aimed to tell consumers about its new, mintier flavour solely by using radio in a £400,000 campaign by the advertising agency, J Walter Thompson. Nestlé Rowntree, Polo's manufacturer, said it could sell the changes using radio alone because the brand was 'iconic' enough to be able to dispense with the visual media. The six radio advertisements say that Polo mints have become 13.063% mintier.

Source: adapted from *The Guardian*, 10.8.2004.

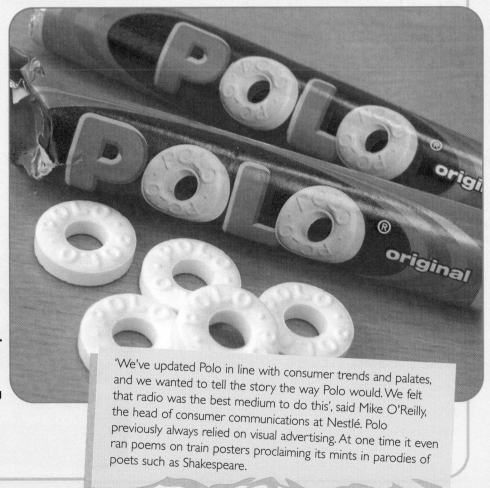

(a) State TWO major differences between audio and visual media. **(2 marks)**
(b) Explain TWO reasons why Nestlé might have switched from using visual to audio media for Polo advertisements. **(6 marks)**
(c) Describe TWO possible risks that the business might be taking by switching advertising media and explain how this might affect the business. **(4 marks)**

'We've updated Polo in line with consumer trends and palates, and we wanted to tell the story the way Polo would. We felt that radio was the best medium to do this', said Mike O'Reilly, the head of consumer communications at Nestlé. Polo previously always relied on visual advertising. At one time it even ran poems on train posters proclaiming its mints in parodies of poets such as Shakespeare.

What is moving image media?

The two main moving image media used for advertising and promotion are commercial television and cinema.

Television advertising This takes the form of brief promotional films that are shown before, during and after programmes broadcast on commercial television channels. There is a wide range of products advertised on commercial television and many different styles of television commercials are used.

To see a range of different commercials, people need only to watch different channels at different times of the day. Different channels often attract different types of advertisers. For example:

- there are likely to be more mass market products being advertised on terrestrial channels such as traditional Independent Television (ITV) stations, Channel Four and Channel Five compared to cable and satellite channels which seem to attract advertisers that have a narrower focus, such as financial products;
- during the daytime more household products aimed at people at home during the day are advertised, compared to late night advertisers who are targeting a different market.

Traditionally, television commercials are usually 30 seconds in length. But as a result of cost constraints, commercials can range from 7 seconds to 30 seconds. Sometimes, a major advertiser will make a much longer commercial for a special occasion or to make a major impact. These may last as long as an entire commercial break in the middle of a programme. It may then be followed by shorter advertisements.

Television advertising will also include 'break bumpers'. This is the showing of an advertising slogan or a branded logo at the start and finish of a programme and each commercial break. This form of television advertising may also be presented as sponsorship of a particular programme, as explained in section 70. Some examples are shown in Table 1.

Ambient advertising and product placement is another common sight on television, as well as the use of chat shows as PR and promotional vehicles for new products such as books and films.

Information on all UK commercial television channels can be found in the *brad* media directory.

Cinema advertising Cinema advertising usually takes the form of a short advertising film, a few minutes long, shown before the main feature in a cinema. Because of the high production values associated with feature films, cinema advertisements often share these same values or they may tend to look inferior in the bold and glossy cinema environment. Sometimes these advertisements are like 'mini films' and may be made by directors that usually make full length feature films. High production costs mean that cinema advertising tends to attract high profile national and multinational brands and products. By booking advertising through the cinema chains, an advertiser can achieve regional coverage or national coverage if required and if the budget allows.

No matter who makes the film or how good it looks, it will only appear if the advertiser buys space or time to have the advertisement shown. In this respect cinema advertising is just like advertising in any other medium.

In contrast to the high profile advertisements, cinemas in the

Figure 1 *Orange cinema advertising*

Orange, the mobile phone company, produced a series of successful and effective high profile cinema advertisements in the early twenty first century. They involved film stars or producers 'pitching' film ideas to Orange and usually ended with a joke relating to the film. Stars or producers included the director Spike Lee and actors Patrick Swayze (Dirty Dancing), Carrie Fisher and the Darth Vader character (Star Wars), Roy Scheider (Jaws) and Sean Astin (Lord of the Rings). At the 2004 British Television Advertising Awards the advertisements won the gold award in the series category.

Source: adapted from *The Guardian*, 11.4.2004.

Table 1 *Television advertisements that have appeared before or after television programmes*

Television advertisements	Programme
Domino's Pizza/Pizza Hut	The Simpsons
Procter & Gamble's Herbal Essences	Desperate Housewives
Direct Line Insurance	Location Location Location
Jacob's Creek wine/Appeltiser	Friends
Allied Domecq's Cockburn's Port	Cold Feet

past have also shown modest advertisements for local businesses, such as 'the chip shop round the corner' or a local taxi service. This illustrates how a powerful medium like cinema can be used in an extremely focused way – advertising a local product to a captive audience with the aim of encouraging the audience to call at the chip shop or use the taxi when they leave the cinema.

Like television advertisements, cinemas show a variety of different advertisements, in different styles, from different businesses. Some advertisers are unique to a particular cinema. There will also be examples in cinemas of ambient advertising and **product placement** in films (see section 74).

Figure 1 shows an example of a successful cinema advertising campaign.

Why use television advertising?

What are some of the positive attributes of this media? They are outlined in Figure 2.

Figure 2 *Reasons for using television advertising*

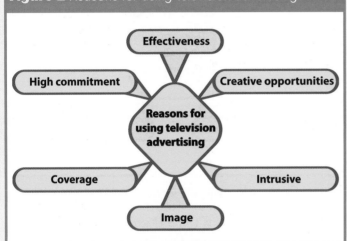

Effectiveness There are many businesses that rely on television advertising to produce consumer sales. The fact that there is no shortage of retailers, manufacturers and services willing to advertise their products on television supports the claim that television advertising really does work and that it is an effective way of providing information and selling products.

Coverage Most homes have one or more television sets that are watched most days. In 2004 the average viewer watched 3.8 hours of television each day. This means that a well-placed television advertisement will be seen by many millions of people.

Image The general consumer perception of television advertisers is that they are big and important. Simply being on television lends them importance and weight. This perception can work to the advantage of advertisers as it can build and enhance the reputation of the business.

Creative opportunities The combination of vision and sound in a short commercial opens up wide creative opportunities. Any commercial break on television will show a variety of advertisements often using the most creative and cutting-edge ideas. Some television commercials are as creative as mini feature films. They attract attention, engage the viewer, tell a story and sell

a product, all within a few seconds. They use a wide range of different production techniques, with photography, film and animation, all being utilised to make the best use of modern technology and sell product.

Intrusive TV viewers cannot fail to be aware of television advertising as it runs between every programme on commercial channels and 'interrupts' every programme that they try to watch.

Demonstrates a high commitment to retail customers If a business is willing to commit the large sums of money required for television advertising, to pay for production and media time, it shows the retail trade that the business is serious and committed to the product. This can be used by advertisers to encourage wider distribution and increased stock levels. Some retailers will not stock a new product unless the manufacturer agrees to support the new product with television advertising. In this situation it not only demonstrates commitment, but should also generate sales to help the retail stocks sell out.

Reasons for not using television advertising

Why might a business decide not to use this media?

Production cost The cost of producing a television commercial is relatively high, usually many thousands of pounds, or even hundreds of thousands for a lavish commercial with high production values. Lower cost commercials can be produced, but will often look cheap when broadcast. They are likely to be more noticeable as most advertisers on television tend to be large, national and multinational businesses that have set high standards for their television commercials, paid for from large marketing budgets.

The relatively high production cost tends to attract advertising from mass market products that will sell in high volumes sufficient to justify the cost. Smaller businesses, with products aimed at small, niche markets, are less likely to choose television advertising for their products because of the relatively high cost of producing a television commercial that is suitable.

Media cost Television media costs tend to be very high compared with other media. But they can usually be justified by the ability to broadcast to a huge audience and achieve national coverage with relative ease. This may suit large businesses that sell mass market products in high volumes. It might not suit smaller businesses with products aimed at niche markets.

However, this situation is changing. The growth in the number of cable and satellite channels has had the effect of expanding the airtime available for television advertising. This has affected the supply of media space, with the result that on some channels the cost of advertising has fallen. The new and expanding number of cable and satellite channels has also had the effect of creating smaller, niche groups of viewers, with tightly defined profiles. This means that cable and satellite television advertising can now be selected and tailored to meet the profile of the target market for a given product, making television advertising more cost-effective for products that may not have been able to afford television advertising in the past.

Coverage Because of its ability reach into most homes in the country, television advertising may be too extensive for advertisers that only operate on a local basis. The country is divided up into television regions. But even one region may be too large and attract customers from outside the advertiser's area of operation or distribution. This may not appear to be too much of a problem as it could provide an opportunity for expanding the business. However, it may also have the effect of annoying and frustrating consumers, whose demands for a product or service has been created by the advertising, only to find that they cannot receive the product or service in their area.

Again, cable channels can overcome this in some areas where their coverage can be limited to smaller areas. The growth of cable and satellite channels has not increased the total number of people that watch television. But it has divided the audience, the total number of viewers, across more channels. The audience for cable and satellite channels has grown at the expense of the audience for terrestrial channels, which has reduced.

Wastage Any given television audience will be made up of people with many different profiles, a range of ages, income groups and interests. This may be appropriate for advertisers with products that have this wide, general appeal. But for most advertisers there will be a degree of 'wastage'. This means there is a number of viewers that are not in the target market for the product being advertised, but are still counted in the overall viewing figures and included in the cost of media. Wastage can be reduced by careful planning to advertise in programmes and at times when the target market tends to be viewing.

Setting a precedence What happens if a business decides not to use television advertising for its next campaign? Once a product is advertised on television, it is hard to turn back. Competition, the trade, the audience and other stakeholders will notice television advertising and they will equally notice if television advertising stops. They may wonder if the business can no longer afford television advertising or if it is in trouble. Even if there are no business problems, stopping television advertising is as significant as starting it.

Competition for attention and viewers' memories Because of the sheer number of advertisements on television any single advertisement has to work hard to attract attention. Viewers are bombarded with many television advertisements. To make an impact on a viewer and to stand out in their memory an advertisement must be really distinctive and memorable. This has resulted in louder soundtracks and more startling visual effects. Alternatively, an advertisement needs to be precisely what the viewer is looking for at that moment in time. Then it will make an impact and be remembered.

Another aspect of competition for attention is the environment in which the television is being viewed. In a busy home there will be many other distractions that can draw attention from what is happening on the screen, especially during the commercial break when many people leave the television to make a drink.

Viewers' interpretation Advertisers cannot control how viewers interpret their television advertising. The classic example of this is the '*Creature Comforts*' campaign run in the 1990s to promote electric central heating. Viewers loved the commercials. However, despite the references to electricity and the use of the

Heat Electric logo, many viewers assumed that the advertisement were promoting gas central heating.

Video, DVD and other recording devices These give viewers the opportunity to skip past advertisement breaks by either fast forwarding or using a recorder that cuts out advertisements. On the other hand, recorders also provide the opportunity for repeat viewing of advertisements and can extend the life of a campaign.

Why use cinema advertising?

What are some of the positive attributes of this media? They are outlined in Figure 3.

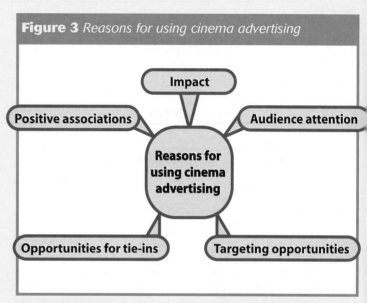

Figure 3 *Reasons for using cinema advertising*

Impact Cinema advertising can be as big, bold and awe-inspiring as the main feature film. It can make the advertiser appear to be much bigger than it really is. This is effective for fighting off competition or trying to make an impact on a market.

Audience attention is high Having paid to go and watch a film, the audience will be extremely receptive to anything that is shown on the screen. Cinema advertising is the only advertising medium where the audience actually pays to go to watch the advertising, as it is part of the cinema-going experience.

Positive associations If an action or adventure film is being shown, it will attract an audience with a profile that is likely to be

Table 2 *Product tie-ins*

Film	Tie-in
Lord of the Rings	Character models
Star Wars	Darth Vader masks, light sabres
Disney films	Toys
Pulp Fiction	Wall posters
Grease, Saturday Night Fever	Music soundtrack

very similar to the market for an action or adventure computer game. Advertising this product when the adventure film is shown will create positive associations with the audience, so long as they like the main film. A risk is that the film may flop and the computer game may be associated with a failure. A similar example would be to advertise lifestyle products when a film is showing that features an attractive and desirable lifestyle. Again, the products will benefit from association with the lifestyle portrayed in the film.

Opportunities for tie-ins Similar to positive associations is the advertising or promotion of products that have a direct link, a tie-in, with a particular film. These are examples of precise targeting and the audience for the film very closely matches the profile of the market for the product being promoted. An example might be Harry Potter books promoted at a cinema showing the films. Tie-ins can also take the form of related products or merchandising. Some examples are shown in Table 2.

Targeting opportunities The cinema audience has a distinct profile. In general it tends to attract young people, with money to spend, who do not watch much television or read many newspapers or magazines. This means that advertisers marketing products to young, relatively high income consumers, who are notoriously difficult to communicate with through other media, can aim their products directly at this elusive market. Similarly, a film aimed at an older audience will have a different but equally defined profile and will attract advertisers with products for this market. Cinema also offers the opportunity for extremely focused local advertising, the 'chip shop round the corner' or the local taxi service. Both are appropriate products for cinema advertisements, as they want a direct response from the audience when they leave the cinema.

Reasons for not using cinema advertising

Why might a business decide not to use this media?

Production and reproduction costs For a cinema advertisement to make an impact and fit with the cinema going experience it will usually need to have high production values. It will also need to be shot on a medium, usually 35mm film stock, that can be projected on the standard equipment in a cinema. This will be the production cost, which involves specialist equipment, skilled technical staff and studios, which are not cheap. Not only that, but a copy of the advertisement will need to be produced and distributed to every cinema that is booked to show the advertisement. This is the reproduction cost. Digital film technology is likely to bring down the cost of shooting, distributing and showing a cinema commercial. But digital technology is not yet used universally by the cinema industry and media owners, the businesses that own and run the cinemas themselves.

Narrow audience profile This may not be a problem for advertisers that have products with a similar profile. However, it is important to research the profile of the cinema audience and compare it with the target market before deciding on a marketing plan that includes cinema advertising.

Small audience/relatively low coverage Compared with television and mass circulation newspapers and magazines, the cinema audience is relatively small. It also requires regular, repeat advertising to buildup coverage that equates to these mass media. This may not be a problem for local advertisers with an extremely local product, as noted in the positive points about cinema advertising.

 Examination practice · MSN television campaign

In 2005, MSN was set to carry out a multi-million pound advertising campaign to promote its new own-brand search engine. For the first time in four years, MSN advertisements would appear on television. They would be complimented by a large on-line campaign reaching 21 million users, accounting for more than 30% of the overall spend. The television commercials featured a search bar that visually mimics unique query terms and showcases how consumers can find anything on MSN Search. The campaign features the slogan 'Find it at MSN.co.uk'.

The TV advertising campaign will be aired on a broad range of channels, including Channel 4 and ITV. The first phase will run from 7 February for a number of weeks with a second phase towards the summer.

The advertisements were positioned to run during television coverage of several high-profile events, including The Brit Awards and the film premiere of Oceans 12. TV advertisements were run in global markets, including the UK, Canada (in English

and French), Australia and Brazil.

Clare Bolton, MSN UK consumer marketing manager said 'This is a fantastic opportunity for MSN to promote one of our most important product launches to date.'

Source: adapted from www.netimperative.com.

(a) **Based on the information, state TWO ways in which running a television advertising campaign at the same time as an on-line campaign might create an effective promotion to reach users of MSN's search engine.** (2 marks)

(b) **Identify TWO factors which may have influenced the business when choosing television as a medium for its advertising and explain how each factor might have affected the business.** (6 marks)

Meeting the assessment criteria

Snappy Toys Ltd produces a range of children's toys aimed at the mass market, with the majority of sales going through supermarkets. Before it takes the latest range into stock, one major supermarket chain insists that the new range is supported by television advertising. Snappy Toys Ltd has never been involved in television advertising before and needs some help understanding certain aspects.

(a) Explain the role that each of the following elements plays in the production of a television commercial.
 - Marketing aims.
 - Script.
 - Budget.

(i) Marketing aims. **(2 marks)**

Expected answers
- *Outlines the business and what it seeks to achieve through application of its marketing plans – identifies how television advertising can play a part in helping the business achieve these aims.*
- *Tells agency/production company what advertiser/client company do/achieve through advertising – specifies how television commercial fits in with marketing aims of business.*

Mark allocation
1 mark for basic role.
1 mark for application to production of television commercial. **(2 marks)**

(ii) Script. **(2 marks)**

Expected answers
- *Document containing the words/images/graphics/look of the proposed commercial – specifies precisely what the production. company/crew/actors have to do.*
- *Defines the look, sound and action in the film – means that each member of the production crew and cast know precisely what they have to do to produce a film that meets clients' specified requirements.*

Mark allocation
1 mark for basic role.
1 mark for application to production of television commercial. **(2 marks)**

(iii) Budget. **(2 marks)**

Expected answers
- *Tells production team the maximum amount of money that client has allocated for production – tells them precisely how much money there is to spend on making the commercial/sets parameters on cost of location/cast/special effects.*
- *Enables the client to plan sales to cover marketing costs – in this case the marketing cost will be for the production of commercial.*

Mark allocation
1 mark for basic role.
1 mark for application to production of television commercial. **(2 marks)**

(b) Explain ONE major difference between advertising on television and advertising in a magazine that is likely to affect the marketing plans at Snappy Toys Ltd. **(3 marks)**

Expected answers
- *Production cost much higher for television than magazines – more people/technology involved – will need a bigger budget.*
- *Media space much more expensive than magazines – as it achieves greater coverage – will need a bigger budget.*
- *TV commercials make a major impact with a large audience – likely to produce high levels of sales – may need to increase production volumes.*
- *Production of commercial involves agencies/film studios/technical experts/scripts – more people/steps involved than producing a magazine advertisement – may need to plan additional time/longer lead times before commercial is ready/product needs to be ready for advertising.*

Mark allocation
1 mark for difference.
1 mark for explanation.
1 mark for application to marketing plans. **(3 marks)**

Ambient and out-of-home media

What is ambient media?

This is a term that is used to describe any of the 'quirky' examples of advertising that are springing up all of the time in the most unlikely places. Rather than being a distinctive and clearly identifiable medium, which is bought, read, watched or listened to, ambient media is part of the day-to-day background to modern life. That is not to say that ambient media are not distinctive or identifiable in their own right. However, they do not fall into the usual classification of mainstream media.

There are many examples as shown in Figure 1. Ambient media is found anywhere that is big or small enough to carry an advertising statement or logo that does not already have an advertisement on it. If it is available, then a creative exponent of ambient advertising should be able to think of a way of exploiting its potential as an advertising space.

There is a close association, and sometimes a crossover, between ambient media and **product placement**. Product placement is where a product or brand signifier appears unconsciously as part of the background in a television programme or a feature film (see section 73). The product placement is designed to work unconsciously on the audience like ambient advertising.

It could be argued that the branding and logos carried on the shirts and other clothing worn by sporting teams, rock bands or racing drivers could be classified as ambient media. This advertising works in a similar way to product placement. It is in the background and a secondary feature to what is actually being looked at, in this case the sports player, musician or driver.

There is a similar close association between ambient media and out-of-home media explained later in this section. A taxi door carrying an advertisement could be classified as ambient media, but it may also be a mobile outdoor poster site. Similarly, a large sticker carrying a brand name or picture of a product could be classified as a mini poster.

To some extent, the definitions of ambient media, product placement or out-of-home media are in the 'eye of the beholder' or the 'mind of the media owner'. For the purposes of marketing planning, it is what the media can deliver in terms of communicating with the target audience that is important, rather than getting hung up on technical terms that are often interchangeable.

Information about ambient and out-of-home media can be found in the *brad* media directory.

Why use ambient media products?

What are some of the positive attributes of this media?

Wide range of quirky and unusual creative opportunities
Ambient media can be used to make a brand statement in unusual places that are not usually thought of for advertising. As a result an advertiser can be perceived to be innovative and original in its creative use of ambient media. This can have a powerful effect on some narrow target markets, such as clubbers, that are not easy to reach by conventional, mainstream media. For example, a manufacturer of clothing aimed at clubbers could produce stickers, cards and other small items to distribute to clubs or decorate walls to promote the brand name.

Relatively low cost The nature of many ambient media means that production costs are relatively low and distribution and placement are also low compared with other media.

Good for supporting a mainstream advertising campaign
Ambient media is rarely used as a primary medium in its own right. However, it is perfect in a secondary role, supporting a mainstream campaign with repeat images or branded logos appearing in unusual places to act as a reminder of the main campaign.

Figure 1 *Examples of ambient media*

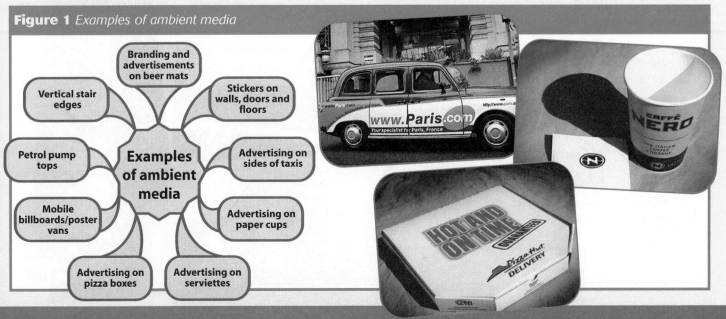

Possible problems with using ambient media

Why might a business decide not to use this media?

Could waste money Although relatively low in cost, there is still a price to pay for ambient media. A business may consider that the marketing budget could be better spent on more traditional media.

Could be lost Given the fight for consumer attention by the mainstream media, and the way that consumers are bombarded with advertising, ambient media can sometimes be lost in the background and barely noticed.

Limited message Most ambient media are either relatively small in size or only seen by the target market for a very short time. This means that the message it can carry is relatively limited. It may be a short message, a brand name or logo, an image or a website address.

Difficult to measure success At best, ambient media provide a low-level background presence. The success of ambient media can be difficult to quantify unless linked to some direct response mechanism that can be counted.

Out-of-home media products

Out-of-home media includes, as the term suggests, examples of advertising media that are seen by the audience when they are outside of their home. Some examples are shown in Figure 2. Out-of-home media can become part of the background to consumer consciousness and could thus be classified as ambient media.

Why use outdoor media products?

What are some of the positive attributes of this media?

High impact Billboards and large poster sites provide the opportunity for making a bold statement that could make a massive impact on the audience. The scale of billboards and poster sites means that any product featured will be larger than life. This can be very impressive for the audience and is likely to

Table 1 *Posters*

Media	Benefit
Posters within a town centre or shopping mall	To direct customers straight to the shop.
Posters in a shop window	Shop puts posters in its own window, directed specifically at customers passing or entering the shop.
Poster sites along a road leading to a town	To advertise historical sites or places to visit within the town. A campaign could be run in just one town, by buying all available poster sites in that town.

Figure 2 *Examples of out-of-home media*

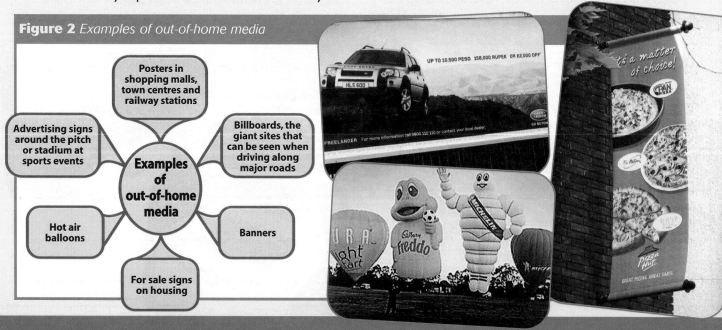

- Posters in shopping malls, town centres and railway stations
- Advertising signs around the pitch or stadium at sports events
- Billboards, the giant sites that can be seen when driving along major roads
- Examples of out-of-home media
- Hot air balloons
- Banners
- For sale signs on housing

make a big impact on their consciousness and hopefully communicate a powerful message or generate sales.

Geographically focused Outdoor posters are perfect for promoting in a tightly defined geographic area. Some examples are shown in Table 1. The versatility of posters means that planning coverage can be very flexible and tailored to precisely the coverage required by the advertiser. They can also be automated or electronic, changing advertisements regularly.

Coverage Posters or banners at a major event, such as a football match that is being broadcast on national and international television, is likely to be seen by a huge audience in addition to the relatively modest audience at the actual event itself. This effect can boost coverage figures and give an advertiser exposure to an international audience and markets beyond the reach of the actual poster or banner itself.

Possible problems with out-of-home media

Why might a business decide not to use outdoor media?

Damage The weather in the UK means there is always the potential for damage to occur to poster sites. Rain can cause outdoor posters to blister and become unstuck. Winds can rip and tear exposed posters. The media owners that manage poster sites are constantly trying to improve the weather resistance of posters. Developments in paper, ink and adhesives have improved the weather resistance, but it remains a potential problem for advertisers. Another cause of damage could be vandalism. Posters are often sprayed with graffiti, written on, or have things thrown at them. Damage could reduce the impact of a poster campaign. It may even cause consumer resistance to the product being advertised if the damage appears to reflect badly on the product itself.

Limited message Depending on the site, the message that can be carried by outdoor media could be limited. Only so much information can be taken in by a driver passing a billboard at high speed. In an underground station, the posters up the sides of the escalators are passed quite quickly by commuters and can only carry a short message or branding statement. The creative treatment of outdoor advertising needs to reflect the problems of situations like these. In contrast, a poster:

- in a railway train carriage;
- in a post office;
- outside an entertainment venue;

where the audience is likely be in front of the poster for a length of time, can carry much more detailed information.

Only seen by passers by This can be an issue when planning coverage of an out-of-home media campaign. Only people passing by will see out-of-home media. This is usually reflected in the cost of outdoor advertising space. The media cost is higher in areas of high traffic and lower in areas where fewer people are likely to pass. It could be argued that this is a problem for any media, i.e. an advertisement in a newspaper is only likely to be seen by someone that buys and reads the newspaper. However, it is a particular problem for out-of-home media because sites are usually prominent, but there is no point being prominent if there is no one around to see it.

Meeting the assessment criteria

Little Alex is a cult band from Aylesbury. The band markets CDs and other merchandise from small advertisements in the *NME* magazine. To update the image of Little Alex the management wants to use as much new media as possible to promote the band to its fan base, which is predominantly males, aged 18-30 years old.

(a) see section 75.
(b) see section 75.
(c) One of the band wants to send stickers with the name of the band and the website address to clubs around England to promote the band. Evaluate this form of ambient media as a way of raising awareness of the band.   **(4 marks)**

Expected answers
Positive points about use of stickers
- *Low cost.*
- *Repeat images reinforce/remind audience of band/website.*
- *Opportunity for lots of them - which should help create awareness.*
- *Use of stickers perceived as anti-establishment fly-posting - could create/reinforce image/cult following.*

Negative points about use of stickers
- *Club owners may not want to put stickers around their clubs.*
- *May be perceived as desperate/tacky and 'uncool'.*
- *Placement of stickers/advertising left to third party – management of band loses control.*
- *Use of stickers perceived as illegal fly-posting - could create legal problems/attract fines.*

(Question based on evaluation – must include both sides of argument.)

Mark allocation
1 mark for each positive point why stickers likely to be effective at raising awareness (maximum 2 marks)
or
1 mark for positive point + 1 mark for developed or applied answer (maximum 2 marks).

1 mark for each negative point why stickers not likely to be effective at raising awareness (maximum 2 marks)
or
1 mark for negative point + 1 mark for developed or applied answer (maximum 2 marks).   **(4 marks)**

Examination practice · **Product placement in I, Robot**

In 2004, it was suggested that product placement reached a new level with Audi's involvement with the movie 'I, ROBOT.' Cars had been associated with movies before, notably the DeLorean in Back to the Future, Aston Martin in James Bond films and the Mini in The Italian Job. Audi has also been involved in films such as Ronin.

In I, Robot it wasn't just a question of promoting the right car in the right movie. It was a custom job. And since this custom job was also a product placement job, the car had to fit into the movie world, while still promoting the Audi brand.

Audi worked with the director of the movie and set designers to achieve a concept that both Audi and the movie people were happy with. The result of the collaborative effort is the futuristic RSQ sports coupe, featuring, spherical wheels, mid-engine design, butterfly-action doors, a colour-changing, luminescent paint job and a low, sleek profile.

Source: adapted from money.howstuffworks.com.

(a) **Give TWO reasons why Audi might use product placement.** (2 marks)
(b) **Evaluate whether the benefits of product placement are likely to outweigh the costs from the point of view of the business promoting its product. (4 marks)**
(c) **(i) State TWO types of out-of-home media which a film business might use to promote its films.(2 marks)**
(ii) In each case, give TWO reasons why this type of media might be effective for promoting the film.
(4 marks)

New media

What are they?

Media technology is changing all of the time. New media refers to all the latest developments in digital media and computer technology that are being used to create innovative and interactive promotional materials. The change is rapid and businesses need to keep up-to-date with current trends and developments. Some examples are shown in Figure 1. New media is usually accessed and distributed on CDs and DVDs or via the Internet, mobile phones, Bluetooth technology and other digital communications media.

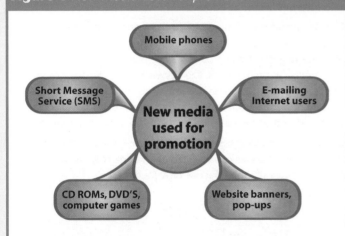

Figure 1 New media used for promotion

Examples of the use of new technology as a promotional media can be seen every time a computer logs onto the Internet. Depending on the website visited, and the level of security being used, people are likely to see and experience many different new media as they appear on the computer screen in the form of;
- banners;
- pop-ups;
- other devices all trying to attract attention and get customers to click and visit the site that is being promoted.

New ideas for promotion using new media are being developed and tried all of the time. These include e-mailing to customers. The use of the Internet for promotion and e-commerce is dealt with in detail in unit 4.

CDs, DVDs, CD-ROMs and computer games discs often carry promotional messages using new media that is adapted to the product it is on and the likely audience that is using the technology. For example, many DVDs include:
- films at the cinema produced by the company selling the DVD;
- other DVDs by the company on sale;
- related products such as computers games or merchandise.
An example is shown in Figure 2.

Mobile phones are being used increasingly for advertising and promotion. Sometimes promotions are funded by consumers entering a competition by dialling a mobile phone number or

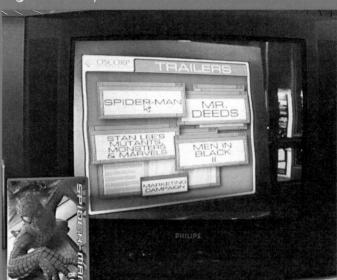

Figure 2 DVD promotions

texting answers. These are all charged at premium rates, or at least a rate that generates some income for the promoter.

Mobile phones are also used for Short Message Service(SMS)/text marketing. This new media service enables the effective targeting of text messages to consumers that are in the target market for the product being promoted. A business will need to conduct research and build its own database or buy one ready-made from a database provider. From this database the business can then launch its campaign. SMS/text marketing is being used to communicate new product news and promotional offers. Other new technology, such as Bluetooth, enables text marketing to become even more targeted as mobile phone messages are broadcast from retail sites and even promotional displays within a retail outlet. Customers walking by will be sent a message from the shop or display to:
- attract them into the shop;
- create awareness of the promotion;
- encourage them to buy.

Why use new media products?

What are some of the advantages of this media?

New and innovative A product being advertised and promoted by new media techniques will benefit from being associated with modern, new media. This will lead some parts of the market to think that if they are using new media then they must be a modern, forward-thinking advertiser. This positive association is being exploited by fashion and lifestyle products and by the music and computer games industries. In the highly competitive world of financial and other banking organisations, a number of businesses are using new media for precisely this purpose, to appear to be modern, with the view of attracting modern, young customers.

Figure 3 *E-mail promotions*

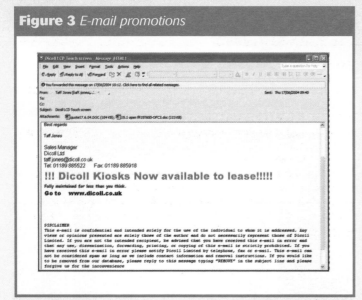

Can reach markets that are normally difficult to reach

This benefit is linked to the profile of some computer and Internet users, who tend to be young and are less likely to see or use traditional mass media. Because they spend a lot of time on the Internet, it is an ideal medium to use to promote products to them, using the medium that they relate to and use. Customers can be directly targeted with e-mail promotions, such as weekly newsletters. An example is shown in Figure 3.

Intrusive This is certainly the case for pop-ups that jump into the computer screen and must be clicked to get rid of them. But even this single click tells the advertiser something about the computer

user, that they are on-line and therefore open to further devices to attract their attention. SMS texts are delivered direct to the target market and must be read or cleared. This means that the message has a high chance of being communicated to the target market.

Why not use new media products?

Why might a business decide not to use this type of media?

Coverage is limited By definition, the coverage of promotions and new media that are on the Internet is limited to computer users. Other new media are equally limited to users of the technology that carries and distributed the new media, such as mobile phones, CD or DVD players. Consumers without access to these new media will be excluded. This may or may not be a problem depending on the profile of the target market, which itself may or may not include consumers who do not have access to new media. It may also become less of an issue as more people have Internet access at home.

Can be annoying The use of pop-ups and other devices that invade computer screens can be irritating for users and may generate negative feelings towards the business that is using these new media. It can be a fine line between pop-ups that are fun and entertaining and those that are just annoying. Getting the balance right takes a lot of skill and planning. Unwanted SMS texts can also be considered to be annoying, as can spam sent to computers.

Difficult to measure success Unless new media promotions and advertising are linked to direct marketing responses, it can be difficult to quantify the effect of new media.

Examination practice · Gizmondo

In March 2005 the new Gizmondo handheld entered the competitive gaming console market at a price of £229. It is a handheld device that runs video games, plays MP3s and MPeg-4 video and contains a 0.3 megapixel camera, a GPS satellite positioning chip and full GPRS phone functionality, although people cannot make voice calls. Industry commentators suggested that it would struggle to compete with Nintendo's DS and Sony's soon to be released PlayStation Portable.

Gizmondo's managing director, Carl Freer, said 'We're not trying to conquer this market ... . We've got an interesting proposition for people who want more than just gaming.' Gizmondo, can download music from the OD2/Loudeye service and music videos. It can play movies pre-loaded on to SD cards, and send cheap SMS and MMS messages.

The price of Gizmondo may drop when 'Smart Adds' is up and running. Smart Adds are targeted advertisements that can be

combined with the GPS location to, for example, offer electronic discount vouchers for Gizmondo owners who walk into particular shops. It is also possible to use the Gizmondo as a car satellite navigation system and to send street-mapping information to it. The business suggests that once 150,000 Gizmondos have been sold in the UK, the Smart Adds' revenue will drive the hardware price down.

Source: adapted from *The Guardian*, 17.3.2005.

(a) **From the information identify and explain TWO factors which are likely to influence the success of this type of promotion.** **(6 marks)**
(b) **Discuss whether sending Smart Adds through to a Gizmondo is likely to be a successful promotional media in future.** **(4 marks)**

Meeting the assessment criteria

Little Alex is a cult band from Aylesbury. The band markets CDs and other merchandise from small advertisements in *NME* magazine. To update the image of Little Alex the management wants to use as much new media as possible to promote the band to its fan base which is predominantly males, aged 18-30 years old.

(a) Give TWO different examples of new media that the band could use to inform fans of new CD releases. Justify why each example would be appropriate.　　**(4 marks)**

Expected answers
- *SMS texts direct to fans' mobile phones – every fan in target age group likely to have/use mobiles.*
- *Website – male fans in this age group likely to have/use computers/the Internet.*
- *Pop-ups on general music websites – will not only inform fans but could generate awareness with people who have never heard of band.*
- *Banner across top of home page on band's website – will immediately alert the casual looker that there is something new/a new CD.*

Mark allocation
1 mark for example of new media.
1 mark for each justification.　　**(1 + 1) x 2 (4 marks)**

(b) Explain ONE problem associated with a reliance on using new media only for promotion.　　**(3 marks)**

Expected answers
- *Not everyone has access to new media - limits the number of people that see advertisement/promotion - could limit/restrict market/sales.*
- *Sometimes seen as peripheral/low key method of promotion - may not generate sufficient volume of sales required/associated with traditional media - may need to consider other methods of promotion.*
- *Does not expose/promote band/business to a wide/mass audience - restricts potential for attracting new fans/customers - need to research market/fan base to identify appropriate media to use.*

Mark allocation
1 mark for basic problem.
1 mark for explanation.
1 mark for applying problem to scenario in question.　　**(3 marks)**

Internal and external constraints

Like all other business activity, promotional activity is usually subject to constraints in one form or another. Constraints can affect decisions regarding the promotional plans of a business. They may:

- restrict the content or extent of promotional activity;
- slow down promotional activity to a rate that can be supported or afforded by the business;
- change planned activity by a business.

This is not necessarily a bad thing. The revised promotional activity that results from constraints can sometimes be better thought through and more focused than the original activity that was planned.

Constraints come in many different forms and have different effects as shown in Figure 1. Internal constraints originate and are applied from **within** the business or organisation itself. They are likely to be set and controlled by the senior management or influential stakeholders of the business or organisation. They may stem from resources available, management decisions or corporate ethos, each can have the effect of slowing, changing or halting promotional plans and campaigns.

The internal constraints that have the most direct effect are based on the resources of the business. These are shown in Figure 2. External constraints originate **outside** the business. They are dealt with in section 77.

Budget and costs

Promotional activity is affected by the costs and budgets of a business.

Figure 1 *Promotional constraints*

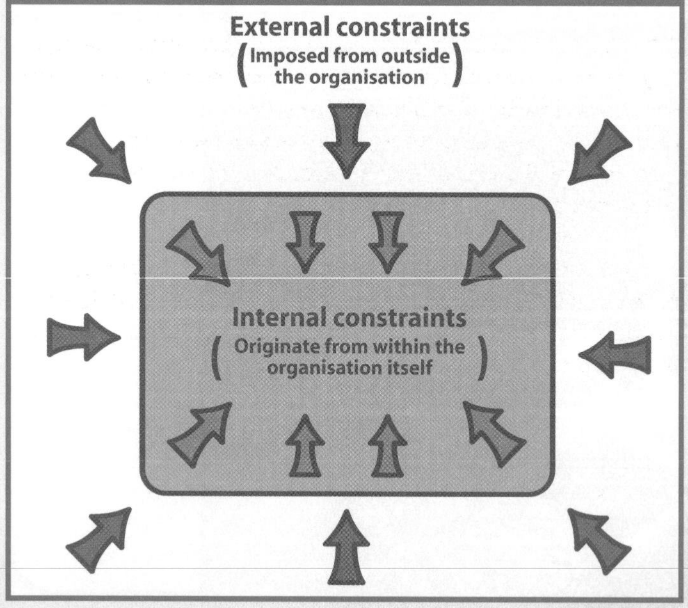

External constraints
(Imposed from outside the organisation)

Internal constraints
(Originate from within the organisation itself)

Figure 2 *Main internal constraints on promotion*

Budget and costs

Time

Internal constraints on promotion

Skills and expertise of staff

Availability of technical resources

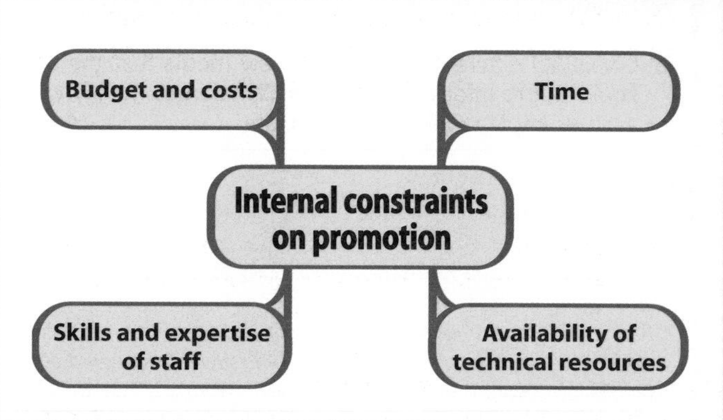

Costs All business activity has cost implications. In a well run business promotional activities are likely to be subject to scrutiny based on:

- the degree to which the promotional activity meets the aims and objectives of the business;
- the cost of the promotional activity required to meet these aims and objectives.

If the promotional activity meets the aims and objectives within a budget that can be afforded, then it is likely to be judged as 'cost-effective'. If it meets the aims and objectives, but at a high cost or at a cost that takes all of the profit that is generated from sales that result from the activity, then it may not be considered to be cost-effective.

However, financial cost is not always the only way to measure promotional activity. It may be designed to meet aims and objectives that are not measured in purely financial terms, such as raising awareness or changing attitudes. In this situation the cost must be weighed against the budget available and what the promotional activity can achieve.

Budgets Financial constraints are usually set by senior management in the form of a budget. A budget is the amount of money that is allocated to an activity such as promotion. A promotional budget can be set in a number of ways.

- It can be based on real, market based costs that are required to be spent on promotion to meet business aims or objectives.
- It may be based on how much an organisation can afford to spend without hurting investors or damaging its viability.
- A more scientific approach to budgeting would estimate the investment expenditure required for a forecast return on expenditure, based on what the promotion is forecast to achieve.

Whichever way a budget is set, it will at some point be a constraint on the marketing mix.

Sometimes a financial constraint may be perceived to be external, for example when a design agency, an advertising production studio or a media owner raises its prices. The constraint is that the allocated budget will not buy as much as had been forecast or expected. However, even though high prices or costs may feel like the constraint is external, the real constraining factor is access to financial resources - the internally set budget.

Financial constraints can sometimes be changed or avoided by reassessing the situation and presenting the case for a change of budget to senior management or the budget controller in the organisation. A business may be more inclined to do this if it is supported by market research or if there is an increased level of probability of achieving the aims and objectives of the promotion.

Time

Time may be an internal constraint when linked to marketing plans and promotional plans for the organisation. Once set, promotional plans will have a time element to them. They have to be developed, launched and completed in line with the aims and objectives that they are designed to achieve. It would be no good running a promotional campaign over a three year period if the business wanted results within a six month period to achieve its budget for the current financial year or to meet the date for the next annual report to shareholders.

Each department within a business will have its own timetable and cycle of time based activities. These may include:
- the sales team producing weekly sales figures;
- the accounts team producing monthly budget reports;
- senior directors producing quarterly management reports for shareholders.

To be effective it is important that marketing and promotional plans are built into the cycle of activities within the business. Some examples are shown in Table 1. This shows that the marketing team should not work in isolation. It needs to plan the timing of promotional activities to make sure that they fit in with

Table 1 *How time and promotional activities affect a business*

Business activity	Effect
Sales team	May need to sell-in a new product before advertising starts. This means that samples and promotional material are needed, which must be produced in advance of the sales activity.
Distribution team	Will need to make sure that customers have stocks before advertising starts.
Production team	Must ensure that stocks are ready for distribution.

the running of the business. If they do not, they may not achieve the set aims and objectives and could waste the budget.

The timing of promotional plans also needs to fit in with cycles in the market place, such as seasonal highs and lows. A budget may be wasted if a promotion is run at a time of the year when most of the target market is on holiday, for example.

Another time constraint is the **lead time** for the development and production of promotional activity. This is the time it takes to actually do it and get it up and running. Again, this could impact on internal time cycles and cycles within the market place. To avoid any problems in this area, it is always advisable to start the planning, development and production required for a promotion well before it is required.

Skills and expertise of staff

A business must make sure that it has the skills and expertise to plan, produce and run a promotional campaign within its own human resources. This can be identified by conducting a **skills audit**. A skills audit is a check on each member of the marketing team and any other team that may be involved in the promotion, such as the sales team or a technical team that is mainly employed in product development.

If people within the business do have the skills, then the business can plan its promotion using existing staff. However, they must be briefed adequately on what is required for the promotion. The business must also be confident that whatever promotional plans are developed internally, they are appropriate for the market place and as good as, or better than, those of competitors.

If a business does not have the right skills and expertise within the organisation, it can 'buy them in' by employing an agency or individual with the appropriate skills. Examples of agencies within the promotion industry would include advertising agencies, promotion agencies and incentive agencies. Buying in skills will be a cost for the business, which could conflict with budgetary and financial plans.

Availability of technical resources

A business may have suitable creative skills internally. However, it may not have the technical skills to produce the support material that is required for promotional activity. For example, it is unlikely that a typical business would have its own skills and resources for the production of audio, film or television commercials, or even design and printing.

For the actual production of promotional material a business could employ the skills of photographic studios, film studios, recording studios, graphic designers, printers, as required. Again, bought in technical resources come at a price, which is a cost for the business.

Meeting the assessment criteria

The social committee at Lea Side School plans to run and promote an end of year dance party aimed at students that are about to leave the school and move to either higher education or into the workplace. The committee wants to use the school's art students to design and produce posters and leaflets for this event.

(a) Apart from budget and financial constraints, give THREE internal constraints that may affect marketing plans to promote the dance party.   **(3 marks)**

Expected answers
* *Design students may not want to do the designs.*
* *Design students may not produce designs that are acceptable to the committee.*
* *School may not have production/reproducing facilities.*
* *Students may not be allowed to use internal notice boards for posters.*
* *Students may not be allowed to distribute leaflets/promotional material.*
* *School staff may not like designs for posters/leaflets and may not allowing them to be displayed.*

Mark allocation
1 mark for each internal constraint.   **(3 marks)**

The social committee thinks that they need to print 100 posters, which will cost £100 in total. Unfortunately they only have £100 in the social account, which also has to pay for the disco which they can hire for a reduced rate of £50 from a friend.

(b) State ONE way that this constrains the marketing plans for the dance party and explain how the constraint you give can be overcome by the committee.   **(3 marks)**

Expected answers
* *Cannot afford to print as many posters – print fewer posters – make them work harder by placing them in better/higher traffic locations*
* *Cannot pay for both full quantity of posters and disco – pay for posters out of funds – pay for disco out of charge at door.*

Mark allocation
1 mark for how marketing plans constrained.
1 mark for how constraint can be overcome.
1 mark for developed answer or application to committee.   **(3 marks)**

(c) Explain ONE way that the financial constraints described in this question can be avoided by the social committee at Lea Side School when they run the end of year dance party next year.   **(3 marks)**

Expected answers
* *Raise funds throughout year – this will result in a bigger kitty/budget – this will mean that there is more to spend on promotion.*
* *Reduce spending on other activities/promotions – save as much of the budget as possible – manage/balance budget better so that all suppliers that will be required next year can be paid for as required.*
* *Negotiate lower printing prices – do this well before posters required – this should help avoid being put under time pressure which can be used by suppliers to raise prices.*

Mark allocation
1 mark for basic way financial constraint can be avoided.
1 mark for explaining how.
1 mark for applying to next year.   **(3 marks)**

Examination practice · FQ

How much does it cost to launch a new magazine? Large businesses often quote figures in the millions. Emap spent £12m plus on *Heat* and Time Warner/AOL spent £7m on *InStyle*. But magazines have been launched with a lot less. It often depends on the magazine and the market.

In May 2003 FQ, the magazine for fathers was launched with a budget of £120,000. 'We've got a magazine that people want to read and that's the main thing,' said the publisher and investor. 'Bigger publishers with larger budgets might print 500,000 copies, but what's the point if people aren't going to buy them?' The magazine aimed to sell around 70,000 copies.

Source: adapted from *The Observer*, 14.9.2003.

(a) From the information, identify ONE internal constraint on the promotion of FQ. Explain how this constraint could affect the publisher of FQ.   (3 marks)
(b) Explain how the human resources in a business might act as a constraint on promotion carried out by (i) a small publisher and (ii) a large publisher. (6 marks)

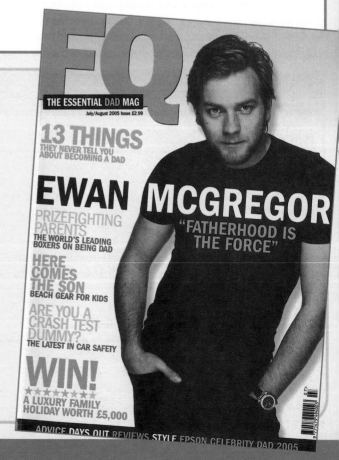

External constraints on promotion

What are external constraints?

The external constraints on promotional activities originate **outside** of the business. They are usually beyond the direct control of a business, but can still affect the promotional plans. They may be set, applied and controlled by a range of organisations, such as:

● the government;
● the European Union (EU);
● or a non-government organisation (NGO) such as a trade or industry association.

In the main, external constraints are designed to protect society and individuals from being offended, cheated, misled or exploited by promotional activity.

The external constraints that are likely to have the most direct effect on promotional activity are shown in Figure 1.

Figure 1 *External constraints on promotion*

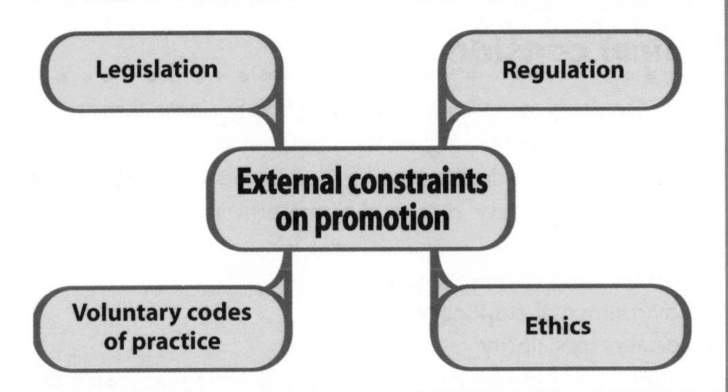

Regulation

Regulation involves standards of operating and operating procedures, such as:

● rules;
● instructions;
● requirements.

They are not explicitly based on legislation, but on executive powers given to a regulator or the organisation that is setting and enforcing the regulations.

There are important regulators in the promotion industry. These organisations constrain marketing plans as they regulate broadcast media and other advertising media.

The Office of Communications (Ofcom) Ofcom is the UK's communications industry regulator. It has wide ranging responsibilities across the UK's communications markets. At the end of 2003 Ofcom inherited the duties of the five existing regulators it replaced - the Broadcasting Standards Commission, the Independent Television Commission, Oftel, the Radio Authority and the Radiocommunications Agency. This is explained in the statement from Ofcom shown in Figure 2.

Figure 2 *The role of Ofcom*

'Consumers will no longer have to juggle with several different regulators in order to get action on misleading, offensive or harmful advertising. An unsatisfactory feature of the former system was the very large numbers who complained to the ASA about TV and radio ads – even though there was nothing we could do to help.

It is important to remember that Ofcom only regulates TV and radio. It does not regulate non-broadcast media. For this reason, Ofcom's contractual relationship is with the separate legal entities ASA(Broadcast) and CAP (Broadcast). The non-broadcast ASA and CAP remain quite independent of any relationship with Ofcom. Formally, this is the Annual Statement of ASA, ASA(Broadcast), CAP (Non-broadcast) and CAP (Broadcast). For more than 40 years, the ASA has regulated non-broadcast advertisements against the CAP Code. Now that model of effective self-regulation is being extended to TV and radio advertisements. The one-stop shop is open for business.'

Source: adapted from www.ofcom.org.uk.

The Committee of Advertising Practice (CAP) The Committee of Advertising Practice publishes the British Code of Advertising, Sales Promotion and Direct Marketing (known as the CAP code). This is the 'rule book' for non-broadcast advertisements, sales promotions and direct marketing communications.

The Advertising Standards Authority (ASA) This is an independent body set up by the advertising industry to police codes, such as the CAP Code and the Radio Code. Since 2004 it has also been responsible for the regulation of broadcast advertising. Details of the regulation of promotion by Ofcom, ASA and CAP can be found at www.ofcom.org.uk, www.asa.org.uk and www.cap.org.uk.

Another example of regulation of promotion would be regulations given to exhibitors at major exhibition halls, which tell exhibitors what they can do, cannot do, must do and must not do before, during and after attending the exhibition. Legislation will always be a back-up option should a business fail to recognise the power of the regulator.

Legislation

There is a great deal of legislation that could affect promotional plans. Most of this legislation has resulted from the objective of protecting consumers. The Trading Standards central website (www.tradingstandards.gov.uk) is a good place to investigate to get some idea of just how much legislation exists to protect consumers, that could affect business and could constrain promotion.

There is no need to learn every part of every piece of legislation for this unit. However, it is useful to understand how the principal pieces of consumer protection legislation can constrain promotion. Some of the main UK legislation is shown in Table 1. Increasingly legislation in the UK is affected by EU legislation (see section 63).

Table 1 *Legislation affecting promotion*

Business activity	Effect
CONSUMER PROTECTION ACT 1987	Prohibits the supply of goods not in accordance with the general safety requirement or are unsafe, and provides for the safety and protection of consumers by enabling regulations or orders to be made controlling consumer goods.
DATA PROTECTION ACT 1998	Affects the collection, storage and use of personal and financial data.
SALE OF GOODS ACT 1979, SALE AND SUPPLY OF GOODS ACT 1994 and SALE OF GOODS (AMENDMENT) ACT 1995	Details the rights of purchasers and the duties of sellers in the sale of goods.
SUPPLY OF GOODS AND SERVICES ACT 1982	Details the rights of purchasers and the duties of suppliers of services.
TRADE DESCRIPTIONS ACT 1968	Prohibits the misdescription on the supply of goods and prohibits false claims for services, accommodation and facilities.

Before any promotional plans and marketing plans are put into practice, a business must check that they comply with current legislation. This will ensure that no offences are likely to occur and no legislation is broken as a result of the plan. Once a potential constraint has been identified, steps can be taken or plans can be changed to avoid or reduce the effect of any constraint and reduce the chance of breaking the law.

The Office of Fair Trading provides very useful general advice on consumer rights in the UK (www.oft.gov.uk).

Voluntary codes

These are terms under which an organisation or industry agrees to operate to reduce the need for legislation or regulation. Different industries may have examples that have a direct effect on promotion. For example:

- the Voluntary Code of Practice for the Fast Food Industry gives options for reducing fast food litter and waste in the local environment;
- the Banking Code is a voluntary code followed by banks and building societies in their relations with personal customers in the United Kingdom.
- a voluntary code covers the promotion of confectionery, crisps, savoury snacks, soft drinks and other processed products containing high levels of fat, sugar and salt, excessive consumption of which are known to be detrimental to children's health;
- the NOAH (The National Office of Animal Health) Code of Practice for the Promotion of Animal Medicines controls the promotion of medicine for animals.

Ethical considerations

These are decisions or ways of conducting business that are based on how an industry or organisation believes that it should be conducting business in the best interests of its customers, employees and society in general. Some ethical considerations include:

- personal and corporate integrity;
- environmental responsibility;
- social responsibility;
- general company policy or code of operating that would be considered to be good behaviour by the industry.

Ethical standards will differ within different industries and different markets. Ethics are covered in more detail in section 14.

The way in which taking an ethical stance constrains promotion should be considered before the promotion is launched. This will make sure that the promotion does not cause offence or lead to other problems that may have a detrimental effect on the ability of the promotion to meet its aims and objectives.

Examination practice · The ASA and mobile phone promotion

The number of complaints about mobile phone advertising has grown as more people buy phones and the industry expands. A common criticism is that pricing is not clear enough, particularly regarding subscriptions. For example, the ASA received a complaint from a parent that their daughter was attracted by an advertisement in a teenage girls' magazine stating '2 Tones for 75p' but did not read the fine print saying the advertisement was for a subscription service. The ASA ordered the advertiser to amend its campaign.

Source: adapted from www.asa.org.uk.

(a) **State why the work of the ASA is an example of an external constraint on promotion by a mobile phone business. (1 mark)**

(b) **State THREE ways in which the actions of the ASA might affect the promotion of a mobile phone business. (3 marks)**

(c) **Explain TWO other external constraints on the promotion of a mobile phone business. (6 marks)**

Meeting the assessment criteria

Many supermarkets use loyalty cards to reward customers for their continued business. Loyalty cards are also used to collect information on customers' buying and spending habits.

(a) (a) State why the use of personal information collected from loyalty cards for promotional purposes is constrained by The Data Protection Act, 1998. **(1 mark)**

Expected answers
- *To protect consumers/customers from having their personal information used/exploited for commercial purposes.*
- *To protect consumers/customers from problems/embarrassment that could occur if personal details become public.*

Mark allocation
1 mark for reason. **(1 mark)**

(b) (i) Describe an example that you have seen or studied of an external constraint changing a promotional plan. (ii) State the external constraint and the effect it had on the promotional plan. **(4 marks)**

Expected answers
- *Studied complaint to ASA about advertisements shown during a break in the film Groundhog Day, on Channel 5 on 3 March 2005 - viewer complained that the advertisements were much louder than the surrounding programme – complaint made to the Advertising Standards Authority (ASA) – complaint was upheld which meant that Channel 5 had to guarantee that the maximum sound level of advertisements would comply with the TV Advertising Standards Code.*
- *Studied Benetton posters which showed violent images – images were considered by some members of the public to be offensive and unnecessary for advertising clothes – complaint made to ASA – complaint upheld and offensive poster was withdrawn which caused promotional plan to be changed in the short term, but the business was soon back with new posters.*

Mark allocation
1 mark for basic example.
1 mark for developed example.
1 mark for stating external constraint.
1 mark for effect on promotional plan. **(4 marks)**

Analysing promotional campaigns

Promotional and advertising campaigns are part of everyday life. However, few, if any, are there for their own sake or for amusement and entertainment. Promotion and advertising costs money and are usually done for business reasons. Sections 78 and 79 examine:

- why a promotional campaign might be run;
- what might be the aims and objectives behind promotional campaigns;
- what businesses might be seeking to achieve from promotional campaigns.

Features of promotional campaigns

How might a business analyse and then evaluate a promotional campaign? To get a feel for the sheer range and breadth of different promotional campaigns, it is important to look at and experience as many as possible. From a range of different media, promotions and advertisements it is possible to identify certain important features, as shown in Figure 1. There are other features of promotions and advertisements, but these will be useful as a starting point for the assessment and evaluation of promotional campaigns.

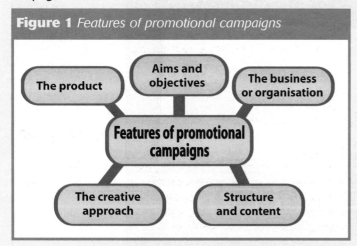

Figure 1 *Features of promotional campaigns*

Aims and objectives What is the point of the promotion? Why is it being run at all? What does the business want to get out of it? These can be difficult to answer without access to the aims and objectives set in the marketing plan. But by analysing the promotional campaign carefully, a business should be able to make some basic assumptions about why it is being run.

The product being promoted The product is the main feature of the promotion or advertisement. What type of product is being promoted? It may be a consumer good, a service, a message or some form of information.

The business or organisation behind the promotion This may be a manufacturer, distributor, retailer or other type of organisation that wants to communicate with the market or a target audience.

Structure and content A promotional campaign may have a particular structure and content.

- Is it a straightforward product description, listing the product features?
- Does it go beyond basic features and start to promote the benefits of the product?
- Is it a promotional offer, such as a discount or other type of price reduction?
- Is it presented as information that is of benefit to the consumer, such as the start date for a sale, the introduction of a new size, or a product improvement?
- Is it factual or does the audience need to study it to understand what is being promoted?
- Is it 'knocking copy' which criticises the competition?

The creative approach It is also useful to analyse how creative the promotion is.

- Does it use straightforward photographs of the product or a highly creative style of photography?
- Does it focus and concentrate on the product or message or does it use some other device, such as an attractive person or location to catch the eye?
- Does it use drawings or cartoons instead of photographs?
- Does it ignore images completely and use words and text to communicate?
- What are the visual and aural stimuli (the shape, the size, the colours or movement, the sound where appropriate)?
- What is it that makes the promotion or advertising memorable?

What the audience remembers from promotion This can take a number of forms, as shown in Figure 2.

Does the creative treatment interfere with the message? Is it clear or confusing to the audience? Will the product be remembered or is it lost within the creative treatment?

The target market What is the target market that the product is aimed at? Is it:

- the consumer market - the people who buy and use the product themselves;
- the trade market, such as buyers or business owners and management?

Does it create desire in one target group, such as children, but has to be bought by another target group such as their parents - so called 'pester power'? Is the promotion or advertising appropriate for the market? If so, why, or if not, why not?

How often promotion takes place What is its frequency of a promotion or advertisement? How often does it appear? It is just once or is it in every newspaper or commercial break? What effect does the frequency have on the target market?

When it can be seen by the target market Is this hourly or more frequently on TV or the radio, such as daily, weekly, monthly? What time of the year does it take place and is this significant?

Figure 2 *What people remember from promotional campiagns*

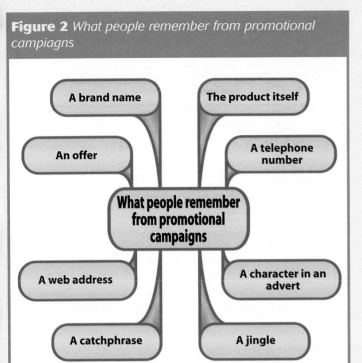

Comparing promotional campaigns

Comparisons can be made from the many promotions and advertisements for products. A starting point may be to identify:
- what they have in common;
- what differences there are in approaches;
- what are the aims and objectives.

Certain products aimed at the same market or market segment will use a similar approach to promotion and advertising because the businesses involved will have conducted marketing research and identified what appeals to the target market. Also, certain media will attract similar advertising from similar manufacturers, retailers and distributors. For example, magazines that are about motor cars are likely to attract advertising from businesses that sell cars, motoring accessories and associated products. These businesses presume that a readership that is interested in cars is likely to be interested and in the market for their products. Fashion magazines will attract advertising from fashion companies supplying and selling fashion clothing and lifestyle accessories.

What about television or radio advertising? Why does advertising on ITV1, a terrestrial channel, during a 'soap' like Coronation Street attract advertisers promoting food and family oriented products, whereas advertising breaks during the 'sit coms' on Paramount Comedy, a cable channel, are filled with advertisers offering loans, credit cards and other financial products? Why is there such a difference in advertisers and products being promoted on different media?

The answers lie in the profile of the audience for each particular media and the matching of target markets with the consumer profile that each medium can deliver for the advertiser. This is done by collecting and analysing market research data. Advertisers will have their own research that profiles their customers. This is likely to be commercially sensitive as it could

provide very useful information to competitors. Media owners will also have their own market research data that is used to attract advertisers by demonstrating that a given medium will attract an audience that matches the consumer profile required for the advertiser. This research is much easier to obtain, as the media owners want to promote their own strengths to potential advertisers. Most media owners will publish 'media packs', which are filled with market research data and are very interesting for anyone studying and assessing promotion. 'Media packs' are also quite widely available by looking at websites produced by media owners to promote their media products.

Considerations when selecting and advertising media and choosing promotions

Sections 71-75 explained a variety of media used to advertise products by businesses. Businesses will take into account many considerations when choosing which are the most effective media to use. These criteria will be similar to those used to select an appropriate promotional campaign.

Aims and objectives The choice of promotion will depend on the aims and objectives of the business. The business will need to consider some of the following questions.
- Are the marketing aims and objectives clear and agreed by all relevant stakeholders?
- Do we need advertising?
- Is it clear what is required from this advertising and this medium?
- How will success or failure be measured?

Appropriateness A business must consider how appropriate the media or promotion are. It might ask some of the following questions.
- Is it affordable and do we have the money?
- Is the cost of production and media space within the approved budget?
- Is it a cost-effective way of reaching the target market?
- Is there a better way of spending this budget that will achieve the aims and objectives better or cheaper?
- Is it appropriate for the product and for the market?
- What effect will it have on competition and how will competition respond?
- Will it provoke the desired reaction from customers and consumers?

Relevance When selecting media or a promotional campaign a business must take into account:
- whether a product should be advertised or promoted in a particular way;
- why a particular medium should be used.

Cost comparisons It can be very difficult to make objective comparisons between different media for example. They all appear to be so different. Each will have its own strengths and weaknesses and each will be considered to be more or less appropriate.

Figure 3 *Cost per thousand of advertisements*

Magazine
A full page advertisement in a magazine costs £15,000.
It has a readership of 120,000.
Cost per thousand is 15,000 ÷ 120 = £125.

Commercial television
A single spot on commercial television may cost £50,000.
It may be watched by 2 million people.
Cost per thousand = 50,000 ÷ 2,000 = £25.

Figure 4 *Coverage of Big L Radio*

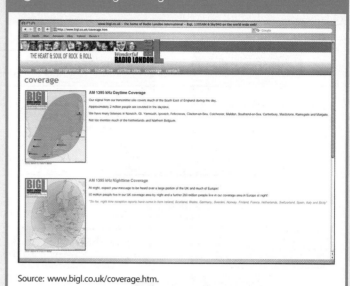

Source: www.bigl.co.uk/coverage.htm.

One way of making a simple, objective comparison, which avoids subjective and quality comparisons, is to look at the 'cost per thousand' (cost per '000) measure. This is the cost of reaching 1,000 people in the target audience. Every advertising product in each advertising medium can be measured on a cost per thousand basis.

In Figure 3 the total cost of advertising in the magazine is a lower figure and may appear to be the cheapest option. However, on a 'cost per thousand' basis it is television that results in the lower cost, although the outlay, the actual cost of advertising, is greater.

Other factors will influence the decision, not just cost. These could include:

- production cost - the advertisement for the magazine will certainly be much cheaper to produce than the television commercial;
- the life of the advertisement - how long the magazine will be read compared with how long the television commercial is shown;
- the impact - a television commercial with its sound and vision is likely to have a greater impact than the magazine advertisement.

The attraction of the 'cost per thousand' measure is that comparison can be made directly. Having considered magazine and television, if radio or cinema advertising is an option, then they too can be measured in the cost per thousand and compared with the magazine and television advertising.

Coverage This is a measure of the proportion of target audience that is able to see or hear an advertisement, programme, commercial or medium. It is an important measure for comparing different advertising media when planning an advertising campaign. Decisions will need to be made to set objectives for coverage, how much/what proportion of the target market to aim for. This is achieved by selecting the media that produce the coverage level to meet the objectives of the business or the particular marketing plan. 100% coverage is rarely achievable and advertisers need to consider carefully the cost of reaching the last few percentages of an market once the bulk of the target market has been reached cost effectively. Figure 4 shows an example of coverage of a radio station.

Penetration Linked to coverage is the measure of penetration. This is the maximum forecast percentage of the population or audience that can be reached by a single broadcaster, publisher or advertising medium. For example, television advertising has virtually 100% penetration of homes. This is because virtually all homes have access to television. In contrast, the penetration of new media will be linked directly to the percentage of homes that has access to the Internet via a computer. Although high at 53% in 2004, this was still lower than television. Newspaper penetration is based on the proportion of the population that buys a newspaper.

Frequency This is how often the target market is likely to see or hear a particular advertisement. As most advertising relies on repeat viewing to reinforce a message or piece of information, how often it can be seen becomes very important when planning. There is no real indication of the 'right' frequency that should be aimed for. Advertisers are advised to aim for the maximum frequency that can be achieved from the budget set for advertising.

Examination practice · Radio Times' promotional campaign

In 2005 the BBC was planning to spend £1 million to promote *Radio Times* in a battle to retain circulation in the TV listings price war. It would involve direct marketing and a promotional campaign in an attempt to combat competition from rivals *What's on TV* and *TV Choice*. The campaign would last four weeks from March 15. Readers would be given the chance to win up to £100,000 to pay off their mortgage and 250,000 readers would receive mailshots through the post. The campaign would be supported by advertisements on Virgin Radio's morning and drivetime shows and on local radio stations, voiced by comedienne and novelist Arabella Weir. *Radio Times'* publisher said she was certain the revamped magazine was 'the right product' and the campaign was the start of a plan to 'shout about it'. Promotion was important to compete with price reductions from competitors. When *What's On TV* cut its cover price by 10p in January to 35p, *TV Choice* responded

with a 10p cut to 30p. *Radio Times* did not follow suit, arguing that price cutting affected the value of products offered.

Source: adapted from *Media Guardian*, 7.3.2005.

(a) **Based on the information, identify the MAIN aim in launching the promotional campaign for Radio Times and explain how the campaign might help the business achieve this aim.** **(3 marks)**

(b) **Other than aims and objectives, identify TWO factors that might have influenced the BBC in its choice of media to use for the campaign and explain how each could affect the business.** **(6 marks)**

(c) **Identify TWO features of the promotional campaign and explain how each will make the campaign effective.** **(6 marks)**

Meeting the assessment criteria

Figures 5 and Figure 6 show the front and back of a promotional leaflet that was included with the monthly statement mailed to all John Lewis account holders at the end of May/beginning of June 2005.

Figure 5 *Front of promotional leaflet*

John Lewis
Clearance
starts Saturday
2 July 2005

50% off selected
lines in our shops
and online

johnlewis.com   John Lewis

Figure 6 *Back of promotional leaflet*

Visit our shops for a full range of products

London
Oxford Street 020 7629 7711
Sloane Square 020 7730 3434
(Peter Jones)
Brent Cross 020 8202 6535
Kingston upon Thames 020 8547 3000

English regions
Bluewater 01322 624123
Cambridge 01223 361292
(Robert Sayle)
Cheadle 0161 491 4914
Cribbs Causeway 0117 959 1100
High Wycombe 01494 462666
(John Lewis Home and Leisure)
Liverpool 0151 709 7070
Milton Keynes 01908 679171
Newcastle upon Tyne 0191 232 5000
Norwich 01603 660021
Nottingham 0115 941 8282
Peterborough 01733 344644
Reading 0118 957 5955

Sheffield 0114 276 8511
Solihull 0121 704 1121
Southampton 02380 216400
Southsea 02392 827511
(Knight & Lee)
Trafford 0161 491 4040
Watford 01923 244266
Welwyn 01707 323456
Windsor (Caleys) 01753 863241

Scotland
Aberdeen 01224 625000
Edinburgh 0131 556 9121
Glasgow 0141 353 6677

Selected lines available at Waitrose Food & Home
Canary Wharf 020 7719 0300
Cheltenham 01242 241425
Rushden 01933 355099
Salisbury 01722 329429
Southend-on-Sea 01702 603403

For opening hours, please visit johnlewis.com/hours

John Lewis department stores
johnlewis.com

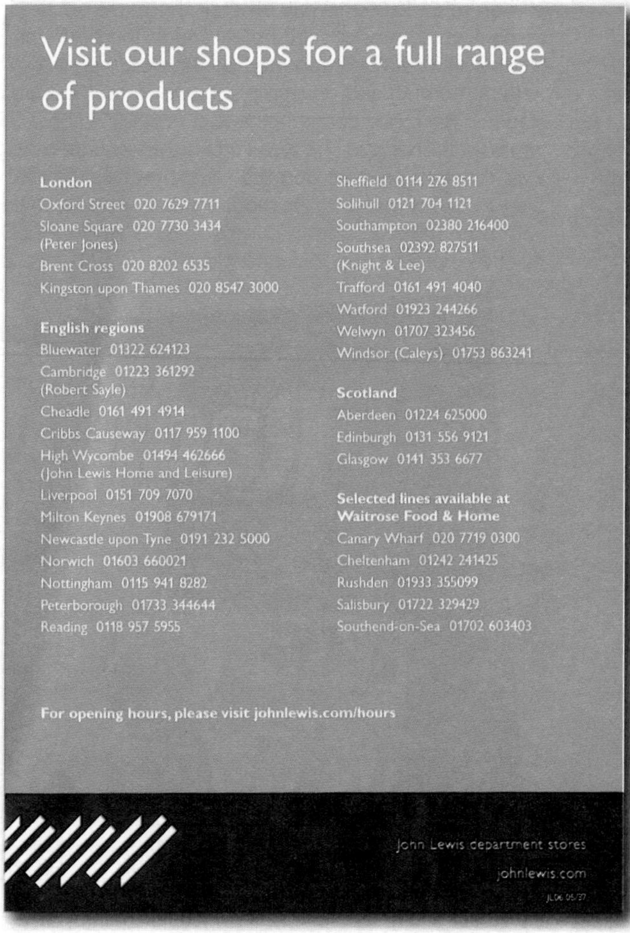

(a) Identify the type of promotion featured on this leaflet.
(1 mark)

Expected answers
• *Sale.*
• *Discount.*

Mark allocation
1 mark for type of promotion. **(1 mark)**

(b) Explain ONE reason why this leaflet is likely to be mailed with account statements. **(3 marks)**

Expected answers
• *Low cost – statement would have occurred anyway – does not attract separate postage charge/budget.*
• *Goes direct to target market – people with an account likely to be existing customers and therefore target market – reduces wastage/increases chance of success.*
• *News of sale offsets any negative feelings about getting statement – sometimes statements can be perceived as a problem for customers as they have to be paid at some point – customers left with positive feeling/something to look forward to.*

Mark allocation
1 mark for reason.
1 mark for application to mailing out with statement.
1 mark for development. **(3 marks)**

Evaluation

Evaluating promotion involves making a judgement on how successful or not a promotional campaign has been. Sometimes the evaluation of promotion, in particular advertising, is subjective. It is based on opinions and views. This can leave it open to interpretation.

However, promotion and advertising is rarely cheap. A business should therefore also be prepared to evaluate in a more objective and quantifiable way before it commits to spending money on promotion and after the promotion. This will help it to judge whether it has achieved the aims and objectives set.

A business will start by setting its marketing aims and objectives before promotion is even considered. Some aims are shown in Table 1. Depending on the business, examples of typical objectives based on these aims are also shown in Table 1.

Whether or not these objectives have been achieved can only be measured effectively by either:

- monitoring and analysing business data, such as sales figures;
- monitoring results and measuring effects, such as actual rate of sales, changes in sales, sales to retailers or sales to consumers;
- collecting primary market research data after the promotion.

The main types of marketing research that can be used to evaluate promotional campaigns are:

- retail audits/auditing;
- pre and post campaign measurement.

Retail audits/auditing

This is the collection of sales data from a panel of retailers that represent the market. Auditors visit shops on a regular, fixed cycle, which may be weekly, monthly or bi-monthly depending on the rate of sale of the goods being audited. The auditors do a stock count and add to this the figures for deliveries from manufacturers and suppliers since the last visit and compare the result with the stock count figure from the previous visit. The difference shows how much has been sold during the period from the last visit, in either units or value terms.

Retail audits are usually carried out for manufacturers and suppliers to obtain market share and rate of sale data about the market, their own goods and competitors' goods. An example is shown in Figure 2. By auditing on a regular basis, any change that occurs during the period of promotion will be seen as a change in market share or rate of sale. This type of research is classified as 'continuous monitoring'.

Continuous monitoring can also be used to detect changes in awareness of a brand name, product or message contained in advertising, or other consumer behaviour, such as product usage or frequency of purchase. This type of research would be conducted by monitoring a panel of consumers, noting their behaviour and changes to behaviour that can be explained as a result of promotion.

Pre and post campaign measurement

This method of market research is based on collecting data on the

Table 1 *Promotional aims and objectives*

Aims	Objectives
To launch a new product.	To gain distribution in X'000 shops.
To send information or a particular message to consumers in the market.	To sign up X'000 new customers as a result of receiving the promotional message, to produce X'00 sales leads.
To meet sales or distribution targets.	To sell X'000 items by the end of the promotion.
To increase market share.	To move market share from 22% to 25%.
To become the market leader.	To overtake competition and increase market share to over 38%.
To let the target market know that the service is now available in this area.	To get 10 phone call enquiries each day and convert at least one of these enquiries into an actual sale.

Figure 2 *Red Agency*

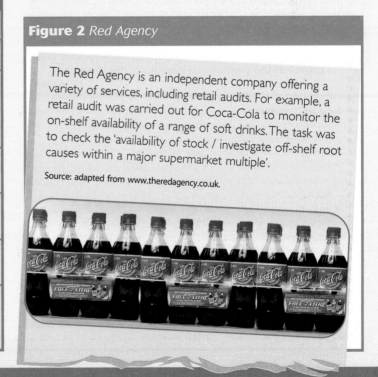

The Red Agency is an independent company offering a variety of services, including retail audits. For example, a retail audit was carried out for Coca-Cola to monitor the on-shelf availability of a range of soft drinks. The task was to check the 'availability of stock / investigate off-shelf root causes within a major supermarket multiple'.

Source: adapted from www.theredagency.co.uk.

target market before promotion starts, then collecting data using the same questions after the promotion has finished. The difference between the two sets of data should show the impact of the campaign on the target market.

An example of this would be to measure what percentage of the target market has heard of a given brand name before advertising starts. When advertising is finished, the same question is asked to measure the percentage that has heard of the particular brand name. The difference in the percentage will indicate how effective the advertising has been.

What is measured pre and post promotion will depend on the aims and objectives that have been set for the promotion.

Evaluating effectively

To be effective, evaluation must be measurable. At the end of the day, any business engaged in promotion needs to answer some very basic questions. These are shown in Figure 3.

Figure 3 *Evaluating promotion – important questions*

Meeting the assessment criteria

Ellis Cycles Ltd is a small specialist business that manufactures fold-up bicycles that are popular with commuters. They are popular because they can be ridden to and from railway stations like a normal bicycle, then folded and carried onto the train without taking up too much room. Ellis cycles are lightweight, which makes them easy to carry when not being ridden.

Ellis Cycles Ltd usually sells 10 bicycles each week. The managing director wants to double sales to 20 per week and decides to advertise for four weeks in the *Metro* newspaper that is given away free to commuters for them to read during their journey.

After the four weeks advertising, sales had risen to 15 per week. In addition, marketing research showed 75% of commuters said that they had heard of Cycles. Research done before advertising started showed that only 25% of commuters had heard of Ellis Cycles.

(a) Explain why the *Metro* newspaper was likely to have been chosen as the promotional medium in this situation. **(3 marks)**

Expected answers
- *Read by commuters – commuters are the target market – therefore well aimed medium/low wastage level.*
- *Newspaper advertisement is ideal medium for descriptive copy – commuters have time to read lots of descriptive copy during journey – technical nature of bicycle may need space/descriptive copy to explain features.*
- *Likely to have greater circulation/ more readers than traditional paid for newspapers – because Metro is free – this means that more people should be able to see the Ellis advertisement which should help increase sales.*

Mark allocation
1 mark for basic reason.
1 mark for application to situation.
1 mark for further explanation. **(3 marks)**

(b) Evaluate the effectiveness of this advertising. **(4 marks)**

Expected answers
Positive reasons
- *Had the effect of raising awareness from 25% of those asked to 75% of those asked.*
- *Increased awareness could result in increased sales in the future/when commuters come into the market for bicycles.*
- *Actually increased sales from 10 to 15 per week although this was lower than the objective set.*
- *Advertising across four weeks is a relatively substantial campaign, will have had the effect of repeating/reinforcing name/branding.*

Negative reasons
- *Did not meet objective to increase sales from 10 to 20 per week.*
- *Newspaper likely to have had high wastage as it is not selected by commuters because they want to read it but given to them free whether they want to read it or not.*
- *Free distribution gives no guarantee that target market will actually see advertisement.*
- *Four week campaign that did not meet sales objectives is likely to have been a costly way of raising sales by just 50%, may have been a better method of promotion that could have been used for same money.*

(Question based on evaluation – must include both sides of argument.)

Mark allocation
1 mark for each positive reason why advertising judged to be effective (maximum 2 marks)
or
1 mark for positive reason + 1 mark for developed or applied answer (maximum 2 marks).

1 mark for each negative reason why advertising judged not to be effective (maximum 2 marks)
or
1 mark for negative reason + 1 mark for developed or applied answer (maximum 2 marks). **(4 marks)**

xamination practice · Cleaver Construction

Cleaver Construction specialises in the assembly of prefabricated buildings. Most of its customers are developers which have bought land and want to build factories, offices and other premises. A large amount of land has become available in its local area recently and planning permission is almost always granted. It also has a small but increasing market from customers who import 'pre-made' houses from abroad and want them assembled. They have been attracted by cases shown on television programmes, such as Grand Designs.

Cleaver Construction has decided that it needs a promotional strategy to take advantage of these trends and expand its customer base. It feels that it offers a unique service and is one of the few businesses in the area to offer such a service. Table 2 shows some examples of its promotional activities.

(a) **Identify TWO aims of the business for its promotional campaign.**

(2 marks)

(b) **Using information from the case study, identify ONE successful method of promotion and explain why it might have been successful for this business.**

(3 marks)

(c) **Identify ONE method of promotion that has not been successful and explain why it might not have been successful.**

(3 marks)

Table 2 *Promotional activities of Cleaver Construction*

Activity	An 'open day' to show clients its services.
Effect	Relatively inexpensive. 1,000 attended, with many leads from both business and individual customers.
Activity	A leaflet sent to 10,000 homes in the local area.
Effect	Less than a 2% response rate.
Activity	An small advert in a specialist building magazine with just a telephone number and e-mail address. No other information included.
Effect	Relatively expensive. 200 phone calls or emails in response, but few actual orders placed.
Activity	A full page advert in a local newspaper with a telephone number and e-mail address and a full description and pictures of the service.
Effect	Relatively inexpensive, around a 10% response rate.
Activity	A 4 page colour brochure sent to businesses identified from a database of names that was bought by the company.
Effect	Relatively expensive, but highly effective. Many leads and firm orders.

The legal status of businesses

In the private sector business organisations are owned by individuals or groups. However, the type of organisation can vary. Some are very small with just one owner, such as a mobile hairdresser. Others are very large, employ thousands of people, market many products and have operations all over the world, such as BP. The ownership of businesses can take different legal forms. Figure 1 shows the different types of business organisation in the private sector, their legal status and the nature of their ownership.

- An **unincorporated** business is where there is no legal difference between the owner and the business. All trading activities are carried out in the name of the owner or owners. These businesses tend to be small and owned either by one person or by partners.
- An **incorporated** business has a separate legal identity from its owners. The business can be sued, taken over and liquidated.

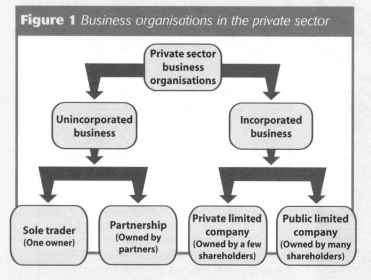

Figure 1 *Business organisations in the private sector*

Features of limited companies

Private limited companies tend to be relatively small, although certain well-known companies like JCB, the excavator manufacturer, and Walkers, the potato crisp producer, are private limited companies. Their business name ends in Limited or Ltd. Such companies are usually owned by a small group of people, family or friends. The name of the company may take on the name of the family or the main shareholder, followed by the word 'Limited'. When forming a limited company a check has to be made to ensure that another company is not already trading under that name. This can be done at Companies House. It is also possible to check on the Internet.

Limited companies have certain features.

Shares Limited companies raise capital by selling shares. People who buy shares are called **shareholders** and they are the joint owners of the company. They are entitled to a share of the profit and they can participate in decision making in the business, although in large companies with many shareholders their role may be limited. Shareholders with the largest number of shares have the most control. In private limited companies, the key shareholders are likely to play an active role in the day-to-day running of the company.

The shares in a private limited company cannot be sold on a stock market. This is perhaps the main difference between a private and a public limited company. Public limited companies tend to be larger organisations with more shareholders, whose shares are traded on stock markets. In private limited companies, shares have to be transferred privately to people who have been approved by the remaining shareholders. This means that a private limited company cannot be taken over by outsiders without the consent of the majority of shareholders.

Share capital When a limited company is formed it has to decide how many shares to issue. It must also decide how much each share will be sold for. If a new company decided to sell 50,000 shares at £1 each, the share capital of the company will be £50,000. This will be used to help set up the business. Once a limited company is trading and becomes established it may issue more shares if necessary to fund expansion. A company may issue different types of shares.

- **Ordinary shares.** These are also called equities and are the most common type of share. They are the riskiest type of share because there is no guarantee that a **dividend** (a share of the profit) will be paid. The size of the dividend depends on how much profit is made. If a company collapses, ordinary shareholders may not receive any of their money back. All ordinary shareholders have voting rights, with the power to elect and dismiss directors. When a share is first sold it has a nominal value, such as £1 in the above example. However, share prices change according to the success of the company and other factors. If they are sold to a new owner, they may be worth more or less.
- **Preference shares.** The owners of preference shares enjoy a fixed dividend. For example, a 4%, £1 preference share will earn 4p every time a dividend is paid to shareholders. They carry less risk because preference shareholders receive their dividend before ordinary shareholders. If the company is liquidated, preference shareholders will receive capital repayments before ordinary shareholders. However, preference shares do not carry any voting rights.

Limited liability One of the advantages of operating as a limited company is limited liability. This means that the amount of money any shareholder can lose from investing in the company is legally restricted. The most any shareholder can lose, if the company collapses, is the amount paid for the shares when they were first purchased. This is different to a sole trader who has unlimited liability. If a sole trader is wound up and still owes money to creditors, the owner can be forced to meet business debts from personal wealth. Limited liability means that people are more likely to buy shares in limited companies. However, money lenders, such as banks, may be less likely to lend because if the company collapses they may not get their money back.

Who runs a limited company?

A limited company is run by a board of directors. The board is led by the chairperson. Directors are elected and the chairperson is usually appointed by the directors. However, in a small private limited company, like a family business, the directors and the chairperson are likely to be key shareholders and appoint themselves. They are also likely to be involved in the actual running of the business. For example, Perkins Ltd, a family engineering business, was set up by Barry and Tessa Perkins. Barry was chairperson and his wife was a director. When the company was set up five people were employed in the firm's factory. Barry was in charge of production and getting new orders. Tessa was responsible for the administration.

If a company has a lot of shareholders, as can be the case in public limited companies, directors are elected by the shareholders who run the company on their behalf. The directors will play managerial roles and are likely to recruit staff and ensure that the company's objectives are being pursued. Alternatively, directors will appoint managers to run the business according to the company's objectives.

Company structure and personnel

A limited company has a formal legal structure. This means that the people who own and run the company have to play a number of important and specific roles. The structure for Perkins Ltd is shown in Figure 2. The number of shares owned by each member of the family is shown in Figure 3. Barry Perkins is the chairperson and owns the most shares. Barry now concentrates on attracting new customers and looking after existing ones. Tessa is the financial director, Carl is in charge of operations and Kim is personnel director. Asif is the company secretary and also works in the finance department. The company employs 40 staff. The roles of the chairperson, directors and secretary are discussed in section 84.

Voting and meetings

Incorporated businesses are required to hold an Annual General Meeting (AGM). All of the company's shareholders are invited to

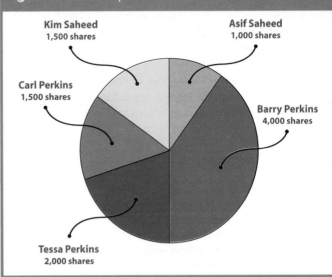

Figure 3 *Ownership of shares in Perkins Ltd*

Kim Saheed 1,500 shares

Asif Saheed 1,000 shares

Carl Perkins 1,500 shares

Barry Perkins 4,000 shares

Tessa Perkins 2,000 shares

attend. AGMs must be held not longer than 15 months apart and a newly incorporated company must hold one within 18 months. The purpose of the meeting is to:
- enable shareholders to discuss current issues with the directors;
- provide an opportunity for directors to put forward resolutions;
- allow shareholders to vote on the directors' ideas;
- declare dividends if appropriate;
- discuss the accounts;
- elect or re-elect directors.

Shareholders do not have to attend the meeting, but can still cast their votes through the post. It is also possible for a private limited company to dispense with an AGM if it obtains an effective resolution. This means that all of the shareholders unanimously agree that such a meeting is not necessary.

Company registration

Before a business can trade as a limited company it has to be registered with the Registrar of Companies. This is a legal requirement and involves registering the name and address of the company and sending a number of documents to Companies House. The main functions of Companies House are to:
- incorporate and dissolve limited companies;
- examine and store company information delivered under the Companies Act and related legislation;
- make this information available to the public.

Once a check has been made to ensure that no other company is trading under the chosen name, the process of registration can begin. Details of the documents that must be submitted to Companies House are explained below.

Memorandum of Association The Memorandum of Association sets out the constitution and gives basic but important details about the company. The **Companies Act, 1985** states that the following details must be included.
- The name of the company.
- The name and address of the company's registered office.
- The objects of the company and the scope of its activities.

Figure 2 *Structure of Perkins Ltd, a private limited company*

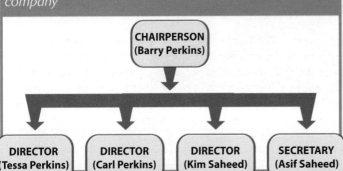

CHAIRPERSON (Barry Perkins)

DIRECTOR (Tessa Perkins)

DIRECTOR (Carl Perkins)

DIRECTOR (Kim Saheed)

SECRETARY (Asif Saheed)

- The liability of its members.
- Details of any share capital.
- Also, in the case of a UK company having share capital, the Memorandum of Association must show the name of each initial member/shareholder (also called 'subscribers') and the number of shares each takes.

Articles of Association The Articles of Association, often just called 'articles', deal with the internal regulation and management of the company. They include details such as the:

- rights of shareholders depending on the type of shares they hold;
- procedures for appointing directors and the scope of their powers;
- length of time directors should serve before re-election;
- timing and frequency of meetings;
- arrangements for auditing the company's accounts;
- procedures for paying dividends;
- procedures for winding up the company.

Statutory declaration One final administrative task when forming a company is to sign a statutory declaration. This is a document which confirms that all the legal requirements relating to the incorporation of a company have been satisfied. It must be signed by a solicitor who is forming the company, or by one of the directors or company secretary. It must be signed in the presence of a commissioner for oaths, a notary public, a justice of the peace or a solicitor. Once all of the above documents have been approved by Companies House a **Certificate of Incorporation** can be issued. This launches the business and permits it to trade as a limited company. The Certificate of Incorporation must be displayed in a prominent place.

Annual legal obligations Limited companies are responsible for delivering information to the Registrar every year. The most important documents required by the Registrar include the following.

- All limited companies, whether trading or not, must keep accounting records and file accounts for each accounting period with the Registrar.
- A directors' report signed by a director or the company secretary.
- A balance sheet signed by a director.
- A profit and loss account (or income and expenditure account if the company is not trading for profit).
- An auditors' report signed by the auditor. This is explained in section 84.;
- Notes to the accounts.

Directors are personally responsible for ensuring that accounts are prepared and delivered to Companies House. Failure to do so may result in a criminal conviction and record for the directors and will result in financial penalties for the company.

Annual returns An annual return is a snapshot of general information about a company, giving details of its directors and secretary, registered office address, shareholders and share capital. Companies House will send a pre-printed annual return form to the company's registered office each year. It details the information already held on the database. The details should be:

- checked closely (and amended if necessary);
- signed and dated;
- returned to Companies House within 28 days of the date shown on the form, with the filing fee.

If the annual return is filed late, or not at all, the company and its directors and secretary can be prosecuted.

Portfolio practice · **Technet**

Technet is a mini company set up by a group of students in Somerset. The mini company produces websites and provides regular updates. They have three designs - Basic, Business and Professional. An example of a basic site designed for a model manufacturer is shown in Figure 4. The company has a formal structure with positions that include Managing Director, IT Director, Financial Director, Productions Director, Marketing Director and Administrator. However, all of the team are involved in the design of the websites.

(a) How might Technet have raised the capital to set up the mini company?
(b) Describe the documents that might have been used when forming the company.
(c) Using this case as an example, explain who is responsible for running a company.
(d) Discuss the legal obligations that a company has once it has been incorporated.

Figure 4 *Basic website design - homepage*

REPLICAZONE

About us

Our products

Order

Choose a limited company in your local area and use the Internet or your own contacts to find out the:
- name of the chairperson;
- names of the directors;
- company's registered address;
- amount of share capital issued;
- company's objectives;
- profit made last year.

Research task

Meeting the assessment criteria

You need to provide evidence of your involvement in setting up the company. You can do this by keeping a diary of your contributions during the launch, planning and running of the company.

Business example - Jewell

Jewell is a mini company set up by students from a Newcastle school. The company designs and makes business and greetings cards and small jewellery items. Products can be personalised to meet the design needs of individuals. Products are priced competitively to allow access to a wider market. The company was formed in 2004 and has 12 members. Glenys Williams is one of the directors. She kept a dairy of her involvement in the forming and launching of Jewell.

Mark Band 1 *Provide outline evidence of your participation in the launch of the company. Use a diary to record the contributions you made in the choice of company name and structure, for example.*

24.9.04 Fifteen students attended this first company meeting. There was a lot of talking and debating but some decisions were made. It was decided to raise £200 by selling shares. It was agreed that no-one could own more than ten shares. Shares would be sold to the company members initially and then to any student in the school that was interested. I volunteered to design some share certificates ready for the next meeting.

30.9.04 The aim of today's meeting (13 attended) was to set up a company structure and allocate roles. We decided to elect a chairperson. Three students wanted the job and each had to give a five minute presentation on why they were suitable. Carlos Dorada was elected. I got the job of marketing director. There are six directors and a company secretary.

6.10.04 Today, ideas for a company name were discussed. A short list of three company names was proposed – Design Ltd, Jewell and CardKraft Ltd. Design Ltd was my idea. In the end the vote was close, but Jewell won by two votes.

Mark Band 2 *Provide detailed evidence of strong participation in the launch of the company. Use a diary to record the contributions you made in the choice of company name and structure, for example.*

24.9.04 This was the first company meeting (15 attended) and was led by our teacher. She explained the process for setting up a company and said that all future meetings would be organised and led by students. It was decided to raise capital by selling 200 £1 shares. However, no single person could own more than 10. This would prevent any single student becoming too dominant. I volunteered to design some share certificates. I could get some ideas for designs from the Companies House website and use my PC to produce the certificates.

30.9.04 The aim of this meeting was to set up a structure for the company. Companies are run by a board of directors. A chairperson was elected after listening to short presentations from three students who wanted the job. Carlos Dorada was elected. He demonstrated good leadership and communication skills. I got the job of marketing director. I argued that the role would suit me because it was my favourite topic and I was going to do some work experience at a market research agency. A total of six directors were appointed and a company secretary.

6.10.04 The name of the company was decided at this meeting. This took ages and lots of different ones were put forward. I suggested that a short list should be drawn up so that we could have a vote. In the end a short list of three was agreed and one of my suggestions was included. The three names were Design Ltd, Jewell and CardKraft Ltd. Design Ltd was my idea. In the end the vote was close, but Jewell won by two votes.

Mark Band 3 *Provide full and detailed evidence of influential participation in the launch of the company. Use a diary to record the contributions you made in the choice of company name and structure, for example.*

<u>24.9.04</u> The first meeting, attended by 15 students, was led by our GCE Applied Business teacher. She explained the process that we would have to follow to form a company. It was also clear that in the future our teacher would only play an advisory role. It was decided to raise £200 by issuing 200 £1 shares. However, it was also decided to limit share holdings to a maximum of 10 per member. This was Jenny's idea and I supported her strongly. We did not want the company to be dominated by a few (or less) individuals. I also said that I could produce some simple share certificates on my PC. I could use examples from the Companies House website.

<u>30.9.04</u> A company structure had to be formed at this meeting. A company is run formally by a board of directors led by a chairperson. The first job was to elect a chairperson. A strong leader was needed. Three students interested in the position gave a five minute presentation about what they would contribute to the company and a vote was organised. Carlos Dorada won easily. He appeared to have good leadership and communication skills. I got the job I really wanted – marketing director. This meant I would be responsible for marketing and also be involved in decision making. I suggested that the role would suit me because it was my favourite topic and I was going to do some work experience at a market research agency. A total of six directors were appointed and a company secretary.

<u>6.10.04</u> The name of the company was agreed today. It took a long time because there were lots of ideas to consider. It was also difficult because we still weren't sure what products or services we were going to sell. I suggested that a short list should be drawn up so that we could have a vote. In the end a short list of three was agreed and one of my suggestions was included. The three names were Design Ltd, Jewell and CardKraft Ltd. Design Ltd was my idea. In the end the vote was close, but Jewell won by two votes. I said this was OK but felt it did not explain exactly what we had to offer and only covered one of our products.

81 Choice of product

Sources of product ideas

A business cannot be launched until an idea for a product or service has been carefully developed. The first stage in that development process is to identify a sound idea that will support the business financially. Business ideas can come from a number of sources.

- Some people learn a skill at work and then decide to set up on their own. For example, a chef might decide to open a restaurant after running a kitchen in a large hotel for 10 years.
- The development of a hobby or interest into a business idea. For example, a collector of football programmes might set up a mail order business buying and selling programmes over the Internet.
- Copying or adapting someone else's idea. For example, setting up a fish and chip shop in a town would not be an original idea. However, it might work if there is sufficient demand or if the service is offered with a slight difference, such as a more extensive menu or very competitive prices.
- Finding a gap in the market. This might be quite difficult but the chances of success might be greater if no-one else is filling the gap. For example, 'new' services in recent years include transport via stretch limousine or upgrading old photographs using computers.
- Market research may be carried out to identify a new business opportunity. Market research may reduce the risk involved when launching a new business. It might help to eliminate ideas that are unpopular with consumers.
- Ideas might be generated when a group of people meet to discuss launching a new business. Such an approach might be used when setting up a mini company at school or college.
- Some product ideas result from technical research and development (R&D). For example, pharmaceuticals companies use R&D to develop new drugs and medicines.

- Some people operate as franchisees. They pay another business (a franchisor) to use an established and proven idea that has already been developed. For example, Domino's Pizzas, Thorntons, Prontaprint and Dyno-rod are run by franchisees.

SWOT analysis

Before committing to a particular business idea it may be useful to evaluate its prospects. One way of doing this is to carry out a SWOT analysis. This involves looking at the internal strengths and weaknesses of a business idea and the external opportunities and threats.

- **Strengths.** These are the things about a new business idea that make commitment to it appealing, such as whether the idea is unique, capable of making a profit or attractive to a potential market. It may also refer to the strengths of the owners involved.
- **Weaknesses.** These are the problems with a new business idea which will have to be overcome, such as high cost of a launch or the inexperience of the owners.
- **Opportunities.** These are the directions the business might take in the future, such as new markets and products.
- **Threats.** These are external factors that might restrict or reverse the progress of the business in the future, such as government legislation, higher interest rates or the strength of competition.

Carrying out a SWOT analysis might result in people dropping a business idea because the threats and weaknesses are too formidable. However, this may be necessary as the cost of business failure, once a start has been made, can be very high.

Figure 1 shows a SWOT analysis carried out by a couple setting up a child minding business. They plan to convert part of their large house into a nursery and look after small children while parents are at work. Once the strengths, weaknesses, opportunities and threats have been identified, they will have to be analysed and evaluated to see whether the business idea is worth pursuing.

Market research

When choosing a product or a service for a business idea it will be helpful to carry out some market research. This might involve gathering information about:

- whether people will buy the product;
- what features about the product they like, dislike or would want to change;
- how much they would pay for the product;
- what competition the product faces;
- what type of people will buy the product;
- the size of the potential market;
- what consumers buy at present.

Market research information can be gathered in a number of ways. For example, it may be possible to use the *Yellow Pages* to find out

Figure 1 *SWOT Analysis carried out by a couple planning to set up a child minding service*

Strengths
Both are qualified, experienced and registered child minders. They know a lot of people who would use their service immediately.

Opportunities
Increased government funding for child minding. Other services such as a breakfast club and an after school club could be offered in future.

SWOT

Threats
Established competition. Increased regulation. Possible reaction by neighbours.

Weaknesses
High set up costs. High level of loans. No experience running a business. A long time before break-even is reached.

Figure 2 *Extracts from market research about car washing*

Four people decided to set up a business providing a car valet service. 300 car owners were questioned. Some of the results are shown below. They helped to convince the group that a car valet service by hand would be popular and to shape the types of services on offer.

How would you prefer to have your car washed?

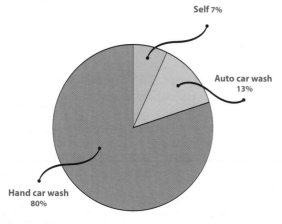

Self 7%

Auto car wash 13%

Hand car wash 80%

Where would you prefer your car to be cleaned?

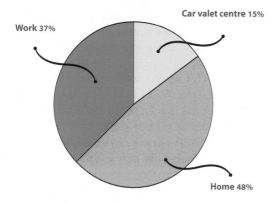

Car valet centre 15%

Work 37%

Home 48%

What sort of service would you prefer?

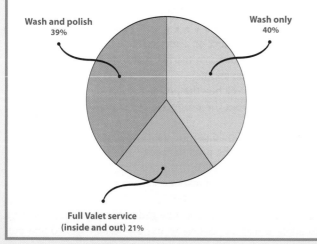

Wash and polish 39%

Wash only 40%

Full Valet service (inside and out) 21%

about the competition a new business idea faces. The Internet might be used to find out about products offered by competitors. Telephone surveys, postal surveys and personal interviews might be used to find out what people think about the new product. Market research techniques are discussed in sections 34 and 35.

Market research will help to ensure that the product matches the needs and wants of consumers more effectively. It will reduce the risk of failure resulting from the launch of a product that no-one wants or one that faces too much competition. Although market research is expensive and the data gathered may be imperfect, many would argue that the benefits outweigh the costs. Market research information can also be used in a business plan.

Figure 2 shows an example of market research into a new car valet service.

Product development

It often takes time to research, design and develop a product before it can be launched. Once a product idea has been agreed a number of development issues have to be considered.

Estimate demand Entrepreneurs will want to be confident that their product is going to sell in sufficient numbers to make a profit. Consequently, it is necessary to estimate potential demand for a new product. This is a difficult task, but important to complete. Demand might be estimated by doing some market research. Alternatively some rough estimates will be needed. They might be based on what similar businesses are selling at the moment or an entrepreneur's 'hunch'. Some entrepreneurs set sales targets which they hope to achieve. However, this is not really the same as estimating what demand is likely to be.

Estimate costs The cost of supplying a product must be calculated otherwise it will be difficult to know how much money to raise for the venture and what price to charge, for example. Figure 3 shows the possible costs that launching a product might incur. If the total cost is known it will also be possible to calculate the break-even point and set budgets. Most entrepreneurs will aim to minimise costs by using cheap resources and efficient operations.

Figure 3 *Costs that must be taken into account when launching a product*

Research and Development
Market research
Design
Prototypes
Test marketing

Production costs
Materials
Machinery
Premises
Labour
Production overheads

COSTS

Marketing costs
Advertising
Promotion
Distribution
Launch

Administration costs
Stationery
Insurance
Telephone charges
Rates

Materials Products can often be made using a range of different materials. For example, it is possible to manufacture a car body using metal or fibreglass. Shoes can be made from leather, canvas or a synthetic material. The same materials can be obtained from many different suppliers. The types of materials selected by a business will depend on the design specifications, the cost of materials, their quality and availability and whether suppliers can meet delivery times.

Resources Resources other than materials will be needed to launch a product. Before production can begin a business will need to find some premises. For example, manufacturers will need to find a factory or workshop and retailers will need to find a shop. Many people who start a new venture begin by operating from home. Entrepreneurs that offer certain services, such as plumbing, decorating and tutoring, can be based at home. Tools, equipment, machinery and a vehicle may also be needed. They could be hired or purchased depending on the financial resources of the business. Some extra staff might also be needed. Help may be required with production and other business functions. Staff may be employed part-time or full-time depending on the needs of the enterprise. Finally, it will be necessary to raise some capital. If a company is set up, capital may be raised by selling shares. It may also be possible to get loans and exploit other sources of finance.

Prototypes When developing a product a prototype may need to be made first. A prototype can be a mock-up, model or actual working version of a technological product. Prototypes are built towards the end of the development process and are used to generate information that will help perfect the final product. For example, UK Design firm PDD has developed a prototype of a new mobile phone. It showed its Helix concept phone at the 3GSM World Congress in Cannes in 2005. While it hadn't been picked up by a mobile manufacturer, the design concept had plenty of tricks, including a rotating screen that flips around when the clamshell is open, as well as a built-in 5-megapixel camera. The Helix could even have 20GB of storage if taken up.

Timescales One of the problems when choosing a product is the amount of time that devlopment takes. Product development can be a lengthy process and if not carefully managed can drag on resulting in a business losing its competitive edge. One way to help overcome this problem is to plan a strict timescale so that the different stages in product development are identified and timetabled. An example of a timescale is given in Table 1.

Table 1 *Timescale for the development of an electronic toy*

20.1.05	Discuss the new toy concepts
25.2.05	Agree on a new toy concept
1.3.05	Begin work on product design
12.6.05	Finalise product design
22.7.05	Complete prototype
27.8.05	Test prototype at a toy fair
10.9.05	Complete modifications
25.10.05	Launch new toy

Use the *Yellow Pages* or a local directory to select one product type or service offered by businesses in your local area. For example you might choose off-licences, restaurants, print centres, sign makers or florists.
1. Identify the number, location, extent and type of competition.
2. Suggest how a new product idea that you might have could be different from others.
3. Examine how your product idea might be successful using SWOT analysis.

Research task

Environmental issues

When choosing what products to supply it may be appropriate to consider environmental issues. Many would argue that a business should aim to be a good corporate citizen and respect and protect the environment in which it operates. How might this be achieved?

- Use recycled materials and other recycled resources to make products.
- Ensure that operations do not create a nuisance in the immediate area. For example, if an event is being organised it is important that visitors do not obstruct residents with their cars when parking.
- Following any environmental legislation regarding emissions and the disposal of waste, for example.

Portfolio practice · TuckIn

TuckIn is a student run tuck shop at a school in Bradford. The enterprise was set up in 2004 when a private company decided not to renew a contract to supply the service. Before opening the directors did some market research to determine what sort of products to stock. About 300 students were questioned. An extract of the results are shown in Figure 4. Fortunately TuckIn was able to buy most of its stock on credit. This meant that the start-up costs would be reduced significantly. It got permission from the Head to set up shop in a classroom at break and lunchtime. It decided to donate 20% of its profits each month to charity.

Figure 4 *An extract from market research carried out by TuckIn*

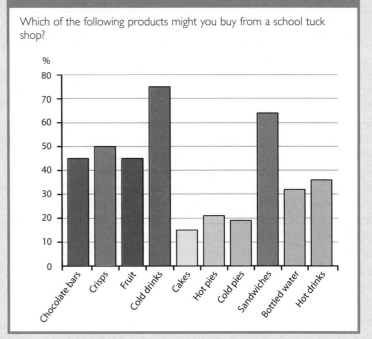

Which of the following products might you buy from a school tuck shop?

(a) (i) **Based on the information in Figure 4, which products might TuckIn decide not to stock? Give reasons for your answer.**
(ii) **State TWO reasons why market research is useful when deciding what products to supply.**

(b) **Describe THREE resources that TuckIn would need to acquire before trading began.**
(c) **Discuss other products that the enterprise might sell in the future if the venture was successful.**

Meeting the assessment criteria

You need to provide evidence of your involvement in setting up the company. You can do this by keeping a diary of your contributions during the launch, planning and running of the company.

Business example - Bookgem

Bookgem is an enterprise run by a group of students in a Southend school. Bookgem has decided to produce yearbooks as its main product. However it will also be selling many other products such as handmade bags and greetings cards for Christmas and birthdays. Bookgem hopes to develop other products in the future. The business also plans to organise events to help generate revenue. It has already organised an open evening raffle and the Bookgem 5-a-side football tournament. It also ran a Bookgem stall at a local fair and plans to have the company represented at the London Craft Fayre in March 2005. Emanuel Segers is one of the directors involved in the enterprise. He kept a diary of his involvement.

Mark Band 1 *Provide outline evidence of your participation in the launch of the company. Use a diary to record the contributions you made in the choice of product or service for example.*

20.9.04 We discussed the products that Bookgem might sell today. Most people were keen to sell hand made products such as bags and greetings cards. They said it would give them something to do at lunch times at school. However, I liked the idea of organising a 5-a-side football tournament. I offered to research the idea.

27.9.04 I reported back to the board about the possibility of organising 5-a-side football tournaments to generate revenue. I showed the others some results from research I did in the school. It suggested that pupils would be prepared to pay for regular tournaments if they were organised properly.

Mark Band 2 *Provide detailed evidence of strong participation in the launch of the company. Use a diary to record the contributions you made in the choice of product or service, for example.*

20.9.04 At the meeting we discussed the products that Bookgem will sell. Most people were keen to sell hand made products such as bags and greetings cards. They said it would give them something to do at lunch times at school. However, I liked the idea of organising a 5-a-side football tournament. I said I would do some market research to see if pupils would be interested. I also offered to look into the possibility of using some of the school's resources to stage such events.

27.9.04 I made a big contribution to the meeting today. I showed everyone my market research results. I used an OHP to show that 79% of the pupils I asked would be interested in taking part. A tournament could raise £80 (less costs) if 16 teams entered and each player paid £1. I also asked how much it would cost to use the sports hall after school. It would be free except we would have to make a donation to charity. I said this would be OK because it would improve the image of Bookgem.

Mark Band 3 *Provide full and detailed evidence of influential participation in the launch of the company. Use a diary to record the contributions you made in the choice of product or service, for example.*

20.9.04 We discussed the products that Bookgem might sell today. The making of products such as bags and greetings cards seemed to be very popular. Everyone said that it would give them something to do at lunch times at school. I said I wasn't very keen on this personally because I think there are easier ways of making money. I suggested organising a 5-a-side football tournament. I thought this would be popular and easy to do. I offered to research the idea and look into whether we could use some of the school's facilities cheaply.

27.9.04 I persuaded everyone today that organising events such as a football tournament would make easy money. I showed everyone my market research results using an OHP. I discovered that 79% of the pupils I asked would be interested in taking part. The 12 to 14 age group showed more interest than others. I also calculated that a tournament could raise £80 (less costs) if 16 teams entered and each player paid £1. Pupils also said they would pay £2 if there was a prize. I also asked the school office how much it would cost to use the sports hall after school. It would be free except we would have to make a donation to charity. I argued that this would be OK because it would improve the image of Bookgem. In the end the board agreed that my idea would be worth pursuing. The more diversified the enterprise, the greater the earning potential, I suggested.

The business plan

It is sometimes said that 'failing to plan is planning to fail'. A business is more likely to be successful if the process of setting up and getting started is planned carefully. This involves identifying some specific objectives and deciding, in advance, what tasks need to be completed in order to achieve them. Many owners produce a document called a business plan. This is a written statement that describes the business, its objectives, its strategies, the market and its financial forecasts. A business plan helps to:

* plot, guide and monitor the development of the business;
* assess the usefulness of the market research/analysis undertaken.;
* clarify the resources needed to achieve the objectives. In particular the money needed to set up the business and become established;
* assess the practical feasibility, financial viability, and probability of success of a new business venture.
* persuade and convince others, particularly banks and investors, to support the new business venture.

The contents of a business plan may vary slightly according to the nature of the business and personal style. However, most plans will contain certain common features as illustrated in Figure 2.

Mission statements

Many companies produce a mission statement. This includes a description of the overall aims of a business and tends to be aimed at stakeholders. They are often found in the Annual Reports and Accounts of limited companies, particularly public limited companies. They include information for all stakeholders including customers, shareholders, suppliers and employees. They usually express the aims of the company in 'qualitative terms', such as emphasising the desire to be 'the best in the industry' or to be the 'best in the field'. Sometimes mission statements are brief, like the ones shown for Boots, the chemist and retailer, and Tate & Lyle, the ingredients manufacturer, in Figure 1.

Mission statements are often displayed in prominent places such as reception areas. They can then be viewed by staff, customers and suppliers, showing what the business is trying to achieve. They can also be placed on company websites. Sometimes more detailed mission statements are produced. These might include details about the aims of the business including its main purpose and how it might evaluate success. In some cases it might give details of specific objectives stating targets or outcomes. It is said that mission statements:

* help the business to focus;
* provide a plan for the future of the business;
* clarify for all stakeholders what the business is trying to achieve.

Figure 1 *Mission statements of Boots and Tate & Lyle*

Boots

'Boots aims to be the place for health and beauty customers. We want to secure market leadership in the UK and build on our brands' growing success internationally.'

Tate & Lyle

Purpose
To create the world's leading renewable ingredients business.

Vision
We will grow by reuniting our businesses and developing partnerships to create the world's leading renewable ingredients business. We will build a consistent global portfolio of distinctive, profitable, high value solutions in products and services for our customers.

Source: adapted from company websites.

Health and safety

When forming a company the health and safety of employees and customers must be taken into account. During the planning stages it is necessary to ensure that the company can provide a safe environment for employees and customers.

What might this involve?

* Obtaining advice on health and safety from local authorities, health and safety executives and business advisory services.
* Taking out adequate insurance.
* Ensuring adequate washing and toilet facilities.
* Obtaining fire certificates for premises, if appropriate.
* Providing protective clothing and safety equipment.
* Providing proper training in relation to health and safety.

Figure 2 *Features of a business plan for OurPetscare*

Executive summary
- Name and address of the company.
- Owners'/directors' names.
- Telephone number.
- E-mail address.
- Legal structure.
- Business start date.

EXAMPLE The company name will be OurPetscare, operating from premises at Unit 6, Kendal Trading Estate, Kendal, Cumbria. It is a limited company with 4 directors.

The product
- The nature of the business idea.
- A description of the product or service.
- Proposed quantities and prices.

EXAMPLE OurPetscare will offer a number of pet related services, including pet care, grooming, training and photography.

Objectives
- What do you plan to achieve in first 6-12 months, e.g. survival, break-even?
- What are your medium-long term objectives, e.g. profit targets, growth targets?
- Objectives should be SMART - Simple, Measurable, Achievable, Realistic and Time related.

EXAMPLE The objective is to build up a loyal clientele in the short-term, particularly in the first six months, to consolidate the business. This will help the business achieve its aim of being profitable within a year of trading.

Market details
- Customers. Who will buy the product? Description of customer profiles. What is the market size? What is the growth rate?
- Competitors. Who are the main competitors? What are their strengths and weaknesses? What is your unique selling point?
- Evidence of Demand. Provide market research details if possible.

EXAMPLE The area around Kendal and the Lake District has many pet owners. Offering some fairly unique services, such as photography, should attract regular customers. Visitors to the area might also make use of some of the kennel facilities.

Marketing and sales processes
- How do you intend to reach customers?
- What methods will be used to promote the product?
- What is the promotion/advertising budget?

EXAMPLE The marketing strategy will be designed to target pet owners through a variety of channels. This will include advertisements in the local newspaper and leaflets in the Cumbria area. The business has also arranged for an interview with local business magazines.

Operational details
- Premises - type, location, size, cost.
- Physical assets - e.g. equipment and vehicles.
- Personnel - numbers and types of staff required.
- Intellectual assets - licences, patents, suppliers contracts, trade endorsements, customer contacts and networks.
- Suppliers' contracts secured.

- Terms and conditions from suppliers - e.g. payment on delivery or 30, 60 days to pay.
- Terms and conditions to customers - e.g. immediate payment or credit.

EXAMPLE Premises are available on the industrial estate to rent. They are large enough to handle expected capacity for the first two years of trading. Two of the directors of the business have worked for grooming kennels before and can provide this service. Another director has worked in the ICT industry and will deal with digital photography and reproduction.

Profit model
- Estimate likely profit based on turnover (price x quantity) and costs.
- Calculation of the break-even point to show the level of output/sales needed to break-even.

EXAMPLE The break-even level of output for the photography service is around 130 units a month at an average price of £12.50 per service. This should give a monthly total sales value of £1,625. The break-even point for the photography service is likely to be achieved fairly quickly because of the low initial costs associated with the activity.

Cash flow forecast
Produce a cash flow forecast statement to show the:
- expected cash inflows
- expected cash outflows
- monthly net cash flows
- expected monthly closing balances.

EXAMPLE Net cash flow will be negative for the first few months of the year. However, the initial cash from the directors and the growing demand estimated for summer should prevent cash flow problems.

Financial requirements
- How much funding is needed?
- What will the money be used for?
- Where will the money come from?
- How long will money be borrowed for?
- What might be used as security?

EXAMPLE Initially two of the directors will each place £10,000 into the business from their own savings.

Source: adapted from www.bplans.com.

Financial planning

Arguably, one of the most important aspects of business planning is financial planning. It is not uncommon for entrepreneurs to overlook the importance of financial planning. This may happen because they become too absorbed in the practical aspects of business start-up. Careful financial planning can help to avoid some common problems such as running out of cash.

Raising capital Once the costs of setting up the business and getting it established have been calculated, the owners can plan how they will raise the money needed. Owners should not attempt to set up a business unless the necessary funding is in place. It would be foolish, for example, to spend £20,000 converting some property into a restaurant and then find out there was no money left for furniture, crockery, glasses and kitchen utensils. The money would be wasted and the business could not open. Owners are likely to raise funds from the following sources:

- owners' capital, proceeds from shares for example;
- loans from friends or relatives;
- bank loans;
- hire purchase;
- bank overdraft;
- other short term sources, such as trade credit, debt factoring or credit cards.

In addition to the amount of money needed to cover the start-up costs, a prudent business owner will ensure that there is some cash left over to meet any unforeseen expenditure. It is very common indeed for start-up costs to exceed planned expenditure. When trying to attract funding, the business plan discussed above will help support any applications. The sources of funds are discussed in section 18.

Cash flow forecasts One of the most useful financial planning aids is a cash flow forecast statement (see section 22). Cash is the lifeblood of business. Without it a business cannot trade. It is important to make sure there is enough cash to meet all the planned expenditure, both during the setting up stages, and once trading begins. Preparing cash flow forecasts makes an important contribution to the planning process. For example, they will show

when a business is going to run short of cash in advance. This gives the owners time to make arrangements for raising additional funds if necessary.

Budgets Budgets are financial plans and force a business to plan ahead (see section 23). This means that owners or managers are more likely to foresee problems before they occur. If budgets were not used managers would be tempted to run businesses on a day-to-day basis. This could result in future problems being overlooked until too late. For example, money might be spent on an advertising campaign when it should have been spent buying some essential materials and components. Variance analysis might also be used to help determine the reasons why actual income and spending is different from the planned levels. Budgets and variance analysis are explained in section 23.

Profit targets One aspect of financial planning may involve setting profit targets. When a company is formed it may not expect to make a profit immediately. However, it is important to set realistic financial targets relating to performance. For example, it might aim to break even in the first trading year. If this is the case then it must calculate the level of sales needed to achieve this target. A break-even chart may be drawn to show this (see section 24). A projected profit and loss account may also be prepared (see section 20). This will show the revenue, costs and profit the company expects to report in the future. One of the advantages of profit targets is that they give the company a point of focus.

1. Find two mission statements from your own research in company reports or on the Internet.
2. Make a comparison and write a brief report commenting on:
- the length of the statements;
- the difference in aims and objectives;
- any similarities;
- whether the objectives are SMART.

Research task

Portfolio practice · Funpaint

Funpaint is a mini enterprise run by a group of students in the South East. They have set up a successful venture providing face painting and body art services. Face painting is done at children's parties, student functions and by appointment. Body art is provided by appointment only. Funpaint has done some research on the designs and Japanese designs have proved very popular indeed. One recent idea which Funpaint has come up with is to visit local football clubs and other sports grounds. It plans to offer supporters face painting in team colours.

Before the business began trading several weeks were spent planning and researching. For example, time was spent allocating roles and jobs to the different members. Funpaint also produced a design brochure for its face paints and body art. As a result of the planning the business was well organised and everyone knew what to do. One important issue in the planning stage was health and safety. Funpaint had to check very

carefully that the paints being used were safe.

(a) Write a short mission statement for Funpaint.
(b) Outline the contents that might be included in a business plan for Funpaint.
(c) Discuss the advantages to Funpaint of producing a business plan.

Meeting the assessment criteria

You need to provide evidence of your involvement in setting up the company. You can do this by keeping a diary of your contributions during the launch, planning and running of the company.

Business example - Helpline

A group of students set up a mini company called Helpline. They planned to sell a variety of products such as handmade scarves, mirrors and badges. They also provide a photography service which involves taking photographs at student events and selling them to students caught on camera. The business has a website which gives information about the company and displays examples of their products. The company donates all their profits to charity – hence the name of the company 'Helpline'.

The company has been very successful. The managing director said 'We spent ages planning our business. We wrote a proper business plan and got our teacher to check it'. The financial director said 'We decided to set financial targets. We aimed to make a profit of £200 during October and November. We did this easily and set a profit target of £300 for December. This is a challenging target, but with Christmas it should be achievable'. Students kept diaries of their participation in the company.

Mark Band 1 *Provide outline evidence of your participation in the launch of the company. Use a diary to record the contributions you made in the planning process.*

6.9.04 We spent another meeting planning again. The business plan is nearly complete now. I wrote a small part of it. This was the section on aims and objectives. I explained that the company aimed to make a profit and donate it all to charity. I also said that Helpline would set SMART objectives.

13.9.04 At last the business plan is finished. The teacher is going to check it for us. The MD said my bit on aims and objectives was OK. We are going to start production next week. I have got to buy some materials at the weekend. We are going to make some badges. The things we need to buy are listed in the business plan. We have a budget of £25. We have to stick to this because budgeting is an important part of running a business.

Mark Band 2 *Provide detailed evidence of strong participation in the launch of the company. Use a diary to record the contributions you made in the planning process.*

6.9.04 Today's meeting focused on the business plan again. I'm writing the section on the market. I am writing a short report based on some market research that I did with two other members. We asked 200 students what sorts of products they would buy from Helpline. We also asked them about the prices they would pay. I presented some of the results in graphs and pie charts using Excel.

13.9.04 The business plan is finished now except that changes may be necessary after it has been checked by the teacher. I helped to put the finishing touches to the document. In addition to my section on the market I helped to plan what resources would be needed for our activities. We plan to start making products next week. We have produced a timetable for the next two months. This will help us to meet deadlines such as making sure we have enough products to sell when we attend trade fairs.

Mark Band 3 *Provide full and detailed evidence of influential participation in the launch of the company. Use a diary to record the contributions you made in the planning process.*

6.9.04 Much of the time recently has been spent planning. Planning is important because it makes us think ahead. We want our business to be successful. The more profit we make the more we can donate to charity. I have been working on the financial section of the business plan. I have prepared a cash flow forecast statement on a spreadsheet. This shows how much cash we expect to flow into and out of the business in the next six weeks. It also shows the expected cash balance at the end of each week. To begin with most of the cash will come from the sale of shares. The rest will come from sales when Helpline starts to sell products.

13.9.04 The business plan was completed today. My section was the longest. I had to produce a cash flow forecast, a projected profit statement and some simple budgets. Each product has been allocated a budget. For example, badges have been given £25. The use of budgets will stop people from spending too much on their product area. I also did some break-even calculations on some of the products. For example, we need to sell 20 mirrors to break-even for that product range. I also agreed some financial targets with the rest of the board. We aim to make £200 during October and November. During December we aim to make £300 profit.

Types of business

There are over four million businesses in the UK. They vary considerably in many ways. Some are huge organisations with millions of shareholders, thousands of employees, production operations all over the world and a wide range of products. For example, Cadbury Schweppes, the confectionery manufacturer, employs over 55,000 staff, has a turnover of over £5 billion, sells products in over 200 countries and owns hundreds of different brands such as Cadbury Crème Egg, Cadbury Dairy Milk, Bassets, 7UP, Canada Dry, Dr Pepper and Trebor. In contrast, Francesca Elliott, who runs a small riding school in Dorset, employs no other staff, rents a stable for £50 a week and has a turnover of £43,000. However, all types of businesses fall into one of the categories in Figure 1.

Figure 1 *Primary, secondary and tertiary sectors*

Primary sector This category includes businesses that take natural resources from the earth, i.e. extracting raw materials and growing food. Businesses involved in mining, quarrying, fishing, farming and forestry fall into this category.

Secondary sector Secondary production involves manufacturing, processing and construction which transform raw materials into goods. Some of the activities included in this sector include:
● textile manufacturing;
● machinery production;
● electrical goods production;
● car assembly;
● refining;
● brewing and distilling;
● printing;

Figure 2 *Business type by sector (gross value added at current basic prices), UK*

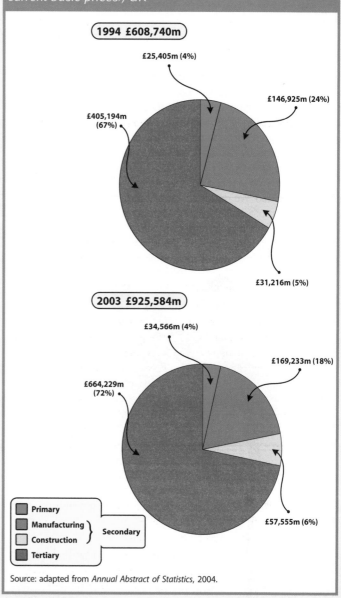

Source: adapted from *Annual Abstract of Statistics*, 2004.

● food processing;
● construction.

Tertiary sector The majority of businesses in the UK fall into this sector. It involves the provision of services. The variety of services in this sector is huge. Some examples include:
● retailing;
● transport such as air travel, bus, coach and train services and taxis;
● personal services, such as hairdressing, beauty treatment and legal services;
● financial services, such as banking, accountancy, insurance, investment and pensions;

- leisure and tourism, such as holidays, hotels, theatre, sport, restaurants and visitor attractions;
- domestic services, such as plumbing, garden design and window cleaning;
- education;
- health care.

Figure 2 shows that primary production makes a relatively small contribution to the UK's total output. Secondary production accounted for around a quarter of total output in 2003, falling as a percentage from 1994. Figure 2 also shows that the tertiary sector grew at the expense of manufacturing, accounting for over 70% of total output in the UK in 2003.

Features of business enterprise

People who set up a business initially are often referred to as **entrepreneurs**. There are certain features associated with business enterprise.

Opportunities People who set up business enterprises are often making the most of an opportunity that has arisen. For example, they may have been made redundant and decide to take the opportunity to work for themselves rather than looking for another job. Alternatively someone might take the opportunity to fill a gap in a market they think exists. Business people are often said to be opportunists. This means that they have the confidence and drive to make the most of an opportunity if one presents itself. They may also be able to spot opportunities that others cannot see.

Risks Entrepreneurs also have to take risks.

- When they set up an enterprise they will probably have to use some of their own money to get it going. Because there is no guarantee that the business will succeed, there is the chance that the money invested by the owner will be lost. If the owner has unlimited liability the financial losses could be much greater than the original amount invested. This could have serious financial implications for the owner's family.
- In some cases entrepreneurs take a risk by leaving a well paid and secure job to start a business. If the business collapses there is no guarantee that the entrepreneur will find such favourable employment again.
- Business failure could affect a person's self-esteem and social standing. To some extent an entrepreneur might be humiliated if their business collapses. Peers may not want to be associated with someone who has failed so publicly.

Innovation and creativity It could be argued that entrepreneurs are innovators. This is because they form a new business where one did not exist before. Innovation involves taking an idea and making it into a commercial success. Even when ideas are copied or adapted, it could be argued that the entrepreneur is being innovative. Some examples of innovators and their innovations are given in Table 1.

Entrepreneurs are often creative people. They may be original thinkers and develop ideas that noone else thought of. This can have an impact on the profit they might make. If a business idea is original, it may be possible to obtain a patent which is a licence which prevents others from copying the idea. This means that an entrepreneur can commercially exploit the original idea without competition for a period of time. Therefore a higher price can be charged and more profit made. Creative entrepreneurs may also

Table 1 *Entrepreneurs and their activities*

Name	Actvity
Stelios Haji-Ioannou	Founder of 'no-frills' air travel, easyJet and other 'easy' businesses.
Rachel Elnaugh	Founder of Red Letter days, a business offering 'unique, never to be forgotten experiences'.
Rupert Murdoch	The first person to supply pay to view TV in the UK, BSkyB.
Richard Reed	The market leader of fruit only (no preservatives) smoothies, Innocent.
Joanne Freer	Founder of CottonBottoms the UK's biggest real nappy provider, which also provides a laundry service for parents.

develop a new concept and exploit it in a wide variety of ways. For example, Stelios Haji-Ioannou has applied his 'no-frills' concept in a number of ways. Some of his 'easy' companies include a cinema, a car hire business, a mini-bus service, cruises and an Internet café. Stelios Haji-Ioannou has been described as a serial entrepreneur.

Entrepreneurship Without entrepreneurs businesses would not exist. They play a crucial role in the development of business activity. In addition to taking risk and being innovators, they have to demonstrate other important skills.

- Organisation. Businesses need resources, such as premises, machinery, tools, equipment, labour, materials and fuel, to operate. Entrepreneurs must acquire the appropriate combination of resources for their chosen business activity. For example, if a venture involves opening a sportswear shop then a suitable retail outlet must be found. It will also be necessary to fit the premises, acquire equipment such as a till and a computer perhaps, buy in stock, recruit some staff and promote the opening of the store. All these activities need effective coordination and good organisational skills. Tasks must be done in the right order so that costs are minimised and the whole operation runs smoothly.
- Leadership. An entrepreneur will also need to be a good leader. They have to support and inspire the whole workforce. It is sometimes said that a person must be a 'jack of all trades' to run a business. Some entrepreneurs underestimate the range of skills needed to run a business effectively.
- Decision making. Entrepreneurs have to make countless decisions when setting up and running a business. The first major decision is deciding what to produce. But many others follow. How should the business be financed? Where should it be located? What resources should be used? Which staff should be recruited? What methods of promotion should be used? Making the right decision will improve the chances of business success. Some entrepreneurs may use quantitative decision making techniques to improve decision making. This involves the use of numbers and formulae to help make decisions. The most important decisions are strategic decisions. These are decisions that can affect the whole direction and progress of the company, such as which products to produce, or, when the company expands, which firms to take over.

Business growth

It is unlikely that a business will remain the same size once established. Many entrepreneurs choose to expand their businesses. There is a number of motives for growth.

Survival It is often argued that unless a business grows it will not survive. Growing might enable it to generate the resources needed to cope with adverse external factors, such as new competition, a downturn in the economy and the threat of a takeover.

Higher profit As a business grows it is likely to make more profit. By growing and selling more output, sales revenue will rise along with profit. This will benefit the owners and there will also be more profit to reinvest.

Economies of scale As a business expands it may exploit economies of scale. This means that the unit costs start to fall. For example, a larger business will need to buy more stock or raw materials. It is generally the case that larger quantities can be purchased for less. Therefore costs will be lower and profits higher.

Increased market share If an enterprise gets bigger it may take a bigger share of the market. The business will have a higher profile and enjoy more publicity. If a company can grow large enough to enjoy some monopoly power it may be able to squeeze competition and eventually raise prices.

Reduce risk It is possible to reduce risk in business by diversifying. Branching out into new markets and developing new products means that if one venture fails there are others to keep the business going.

Limitations to growth

In some cases entrepreneurs are not able to grow their businesses. There is a number of restrictions that prevent business expansion.

Market limitations Some markets are very small and it is not possible to sell very large quantities. For example, the market for a village shop is likely to be restricted to villagers, a small amount of passing trade and immediate outlying rural areas. There would be no point in developing a huge grocery store in these circumstances. There would not be enough customers.

Lack of finance Many entrepreneurs want to grow but cannot raise the money to fund the growth. They are frustrated in their efforts. Money lenders and investors are often reluctant to fund small enterprises. They consider them too risky.

Diseconomies of scale In some cases a business that is already large cannot grow any more without experiencing rising costs. This is called diseconomies of scale. Certain costs, such as staff supervision, communication costs and coordination, may start to rise if a large company grows any bigger.

Geographical limitations Some products, such as crisps, bread and beer, are low value and very bulky. Consequently it costs too much to transport them beyond local markets. However, with improved distribution networks and more efficient logistics, some national suppliers of these products do exist. Also, the provision of many services, such as personal, domestic and retail, is confined to local geographical markets because customers will not travel.

In some cases an entrepreneur may decide that growth is not an

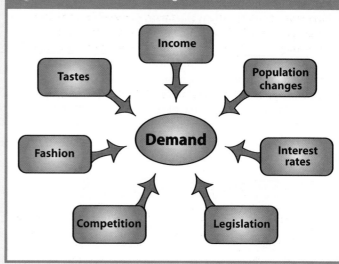

Figure 3 *Factors influencing demand*

objective. Some owners may not want to take on the extra work and responsibilities that come with growth. They may want to remain below the VAT threshold to avoid the need to charge customers more and complete regular VAT returns. They may also be content with the amount of profit they are currently making.

The impact of market forces

Businesses operate in a dynamic environment where a wide range of factors can influence the markets in which they operate. For example, Figure 3 shows some of the factors that might influence the demand for a firm's product.

The degree to which each of these factors can influence demand will depend on the nature of the product. For example, changes in:

- income will tend to affect the demand for non-essential products like holidays and computer games;
- interest rates are likely to affect demand for products that are purchased using loans and credit cards, such as consumer durables and houses;
- legislation has led to an increase in demand for child minding and nursery facilities in recent years;
- the number of people in the over 60s age group has led to increase in demand for health care;
- fashions and trends can affect the demand for products, such as clothes and holidays;

1. Using the *Yellow Pages* for your local area or a local business directory, calculate the percentage of businesses which operate in the:
   - primary sector;
   - secondary sector;
   - tertiary sector.
2. Compare your results with the pie charts on page 374 and:
   - comment on the main types of business in your area;
   - account for any differences between your results and those on page 374.

Research task

the activities of competitors can affect any business. They may bring out new products or change their prices, for example. Businesses often attempt to increase demand for their own products to ward off competitors. They may do this by advertising, using promotions, improving the product, improving after-sales service, lowering the price or developing new products.

Changes in other markets will also affect businesses. For example, movements in the labour market might make labour more scarce and expensive. Oil prices often increase significantly. This can affect businesses that rely on oil as a key raw material. The market for land and business premises may also be important. In recent years the price of land and property has escalated, making it expensive to buy or rent premises.

Portfolio practice · Take It All

After leaving university, John Mycroft and Beth Montague set up an enterprise selling takeaway food. In their local town they persuaded four take away restaurants to supply food that they planned to deliver. They drew up a menu offering Indian, Chinese, Mexican and Thai meals delivered to the door. This meant that if a family, for example, wanted different types of ethnic food, it could all be delivered together. A flier, promoting the new service with detailed menus and prices, was posted to all houses in the town. Orders were received on mobile phones and relayed to the restaurants immediately. John and Beth used scooters to transport the meals and collect payment. John and Beth thought their idea was innovative because no one else offered this service. They were convinced it would work and risked £2,000 each of their own money in the venture.

(a) **Describe the type of business set up by John and Beth.**
(b) **Describe the features of enterprise highlighted by this case.**
(c) **John and Beth aim to grow Take It All once people become accustomed to their service. Discuss the factors that might limit their growth.**
(d) **Evaluate the extent to which Take It All might be affected by market forces.**

Meeting the assessment criteria

The **NewZ**

Are we overspending?

You need to provide evidence of your involvement in setting up the company. You can do this by keeping a diary of your contributions during the launch, planning and running of the company.

Business example - The Newz

The Newz is a magazine published by a group of students for other students at a Leeds college. It contains a variety of news reports, features and articles, such as college issues, editorial, pop reviews, sports stories, dates of events, gossip, letters, teacher interviews, puzzles, quizzes, competitions and adverts. An opportunity for this sort of venture arose when the college itself stopped producing a weekly newsletter for students. So far ten issues have been published and a small profit has been made on every issue. Students kept diaries of their participation in the magazine.

Mark Band 1 *Provide outline evidence of your participation in the running of the company. Use a diary to record the contributions you made in the running of the business.*

4.2.05 I spent all lunch time today selling copies of The Newz around college. I managed to sell my full allocation of copies. I also helped to count all the money and check that none had gone missing. We made £60 in revenue today and I went with Trena to pay the money into the college office.

19.2.05 I tried to write an article for The Newz but got bored. Instead I helped design a quiz based on the Champions League. I think this will get published because it is topical.

Mark Band 2 *Provide detailed evidence of strong participation in the running of the company. Use a diary to record the contributions you made in the running of the business.*

6.2.05 Tonight I wrote some replies to letters received by The Newz from students. Most of them are about relationships. I share this job with another member of the group. We have to meet tomorrow and choose the five best replies out of the ten that we have written.

20.2.05 At the editor's meeting today we discussed some ideas for a new feature in The Newz. We broke up into pairs to consider our ideas. We then pooled our ideas to draw up a short list. Our idea for a review of local night spots was put on the short list. We will have a vote on the best new feature next week. I also volunteered to do some design work for a new advert. We raised £45 in advertising revenue in the last issue and the editor is keen to allocate more space to adverts.

Mark Band 3 *Provide full and detailed evidence of influential participation in the running of the company. Use a diary to record the contributions you made in the running of the business.*

6.2.05 I prepared for an interview with one of the teacher tomorrow. The regular feature of teacher interviews in The Newz is very popular. I try to ask amusing questions and make the interviews a bit different. I dig as deep as I can without being too personal. I am also the assistant editor. Part of this job involves short listing articles for the editor. At our meeting today I stressed how important it was to de with issues such as non-smoking in public places. She felt that students may not be too interested. But I showed her news coverage recently of this issue and examples of businesses and whole towns that had banned or were considering such a ban on smoking in public places. My arguments convinced her. Regular features are likely to be included in future.

20.2.05 After the editor's meeting today I have a lot to do. The editor and I have also discussed including some articles which address sensitive areas, such as environmental issues. I have argued strongly that our strategy should be to take the magazine into important areas. However, I have stressed that we must be careful to include all sides of any argument about a sensitive issue so students can make up their own minds. So far we have only had one meeting about publishing such material. However, I have argued strongly that it will sell more copies. I have also got to find someone to draw cartoons to illustrate the issues in a hard-hitting way. I will consider some drawings tomorrow, but they must make the impact which I feel will attract readers.

Who runs a limited company?

A limited company is run by a board of directors headed by a chairperson. The board, which is elected by the shareholders, makes the important decisions for the company. In certain very important situations, such as whether a company should be taken over, the shareholders will decide. The main job of the board is to oversee the day-to-day running of the company by senior management. The board defines and enforces standards of accountability to ensure that the senior management team run the company in the interests of shareholders. The main responsibilities of the board of directors are shown in Figure 1.

In private limited companies the chairperson and board of directors may also be key shareholders and involved in the day-to-day running of the business.

Chairperson

The chairperson's main role is to ensure that the board is effective in setting and implementing the company's direction and strategy. The chairperson is appointed by the board. The post may be full-time or part-time. The chairperson takes 'the chair' at general meetings and board meetings. The chairperson is the company's leading representative and is responsible for presenting the company's aims and policies to the outside world. It is possible for someone to be a chairperson of more than one company. A chairperson is accountable to the shareholders of a company. In 2005 Jacques Gounon was chairperson of Eurotunnel, the channel tunnel operator. Figure 2 identifies the responsibilities of this job.

Skills and qualifications - chairperson

In practice, one company chairperson is likely to have a different approach to another and therefore is likely to have different skills

Figure 2 *The responsibilities of the Eurotunnel chairperson in 2005*

- Provide leadership to the board.
- Take responsibility for the number and type of directors on the board.
- Ensure proper information is provided to the board.
- Plan and conduct board meetings effectively.
- Get all directors involved in the board's work.
- Ensure the board focuses on its key tasks.
- Engage the board in assessing and improving its performance.
- Oversee the induction and development of directors.
- Support the Chief Executive Officer (CEO) or the managing director.

Source: adapted from www.eurotunnel.co.uk.

and qualities. Sir Richard Greenbury, the ex-chairperson of Marks & Spencer, says: 'There is no rule, no one way of doing things. It depends on the individuals, the cultures and histories of the company.' Michael Knight, partner of the head-hunter, CCG Ward Howell International, and industrial psychologist Brenda Bell, asked 400 directors of Britain's top companies what they believed were the most desirable qualities in a chairperson. Four 'preferred profiles' emerged from the research - the Facilitator, the Thinker, the Driver and the Integrator. The qualities valued most by the 400 directors questioned were as follows.

- Nearly a third of the directors who responded chose the Facilitator. Such people are detached, visionary and focused, low on ego and do not indulge in power struggles with his or her chief executive. They are seen as low-key and hands-off, with wisdom and judgment. They foster unity and commitment and are particularly popular with chief executives.
- A quarter of respondents went for the Thinker - shrewd, visionary and detached. Such people work through a chief executive but have no doubts about their power. They are challenging and analytical.

Figure 1 *The responsibilities of the board of directors*

- Overseeing the running of the business, ensuring that it is managed in the interest of shareholders.
- Appointing a chief executive to be responsible for the day-to-day running of the business and to monitor their progress.
- Reviewing, approving and monitoring the company's strategic plans and objectives.
- Monitoring the company's accounting and financial reporting practices and reviewing the company's financial and other controls.
- Overseeing the company's compliance with laws and regulations.
- Overseeing the processes designed to protect the company's assets and guard against unnecessary risk.

- The Driver came next with 23 per cent. Such people are directive, passionate and focused. They are charismatic leaders who tower over others on the board.
- The last, the Integrator, sets out to win hearts and minds, has insight and is visionary and passionate. Intellectually brilliant, such people have a flair for communication and relationships. Although least popular overall, they are a hit with non-executive directors.

In small limited companies, where the chairperson is involved in the day-to-day running of the business, different qualities will be needed. They will need more practical business skills in addition to leadership qualities, drive and ambition.

Directors

Company directors are appointed by the shareholders and look after the affairs of the company. They are in a position of trust and must be careful not to abuse their position in order to profit at the expense of the shareholders. Consequently, the law imposes a number of duties, burdens and responsibilities upon directors, to prevent abuse. There are two types of directors - executive and non-executive. There is no legal distinction between the two and both have the same legal obligations. The difference is in their roles.

Executive directors They are actively involved in the running of the company. They are the senior managers in the business. They are likely to be specialists in fields such as accounting, production, marketing and personnel. They will also have a greater intimate knowledge of the company than non executives. Executive directors determine the objectives, direction and policy of the company. One of these executive directors will be the appointed Chief Executive Officer (CEO). This role involves leading the team of directors to run the business and working closely with the chairman. An example of a job description for a CEO is shown in Figure 3.

Non-executive directors They are recruited to monitor the performance of the company as a whole and the performance of the executive directors. This should be accomplished by non-executives serving on appropriate committees and reporting regularly to the board. The main committees include the audit committee, remuneration committee, the health and safety committee and the nominations committee (responsible for monitoring the size and structure of the board).

Directors' legal responsibilities include:
- keeping proper books of accounts and preparing accounts for presentation to the company's shareholders;
- filing accounts and returns annually with the Registrar of Companies;
- informing the Registrar of Companies of the appointment or retirement of any director or the company secretary;
- informing the Registrar of Companies of any change in the situation of the company's registered office;
- appointing auditors;
- calling and holding annual general meetings (at which annual accounts are presented);
- making sure that the company acts strictly in accordance with the powers and rules set out in its Memorandum and Articles of Association.

Skills and qualities - directors

Executive directors need to be experienced in running a business at a senior level. They are likely to be specialists and responsible for a certain part of the organisation. For example, the Finance Director will be responsible for the accounting function in the business. They will need to demonstrate the ability to lead and motivate a large team of staff and have strong interpersonal, organisational, analytical and communication skills. Executive directors may be promoted from within the company or recruited from outside on the basis of a proven record.

Figure 3 *An example of a job description for a CEO of a large multinational business*

Job title: Chief Executive Officer.

Function:
- To implement the strategic goals and objectives of the organisation.
- With the chairperson, to enable the board to fulfil its governance function.
- To give direction and leadership toward the achievement of the organisation's philosophy, mission, strategy and its annual goals and objectives.

Reports to: Board of directors.

Major functions/accountabilities:
- Board administration and support supports operations and administration of the board by advising and informing board members, interfaces between the board and staff and supports the board's evaluation of chief executive.
- Program, product and service delivery oversees the design, marketing, promotion, delivery and quality of programs, products and services.
- Financial, tax, risk and facilities managementrecommends yearly budgets for board approval and prudently manages the organisation's resources within those budget guidelines according to current laws and regulations.
- Human resource management - effectively manages the human resources of the organisation according to authorised personnel policies and procedures that fully conform to current laws and regulations.
- Community and public relations - assures the organisation and its mission, policies, products and services are presented consistently and positively to the company's stakeholders.

Non-executive directors should be independent, totally honest and conscientious. They should also be people with sound business experience or professionals with exposure to business matters. They might include solicitors, accountants, management consultants and academics for example. Since non-executives are required to sit on specialist committees it is desirable that they are appropriately qualified. For example, a non-executive director sitting on the audit committee should be a qualified and experienced accountant or financial analyst. Figure 3 is an example of a job description for a CEO for a large multinational business.

Company secretary

In the UK a company must appoint a company secretary and have a minimum of one director/shareholder. The company secretary and the company director cannot be the same person. The secretary may be criminally liable for defaults committed by the company, such as failure to file any change in the details of the company's directors and secretary and the company's annual return. Although the law does not lay down the specific duties of a company secretary, there are some generally agreed responsibilities.

- Maintaining the statutory registers, for example the register of members, the register of directors and secretaries and the register of directors' interests.
- Ensuring that statutory forms are filed promptly, for example, using the appropriate form to notify the Registrar of a change in the company's registered office.
- Providing members and auditors with notice of meetings, for example, the secretary must give shareholders 21 days written notice of an Annual General Meeting.
- Sending the Registrar copies of resolutions and agreements, for example, special and extraordinary resolutions must be sent to the Registrar within 15 days of them being passed.
- Supplying a copy of the accounts to every member and debenture holder of the company. Accounts must be sent at least 21 days before a meeting at which they are to be laid.
- Keeping, or arranging for the keeping, of minutes of directors' meetings and general meetings.
- Ensuring that people entitled to do so can inspect company records, for example, members of the company are entitled to inspect the minutes of its general meetings.

Skills and qualifications – company secretary

For a private limited company the secretary needs no formal qualifications. However, for a public limited company the directors must ensure that the secretary has the knowledge and experience to carry out the functions detailed above. According to the **Companies Act, 1985**, the secretary must also be a person who:
- is a member of a professional body such as the Institute of Chartered Accountants in England and Wales or the Institute of Chartered Secretaries and Administrators; or
- held the office of secretary of the company on 22 December 1980; or
- held the office of company secretary of a company (except a private company) for at least 3 out of the 5 years immediately before his or her appointment as secretary; or
- is a barrister, advocate or solicitor called or admitted in any part of the UK; or

- is a person who appears to the directors to be capable of carrying out the functions of company secretary, because he or she holds, or has held, any other similar position or is a member of any other body.

Accountants

Large limited companies are likely to employ their own team of accountants. **Financial accountants** are responsible for preparing the financial statements that are required to be filed with the Registrar every year. Generally, accounts must include:
- a profit and loss account (or income and expenditure account if the company is not trading for profit);
- a balance sheet signed by a director;
- an auditors' report signed by the auditor;
- a directors' report signed by a director or the secretary of the company;
- notes to the accounts; and
- group accounts (if appropriate).

A company may also employ **management accountants**. These are more concerned with the future and are involved in decision making and problem solving. They are responsible for producing financial reports, interpreting financial statements and preparing forecasts and budgets. They act as information 'servants' to the management team.

Small limited companies will not be able to afford a full time team of accountants to produce the annual accounts. They will employ a firm of chartered or certified accountants to prepare their accounts from their financial records. Businesses are obliged to keep records of all their transactions from which accounts can be prepared.

Skills and qualifications - accountants

Financial accountants employed by a company have to be fully qualified. They have to be in possession of relevant professional qualifications. Most qualified accountants are members of professional bodies such as the Institute of Chartered Accountants or the Institute of Certified Accountants. In addition to accountancy qualifications, management accountants may also have training in economics and management science.

Auditors

An auditor is a person who makes an independent report to a company's members as to whether its financial statements, such as the profit and loss account and balance sheet, have been prepared in accordance with the law. Companies with a turnover of over £5.6m or a balance sheet total in excess of £2.8m (after March 31 2004) must have their accounts audited. It is the responsibility of the directors to appoint auditors.

The auditor will check the accounts and accounting records of the company and prepare a report for the company's members. The report will say if the company's annual accounts have been properly prepared in accordance with the Companies Act and if they give a true and fair view of the company's financial affairs. The auditor will also consider if the information given in the directors' report is consistent with the annual accounts. If, in the auditor's opinion, the accounts or directors' report does not comply with the Companies Act, the auditor will say so in the report. An auditor must be independent of the company. Therefore, a person cannot be appointed as an auditor if they are an officer or employee of the company or an associated company. Auditors tend to be chartered or certified accountants. However, they must hold an audit-practising certificate issued by a recognised supervisory body such as the Institute of Chartered Accountants.

1. Using a copy of an Annual Reports and Accounts for any company, identify the following:
- chairperson;
- executive directors;
- non-executive directors;
- chief executive;
- auditors.
2. Write a brief description of what the auditor's report contains in the accounts.

Research task

Portfolio practice · **Marks & Spencer plc**

Stuart Rose (Chief Executive)
Stuart Rose is 56 years old and was appointed as chief executive in May 2004. He first joined M&S in 1972. However, he moved to the Burton Group in 1989 and became chief executive in 1994. He joined Argos as chief executive in 1997 to defend the takeover bid from GUS. He then became chief executive of Booker plc, which later merged with Iceland. He joined Arcadia as chief executive and left in 2002 when it was acquired. Stuart Rose is also a non-executive director of Land Securities and chairman of The British Fashion Council.

Steven Holliday
Steven Holliday was appointed as a non-executive director in July 2004. He is 48 and also an executive director of National Grid Transco. He was formerly an executive director of British Borneo Oil and Gas. Prior to that, he spent 19 years with Exxon Group. His international experience includes four years in the US.

Source: adapted from Marks & Spencer, *Annual Report and Accounts*, 2005.

(a) **Who is responsible for running a company like Marks & Spencer?**

(b) **Explain the possible differences between the roles of chief executive and non-executive director held by the above personnel at Marks & Spencer.**

(c) **Describe the skills and qualifications that may be necessary to hold the positions described above.**

Meeting the assessment criteria

You need to produce an individual report describing the roles and responsibilities of the officers involved in the launch, planning and running of the company.

Business example - Sparkle

Sparkle is an enterprise set up by a group of students to make jewellery and other fashion accessories. The company has a formal structure with a chairperson, seven directors and a company secretary. The company is owned by 40 shareholders who are mainly pupils of the school. However, 60% of the shares are owned by members of the board. The company began making jewellery four months ago and has made a sound start. At a local trade fair, just before Xmas, £310 of jewellery was sold. The board decided that 50% of any profit made by Sparkle would be donated to a local charity.

SPARKLE

Job Description: Secretary
The Secretary will:-
Act as a point of contact with all outside organisations and individuals.
Prepare the Agenda for Board Meetings.

Mark Band 1 *You need to provide a basic report which identifies some other roles and responsibilities of officers in the company. (In this example the focus is on the directors.)*
The board of directors at Sparkle run the company. There are seven directors in total, all of whom are involved in the running of the company. They would be regarded as executive directors. In a 'real company' directors have legal responsibilities such as keeping proper financial records and providing accounts for the shareholders. In the case of Sparkle the directors met regularly to make decisions about running the company. For example, at one meeting a decision was made about what to do with the profit. It was decided to give half of it to a local charity.

Mark Band 2 *You need to provide a sound report which describes most other roles and responsibilities of officers in the company. (In this example the focus is on the company secretary.)*
At the first board meeting held by Sparkle a company secretary was appointed. Only one person wanted the job but he did seem suitable. He was well organised and had good administrative skills. He kept the minutes at the meetings, notified people about the timing and venues for meetings and circulated important company information whenever necessary. He also communicated with people outside the company. In a limited company the secretary is responsible for making sure that the business complies with company law. For example, the company secretary must maintain the statutory registers such as the register of members and the register of directors and secretaries. He must also ensure that the statutory forms are filed promptly. No formal qualifications are necessary to become a company secretary of a private limited company. However, in the case of a plc the secretary must be a member of a professional body such as the Institute of Chartered Accountants.

Mark Band 3 *You need to provide a comprehensive report which describes all other roles and responsibilities of officers in the company. (In this example the focus is on the chairperson.)*
The chairperson's main role is to ensure that the board is effective in setting and implementing the company's direction and strategy. Our chairperson was appointed by the board of directors after a vote. She won unanimously. She takes the chair at all meetings and sets the agenda. She is the company's leading representative and is responsible for presenting the company's aims and policies to the outside world. She spoke to all the pupils in the school at an assembly. She told them about our company and its products and asked the school to support us by buying our products.

The chairperson is accountable to the shareholders and is responsible for tasks such as providing leadership to the board, taking responsibility for the board's composition and development, getting all directors involved in the board's work and ensuring that the board focuses on its key tasks. Our chairperson has a number of suitable qualities. She is confident and expresses herself well. She is shrewd, visionary and analytical. She has the respect of all the directors and is very professional in her role.

Team working

It is common for businesses to organise their staff into teams in the work place. This is because teams of staff tend to be more productive and better motivated. Teams are often given the power to organise how they work and solve any problems that arise. A group of workers is likely to develop a team spirit and support each other. The advantages and disadvantages of team working are shown in Figure 1.

Decision teams and work teams

It is useful to distinguish between decision teams and work teams.

Decision teams A decision team might be a senior management team, a remuneration committee, a university academic department or a group of professionals, such as doctors or lawyers. The main function of such a team is to make decisions. The team members may not rely on each other to carry out individual tasks, but do make decisions that are important for the welfare of the organisation.

Work teams In contrast a work team must work to together to accomplish a goal. It must co-ordinate its efforts constantly, for example, as might a team of workers in a cell making a family of products. Such a work group will contain workers with a variety of skills who will be committed to the aims of the cell.

In a company the board of directors is good example of a decision team (see unit 84). It is responsible for setting the objectives of the company and implementing policies that will help to meet those objectives. It is important that the board of directors works as a team. Directors should support each other, but also challenge ideas and think critically. When a company is being formed it is likely that the board will have to meet on a very

regular basis because there will be a lot to discuss during the planning stages.

A number of crucial decisions have to be made that could affect the plight of the company long into the future, such as where to locate the business. A committed team approach will help to reap some of the benefits of team working described in Figure 1. For example, each director, whether executive or non-executive, is likely to have a different range of skills and experiences which will help in the decision making process.

Once a company is established, a number of other teams are likely to be formed. Examples might be:
- functional departments, such as marketing, finance and production;
- specialist committees, such as the audit committee, the remuneration committee and the health and safety committee;
- working parties, such as one set up to explore ways of saving fuel and energy in the business.

Team building

Some companies think that team working is so important that they take special measures to build teams. They may do this by organising exercises to help group members:
- develop trust;
- open up communication channels;
- understand the group goals;
- improve group decision making;
- prevent domination by one member;
- openly examine and resolve conflicts;
- review work activities.

Such exercises often involve taking groups to outdoor locations and setting them problems to solve, such as building a raft from limited resources to cross a river. In many cases these exercises

---

Figure 1 *Advantages and disadvantages of team working*

Advantages
- Greater productivity due to pooled talents.
- Increased flexible working as team members bring a range of different jobs and skills and are able to cover for each other.
- More ideas may be created by a team.
- Responsibility is shared and is therefore less of a burden.
- People can specialise and draw on the skills and knowledge of their colleagues.
- Greater ability to solve problems.

Disadvantages
- There may be too much emphasis on harmony. It is often argued that teams work better when there is some lively debate and disagreement.
- Serious conflict between individuals in the team may cause too much tension and a break down in team spirit.
- An over-reliance on teams could be counter-productive if a particular task is better undertaken by an individual.
- Teams that organise meetings too frequently may waste valuable time.
- Teams might be ineffective if they are not given any power.

help to motivate groups of people, develop a strong team spirit and eventually improve their performance at work.

Communication

Effective communication is very important when launching and running a company. This is because poor communication can result in a wide range of problems for a business. For example, if the sales team fails to notify the production team that a customer has doubled the order size, it may not be possible to meet the order. This could result in a disgruntled customer who may find an alternative supplier. When forming a company a great deal of communication must take place.

Figure 2 shows the different groups that might exchange information with the board of directors. It also shows that members of the board also need to communicate with each other.

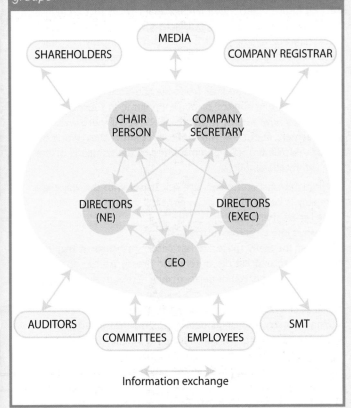

Figure 2 *Communication between the board and other groups*

Information exchange

Internal communication between board members

Since the board of directors is responsible for running the company, it is vital that they communicate openly. Formal communication will usually take place at board meetings where an agenda will be followed and minutes kept by the secretary. There may also be formal meetings between members of the board. For example, the chairperson is likely to meet with the CEO on a regular basis to discuss the progress made by the company and any problems that may have arisen. There will also be informal communication when executive directors, who are involved in the day-to-day running of the business, exchange information using the telephone or e-mail, or face-to-face communication.

External communication

The board of directors has a duty to communicate with certain groups outside the business.

Shareholders Since shareholders are the owners of the company they have a right to be informed about its progress. This is the responsibility of the chairperson and every year the chairperson addresses the shareholders at the Annual General Meeting. He or she reports on performance and progress of the company and takes questions from the floor. The chairperson also writes a report on the company's performance, which appears at the front of the annual reports and accounts. All shareholders by law receive a copy. A chairperson will also speak to individual shareholders personally if necessary or by telephone. Finally, the annual report and accounts also contain a directors' report. This is similar to the chairperson's report, but contains more detail, particularly about the operations of the company.

Registrar of Companies Legally, a company has to maintain communications with the Registrar of Companies. This is the responsibility of the company secretary. For example, the secretary must send copies of the annual accounts and notify them of any changes in the company's circumstances, such as change in the directors.

Media Newspapers, magazines and television and radio companies often need information from businesses for their reports, articles and programmes. It is often in the interests of companies to supply such information. Some companies employ a press officer or

Figure 3 *A spokesperson's announcement to the media*

In 2005 it was announced that Nokia had agreed to work with Microsoft's Windows Media Player technology so that digital music could be played on both PCs and Nokia phones and tracks could be moved between the two. "We are enabling Windows Media Audio files to be played on the Nokia music player' explained a Nokia spokesperson. That means that a large number of CDs can be easily downloaded on to a PC and into a phone. Microsoft will support open standards digital rights management technology. 'So if you purchase a song from one of the operators' music stores, you can listen to the music on your PC' he said.

Source: adapted from *The Guardian*, 16.2.2005.

spokesperson who takes responsibility for this task. However, sometimes, a member of the board might be involved directly in such communication. For example, the media might interview a company chairperson about an important development in the company. An example of an announcement is shown in Figure 3.

Senior management team (SMT) If the board is not directly involved in the running of the company, it will need to communicate with the senior management team. It will have to discuss whether the board's policies are being implemented effectively and whether performance targets are being met. This may be done by consulting the CEO or arranging a meeting with the SMT or its representatives.

Auditors When the auditors carry out their work they will need access to documents and other information belonging to the company. Communication channels must be kept open so that auditors can gather whatever information they need. Interviews with staff may be necessary and access to computer records. Inevitably there will be a great deal of communication between the company's accountants and the auditors.

Committees The board will need to communicate with the audit, remuneration, health and safety and nominations committees when necessary. It is likely that meetings will be organised so that the groups can meet formally. The various committees might also produce reports for the board which outline any recommendations for action. For example, the remuneration committee might prepare a report outlining their proposals for directors' salaries and other payments.

Employees Effective communication between the board of directors and the employees is vital for the success of a business. The board may want to tell employees about its plans for the future of the company, for example. This is likely to be accomplished formally. For example, a newsletter might be published or a member of the board may address the workers at an assembly. Alternatively the board may meet formally with employee representatives. In some organisations employees may also be members of the board.

Evaluating individual roles

Everyone employed by a company is accountable. This includes the chairperson, directors and other officers. The contribution made by each of the officers has to be acceptable or they may lose their positions. The performance and contribution made by each individual could be evaluated in a number of ways.

Target setting One way of evaluating individual performance is to set targets and measure the extent to which they are met. For example, the sales director may be responsible for seeing that the company achieves a certain level of sales. If the target is missed by a significant distance then the sales director may face individual criticism. It is possible that shareholders want the board to deliver a particular rate of growth for the company or a particular return on capital employed. The board may be collectively responsible for this, but if targets are missed it may be possible to single out poor performing individuals.

Non-executive directors The role of non-executive directors is to scrutinise the performance of executive directors and other senior managers. They must ensure that they are acting in the interests of shareholders. Non-executive directors are likely to do this by agreeing goals and objectives with board members and

measuring the extent to which these are achieved.

Nominations committee The nominations committee will play a role in the evaluation of individual performance. It reviews the structure, size and composition (including the skills, knowledge and experience) of the board and makes recommendations with regard to any changes. The committee must also review the performance of non-executive directors before their period of office ends.

Remuneration committee The main duty of the remuneration committee is to determine the amount of money that directors receive for their services to the company. The committee is likely to evaluate the performance of individuals when making decisions about directors' payments.

Appraisal A company may have a system of appraisal established. This involves discussing with an employee the contribution made to the running of the company and how well the individual has performed during the year. Appraisal can be used to assess and improve performance, provide feedback, increase motivation and set out future objectives. If an appraisal reveals that an individual's performance has not been satisfactory, further action might be necessary. For example, if it is clear that a company secretary has been neglecting important duties, it may be necessary to replace that person.

Auditors Once an auditor has been appointed by the board, it is common for that auditor to be reappointed in subsequent years. However, a new auditor might be appointed if there was a disagreement about the way auditors conduct their work, or about the true financial circumstances of the company or the price charged by the auditors.

Ultimately, if shareholders are not happy with the way their company is being run they can either:
● sell their shares; or
● dismiss the directors at the AGM.
However, for many, these are last resort measures. It may be preferable to express discontent and pressurise the board into raising their standards of performance. Collectively, media pressure and shareholder discontent can lead to a chairperson being replaced if a company is not doing very well.

Finally, interrelationships between company officers are important. A company is more likely to be successful if all the company officers work as a team, support each other and get on well. The relationship between the chairperson and the CEO is particularly important. Conflict between the two could result in the company being stretched in two directions. It may also lead to confusion about the aims and objectives of the company amongst subordinates. Trust, respect and confidence in each other's abilities will all help to improve working relationships between company officers and maintain open communication.

1. Find out the names of some companies that offer team building courses.
2. Write a brief report explaining:
   ● what they comprise of;
   ● what they aim to achieve;
   ● how much they charge.

Research task

Portfolio practice · **Next plc**

CHAIRMAN'S STATEMENT

I am pleased to report that NEXT has had a very satisfactory first half for 2004. We achieved a 15% increase in turnover and a 30% increase in pre-tax profit. Earnings per share increased by 36%. The interim dividend is being increased by 2p to 13p per share. At the Annual General Meeting on 13 May 2004 two of our non-executive directors retired from the Board and at the same time Jonathan Dawson was appointed. We intend to make another non-executive appointment in due course.

We continue to put all of our energy into providing well styled, good quality, value for money products to our customers in the core markets of the UK and Eire. Whilst the trading environment may become more difficult I am confident that NEXT has the strategy and the people to continue to take the company forward.

David Jones, C.B.E.

Source: adapted from www.next.co.uk.

(a) **State TWO external groups that might be interested in the above statement.**

(b) **Explain why it is important for the chairperson to communicate with external groups.**

(c) **How might the performance of directors at Next be evaluated?**

Meeting the assessment criteria

You need to write a report assessing the contribution made by the officers of the company.

Business example - Game Exchange

Game Exchange is a student-run enterprise which buys and sells second-hand computer games. It has a company website where computer games can be bought and sold on-line. However, the company also trades on the school premises at lunch times and attends local trade fairs, jumble sales and fetes. At a recent board meeting it was decided to extend trading to CDs and DVDs. The company has been very successful and one of the main reasons is due to the strong leadership shown by the chairperson.

Mark Band 1 *You need to write a report which assesses the contribution made by some of the officers in the company.*

The chairperson was a good leader. He was well liked and got things done. He also let everyone know what was going on. He worked hard and expected everyone else to do the same. The shareholders liked him because the company made good profits.

The marketing director was not as good. She was not a team player. She preferred to work on her own. She had some good ideas but often caused disputes and also let people down. She went missing a lot and people did not know what was going on.

Mark Band 2 *You need to write a sound report, supported with relevant examples, which assesses the contribution made by some of the officers in the company.*

The chairperson of our company has done a good job. He was a firm leader and a good team worker. He communicated well and kept everyone informed. The meetings were orderly and everyone got the chance to speak. He appeared to understand the role of chairperson and carried out the duties effectively. For example, he wrote a newsletter every half term for the shareholders. He commented on the progress of the company and thanked everyone for their support.

The marketing director of the company was criticised a number of times. She tended to go off and do things herself without telling everyone else. For example, she raised the prices of some games without telling anyone. This led to some disputes with customers and possibly some lost sales. She tended to work in isolation and frequently missed board meetings. She tended to neglect her responsibilities as a director.

Mark Band 3 *You need to write a comprehensive and objective report, fully supported with examples, which assesses the contribution made by other officers in the company.*

The chairperson of the company performed very well indeed. He was very professional and took his role seriously. He was an excellent communicator. For example, he wrote a regular newsletter for shareholders informing them about the progress of the company. He also took the trouble to speak to individual shareholders when asked to. He worked particularly well with the rest of the company officers and helped to generate a really good team spirit. It was good fun being part of his team. He led by example and worked very hard. This helped to motivate the rest of team and contributed significantly to the success of the company.

The main strength of the marketing director was her ideas. For example, it was her idea to extend the product range and visit trade fairs at weekends. Although this was hard work, we made a lot of money. However, unfortunately she was not a good team member. She liked to work independently. This led to communication problems because we were often unaware of her intentions. For example, she increased the prices of some products without telling anyone. This caused a problem with some customers and possibly resulted in some lost sales. She also failed to attend several important meetings and she did not always know what was going on.

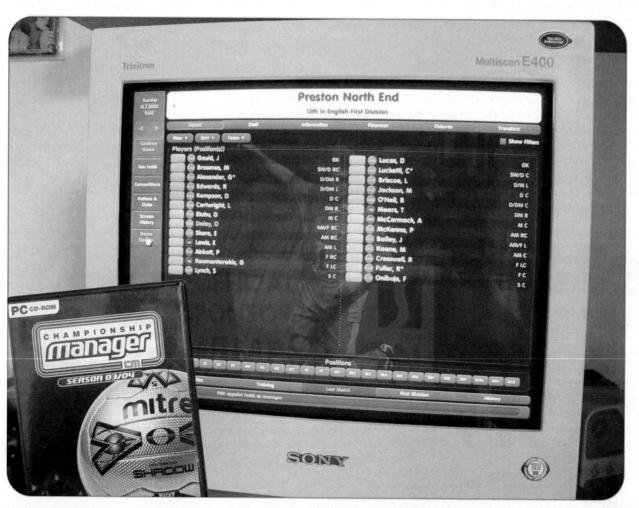

The need for monitoring

Once a company has been incorporated, monitoring its performance is essential. This might be done by assessing the performance of the functional areas. By evaluating the performance of different areas in the business such as the Production, Marketing, Human Resources and Finance Departments, it may be possible to improve the performance of the company as a whole. The performance of the whole company is usually reflected by the amount of profit made. However, the amount of profit made will not show how well each functional area is performing. For example, if profit starts to fall it could be due to:

- inefficient production methods;
- poor sales performance;
- poor quality staff caused by ineffective recruitment;
- overspending due to poor financial management;

Constant monitoring of functional areas is needed to identify weaknesses and inefficiencies. Once they have been identified corrective action can be taken and improvements made. This section looks at how the Human Resources (HR) function might be monitored.

Human resources

The human resources of the business are the people employed to help produce goods and services. In a small organisation, such as a mobile PC engineer, the owner might be the only human resource. He or she will carry out most, if not all, of the tasks. However, in a large company such as Vodafone, thousands of people are employed. As companies grow, and more people are employed, it is common for a business to set up a human resources (HR) department. To ensure that the HR department is performing well

constant monitoring will be necessary.

Figure 1 shows the role of the HR department at Vodafone.

Team working

Section 00 looked at the importance of team working in companies. There are significant benefits from organising staff in teams such as flexibility and improved motivation. However, a business still needs to monitor the contribution made by teams in the business. It might do this by setting targets for each team. For example, a bank might set targets for each branch such as the number of new mortgages sold. The HR department is likely to be involved in the gathering and evaluation of data regarding team performance. It may write reports or give presentations to senior managers or the board of directors showing how teams have performed.

The department will also be required to give **support** to teams and help to **motivate** them. The quality of such support will have an effect on the team's performance and level of motivation. For example, if the HR department fails to deal with staff queries effectively, or provide poor quality training, teams may be less motivated and less productive. The quality of support given to teams by the HR department may be monitored, by asking staff to fill in questionnaires about the service and training they have experienced.

Communication

The HR department will play a key role in the communication of information in a company. Good communication in an organisation will help improve performance. It is therefore important to monitor how well the HR department communicates information.

Figure 1 *HR management at Vodafone*

The HR mission at Vodafone is 'To provide leadership, processes and expertise in order to improve organization and people capability and create a sustainable competitive advantage'. The HR Department is 'responsible for recruiting, selecting, retaining and developing talented individuals'. The functions of the department include:

- organisational capability – providing effective organisational structure, job roles, responsibilities and culture;
- resourcing and talent management – developing talent and ensuring vacancies are filled internally;
- communications and employee relations – providing advice to employees and feedback from employees;
- policy and practices – meeting legal requirements and providing best practice in areas such as pay and work time;
- compensation and benefits – providing pensions, maternity pay and share schemes, for example;
- people development and succession – providing training and leadership and recognition programmes.

Source: adapted from www.vodafone.com.

This might be done by looking at how effective information is communicated formally using the following methods.

Meetings Most businesses use meetings to communicate. For example, they are used to generate ideas, exchange information, negotiate deals, inform people of changes and obtain feedback. It is important that meetings are efficient and achieve their aims. Meetings will tend to be more effective if there is a proper agenda and firm leadership. On the other hand, meetings can waste valuable company time if they are dominated by one person, do not stick to the agenda, go on for too long or fail to reach meaningful conclusions. The effectiveness of meetings may be difficult to measure. However, if a company holds too many or too few meetings, this would be considered ineffective. The HR department must also ensure that minutes of meetings are kept when appropriate. They must also be made available to those who are entitled to access. Company meetings might be evaluated by using staff questionnaires. Finally, meetings should result in action. If meetings fail to result in outcomes, it might be argued that there is little point in having meetings.

Notices An easy way of communicating information is to use a notice board. It is cheap and can be used to pass on information to large numbers of people. However, there is no guarantee that everyone will read the notice and it does not allow any feedback. Again, it is difficult to monitor the effectiveness of notices as a means of communication. But if the notice board is kept tidy, up to date and relevant, people will get into the habit of reading notices and benefit from the method.

ICT An increasing amount of information is transferred using information and communication technology. Examples of electronic media include e-mail, mobile phones, answerphones, paging devices, videoconferencing and teleconferencing, laptop computers, the Internet and fax machines. These can be used for both internal and external communication. The rapid development in such technology has improved business communications significantly. However, there are also problems with technological methods of communication. For example, if it breaks down there may be a complete stop to communication for a while. There may also be a problem from staff abuse. Some businesses have found that some staff use the technology for their own personal use. For example, company time has been wasted when staff use the Internet when they should be working. The HR department may be responsible for monitoring Internet use in organisations. In some cases companies have withdrawn or restricted Internet access to staff.

Written communication All companies transmit information using letters, reports, forms and memos. Monitoring this type of communication may involve reviewing the design of standard letters and forms for example. Written information should be concise and clear. Over lengthy reports and poorly written letters should be avoided for example.

Face-to-face communication In addition to meetings, information will be passed on verbally by people. For example, staff will have to discuss progress, problems and methods relating to their work. Working in teams requires a lot of face-to-face communication for example. The problem for companies is to ensure that staff are talking about work and not spending too much time discussing non-work matters. This is difficult to monitor

but the productivity of teams and individuals may serve as a guide to how much time is being wasted.

Methods of reviewing and monitoring the HR function

To monitor the performance of the HR department it is necessary to gather data. The methods of monitoring can be quantitative, measurable in numbers, or qualitative, assessed by opinions. Examples of methods that might be used are shown in Figure 2.

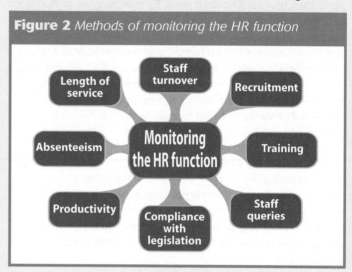

Figure 2 *Methods of monitoring the HR function*

Monitoring the HR function

- Length of service
- Staff turnover
- Recruitment
- Absenteeism
- Training
- Productivity
- Compliance with legislation
- Staff queries

Staff turnover This measures the number of people that leave a business during the year as a percentage of the total number of people employed. It is important to keep staff turnover low because it is expensive to recruit and train new staff. If staff turnover is low this might suggest that the HR department is doing a good job – recruiting the right sort of people, supporting them and providing sufficient motivation. An example is shown in Figure 3.

Figure 3 *Staff turnover at Volkswagen Group UK*

Volkswagen Group UK employed 508 staff in 2004 and had a staff turnover of 6%. This means that about 30 staff left during the year.

Source: adapted from *The Sunday Times*, 6.3.2005

Cost and speed of recruitment The cost of recruitment might reflect how well the HR department is performing. If the department is inefficient the cost of recruitment per worker will be high. Also, if positions are vacant for a long time, this could also reflect badly on the department.

Length of service If employees are happy at work they are more likely to stay with the company. The average length of service may reflect the performance of the HR department. If it supports staff effectively, keeps people informed, provides good induction and training and pushes for good working conditions, employees are likely to stay for longer.

Cost and quality of training The HR department is usually responsible for meeting the training needs of employees. If the training budget is used effectively and staff benefit from the training organised this will reflect well on the HR department. The quality of training may be monitored using staff questionnaires after training sessions. A lot of training is to do with health and safety. As a result the number of reported accidents might reflect the performance of the department.

Absenteeism The number of days taken off by staff for sickness and other reasons might reflect on the HR department. This is an easy record to monitor but may not reflect accurately the performance of the HR department. A wide range of factors might result in high absenteeism rates, such as the culture of the organisation.

Labour productivity Since the HR department is responsible for recruiting good quality staff and training them, it could be argued that their performance affects labour productivity in the company. If labour productivity starts to fall it could be because the staff recruited are not suitable. This would reflect badly on the department.

Dealing with staff queries The amount of time the HR department takes to deal with staff queries would be a way of monitoring its performance. For example, if staff find that the department is slow to deal with queries on payslips this may lead to frustration and anxiety. Staff might complain and the number of complaints would be a reflection of the department's performance. If complaints are recorded, this would provide evidence of performance.

Compliance with employment and health and safety legislation It is likely to be the responsibility of the HR department to ensure that the company complies with all employment and health and safety legislation. Employees have certain rights and are entitled to a contract of employment and safe working conditions, for example. The number of disputes and the amount of time and money spent fighting legal battles might be a way of monitoring the HR department's performance in this respect.

Compliance with the Data Protection Act The HR department is likely to hold a lot of information about employees on computer. In holding this information they must comply with the **Data Protection Act, 1998**. For example, the data held must be adequate, relevant and not excessive. Any failure to comply under this Act would reflect badly on the HR department.

Although it might be possible to monitor the performance of the HR department using some of the above indicators, it must be remembered that other factors might also influence those same indicators. For example, labour productivity is affected by a range of factors such as the quality of tools and equipment provided, the incentive schemes employed and the quality of leadership. It may be difficult to separate out the contribution made by the HR department when monitoring its performance.

Personal reviews

In addition to monitoring the performance of the company and its functional areas, it is common to assess or review the performance of individuals. In many organisations it is the job of a line manager to monitor the progress made by individual members of staff. For example, a line manager might write an annual report commenting on the contribution made by individual members of staff.

An increasingly common method is to use **appraisal**. This is where an employee meets with a manager to discuss their progress over the last year, for example. The purpose of appraisal is to find out the qualities, usefulness or worth of its employees. It is an opportunity to have a frank discussion about the contribution made by an individual to the running of a business. The topics of discussion might be whether work targets have been met and what targets will be set for next year. The training needs of individuals and promotion prospects might also be discussed. Sometimes appraisal might form the basis of pay awards. Appraisal systems tend to be more effective if they are open and interactive. Sometimes self appraisal or peer appraisal might be used to review individual contributions.

1. Obtain permission to question one or two employees in a large company near where you live. Design a questionnaire that could be used to evaluate the performance of the HR department. You could ask questions about:
   - the quality of induction;
   - the amount and quality of training;
   - how quickly staff queries are dealt with;
   - what support the department gives to staff;
   - how well information is communicated;
   - whether staff work in teams;
   - how often meetings are held and whether they are useful.
2. On the basis of the answers write a brief report commenting on how well you think the company's HR department is performing.

Research task

Portfolio practice · Botanic Inns and Lindum Group

Botanic Inns

Botanic Inns runs 10 bar-restaurant-pubs, a hotel and two off-licences. It is based in Belfast and employs 467 staff, 55% of whom are male. Staff turnover is quite high at 72%. But employees enjoy a number of benefits, such as competitive rates of pay, a contributory pension scheme, company sick pay, four week's paid holiday, flexible working options, childcare vouchers, a company gym and life assurance. The training provided for new recruits is excellent. Stephen Magorrian, managing director, gives an induction speech and a flash dedicated training bar with reflective mirrors is used in a purpose built training area. About £138,000 was spent funding off-the-job training in 2004. More then 75% of staff say they get the support they want to learn new skills.

Lindum Group

Lindum Group is a construction company based in Lincoln. It is chiefly a house-builder but does have a number of other land and construction interests. Lindum employs 500 staff, 84% of whom are male. In 2004 its staff turnover was 3% and, according to a survey published by *The Sunday Times*, was the 30th best company to work for in the UK. All staff have a personal development plan. 70% of them say that their work is stimulating and 79% said they would not leave tomorrow if offered another job.

Source: adapted from *The Sunday Times*, 6.3.2005.

(a) What is meant by staff turnover?

(b) How might the performance of the HR function account for the different staff turnovers in the above companies?

(c) Discuss other ways in which the performance of the HR function might be monitored in the above businesses.

Meeting the assessment criteria

You need to prepare a group presentation and report which explains the planning and preparation that went into the launch of the company. You also need to assess the issues involved in the day-to-day running and monitoring of the business. In this section the focus will be on human resource issues.

Business example - Chill Out

Chill Out is an enterprise run by students who plan to sell a range of products designed to reduce stress. Its range of soothing and calming products aims to relax the user and give them an energising boost. Examples of the products include the following:

- **Lip Balm (£3.00)** Lip balm in two flavours - milk chocolate and chocolate orange - packaged in a chocolate or orange coloured container.
- **Cooling Eye Masks (£6.00)** Reusable, relaxing eye masks designed to prevent irritated eyes.
- **Ice Lolly Soaps (£3.75)** Scented novelty soaps.
- **Bath Confetti (£4.20)** Rose scented bath confetti in 'designer' packaging.

Chill Out sells its products at school on Wednesdays and Thursdays and also sets up stalls at local trade fairs.

Mark Band 1 *Provide evidence of a basic contribution to the group presentation and report.*

Communication, team work and personal reviews

One of the strengths of the company was the way in which everyone worked together as a team. Everyone was excited about the prospects of the company and worked hard to make it a success. All team members were well motivated and communicated effectively. However, we seemed to have a lot of meetings which took up a lot of time. I was responsible for taking the minutes because I was company secretary. However, I kept them brief because it was difficult to keep a record of what everyone was saying. Peer appraisal was used to review personal contributions to the running of the company.

Mark Band 2 *Provide evidence of a sound contribution to the group presentation and report.*

Communication, team work and personal reviews

The team running the company were very well motivated and worked hard for each other. There was rarely any conflict and decisions were usually made swiftly without any serious disagreement. This meant that meetings went quite smoothly and not too much time was wasted. However, there did seem to be a lot of meetings and sometimes they may have been a little unnecessary. Communication between team members was also good. Most internal communication was face-to-face because we all saw each other at school every day. However, e-mails were used quite regularly and we often kept in touch using mobile phones, particularly when working out of school. Everyone seemed to know what was going on. Personal contributions to the running of the company were reviewed using peer appraisal. This was OK but I don't think we were sufficiently critical of each other.

Mark Band 3 *Provide evidence of a substantial contribution to the group presentation and report.*

Communication, team work and personal reviews

The team running the company operated as a cohesive unit. At meetings there was a lot of good ideas and meaningful discussion. The meetings were well led although they did tend to go on for longer than planned. Minutes were kept but tended to be brief. Team members communicated openly and everyone understood each other's roles and responsibilities. Most communication was face-to-face because we saw each other every day. However, at weekends we used e-mails and mobile phones. Mobile phones were particularly useful when organising trade fairs at weekends. As sales director I had to keep the purchasing officer informed about how much needed to be bought. I spoke to her nearly every day. We were determined not to let any customers down by running out of stock. The contribution made by each member of the team was reviewed using peer appraisal. This was quite useful. We were able to talk openly about each other. However, it could be argued that many of our comments and conclusions lacked constructive criticism. We could be accused of being 'self-congratulatory'. This may have been because most of us were friends anyway.

Production

Production involves transforming resources such as materials and components into useful products. For example, production at Cadbury Schweppes might involve using milk, sugar, cocoa and other ingredients to make chocolate bars. However, production also includes the provision of services. This is where resources such as labour and tools are used to carry out a useful task for a customer. For example, a market research agency might employ a team of people to carry out a telephone survey to gather information on people's drinking habits for a pub chain. For most businesses production is the most important function. It uses the most resources and takes up most of the company's time. This means that careful monitoring is necessary to ensure that:

- production targets are met;
- quality is maintained;
- resources are not wasted;
- the production environment is safe.

How are production levels set?

Most businesses will set targets for production levels, perhaps daily or weekly. Figure 1 shows the factors that might influence these levels.

Demand The whole production function will be driven by demand. The nature of the products or services required by consumers, and the amounts required, will be determined by the orders or expected orders placed by customers. For example, ice-cream manufacturers expect demand for their products to rise in the summer, therefore they may have to increase production.

Capacity Production levels are restricted by the total capacity of the production unit. A business cannot produce more than its current resources will allow. For example, a small car manufacturer may be able to produce a maximum of 14 cars a week when working at full capacity. It cannot produce any more because it does not have the space, labour and machinery to cope with higher production levels.

Productivity Although a business may have a restricted capacity, production levels can vary according to the efficiency or productivity of its resources. For example, by offering incentives to workers it may be possible to raise output levels.

Quality It could be argued that products with demanding quality specifications take longer to produce. For example, it takes longer to produce a high quality suit than a cheaper inferior one. Sometimes the standard of work required when making high quality products or supplying high quality services means that production levels are lower.

Stock levels The amount a business plans to produce will also depend on stock levels held. If stock levels are currently high production levels may be set lower. This is because stock is often expensive to hold.

Monitoring and controlling production

Production will tend to be more efficient if it is carefully planned, controlled and monitored. The diagram in Figure 2 shows the various stages that might be involved in the planning and monitoring of production.

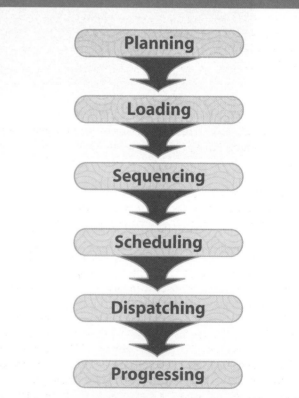

Figure 2 *Stages in the planning, monitoring and controlling of production*

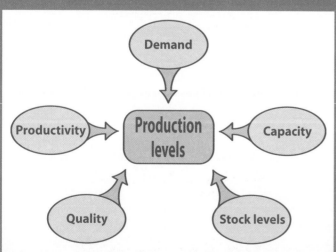

Figure 1 *Factors influencing production levels*

Planning This involves setting the production total or target for the day or week and making sure that the production unit has sufficient resources to meet that target. The target set will depend on the factors discussed above. In many cases production might involve producing lots of different products, with different specifications and at different times. For example, the bakeries in supermarkets produce a wide range of different sorts of breads, rolls, buns, cakes and muffins, for example. Planners must decide the order in which the different products are made.

Loading This involves deciding which 'work centres' will carry out which tasks. A work centre might be an employee, a machine, a production cell or a process such as painting.

Sequencing Most production requires tasks and processes to be carried out in a particular sequence. For example, when building a house the foundations must be laid before bricklayers can begin their task.

Scheduling The production schedule will show times when particular tasks and processes start and finish. This is particularly important when organising large production projects such as in construction. The aim of scheduling is to ensure that resources are not idle waiting for the completion of a previous task. It is obviously wasteful if a newspaper editor is kept waiting because an article or report is not finished by the agreed deadline.

Dispatching This involves giving instructions about tasks to the workforce. They may be given daily or weekly and can be written or verbal.

Progressing This is an ongoing monitoring process. It requires supervisors, teams or managers reporting on the progress of their jobs. Managers or teams may help to solve problems that arise during production. They will also encourage staff to work more quickly if targets are not being met.

Companies are likely to compare the production totals each day or week with the targets set. If targets are not met there may be a need for an investigation to find out the reasons why. Once these have been identified corrective action might be necessary. For example, if production has been held up because machinery keeps breaking down, it may be time to invest in new machines.

Quality control

Businesses are generally under pressure to supply customers with high quality products. Failing to meet the quality needs of customers will eventually result in lost orders. Poor quality also results in other costs, such as waste resources and rework. Most businesses recognise that quality is needed in the final product, production processes and customer services. There is a number of approaches to ensure that quality is monitored carefully throughout the company.

Total quality management (TQM) TQM is an approach to quality control which aims to prevent errors and poor quality before they happen. It is a philosophy in business where the entire workforce is responsible for quality. Every single employee in the organisation is trained to check, inspect and improve their work all of the time. One of the key features of TQM is strict monitoring. Many businesses use statistical process control (SPC) to monitor quality. This involves collecting data relating to the performance of a process (a production process such as forming, shaping or welding in this case) and analysing it in detail. SPC can help to identify variability in processes. Variability is often the cause of

poor quality and SPC will help to eliminate it.

Quality assurance Quality assurance attempts to guarantee that quality has been maintained at all stages in the production process. Again, the aim is to prevent problems before they arise not after they occur. This method of ensuring quality takes into account customers' views in the production process. Sometimes they may even be consulted during planning.

Independent bodies One common approach to monitoring quality is to involve an independent body to check for quality. For example, the British Standards Institution (BSI) is an independent organisation that attempts to set quality standards in industry. The BSI will check for quality by making regular inspections of production processes. Companies seeking certification must show that their processes meet the recognised standards set by the BSI. Once a business has demonstrated it is capable of reaching and maintaining the BSI standards, it is awarded a certificate, such as BSI EN ISO 9000. However, regular inspections are continued indefinitely by the BSI to monitor standards.

Monitoring complaints The number of complaints received by a business will reflect the quality of its products and services. Some businesses keep detailed records of complaints. These can be used to help make improvements in the future. Dealing with complaints effectively will help protect the image of the company. Learning from mistakes will also improve performance in the future.

Purchasing

Purchasing involves acquiring the resources such as materials, components, fuel, tools, equipment, machinery, stationery and services that are needed by the business. Some of these will be bought outright others will be leased or hired. Figure 3 shows the stages in the purchasing process.

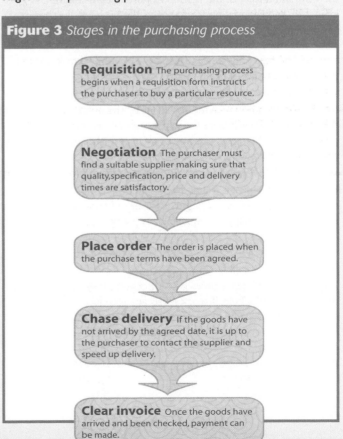

Figure 3 *Stages in the purchasing process*

Requisition The purchasing process begins when a requisition form instructs the purchaser to buy a particular resource.

Negotiation The purchaser must find a suitable supplier making sure that quality, specification, price and delivery times are satisfactory.

Place order The order is placed when the purchase terms have been agreed.

Chase delivery If the goods have not arrived by the agreed date, it is up to the purchaser to contact the supplier and speed up delivery.

Clear invoice Once the goods have arrived and been checked, payment can be made.

Figure 4 *A vendor rating form*

Criteria	Importance	Vendor A *	**	Vendor B *	**	Vendor C *	**
Costs	1.0	2.5	2.5	1	1.0	2.5	2.5
Product/service quality	1.2	2.5	3.0	1	1.2	1	1.2
Warranty	0.8	2.5	2.0	1	0.8	1	0.8
Reputation/references	1.2	1	1.2	2.5	3.0	1	1.2
Financial stability	1.0	1	1.0	2.5	2.5	0.5	0.5

Importance values		Vendor score values	
Very high	1.2	Excellent	2.5
High	1.1	Good	2.0
Moderate	1.0	OK	1.0
Low	0.8	Poor	0.75
Very low	0.5	Very poor	0.5

Vendor rating 9.7   **Vendor rating** 8.5   **Vendor rating** 6.2

* This column is the actual value assigned this rating.

** This column is the adjusted value of the rating based on the importance of the criterion.

Source: adapted from Mikulak Consulting.

Monitoring purchasing

For businesses that buy lots of different resources, such as manufacturers, purchasing is an important function. This is because the cost and quality of the resources purchased can have a large impact on the financial performance of the business. Purchasers need to get the best possible quality and the lowest possible cost. They also need reliable suppliers that can deliver resources when needed. The following approaches might be used to monitor the performance of purchasers.

Purchases budgets The use of budgets in purchasing may help to control the amount of money spent by the purchasing department. This will exert some pressure on the department to buy prudently. If budgets are overspent, this might suggest that the resources purchased are too expensive.

Vendor rating If purchasers use a vendor rating system it is likely that their performance will be better. Vendor rating involves comparing suppliers according to a variety of criteria such as quality, price, reliability and flexibility. By giving suppliers a 'score' or vendor rating, only the best suppliers will be selected. Figure 4 shows a possible form that may be used. Vender A is the highest rated vender in the example.

Stock levels The performance of purchasers may be reflected by the level of stocks held. If stock levels are too high, excessive storage costs might be incurred such as warehousing, handling and opportunity cost. On the other hand, if the production department runs out of stocks of materials and components, production might be delayed and customers let down. The purchasing department must ensure that the 'right' level of stocks is maintained consistently over time.

Waste levels The amount of materials and other resources wasted in production might reflect the performance of purchasers. Poor quality materials often results in more waste. For example, if cheap paper is used in a printer, it may jam more often and be wasted. It may also damage the printer.

1. Visit a local supermarket to see how it monitors and deals with complaints. You could use a short questionnaire to find out:
   - how often complaints are made;
   - what the complaints are usually about;
   - how the supermarket compensates customers;
   - how complaints are recorded;
   - how the supermarket learns from complaints.
2. Write a brief report outlining your findings and suggest whether, in your opinion, the supermarket is monitoring quality adequately through its complaints procedure.

Research task

Portfolio practice · Armadillo

Armadillo produces simple knitwear products – scarves, woolly hats and sweaters. The company owns a second-hand knitting machine which was purchased cheaply from a factory sale. The production team are set weekly targets by the production manager who has to decide how many of each product should be produced. The production manager is also responsible for monitoring production. He does this by:

- comparing the weekly production totals with the targets. Table 1 shows production targets and actual production levels at Armadillo for the last six weeks;
- recording the amount of waste;
- recording 'downtime', i.e. the amount of time wasted when production stops due to machinery breakdowns;
- recording the output of different operatives.

In recent weeks the amount of downtime due to machinery breakdowns has increased significantly. Problems with the knitting machine have also resulted in an increase in waste.

Table 1 *Production at Armadillo for a six week period*

Week	1	2	3	4	5	6
Production targets						
Scarves	20	20	25	25	28	28
Hats	30	30	30	30	30	30
Sweaters	40	40	40	40	40	40
Production totals						
Scarves	18	19	21	20	22	23
Hats	28	31	32	24	32	28
Sweaters	30	35	32	40	33	36

(a) State THREE factors that will influence the production targets set by Armadillo.

(b) (i) Describe how production is monitored by Armadillo.

(ii) Evaluate the performance of the production function at Armadillo.

(c) How might the performance of the production function be improved at Armadillo?

Meeting the assessment criteria

You need to prepare a group presentation and report which explains the planning and preparation that went into the launch of the company. You also need to assess the issues involved in the day-to-day running and monitoring of the business. In this section the focus will be on monitoring production, quality and purchasing.

Business example - Trinkets 4U

Trinkets 4U is a small student company which makes and sells jewellery such as bracelets, earrings, brooches, bangles, rings and small fashion accessories. Production is an important part of the venture. The company started by making standard pieces of jewellery. However, a lot of customers now want pieces made to order. The move towards 'one-off' pieces meant that quality was more difficult to maintain. Consequently the board of directors, following the advice of the production manager, created the post of Quality Supervisor. The Quality Supervisor was responsible for training the jewellers in quality matters and checking their work. The supervisor also worked closely with the purchaser to ensure that good quality materials were purchased.

Mark Band 1 *Provide evidence of a basic contribution to the group presentation and report.*
It was important to monitor quality in our enterprise. People like attractive jewellery and sometimes, when we were busy,

the work was rushed and some of the jewellery came apart. This was costly to the business because it had to be either repaired or replaced. However, when the quality supervisor was created, quality improved. We were encouraged to make the jewellery more carefully and check each other's work. The number of returns and complaints fell after this. I was a member of the production team and helped to raise the quality of jewellery.

Mark Band 2 *Provide evidence of a sound contribution to the group presentation and report.*
Everyone in the company recognised that quality was important. The type of jewellery made by Trinkets 4U was similar to a lot of other jewellery on sale in the local area, at market stalls for example. However, when the production team was busy, trying to meet difficult production targets, quality sometimes suffered. As a result the board appointed me as quality supervisor to take responsibility for quality. I set some quality standards and trained the production team in quality. I tried to implement a TQM approach in the company where everyone understood the importance of quality and knew how it could be delivered. I encouraged production workers to check and inspect each other's work. This proved to be a good move because the number of complaints and returns fell by 80% after this.

Mark Band 3 *Provide evidence of a substantial contribution to the group presentation and report.*

Trinkets 4U operates in a highly competitive market. The sort of jewellery made by the company can be bought from a range of outlets such as markets and street vendors. Trinkets 4U decided to produce high quality jewellery to get a competitive edge. However, quality began to suffer when demand grew. The production team found it difficult to cope with the production targets and some of the quality of work was not up to standard. Consequently the board decided to appoint a quality supervisor. The supervisor encouraged the production team to take pride in their work. They were trained to check and inspect each others work and take responsibility for quality. Some quality standards were also set, and as a result, returns and complaints fell by 80%. As the main purchaser, I worked closely with the quality supervisor. We started to buy better quality materials from some new suppliers. However, to monitor purchasing I had to stick to a budget. This was to make sure that I did not overspend. We also noticed that waste was reduced when we started buying better quality materials. They were more robust and did not break in production.

The need for financial monitoring

It is important to monitor the financial performance of a business. By keeping a regular check on certain financial performance indicators, a number of serious pitfalls can be avoided. Monitoring financial performance might help to achieve the following aims.

Maintain adequate cash levels The worst thing that could probably happen to a successful business is for it to run out of cash. Without cash, a business cannot trade. For example, if there is not enough cash to pay staff they will not work and the business could not function effectively.

Keep costs down If a business can keep costs down it will make more profit. Spending too much on resources, or buying resources that are not really necessary, will result in escalating costs. For example, if a business buys a machine that is only used for six hours a week, this may be considered wasteful if the machine could be hired for six hours.

Avoid over-borrowing Businesses often have to borrow money. For example, they might go overdrawn at the bank. However, by restricting the amount and frequency of borrowings, unnecessary interest payments can be avoided. This will reduce the debt burden and raise profits.

Maintain strict credit control The finance department is often responsible for making sure that customers pay their debts on time. It is important to monitor customer payments to ensure that customers pay what they owe. Failure to collect debts when they are due can result in cash flow problems and bad debts.

Achieve profit targets Many businesses set profit targets. When a company first starts trading it might aim to break-even. However, once it is established it will aim to make a profit. The board may set profit targets based on the amount of money invested in the business or aim to achieve certain profit margins based on sales.

A business can monitor its cash position using cash flow forecasts and bank reconciliation statements.

Cash flow forecasts

A company is likely to use a cash flow forecast to monitor its cash position (see section 22). This shows the expected monthly flows of cash into and out of a business for a future time period. It also shows the expected net cash flow and the cash balance at the end of each month. The forecast will serve as a warning to prepare for the months when cash is going to be short.

Table I shows the cash flow forecast for Timmings Ltd, a CD store. The cash position does not look very good for much of the future time period. It is expected to be negative for four of the six months. The business will need to get some cash from somewhere to carry on trading.

Table 1 *Cash flow forecast for Timmings Ltd (£)*

	June	July	Aug	Sep	Oct	Nov
Receipts						
Cash sales	17,000	15,000	15,000	18,000	24,000	23,000
Tax refund						3,400
Total cash receipts	17,000	15,000	15,000	18,000	24,000	26,400
Payments						
Wages	5,000	5,000	5,000	5,250	5,250	5,250
Rent	2,000	2,000	2,000	2,000	2,000	2,000
Stock purchases	6,500	7,000	7,500	8,000	8,000	8,000
Motor expenses	500	500	700	500	700	1,000
Other expenses	2,500	2,500	3,000	3,000	6,500	3,000
Total cash payments	16,500	17,000	18,200	18,750	22,450	19,200
Net cash flow	500	(2,000)	(3,200)	(750)	1,550	7,150
Opening balance	1,200	1,700	(300)	(3,500)	(4,250)	(2,700)
Closing balance	1,700	(300)	(3,500)	(4,250)	(2,700)	4,450

Bank reconciliation statement

A business will also monitor its cash position by regularly checking the bank balance on a statement. Businesses keep a record of all payments and receipts in a cash book. From these records they can calculate their cash position. However, the balance in the cash book is not likely to be the same as the balance on the bank statement. Consequently their true cash position will be unclear. There is a number of reasons for this.

Unpresented cheques Cheques take at least three working days to 'clear'. Clearing is the term used in banking to describe the transfer of funds from one bank account to another. This means that cheques posted to suppliers may not appear on the bank statement for many days. Since these unpresented cheques have not been cleared, the bank balance will be inaccurate. It will overstate the amount of money in the bank.

Uncleared lodgements It also takes time for money deposited in a bank to appear on the bank statement. If these uncleared lodgements do not appear on the bank statement, the actual bank balance will be understated.

Omissions from records Some payments and receipts may be omitted from a company's cash book and will not come to light until a bank statement is received. These transactions include bank charges, interest and direct transfers such as direct debits and standing orders. Companies usually wait for a bank statement until recording them in the cash book. Consequently, the balance in the cash book will be different from the balance on the bank statement.

Errors It is possible that bookkeeping errors could result in a difference between the balance in the cash book and the balance on a bank statement. For example, if a payment made is omitted from the company's records, the balance in the cash book will be overstated.

Dishonoured cheques It is possible for a customer's cheque to 'bounce'. This means that a customer's bank refuses to transfer funds from the customer's account when the cheque is paid in. Banks may refuse to honour cheques for a number of reasons. For example, the customer may not have any funds in the bank or there may be a mistake on the cheque. If a customer's cheque is dishonoured the balance in the cash book will be overstated.

Because of the difference between the balance in the company's cash book and the balance on the bank statement (caused by the issues above) it is necessary to reconcile the two. Once this has been done the true cash position of a business can be determined. A bank reconciliation statement is used for this purpose.

How is a bank reconciliation statement prepared?

To prepare a bank reconciliation statement the following information is needed:
- balance on the bank statement;
- details of any uncleared lodgements;
- details of any unpresented cheques;
- balance in the cash book.

This information can be provided by bookkeepers by checking entries made in the cash book against entries on the bank statement. Part of the checking process will also involve bringing the company's cash book up to date by entering transactions such as bank charges and direct debits listed in the bank statement. A bank reconciliation statement is shown for H Manning Ltd, a small construction company, in Table 2.
- The first entry shows the balance from the bank statement. In this case it is £3,200. However, this does not represent the amount of money the business has available to spend.
- The company has paid £850 into the bank which has not yet shown up on the statement. This must be added to the bank

balance making a total of £4,050.
- It is also necessary to subtract the value of any unpresented cheques. According to the reconciliation statement, £3,100 of cheques have not yet been cleared.
- When the value of unpresented cheques are subtracted from the total, the actual amount of money the business has available to spend is shown. In this case it is £950.

The bank reconciliation statement plays an important role in the monitoring of cash in the business.
- It shows exactly how much cash a business has to spend and therefore helps a business to avoid overspending.
- Dishonoured cheques will be identified because they won't appear on the bank statement.
- It provides a check for dishonesty. For example, if a business cheque is dishonestly made payable to an employee it will eventually appear on the bank statement even though it will be missing from the company's cash book.

Table 2 *Bank reconciliation statement for H Manning Ltd*

H Manning Ltd
Bank Reconciliation Statement as at 31.7.05

	£
Balance as per bank statement	3,200
Add uncleared lodgement	850
	4,050
Less unpresented cheques	3,100
Balance as per cash book	**950**

Monitoring profit levels

The amount of profit made by a company is one of the most important indicators of financial performance. It is common for businesses to set targets for profit. If profit targets are met then this suggests that a company is matching the expectations of owners and managers. A business may use a break-even chart to monitor profit levels. For example, it can be used to see the different profit levels that can be made at various levels of output.

Figure 1 shows a break-even chart for Tulip, a mini enterprise that sells student stationery packs. It shows the profit the enterprise would make depending on the number of packs sold. The enterprise incurs fixed costs of £60 and charges £5 per pack. The variable costs per pack are £3. The enterprise breaks even when 30 packs are sold. The chart shows that as more packs are sold the amount of profit made rises. For example, if 80 packs are sold the profit is £100.

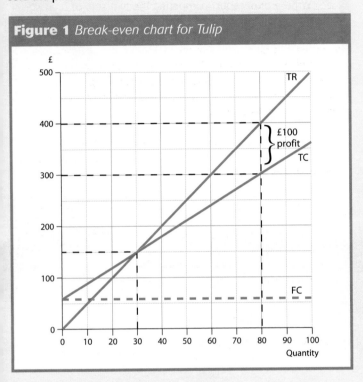

Figure 1 *Break-even chart for Tulip*

Monitoring profit margins

Some companies monitor the performance of a company by analysing profit margins. One approach is to look at the gross profit margin. This measures the profit before overheads as a percentage of turnover. The gross profit margin, sometimes known as the mark-up, is shown in Figure 2.

Higher gross margins are more favourable and they vary significantly between different industries. A company can increase gross margins by lowering cost of sales or raising prices.

Figure 2 *Gross profit margin*

$$\text{Gross profit margin} = \frac{\text{Gross profit}}{\text{Turnover}} \times 100$$

Figure 3 *Net profit margin*

$$\text{Net profit margin} = \frac{\text{Net profit}}{\text{Turnover}} \times 100$$

A company might also monitor the net profit margin. This helps to measure how well a business controls its overheads. The net margin calculation is shown in Figure 3.

Table 3 shows the gross and net profit margins for a DIY retailer for a four year period. The information shows that gross profit margins rise over the time period from 14.43% to 21.34%. However, although net profit also rises over the same period, the net profit margin actually falls. In 2002 the net margin was 5.43% but in 2005 it has fallen to 4.78%. This suggests that the business has not been able to keep overheads under control. By monitoring these margins a company will be able to identify poor financial performance.

Table 3 *Gross and net profit margins for a DIY retailer*

	2002	2003	2004	2005
Turnover (£)	187,000	210,000	231,000	253,000
Gross profit (£)	27,000	33,000	39,000	54,000
Net profit (£)	10,000	11,000	11,100	12,100
Gross profit margin	14.43%	15.71%	16.88%	21.34%
Net profit margin	5.34%	5.23%	4.81%	4.78%

Monitoring customer payments

One of the most important jobs in the finance department is monitoring customer payments. This involves making sure that customers pay for what they have bought. A lot of businesses offer **trade credit**, which means customers buy goods and pay for them later. They may be allowed up to 90 days to settle their accounts. Credit controllers in the finance department must ensure that customers pay on time and 'chase' debts if customers are slow to pay. One way of monitoring the performance of credit controllers is to calculate the debt collection period. This is the amount of time customers take to pay their bills. The formula is shown in Figure 4.

Figure 4 *Debt collection period*

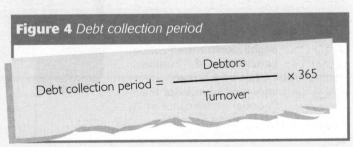

$$\text{Debt collection period} = \frac{\text{Debtors}}{\text{Turnover}} \times 365$$

Table 4 shows the debtors, turnover and debt collection period for Patel & Co, a fruit and vegetable wholesaler. The company allows customers 30 days' credit. According to the information in the table, over the last four years, customers have generally settled their debts when they were due. This is good for the company and suggests that the credit controllers are performing well. It is often the case that customers settle their debts well after their permitted credit period.

Table 4 *Debt collection period for Patel & Co*

	2002	2003	2004	2005
Turnover	£97,500	£89,400	£93,200	£94,200
Debtors	£7,747	£7,593	£8,170	£7,484
Debt collection period		29 days	31 days	32 days	29 days

1. Obtain the annual reports of two companies which are retailers and calculate the following:
   - gross profit margin;
   - net profit margin;
   - debt collection period.
2. Write a brief report comparing the two sets of results and suggest which of the two companies has the best financial performance. You can also compare the progress made by each company by calculating the margins for each year.

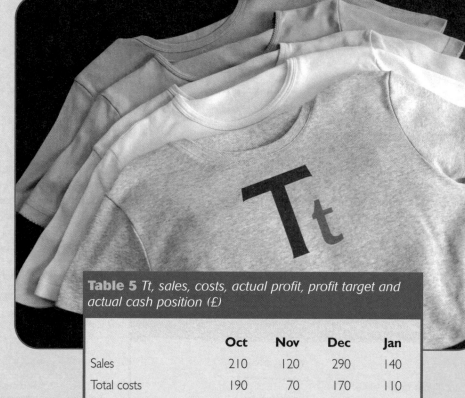

Research task

Portfolio practice · Tt

Tt is an enterprise run by a group of students in Cheshire. The company prints patterns, logos and other images and messages onto T-shirts. Most of the sales are generated at school during lunch times. However, the company have recently visited youth groups and other schools to generate sales. The quality is quite good and some of the designs developed by the design team have been very popular.

Unfortunately, the company was closed down for a couple of weeks in November because the printing machine broke down. Table 5 shows some financial information for a four month period.

(a) **State THREE ways a business might monitor the financial performance of a business.**

(b) **Explain why it is so important to monitor the financial performance of Tt.**

(c) **Evaluate the financial performance of Tt.**

Table 5 *Tt, sales, costs, actual profit, profit target and actual cash position (£)*

	Oct	Nov	Dec	Jan
Sales	210	120	290	140
Total costs	190	70	170	110
Actual profit	20	50	120	30
Profit target	0	100	200	100
Cash balance	20	50	130	230

Meeting the assessment criteria

You need to prepare a group presentation and report which explains the planning and preparation that went into the launch of the company. You also need to assess the issues involved in the day-to-day running and monitoring of the business. In this unit the focus will be on monitoring the financial performance of the company.

Business example - CaneCo

CaneCo is a student company which makes coffee tables from bamboo canes. The table top is made of glass and the canes are bound together with a natural binding material. The cane structure is strong and the tables have proved popular. The tables are sold at trade fairs and local fetes for £20 each. Fixed costs are £50 and variable costs are £15 a table.

Figure 2 shows a break–even chart used by CaneCo. The company aimed to break-even by the end of November. On December 2nd, the sales director informed the board that 15 tables had been sold. Just before the company was wound up in May, a total of 25 tables had been sold. However, it was hoped that a profit of £150 would have been made.

Mark Band 1 *Provide evidence of a basic contribution to the group presentation and report.*
The company's financial performance was quite good. The first financial target was to break-even by the end of November. According to the break-even chart CaneCo needed to sell 10 tables to break-even. On December 2nd, the sales director announced that 15 tables had been sold. This means that the financial target was exceeded. The sale of 15 tables generated a profit of £25. This is shown on the break-even chart. Another profit target of £150 was set before the company was wound up. However, this was missed because sales were not high enough.

Mark Band 2 *Provide evidence of a sound contribution to the group presentation and report.*
One obvious way of monitoring the financial performance of a company is to focus on profit. However, it is helpful if profit

targets are set. If reasonable targets are set it is easier to evaluate the performance of a company. For example, in this case the company wanted to break-even by the end of November. This target was easily exceeded. Sales of 10 tables were needed to break-even but 15 tables were sold. This generated a profit of £25. The total revenue from selling 15 tables was £300 and the total cost was £275. As a result it could be concluded that the company has performed well. Unfortunately the company was not able to meet its final profit target. It was hoped that a profit of £150 would be made before the company was wound up. However, by the end of May only 25 tables were sold which generated a profit of just £75. Total revenue was £500 and total costs were £425.

Mark Band 3 *Provide evidence of a comprehensive contribution to the group presentation and report.*
The financial performance of a company can be monitored in a number of ways. First of all it is important to constantly monitor the cash position of the business. This is because if the company runs out of cash it cannot trade. The cash position of CaneCo was monitored using a cash flow forecast. However, most managers and owners are most interested in the profit made by a business.

In the short life of CaneCo, two important profit targets were set. The first was to break-even by the end of November. This target was exceeded. According to the break-even chart it was necessary to sell 10 tables to break-even. On December 2nd the sales director informed the board that 15 tables had been sold. This resulted in a small profit of £25. Sales of 15 tables generated £300 revenue whilst the total costs were £275.

Unfortunately the financial performance was not really sustained. The second profit target set by the board was to make £150 before the company was wound up in May. However, the final profit was only £75 which resulted from the sale of 25 tables. Total revenue was £500 and total costs were £425. It was felt that the target was missed because some members of the team lost interest in the enterprise towards the end of the venture.

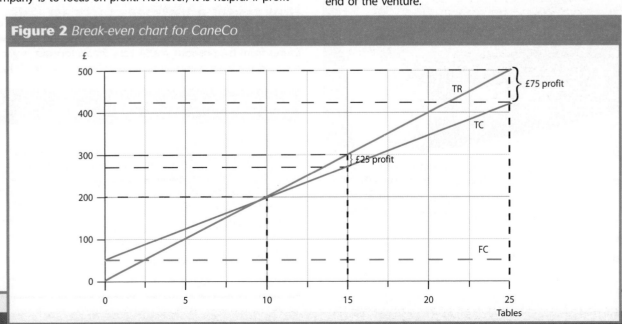

Figure 2 *Break-even chart for CaneCo*

Sales targets

The performance of a company can be measured by the level of sales it generates. Most companies aim to sell as much as they can. However, they are likely to set targets for sales staff. The sales targets may be expressed in units or financial terms.

Some companies, such as supermarkets for example, may set sales targets for each of its stores, each of its departments or each of its product ranges. The targets are likely to be expressed in revenue terms. The use of sales targets provides an effective way of monitoring the company's performance. Targets need to be clear and are often linked to incentives such as commissions and bonuses. This helps to motivate sales staff and provides them with a clear indication of the kind of performance expected of them. The targets set also need to be closely linked with the overall strategy of the business and fit in with production capacity, for example.

Figure 1 Sales forecasts

In June 2005 Intel, the world's largest producer of semi-conductors raised its sales forecast as a result of strong demand for chips used in laptops. It expected sales of between $9.1-9.3 bn for the quarter (around £5.25bn), compared to consensus estimated sales revenue of $8.89 bn.

Source: adapted from http://money.cnn.com.

Setting targets

Businesses may set SMART sales targets. This means that targets will be specific, measurable, agreed, realistic and time specific. This is explained in more detail in unit 17. SMART sales targets are likely to help staff to understand clearly what is expected of them. Sales targets may be broken down into different areas. The following breakdown is an example.

New sales A company will normally want to grow. This involves attracting new customers and sales targets must take growth into account. However, the changing market and economic conditions will also have to be taken into account before the final target is set. It is obviously difficult trying to generate new sales if the market is shrinking.

Renewals Sales staff need to understand that selling isn't just about new business. It is also about retaining existing customers. Obtaining new customers is far more expensive than retaining existing ones. A typical renewals rate is about 60 to 70%.

Lapsed customers Another aspect of selling is trying to recover past customers who have not bought from the company for some time. Again, it is cheaper to make a sale to a lapsed customer than a new one.

Sales forecasting

Before staff sales targets can be set it is necessary to forecast sales for the whole company, as shown in Figure 1. This is usually done once a year and forms the basis of financial and production plans for the year ahead. For example, a month-by-month sales forecast may be used to prepare the sales budget which has an influence on all other budgets in the business. Accurate sales forecasts can help a company avoid cash flow problems and manage its production, staff and financing needs more effectively. Figure 2 shows an example of adjusting sales to meet changing conditions.

How might a business forecast sales?

Extrapolation Many sales forecasts start with the actual sales figures from the previous year. A very simple forecast might look at the sales levels for a certain time period in the past and then just

Figure 2 Sales targets at Unilever

In February 2004 it was predicted that Unilever would cut its sales forecasts greatly and set sales growth targets at 3 to 4%. That compared with a 6% target set when Unilever acquired America's BestFoods. One of the factors leading to this revision was a fall in sales at its Slim-Fast business, which had been hit by the popularity of Atkins, as well as a poor performance in perfumes and the home care business.

Source: adapted from The Observer, 8.2.2004.

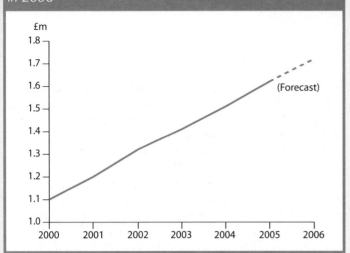

Figure 3 *Sales forecast for an ice-cream manufacturer in 2006*

extrapolate the trend. For example, Figure 3 shows the sales levels for an ice-cream manufacturer between 2000 and 2005. Sales have risen steadily from £1.1m in 2000 to £1.62m in 2005. By extending the sales line shown on the graph at the same gradient, the sales figures for 2006 can be estimated. The dotted line shows that sales are expected to rise to £1.72m in 2006. This method of forecasting is called extrapolation. However, although it is simple it ignores a number of other important factors. These are shown in Figure 4.

Assumption-based forecasting A more accurate way to forecast future sales is to make some assumptions about the factors that influence sales levels. Figure 4 shows some of the main factors that might affect future sales levels.

- Market state. If a market is expanding, such as the market for long haul air travel, it is reasonable to assume that an airline company could sell more seats to long haul destinations. On the basis of this it might raise its sales forecasts for the next year. On the other hand, if the market is nearly saturated, like the market for mobile phones, it might be unrealistic for a mobile telephone retailer to forecast large increases in sales. Information about the size and state of markets can be obtained using market research.
- Competition. The activities of competitors are bound to affect future sales forecasts. If competition is strengthening, it is reasonable to assume that raising sales in the future will be difficult. For example, supermarkets such as Sainsbury, Morrisons and Asda may find it more difficult to raise sales if Tesco becomes stronger and more dominant.
- Promotion. The amount of money spent on promotion and its effectiveness will affect future sales levels. If a company decides to invest in an expensive TV advertising campaign, it would expect future sales to rise.
- New products. When companies introduce new products they are optimistic that sales levels will increase. For example, when a publisher publishes a new book it does not necessarily expect sales of its existing books to fall. As companies continually expand their product range they would expect future sales to rise.
- Capacity. The amount of resources a company has will restrict sales to some degree. Once a company is working at full

capacity it cannot produce any more in the short run. Therefore it is not able to sell any more.
- Staff performance. The performance of sales staff can affect future sales levels. To improve performance staff need effective training, adequate support, sound incentives and realistic targets.

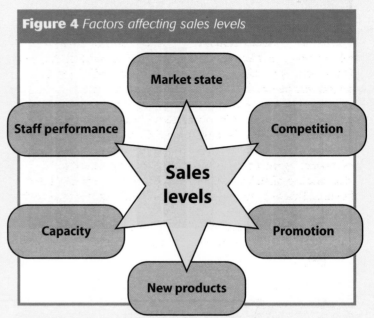

Figure 4 *Factors affecting sales levels*

Measuring the performance of sales staff

It is important to monitor the performance of staff in the sales team. The extent to which they meet sales targets is likely to be the main measure used. This should be fairly easy to monitor in a variety of different business circumstances. For example, the following could be measured quite easily:

- the number of insurance policies sold by a sales person working in a call centre. It is common for call centres to record all calls handled by staff to help monitor performance;
- the number of new cars sold by a car sales person in a dealership;
- the number of new accounts opened by a bank teller;
- the value of sales achieved by a branch in a clothes chain;
- the value of holidays sold by a travel consultant in a travel agents.

A company might also analyse **conversion rates** for sales staff. This is the number of visits, contacts or phone calls it takes to achieve one sale to a customer. Depending on the nature of the business, there may be a standard or average number which is thought to be satisfactory.

A company might also monitor the quality of customer service provided by sales staff. This might be done using customer questionnaires. If sales performance is disappointing or inadequate a company should explore the reasons why. Poor performance may be caused by incompetence or a lack of effort. However, it may result from factors beyond the control of the sales person. For example:

- there may be problems with the product;
- the sales territory may be too wide or difficult;
- there may be a slump in the market;
- sales staff may lack support from the marketing department.

By monitoring sales performance it may be possible to identify problems and eliminate them before there is a serious adverse effect on sales levels.

Figure 5 *An example of scientific research to measure the effect of using TV and magazine advertisements together*

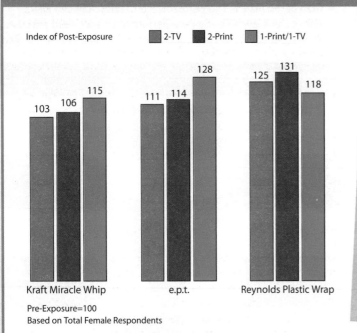

Index of Post-Exposure
- 2-TV
- 2-Print
- 1-Print/1-TV

Kraft Miracle Whip: 103, 106, 115
e.p.t.: 111, 114, 128
Reynolds Plastic Wrap: 125, 131, 118

Pre-Exposure=100
Based on Total Female Respondents

A study funded by MPA (Magazine Publishers of America) looked at the effect of using TV and magazine advertisements together. One aspect of the research looked at the effect on brand selection. The purpose of most advertising is to persuade a consumer to select one brand over another. The survey found that in most cases, the combination of print and television produces higher levels of brand selection than either medium separately. Kraft Miracle Whip and e.p.t. (a home pregnancy testing kit) both had considerably higher indices when television and print were used together. Reynolds Crystal Colour Plastic Wrap had a greater index in the 2-print group. All indices are over 100 because after exposure to the advertisements, brand selection improved in all three groups.

Source: adapted from www.magazine.org.

Promotion strategies

Promotion is the way businesses make customers aware of their products. Generally, the aim of promotion is to obtain and retain customers. However, some specific objectives of promotion can be identified.
- To raise or increase awareness of a product or corporation.
- To reach a target audience which might be geographically dispersed.
- To remind customers about a product by encouraging them to purchase it again.
- To enhance brand loyalty by reassuring customers.
- To improve the image of the company.
- To show that a product is superior to that of a competitor.

A wide range of different promotion methods can be used by a company. They are dealt with in unit 6.

Monitoring promotion

In 2003, over £17,000 million was spent on advertising in Britain. 76% of this was spent on display advertising of products in the press, on television, radio, posters, direct mail, cinema and the Internet. The remaining 24% bought classified advertising (small ads), financial and legal notices, company announcements, recruitment advertising (job ads) and advertising in the business and professional press. Since such huge amounts of money are spent by companies, it is important to monitor the effectiveness of such expenditure. Some examples of methods that companies might use are outlined below.

Market research Some companies may take a scientific approach and employ market researchers to measure the impact of various promotions, such as an advert in the national press or a TV advertisement. Statistical methods may be used to measure the increase in sales resulting from the use of certain advertising media. An example of some scientific research is shown in Figure 5.

Comparing sales levels The effectiveness of promotion can be monitored by comparing sales levels before and after a promotion. For example, sales levels in the month after a TV campaign could be compared with the month before the campaign, or with the same calendar month in the previous year.

Past records Companies may keep a record of how new customers have found out about their services. For example, an insurance company using a call centre to sell premiums may ask new customers how they heard about the company.

The Internet Companies with websites may be able to measure the effect of promotions by recording the number of 'hits' on their site after a promotion or by asking customers to complete questionnaires. Developments in ICT have made it easier to communicate with customers and gather information from them.

Loyalty card information Some companies, such as supermarkets, use loyalty cards which store lots of data about consumer purchases. This could be analysed to see the effect of any promotions.

1. Carry out your own market research to test the effectiveness of TV advertising amongst students at your school or college. You could do this by briefly describing 5 to 10 advertisements that currently appear on TV and then ask respondents which products are being advertised.
2. Present your results using an appropriate charts and graphs and comment briefly on them.

Research task

Problems with monitoring promotion

Monitoring promotion can have some problems.

- Monitoring the effectiveness of different promotions can be time consuming and expensive. For example, the type of scientific research explained in Figure 5 could cost thousands of pounds.
- Quite often a company uses more than one type of promotion method at the same time. Consequently it may be difficult trying to determine which particular method has been the most successful. For example, a toiletries manufacturer may advertise a brand of shampoo on the TV and in magazines and also use point of sale materials. It could be difficult to find out which of the methods was the most effective.
- External factors are also likely to affect sales levels at the same time as promotions. For example, if sales of ice-cream rose sharply following a promotion which coincided with a spell of good weather, it could be difficult to determine whether the increase was due to the promotion or the favourable weather conditions.
- When using market research to monitor the performance of promotions it is possible that the data collected is inaccurate. For example, the sample used may not be representative.

Meeting the assessment criteria

You need to prepare a group presentation and report which explains the planning and preparation that went into the launch of the company. You also need to assess the issues involved in the day to day running and monitoring of the business. In this unit the focus will be on monitoring sales and promotion.

Business example - Gloworm

Gloworm was a mini enterprise run by students in a Gloucestershire school. They sold a range of glow products such as glow sticks, glow bracelets and glow necklaces. The company employed a team of seven sales staff. Each seller was allocated a year group in the school to target. To encourage sales the company used an incentive scheme. It involved setting targets and rewarding sales staff for meeting them and exceeding them. For every 15 items sold per week a sales person received £1. If a further 5 were sold another £1 was given. In November, a weekly target of 100 units was set by the company. Unfortunately it only sold 57. However, after a board meeting it was agreed that not enough promotion had been done around the school to raise students' awareness of the enterprise and its products. As a result some posters were made and displayed around the school. The chairperson also spoke to students in an assembly, explaining that the purpose of the enterprise was to help raise money for the new swimming pool fund. In December the sales target was reduced to 80 and actual sales were 102.

Mark Band 1 *Provide evidence of a basic contribution to the group presentation and report.*

The company monitored sales by setting weekly targets. In November the board decided to set a weekly target of 100 units. Unfortunately, these targets were not met. Many of the sales staff were disappointed because they were not able to meet their personal targets. Consequently they did not get their bonus payments. However, after some promotion, new sales targets were set and actual sales levels exceeded them. Since the new targets were more achievable, the sales team was better motivated and sold more.

Mark Band 2 *Provide evidence of a sound contribution to the group presentation and report.*

The use of sales targets provides an effective way of monitoring the company's performance. Targets need to be clear and are often linked to incentives such as commissions and bonuses. This helps to motivate sales staff and provides them with a clear indication of the kind of performance expected of them. Gloworm set targets for the company and its sales team. The first target was set in November when it was hoped to generate sales of 100 units per week. However, this proved to be too challenging and after a board meeting it was agreed that there had not been enough promotion. The company used posters and a presentation in assembly to promote the company and its products. This seemed to have a positive effect on sales. In December, new weekly targets were set and exceeded. This meant that most sales staff got their bonus payments and were happy to carry on selling for the company.

Mark Band 3 *Provide evidence of a comprehensive contribution to the group presentation and report.*

One of the best ways to gauge how well a company is progressing is to monitor sales levels. However, the level of sales alone does not provide an accurate guide unless set against some sales targets. Gloworm set weekly sales targets for its glow products. When the company was first launched in November weekly targets of 100 units were set. An incentive scheme was also used to help motivate sales staff. If their personal target of 15 units per week was met, a payment of £1 was made. A further £1 was paid if 20 were sold. Specific and achievable targets are likely to achieve results. However, the targets proved to be unattainable for many staff. It was agreed that this was not due to the poor performance of the sales staff. It was felt that insufficient promotion had been undertaken. As a result some colourful posters were designed and displayed around the school. The chairperson also gave a presentation in an assembly. He explained what the aims of the company were and when products would be on sale. In December the sales targets were revised downwards to 80 units per week and actual sales levels rose to 102 units. By monitoring sales performance Gloworm was able to identify a problem and take action to resolve it.

Portfolio practice · **MoroccoHols**

MoroccoHols is a specialist holiday company providing a range of different Moroccan holidays. It markets holidays using a brochure which is distributed around the country's travel agents. It also has a website where information about the country, the company's holidays and customer feedback can be viewed. Morocco Ltd places small ads in a variety of newspapers on a regular basis. When taking bookings, MoroccoHols keeps a record of how customers found out about the company. Some responses for January 2005 are shown in Figure 6. MoroccoHols spends nearly £15,000 every year on advertising and it is keen to find out where it gets the most response.

(a) How might MoroccoHols use the information in Figure 6?

(b) Why do you think it is important for MoroccoHols to keep records like the ones shown in Figure 6?

(c) Explain the problems of monitoring the effects of promotion.

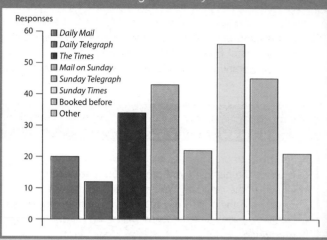

Figure 6 *Customer responses to 'Where did you hear about us before booking?' (January 2005)*

Why are companies wound up?

One of the advantages of operating as a limited company is that it cannot 'die'. It has continuity. This means that members who want to withdraw their interest whilst the company is still trading can do so by selling their shares. In the case of a public limited company the shares can be sold on the open market. With private limited companies shares are transferred to a new owner with the consent of the remaining members. This means that companies can trade indefinitely. Some examples of long established companies are shown in Figure 1.

A limited company will carry on trading until it:
- goes into liquidation. This happens when it becomes insolvent and does not have enough money to pay its debts. A company may go into liquidation voluntarily or it could be forced by creditors;
- is taken over by another company;
- is wound up by the owners voluntarily.

This section is concerned with the voluntary winding up of a company, where the owners decide to cease trading. A private company that is not trading may apply to the Registrar to be 'struck off' the register. It can do this if the company is no longer needed. Why might the owners wind up a company voluntarily?
- The active directors may wish to retire and there is no-one to take over from them.
- The company is a subsidiary whose name is no longer needed.
- It was set up to exploit an idea that turned out not to be feasible.

Planning for winding up

A company can only be wound up if it has not traded for at least three months. Therefore, the directors must plan ahead and decide when the business will cease trading before it can be wound up. There are also a number of important issues to consider during the winding up process. Figure 2 shows some examples.

The first thing that directors must decide is when exactly they propose to terminate the company. Once a date for termination has been chosen, an action plan can be drawn up to help the winding up process run smoothly.

Figure 1 *Examples of long established companies*

- Youngs, the London brewer, was established in 1675.
- Aston Villa FC, the quoted Premier League football club, was founded in 1874.
- Marks & Spencer was formed in 1894.

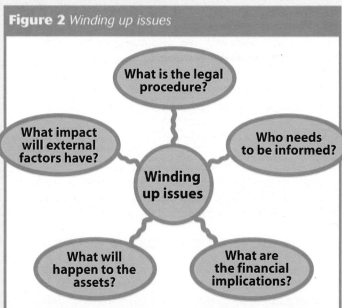

Figure 2 *Winding up issues*

- What is the legal procedure?
- What impact will external factors have?
- Who needs to be informed?
- Winding up issues
- What will happen to the assets?
- What are the financial implications?

Closing down trading activities

Before the legal process of winding up a company can be begin, it has to cease trading. A number of measures need to be taken before this can happen. To avoid inconvenience and hardship, and to ease the administrative strain, various stakeholders need to be informed of the company's intentions. The way in which a company goes about this might depend on the nature and size of the business. It might be assumed that since the company was about to be wound up, the extent of its trading activities would be limited. However, this may not necessarily be the case. Figure 3 shows some of the stakeholders and authorities that would need to be told that the company was going to cease trading.

Figure 3 *Who must be notified that a company is to cease trading?*

Announcing the closure of a business may be a sensitive issue, particularly if it is unexpected. For example, employees rely on the company for their income and livelihood. Suppliers will also depend on the business provided by the company and customers may depend on its products or services. Important stakeholders, such as employees, would need to be told in advance. This would give them the chance to prepare for the closure. For example, they can start to look for a new job and perhaps make some financial arrangements if they expect to be unemployed for a while.

In addition to informing stakeholders and the authorities, before a company actually closes down it will be necessary to undertake the following tasks.
- Sell off stocks of finished goods (if appropriate). For example, a retailer might do this by organising a closing down sale.
- Sell off the physical assets of the business.
- Collect all of the business debts, from customers for example.
- Comply with any legal requirements to staff redundancies and make any redundancy payments.

What is the legal process for winding up?

Companies have to make a formal application to the Registrar to be struck off. According to company law, a private company that is not trading may apply to the Registrar to be struck off the register.

A private company can apply to be struck off if, in the previous three months, it has not:
- traded or otherwise carried on business;
- changed its name;
- undertaken any business transactions resulting in a financial gain for the company. However, this does not include any assets that were used by the business such as plant, machinery and premises. These may be disposed of in the three months leading up to closure;
- been involved in any other business activity except one necessary for making a striking-off application, settling the company's affairs or meeting a legal requirement such as seeking professional advice on the application and paying the costs of copying the Form 652a. However, a company can apply for striking off if it has settled trading or business debts in the previous three months.

A company cannot apply to be struck off if it is subject to any insolvency proceedings. This is where a company may have to close because it is in serious debt. If a company is insolvent it can be forced to close down by its creditors.

Legal safeguards There are safeguards for those who are likely to be affected by the winding up of a company. Creditors, shareholders, directors and managers or trustees of any employee pension fund have to be informed before an application to wind up is submitted. These parties may be entitled to object to the winding up of the company. Also, any loose ends, such as closing the company's bank account, should be dealt with before an application is made.

It is also advisable to notify any other organisation or party who may have an interest in the company's affairs, otherwise they might later object to the application. Examples include local authorities, especially if the company is under any obligation involving planning permission or health and safety issues, training and enterprise councils and government agencies.

Form 652a The application to wind up a company is made using Form 652a. It can be obtained from the Registrar. The form must be signed and dated by:
- the sole director, if there is only one;
- by both, if there are two; or
- by the majority, if there are more than two.

The name, address and telephone number of the person Companies House should contact about the application should also be given. A charge of £10 is made by the Registrar for processing the form. This payment should be sent along with Form 652a to the Registrar. Within seven days of posting the form copies must be provided for:
- members, usually the shareholders;
- creditors;
- Inland Revenue, DSS and Customs & Excise if there is any money owed;
- employees;
- managers or trustees of any employee pension fund;
- any directors who have not signed the form.

All VAT-registered companies must notify the relevant VAT office (**Finance Act, 1985**). Finally, anyone who becomes a member, creditor after the application must also be sent a copy of the form within seven days.

Formal winding up The Registrar will advertise and invite objections to the proposed striking-off of a company. If there are no objections within three months of the notice the Registrar will strike the company off the register provided there is no other reason to do otherwise and the application has not been withdrawn. The company will be dissolved when the Registrar publishes a notice to that effect. At the time of striking-off, a letter will be issued to the contact name on Form 652a confirming the proposed date of dissolution.

Distribution of assets

An important part of the winding up process involves selling off the company's physical assets. Most companies will have premises and a variety of other assets such as plant, machinery, tools, equipment, furniture, vehicles, fixtures and fittings and stock that have to be disposed of. Companies will aim to maximise the amount of money that can be raised from the sale of these assets. If the winding up of the company has been well planned in advance a business is likely to get more for its assets. This is because it can spend more time preparing the assets for sale and be more selective when accepting offers. How might assets be sold?

Agents A company might use specialist agents to help dispose of physical assets. For example, estate agents are likely to be used to sell premises and other property owned by the company.

Auction It may be possible to organise an auction of some, or all, of the physical assets belonging to the company. This might be quite an efficient way of disposing of assets. They might all be sold on the same day.

Privately Many companies will sell unwanted assets by advertising their sale using appropriate media. For example, a farmer might advertise the sale of his plant and machinery in the *Farmers Weekly* magazine.

A company will find that most of its assets can be sold fairly easily provided they are in reasonable condition. Many assets, like vehicles for example, may attract a lot of interest and can be sold quite quickly. However, some assets like specialised machinery may be difficult to dispose of. This is because the number of buyers in the market for highly specialised machinery will be small. Finally, a company's stock can be sold to existing customers. Alternatively a sale might be organised to get rid of it quickly.

Financial implications

There are certain financial implications for a business when winding up.

Distribution of cash What happens to the cash raised from the sale of assets? A proportion of the cash will be used to pay off creditors. Money may be owed to suppliers, employees, bankers, credit card companies, utilities, the Inland Revenue and Customs & Excise for example. The Inland Revenue need to know that a business has ceased trading to organise a final tax demand. A provision must also be made for any administration costs incurred when winding up the company. After this, any money left over belongs to the owners of the business. In the case of a company this will be the shareholders. The money is likely to be given back to the shareholders in proportion to the number of shares owned. However, from the date of dissolution, any assets held by a

dissolved company will belong to the Crown. The company's bank account will be frozen and any credit balance in the account will be passed to the Crown.

Cessation accounts A company is likely to produce some cessation accounts. These are the final set of accounts ever produced by a company. They cover the trading period from the end of the last financial year to the day the company formally ceases trading. These accounts are necessary to calculate the amount of tax the company is liable to pay.

Tax implications When a company is wound up and money is returned to the owners, shareholders may need legal advice to determine:

- whether retained profits are best extracted prior to winding-up, as salary, dividends, or pension contributions, or left within the company to create a revenue or capital distribution upon winding up;
- whether it is beneficial to repay capital in more than one payment; typically either side of 5th April, to make use of 2 years' capital gains tax annual exemptions.

External factors

When a company ceases trading it may have an impact on the external environment.

Employees Employees are likely to be affected adversely. They will lose their jobs and income. They may receive redundancy payments but they will eventually have to find another job. This may be difficult and it may be necessary for them to retrain. In extreme circumstances, if unemployment is high for example, it may take a very long time to find a new job and people may endure some hardship.

Customers Customers may be disappointed and inconvenienced when a business ceases trading. For example, if a village shop or post office closes down customers may have to travel further afield to buy goods or services. Some people are often dependent on local business services and may suffer hardship if they cannot be provided anymore.

Competitors Competitors are likely to benefit when a company ceases trading. This is because they would expect to win some of their rival's customers when the business closes down.

The environment The environment might benefit from the closure of a business. For example, a manufacturer may cease to pollute the atmosphere when emissions are stopped. There may also be less noise and congestion for people who live near to a business. However, there may also be drawbacks. For example, business premises may be left derelict for many years when a company is wound up. This is a waste of resources and may look unsightly.

Government The government is unlikely to welcome the winding up of a company. Businesses provide employment, produce useful goods and services, pay taxes and generate wealth. The government would prefer more businesses not less.

In practice the number of companies that are wound up voluntarily is quite small. Companies that are successful and profitable are not likely to be wound up at all. Those that are wound up are possibly insignificant in terms of their contribution to output and employment in the economy.

1. Find a business in your local area that is closing down. They may be identified by sale notices in the window. Otherwise you may need to ask local business people if they know of any. Using a short questionnaire find out:
   - the reason for closure;
   - if they are following a legal process;
   - how they propose to sell the assets of the business;
   - what effect the closure might have in the local area.
2. Present your findings in a brief report.

Research task

Portfolio practice - Braithwaite's

Albert Braithwaite set up Braithwaite's in 1967. It was a business which repaired metal items for customers, such as metal gates, and made metal products such as pokers. It operated from leased premises in Southend. The company, which made its name for the quality of its work over many years, was finally closed in May 2005.

After 38 years of trading Albert believed that there was no longer sufficient demand for his products and services. The business employed four staff, two of whom had been with the company for over 25 years. Albert had tried to sell the business in the last two years, but the accounts for those two years did not suggest that the business was worth buying.

Albert laid off his staff in February and applied to the Company Registrar for a formal winding up a few weeks later. He expected the sale of stock and assets to realise just enough cash to pay off suppliers, staff and the authorities.

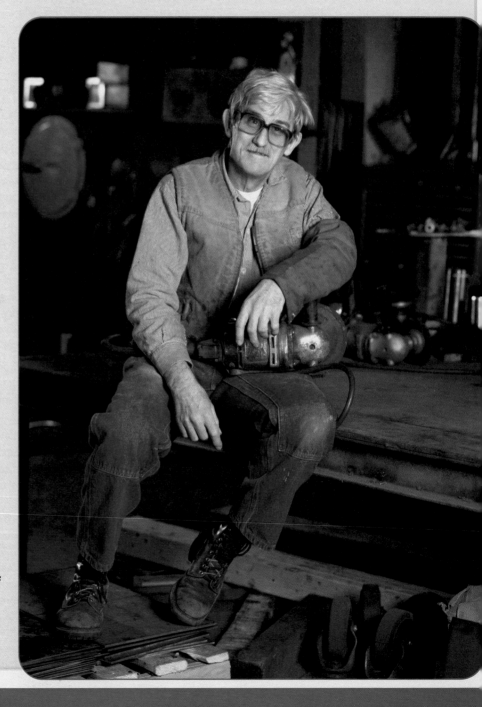

(a) **State FOUR parties that would need to be informed of the closure of Braithwaite's. Give reasons for your answer.**
(b) **Explain the legal process that Albert would have to follow when winding up his business.**
(c) **How might Albert dispose of his stock and assets?**
(d) **Evaluate the impact the winding up of Braithwaite's might have on external factors.**

Meeting the assessment criteria

You need to prepare a group presentation and report which explains the planning and preparation that went into the launch of the company. You also need to assess the issues involved in the day-to-day running and monitoring of the business and the winding up of the company when it ceases to trade. In this unit the focus will be on the winding up of the company when it is formally closed down.

Business example - The Action Station

The Action Station is a youth club for 12 to 14 year old youngsters. It is run as a mini company by a group of sixth form students at a school in Milton Keynes. The Action Station operates in a school building which is rented for £20 a week. It was set up in October 2003 and because the students are now due to complete their studies it must be wound up. The club raises revenue by:
- charging a weekly subscription of £1 per person;
- selling refreshments;
- organising the occasional disco;
- organising trips to places of interest.

The company owns a number of assets, such as table tennis equipment, footballs, a CD and MP3 player, some CDs and DVDs, a Karaoke machine and a pool table. When the company was set up the directors decided that any money left over at the end of the venture would be donated to charity.

Mark Band 1 *Provide evidence of a basic contribution to the group presentation and report.*
Winding up the Action Station was a sad activity. It had been a success and everyone was disappointed, particularly the youngsters who attended regularly. A big party was organised before trading ceased. This was hugely enjoyable and helped to boost revenue by £200. In the last week before the company was finally wound up a number of tasks had to be completed. The assets were sold off at an auction held in the school hall. This raised £260. The stock of confectionery was sold off to pupils at lunch times and letters were sent to suppliers, helpers and other external groups involved in the venture, thanking them for their support. The Finance Director produced some cessation accounts and £550 was given to charity.

Mark Band 2 *Provide evidence of a sound contribution to the group presentation and report.*
After 18 months of trading the Action Station had to be formally wound up. This involved a number of important tasks. It was decided to hold a party for all the people involved in the running of the youth club and all the youngsters who had attended. In addition to being a thoroughly enjoyable event £200 was generated in revenue. Everyone said that the Action Station would be missed by the local youth in the community. This was one of the negative impacts of winding up. One important task in the winding up process was to sell off the assets belonging to the company. It was decided to hold an auction in the school hall to sell off assets like sports equipment,

the MP3 player, CDs, DVDs, the Karaoke machine and other things. The auction raised £260. The Finance Director produced some cessation accounts. This was the last set of accounts before the company was wound up. The day after the company was formally closed a cheque for £550 was given to a local children's charity. A number of letters were also sent out to helpers, suppliers and other groups involved in the Action Station to thank them for their support over the last 18 months.

Mark Band 3 *Provide evidence of a comprehensive contribution to the group presentation and report.*
The winding up of a company is an important process and a number of tasks have to be undertaken to formally close the company down. The winding up process should be planned so that it runs smoothly. To avoid inconvenience and hardship, and to ease the administrative strain, various stakeholders need to be informed of the company's intentions. In this case a letter was sent to suppliers, helpers and other groups involved in the running of the Action Station. The letter thanked them for their support and explained why the Action Station was closing down. A week before the company was formally wound up a big party was held for all the people involved in the running of the youth club and the youngsters who had enjoyed the activities provided. This was an enjoyable event and well attended. Indeed a further £200 of revenue was generated for the company.

Before a company can be wound up its assets must be liquidated. This means they must be sold for cash. The equipment used by the Action Station and other assets belonging to the company were sold off at an auction in the school hall. This raised £260 in cash. The stocks of confectionery were sold to pupils at the school during lunch times. The financial director produced some cessation accounts and a total of £550 was handed over to a local children's charity.

Finally, the winding up of the company had an impact on a number of external groups. It was said, for example, that the local community would miss the Action Station because it had provided youngsters with somewhere to go at nights. Some small suppliers might also miss its business.

How can the success of an enterprise be evaluated?

To evaluate the success of a business enterprise it is necessary to determine whether or not it has achieved its aims and objectives. Many companies set targets which they hope to achieve. The extent to which these targets are met will help determine whether or not the company has been successful. For example, if a company aims to increase profit by 10% in the next trading year, it would be considered successful if profit actually rose by 12.5%. This measure focuses on the financial performance of the company. However, it is likely that a company will look at a range of other performance indicators such as customer service, labour turnover, environmental performance, wastage and staff development, for example. The success of an enterprise is not just about profit.

Evaluating financial success

Some stakeholders would argue that the success of a company is determined by its financial performance. The financial management of the company is often seen as the most important aspect of running a company. Financial success might be evaluated using the performance indicators shown in Figure 1. Figure 2 shows an evaluation of the financial performance of Wolverhampton & Dudley, the brewer.

Evaluating the success of staff

The people employed in a business are very important. Staff in a successful enterprise will work effectively in teams, communicate openly and respond positively to new initiatives such as a change in working practices. If staff are well motivated they are likely to be more productive, provide better customer service and are less likely to leave the company. When reviewing and evaluating the

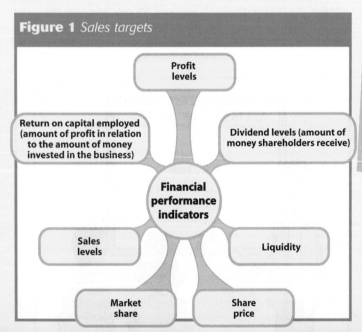

Figure 1 *Sales targets*

Figure 2 *Analysing the financial performance of Wolverhampton & Dudley*

Financial information can be used to evaluate the financial success of the company in 2004. The level of sales generated by the brewer has increased from £491m to £514m over the time period. This is a small increase of 4.7%. However, in such a competitive industry this may be considered favourable. Profit before tax has risen by £10.6m, an increase of 17.8%. This is quite a significant increase in profit. Dividend per share has gone up by 10% from 32.1p per share to 35.3p. Again this is a very healthy increase. The amount of cash held by the company has also risen from £11.9m to £16.2m. This is obviously good, but does not reflect entirely the liquidity of the company. This is because companies hold other types of liquid assets, such as debtors, and the value of current liabilities needs to be taken into account. Finally, the company's share price has increased significantly by 18%. To conclude, it could be argued that Wolverhampton & Dudley has enjoyed a very successful year in 2004. The shareholders would be particularly pleased with the healthy increase in profits, dividends and the share price. However, a more accurate evaluation might involve comparing these financial results with any targets set by the company and the results of other brewers.

Financial information for Wolverhampton & Dudley 2003 and 2004

	2003	2004
Turnover	£491m	£514m
Profit before tax	£59.6m	£70.2m
Dividend per share	32.1p	35.3p
Cash	£11.9m	£16.2m
Share price (approx)	720p	850p

Source: adapted from Wolverhampton & Dudley, *Annual Reports and Accounts*, 2004.

success of the workforce the following indicators may be used.
- Labour productivity.
- Staff turnover.
- Punctuality.
- Absenteeism.

These indicators can all be quantified. For example, the labour productivity can be calculated using the formula shown in Figure 3.

Figure 3 *Formula for calculating labour productivity*

$$\text{Labour productivity} = \frac{\text{Output}}{\text{Number of employees}}$$

If a car assembly plant employed 1,500 workers and produced 12,500 cars during a year the labour productivity would be:

$$\text{Labour productivity} = \frac{12,500}{1,500} = 8.33$$

This level of productivity can be compared with any targets set by the company and productivity levels in other car assembly plants to evaluate its success.

Evaluating teamwork and communication

Although the success of the workforce can be evaluated using quantitative techniques, such as labour productivity shown above, some aspects of staff performance are more difficult to assess. For example, the quality of communication in a business and how effectively people work together as a team are important but may be more difficult to evaluate. The quality of communication might be reviewed by looking at the:

- number of complaints received from customers relating to communication;
- morale of staff (good staff morale is often a symptom of good communication);
- effectiveness of meetings in the organisation;
- use made of ICT in the business.

It may be possible to evaluate the success of team working by looking at:

- whether there has been any conflict or disputes between team members;
- the morale of staff (staff morale will tend to be higher if team members get on well with each other);
- the quality of team leaders (good team leaders will motivate the rest of the team).

Gathering information to evaluate team working and communication may be time consuming. A company might use an appraisal system, where staff are interviewed individually to review their progress at work. At an interview staff might be encouraged to talk about team working and communication. Questionnaires might be used where staff are asked a range of questions about how they feel about the relevant issues. Some companies might ask teams and departments to carry out annual reviews where such issues are discussed in detail by all members of a team in an open meeting. This might be the best way because open discussions are more transparent. The team leader would then have to write a report for the senior management team. After the reviewing process it may be possible to make changes which can improve team working and communication in the future.

Evaluating marketing and sales

The relationship between marketing and sales is likely to be very strong. If marketing is effective then sales should be higher. It is common for a business to review its marketing activities to see if the marketing mix that it currently uses is the best for the prevailing circumstances. A company may base its evaluation on the 4Ps shown in Figure 4.

A business might evaluate its marketing activities in a number of ways.

Market research Some companies may take a scientific approach and employ market researchers to measure the impact of various promotions such as an advert in the national press or a TV advertisement. Statistical methods may be used to measure the increase in sales resulting from the use of certain advertising media.

Promotion The effectiveness of promotion can be monitored by comparing sales levels before and after a promotion. For example, sales levels in the month after a TV campaign could be compared with the month before the campaign, or with the same calendar month in the previous year.

Records Companies may keep a record of how new customers have found out about their services. For example, a holiday company might ask customers when they book or how they found out about the particular holiday.

Websites Companies with websites may be able to measure the effect of promotions by recording the number of 'hits' on their site after a promotion or by asking customers to complete questionnaires. Developments in ICT have made it easier to communicate with customers and gather information from them.

Customer feedback Companies may keep records of customer feedback. For example, they may monitor complaints which can be used in an evaluation process. Many companies, such as hotels and retailers, invite customers to complete questionnaires designed to find out what they liked or disliked about the service. An example is shown in Figure 5.

Stock If a company misses its sales targets and is left with lots of stock, this suggests that something is wrong. Either the product is weak relative to its competitors or the marketing mix is wrong.

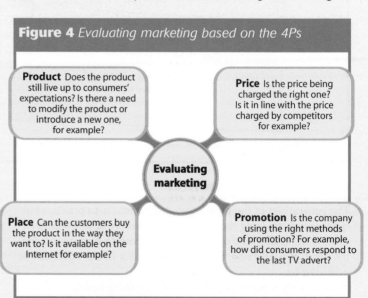

Figure 4 *Evaluating marketing based on the 4Ps*

Product Does the product still live up to consumers' expectations? Is there a need to modify the product or introduce a new one, for example?

Price Is the price being charged the right one? Is it in line with the price charged by competitors for example?

Evaluating marketing

Place Can the customers buy the product in the way they want to? Is it available on the Internet for example?

Promotion Is the company using the right methods of promotion? For example, how did consumers respond to the last TV advert?

Figure 5 *A questionnaire used to evaluate customer satisfaction for a retailer*

Dear customer,

As manager of Westoms, I want to thank you for giving us the opportunity to serve you. Please help us serve you better by taking a couple of minutes to tell us about the service you have received so far. We appreciate your business and want to make sure we meet your expectations.

Sincerely,
M. Tiler
Manager

Please indicate your opinions about each of the following statements.

	Very Strongly Agree	Strongly Agree	Agree	Disagree	Strongly Disagree	Very Strongly Disagree
Stores are conveniently located.	☐	☐	☐	☐	☐	☐
Store hours are convenient for my shopping needs.	☐	☐	☐	☐	☐	☐
Store atmosphere and decor are appealing.	☐	☐	☐	☐	☐	☐
A good selection of products was present.	☐	☐	☐	☐	☐	☐
Westoms has the lowest prices in the area.	☐	☐	☐	☐	☐	☐
Merchandise sold is of the highest quality.	☐	☐	☐	☐	☐	☐
The merchandise sold is good value for the money.	☐	☐	☐	☐	☐	☐
Merchandise displays are attractive.	☐	☐	☐	☐	☐	☐
Advertised merchandise was in stock.	☐	☐	☐	☐	☐	☐
Overall, I am satisfied with the store.	☐	☐	☐	☐	☐	☐
I am very satisfied with the price I paid for what I bought.	☐	☐	☐	☐	☐	☐

Source: adapted from www.questionpro.com.

Evaluating production

The general aim of the production department is to produce high quality products using the least possible resources. To evaluate its success the quality of the product would have to be analysed and the costs of production measured. The quality of a product can be evaluated by:
- comparing it with competitors, perhaps using a benchmark;
- comparing to industry standards, such as BSI;
- analysing customer feedback.

Production costs are likely to be monitored by financial managers. However, production staff will be under pressure to minimise costs. The success of the production department might be evaluated by looking at:
- total production costs;
- production cost variances (see section 23);
- waste, such as rework, arising from mistakes in production.

Evaluating interrelationships

The success of a company will depend upon how everyone in the organisation works together. It is important that all the different teams or departments pursue the same objectives. This requires strong leadership, extensive cooperation across departments and a positive corporate culture. The workforce needs to be highly trained and encouraged to support all of their colleagues.

Conflicts, if they arise, need to be settled quickly without ill feeling and information must be communicated effectively to everyone in the organisation. How might interrelationships be evaluated?

- Obtaining staff feedback from an appraisal system or staff suggestion schemes.
- Monitoring and assessing the number of conflicts.
- Monitoring and assessing the quality of meetings.
- Analysing customer feedback. Customers can often tell if an organisation is working together well.

Interview a company manager from your contacts. Design a questionnaire to identify:
- the successes of the company;
- areas of improvement over the last year.
OR
Obtain a set of annual reports from any plc. Look at the managing director's report towards the beginning of the document (not the chairperson's report). To what extent is the report an evaluation of the company's success?

Research task

Portfolio practice · Dawkings Ltd

Dawkings Ltd was set up in Hereford in June 2003 to manufacture cakes for local businesses. After the first year of trading the two partners met to evaluate the success of the enterprise. They agreed on the following.

- Financially Dawkings was just keeping its head above water. The aim was to break even in the first year but in fact a loss of £3,700 was made. This was due to some unforeseen expenditure when converting the premises.
- The amount spent on marketing was not adequate. The advertising budget would have to be increased and some imaginative marketing methods would have to be used. For example, leaflets could be produced showing unusual cake designs that shops could buy .
- One of the great strengths of the company was the workforce. The partners had recruited some excellent staff who were flexible, highly motivated, loyal and reliable. Staff

worked as a cohesive team and communication was genuinely open.
- There would be a need to cut down on waste. Food was often wasted due to poor portion control, for example. There was also a lot of spillage which could be reduced if work areas were increased. This is something which would have to be addressed.

(a) **Using this case as an example, explain how the financial success of an enterprise can be evaluated.**
(b) **How do you think the partners may have come to the conclusion that the workforce was one of the key strengths of the business?**
(c) **How might the partners benefit from the evaluation of Dawkings Ltd?**

Meeting the assessment criteria

You need to write an individual report reviewing and evaluating the success of the whole enterprise. You need to consider issues such as team working, communication, financial management, marketing, sales, production and their interrelationship.

Business example - ZapCo

ZapCo was a student run enterprise based in a Bristol school. The mini company produced personalised products such as mousemats, mobile phone covers, door signs and key rings. The products were well liked and pupils in the school were impressed with their quality and originality. ZapCo was wound up in March 2005 and the following financial information was provided.

	Target	Actual
Sales	£1,000	£743
Profit	£500	£548

Generally the company was a success. However, there were one or two problems.
- There was often conflict between the sales team and the production team. This was usually because the production team were unable to deliver products on the days the marketing team had promised customers. The delays were often due to breakdowns in communication between the two teams.
- The marketing was a bit weak. The posters used to promote products were hand drawn and looked unprofessional.
- The winding up of the company was not completed very successfully. The cessation accounts were inaccurate and there were still quite a lot of raw material stocks the day the company was formally wound up.

Mark Band 1 *Provide a basic individual report reviewing and evaluating the success of the whole enterprise.*

ZapCo was a great success. It made £48 more profit than was expected. Everyone liked the products and demand was so great it was often difficult to meet customer orders. However, at times there were disagreements between different people. For example, the production manager was often arguing with the marketing manager. This was usually because the marketing manager was a bit vague about when customers expected to receive their products which they had paid for in advance. Sometimes customers would go and complain to the

production manager about late delivery and it may not have been her fault. You could say there was a breakdown in communication at times. But generally everyone worked quite well together as a team.

Mark Band 2 *Provide a sound individual report reviewing and evaluating the success of the whole enterprise. Draw some conclusions and make recommendations.*

Being involved in the running of ZapCo was an enjoyable and rewarding experience. It could be argued that the company was a success. Financially the profit made by ZapCo exceeded the target set at the beginning. However, sales were not as high as it was hoped. The marketing used by the company could have been better. The posters used to promote the products were hand drawn and looked unprofessional. Some more effective marketing may have helped to lift sales closer to the target of £1,000. Profit was higher because some of the costs were lower than expected. Communication in the organisation was generally good, but a problem did exist between the marketing and production department. Communication broke down when customer orders were verbally sent to the production department. There was sometimes confusion about when customers wanted their products. In future a recommendation might be to write down clearly the dates when customers would get their products. Finally, it could be argued that the winding up of the company was not taken seriously. Everyone seemed to lose interest and the job was not done properly. For example, the cessation accounts were inaccurate and some stock was left over.

Mark Band 3 *Provide a comprehensive and detailed report reviewing and evaluating the success of the whole enterprise. Use relevant examples to analyse the enterprise and include fully supported and justified conclusions and appropriate recommendations.*

From a financial perspective it could be argued that ZapCo was successful. It made £548 profit, which exceeded the targets set at the beginning. Although sales were less than forecast, they were still quite high at £743. One reason why the sales target was not met was because of the marketing methods employed. Hand drawn posters were used to promote the products and they looked unprofessional. They could have been produced using a computer. Alternatively some professional posters could have been produced by a local printer. It may also have been appropriate to use other methods of promotion to support the poster campaign. For example, some leaflets could have been handed out to pupils at the school offering them a discount on a product if they produced the leaflet when making a purchase.

Although everyone worked enthusiastically as a team communications were sometimes vague. The verbal system used to inform the production department about delivery dates was obviously flawed. People forgot dates and it would have been so easy to write things down. The interrelationship between the marketing department and the production department was often strained as a result. However, company meetings were conducted in an orderly fashion and everyone wanted to make contributions. Morale was generally high.

Finally, when the company was wound up in March the job was rushed. No-one was really interested in the paperwork involved and the cessation accounts contained a number of errors. There was also some stock left over which could have generated some more cash if a proper sale had been organised.

Index

A

ABCIs 148
Absenteeism 391, 414
    and monitoring customer service 280
    and motivation 45-46
ACAS 71-72
Access
    and sponsorship 324
Accountants 381
Accounting equation 94
Accounting software 116
ACORN 148
Administration
    and ICT 111
    as business function 17
Administration Department
    as internal service provider 239
Adobe GoLive 214, 230
Adobe Photoshop 230
Adverse variances 103
Advertising 184, 308-312
    and attracting visitors 309
    and changing image 309
    and jobs 33
    and promoting 309
    as communication method 267
    as promotional tool 302
    brand 309
    budget 310
    direct sell 308
    controls on 311
    costs of a website 214
    factors affecting 310-311
    informative 308
    media 310
    objective of 308
    radio 331
    reasons for 308-309
Advertising Standards Authority (ASA) 72, 186, 292, 311, 349
    as constraint on marketing 190
Age
    and discrimination 43
    and needs of customers 244-245
    and segmentation 148
Age concern 11
Age discrimination 43
Age restrictions
    on consumer service 292

Agents
    and place/distribution 180
Aims 5
    and an on-line presence 197
    and improving profitability through marketing 130
    and planning 77
    corporate image 7
    growth 6
    in primary industry 10
    in secondary industry 10
    in tertiary industry 10
    market share 6
    profit maximisation 6
    quality 7
    sales 5-6
    survival 7-8
Aims and objectives
    and promotional campaigns 353
Air pollution 59
Air Quality Limit Regulations 60
Ambient media 339-340
    problems of 340
    reasons for 339
Analysing
    customer service data 286
    promotional campaigns 352-356
Animal rights 63
Annual General Meeting (AGM)
    and company formation 361
    and websites 201, 218
Annual legal obligations
    of companies 362
Annual reports and accounts 161-162
Annual returns
    of companies 362
Ansoff Matrix 127, 141
Anti-virus protection 213-214
Appearance
    of staff and effective customer service 255
Application form 32-33
Appraisal
    and monitoring customer service 280
    and role evaluation 386
Apprenticeships 38, 39
Appropriation account
    of profit and loss account 91
Appropriateness
    and sponsorship 324, 425
    of promotional campaigns 353

    of radio media 332
Aptitude tests 34
Articles of Association 13, 362
Assets 89
    and balance sheet 94
Associated products
    and promotion using radio media 332
Association
    and sponsorship 324
Association of the British Pharmaceutical Industry 64
Association of British Travel Agents (ABTA) 291
Assumption-based sales forecasting 405
Attitudes
    and effective customer service 256
    and segmentation 150
Audio media 331-333
    problems of 332
    reasons for 331-332
Auditing 17
Auditors 381-382
    and communication with enterprises 386
    and role evaluation 386
Auditors' report
    of companies 362
Audits
    and primary research 156
    and product failure 127
Awareness
    and sponsorship 323

B

Back ups
    and ICT 119
Bad publicity
    and sponsorship 324
Balance sheet 89, 94-97
    limitations of 96
    limited company 95-96
    structure 94-95
    uses of 96
Bank reconciliation statements
    monitoring in enterprise 399, 400
Banking code 350
Banners
    and websites 231
BazaarBuilder 215

BCAP Radio Advertising Standards
Code 311
BCAP Television Advertising Standards
Code 311
Behavioural management 48
Benchmarking
as measure of customer service
277, 286-287
Benefits
and motivation 53
Bias in research 156, 163
Billboards 184
as communication method 267
Bluetooth
as promotional media 343
Board of directors
in hierarchy 22
BOGOF (buy one get one free) 303
Bookmarks
and websites 231
Books 327-330
Bot networks 222
Brad media directory 328, 331, 334, 339
Brand advertising 309
Brand awareness 143-146
and sponsorship 185, 324
Brand image 143
Brand name
and market share 141
Brand share 137
Branding 143-146
and aim of business 7
and place/distribution 181
as ambient promotional media 339
Brands 143-146
Break-even 106-110
and spreadsheets 112
calculating 106-107
limitations of 108
Break-even charts 107-108
Break-even output 106, 107
Break-even point 106, 107
Breaking-even 106-110
Break bumpers 334
British Code of Advertising, Sales
Promotion and Direct Marketing
287-288, 306, 311
British Electrotechnical Approvals
Board 296
British Standards Institution (BSI) 395
British Toy and Hobby Association
(BTHA) 296
Broadband
and communication 201
Brochures 327-330
Browsers 213
Budget 102-105
advertising 184, 309
for a websites 229

Budgetary control 103
Budgeting 102-105
Budgets 102-105
and starting a new business 372
as internal constraint on
promotion 346
purpose of 102-103
types of 102
Business
departments 16
functions 16-19
setting up a 73-76
Business advice 75
Business Bridge 75
Business customers
as external customers 240
Business ethics 63
see also ethics
Business growth
and new businesses 376
limitations to 376
Business Links 75
Business plan 370, 371
Business planning 77-80
and aims and objectives 77
and performance 77
key elements of 78-79
Business resources 81-84
Business to business (B2B) products
and direct marketing 391, 320

C

Cable television
and advertising 335-336
Cables and wires
and website costs 213
CAD
and ICT 117
CAP code 287-288, 306, 311
Capital
and balance sheet 94
Capital and reserves 95
Capital expenditure budgets 102
Cash budgets 102
Cash flow 98-101
and planning 78
improving 99
Cash flow forecasting 98-101
Cash flow forecasts 98-99
and new enterprises 372
benefits of 99
interpreting 99
limitations of 99-100
monitoring in enterprises 399
Catalogues 318, 327-330
CDs
as promotional media 343

Cells
and spreadsheets 111
Census 149
Certificate of incorporation 362
CFCs 61
Chairperson 379-380
Chambers of Commerce 75
Chat shows
as promotional media 334
Children and Young Persons (Tobacco)
Act 292
Choice
of product for a company 365-369
Cinema advertising 184, 334
benefits of 336
problems of 337
Civil law
and customer service 294
Clean Air Act 75, 298
Closed questions
and interviews 34
Closing balance
and cash flow 98
Closing capital
and balance sheet 95
Closing down a company
see winding up a company
Coaching 38
Co-operatives 14
Code of practice
and sales promotion 306
Code of Practice for Commercial
Leases in England and Wales 287
Codes of practice 63-64
and e-business 210-211
Coldfusion 230
Collusion 68
Columns
and spreadsheets 111
Comics 327
Comment boxes 280-281
Comment cards 282
Commercials 334
Committee of Advertising Practice
(CAP) 305, 311, 349
Communication
and e-business 195
and effective customer service 256,
266-270
and enterprises 385-386
and ICT 111
methods of 266-268
Community
and ethics 66
Companies 13
Act 361
House 361, 362
incorporated 360
limited 360

private limited 13, 360
public limited 13, 360
unincorporated 360
Companies House 13
Company
 formation 360-364
 officers 379-383
 secretary 380-381
 structure 361
 see also companies
Company cessation
 see winding up a company
Company liquidations 9
Competition
 and brand awareness 145
 and effects of website trading 206
Competition Act 68, 294
 and e-business 209
Competition Commission (CC) 68, 294
 as constraint on marketing 190
Competition law 68
Competitions 185
 as sales promotion 305
Complaints
 and effective customer service 256
Complaints records 282
Computer passwords 119
Computer viruses 119
Computers
 as a website cost 213
Confidence levels 156
Confidentiality
 and ICT 118-119
Conflict
 between customer service and
  needs of the organisation 271-
  272
Congestion charge 61
Consent forms
 and e-business 210
Constraint
 legislation as a 68
Constraints
 on marketing (other) 189-192
Consumer co-operative 14
Consumer Credit Act 293
 and e-business 209
Consumer data 162
Consumer driven product approach
 172
Consumer expectations
 and place/distribution 181
 and pricing 175, 176
Consumer panel 156
Consumer profiling
 and websites 202-203
Consumer protection 69
Consumer Protection Act 293, 294, 350

Consumer Protection (Distance Selling)
 Regulations 292
Consumer research 127
 and product failure 127-128
Consumer rights
 and e-business 209
Consumers 121, 234
 as external customers 240
Content
 of websites 226
Contract of employment 55
Contribution
 and break-even 106
Control of Misleading Advertisements
 Regulations 210
Control of Substances Hazardous to
 Health (COSHH) Regulations 297,
 299
Conversion rates 405
Corporate image
 and an on-line presence 197
 as a business aim 7
 opportunities to promote through
  e-business 218
Corporate social responsibility
 and customer service 287
Cost
 of ambient media 339
 of audio media 331
 of cinema advertising 337
 of print media 329
 of promotional campaigns 353
 of sponsorship 324
 of television advertising 335
Cost of sales 90, 91
Cost per 000 measure
 of promotional campaigns 354
Cost price 175
Costs
 and break-even 106-107
 as internal constraint on
  promotion 346
 effects of a website on 202
 of a website 213-216
 reducing to improve profitability
  131-132
 reducing with an on-line presence
  198, 218
Countryside
 damage to 61
Countryside Alliance 11
Couples
 and needs as customers 244
Coupons 185
Coverage
 and new media 344
 and promotional campaigns 354
 of cinema advertising 337
 of out-of-home media 341

of radio media 332
 of television advertising 335
Crackers 222
Creative challenge
 of radio media 332
Credit cards 82
 and ordering on-line 219
Criminal law
 and customer service 294
Culture
 and needs of customers 246
Current assets
 and balance sheet 94, 95
Current liabilities
 and balance sheet 94, 95
Curriculum vitae 33
Customer
 characteristics 244
 charters 272, 273
 complaints 282, 287
 interviews 282
 lifetime value 272
 needs and wants 121-124
 observation 282
 pledges (see pledges)
 pressure groups 282
 receptions 185
 questionnaires 282
 safety 296-300
 satisfaction questionnaire 416
 segmentation 122
 surveys 282
 see also customer service,
  customers
Customer expectations 250
 before, during and after the
  product is bought 252-253
 and complexity of product 251
 and essential nature of product 251
 and how long product lasts 251-
  252
 and place 250-251
 and price 250
Customer payments
 monitoring in enterprises 401
Customer Protection (Distance Selling)
 Regulations 251
Customer service 234-300
 analysing data 286
 and appearance 255
 and attitude 256
 and communication 256, 266-270
 and complaints 256
 and external customers 18
 and handling difficult customers
  256
 and health, safety and security 296-
  300

and internal customers 18
and inter-personal skills 256
and premises 260-261
and product knowledge 256
and product quality and knowledge
    262-263
and staffing 255-259
and teamwork 257
and timekeeping 256
and training 257
and websites 203
as business function 18
balanced against the needs of the
    organisation 271-275
degree expected 250-255
desk 266
effects of good 235
effects of poor 235
impact of ineffective 273-274
importance of 234-236
improving 286-290
improving through an on-line
    presence 199
internal 253
legislation 291-295
levels of 235
maintaining 286-290
measuring the quality of 276-279
monitoring methods 280-285
to old and new customers 235
see also customer, customers
Customers 121, 234
and age 244
and culture and language 246
and employment 243
and ethics 65
and gender 244-245
and income 246
and interests, lifestyle and
    personality 247
and websites 205
characteristics 244
departments as internal 238-239
disabled 245-246
employees as internal 237-238
external 121, 240-241
importance of 234-235
internal 121, 237-240
internal and external 237-243
managers as internal 238
needs of different 244-249
old and new 235
owners and shareholders as
    internal 238
see also customer, customer
    service

D

(DAB) Digital Audio broadcast radio
    331, 332
Daltons Weekly 329
Data
    and spreadsheets 111
Data protection 118
Data Protection Act 297, 350
    and e-business 209, 210, 223
    and monitoring human resources
    391
Database marketing 318
Databases 112-113
    and direct marketing 318
    and on-line shopping 194
    and promotion 185-186
De-motivation 45-47
    and staff turnover 28
    of customers 237
    see also motivation
Decision teams 384
Defensive reasons
    for promotion 301, 302
Defra 72
Delayering
    and recruitment 31
Deliveries
    and measuring customer service
    277
Demand
    and effect on price 177
Demographic segmentation 122, 148-
    149
Demonstrations
    as direct marketing 320
Department of Trade and Industry 38
Departmental manager
    in hierarchy 22
Departments
    as internal customers 238-239
    in business 16-19
Design and construction costs
    of a website 214
Desk research
    see secondary research
Developing new products 125-129
Development of Tourism Act 293
Dichotomous questions 156
Different customers
    and their needs 244-249
Difficult customers
    and effective customer service 256
Difficult markets
    and new media 344
    and radio media 332
Digital audio broadcasting 332

Digital cameras
    and website costs 213
DINKS 244
Direct costs
    and pricing 175
Direct e-mailing 185
Direct mailing 185-186
Direct marketing 317-322
    and catalogues 318
    and database marketing 318
    and direct response advertising 321
    and door to door selling 318-319
    and e-mail marketing 319
    and e-tailing 321
    and field marketing 319-320
    and home shopping 318
    and short message service (SMS)
    319
    and telemarketing 319
    and telesales 319
    and websites 321
    as promotional tool 302
    factors affecting 321
    reasons for 317
Direct Marketing Association (DMA)
    211, 317, 321
Direct response advertising 321
Direct sell advertisements 306
Direct questioning 154-155
Direct selling 180, 181
Directive on Privacy and Electronic
Communications 210
Directories 184, 327-330
Directors 24
    of companies 361, 362
    report 362
    rolls and skills of 380
Disability
    and needs of customers 245
Disability discrimination 41, 42-43
Disability Discrimination Act 43
    and needs of customers 245
    and e-business 210
Disability Rights Commission 43
    and needs of customers 245
Disabled customers 245-246
Discipline
    and legislation 57
Discrimination 41-44
    age 43
    disability 42-43
    gender 41
    race relations 42
    reasons to prevent 43
    sexual orientation 43
    types of 41
Dishonoured cheques 400

Dismissal
and legislation 57
and staff turnover 28
Distance Selling Regulations 292
and e-business 209-210
Distribution
see place
Distribution and Logistics
as business function 18
Distribution margins
and pricing 175, 176
Distribution of assets 411
Diversification 127, 140-142
Dividends 360
and profit and loss account 91
Division of organisational structure
by function 21-22
by product 21
geographical 21
Domain name 214
Door-to-door selling 318-319
Dreamweaver 214
Drills
for safety 298
Drive time 332
DVD
as method of communication 267
as promotional media 343
DVD recording devices 336

E

E-business 193-233
and a responsive service 195
and attracting new staff 198
and automated processes 218
and business aims and objectives
197-200
and codes of practice 210-211
and communication 194
and competitors 221
and consumer rights 209
and crackers 222
and Data Protection Act 209-210
and Distant Selling Regulations 209
and flexibility of location 195
and global perspective 194
and hackers 222
and improved communication 218
and improving corporate image 197
and improving customer service
199
and increasing efficiency 199
and increasing sales 197
and information 194
and legislation and industry
standards 209-212

and new services 195
and on-line ordering 219
and opportunities in global markets
217-218
and opportunities to promote a
corporate image 218
and personalised marketing 219
and phishing 222
and reaching new markets 197
and reducing costs 198, 218
and removing a layer of the supply
chain 218
and scams 222
and secure payments 219
and shrinking the competition gap
219
and spam 222
and spyware 222
and targeting customers 197
and threat of global trading 221
and Trojan horses 222
and updating 203, 222
and viruses 221-222
and worms 222
examples of 193
growth of 193
opportunities for 217-220
reasons for 194-195
threats to 221-224
see also e-commerce, websites
E-commerce 118, 193
and direct marketing 319-319
as electronic communication 268
see also e-business, websites
E-mail 117-118, 205, 210, 213, 221, 222,
226, 231
and communication 267
as electronic communication 268
as promotion 185, 343
E-tailing
and direct marketing 321
Economic constraints on marketing 190
Economic growth
as constraint on marketing 190
Effective websites 225-228
Efficiency
and an on-line presence 199
and ICT 113
Electronic business
see e-business, websites
Electronic Commerce (EC Directive)
Regulations 210
Electronic communication 268
Electronic transactions 193
Employee rights
and ethics 63
Employees 27
and ethics 64-65
and expanding businesses 27-28

and retirement 28
and staff turnover 28
and starting a business 27
and their well-being 55-58
as customers 237-238
needs and expectations as
customers 238
Employment
and needs of customers 247
Employment Act 56, 57, 71
and setting up a business 75
Employment Equality (Religion and
Belief) Regulations 42
Employment Equality (Sexual
Orientation) Regulations 43
Employment Framework Directive 43
Employment protection legislation 69-
70
see also individual Acts
Employment Relations Act 57, 71
Employment Rights Act 55, 57
Ending a company
see winding up a company
Enterprise 73
starting and setting up 360-418
Enterprise Act 68
and e-business 209
Enterprise agencies 75
Enterprise resources planning software
116
Entrepreneurs 73
Entrepreneurship 73, 375
Environment Act 60, 63
Environmental issues 59-62
and ethics 63
and new product ideas 366
as constraint on marketing 190-191
EPOS
as electronic communication 268
Equal opportunities 41
Equal Opportunities Commission 42
Equal Pay Act 42
Equal Pay Directive 42
Equal Treatment Directive 41-42
Equipment
as a resource 82
Establishing a website 229-233
Estate Agents Act 293
Ethical issues 63-67
Ethics 63
and discrimination 41-44
and stakeholders 64-66
as constraint on marketing 189
as constraint on promotional
activity 350
see also business ethics
European Commission 68
European Court of Justice 42
European Work Time Directive 55, 56

European Year of Disabled People
aim and objectives 5
Evacuation procedures 298
Evaluating
financial success 414
interrelationships 417
marketing and sales 415
production 416
promotional campaigns 357-359
staff 414
success of a company/enterprise
414-418
teamwork 415
Exchange & Mart 329
Executive directors 380
Exhibitions
as direct marketing 320
Exit interviews
see staff exit interviews
Expenses 90
Explorer
see Internet Explorer
External
customers 18, 121
recruitment 27
External constraints
on marketing 189-191
on promotion 349-351
External customers 240-241
and premises 260, 261
monitoring customer service 281-
284
External factors
affecting winding up a company 411
Extra product free
as sales promotion 303
Extranet
and communication 201
Extrapolation
of sales 404-405

F

Face-to-face communication 267
Facsimile
as electronic communication 268
Factoring 82
Fads 126
Families
and needs as customers 244
Family commitments
and staff turnover 28
Family status
and needs of different customers
244
Farm Assured British Pigs 288

Farming
and job roles through
diversification 29
as part of primary industry 10
Fashions 126
Favourable variances 103
Federation of Small Business 75
Federation of the Electronics Industry
(FEI) 291
Field marketing 319-320
Field merchandising 320
Field research
see primary research
Fields
and databases 112
Film
as method of communication 267
Finance 81-82
and ICT 111
and legislation on consumer
service 293
as constraint on marketing 189
as function of business 16, 17
Finance Act 410
Finance Department
as internal customers 239
Financial accounting 17
Financial constraints
see costs
Financial costs
of a website 213-216
see also costs of a website
Financial documents
and communication 267
Financial implications
of winding up a company 411
Financial performance
monitoring in enterprise 399-403
Financial planning
and starting a new enterprise 372
Financial resources 81-82
Financial Services and Markets Act 293,
297
Financial Services Authority (FSA) 293,
297
Financiers
and ethics 64
Firewalls 213-214
Fishing
as part of primary industry 10
Fitness Industry Association 64
Fixed assets
and balance sheet 94, 95
Fixed costs
and break-even 107, 108
Fixed overhead variance 104
Flat structure 21-22
Flexibility at work
and legislation 56-57

Focus groups 155, 282
Food Safety Act 63, 291, 292, 294, 296
Forestry
as part of primary industry 10
Form 652a 410
Formulae
and spreadsheets 111
Franchisee 13
Franchising 13-14
and setting up a business 74
Franchisor 13
Free gifts 185
as sales promotion 304-305
Free offers 185
as sales promotion 304-305
Freehand 230
Frequency
of promotional campaigns 354
Friends of the Earth 60
Functional division of organisations 21-
22
Functions
of business 16-19
working together 19

G

Gap in the market 365
Gender
and needs of customers 244
see also sex
Gender discrimination 41-42
see also sex discrimination
General staff 24
Geographic segmentation 122, 147
and market share 136
Geographical division of organisation
21
Global trading
and e-business 194, 217
Global warming 61
Golden hello 235
Government
and setting up a business 75
as business customer 234
data 162
finance 82
loans 82
Grapevine
and monitoring customer service
281
Greenpeace 60
Grievances
and legislation 57
Gross profit 90, 91
improving through marketing 130-
132
monitoring in enterprises 401

Gross profit margin 91
Growth
    as a business aim 6
    see also business growth

H

Hackers 222
Hall tests 155
Halo effect 332
Hardware costs
    of a website 213
Headhunting 33
Health and Safety 70
    and customer service 296-300
    and ICT 118
    and starting a new enterprise 370-
    371
Health and Safety at Work Act 70, 299
    and setting up a business 75
Health and Safety Commission 70
Health and Safety (Display Screen
    Equipment) Regulations 118
Health and Safety Executive 70
Herzberg, Frederick 49
Hierarchy of needs 49
Hire purchase 81, 82
Home shopping
    and direct marketing 318
Human resources
    and communication in enterprises
      389-390
    and team working in enterprises
      389
    as business function 16-17
    as business resources 83
    methods of monitoring in
      enterprises 390-391
    monitoring in enterprises 389-393
Human Resources Department
    as internal customers 239
Hunches
    and new product ideas 366
Hygiene factors 50
Hyperlinks 226

I

Icons
    and websites 226
ICT
    as business function 18
    role in business 111
    to improve efficiency of business
      113

ICT Department
    providing services for a business
      239
ID checks 297-298
ID numbers 297
Image reading 230
Improving profitability
    and marketing strategies 130-134
In-house training 38
Incentives
    and motivation 53
Income
    and needs of customers 246
Independent bodies
    controlling quality 395
Independent Television (ITV)
    as promotional media 334
Independent Television Commission
    (ITC) 291
Indirect costs
    and pricing 175
Individuals
    and needs as customers 244
Industrial action 71
Industrial information
    and security on websites 222
Industrial sectors 10
Inflation
    as constraint on marketing 190
Informal meetings
    and monitoring customer service
      281
Information
    and e-business 194
    and legislation on consumer
      service 292-293
Informative advertising 308
Innovation
    and de-motivation 46
    and new enterprise 375
    and setting up a business 73
Inputs
    to production function 16
Institutional investors 13
Intangible products
    and websites 205
Inter-personal skills
    and effective customer service 256
Interactive Media in Retail Group
    (IMRG) 217-218
Interest
    and needs of customers 247
    on profit and loss account 91
Interest rates
    as constraint on marketing 190
Interests
    and segmentation 149
Internal
    customers 18, 121

    promotion 28
    recruitment 27
Internal business data 161
Internal constraints on marketing 189
Internal constraints on promotion 346-
    348
Internal customer service 253
Internal customers 237-240
    and premises 260, 261
    importance of 237
    monitoring service 280-281
Internal service providers 239
Internal sources of data 161
Internet 117
    and secondary research 162
    as promotional media 343
    see also e-business, websites
Internet advertising 184
Internet Explorer 213
Internet Service Provider (ISP) 214, 225
Internet shopping
    see on-line shopping
Interviews 33-34
    and primary research 155
Intranets 117-118
Investors in People 39
ISO 9000 85-86, 296, 395

J

Job description 31-32
Job roles 23, 29, 31
Junk mail 318

K

Kyoto Protocol 61
    as constraint on marketing 191

L

Labour budgets 102
Labour productivity 391, 415
Labour variance 104
Landfill tax 60
Language
    and needs of customers 246
Launches
    as promotion 185
Layout and design
    of websites 226
Layout of premises
    and effective customer service 261
Lead time
    and promotional activities 347

Leaflets 185, 327-330
  and direct marketing 318
Learning and Skills Council 39
Leasing 82
Leave
  and legislation 56
Legal contracts
  and communication 267
Legislation
  and customer service 288
  and discrimination 41-44
  and e-business 205
  and effects on needs of disabled
    customers 245
  and employees' well-being 55-58
  and performance of a business 87
  and setting up a business 74-75
  and websites 231
  as constraint on business 68-72
  as constraint on marketing 190
  as external constraint on
    promotion 349-350
  see also individual Acts
Letter of application 32-33
Liabilities 90
Licences
  and setting up a business 74
Licensing (Young Persons) Act 292
Lifestyle
  and needs of customers 247
  and segmentation 149
Likert scale 157
Limited company
  and setting up a business 74
  balance sheets 95
Limited liability 13, 360
Liquidations 9, 409
Liquidity
  and profitability 89
Loan
  bank 82
  government 82
  long term 81
  secured 81
  unsecured 81
Lobbying
  and PR 314
Local community
  as business customers 234
Location
  and e-business 195
Location of premises
  and effective customer service 260
London Underground 12
Long term liabilities
  and balance sheet 94, 95
Long term loan 81
Long term sources of finance 81-82

Loss
  and break-even chart 107
Loyalty cards 185
  as sales promotion 303

M

Macromedia Dreamweaver 214, 230
Macromedia Flash 230
Magazines 327-330
Mail order
  and direct marketing 318
Management information systems 116
Managers 24
  as internal customers 238
Manual Handling Regulations 299
Margin of safety 107
Market development 127, 141
Market forces
  and new enterprise 376
Market niche 150-151
Market orientated goods and services
  234-235
Market orientation 172
Market penetration 127, 141
Market place pricing 175, 176
Market research
  and developing a product 172
  and product ideas 365-366
  and setting up a business 73
  see also primary research,
    secondary research
Market research reports 162
Market segmentation 147-153
Market share 135-139
  as a business aim 6
Market size 135-136
Market testing 128
Marketing budgets 102
Marketing Department
  as internal customers 239
Marketing mix 166-170
  and brands 143
  changing to improve profitability
    132
Marketing research
  see primary research, secondary
    research
Maslow, Abraham 49
Mass marketing 151
Materials
  as a resource 82
Materials variance 104
Matrix structure 23
Mayo, Elton, 48
McGregor, Douglas 49
Me-too products 126

Measuring quality of customer service
  276-279
Media
  and communication with
    enterprises 385-386
Media relations 313
Media reports
  and monitoring customer service
    283
Medicines (Advertising) Regulations
  210
Memorandum of Association 13, 361-
  362
Memorandums 267
Mentoring 38
  and sponsorship 324
Menus 226
Merchandising
  as direct marketing 320
Meta Tags 231
Methods of communication 267-268
Milk round 33
Minimum Wage Act 56, 63
Minimum wages 56
  and motivation 48
Mining
  as part of primary industry 10
Mission statements 5, 370
  and customer service 272
Mobile phones
  as promotional media 343
Modem 213
Money-off purchases 185
Monitoring
  financial performance in enterprises
    399-403
  human resources in enterprises
    389-393
  production in enterprises 394-398
  sales and promotion in enterprises
    404-408
Monitoring complaints 282
Monitoring customer service 280-285
Monopoly 68
Montreal Protocol 61
  as constraint on marketing 190
Mortgage 81
Motivation 45-47
  and legislation 55-58
  effects of poor 45
  methods of 52-54
  positive effects of 46
  theories of 48-51
Moving image media 334-338
  cinema 334, 336-337
  television 334-336
Motivators 50
Motor Vehicles (Safety Equipment for
  Children) Act 296

Multi-choice questions 156, 157
Multi-packs
    as sales promotion 304
Multi-skilling
    and training 36

Mystery shoppers 320
    and monitoring customer service
        284

N

Narrow product range 171
National Lottery Act 292
National Office of Animal Health
(NOAH) 350
National Readership Survey
    and segmentation 148
National Society for Clean Air 60
National statistics socio-economic
    classification 149
Navigation routes
    and websites 225-226
Needs 121
    of different customers 244-249
Negative association
    and sponsorship 324
Net assets
    and balance sheet 95
Net cash flow 91
Net current assets
    and balance sheet 95
Net profit 90, 91
    improving through marketing 130-
        132
    monitoring in enterprises 401
Net profit margin 91
Netscape Navigator 213
New customer profiles
    and e-business 219
New markets
    and brand awareness 145
    reaching through an on-line
        presence 197
New media 343-345
    problems of 344
    reasons for using 343-344
    types of 343
New products 125-129
    and brand awareness 145
New services
    and e-business 195
Newspapers 327-330
Newspaper advertising 184
Newspaper circulation
    and market share 136
Niche marketing 150-151

Noise pollution 60
Nominations committee
    and role evaluation 386
Non-executive directors 380
Non-profit making businesses 10-11
Not-for profit businesses 11
Nursing staff
    and motivation 46

O

Objectives 5
    and an on-line presence 197
    and improving profitability through
        marketing 130
    and planning 77
    see also aims
Observation 154
    of customers 282
ODS 61
Ofcom 68, 349
    and advertising 311
    as constraint on marketing 190
    as radio media 332
Off-site training 38
Off-the-job training 37-38
Offers
    see free offers
Office of Fair Trading (OFT) 68, 294
    as constraint on marketing 190
Offices
    of companies 379-383
Ofgem 68, 293
Oftel 293
Ofwat 68, 293
    as constraint on marketing 190
OHP
    as method of communication 267
Ombudsmen 282
Omnibus surveys 155
On-going training 38
On-line catalogues 205
On-line ordering 219
On-line payment 214-215
On-line presence
    see e-business, websites
On-line shopping
    growth of 218
    see also e-business, websites
On-line surveys 155
On-line trading
    see e-business, websites
On-site training 38
On-the-job training 37
Open-ended questions 156, 157
Open days 185

Open questions
    and interviews 34
Opening balances
    and cash flow 98
Opening capital
    and balance sheet 95
Operating profit 91
Operatives 24
Opinions
    and segmentation 150
Opportunities
    and e-business 217-220
    and new enterprise 375
Ordinary shares 360
Organisation chart 21
Organisational structures 21-26
Orr 68, 293
Out-of-home media 340-341
    problems of 341
    reasons for 340-341
Output
    of production function 16
Overdraft 82
Overheads 90
Owners
    and ethics 64
    as internal customers 238
Ownership 10-14
    and setting up a business 73-74
Ozone layer 61

P

PA system
    as electronic communication 268
Paper based operations
    and websites 203
Part-Time Workers (Prevention of Less
    Favourable Treatment) Regulations
    56
Partnership
    and setting up a business 74
Partnerships 12-13
Passwords 297
    see also computer passwords
Payments
    and cash flow 98
    and legislation on consumer
        service 293
    on-line 214-215, 219, 231
    safety of 297
PayPal 195, 214-215, 219
Performance 86
    improving 87
Person specification 32
Personal hygiene
    and effective customer service 255

Personal interviews 391
Personal support
    and sponsorship 324
Personalised marketing
    and e-business 219
Personality
    and needs of customers 247
Personnel
    safety 298-299
    see also human resources
Phising 222
Photoshop
    see Adobe Photoshop
Physical resources 82-83
Piece rates
    and motivation 48
PIN numbers 297
Place 180-183
    and marketing mix 166, 167
    and price 182
    and promotion 162
    customer expectations of 250-251
Planning
    and starting an enterprise 370-373
    see also business planning
Pledges
    customer 273
Political constraints on marketing 189-190
Pollution 59-60, 62
Pop-ups 231
    as promotional media 343
Population
    and samples 156
Positioning
    and place/distribution 181
Positive associations
    and sponsorship 323, 324
Post-it notes 267
Postal surveys 155
Posters 184
    as communication method 267
    as out-of-home promotional media 339-340
PowerPoint
    as method of communication 267
Pre and post campaign measurement 358
Preference shares 360
Premises
    and effective customer service 260-261
    and measuring customer service 277
    as a resource 82
    as method of visual communication 267
Press receptions 185
Press releases 313

Pressure groups 65-66
Print media 327-330
    problems of 329-330
    reasons for 327-330
Price 175-179
    and marketing mix 166, 167
    customer expectations of 250
    raising to improve profitability 131
    reduction as sales promotion 303-304
Prices Act 293
Pricing
    and effect on website trading 206
    and legislation on consumer service 293
    strategy 176-177
Primary data 154
Primary industry 10
Primary research 154-160
Primary sector 374
Prince's Trust 75
Privacy
    and e-business 209-210, 219
Private limited company 13
    and setting up a business 74
Private sector 11, 12-14
Producer co-operative
    see worker co-operative
Product 171-174
    and effective customer service 262-263
    and marketing mix 166, 167
    as method of visual communication 267
Product brief 172
Product development 127, 141
    and new product ideas 366-367
Product endorsements 185
Product failure 127
    methods of reducing 127-128
Product ideas 365
Product improvements 125
Product knowledge
    and effective customer service 256
Product launch
    and developing a product 172
Product launches 314
Product life cycle 126-127
Product management 173
Product orientated goods and services 235
Product orientation 172
Product placement 185, 335, 339
Product range 171
Product re-launch 127
Product research
    and product failure 128
Product specification 171

Product standards
    and customer service 291
Product tie-ins 336-337
Production
    as function of business 16
    levels 394
    monitoring in enterprises 394
Production budgets 102
Production Department
    as internal customer 239
Products
    and customer safety 296
Professional staff 24
Professional standards
    and primary research 158
Profiling
    of customers 123
Profit
    and break-even chart 107
    as a measure of performance 87
    gross 90, 91
    improving through marketing 130-132
    margins 91
    net 90, 91
    operating 91
Profit and loss account 89-93
    and limited companies 90-91
    and sole traders 90
Profit and loss budgets 102
Profit making businesses 10-11
Profit margins
    monitoring in enterprises 401
Profit maximisation
    as a business aim 6
Profitability
    and liquidity 89
    and marketing strategies 130-134
Profits
    monitoring in enterprises 400-401
Project groups
    and matrix structures 23
Promotion 184-188, 301-359
    aggressive reasons 301, 302
    and customers' wants and needs 301
    and marketing mix 166, 168
    and websites 231
    defensive reasons 301, 302
    external constraints on 349-351
    factors influencing 186
    important questions on 301
    internal constraints on 346-348
    monitoring in enterprises 404, 406, 407
    of internal staff 28
    reasons for 301-302
    sales 184-185, 303-307

use by businesses 301-302
  see also advertising marketing
Promotional campaigns
  analysing 352-356
  comparing 353
  evaluating 357-359
  factors affecting choice of 353-354
  features of 352
Promotional lines 126
Promotional media 327-345
Promotional support
  and sponsorship 324
Promotional tools 302
Prompt service
  and effective customer service 256
Prompted brand awareness 144
Protection
  of customer information 297-298
Protection of Children (Tobacco) Act
  292
Prototypes 172, 367
Psychographic segmentation 122, 123
Psychometric tests 34
Public address system 331
Public liability 298
Public limited company 13
  and setting up a business 74
Public opinion
  and PR 314-315
Public private partnerships 12
Public relations (PR) 185, 313-316
  and changing an image 314
  and lobbying 314
  and media relations 313
  and product launches 314
  and public opinion 314-315
  and research reports 314
  and spin 316
  as promotional tool 302
  events 314
  factors affecting 315-316
  types of 313
Public sector 11-12
Public utilities
  price controls 293
Published standards
  and customer service 287
Punctuality
  and effective customer service 256
  measurement 276
Purchasing 395, 396
  budgets 102, 396

Q

Qualitative data 154, 161
Quality 85-86

and effective customer service 262
  as a business aim 7
  assurance 395
  control 395
Quality assurance 85
Quality chains 86
Quality circles
  and matrix structures 23
Quality control 85
Quality of products
  and measuring customer service
    277
Quantitative data 154, 161
Questioning
  see direct questioning
Questionnaires 155, 156-158

R

Race relations
  and discrimination 41, 42
Race Relations Act 42
Race Relations Amendment Act 42
Radio
  as promotional media 331-333
Radio advertising 184
Raising capital
  for a new enterprise 372
Ramblers' Association 11
Range proliferation
  and segmentation 150
Receipts
  and cash flow 98
Recruitment 27-29
  and monitoring human resources in
    enterprises 391
  external 27
  internal 27
  process 31-34
  using an on-line presence 198
Recycling 60-61
Redundancy
  and legislation 57
  and staff turnover 28
Registrar of Companies 361
  and communication with
    enterprises 380
Regulation
  of promotion 349
Regulatory bodies
  and monitoring customer service
    282-283
Regulatory watchdogs 68
Remuneration committee
  and role evaluation 386
Renewable resources 61

Research and development (R&D)
  and ICT 111
  and product ideas 365
  as function of business 17, 18
Research reports
  and PR 314
Reserves
  and balance sheet 95
Resources
  and business planning 77
  and sponsorship 325
  financial 81-82
  human 83
  physical 82-83
  using up of 61
  see also business resources
Respondents 154
Retail audits 357-358
Retail co-operative
  see consumer co-operative
Retail selling price 176
Retailers
  and place/distribution 180-181
Retained profit
  and the profit and loss account 91
  as source of finance 82
Retirement 28
Revenue
  and break-even 106-107
Risk
  and diversification 141
Risks
  and new enterprise 375
Roadshows
  as direct marketing 320
Road Traffic Act 291
Role evaluation
  in enterprises 386
Running costs 90

S

Safety
  of customer information 297-298
  of customers 296-300
  of personnel 298-299
  of products 296
  of services 297
  of visitors 298
Safety of products
  and effective customer service 262
Sale and Supply of Goods Act 293, 294,
  350
Sale and Supply of Goods to
  Consumers Regulations 209, 293,
  294
Sale of Goods Act 291, 292, 294, 350

Sale of Goods (Amendment Act) 350
Sales
    as a business aim 5-6
    monitoring in enterprises 404-408
    targets 404
    forecasting 404, 405
Sales budgets 102
Sales promotion 184-185, 303-307
    factors affecting 305-306
    planning 305-306
    reasons for 303
Sales records
    and monitoring customer service
        282
Sales staff
    measuring performance of 405
Sales value
    and market share 135
Sales volume
    and market share 135
Sales variance 103-104
Sample 156
Sample size 156
Samples
    as sales promotion 305
Sampling 156
Satellite television
    and advertising 335-336
Satisficing
    as a business aim 5
Scaling questions 156-157
Scams 222
Scientific Management 48
Search engines 194, 214, 221, 226
Secondary data 161
Secondary industry 10
Secondary research 161-165
    benefits of 162-163
    limitations of 163
Secondary sector 374
Secure on-line payment 219
Secured loan 81
Security
    and website design 231
    and websites 214, 223
    checks 297-298
    of customers (see safety)
    of information (see safety)
Security of products
    and effective customer service 262-
        263
Segmentation 147-153
    and advertising 310
    and brand awareness 145
    benefits and problems 150
    demographic 148-150
    geographic 147-148
    of customers 122-123
    psychographic 149-150

Segmenting
    a market 147
Self-assessment
    and monitoring customer service
        280
Self-employed 27
Self-liquidator 305
Self regulation
    and e-business 210
    by businesses 68
Selling price 175
Senior management
    in hierarchy 22
Senior management team
    and communication with
        enterprises 386
Services
    safety for customers 297
Setting up a business 73-76
Sex
    and discrimination 41-42
    and segmentation 148
    see also gender
Sex discrimination 41-42
Sex Discrimination Act 42
Share capital 81, 360
Shareholder feedback
    and monitoring customer service
        281
Shareholders
    and communication in enterprises
        385
    and company formation 360
    as internal customers 238
Shareholders' funds
    and balance sheet 95
Shares 360
Shopping trolley 214
Short listing 33
Short message service (SMS)
    and direct marketing 319
    as promotional media 343, 344
Short term sources of finance 82
Sickness
    and monitoring customer service
        280
Signage 267
Site map 225-226
Skills
    as constraint on marketing 189
    as internal constraint on
        promotion 347
    audit 347
Skills Academies 39
Skills strategy 39
Small businesses
    and sponsorship 324
Small Business Research Initiative 75
Small Business Service 75

SMART objectives 77-78
SMART targets 404
Social issues 63-67
Social responsibilities 63
Society
    as external business customer 241
Socio-economic groupings 148
Software costs
    of a website 213, 214
Software protection 231
Soil Association 7
Sole trader 12
    and setting up a business 73-74
Solvency 86
Sources of finance 81-82
Spam 222
Span of control 22-23
Special terms
    as promotion 185
Specialist software 116-120
Spin
    and PR 315
Sponsorship 186, 323-326
    as promotional tool 302
    dangers of 325
    factors influencing 325-326
    reasons for 323-324, 324-325
Sports events
    and sponsorship 323-324
Spreadsheets 111-112
    advantages of 112
Spyware 222
Staff
    and an on-line presence 198
    and effective customer service 255-
        259
    and measuring customer service
        277
    as business customers 234, 237-238
    benefits 237
    canteen 237
    exit interviews 280
    in hierarchy 22
    needs and expectations as
        customers 238
    queries 391
    surveys 280
    turnover 280
Staff turnover 28, 30, 390
    and de-motivation 28
    and dismissal 28
    and family commitments 28
    and motivation 46
    and promotion externally 28
    and promotion internally 28
Stakeholders 74
    and sponsorship 324
Start-up costs 90
    of website 202

Statutory declaration 362
Statistical process control (SPC) 395
Stickers
    as ambient promotional media 339
Stock Exchange
    and plcs 13
Stock levels
    and monitoring production 394
    and purchasing 396
Structure
    see organisation structures
Suggestion boxes
    and motivation 46
Sunday Trading Act 190
Supermarket shopping
    and on-line presence 197
Supervisors 24
    in hierarchy 22
Suppliers
    and effect of website trading 206
    and ethics 64
    as business customers 234, 240-241
Supply
    and effect on price 177
Supply chains 180
Supply of Goods and Services Act 291,
    297, 350
Surveillance cameras
    as electronic communication 268
Survey 154
Survival
    as a business aim 7-8
SWOT analysis 365
    and e-business 217

T

Tall structure 22
Tannoy
    as electronic communication 268
Targeting
    of customers 123
    using cinema 337
    using print media 328
    using radio media 332
    see also segmentation
Targeting customers
    using a website 227
Task groups
    and matrix structures 23
Tastes
    and segmentation 150
Taxis
    as ambient promotional media 339
Taylor, F.W. 48
Team building 384-385

Teamwork
    and new enterprises 384
    and TQM 86
    as effective customer service 257
Technical resources
    as internal constraint on
        promotion 347
Technology driven product approach
    172
Telemarketing 319
Telephone
    as electronic communication 268
Telesales 319
Television
    as method of communication 267,
    268
Television advertising 184, 334-336
    benefits of promotion on 335
    problems of promotion on 335-336
Tertiary industry/sector 10, 374-375
Test marketing 155
Text
    as electronic communication 268
Text marketing 319
The State
    as external business customer 241
Theory X 49
Theory Y 49
Threats
    and e-business 221-224
Three clicks 226
Three for price of two offers 304
Time
    as internal constraint on
        promotion 347
Time spent at work
    and legislation 55-56
Timekeeping
    and effective customer service 256
Timing
    and sponsorship 325
Total cost function
    and break-even 107
Total quality management (TQM) 85,
    86, 395
Total revenue function
    and break-even 107
Toys (Safety) Regulations 296
Trade Associations 75
Trade audits
    and primary research 156
Trade credit 82, 401
Trade Descriptions Act 75, 293, 294,
    311, 350
    and e-business 210
Trade journals 162, 184
Trade Marks Act 293, 294
Trade media 329

Trade restrictions 294
    as constraint on marketing 190
Trade Union Reform and Employment
    Rights Act 71
Trade unions 70-71
Trading account
    on profit and loss account 91
Trading policies
    and ethics 63
Trading standards 349
Traffic congestion 61, 62
Training 36-40
    and effective customer service 257
    government schemes 39
    reasons for 36-37
    types of 37-38
Trojan horse 222
Trust
    and websites 205
Trust UK 211
Turnover
    and the profit and loss account 90,
    91
    see also staff turnover
Twenty four hour service
    and e-business 194

U

Un-prompted brand awareness 144
Undeclared lodgements 400
Unfair Commercial Practices legislation
    292
Unfair Contract Terms Directive 293
Unfair dismissal 28
Unfair Terms in Consumer Contracts
    Regulations 209
Unilever 18
Unison 45
Unique selling point
    and e-business 221
Unpresented cheques 400
Unsecured loan 81
Unsolicited Goods and Services Act
    292
Updating
    websites 203, 222

V

Vacancies 27, 31
Value for money
    and effective customer service 262
Value offers 185
Variable costs
    and break-even 107

Variance analysis 103-104
Variances 103-104
VAT
  and pricing 176
Vendor rating 396
Venture capital 81-82
Venture capitalist 81-82
Video recording 336
Virus 213-214, 222
Virus protection 231
Viruses
  see computer viruses
Visual communication 267-268
Voluntary codes of practice 71
  as constraint on marketing 191
  as external constraint on
    promotion 350
Voluntary Code of Practice for the Fast
  Food Industry 350

W

Wages Act 55
Wants 121-122
Warnings
  and website design 231
Wastage
  and print media 329-330
  and television 336
Waste control and management 60-61,
  62
Waste creation 60
Waste levels
  and purchasing 396
Waste Watch 60
Water pollution 59-60
Web authoring software 214

Web authoring tools 230
Webcasting 218
Websites
  and business aims and objectives
    201
  and communication 201-202
  and consumer profiling 202-203
  and customer service 203
  and direct marketing 321
  and ease of use 226
  and effects on costs 202
  and hardware costs 213
  and identifying customers 229
  and identifying purpose 229
  and navigation routes 225-226
  and other costs 214
  and paper based operations 202
  and personalised shopping 206
  and personnel 214-215
  and personnel management 202
  and pricing 206
  and promotion 231
  and reaching target customers 227
  and security in design 231
  and site maps 225-226
  and software costs 213-214
  and speed of use 225
  and use of media 226
  and user interface 226
  and web authoring tools 230
  budgets 229-230
  content of 226
  costs of 213-216
  design 230
  effective 225-228
  effects of not updating 203
  establishing 229-233
  features of a good 225

  impact on a business 201-204
  impact on competitors 206
  impact on customers 205
  impact on stakeholders 205-208
  impact on suppliers 206
  nature of 201
  poor design 222-223
  problems of not updating 203, 222
  revue and evaluation 231
  setting up 229
  short term and long term effects
    203
WebTrader UK 211
Weights and Measures Act 291
Well-being
  see employees and their well-being
Whitbread plc 58
Wholesalers
  and place/distribution 180-181
Wide product range 171, 172
Wider business issues
  and starting a new enterprise 374-
    375
Winding up
  a company 409-413
Word processing 112
Work teams 384
Worker co-operative 14
Workers
  see employees
WorldPay 215, 219
Worm 222
Written communication 267

y

Young Enterprise 75